INTERNATIONAL INSIDER DEALING

INTERNATIONAL INSIDER DEALING

General Editors
Mark Stamp
Carson Welsh

LAW & TAX

© Pearson Professional Limited 1996
except Singapore, Indranee Rajah and Gary Pryke
Australia, Blake Dawson Waldron

Mark Stamp, Carson Welsh and the contributors have asserted their right
under the Copyright, Designs and Patents Act 1988 to be identified as the
authors of this work

ISBN 0 75200 1795

Published by
FT Law & Tax
21–27 Lamb's Conduit Street
London WC1N 3NJ

A Division of Pearson Professional Limited

Associated offices
Australia, Belgium, Canada, Hong Kong, India, Japan, Luxembourg,
Singapore, Spain, USA

Printed in Great Britain by Biddles Ltd, Guildford

CONTENTS

PREFACE

Given the globalisation of the world's various stock exchanges it is becoming increasingly important for those who are involved in advising international companies or who deal on such exchanges to have an understanding of the law of insider dealing in all those countries in which they operate. The purpose of this book is to provide the reader with a clear and practical guide to the law of insider dealing in those countries where the top 20 stock exchanges of the world are located. In addition, five emerging market jurisdictions (China, India, Indonesia, the Philippines and Russia) have been included since it seems likely that a number of the stock exchanges located in these jurisdictions will be in the top 20 within the next ten years or so.

This is not the first book on the market to review insider dealing legislation in a number of countries. However, the editors have attempted to distinguish it from its potential rivals by emphasising a practical approach to the subject and so avoiding an academic consideration of the law. Consequently, if we have achieved our aim the book will be of some value not only to lawyers but also to bankers, brokers and other financial intermediaries. In addition, the style of the book is designed to enable the reader to gain an understanding of the relevant legislation without reading great volumes of material. Each chapter is prefaced by a flow diagram which provides an overview of the relevant law and allows the reader to understand, at the outset, the necessary components that need to be established before a charge of insider dealing can be brought. The flow diagram contains cross references to appropriate parts of the text to allow particular areas to be quickly pinpointed. In the chapters themselves, use of boxes to highlight important areas are used—again to allow the reader to gain familiarity with the subject without having to become fully immersed in the text.

We have attempted to use as many practical examples as possible, highlighting these in the text. There are, by necessity, fewer examples in those markets where financial protection for investors is still at an early stage since the law is not designed to deal with many of the nuances found in more developed jurisdictions. In addition, to enable an easy comparison to be made between the different jurisdictions a case study is found at the end of each chapter together with a suggested solution. The case study is based on substantially the same facts in each jurisdiction and accordingly, this enables the reader to compare jurisdictions at a glance.

Our contribution to this work has been modest compared to the collective contributions of the other authors—it is thanks to them that we have produced a book at all. In addition, we would like to take this opportunity to thank a succession of our trainees for their hard work and organisational skills without which we would have aggravated our publishers even more than we did. In particular we would like to thank James Dawson for his masterful creation of the flow diagrams for each chapter and David Walsh for his unstinting effort and good humour throughout the project. Finally, our thanks must go to the publishers whose patience and understanding were tested on more than one occasion but who never failed to give us the necessary support and encouragement at all times.

MAS

CJW

The law is stated as at 1 January 1996

INTRODUCTION

One thing is apparent from a review of the insider legislation contained in this book—in most jurisdictions the law is just not working. While almost all countries have criminal sanctions to deal with insider dealing it appears to remain prevalent, in one form or another, in most of them. The real test in judging whether insider dealing legislation is effective is by reference to the manner by which it is enforced. After all, having sophisticated provisions to catch the seasoned and intuitive insider dealer is not, in itself, enough—this has to be combined with both the political and judicial will to implement and enforce the legislation. It is difficult to see how the legislation can be seen as a deterrent if there is not a system for detecting the offence in the first place and the will to prosecute subsequently.

The reasons for few prosecutions being brought are varied. In a number of common law jurisdictions, such as the UK, Australia and Hong Kong the failure to prosecute can, in part, be attributed to the failure by the legislature to get the balance right in drafting the legislation so that the burden of proof on the prosecution is onerous, making it difficult to secure a conviction. In other jurisdictions, notably Japan and South Korea, this problem is exacerbated by the legislatures' attempt to provide an exhaustive list of categories of information which are to be treated as inside information which can be exploited by the experienced insider dealer. On the other hand, in a number of other countries, principally in countries in the Far East, there is no real political will to enforce the legislation. The insider dealing provisions in those countries were, on the whole, introduced to give credibility to the relevant market but without putting in place the necessary detection or enforcement mechanisms to enable the legislation to be effectively enforced. As a more general point, there are few countries where the level of any penalty imposed on the insider dealer is dependent upon the amount of profit made, thus allowing an insider to risk prosecution if he considers the gains to be sufficiently worthwhile.

In contrast, there are two jurisdictions which the insider dealer would be well advised to avoid. Not surprisingly, the US has a determined policy to eradicate insider dealing. Rather ironically, the US has no tailor-made insider dealing legislation, relying instead on general provisions of its 1934 Securities Exchange Act for prosecution of insiders. What sets it apart from other jurisidictions are its proactive judiciary who do not shy away from developing the limited legislation into an effective weapon against the insider and the vigilance of the SEC in pursuing insider dealers.

Perhaps more surprising is the success which the French authorities have had in combatting insider dealing. There have been a number of successful, high profile prosecutions brought in France. One of the principal reasons for this is the reversal of the burden of proof when it comes to the prosecution having to establish certain elements of the offence. For example, there is a presumption that certain insiders have knowledge of the price-sensitive information and a presumption that the accused based his decision to trade on his knowledge of inside information. This puts the onus on the accused to establish that these elements of the offence were missing.

In conclusion, it is clear that a number of jurisdictions are either not interested in, or are not prepared to devote the necessary resources to, implementing their insider dealing legislation and until there is a change of policy the insider dealer can continue to trade at his leisure. In those countries where there is the political will to tackle the insider dealing issue then, aside from a radical overhaul of securities legislation to create a regulatory body equivalent to the SEC in the US, it would seem a sensible step to consider reversing the burden of proof on certain elements of the relevant offences, particularly those where the subjective knowledge of the accused is involved, since this will give the prosecuting authorities in those jurisdictions a better chance of securing a successful conviction.

MAS

CJW

PART I

North/South America

UNITED STATES
CANADA
MEXICO
BRAZIL

United States

Edward F Greene and David A Christman*,
Cleary, Gottlieb, Steen & Hamilton, London

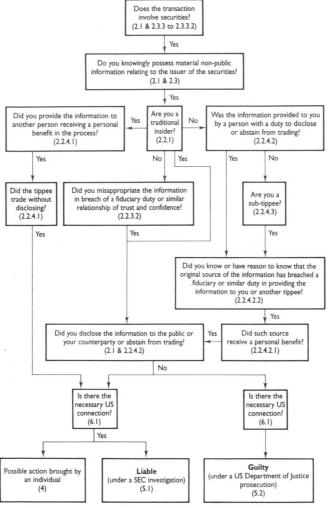

Note: The SEC may bring tipper actions where the tippee abstains from dealing (2.2.4.1).

* Mr. Greene is a partner, and Mr. Christman an associate, with the London office of Cleary, Gottlieb, Steen & Hamilton. The authors wish to express their gratitude to Richard F Ziegler of Cleary's New York office and Daniel A Braverman and Manley O Hudson, Jr of Cleary's London office for their insightful comments on the many drafts of this chapter.

1 INTRODUCTION

1.1 STATUTORY SCHEME

Unlike most European countries, US laws against insider trading do not consist of statutes defining certain prohibited activities. Instead, the US insider trading scheme is very much the product of a common law system, shaped in large measure by judicial interpretations of several overlapping statutory and regulatory prohibitions. These statutes and regulations may, on their face, appear surprisingly vague to someone familiar with European insider trading laws. For instance, r10b-5, which, as described below, is the centrepiece of the US insider trading laws, does not define or even mention insider trading as such but rather prohibits fraudulent and deceptive practices in connection with the purchase and sale of securities generally.

Various comprehensive schemes have been proposed by academics and lawmakers as alternatives to the current laws. However, the US Securities and Exchange Commission (the 'SEC') has resisted the enactment of a statutory scheme defining the offence, believing that the current rather loosely-worded statutes and rules provide the flexibility necessary to deal with changing market practices and problems. This approach, of course, complicates the job of US legal advisors to securities issuers and their insiders, since with flexibility comes a degree of uncertainty regarding activities and issues not previously considered by the SEC or the courts. A happy by-product of the system, so far as the SEC is concerned, is that this lack of predictability results in a cautious form of self-policing amongst persons with access to inside information.

The general statutory framework of the US insider trading laws is described below. Some of these statutes were enacted by the US Congress either as part of, or as amendments to, the two principal US securities law Acts. Others were promulgated by the SEC pursuant to powers granted to it by the Congress. Despite this distinction, there is no practical difference in the enforcement or application by US courts of these statutes and rules.

1.1.1 Rule 10b-5

Rule 10b-5 was promulgated under s 10 of the Securities Exchange Act 1934 (the 'Exchange Act'). Section 10 contains the Exchange Act's general anti-fraud provisions. Rule 10b-5 states that:

> It shall be unlawful for any person, directly or indirectly, by the use of any means or instrumentality of interstate commerce, or of the mails, or of any facility of any national securities exchange:
> (1) To employ any device, scheme or artifice to defraud,
> (2) To make any untrue statement of a material fact or to omit to state a material fact necessary in order to make the statements made, in the light of the circumstances under which they were made, not misleading, or

(3) To engage in any act, practice, or course of business which operates or would operate as a fraud or deceit upon any person,

in connection with the purchase or sale of any security.

As noted above, r10b-5 makes no explicit mention of insider trading. None the less, it is the linchpin of the US insider trading laws. Rule 10b-5 is relied on not only by the SEC in bringing its enforcement actions, but has been interpreted by the courts as creating a right on the part of private individuals to bring suit against persons and entities who have engaged in insider trading, subject to certain conditions more fully described below.

1.1.2 Section 17

Section 17 of the Securities Act 1933 is a near mirror-image of r10b-5, except that s 17's prohibition operates in connection with only the 'offer or sale' of a security and not the 'purchase and sale' of any security as does r10b-5's. Section 17 is principally relied upon by the Department of Justice and the SEC in criminal and enforcement proceedings. Nearly all federal courts have held that s 17 does not create a right of action on the part of private litigants.

1.1.3 Rule 14e-3

Rule 14e-3 was promulgated under s 14 of the Exchange Act and deals with insider trading in the context of a tender offer (it does not apply in the context of a merger or consolidation). Like r10-5b, r14e-3 has been interpreted as creating a private right of action.

1.1.4 Section 20A

Section 20A was enacted by the US Congress as part of the Insider Trading and Securities Enforcement Act 1988. Section 20A creates a private right of action for individuals who traded contemporaneously with insiders who have traded in violation of the judicial interpretations of r10b-5. Section 20A does not itself define the elements of the insider trading offence, but allows private plaintiffs to recover damages from insider traders without proof that the defendant directly caused the plaintiff's loss. However, because s 20A limits the amounts that may be recovered by most such private plaintiffs, its enactment has not created a significant role for private actions in US insider trading law. See 5.3

1.1.5 Section 16(b)

Section 16(b) of the Exchange Act is a specialised insider trading statute which enables a company to recover any profits realised by an officer, director or 10 per cent-or-greater shareholder on any purchase and sale (or sale and purchase) of such company's stock by such person within any six-month period. Section 16(b) applies regardless of whether the person who made the profit used or possessed material non-public information in trading. Furthermore, under s 16(b), a 'profit' is earned any time a person buys at one price and sells at a higher price (even if the sale at the higher price occurred before the lower priced purchase), regardless of the number of transactions effected during the period. Suit to recover such profits can be brought by the company or by any shareholder acting on behalf of the company.

Section 16(b) represents a specialised and highly technical aspect of the US insider trading laws and for that reason is not discussed further in this chapter. Among other things, numerous regulatory exceptions and provisos to s 16(b) exist. Thus, the foregoing summary of the central concepts underlying the section should be taken merely as a starting point in exploring the statute. Additionally, it should be noted that s 16(b) is not generally applicable to directors and officers of non-US companies.

As indicated above, judicial interpretation has played a significant role in the development of US insider trading law. Moreover, because the US federal courts are divided into ten different geographic 'circuits', the law on insider trading in the US has developed unevenly and differences may exist between the various circuits.

1.2 OVERVIEW OF ENFORCEMENT MECHANISMS

There are three principal mechanisms through which the US insider trading laws are enforced. First, civil proceedings can be brought by the US SEC using its broad investigatory and enforcment powers. Enforcement actions by the SEC take the form of administrative proceedings, which are appealable to the US federal courts, or judicial proceedings in the US federal courts. Either type of enforcement proceeding can result in orders against future conduct, disgorgement of profits made or losses avoided, and the imposition of monetary penalties. Second, upon recommendation by the SEC, or on its own initiative, the US Department of Justice (or state prosecutorial agencies) can institute criminal proceedings. Such proceedings may be based on violations of the securities laws but may also include charges based on violation of applicable wire and mail fraud statutes. Finally, certain of the statutes that deal with insider trading permit individuals to bring actions, either on their own behalf or derivatively on behalf of the corporation, under certain circumstances.

2 BASIC ELEMENTS OF INSIDER TRADING

2.1 THE 'ABSTAIN OR DISCLOSE' RULE

The basic rule of US insider trading law as developed in numerous judicial proceedings is that certain individuals who are knowingly in possession of material non-public information relating to a company must disclose such information prior to trading in the company's securities. If the individual is not able to make the required disclosure (eg due to such individual's fiduciary duties to the company) or is unwilling to do so, the law requires that the individual refrain from trading. This obligation has been described as a duty to 'abstain or disclose' (see *Re Cady, Roberts & Co*, 40 SEC 907 (1961)).

A key difference between insider trading law as applied by the SEC and the law as applied in most European countries is that, in the US, the SEC has taken the view that trading while *knowingly in possession* of material non-public information is, on its own, enough to create liability. For example, in a recent SEC enforcement action, *SEC v Baker*, 93 Civ 7398 (RWS), Litigation Release No 13850 (1993), the SEC accepted the defendant's contention that he had made a decision to trade prior to being made privy to material non-public information but initiated proceedings against the defendant none the less. The defendant agreed to disgorge his trading profits plus interest and to pay a civil penalty. In England, by contrast, an insider can establish a complete defence to an insider trading charge if he or she can establish that the same trades would have been made even in the absence of non-public information. No US court has been asked to rule directly on whether trading while 'knowingly in possession' of non-public material information is enough to create liability. Despite some arguable tension between the *knowingly in possession* standard and the view of the US courts that a violation of r10b-5 must be premised on a breach of fiduciary duty, at least one US circuit court has indicated that, if faced with the question, it would employ the 'knowingly in possession' standard (see *United States v Teicher*, 987 F 2d 112 (2d Cir), *cert denied* 114 S Ct 467 (1993)).

A more subtle difference is the fact that, because of the significant role of judicial interpretation in the development of US insider trading law, at least some knowledge of the history of the law, especially of the ever-evolving role of r10b-5 in the area, is essential to gaining an informed understanding of the current state of the law and the directions in which it is likely to move in the future.

Two primary forces have shaped US insider trading law. First, the SEC, which has continually attempted to expand the universe of persons falling within r10b-5's prohibitions. The SEC's aggressiveness stems from its traditional view of r10b-5 as a tool for ensuring that 'all investors trading . . . have relatively equal access to material information': *SEC v Texas Gulf Sulphur Co*, 401 F 2d 833, 848 (2d Cir 1968), *cert denied* 394 US 976 (1969)). Given its druthers, the SEC would find a violation of r10b-5 any time a person traded while knowingly in possession of information unavailable to the rest of the market. Second, the US federal courts, which have been unwilling to endorse the SEC's more aggressive uses of r10b-5. Instead, mindful of r10b-5's stated purpose as an anti-fraud provision, the courts have continually looked to common law concepts of fraud in interpreting the contours of the rule, requiring that there be some form of wrongful behaviour before finding that the rule has been violated.

In large measure, the judicial history of r10b-5 has been forged by the efforts of the SEC to apply the rule's prohibitions to an ever-widening circle of persons into whose hands material non-public information may fall.

2.2 PERSONS WHO MUST 'ABSTAIN OR DISCLOSE'

As US insider trading law has evolved, several groups of persons have been identified as potentially being able to benefit improperly from material non-public information. As more fully described below, various legal theories have been employed by the SEC in its efforts to hold these persons accountable. The US courts, however, have resisted some of the SEC's most aggressive efforts, taking the view that in order to find a violation of r10b-5 it is necessary that the information have been used in (or obtained as the result of) a breach of a fiduciary or similar duty.

2.2.1 Traditional insiders

The first such group is traditional insiders; the directors, officers and controlling shareholders of a company. These individuals have a well-established common law fiduciary duty to the corporation and its shareholders not to use corporate information for personal gain. Thus, it has long been acknowledged that such individuals violate their fiduciary duty to shareholders when they trade in the company's equity securities while knowingly in possession of material non-public information. Spouses and other immediate family members of such persons are also treated as insiders. Additionally, because an issuer repurchasing its shares in the market owes a fiduciary duty to its shareholders, it violates US insider trading law when it makes such purchases without disclosing material non-public information.

Problem Area 1

Larry, a senior officer with Four Wheels Inc, a small specialty automobile manufacturer, learns that the company is about to announce a huge recall program, the cost of which will require previous profit forecasts to be substantially revised. Larry calls his broker and orders all of his Four Wheels shares sold. The following morning, after the announcement of the recall program, Four Wheels' share price plummets by 40 per cent. In enforcement proceedings brought by the SEC, Larry attempts to argue that because the buyers of the shares were not existing shareholders of Four Wheels at the time of his trades, he had no fiduciary duty to such persons. Thus, he argues, he was free to trade with them without disclosing the material non-public information in his possession.

Larry's argument points up a conceptual problem in the law as applied to traditional insiders. In the US, a person who fails to disclose material information prior to the consummation of a trade commits fraud when he is under a duty to disclose. If the duty to disclose only arises as a result of a fiduciary relationship with the corporation, and is thus owed to the corporation and its shareholders, the sale to a non-shareholder arguably does not trigger the duty. Obviously, however, a rule which prohibits an insider from buying shares while knowing positive material non-public information but *permits* an insider to *sell* shares while knowing negative material non-public information would be inequitable. Thus, the law has been extended to reach the selling insider as well as the buying insider (see Re *Cady, Roberts*, 40 SEC 907 at 914 n 23 (1961)).

2.2.2 Temporary insiders

It should be noted at this point that a variety of otherwise independent persons may be viewed as insiders in situations in which they are rendering professional services to a corporation. Such persons, known as 'temporary' insiders, may include underwriters, lawyers, accountants, financial advisors and other consultants to a corporation. The US Supreme Court has acknowledged that such persons may be treated as insiders for purposes of insider trading laws where (1) a special confidential relationship exists pursuant to which the advisor has access to information which is being provided to him or her solely for corporate purposes and (2) where there is an expectation (implicit or explicit) that the information will be kept confidential (see *Dirks v SEC*, 463 US 646, 655 n 14 (1983)).

2.2.3 Non-insiders

In addition to the problem of trading by traditional and temporary insiders, the SEC has confronted a variety of situations in which persons owing no fiduciary obligation to the company or its shareholders have become privy to, and traded upon, material non-public information.

In 1961, in Re *Cady, Roberts*, the SEC considered the case of a broker who was given inside information by one of his partners in the brokerage house. The partner had obtained the information by virtue of being a director of an unrelated corporation. This situation created a modest dilemma in that the person who had actually traded was not in a fiduciary relationship with the corporation. However, the SEC determined that the abstain or disclose duty could be applied to a larger group than those owing a traditional common law fiduciary duty to the corporation and its shareholders.

The doctrinal basis for the SEC's view and the nexus the SEC saw to r10b-5 in the non-insider context was not very clearly articulated in *Cady, Roberts*. According to the SEC, the abstain or disclose obligation was 'based on two principal elements: first, the existence of a relationship giving access, directly or indirectly, to information intended to be available only for a corporate purpose and not for the personal benefit of anyone, and second, the inherent unfairness involved where a party takes advantage of such information knowing that it is unavailable to those with whom he is dealing': *Re Cady, Roberts*, 40 SEC 907 at 912 (1961). Since the defendant had gained the information from an insider of whom he was a business partner, the defendant shared in the insider's abstain or disclose obligation.

In a later case, *SEC v Texas Gulf Sulphur Co*, a US circuit court endorsed the application of the abstain or disclose duty to persons both within and without the traditional fiduciary circle of officers, directors and controlling shareholders. However, in doing so, the court seemed to rely most heavily on the second of the two principles enunciated in *Cady, Roberts*, stating that r10b-5 is 'based in policy on the justifiable expectation of the securities marketplace that all investors trading . . . have relatively equal access to material information': *SEC v Texas Gulf Sulphur Co*, 401 F 2d at 848 (2d Cir 1968). In short, the court and the SEC were operating on the assumption that it was the counterparties' inability to obtain the information in the traders' possession that was driving the duty on the part of the traders to disclose, rather than the existence of some sort of special relationship between the traders and the corporation.

Developments in the non-insider area of the law eventually revealed a significant tension between the view of the SEC and that of the Supreme Court regarding the appropriate scope of r10b-5's application. After *Cady, Roberts* and *Texas Gulf Sulphur*, the SEC and some federal courts took a broad view of r10b-5; interpreting the rule as requiring equal access to information between parties to securities transactions generally. The SEC attempted to use the rule in a wide variety of situations in which individuals traded while in possession of material non-public information. The US Supreme Court would ultimately reject this broad approach, however, holding that the duty to abstain or disclose does not arise in every instance in which an individual has material non-public information but rather only where the individual has obtained the information as the result of a breach of a fiduciary (or, in certain instances more fully discussed below, a similar) duty.

2.2.3.1 United States v Chiarella

In *United States v Chiarella*, 445 US 222 (1980), the US Supreme Court considered the case of an employee of a financial printing shop who, in violation of workplace rules, had deduced from documents being prepared in the shop the identities of several companies being targeted for takeovers. The employee bought shares in the companies, selling at a profit after the takeover attempts became public. The employee was subsequently forced to disgorge his profits after settling an enforcement action brought by the SEC and was convicted of criminal violations of r10b-5 and sentenced to a jail term.

On appeal, the Supreme Court reversed the criminal conviction, holding that because the print shop employee was not in a fiduciary relationship vis-à-vis the target companies, he had been under no duty to 'abstain or disclose' before trading. In so holding, the court emphatically rejected the SEC's position, accepted by the lower court, that '[a]nyone—corporate insider or not—who regularly receives material non-public information' is liable if he or she 'use[s] that information to trade in securities' without disclosing such information. The court (see Chiarella, p 231) would later note that the Chiarella decision 'repudiat[ed] any notion that all traders must enjoy equal information before trading': Dirks v SEC, 463 US 646 at 657 (1983).

The Chiarella court, however, suggested in dicta that the conviction might have stood had the jury been instructed on an alternative theory of r10b-5 liability. Specifically, the court seemed to acknowledge that a duty to abstain or disclose might arise where a person 'misappropriates' material non-public information from his or her employer or the employer's client. The SEC and some US federal courts quickly seized on this 'misappropriation theory' of insider trading.

2.2.3.2 Misappropriation theory

Under the misappropriation theory of insider trading, which has been accepted in several US judicial circuits, a person violates r10b-5 'when such person misappropriates material non-public information in breach of a fiduciary or similar relationship of trust and confidence' and engages in securities transactions while knowingly in possession of such information: United States v Chestman, 947 F 2d 551, 566 (2d Cir) (en banc), cert denied 112 S Ct 1759 (1992). Liability can attach even though the source of the information is unaffiliated with the buyer, seller or issuer of the securities in question.

The misappropriation theory was brought to bear in a virtual repeat of the Chiarella case, SEC v Materia, 745 F 2d 197 (2d Cir 184), cert denied 471 US 1053 (1985), in which the US Second Circuit affirmed the conviction of a printshop employee who had traded after learning of certain corporate transactions involving his employer's clients. However, in a recent decision, United States v Bryan, 58 F 3d 933 (4th Cir 1995), the US Fourth Circuit rejected the misappropriation theory as a basis for liability under r10b-5. The defendant in Bryan was a high-ranking state lottery official who was convicted of violating r10b-5 after he purchased securities of firms which were going to be awarded lucrative government contracts in connection with the lottery. The Bryan court held that r10b-5's prohibition against 'fraud . . . in connection with the purchase or sale of any security' means that the fraudulent act must be perpetrated upon the counterparty to the securities transaction. According to the Bryan court, the misappropriation theory improperly bifurcates these elements, creating liability where the fraud (ie the breach of a fiduciary or similar duty) is perpetrated against one individual (eg a printshop worker's employer) while the purchase or sale of the securities involves another individual to whom no duty is owed.

Prior to the *Bryan* decision, the misappropriation theory had been given a limited endorsement by an evenly divided US Supreme Court in *Carpenter v United States*, 791 F 2d 1024 (2d Cir 1986), *affd* 484 US 19 (1987) (affirmed by 4-4 decision). Under US law, however, an affirmation by an evenly divided Supreme Court is not binding precedent on a lower court that subsequently considers the same issue. The 'split' that now exists among the federal circuits with respect to the legitimacy of the misappropriation theory increases the likelihood that the US Supreme Court will revisit the issue in the not too distant future. In the meanwhile, it is highly likely that the SEC will continue to use the misappropriation theory as a basis for liability and that the US Department of Justice will continue to prosecute actions based on the theory in judicial circuits other than the Fourth Circuit.

2.2.3.2.1 Fiduciary duty
Unlike the fiduciary duty contemplated by the original 'abstain or disclose' cases, the fiduciary or similar duty that is contemplated by the misappropriation theory can include a duty to one's employer or the clients of one's employer. The breach of a duty to protect an employer's confidences (or the confidences of the employer's clients) can trigger an insider trading action based on misappropriation. Presumably, a consultant or other independent contractor owes such a duty to a company to which he or she renders services.

2.2.3.2.2 Breach of fiduciary duty
Under common law principles, a fiduciary duty is 'breached' when the person to whom the duty is owed is injured as a result of the fiduciary's deliberate or reckless actions. In the misappropriation context, in judicial circuits accepting the theory, injury can be either pecuniary or to the professional reputation of the person to whom the duty is owed. For example, an employee has been found to have breached a fiduciary-like duty to his employer, an investment bank, because the employee's trading threatened to undermine client confidence in the security of information held by the bank (see *United States v Newman*, 664 F 2d 12, 17 (2d Cir 1981), *cert denied* 464 US 863 (1983)).

Problem Area 2

Imelda is the chief executive officer of Planet Inc, a publicly-traded supplier of genetically engineered bio-technical products. Planet is engaged in discussions with Company X regarding a joint venture that would be highly beneficial to Planet's balance sheet. Imelda tells her husband, Tom, about the venture over dinner, admonishing him to keep the information confidential. Tom, in turn, tells his sister, Sally, who repeated the news to her husband, Harold. Later in the day, during a therapy session with his psychiatrist, Sigmund, Tom describes the impending joint venture while explaining why he believes that Imelda's job is more important to her than he is. Before news of the joint venture is announced, Harold and Sigmund purchase shares of Planet Inc which increase sharply in value when the venture is made public.

In each instance, the key issue is whether a fiduciary or similar duty was breached in, or by, the trading which would give rise to an action based on the misappropriation theory. Under the misappropriation theory of insider trading, which has been accepted in several (but not all) of the US judicial circuits, a person violates r10b-5 when such person misappropriates material non-public information in breach of a fiduciary or similar relationship of trust and confidence and trades while knowingly in possession of such information.

In Harold's case, there is probably no such breach because neither a marital nor a family relationship, standing alone, is generally regarded as creating a fiduciary-type obligation of confidentiality. Thus, Harold's use of the information would not breach any duty and no liability would attach as a result of his trade (see *United States v Chestman*, 947 F 2d 55 at 566 (2d Cir) (en banc), *cert denied* 112 S Ct 1759 (1992)). Note, however, that fiduciary-like obligations may be imposed on Tom if the family members had frequently shared business-related information amongst one another.

Note that Harold's trading is not prohibited based on standard tipper/tippee analysis, see 2.2.4, since Imelda's provision of information to Tom was not improper (ie, not done for Imelda's personal benefit).

Sigmund, however, could be found to have violated insider trading laws. A psychiatrist-patient relationship has been held to give rise to a fiduciary-type obligation of confidentiality on the part of the psychiatrist (see *United States v Willis*, 737 F Supp 269 (SDNY 1990)). Although Sigmund may argue that he cannot be treated as having breached a duty in the absence of any injury to Tom, US courts have been willing to hold up even mild injuries as evidence of a breach of fiduciary or similar duty. Tom may have to incur extra expense in obtaining the services of a new psychiatrist, which could constitute a pecuniary injury. Additionally, the publicity surrounding the case may have made many of Tom's friends aware that he is being treated by a psychiatrist, which may constitute an injury to Tom's reputation.

2.2.3.2.3 Private plaintiff context

The misappropriation theory was originally held to be unavailable to private plaintiffs bringing suit against persons who traded while in possession of misappropriated information. In light of the *Chiarella* decision, the US courts that had accepted the misappropriation theory took the view that even though a breach of a fiduciary or other special relationship owed to a non-insider's employer could be the basis for a civil or criminal r10b-5 proceeding by the government, the breach of such a duty could not in turn create a duty of disclosure in favour of an otherwise unrelated trading counterparty (see *Moss v Stanley*, 719 F 2d 5 (2d Cir 1983), *cert denied* 465 US 1025 (1984)). Since a non-insider owes no disclosure duty to a buyer or seller of securities, the fact that information might have been misappropriated could not create such a duty and therefore the non-insider could not be sued by those trading at the same time he or she was buying or selling securities.

The Congress, however, viewed the denial of a private right of action in such circumstances as unfair. In response, the Congress enacted s 20A of the Exchange Act as part of the Insider Trading and Securities Enforcement Act 1988 ('ITSFEA'). Section 20A created a remedy for a private plaintiff who loses money while contemporaneously trading with a person who violates the Exchange Act by engaging in securities transactions while in possession of material non-public information. Thus, to the extent that trading on 'misappropriated' information is a violation of the Exchange Act, a question which may ultimately have to be resolved by the US Supreme Court, a private right of action exists.

2.2.3.2.4 Information not company specific

In some situations, information is obtained which, although not directly related to a given company, is material in relation to the company none the less. For instance, information regarding an impending rate increase by the US Federal Reserve might have a disproportionate impact on lending institutions. An employee of the Federal Reserve in possession of such information would only be liable for trading in the stock of lending institutions based on the misappropriation theory, since such an employee would owe no duty to the lending institutions under more traditional insider trading analysis.

Problem Area 3

Mary is a reporter for *The Daily Blatt*, a well-respected newspaper with extensive coverage of the markets in the US and abroad. As part of her duties, Mary writes, for publication each Tuesday, the *Blatt*'s 'Word on Wall Street' column. Although the information contained in the column is publicly available, the market's perception of the *Blatt* as a highly informed and reliable publication frequently results in an increase in the share price of companies which are featured in a positive light in the column. Sensitive to the impact of its column on trading and share prices, the *Blatt* has a policy which prohibits employees from trading in securities of companies that will be featured in the column. On a number of occasions, in violation of *Blatt* policy, Mary purchases shares in a company which will be favourably depicted in a forthcoming edition of the *Blatt*. In an enforcement proceeding brought by the SEC, Mary argues that she cannot have violated US insider trading law, even under the misappropriation theory, because, unlike the printshop employees in *Chiarella* and *Materia*, neither she nor the *Blatt*

owed any duty to the companies featured in the column or to the shareholders of such companies.

Mary may have violated US insider trading laws. Under the misappropriation theory of insider trading, which has been accepted in several (but not
all) of the US judicial circuits, a person violates r10b-5 by misappropriating
material non-public information in breach of a fiduciary or similar relationship of trust and confidence and engaging in securities transactions while
knowingly in possession of such information. By violating *Blatt* policy regarding trading in companies to be featured in the column, Mary has arguably
injured the paper in a number of ways. First, she has injured the *Blatt's* reputation as an impartial voice in the world of financial journalism. Second, she
has taken intellectual property that belongs to the *Blatt*. The breach of duty
owed to her employer is probably sufficient to support an insider trading
charge based on misappropriation in a federal judicial circuit that accepts the
theory. On essentially identical facts, the US Second Circuit affirmed the
conviction of a reporter for the Wall Street Journal (see *Carpenter v United
States*, 791 F 2d 1024 (2d Cir 1986), *affd* 484 US 19 (1987)).

Mary's argument, however, points up a weakness in the misappropriation
theory when applied to persons who trade in the shares of a company not
associated with the trader's employer. What would happen if the *Blatt* had
no policy against trading by employees or even encouraged such trading as
creating an incentive for reporters? Mary would not have breached a duty
and her trading would not be prohibited. Thus, even in jurisdictions that
accept the misappropriation theory, its availability may depend to a large
extent on the policies of entities which have no relationship with the traded
corporation.

2.2.4 Tippers and tippees

Another area in which insider trading liability may attach, and another area of
tension between the views of the SEC and the US Supreme Court, is where non-
insiders are 'tipped' to material non-public information by insiders and others with
access to inside information. The SEC has aggressively pressed enforcement actions
against people who pass such information to others, referred to as 'tippers,' and
the recipients of such information, referred to as 'tippees'. The US Supreme Court,
however, has declined to require that every tippee, regardless of the circumstances
surrounding his or her receipt of inside information, abstain or disclose. The duty
attaches only where the source of such information is subject to that duty and the
tippee is aware that the tipper is breaching a duty in making the tip.

2.2.4.1 Tipper liability

Under US law, a person who passes on material non-public information may be
liable for violating r10b-5 even if he or she does not personally trade on the

information. The US Supreme Court has held that such liability exists where inside information is *improperly* made available to another person and such other person trades on the information. The court has indicated that the question of whether information is improperly provided depends upon the purpose of the insider's disclosure. If the disclosure is made for corporate purposes, and not for the tipper's 'direct or indirect personal benefit', no liability under r10b-5 can attach. However, where the disclosure is made for the insider's personal benefit, or where a combination of legitimate corporate purpose and personal benefit are involved, the passing of inside information can result in liability.

According to the Supreme Court, an insider can receive a 'personal benefit' not only where he or she receives money (eg a portion of a tippee's profits or losses avoided), but where the insider gains a 'reputational benefit that will translate into future earnings'. Likewise, a personal benefit accrues to the insider where the passing of information operates as a 'gift' from the insider to another person; the 'tip and trade resemble trading by the insider himself followed by a gift of the profits to the recipient': *SEC v Dirks*, 463 US 646, 664 (1983). Presumably, an insider could receive such a benefit even where the material information in such person's possession is not disclosed to the tippee (ie where the insider merely urges another person to buy or sell the company's shares and such person knows generally of the insider's access to material information).

Some uncertainty surrounds the question of whether a tippee must actually trade in order for liability to attach to the tipper. Since r10b-5 prohibits fraud in connection with the 'purchase or sale' of a security, the better view is that if no purchase or sale has occurred, there can be no tipper liability. In light of the narrow view that the US Supreme Court has adopted regarding the application of r10b-5 in other insider trading contexts, it seems unlikely that the court would uphold a finding that r10b-5 was violated where no purchase or sale occurred. However, it should be noted that, in the past, the SEC has taken the view that a tipper is liable whether or not his tippee actually trades, assuming it was reasonably foreseeable at the time the information was provided that the tippee would trade. The SEC has incorporated this approach into r14e-3, which it promulgated to prohibit insider trading in the tender offer context. Under r14e-3, the communication of inside information is prohibited where it is reasonably foreseeable that the communication is likely to result in a violation of the rule. However, r14e-3 was intended to fill certain perceived gaps in the law in the aftermath of the *Chiarella* decision. It remains to be seen whether, under the current state of the law, tipper liability would attach under r10b-5 where no tippee trades.

Regardless of the disposition of the 'non-trading tippee' issue, even under the current state of the law it seems clear that there need not be a *violation* of r10b-5 by a tippee for liability to attach to the tipper. For instance, where the tippee trades without knowing that the information in his possession is material non-public information, the tippee is not liable. However, because the 'purchase or sale' of a security element of r10b-5 is satisfied by the tippee's transaction, the tipper may be liable.

2.2.4.2 Tippee liability

A tippee is subject to a derivative 'abstain or disclose' duty when knowingly in possession of material non-public information which (1) the tipper has acted improperly in passing to the tippee (ie, in breach of a fiduciary or similar duty) and (2) the tippee knows or should know was passed in violation of such a duty. Both elements must be satisfied before the tippee can be held liable.

2.2.4.2.1 Fiduciary breach by a tipper

The US Supreme Court has taken the view in the r10b-5 context that an insider breaches his or her fiduciary duty by passing material non-public information only where the insider receives a direct or indirect 'personal benefit' as a result of his or her disclosure. This view was first enunciated in the case of *Dirks v SEC*.

Dirks is one of two cases (the other being *Chiarella*) in which the Supreme Court has significantly limited the SEC's use of r10b-5 in the insider trading context. In *Dirks*, a company employee provided an investment analyst with material non-public information in order to expose fraudulent business practices by his employer. Although the analyst did not trade on the information, he mentioned it to several others who sold their holdings in the company, avoiding losses they would have otherwise suffered when the fraud was publicly exposed. The SEC determined that the analyst and his tippees had violated r10b-5.

The US Supreme Court reversed the SEC's finding, rejecting the view that the analyst, simply by virtue of having been given the information, 'inherited' the insider's duty to abstain or disclose. In so doing, the court rejected an argument similar to the one the SEC had put forward in *Chiarella*; namely that the mere possession of information, regardless of source, may create a duty to abstain from trading or disclose the information. As in *Chiarella*, the court saw a need to find a nexus between the information in the tippee's possession and a breach of duty on the part of the insider. As discussed above, the court held that only information passed for the tipper's, rather than the corporation's, benefit creates a duty on the part of the recipient to abstain or disclose. The fact that the analyst may have received a 'personal benefit' by virtue of having passed on the information is irrelevant if the original source of the information did not act improperly. Because the employee in *Dirks* provided the information in order to expose the fraud (and thus had acted for the company's benefit and not for any personal benefit), there had been no breach of fiduciary duty and thus no derivative r10b-5 liability could attach to the analyst (or to those who traded based on the information he provided them).

Problem Area 4

Linda is the chief executive officer of Holodyne Inc, a publicly-traded company involved in developing 'virtual reality' technology for home use. Holodyne has only recently become a public company and Linda is not familiar with the ways of financial analysts following companies such as Holodyne. On one occasion, she inadvertently angered analysts by refusing to discuss the company's limited sales forecasts with them.

Linda learns that some of Holodyne's newest technology is going to be licensed by and incorporated into a new product by Big Games Inc, one of the leading game manufacturers in the world. Linda calls two analysts, Hal and Mal, to inform them of the news. Linda sees herself as accomplishing two tasks with this call. First, she has informed the market of the news, which she assumes will be quickly disseminated once Hal and Mal began advising their clients of the development. Second, she has taken steps to improve relations with the two analysts, since being first to market with the news will certainly be a feather in the caps of Hal and Mal. Although Hal and Mal do spread the news, resulting in it being widely disseminated within 48 hours, each first purchases shares of Holodyne on behalf of several of his clients, as Linda assumed they would. The SEC brings an enforcement action against Linda, alleging that she 'tipped' Hal and Mal to material non-public information in violation of r10b-5.

Since *Dirks*, the SEC has taken an especially broad view of the concept of 'reputational benefit', apparently satisfied that almost any enhancement of one's reputation will eventually 'translate into future earnings' and thus constitute a personal benefit. In Linda's case, the SEC would probably view her provision of information as an effort to polish a poor reputation with securities analysts which might otherwise have threatened her earning power. Thus, the passing of the information would constitute a violation. The SEC successfully prosecuted a senior executive on similar facts in *SEC v Stevens*, 91 Civ 1869 (CSH), Litigation Release No 12,813 (1991).

Since Linda passed the information 'improperly', Hal and Mal's trading would be illegal *if* they knew that Linda's tip was given in violation of her fiduciary duty (ie for her personal benefit as opposed to purely for the corporation's benefit). The analysts in the *Stevens* case were not prosecuted.

It should be noted that the SEC would almost certainly premise its action against Linda on the notion that Linda's conduct, standing alone, constituted a violation of r10b-5, rather than alleging that Linda 'aided and abetted' a violation of the rule by Hal and Mal. A recent US Supreme Court decision, *Central Bank of Denver, NA v First Interstate Bank of Denver, NA*, 114 S Ct 1439 (1994), held that private plaintiffs could not bring civil suits alleging that the defendant aided and abetted another person's violation of r10b-5. However, the decision was so broadly worded as to put into significant doubt the

SEC's ability to pursue civil enforcement actions based on aiding and abetting. Note, however, that aiding and abetting remains a viable charge in a criminal case brought by the US Department of Justice due to the explicit statutory prohibition against aiding and abetting criminal conduct found in s 2 of ch 18 of the United States Code.

The SEC's expansive view of personal benefit makes it difficult for issuers and their insiders to determine when information can appropriately be provided to financial analysts without disclosing such information through general public announcements. Although the SEC and the US courts have acknowledged that analysts and other market professionals play an important role in ferreting out and disseminating information regarding issuers and their securities, the SEC's aggressive prosecutions of both insiders and analysts requires insiders to be extremely cautious in providing information to analysts. As a rule, material information regarding a company should be released through general channels only and should not be provided to analysts on a selective basis.

A weakness in the US approach is that liability for a tippee's trading depends upon the motive of the tipper who originally provided the information. Where a corporate insider provides a piece of material information to an analyst believing his/her actions to be solely for the corporation's benefit, the analyst can *trade* on the information without incurring liability. An alternative to this approach can be found in the insider trading law of England. There liability attaches if the recipient knows he/she is receiving price-sensitive, non-public information from an insider, regardless of the motivation of the person providing such information.

2.2.4.2.2 Tippee's knowledge

The second prong of the tippee liability test is that the tippee must have known or had reason to know of the tipper's breach of fiduciary duty. Obviously, where there is a *quid pro quo* for the information (eg the tippee is expected to share profits with the tipper, reciprocate with information regarding his or her own company or make available a favourable business deal for the tipper), the knowledge prong is easily established; the tippee clearly knows that the tipper will be receiving a personal benefit.

A more difficult question is presented where there is no *quid pro quo* for the information provided (eg where the insider's personal benefit is the pleasure he or she has received in having made a 'gift' of such information). However, US courts have permitted fact-finders to draw inferences regarding knowledge based on objective factors. Among them are, first, the significance of the information passed to the tippee. The more important the information, the more likely that the tippee knew the tipper was passing the information in violation of the tipper's duty to the company. Second, the level of sophistication of the tippee may also play a role in fact-finding. The passing of information to a shrewd market player may satisfy the knowledge prong notwithstanding the fact that an unsophisticated investor might not have recognised that the same information was significant.

Problem Area 5

Jeremiah is the president of Fastener Co, a publicly-traded company which manufactures and sells metal fasteners for use in aircraft. Fastener Co enters into a sale contract with an aircraft manufacturer that will result in a four-fold increase in its sales for the year. By agreement with the purchaser, the existence of the contract is to be kept secret until the manufacturer unveils a prototype of the new product in which Fastener Co's products will be used.

Before the prototype is unveiled, Jeremiah calls Bill, the contractor who is remodelling the kitchen of Jeremiah's home. Jeremiah tells Bill of the impending announcement and urges him to buy shares in Fastener Co. Bill agrees to reduce his fees for the work on Jeremiah's kitchen in exchange for the information. Next Jeremiah calls Alexandria, a stock broker and a close personal friend, and tells her of the contract. Meanwhile, unbeknownst to Jeremiah, his conversations have been overheard in part by Eve, who is using the pay phone next to his. Although Jeremiah refrains from trading, Bill, Alexandria and Eve all purchase shares of Fastener Co and realise profits when the prototype is unveiled and the existence of the contract made public.

Jeremiah has violated the insider trading laws by providing material non-public information to Bill and Alexandria. By tipping Bill, Jeremiah is receiving a pecuniary benefit, albeit in the shape of debt reduction. By tipping Alexandria, he is getting a more subtle but still actionable personal benefit since the tip to Alexandria acts, in effect, as a gift of whatever profits she realises. The US Supreme Court has indicated that a tip given as a 'gift' creates a personal benefit for the tipper. Thus, regardless of the fact that he did not trade, in each instance, Jeremiah could be prosecuted as a tipper since each of his tips gave him a personal benefit and resulted in a purchase of securities. Note that if the US Department of Justice elected to bring criminal charges against Jeremiah, he could also be prosecuted for aiding and abetting a violation of the law.

Bill, as a tippee, has violated the insider trading laws. The rule is that tippee liability exists where the tipper has acted improperly in passing material non-public information to the tippee (ie to obtain a personal benefit) and the tippee knows or should know that the information was improperly passed. Here, Jeremiah received a personal benefit for providing the corporate information to Bill. Furthermore, Bill was clearly aware that Jeremiah was receiving such a benefit (and thus had at least constructive knowledge of the fact that Jeremiah was breaching a fiduciary duty).

Alexandria, as a tippee, has violated the insider trading laws. Under the circumstances, it is clear that Alexandria knew or should have known that Jeremiah was breaching a fiduciary duty to the company. First, Alexandria is a sophisticated market player. Second, she was aware of Jeremiah's position at Fastener Co.

Whether Eve has violated the insider trading laws depends on how much she has been able to glean from Jeremiah's conversations. Jeremiah has clearly breached his fiduciary duty in providing the information. The important question is whether Eve is aware that he has done so. If, for instance, Eve overheard Jeremiah tell Bill that 'As a director of Fastener Co, I could be in big trouble for telling you this . . .' then she would be on notice that the information is the result of a breach of duty. To the extent that Eve does not know of Jeremiah's position and hears only that Fastener Co is about to announce a sizeable contract, the tip is more akin to a rumour and liability is unlikely to attach.

It bears mention that had Eve overheard a conversation in which news of the contract was being discussed properly (ie not in connection with an improper tip), no liability would attach even if she knew the speaker's position and was aware that the information was non-public. In *SEC v Switzer*, 590 F Supp 756 (WD Okla 1984), the defendant was acquitted of insider trading based on a discussion he had overheard, between a company director and the director's wife, while seated in a public place.

2.2.4.3 Sub-tippees

If a tippee in turn passes information and the recipient knows or reasonably should know that such information originated with an insider in breach of a fiduciary duty, the 'sub-tippee' is quite likely to be liable if he or she trades upon the information. However, to the extent that the nature and source of inside information becomes less distinct as it travels down the sub-tippee chain, it becomes less likely that insider liability will attach to the more remote sub-tippees. For instance, no insider trading liability attaches to a person who trades based solely on 'rumours', (eg the suggestion by a person unaffiliated with a company that its stock is a 'good buy' or that material information is about to be released regarding such company).

Recent enforcement actions by the SEC point up both the agency's vigilance in pursuing sub-tippees and the circumstances under which even sub-tippees far from the original source of insider information can be liable. In one case, involving the acquisition of the 'Motel 6' hotel chain, the SEC was able to trace the passing of material non-public information, which originated with an officer of the target company, to a seventh generation sub-tippee. The SEC's ability to investigate such a case effectively is aided by the eagerness of those incriminated to implicate others in an effort to gain lenient treatment. Moreover, because tippees usually wish to ascertain that the tip they are receiving is genuine, frequently by pressing to learn the original source of the information and how the information came into their tipper's hands, it is generally quite easy for the SEC to establish that the tippee knew or should have known that the information was passed in violation of a fiduciary duty.

2.3 'MATERIAL NON-PUBLIC INFORMATION'/TRADING

As discussed above, the basic rule of US insider trading law is that certain individuals who are knowingly in possession of material non-public information relating to a company must disclose such information prior to trading in the company's securities. This section describes what is meant by 'material non-public information' and discusses the scope of the restriction on trading while in possession of such information.

2.3.1 Material information

Information is considered 'material' for purposes of US securities' laws if there is 'a substantial likelihood' that the disclosure of the information would be 'viewed by the reasonable investor as having significantly altered the "total mix" of information made available': *TSC Industries Inc v Northway*, 426 US 438 (1976); *Basic Inc v Levinson*, 485 US 224, 232 (1988). Although the US Supreme Court has not defined materiality in the insider trading context, the appropriate enquiry would likely be whether there is a substantial likelihood that the reasonable investor would consider the information important in making an investment decision or whether there is a substantial likelihood that the information would result in a significant change in the price of the security. Obviously, where a sharp increase or decrease in stock price follows a company announcement, there will be a strong presumption that the information contained in the announcement was 'material.'

The materiality assessment is made in light of all other publicly available information. For example, assume that Director Jones tells a friend that the Smith Co, net value $500 million, has just purchased, for $1 million, a working mine capable of producing 1000 tons of Factor X per year. In the absence of other information, the reasonable investor would be unlikely to consider the information important in making an investment decision regarding Smith Co stock. If, however, Factor X can be converted through a simple process into Factor Y, a key component in Smith Co's main product line, and the company's inability to obtain steady supplies of Factor Y has resulted in lost sales in recent months, the purchase of the mine and a ready supply of Factor X is likely to be material.

The common-law development of a materiality standard should be contrasted with the law of other countries. In England, for instance, the functional equivalent of materiality is a determination of whether the information in question was 'price-sensitive'. For practical purposes in the US, however, price sensitivity is a key concern as well, since insider trading prosecutions are generally only brought where there is a movement in stock price after information became public.

2.3.1.1 Probability and magnitude analysis

Information can be considered material even though it suggests only some level of probability of a certain event occurring. In the seminal insider trading case *SEC v Texas Gulf Sulphur Co*, the appeals court overturned a finding that a favourable drilling report from a mineral field was not material. The lower court had ruled that information regarding the uncommonly strong tests results was 'too remote' to have any significant impact on the company's securities. The appellate court reversed, stating that the materiality of information regarding a specific event depends 'upon a balancing of both the indicated *probability* that the event will occur and the anticipated *magnitude* of the event in light of the totality of the company . . .' (emphasis added). Under the circumstances, the court ruled, knowledge of the possibility of a major mineral strike would have been important to a reasonable investor.

It is typically the case, as it was in *Texas Gulf Sulphur*, that the defendant's claims of immateriality of information are undercut by the fact that the defendant immediately issued buy or sell orders upon obtaining the information.

2.3.2 Non-public information

Information is considered non-public until the relevant markets have had an opportunity to fully 'digest' the information. In a heavily traded issue, this is usually said to occur once the price of the company's stock has stabilised after the initial disclosure of the information.

There is some uncertainty as to whether information must have been made available to all corners of the market in order to be regarded as having become 'public'. Taking their cue from the efficient capital markets hypothesis, some US courts have suggested that, assuming a highly efficient market for a company's shares, the issue would not be 'the number of people who possess [the information] but whether their trading has caused the information to be fully impounded into the price' of the shares: *United States v Libera*, 989 F 2d 596, 601 (2d Cir 1993). The SEC has espoused a contary view, suggesting in *Re Faberge Inc*, 45 SEC 249, 256 (1973), that information must be disclosed 'by a public release through the appropriate public medium' in order to become 'public'. In *SEC v MacDonald*, 568 F Supp 111 (DRI 1983), *affd* 725 F 2d 9 (1st Cir 1984), the court held that the price of a thinly-traded company's stock did not stabilise until several days after a *Wall Street Journal* article appeared, notwithstanding the fact that the press release on which the *Journal*'s story was based had been released by the company over two weeks earlier.

In the tender offer context, r14e-3 under the Exchange Act requires that any person subject to the rule's prohibitions must disclose any material information in his or her possession, and the source of such information, to the public through a 'press release or otherwise' and that such disclosure must be made 'a reasonable time' before such a person can trade.

Problem Area 6

Marina and Thomas are independent, non-executive directors of Trident Corp, a company principally involved in the production of pet food, whose stock price has been depressed by well-publicised financial problems. Marina, a marine geologist and environmental expert, sits on the board's environmental committee. Thomas, an accountant, sits on the audit committee. As the result of research she is conducting with a group of friends in her spare time, Marina determines that large oil deposits exist beneath the sea beds along a stretch of the local coast. One Sunday, Marina sees two boats equipped with sampling gear heading towards the oil-rich stretch. She learns from the port register that both vessels are leased to Petro Co, a small subsidiary of Trident Corp. Later that same day, at an emergency meeting of the Trident Corp audit committee, Thomas learns that the results of offshore testing by Petro Co have been completed and that a major oil find is imminent. The committee is told that the company's financial woes will soon be 'a thing of the past'. The following morning, Marina and her friends purchase shares in Trident, as does Thomas. A few weeks later, Trident's Petro Co subsidiary announces a major new offshore oil find and Trident's shares triple in value.

Each of Marina's and Thomas's information is 'material' for purposes of the US insider trading laws. The standard is whether a reasonable investor would find the information important in making an investment decision regarding Trident. Thomas knows for certain that oil has been found. The sharp increase in Trident's share prices after the announcement amply demonstrates that a 'reasonable investor' would find this information important. Marina has information suggesting a level of probability regarding an oil find. Under US law, information can be considered material even though it suggests only a probability of an event occurring.

The information Marina has obtained, however, would not be viewed as 'non-public' for purposes of the US insider trading laws. US law views independent research as important to the efficient operation of the capital markets and seeks to encourage such activity. Thus, information obtained by independent means is not regarded as falling under the category of 'non-public' information for purposes of insider trading law. Marina, therefore, has no liability for having traded without disclosing the information in her possession. Note, however, that most corporations have some requirement that dealings in shares by insiders be approved prior to execution. Under the circumstances described here, Marina would probably not have been permitted to buy shares.

The information Thomas has obtained, on the other hand, *would* be viewed as non-public. Thomas has only obtained the information as a result of his fiduciary relationship with Trident Corp and not as the result of any independent investigation. Since he was in possession of material, non-public information, Thomas had a duty to the shareholders of Trident from whom he purchased his shares to either disclose the information or abstain from trading. Thus, Thomas is liable for insider trading.

Thomas might try to argue that the information became public by virtue of having been obtained by Marina and her friends. However, under US law, information is not regarded as becoming public until it has been digested by the markets. Thomas's argument would likely fail since the *market* did not respond at the point Marina and her friends became aware of the information but did respond when Petro Co's announcement was made.

2.3.3 Trading

Unlike the insider trading laws of some European countries, the US laws contain no requirement that securities be traded or listed on an exchange in order to subject an insider trader in such securities to liability. The judicial interpretations of the relevant insider trading statutes have not been in complete accord as to the specific types of securities to which the insider trading prohibitions apply. While the prohibitions are clearly applicable to equity securities of all varieties, the applicability of the insider trading laws to debt securities and options is less certain and merits separate discussion.

2.3.3.1 Debt securities

There has been considerable uncertainty regarding the application of the US insider trading laws to persons dealing in debt securities. The basic 'abstain or disclose' rule is, as described above, premised largely on the fiduciary duty an insider owes to a company and its shareholders. Under US corporate law, the duty that is owed to bondholders and other creditors is a contractual duty rather than a fiduciary one. Thus, more than one court has held the basic prohibition against insider trading inapplicable where trading in debt securities is alleged. However, several alternative bases on which insider trading liability has been premised in other situations, notably the misappropriation theory discussed in 2.2.3.2 and r14e-3 under the Exchange Act, are generally viewed as successfully closing this conceptual gap in the law.

2.3.3.2 Options

Prior to the enactment of s 20(d) of the Exchange Act, the SEC's ability to act successfully against insider traders in options was hampered by the fact that an

...er's counterparty in an option transaction is not a shareholder of the company whose shares underlie the option. In light of the *Chiarella* and *Dirks* decisions, which had held that a r10b-5 action could only be premised on a breach of a fiduciary or similar duty, some US courts, seeing no fiduciary or similar duty owed by an insider to his or her option counterparty (who is not a shareholder of the company), declined to find an 'abstain or disclose' duty on the part of insiders involved in such transactions. The US Congress decided to act, however, recognising that such an approach would leave insiders free to profit on the options market—an increasingly important part of the US capital markets: it adopted s 20(d) of the Exchange Act as part of ITSFEA. Section 20(d) closed the 'options gap' in the US insider trading law by making it illegal to trade in options (including indexed options) where trading in the securities underlying such options while in possession of material non-public information would violate any other provision of the Exchange Act, including r10b-5.

2.4 SCIENTER

Under US law, for an individual to be prosecuted for fraud, there must be some showing of scienter (ie intent to defraud).

As discussed more fully in 2.1, the SEC has taken the view that trading or tipping while 'knowingly in possession' of material non-public information satisfies the scienter requirement. No US court has been squarely faced with the question of whether the *knowingly in possession* standard is compatible with accepted concepts of scienter. However, one US circuit court has suggested that it would accept 'knowingly in possession' as meeting the scienter requirement under r10b-5 (see *United States v Teicher*, 987 F 2d 112 at 120–121) (2d Cir), *cert denied* 114 S Ct 467 (1993).

2.4.1 'Chinese Wall' procedures

The SEC's endorsement of a 'knowing possession' standard raises serious concerns for many financial institutions. For instance, a diversified investment banking firm may be considered a temporary insider of a client (eg in connection with the client's proposed acquisition of another company). At the same time, the investment bank's asset management team may be taking positions or advising others to take positions in the client's or the target company's securities. A strict application of the 'knowing possession' standard could be argued to subject the firm to insider trading liability based on the actions of the asset management team, since they were trading while the firm was knowingly in possession of material non-public information.

One solution to this problem is to erect a so-called 'Chinese Wall' between the group advising the client on its acquisition and the asset management group. A Chinese Wall is a set of procedures designed to restrict the flow of inside information within a company. Chinese Wall procedures can include restricted interdepartmental communication (including, if necessary, separate physical work areas and facilities), the use of project code words, and strict control of drafts and other documentation relating to client activities.

The SEC has recognised that aggressive application of insider trading laws may inhibit the activities of financial institutions and has endorsed the use of Chinese Walls as a means of preventing research and trading departments from becoming tainted by material non-public information possessed by other departments within the institutions. Rule 14e-3 under the Exchange Act, which incorporates the 'knowing possession' standard in its prohibition of insider trading in the tender offer context, creates a safe harbour for transactions executed on behalf of a company where (a) the person making the transaction decision was not in possession of inside information and (b) the company had implemented 'One or a combination of policies and procedures' to ensure that the decision-maker does not violate the rule; these procedures can include the use of a Chinese Wall.

Chinese Wall procedures may also be utilised by an institutional investor which holds debt in a bankrupt entity and which, as a creditor of the bankrupt, serves on the creditors' committee in connection with the bankruptcy proceeding. In such a situation, the institution may be privy to material non-public information. By using Chinese Wall procedures, the trading department of such an institution has no access to information coming out of the creditors' committee and can continue to trade in the debtor's securities in the normal course of its business. Such arrangements have been approved by US bankruptcy courts (see, eg *Re Federated Department Stores Inc*, No 1-90-00130 (Bankr SD Ohio, 1991)).

2.4.2 Other procedures

Financial institutions may also adopt self-policing procedures intended to prevent insider trading. These procedures include the maintenance of 'watch lists' and 'restricted lists'. These are lists containing the names of issuers which are either clients of the institution or which are or may become involved in transactions with such clients. When such a firm institutes a restricted list policy, it curtails all activities throughout the firm with respect to the securities of issuers on the list. This typically occurs once information regarding a client's activities becomes (or is about to become) known to the entire institution. When such a firm institutes a watch list policy, common where Chinese Wall procedures are in effect with respect to a client, it typically monitors the activities of its various divisions with respect to issuers on the list and investigates any unusual trading in such issuers' securities.

The US Congress has expanded insider trading liability to force financial and securities institutions to be more vigilant in such self-policing efforts. As part of ITSFEA, the Congress adopted s 15(f) of the Exchange Act which requires broker-dealers to 'establish, maintain, and enforce written policies and procedures reasonably designed . . . to prevent the misuse of material non-public information.' A

US registered broker-dealer which fails to maintain such policies and procedures can face civil penalties if the lack of such policies and procedures substantially contributes to the occurrence of insider trading. A similar rule applies to investment advisers registered under the US Investment Advisers Act 1940.

The New York Stock Exchange, the National Association of Securities Dealers and the SEC have all established certain minimally acceptable policies and procedures in this respect.

3 SPECIALISED STATUTES

In addition to encouraging the use of Chinese Wall procedures as described above, the SEC and the Congress have, on a number of occasions, sought to remedy gaps in the insider trading law. Frequently, these are gaps that have been revealed by—or, depending on one's perspective, caused by—the decisions of the US federal courts.

3.1 RULE 14E-3

Rule 14e-3, which deals with insider trading in the context of a tender offer, was promulgated by the SEC under s 14 of the Exchange Act, partially in response to the US Supreme Court's decision in the *Chiarella* case, which is discussed in 2.2.3.1. After *Chiarella*, the SEC realised that specialised rules would be necessary in the context of a tender offer since neither a tender offer bidder nor any of the bidder's tippees owe a duty to the target company or its shareholders.

In contrast to much of the US law regarding insider trading, r14e-3 sets out fairly specific prohibitions. Under the rule, if substantial steps have been taken toward the commencement of a tender offer, it is a violation of s 14 of the Exchange Act for any person (other than the bidder or a person acting on the bidder's behalf) who possesses material non-public information, which such person knows or has reason to know is non-public and which such person knows or has reason to know has been acquired from the target or the bidder (or any agent of either), to trade in the target's stock without disclosing the information possessed. Once a tender offer has actually been commenced, special rules, including disclosure requirements, apply to the actions of the bidder. However, prior to that point, r14e-3's prohibitions do not prevent a potential acquiror (or a person authorised to act on behalf of a potential acquiror) from purchasing shares without disclosure.

Rule 14e-3 is considerably more restrictive than the general insider trading law that has developed under r10b-5. For instance, liability can exist under r14e-3 without a showing that a fiduciary or similar relationship existed or was breached. Furthermore, the rule adopts the 'knowing possession' standard of scienter, the appropriateness of which has not yet been endorsed by the US courts in the r10b-5 context. On the other hand, r14e-3 permits a company to establish a defence based on the establishment of a Chinese Wall arrangement.

Rule 14e-3 casts a wide net where tippers are concerned, making it a violation of s 14 of the Exchange Act for any person who obtains material non-public information, directly or indirectly, from a bidder or target (or the agent of either) to communicate such information to another person under circumstances in which 'it is reasonably foreseeable that such communication is likely to result in a violation' of the rule's trading restrictions.

The SEC frequently brings enforcement actions based on violations of both r10b-5 and r14e-3. Furthermore, r14e-3, like r10b-5, has been interpreted to provide a right of action for private litigants injured as the result of insider trading.

It should be noted that r14e-3 applies only in the context of a tender offer and not in the context of a standard merger or consolidation. Actions brought in respect of insider trading in connection with a merger or consolidation are typically brought under r10b-5.

3.2 ITSFEA

The US Congress also responded to perceived inadequacies in the existing insider trading scheme by passing the Insider Trading and Securities Enforcement Act 1988 ('ITSFEA'). ITSFEA enabled the SEC to seek significant penalties against officers, managers and other supervisory personnel in certain situations in which such persons knew there was a likelihood (or recklessly disregarded the likelihood) that a subordinate would trade on material non-public information gleaned as a result of employment and such trading occurred.

ITSFEA created s 20A of the Exchange Act, which provides a private right of action for individuals who traded *contemporaneously* with insider traders. See 4.2.2.1.

ITSFEA also overturned case law to permit a private litigant to whom no fiduciary duty was owed by an insider trader to rely on the misappropriation theory when suing under r10b-5. See discussion in 2.2.3.2.3.

Additionally, ITSFEA, partially in an effort to stem the flow of 'strike suits' (ie suits of questionable merit brought against corporations and their insiders in an effort to coerce a settlement with the threat of protracted litigation), limited the recovery to which a private litigant alleging losses due to contemporaneous trading with insiders is entitled.

4 PRIVATE RIGHT OF ACTION

Under certain circumstances, the US insider trading laws permit a private individual to bring a civil action against an insider trader (either in the individual's own name or on behalf of a corporation in which the individual owns shares). This section discusses the differences which exist between the ability of individuals on the one hand, and the government, acting in either a civil enforcement or criminal proceeding capacity, on the other, to bring insider trading actions.

4.1 STANDING TO SUE

The US courts have interpreted r10b-5 to permit suits by private plaintiffs against persons who engage in insider trading. The courts have also afforded standing for private litigants under r14e-3 under the Exchange Act, which contains special insider trading restrictions in a tender offer context. In addition, s 20A of the Exchange Act creates an express private right of action for persons trading contemporaneously with insider traders.

4.2 CAUSATION

Generally speaking, in order to bring a private claim under US insider trading law, a plaintiff must allege that he or she (or the corporation on behalf of which suit is brought) suffered injury due to the insider trading of the defendant.

4.2.1 Purchase or sale

The prohibitions of r10b-5 operate 'in connection with the purchase or sale of [a] security'. A private plaintiff bringing a claim under r10b-5 must establish, therefore, that he or she either purchased or sold securities and suffered an injury as a result thereof. The plaintiff cannot support such a claim by alleging that he or she lost money because they decided not to purchase or sell securities: *Blue Chip Stamps v Manor Drug Stores*, 421 US 723, 731 (1975).

4.2.2 Privity

In the modern marketplace, securities transactions take place on an impersonal, anonymous basis. Sellers do not know the identities of their buyers and vice versa. This lack of identifiable privity between counterparties presents a theoretical stumbling block to the plaintiff who wishes to establish that the defendant's insider trading caused the plaintiff's injury.

Private plaintiffs in the US and the US courts, have responded creatively to this theoretical problem. Under US law, a plaintiff can allege injury based on the defendant's trading where the plaintiff can establish that both parties traded in the securities in question 'contemporaneously' (see eg *Wilson v Comtech Telecommunications Corp*, 648 F 2d 88 (2d Cir 1981)). As described in 3.2, the availability of this approach for private litigants was codified in s 20A of the Exchange Act as part of ITSFEA.

4.2.2.1 'Contemporaneously'

In keeping with the basic approach of the US securities fraud laws, s 20A of the Exchange Act leaves the courts to define 'contemporaneously'. The current view is that, in a widely traded security, contemporaneous trading by a plaintiff is trading that takes place within a few days of the insider's trading activities. At least one court has indicated that trading would have to take place within one day to be contemporaneous. The definition is likely to continue to evolve as more courts consider the question.

4.2.3 Aiding and abetting

A private plaintiff cannot sue a non-trading tipper under r10b-5. The most likely avenue for such a suit, a claim that the tipper 'aided and abetted' a violation of r10b-5, was recently foreclosed by the US Supreme Court. The court held that there is no private right of action for aiding and abetting such a violation (see *Central Bank of Denver*, 114 S Ct at 1448).

5 CONSEQUENCES OF INSIDER TRADING

5.1 CIVIL PENALTIES

Under s21A of the Exchange Act, the SEC can bring a civil action for injunction and 'disgorgement' of profit gained (or loss avoided) against persons who communicate or trade while knowingly in possession of material non-public information in violation of a provision of the Exchange Act. A court, at the SEC's behest, can impose civil penalties of up to three times the profit gained (or loss avoided) as a result of the violations. Profits (or losses avoided) are measured by reference to the price at which the securities were trading at the point the material non-public information had been digested by the market (without regard to how the price behaved subsequently).

The SEC may also seek civil penalties up to the greater of $1 million (approximately £650,000 STG) and three times the profit gained (or loss avoided) against 'controlling persons' (eg the employer, including officers, managers and other supervisory personnel, of an insider trader) in certain situations in which (1) such persons knew there was a likelihood, or recklessly disregarded the likelihood, that a subordinate would trade on material non-public information gleaned as a result of employment and such trading occurred or (2) the control person is a broker-dealer or investment adviser and knowingly or recklessly failed to establish, maintain or enforce the 'Chinese Wall' procedures required by the Exchange Act and the Investment Advisers Act 1940. See 2.4.1 *above*.

5.2 CRIMINAL PENALTIES

Upon referral by the SEC, or on its own initiative, the US Department of Justice can bring criminal proceedings against any person who wilfully violates the US insider trading laws (or any other US federal securities laws). Pursuant to s32 of the Exchange Act, a conviction can result in fines of up to $1 million (approximately £650,000 STG) and/or imprisonment of up to ten years for natural persons or fines of up to $2,500,000 (approximately £1,623,000 STG) for violations by a company or other entity. Such penalties apply for each 'count' of criminal misconduct; separate trades can be prosecuted as separate counts of misconduct.

The US courts have defined 'wilfully' rather broadly. Generally speaking, a defendant can be convicted even without having known of specific provisions of the Exchange Act which his or her conduct violated. It is enough that the defendant have known generally that his or her conduct was wrongful. Under s 32 of the Exchange Act, no person can be imprisoned for a violation of any rule or regulation if they can prove that they had no knowledge of such rule or regulation.

5.3 RECOVERY BY PRIVATE PLAINTIFFS

Under s 20A of the Exchange Act, which creates a right of action for persons who trade contemporaneously with an insider trader, a private plaintiff's recovery is limited to the profit gained (or loss avoided) by the defendant in the transactions that are the subject of the violation. Additionally, the plaintiff's recovery is reduced by any amount the defendant is required to disgorge pursuant to an SEC action to enjoin the transactions that are the subject of the defendant's violation.

Although the express remedy available under s 20A does not supplant the implied common-law remedy for insider trading under r 10b-5, the remedies cannot be pleaded in the alternative since s 20A has a limitation on the recovery of damages. Where a plaintiff alleges injury based on contemporaneous trading, s 20A governs the recovery: *T Towe Price New Horizons Fund Inc v Preletz*, 749 F Supp 705, 709–710 (D Md 1990).

5.4 CORPORATION'S LIABILITY FOR INSIDER TRADING

A corporation can be prosecuted and subject to penalties for insider trading just as an individual can. However, a corporation only 'acts' through its officers, directors and other agents. Thus, the central issue where corporate liability is considered is whether the corporation can disavow the agent's actions because such actions were improper or unauthorised. Typically, three elements are considered in such an analysis: (1) whether the agent was acting to benefit the corporation, (2) whether the agent was working within the scope of his or her duties in taking the action, and (3) whether the agent had authority (either actual, implied or apparent) to so act.

6 OTHER CONSIDERATIONS

6.1 TERRITORIAL SCOPE

The US insider trading laws are viewed as having extraterritorial effect where conduct which violates the law has an impact on US investors or markets. Such a view is a virtual necessity in light of the globalisation of the securities markets; US investors and markets can be easily affected by conduct occurring outside its borders. Extraterritorial application of the law is necessary to 'protect domestic investors who have purchased foreign securities on American exchanges and to protect the domestic securities market from the effects of improper foreign transactions in American securities': *Schoenbaum v Firstbrook*, 405 F 2d 200, 206 (2d Cir 1968).

The SEC will bring actions based upon, and the US courts will enforce, the US insider trading laws against non-US persons who trade in the US markets, even if such trades are effected in the securities of *non*-US issuers through a foreign intermediary. However, before attempting to enforce the US laws against non-US persons, the court must determine that it can fairly exert personal jurisdiction over the defendant. Jurisdictional analysis under US law is too complex to address at length here but, put simply, it requires that a significant enough connection between the defendant and the state where the action is brought exist such that US constitutional due process standards are not violated by requiring the defendant to stand trial in the US court.

SEC v Wang, 699 F Supp 44 (SDNY 1988), illustrates the assertion of US judicial power in connection with insider trading laws. There, the court issued an order against a Hong Kong bank, freezing the funds of a non-US depositor who, the SEC alleged, had traded on non-public information provided to him by an employee of an investment bank in New York. The court ordered the bank, which had a branch in New York (which provided the required connection to the US), to pay the amount on deposit in Hong Kong into the court's registry in New York.

6.2 NON-STATUTORY REGULATION

Issuers, broker-dealers and other market participants may violate the rules of the National Association of Securities Dealers and of the various US securities exchanges if they engage in, or permit or assist others to engage in, insider trading.

7 CONCLUSION

Although US insider trading law lacks the statutory cohesion of some other countries' law on the subject, the number of successful prosecutions brought in the US is relatively high. For instance, according to its Annual Report for 1994, the SEC brought 45 cases alleging insider trading violations during that year. In 1993 and 1992, the SEC reported having brought 34 and 41 such cases, respectively. The relatively high number of prosecutions brought by the SEC is largely a function of the agency's vigilence in policing insider trading. Also, the high rate of success in such prosecutions is, at least in part, attributable to the fact that many defendants are eager to settle SEC charges in order to avoid the potentially burdensome legal and intangible personal costs of prolonged litigation. During 1993, the SEC issued disgorgement orders in connection with insider trading cases requiring the payment of approximately $12 million (approximately £7,790,000 STG). In 1992, such disgorgement orders required the payment of $51 million (approximately £33,108,000 STG).

CASE STUDY

Splash Plc, a company listed on the New York Stock Exchange, manufactures rainwear and umbrellas. Alan, a weather forecaster, on discovering that there is an unseasonable amount of rain due in the next three months, instructs his broker to buy shares in Splash. Meanwhile, Charles, an analyst of the company's shares, is told in a conversation with Jeremy, one of the directors, that the Chairman is expected to be paid a salary of $500,000. Charles knows from his knowledge of the Chairman's service contract (which is available for public inspection) that this salary could only be paid if the company achieved profit in excess of $20 million. Charles revises his profit forecast for the company but before he publishes it he cancels instructions which he had previously given to his broker to sell his Splash shares. Charles also tells his girlfriend, Maggie, that 'things are looking up' for Splash. Maggie then buys shares in the name of her father from an old friend of hers who wanted to sell Splash shares off market to save the payment of a broker's commission. In addition, Owen, an employee of the contracting firm which cleans Splash's offices, finds a draft of the latest management figures, which demonstrate Splash's high profitability in a wastepaper bin. He immediately buys shares.

Alan
Alan is not guilty of insider trading. The threshold issue is whether Alan's knowledge of expected rainfall is 'material non-public' information for purposes of the US insider trading laws. Because the US law views private research as helping to create efficient markets, independently obtained information, even when not widely disseminated, is not considered to be 'non-public' for purposes of insider trading laws. Although a court would be unlikely to take the inquiry beyond this threshold question, it bears mention that in order to find a violation of the insider trading laws in the US it must be established that the information originated with, or was obtained as the result of, a breach of a fiduciary or similar duty. Since the information regarding rainfall did not originate with a breach of fiduciary duty, there can be no violation of insider trading law.

Jeremy
Jeremy may be liable for having violated US insider trading law by 'tipping' Charles to inside information. Assuming that a $20 million profit would be material to Splash Plc, the information regarding Jeremy's salary would be

considered 'material' since the materiality analysis is made in light of all pub-licly available information regarding the issuer. Two key issues emerge: first, a threshold question, whether Jeremy can be liable for tipping Charles even though Charles did not ultimately trade. Second, whether Jeremy acted 'improperly' in giving the information regarding his salary to Charles.

The first issue remains an open question under US insider trading law. Because r10b-5 speaks to fraud in connection with the 'purchase or sale' of a security, the better view is that liability cannot attach to a tipper if his/her tippee does not trade. However, the SEC has in the past taken a more aggressive view and, based on its pre-*Chiarella* perspective, might attempt to proceed against Jeremy if his provision of information to Charles was in breach of a fiduciary duty.

Assuming trading by Charles is not a necessary element of Jeremy's potential tipper liability, Jeremy's status would depend upon whether he acted 'improperly' in providing the information to Charles. The US Supreme Court has held that an insider acts improperly when information is provided to another person for the insider's 'personal benefit'. Ultimately the ques-tion for the court will be what Jeremy's motive was in providing the infor-mation to Charles. For instance, if Jeremy believed he was providing non-material information that would enhance Charles's understanding of Splash's philosophy of rewarding strong performance and did not realise the significance of the chairman's salary in light of other available information, he would not have acted improperly for the purposes of r10b-5 (though he may be guilty of an innocent breach of fiduciary duty) and no liability can attach. On the other hand, if Jeremy was well aware of the significance of his remarks and intended them as a gift to Charles or expected that Charles would reciprocate with information regarding other issuers, then he did act improperly and he is liable.

Charles
Charles's decision to refrain from selling his Splash shares does not consti-tute a violation of US insider trading laws. Rule 10b-5 applies in connection with the 'purchase or sale' of securities. Charles's decision not to trade, even if based on material non-public information, cannot constitute a violation. Charles may, however, have liability as a result of having 'tipped' Maggie. Such liability would probably depend on (a) whether Charles was under a duty to keep the information confidential, and (b) what his expec-tation was regarding Maggie's use of the information.

Under the circumstances described in the case study, Charles's duty to keep the information confidential could likely arise in one of two ways. First, if Charles knew that Jeremy 'improperly' provided him with material, non-public information (see the discussion of Jeremy's liability above) then Charles would be subject to a derivative 'abstain or disclose' obligation. Second, Charles would then be under the same obligation if he has 'misappropriated' the information. Under the misappropriation theory, which has been accepted in several (but not all) of the US judicial circuits, a person violates r10b-5 when such person misappropriates material non-public information in breach of a fiduciary or similar relationship of trust and confidence. Such a duty can include a duty to one's employer. If Charles's employer had a policy requiring employees to keep any information obtained in their employment confidential, then Charles may be said to have misappropriated the information by using it to tip Maggie.

Assuming Charles has a duty to keep the information confidential, if he provides the information to Maggie with the expectation that she will trade on it, he would be likely to have tipper liability. If, however, he has provided the information to Maggie with no such expectation (eg to allay her concerns about her close friend Jeremy who has been depressed about Splash's recent performance), he would not be viewed as a tipper.

In neither case will Charles's liability depend upon whether Maggie herself has violated the insider trading laws by trading. The SEC has taken the view that tipper liability can exist under r10b-5 even where the tippee's trading on the information does not constitute a violation.

Maggie

Whether Maggie, a 'tippee', has violated the US insider trading law depends on whether (1) Jeremy, the original 'tipper', acted improperly in providing the information to Charles and (2) whether Maggie knew or should have known that the information provided to her originated with a breach of an insider's fiduciary duty. Even assuming Jeremy acted improperly in tipping Charles, under the circumstances it appears that Maggie was not aware of the breach of fiduciary duty since Charles provided no details regarding his tip and did not identify the source of his information. However, if Maggie had reason to know of the source of the information (eg Charles had earlier indicated that he had an 'inside line' with a director at Splash) then she may be liable. The fact that Maggie carried out the trades on behalf of someone else or that the trades were conducted off-market does not affect the analysis.

Owen

The question of Owen's liability turns on whether he 'misappropriated' material non-public information. In the absence of the misappropriation theory, Owen would not be liable for insider trading, since Owen owes no fiduciary duty to Splash or its shareholders. Thus, he would not have a duty to 'abstain or disclose'. However, if as is likely, Owen's employer had a policy requiring employees to keep any information gleaned from their employment confidential, then Owen has misappropriated the information and may be liable for having traded based upon it.

Canada

Peter E S Jewett and Darren Sukonick,
Tory Tory DesLauriers & Binnington, Toronto

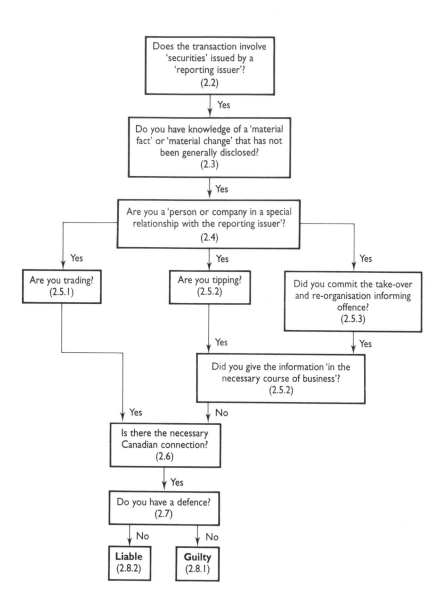

1 INTRODUCTION

Canada is divided into ten provinces and two territories. (The territories are located in the Arctic regions of Canada and are very sparsely populated.) Legislative bodies exist at both the federal (Canadian) level and the provincial and territorial level.

The regulation of securities transactions is currently a matter of provincial jurisdiction. Each of the ten provinces has a Securities Act and regulations thereunder which embody the principal laws dealing with insider dealing. The two territories also have Securities Acts but these Acts do not contain insider dealing provisions. In Canada, insider dealing is commonly referred to as 'insider trading', although the laws also cover the improper passing on of inside information even if no actual trade takes place and provide for a system of reporting the holdings of and trading in securities by insiders of the relevant issuer.

This chapter focuses on the provisions of the Securities Act (Ontario) (the 'OSA') and the regulations thereunder since Ontario is generally regarded as the province with the most active securities markets and securities commission in Canada. Recently, there have been discussions between the Canadian government and most of the provincial governments about the possibility of establishing a Canadian Securities Commission and enacting a Canadian Securities Act which would effectively replace the Securities Acts of most of the provinces. If this effective change in jurisdiction takes place, it is unlikely that it would result in significant changes to the laws dealing with insider trading.

In addition to the provisions of the various provincial Securities Acts referred to above, insider trading is also regulated by the statutes under which Canadian corporations are incorporated. Such statutes exist at the federal, provincial and territorial levels. There are also certain specialised pieces of legislation under which a specific type of corporation can be incorporated. For example, at the federal level, these include the Bank Act, Insurance Companies Act, Trust and Loan Companies Act and Cooperative Credit Associations Act. Each of these statutes contains provisions dealing with insider trading with respect to securities issued by corporations incorporated under the particular statute. There is similar specialised legislation at the provincial level.

The insider trading provisions of the provincial securities statutes generally apply to situations involving a 'reporting issuer' under those laws. A reporting issuer is, in general terms, a corporation the securities of which are recognised to be publicly traded in the particular jurisdiction. The insider trading provisions of the provincial corporate statutes generally apply to corporations incorporated under those statutes which are not reporting issuers. The insider trading provisions of the federal corporate statute apply to corporations incorporated under that statute whether or not they are reporting issuers.

The Canadian Criminal Code does not contain provisions dealing with insider trading as such. However, there have been convictions under the general fraud section with respect to particularly egregious cases of trading in circumstances where one party to the trade has actively misled the other party.

The stock exchanges in Canada do not have rules as such against insider trading, presumably because the exchanges are satisfied that the relevant securities and corporate laws provide adequate prohibitions and remedies. The exchanges do, however, draw listed companies' attention to the applicable prohibitions and recommend that listed companies adopt internal policies aimed at limiting the possibility of the improper use of confidential information.

Breach of the insider trading laws in Canada can give rise to both criminal and civil liability. The securities regulators are also empowered to impose administrative sanctions in respect of insider trading, informing or reporting contraventions in order to maintain the integrity of and confidence in the Canadian capital markets. Unlike the experience in the United States, very few criminal cases, and virtually no civil cases relating to insider trading or informing are brought to the courts in Canada. Almost all proceedings are administrative proceedings before one of the provincial securities commissions. While some of the more precise distinctions drawn in this chapter, between conduct which is in breach of the applicable laws and conduct which is not, may be persuasive in court proceedings, it should be expected that the fine distinctions may be less conclusive in regulatory proceedings since the regulatory bodies are concerned predominantly with overall confidence in the capital markets.

Proceedings before securities regulators are usually initiated by the relevant regulator's staff. If administrative sanctions are sought the proceedings will be brought before the securities regulator, but decisions of the regulator may be appealed as of right to the courts of that province. If the regulator's staff wishes to seek a fine or other criminal sanction, the proceedings must be brought in the courts in the first instance. There have been cases in which administrative sanctions have been sought even though an attempt to impose criminal sanctions based on the same set of facts has failed.

The provincial securities laws apply with respect to activities which take place in whole or in part within the particular province or which might impact on the integrity of the capital markets in the province. Court proceedings with respect to a corporation incorporated under a provincial corporate statute would be brought in the courts of that province, except for proceedings between persons seeking civil damages which may be brought in the courts of a province convenient to the parties. Court proceedings with respect to a corporation incorporated under a federal corporate statute or proceedings under the Criminal Code could be brought in the courts of any province, provided such courts were convenient to the parties in the particular case.

These multiple layers of laws dealing with insider trading are far-reaching and complex. For the sake of clarity, some of the more esoteric details have been left out of the following description. The discussion begins with a consideration of the provincial securities laws and then goes on to consider the provincial and federal corporate laws.

2 PROVINCIAL SECURITIES LAWS

2.1 SUMMARY

The OSA contains prohibitions against insider trading and informing (or 'tipping'). It also contains a reporting regime under which an insider is required to file reports disclosing the insider's holdings of and trading in securities of the reporting issuer with respect to which he is an insider. The prohibitions set out in the OSA relate only to the securities of certain types of issuer.

2.2 TO WHICH SECURITIES DOES THE OSA APPLY?

2.2.1 Definition of 'securities'

The OSA prohibitions apply in the context of securities issued by a reporting issuer. The OSA gives 'securities' a wide and non-exhaustive definition. It includes, for example, any document commonly known as a security and is deemed to include a put, call, option or other right or obligation to purchase or sell securities of the reporting issuer, as well as a security the market price of which varies materially with that of the issuer's securities. This would include puts, calls, options and any other rights or obligations to purchase or sell securities written by parties other than the reporting issuer. The securities themselves do not have to be listed on any stock exchange.

2.2.2 Who is a 'reporting issuer'?

Table (1) below sets out details of who, in the context of Ontario, is a 'reporting issuer'.

TABLE (1)

A 'reporting issuer' is:
- an issuer of securities in respect of which a prospectus was filed in Ontario
- an issuer which has made a securities exchange take-over bid in Ontario
- an issuer which has securities listed on the Toronto Stock Exchange
- an issuer incorporated under the Business Corporation Act (Ontario) which, for the purposes of that Act, is offering its securities to the public

This definition of reporting issuer is clearly specific to Ontario. The definitions of 'reporting issuer' in the Securities Acts of other provinces vary to take into account the different jurisdictions. However, in general terms the concept covers corporations incorporated in that jurisdiction and corporations the securities of which are recognised to be publicly traded in that jurisdiction.

2.3 WHAT IS INSIDE INFORMATION?

The insider trading prohibition set out in the OSA applies where the 'accused' has knowledge of a 'material fact' or 'material change' with respect to the reporting issuer which has not been 'generally disclosed'. These individual elements are considered in turn.

2.3.1 'Material fact'

A material fact is one that significantly affects, or would reasonably be expected to have a significant effect on, the market price or value of a security. This concept includes a fact which is not specific to the particular reporting issuer (for example, industry-wide information) although the prohibition against insider trading applies only with respect to persons in a special relationship with the reporting issuer and only with respect to facts which have not been generally disclosed. While there is no case law to confirm the point, the common meaning of the word 'fact' points to the conclusion that a 'material fact' does not include a false market rumour. There are however other prohibitions against manipulating the market for a security.

2.3.2 'Material change'

A material change is one in the business, operations or capital of an issuer that would reasonably be expected to have a significant effect on the market price or value of any of the securities of the issuer and includes a decision to implement such a change made by the board of directors of the issuer or by senior management who believe that confirmation of their decision by the board of directors is probable.

2.3.3 'Generally disclosed'

The prohibitions in the OSA do not apply with respect to information which has been generally disclosed. For a material fact or material change to be considered to have been generally disclosed, it must have been disclosed publicly, usually by press release issued to the major newspapers and news wire services in Canada, and sufficient time must have passed after its release to allow the news to be disseminated in the market place for the securities of the issuer in question. This means that there must have been an opportunity for the news to have appeared over the media of widest circulation and the relevant trading public must have had the news in its possession long enough to digest the information, taking into account its nature and complexity. It is generally considered that at least one full trading day should pass after the release of the relevant information before any insiders trade.

Problem Area 1

GENERALLY DISCLOSED

Angela is a director of SmallCo Inc. Amalgamations Ltd has proposed a merger with SmallCo Inc. Upon the merger, the shareholders of SmallCo Inc will receive a certain number of Amalgamations Ltd's shares, based on a conversion formula. The majority shareholder is pleased with the arrangement and it is likely to go forward. Angela is confident that the synergies between these two companies will result in a profitable merged entity, and is eager to buy SmallCo Inc shares. Angela is also anxious to tell her best friend about this opportunity. Will Angela be liable for insider trading or tipping in the following situations?

(1) SmallCo Inc issues a press release describing the proposed merger at 9.00 am and Angela places an order to buy shares and informs her friend at 9.30 am;

(2) SmallCo Inc issues the press release at 9.00 am and Angela places an order to buy and informs her friend immediately before the close of trading on the same day;

(3) An officer of SmallCo Inc has been interviewed by a trade magazine with relatively limited circulation, and discloses the proposed merger. The magazine carries a story describing the merger in its issue released on Monday and Angela places an order to buy and informs her friend on the following Monday.

Before the press release is issued or the interview takes place, Angela has knowledge of an undisclosed material fact. There must be some interval between the initial release of the information and the time at which she can trade. The situation in (1) is prohibited. The mere act of issuing a press release does not meet the requirement that information be 'generally disclosed'. The situation in (2) is somewhat problematic. A working rule is that there should be a minimum of one full trading day after the release of the information. However, the information in this case is quite complicated, involving (a) the fairness of a share conversion formula, and (b) the future profitability of the merged entity. It may take more time for the trading public to digest the information and appreciate its significance. In (3), there is a problem regarding the manner of dissemination. Information must be distributed to the trading public. This test is probably not met by the publication of the trade magazine. Despite the length of the interval before Angela trades or informs, the information is probably not 'generally disclosed'.

2.4 WHO IS AN INSIDER?

The provisions of the OSA apply to any 'person' or 'company' who is 'in a special relationship with a reporting issuer'. Again, these elements are considered in turn.

2.4.1 Person or company

In contrast to some jurisdictions, for example the United Kingdom, the insider dealing prohibitions set out in the OSA apply, not only to individuals, but also to companies and other entities. A 'person' is widely defined as not only an individual but also a partnership, unincorporated association, unincorporated syndicate, unincorporated organisation, trust, trustee, executor, administrator or other legal representative. A 'company' is defined as any corporation, incorporated association, incorporated syndicate or other incorporated organisation (incorporated in any jurisdiction).

2.4.2 Special relationship

Only a person or company in a special relationship with a reporting issuer can be liable for a breach of the provisions in the OSA. Table (2) *below* sets out the categories of persons and companies who are considered as having such a relationship.

TABLE (2)

The following are in a special relationship with a reporting issuer:
- an insider, affiliate or associate of the reporting issuer as such terms are defined in Table (3)
- an insider, affiliate or associate of a person or a company proposing to make a take-over bid (tender offer) for securities of the reporting issuer
- an insider, affiliate or associate of a person or company that is proposing to become a party to a reorganisation, amalgamation, merger, arrangement or a similar business combination with the reporting issuer or to acquire a substantial portion of its property (a 'business combination')
- a person or company that is engaging in or proposes to engage in any business or professional activity with or on behalf of the reporting issuer or of a person or company proposing to make a take-over bid or to become a party to a business combination
- a person who is a director, officer or employee of the reporting issuer or of a person or company proposing to make a take-over bid or to become a party to a business combination or of a person or company that is engaging in or proposing to engage in any business or professional activity as described above

- a person or company that learned of the material fact or material change with respect to the reporting issuer while the person or company was a person or company as described above; or
- a person or company that learns of a material fact or material change from any other person or company described in this definition, and knows or ought reasonably to have known that the other person or company is such a person or company.

Table (3) *below* sets out some relevant definitions.

TABLE (3)

'insider of an issuer'	• every director or senior officer (as defined *below*) of the issuer • every director or senior officer of a company that is itself an insider or subsidiary of the issuer • any person or company who beneficially owns, or exercises control or direction over, voting securities of the issuer carrying more than 10 per cent of the voting rights attached to all-voting securities of the issuer
'senior officer'	• the chair or vice-chair of the board of directors, the president, a vice-president, the secretary, the treasurer or the general manager, or any person performing any of the foregoing functions • each of the five highest paid employees, whether or not the employee is one of the above officers
'affiliate of an issuer'	• a company which is a subsidiary of the issuer • a company of which the issuer is a subsidiary • a company which is a subsidiary of the same company of which the issuer is also a subsidiary • a company that is controlled by the same person or company which controls the issuer (for this purpose control means the ownership of securities carrying more than 50 per cent of the votes for the election of directors)
'associate of any person or company'	• any company of which such person or company beneficially owns voting securities carrying more than 10 per cent of the voting rights attached to all voting securities of the company • any partner of such person or company • any trust or estate in which such person or company has a substantial beneficial interest or as to which such person or company serves as a trustee

- any relative of that person who resides in the same home as that person
- any person of the opposite sex who resides in the same home as that person and to whom that person is married or with whom that person is living in a conjugal relationship outside marriage
- any relative of a person mentioned in the preceding clause who has the same home as that person

As can be seen from the definitions set out in Tables (2) and (3), the prohibition against insider trading is very broad and complex, covering a wide range of persons (going well beyond those persons who are 'insiders' as defined). For example, the last element of the definition of 'in a special relationship with a reporting issuer' sweeps into the prohibition so-called 'tippees'; that is, anyone who learns of undisclosed material information from someone whom that person ought to know is someone who is included in the definition, including another tippee. Problem Area 2 illustrates just how broad this concept is.

Problem Area 2

TIPPEE OF A TIPPEE

Fiona, a director of Go-Ahead Inc, reveals a material fact about the company to Carol, her golfing partner, who knows that Fiona is a director of Go-Ahead Inc. Carol passes the information to her husband Greg. Is Greg 'in a special relationship with' Go-Ahead Inc? Carol is in a special relationship because (a) she learned of a material fact from Fiona, who, as a director, is in a special relationship with Go-Ahead Inc, and (b) Carol knows that Fiona is in this special relationship. Regarding Greg, the issue is whether Greg knows or ought reasonably to have known that Carol is 'in a special relationship'; in other words, that she must have received the information from someone else who is in a special relationship with Go-Ahead Inc.

Consider the following situations:

(1) Greg knows that the source of the information is Fiona, who is a director of Go-Ahead Inc;

(2) Greg knows that the source of the information is one of Carol's friends, who is a director of some company; or

(3) Greg knows that several of Carol's friends are company directors, including directors of Go-Ahead Inc, but he does not know where Carol got the information.

In (1), Greg has actual knowledge that Carol is 'in a special relationship' and he too will therefore be 'in a special relationship'. In (2), it might be argued that Greg ought reasonably to have known that Carol received her information from one of her friends who is a director of Go-Ahead Inc and is therefore herself 'in a special relationship with' Go-Ahead Inc. This argument is likely be more persuasive in regulatory proceedings than in a court proceedings. In (3), there is only a tenuous link between Carol's information and anyone 'in a special relationship'. It may be argued that Greg ought not to be expected to have deduced this link although it should be expected that securities regulators may be quite strict in what one ought reasonably be expected to know in situations where the information is clearly confidential and is unlikely to have originated from anywhere other than a source inside the company.

An interesting variation on the above facts is the case in which Carol does not pass on the material information to Greg, but merely suggests to him that he buy or sell shares of Go-Ahead Inc with no explanation as to why. Technically, it could be argued that Greg falls outside the definition of 'in a special relationship with' because he has not learned of a material fact or a material change. As noted elsewhere, however, even if this type of precise line-drawing were to be successful in court proceedings, it would be unlikely to succeed in regulatory proceedings before a securities commission which will be concerned about the integrity of and confidence in the capital markets.

Problem Area 2 illustrates how far-reaching the concept of a 'tippee' can be. It would be open to a regulator or a court to find that just about anyone who becomes aware of clearly undisclosed inside information ought to have known that it was being passed on by someone who was in turn a 'tippee'. A broad interpretation of this kind would make many of the other elements of the definition of 'in a special relationship with' (such as the definition of 'associate') unnecessary since it would be difficult to identify an 'associate' which was not also a 'tippee'. Nevertheless, it is assumed that there are some examples of a person obtaining undisclosed material information which a securities regulator or a court would decide did not involve the person becoming a tippee. An example might be a person finding a piece of paper on the street containing the information without there being any evidence as to from where the piece of paper originated, or a person overhearing a conversation in a restaurant without knowing who the people engaging in the conversation were.

It should be noted that the insider trading prohibition applies to a director, officer or employee of a person or company proposing to make a take-over bid or to become a party to a business combination or to any 'tippee' who learns of the proposed bid, but does not apply to the person or company itself. A potential offeror is, therefore, not prohibited by these rules from purchasing securities of a target before the proposed transaction is publicly announced, although such purchases would have to be carried out in compliance with the applicable take-over bid rules.

As can be seen from Problem Area 3 *below*, the definition of 'associate' is particularly broad in scope. In many cases it is academic for the purposes of the insider trading prohibition whether or not a person is an 'associate' of another person since in most cases the person in question will be caught by the 'tippee' concept. However, as Problem Area 3 shows, the concept of 'associate' does not depend on what the alleged associate knew or reasonably ought to have known; the relationship alone is enough.

Problem Area 3

RESIDING IN THE SAME RESIDENCE

Kathy and Steve have been involved in a serious relationship for several years, although they are not yet married. Steve is a director of Success Corp. Kathy's cousin, Brandon, has taken up residence in Kathy and Steve's home for the past two months. Brandon does not know anything about Steve's occupation or involvement with Success Corp. One night, Steve tells Kathy that Success Corp will soon publish its financial statements which will show outstanding profits compared to previous years. The next morning, Kathy mentions to her cousin Brandon that Success Corp had an extremely profitable year. Before the financial statements are released, Brandon buys shares in Success Corp.

Since Kathy and Steve are living in a conjugal relationship, Kathy is an associate of Steve. Since Brandon is a relative of Kathy and currently has the same home as Kathy, Brandon is also an associate of Steve. Since Brandon is an associate of Steve, Brandon is an associate of a director of Success Corp, and hence, is 'in a special relationship with' with Success Corp. He is not permitted to use his knowledge of the undisclosed material fact (that Success Corp had an extremely profitable year) to purchase or sell securities. It is not relevant that Brandon did not know of Steve's connection to Success Corp.

2.4.3 Deemed insiders

Under the OSA, if an issuer acquires 10 per cent of the voting rights attached to securities of a reporting issuer, a director or senior officer of the issuer is deemed to have been an insider of the reporting issuer for the previous six months. Similarly, if the acquiror is itself a reporting issuer, the directors and senior officers of the acquired reporting issuer are deemed to have been insiders of the acquiring reporting issuer for the previous six months.

Presumably, these deeming provisions are intended to support the insider reporting provisions of the OSA, described at 2.9 *below*, by requiring the directors and officers who are deemed to have been insiders to file initial reports disclosing their ownership of securities of the acquiring or acquired reporting issuer. The deeming language does not, however, limit the deeming to the insider reporting requirement. If the deeming language were to be interpreted literally, it would lead to the anomalous situation in which a person might be retroactively caught by insider trading or tipping liability when the corporation of which the person is a director or officer makes an investment in, or is invested in by, another corporation even though the investment was not even contemplated at the time when the trading or tipping which gives rise to the concern took place. One would expect that a court or a securities regulator would not impose liability in such a case.

2.5 WHAT ARE THE OFFENCES?

Section 76 of the OSA contains prohibitions—trading and informing which are considered in turn below.

2.5.1 Trading

Section 76(1) of the OSA prohibits any person or company *in a special relationship with* a reporting issuer from purchasing or selling securities of the reporting issuer with knowledge of a material fact or material change with respect to the reporting issuer that has not been generally disclosed.

The purchasing or selling referred to in the prohibition is any purchase or sale of the securities, whether or not the purchase or sale takes place on a recognised securities exchange. There must, however, be an actual transfer of property; an agreement to purchase or sell would not of itself attract liability, although a transfer of a security which is a right or obligation to purchase or sell could attract liability. There is also case law to the effect that in an agency situation both the principal and the agent can be liable for a breach of the prohibition.

2.5.2 Informing ('tipping')

Section 76(2) of the OSA contains the anti-tipping prohibition. It provides that no reporting issuer and no person or company *in a special relationship with* a reporting issuer shall inform, *other than in the necessary course of business,* any other person or company of a material fact or material change with respect to the reporting issuer before the material fact or material change has been *generally disclosed.* There has been no judicial or regulatory interpretation of the phrase 'in the necessary course of business' in this context. However, it is generally considered to include disclosing information, subject to normal confidentiality restrictions, to parties who may be interested in acquiring the reporting issuer or a significant part of its business and to financial and legal advisers and bankers.

2.5.3 Proposed take-over bids and re-organisations

Section 76(3) of the OSA contains an extension of the 'tipping' prohibition. It prohibits any person or company proposing to make a take-over bid for securities of a reporting issuer, proposing to become a party to a business combination with a reporting issuer, or proposing to acquire a substantial portion of the property of a reporting issuer from informing any other person or company of a material change or material fact with respect to the reporting issuer before that material change or material fact has been generally disclosed, except where the information is given in the necessary course of business to effect the proposed take-over bid, business combination or acquisition. A take-over bid is an offer to acquire voting or equity securities of a class of securities where the offer is made to any person or company in Ontario if the securities subject to the offer, together with securities already owned by the offeror, would aggregate 20 per cent or more of the outstanding securities of that class. An equity security is defined as a security that carries a residual right to participate in the earnings of an issuer or in its assets upon liquidation or winding-up.

Problem Area 4

PROPOSED TAKE-OVER BID

Gary is the sole shareholder and director of AcquireCo Ltd. AcquireCo currently owns 19.9 per cent of the shares of the public company, Target Corp. Gary is preparing to launch a formal take-over bid for all of the outstanding shares of Target Corp. The day before he announces the bid, he speaks to the following people:

(1) Abby, his investment banker, who has advised him with respect to the bid and the initial bid price per share;
(2) Karen, a good friend, who has recently completed a successful take-over bid. At their weekly lunch, he asks her if she has any practical advice for his upcoming bid for Target Corp; and
(3) Mac, the security guard who works in the lobby of the building in which AcquireCo has its head offices. Gary tells Mac that there will be much activity in the building because of his upcoming bid for Target Corp.

Gary is proposing to make a take-over bid for Target Corp and has informed other people of a material fact regarding Target Corp: that it will be the subject of a take-over bid. He has violated the prohibition in s 76(3) of the OSA unless the information has been given in the necessary course of business to effect the take-over bid. In (1), Abby has been retained by Gary to provide professional services in respect of the take-over bid. Any communication with her in this regard is permitted. (Of course, Abby is in a special relationship with Target Corp and is herself subject to the insider trading and tipping prohibitions.) In (2), although Karen may have provided some practical advice, given the social context of the communication, it is uncertain whether the information was given in the 'necessary course' of the take-over bid. In (3), although Gary was justified in advising Mac of the anticipated night-time activity, it was unnecessary to disclose the existence of a proposed take-over bid and the proposed target. This would certainly be considered to be tipping.

2.6 WHAT IS THE TERRITORIAL SCOPE OF THE OSA?

The OSA and the other provincial securities laws apply with respect to activities which take place in whole or in part within the particular province, and to activities which have a sufficient connection to the province to warrant intervention to protect the integrity of the capital markets in the province. For example, it can be expected that in any province the securities regulators would consider taking action in connection with insider trading between parties who are outside the province and who trade outside the province but with respect to securities of a corporation which is a reporting issuer in the province.

2.7 WHAT ARE THE DEFENCES?

2.7.1 Defences to criminal and civil liability

2.7.1.1 General disclosure

Section 76(4) of the OSA provides that no person or company shall be found to have contravened the insider trading or tipping prohibitions if the person or company reasonably believed that the material fact or material change in question had already been generally disclosed.

2.7.1.2 Equivalent information

The Regulation under the OSA also exempts a person or company from the insider trading and tipping prohibitions if the person or company proves that the person or company reasonably believed that the other party to the purchase and sale transaction, or the person or company informed, already had knowledge of the material fact or material change in question.

2.7.1.3 Specific defences

In addition to the defences in 2.7.1.4 *below*, certain trades are exempt from the insider trading prohibition. These include trades entered into as an agent pursuant to a specific unsolicited order, trades made pursuant to an automatic trading plan (such as a dividend reinvestment plan) established prior to the acquisition of the inside information, and trades made to fulfil a legally-binding obligation entered into prior to the acquiring of the insider information. It should be noted that these exemptions do not include the exercise of pre-existing stock options even where the exercise price was established before the insider acquired knowledge of the inside information.

2.7.1.4 Investment dealers

The insider trading and tipping prohibitions present particular problems for integrated investment dealers which will have research, corporate finance and mergers and acquisitions staff in contact with issuers at the same time as trading staff are actively executing trades in securities on behalf of clients and on behalf of the investment dealer itself. The policies published by the Ontario Securities Commission include policies and guidelines to be followed by investment dealers (and businesses facing similar information control problems) to prevent and detect insider trading and tipping.

These policies are designed to encourage the establishment of procedures to take advantage of a defence (the so-called 'Fire Wall' defence) set out in the Regulation to the OSA under which it is a defence to the prohibition against, and civil liability for, insider trading for the person or company to prove that:

(a) no director, officer, employee or agent of the person or company who made or participated in making the decision to trade in the securities had actual knowledge of the relevant material fact or material change; and

(b) no advice was given with respect to the purchase or sale to the director, officer, partner, employee or agent who made or participated in the making of the decision to purchase or sell by a director, partner, officer, employee or agent who had actual knowledge of the material fact or the material change.

This defence applies to all companies but is of particular relevance to market dealers and other market participants.

The Ontario Securities Commission's policies require dealers to have written procedures in this area covering education of employees, containment of information, restrictions on transactions, and compliance. The policies depend heavily on establishing a 'Fire Wall' between the research, corporate finance and mergers and acquisitions staffs on the one hand, and the trading staff on the other. This is designed to prevent undisclosed material information obtained by one part of the business from being transferred to the trading part of the business. The policies also suggest the establishment of 'gray' lists and 'restricted' lists: a gray list being a confidential list of issuers about which the dealer has inside information and in respect of which trading will be closely monitored; and a restricted list being a list of issuers the securities of which should not be traded except for the execution of unsolicited and pre-arranged orders. When the investment dealer finds itself in a special relationship with a particular reporting issuer (eg when the dealer is engaged by the reporting issuer on a specific retainer) and in possession of undisclosed material information, that issuer should be added to the restricted list.

2.7.2 Defences to civil liability

It is a defence to civil liability for insider trading or tipping for the accused to prove that he reasonably believed that the relevant material fact or material change had already been generally disclosed, or that the material fact or material change was known or ought reasonably to have been known to the other party to the purchase and sale transaction. In this regard, the other party does not have a positive duty to inquire diligently as to the existence of material undisclosed information. However, the other party will not be able to enforce a claim if, given the surrounding circumstances, it would have been reasonable for the party to inquire and the party would have been made aware of the information if an inquiry had been made.

It should be noted that it is not a defence to liability for tipping that the tipper did not expect the tippee to deal in the relevant securities.

It is a defence to civil liability to the reporting issuer itself for the person or company to prove that the person or company reasonably believed that the material fact or material change had already been generally disclosed.

2.8 WHAT ARE THE PENALTIES AND CONSEQUENCES OF INSIDER TRADING?

2.8.1 Criminal liability

Under the OSA, anyone who contravenes the insider trading or tipping prohibitions is guilty of an offence and on conviction is liable to imprisonment for a term of up to two years and/or to a fine of not less than the profit made or loss avoided by reason of the contravention, and not more than the greater of (a) Cdn$1 million (approximately £471,000 STG), and (b) three times the profit made or loss avoided. (In Quebec, the limit is four times the profit made or loss avoided.)

It is not necessary to have benefited personally from the misuse of the material undisclosed information in order to be guilty of committing an offence. For example, the OSA prohibits tipping even though the tippee, and not the tipper, later benefits. Similarly, if an insider has knowledge of material undisclosed information and trades for someone else's benefit, the insider is still caught under the prohibition. In a recent case in Ontario, an insider effected a trade to benefit a friend who had lent money to the insider's failing company. At trial, the insider was fined Cdn$15,000 (approximately £7,000 STG). This fine was replaced, however, on appeal by a sentence of 90 days' imprisonment in view of the fact that there had been repetitive trading pursuant to a fully thought-out plan (R v Plastic Engine Technology Corp (1994) 88 CCC 287 (Ont CJ)).

Securities regulators may apply administrative sanctions as well in response to insider trading violations. Under the OSA, the Securities Commission has the power to order that trading in respect of specific securities cease, to order that certain trading exemptions set out in the OSA not apply to a specific person and to suspend, cancel, restrict or impose terms and conditions upon the registration of a participant (dealer, salesperson, underwriter or adviser) in the capital markets. Each of these powers could be used effectively to deny the realisation of a profit from improper insider trading or, in order to protect the integrity of the capital markets, to sanction a person who has breached the insider trading or tipping prohibitions.

2.8.2 Civil Liability

Section 134(1) of the OSA provides that anyone in a special relationship with a reporting issuer who purchases or sells securities of the reporting issuer with knowledge of a material fact or material change with respect to the reporting issuer which has not been generally disclosed is liable to compensate the seller or purchaser for damages as a result of the trade.

Similarly s 134(2) of the OSA provides that anyone who breaches the tipping prohibition is liable to compensate anyone who thereafter sells securities of the reporting issuer to, or purchases such securities from, the person or company that received the information.

In assessing damages and in establishing the level of fines, the discrepancy between the price at which the transaction in question took place and the average market price of the security in the 20 trading days following general disclosure of the material fact or material change, will be considered.

In addition to the above civil liability, every person or company who is an insider, affiliate or associate of a reporting issuer, and who breaches the insider trading or tipping prohibitions with respect to the reporting issuer, is accountable to the reporting issuer for any benefit or advantage received or receivable by the person or company as a result of the purchase, sale or communication. The effect of this provision is to create the possibility of being liable for double damages.

Anyone who has access to information concerning the investment programme of a mutual fund in Ontario or the investment portfolio managed for a client, and uses that information for his, her or its direct benefit or advantage in purchasing or selling securities included in such investment programme or portfolio, is accountable to the mutual fund or the client for any benefit or advantage received or receivable as a result of such purchase or sale.

If more than one person is liable to pay damages under these provisions as a result of the same transaction or series of transactions, their liability for damages is joint and several.

In a recent situation being investigated by the Ontario Securities Commission, insiders of a corporation were alleged to have sold shares short when they had knowledge of material facts about the corporation which had not been generally disclosed. As a result of closing out their short position, they realised a gross profit of approximately Cdn$16.5 million (approximately £7,778,000 STG). The insiders denied having any material undisclosed information but agreed, as a settlement, to pay (i) Cdn$18 million (approximately £8,485,000 STG) into a fund to be distributed to any person who could prove that they had traded during the period of the alleged violations, and (ii) Cdn$5 million (approximately £2,357,000 STG) to the Securities Commission: (Re Seakist Overseas Limited (1993) 16 OSCB 1959).

2.8.3 Limitation periods

A proceeding under the OSA to impose penalties for breaches of the insider trading or tipping prohibition must be commenced within five years after the date of the occurrence of the last event on which the proceeding is based.

An action to recover damages under the civil liability provisions of the OSA must be commenced within the earlier of (a) 180 days after the plaintiff first became aware of the facts giving rise to the cause of action, and (b) three years after the date of the events that gave rise to the cause of action.

2.8.4 Liability of corporations for actions of their employees

A corporation may violate the insider trading and tipping prohibitions through the actions of its employees with resulting civil and criminal liability. Normally, under Canadian law, only the acts of persons in authority, sometimes called 'the directing mind' of the corporation, can lead to criminal responsibility for the corporation. The class of persons who may bring criminal liability upon the corporation can be expanded to the extent that authority is delegated to employees. In a civil suit, a corporation will be vicariously liable for the illegal acts of its employees acting within the scope of their employment. The employer has a responsibility to supervise its employees properly and to ensure that appropriate institutional safeguards are in place.

Any company which establishes 'reasonable policies and procedures' to safeguard confidential information in the possession of certain of its employees, as described in 2.7.1.4, is entitled to have this taken into account in determining whether it has contravened the insider trading and tipping provisions of the OSA. The extent to which such policies and procedures will provide an effective defence is, however, difficult to assess.

2.9 INSIDER REPORTING

Section 107 of the OSA requires that any person or company who becomes an insider (see Table (3)) of a reporting issuer must file a report with the Securities Commission disclosing his, her or its ownership of or control over securities of the reporting issuer. This report must be filed by the tenth day of the month following the month within which the person or company became an insider. Any changes to the information reported must in turn be reported by the tenth day of the month following the change. The Securities Commission publishes regularly the information contained in insider reports.

It should be noted that these reporting requirements apply to insiders only and not to all persons who are in 'a special relationship with' a reporting issuer. However, the definition of insider includes those deemed insiders referred to at 2.4.3 *above*.

3 CORPORATE LAWS

3.1 PROVINCIAL

The securities law prohibitions against insider trading and tipping apply with respect to *reporting issuers*. The Business Corporations Act (Ontario) (the 'OBCA') provides for civil liability with respect to insider trading in securities of any corporation incorporated under the OBCA which is not a reporting issuer, and in securities of companies which are subsidiaries of such a corporation or of which such a corporation is itself a subsidiary or under common control. Most of the corporate statutes of the other provinces and territories and statutes under which specific special types of corporations are incorporated contain substantially similar provisions.

The OBCA provides that an 'insider' who '*makes use of*' any '*specific confidential information*' for the insider's '*own benefit or advantage*' that, if generally known, might reasonbly be expected to affect materially the value of the security traded, (a) is liable to compensate any person for direct loss suffered by that person as a result of the trade, and (b) is accountable to the corporation for any direct benefit received by the insider as a result of the trade. It is a defence to the liability to other persons to show that the information was known or should have been known, in the exercise of reasonable diligence, to that person.

These provisions apply to 'specific confidential information'. 'Specific' is used in contradistinction to 'general'; however, it need not be precise or extensively detailed. Examples of information which have been held to be specific are: that a company will report a loss even though the exact amount of the loss is unknown; that there is a letter which states that a person is tentatively interested in purchasing a company at a given price; and that negotiations are underway for a takeover and that two days have been set aside for the final talks even though the potential bid price is unknown. Confidential information is information which has not been generally disclosed as described earlier in this chapter at 2.3.3.

The provisions also require that the insider 'make use of' the information in order to be held liable. This concept is a significant distinguishing feature between the OBCA insider trading provisions and those in the OSA. The burden of proof rests on the insider to show, on a balance of probabilities, that the insider did not make use of the information and that it was not a factor in the insider's decision to trade (*Green v Charterhouse* (1976) 12 OR (2d) 280 (CA)). The information must be a motivating or influencing factor, either by inducing the person to enter into the transaction or by assisting the person or otherwise influencing the person in the manner in which the person performs the transaction. The insider may, therefore, be held not to be liable in a case where the trading took place after the insider became aware of the confidential information but pursuant to arrangements put in place prior to the insider becoming aware of the information.

Problem Area 5

'MAKES USE OF'

As of 1 January, Lawrence and Natasha each held shares in Tension Corp. Lawrence and Natasha were also directors of the company. In mid-January, the relationship between Lawrence and Natasha deteriorated and they discussed the possibility of Lawrence 'buying out' Natasha's interest. These discussions and negotiations continued until March and the two had almost decided on the final price. On 29 March, Lawrence received information that Tension Corp would be awarded a large and lucrative government contract. On 30 March, before Lawrence had taken any action, Natasha phoned and asked whether Lawrence was willing to buy at the last price they had discussed. Lawrence said he was and he completed the purchase of Natasha's shares soon afterwards. Given that Lawrence was an insider and, therefore, in a special relationship, and had knowledge of an undisclosed material fact, did he violate any insider trading prohibitions?

(1) If Tension Corp is a reporting issuer so that the insider trading provisions of the OSA apply, Lawrence is liable if he purchased or sold shares with knowledge of an undisclosed material fact. It is irrelevant whether the undisclosed information played any role in his decision. Therefore, Lawrence violated the OSA prohibition.

(2) If Tension Corp is incorporated under the OBCA but is not a reporting issuer so that the insider trading provisions of the OBCA apply, Lawrence is only liable if he 'made use of' any specific confidential information. Lawrence might argue in this case that he did not make use of the information in deciding to buy the shares and is therefore not liable. It is unclear whether this argument would succeed.

Finally, the provisions of most corporate statutes require that, in order to be held liable, the insider must have used the confidential information for the insider's 'own benefit or advantage'. Problem Area 6 illustrates this concept.

Problem Area 6

INSIDER'S OWN BENEFIT OR ADVANTAGE

Joann is a director of Down-The-Tubes Inc ('DTT'). Marcel and Joann are good friends. In fact, Marcel has granted to Joann authority to execute trades on his behalf. At Joann's request, Marcel has lent DTT a large amount of money. Joann has confidential information that DTT is doing very poorly and that Marcel will likely be unable to recover his loans. Joann feels badly about this and executes a short sale on Marcel's behalf without telling Marcel about the trading or DTT's situation. Given that Joann is an insider of DTT (and, hence, is in a special relationship with DTT) and had specific, confidential information, did she violate any insider trading prohibitions?

(1) If the provisions of the OBCA apply, under the OBCA, an insider is prohibited from trading for the insider's own benefit or advantage. Since Joann's actions benefited Marcel, she would not be liable.

(2) If the provisions of the OSA apply, under the OSA (and most other provincial securities Acts) an insider is prohibited from purchasing or selling securities. There is no requirement that the trade be effected for the insider's own benefit. Accordingly, Joann will have breached the insider trading prohibition.

In this example, there is a theoretical issue as to whether Joann has actually traded since the sale she executed was executed on Marcel's behalf. There is case law supporting the proposition, however, that effecting a trade in this manner will fall within the terms 'trading' or 'purchase and sale' as they are used in the insider trading provisions.

The civil liability provisions of the OBCA apply to 'insiders'. 'Insider' is defined more broadly than in the OSA but more narrowly than the OSA's concept of 'a person in a special relationship with' a reporting issuer. The definition of 'insider' in the OBCA is summarised in Table (4).

TABLE (4)

Definition of insider under the OBCA
In relation to a corporation, an insider is:
- the corporation
- a subsidiary of the corporation, or a company of which the corporation is a subsidiary or under common control, or a director or officer of such other company
- a director or officer of the corporation
- a person who beneficially owns, directly or indirectly or exercises control or direction over more than 10 per cent of the voting securities of the corporation

- a person employed or retained by the corporation
- a person (a 'tippee') who receives specific confidential information from a person described in this definition (including another tippee) and who knows that the person giving the information is a person described in this definition

As under the OSA, under the OBCA a director or officer of Company A is deemed to have been an insider of Company B for the previous six months where Company A becomes an insider of Company B, and the directors and officers of Company B are deemed to have been insiders for the previous six months of Company A. The OBCA extends this deeming provision somewhat further by also deeming a 10 per cent shareholder of Company A or Company B to have been an insider of Company B or Company A, respectively, and by covering cases where Company A enters into a business combination with Company B as well as where Company A becomes an insider of Company B.

Actions to enforce civil liability under the OBCA must be commenced within two years after the discovery of the facts which give rise to the cause of action.

3.2 FEDERAL

The Canada Business Corporations Act (the 'CBCA') imposes civil liability for insider trading, on substantially the same terms as the civil liability imposed under the OBCA, in respect of a corporation incorporated under the CBCA and subsidiaries of such a corporation and companies of which such a corporation is itself a subsidiary or under common control. The only significant difference between the two statutes is that under the CBCA an action to enforce the civil liability must be brought (a) within two years after the discovery of the facts that give rise to the cause of action, or (b) within two years after the filing of the report of the trade in question under the CBCA if the trade was required to be so reported. The CBCA contains insider reporting provisions substantially similar to those contained in the OSA. See 2.9 *above*. The CBCA insider reporting provisions apply to insiders of corporations incorporated under the CBCA which distribute securities to the public.

As noted earlier, the rules under the CBCA apply to a corporation incorporated thereunder whether or not it is a reporting issuer. In the case of a reporting issuer in Ontario which is incorporated under the CBCA, the insider trading provisions under both the CBCA and the OSA apply, whereas in the case of a reporting issuer incorporated under the OBCA, the insider trading provisions under only the OSA apply.

Insider trading liability provisions, similar to those in the CBCA, are contained in various federal statutes under which specific types of corporations are incorporated such as banks, insurance companies, trust companies, loan companies and co-operative credit associations.

4 CRIMINAL LAW

There is the possibility of a prosecution under the general fraud section of the Criminal Code with respect to certain egregious cases of insider trading. Section 380 of the Criminal Code provides that every person who, by deceit, falsehood or other fraudulent means defrauds any person of any property, money or valuable security, is guilty of an offence and is liable to imprisonment for up to ten years (two years if the subject matter of the offence does not exceed Cdn$1,000 (approximately £500 STG)). The section also makes it an offence, punishable by up to ten years' imprisonment, to affect the public market price of stocks or shares, by use, with intent to defraud, of deceit, falsehood or other fraudulent means. Section 725 of the Code gives the court the power to order the accused to compensate the victims of a fraud.

An example of a prosecution under the Criminal Code relating to an insider trading situation was a case in which an insider of a target company purchased shares at well below the offer price knowing that an offer was imminent. The insider also denied that he had any intention of selling his shares when the vendor questioned him about a rumoured take-over. The insider insisted that he was buying the shares for his sons to keep control of the target company within his family. The insider was convicted of fraud and was sentenced to five years' imprisonment (reduced to two years on appeal) and was ordered to compensate the victim: (R v Littler (1974) 65 DLR (3d) 443, 467 (Que CA)). Of course this case involved specific misrepresentations to the other party to the trade. It is unclear whether a prosecution under the Criminal Code would have taken place if the insider had simply completed the purchase without making any representations to the vendor.

CASE STUDY

Splash Inc, a company listed on the Toronto Stock Exchange, manufactures rainwear and umbrellas. Alan, a weather forecaster, on discovering that there is an unseasonable amount of rain due in the next three months, instructs his broker to buy shares in Splash. Meanwhile, Charles, an analyst who follows Splash, is told in a conversation with Jeremy, one of the directors of Splash, that the president of Splash is expected to be paid a salary of Cdn$1 million. Charles knows from his knowledge of the president's employment contract (which is available for public inspection) that this salary could be paid only if Splash achieved profit in excess of Cdn$40 million. Charles revises his profit forecast for Splash but, before he publishes it, he cancels instructions which he had previously given to his broker to sell his Splash shares. Charles also tells his girlfriend, Maggie, that 'things are looking up' for Splash. Maggie then buys shares on her father's account from an old friend of hers who wanted to sell Splash shares off the market to avoid paying a brokerage commission. One day after the new profit forecast is published, Charles places an order to purchase additional Splash shares. Owen, an employee of the contracting firm which cleans Splash's offices, finds a draft of the latest management figures in a wastepaper bin; these figures demonstrate Splash's high profitability. He immediately buys shares.

Alan

On these facts, Alan is not in a special relationship with Splash. He is therefore not caught by the insider trading prohibition. It is also highly unlikely that the rainfall information would be held to be a material fact about Splash in much the same way that world gold prices would not be held to be a material fact about a gold producing company.

Jeremy

As a director of Splash, Jeremy is an insider of the company and is, therefore, in a special relationship with Splash. There is an issue as to whether the president's salary is a material fact. It would be a material fact if it was held that if the fact was known, investors would be reasonably expected to draw the conclusion about Splash's profitability and this conclusion could reasonably be expected to have a significant effect on the market price or value of Splash's shares. Certainly, the information has not been generally disclosed. If the president's salary is determined to be a material fact, Jeremy has violated the tipping prohibition by informing Charles of a material fact before the fact has been generally disclosed. Jeremy's only defence would be that he disclosed the fact in the necessary course of business. In this situation, it would be difficult to maintain that Jeremy informed Charles in the necessary course of Splash's business.

Charles

Assuming the president's salary is a material fact, Charles learned it from an insider. If Charles knew or ought reasonably to have known that Jeremy was an insider (or was otherwise in a special relationship with Splash) then Charles is also in a special relationship with Splash. Before Charles published his revised forecast, he cancelled an order to purchase shares. Although Charles had knowledge of a material fact that was not generally disclosed and was in a special relationship with Splash, he neither purchased nor sold shares. Charles might argue that he could therefore not have breached the insider trading prohibition because there was no trade. While this argument might succeed in a court proceeding, the securities regulators would be concerned that his conduct could adversely affect the integrity of the capital markets. Since Charles is a participant in the securities industry the regulators could apply severe administrative sanctions against him. After Charles published his revised foreast, he waited a day and then purchased shares. There must be some interval between the time at which material information is released and the time at which a person in a special relationship with the issuer can trade. As a rule of thumb, one trading day will usually suffice. However, Charles might have acted too quickly depending upon the dissemination of his forecast. The information may not have been widely disseminated in which case the material fact would not be considered to have been generally disclosed. Charles may also have breached the insider tipping prohibition, although he did not inform Maggie of the specific material undisclosed information. Notwithstanding this technicality, the securities regulators, and probably a court, would strain to conclude that he did breach the prohibition.

Maggie
There is the same issue as to whether Maggie has learned of a material fact. She was told that 'things are looking up' for Splash. This information is quite general although it might be expected to affect the market price or value of Splash's shares. Even assuming the information is a material fact, there is a question as to whether Maggie is in a special relationship with Splash. She learned of the material fact from Charles. Charles was in a special relationship with Splash because he learned his information from an insider. It is, however, debatable whether Maggie knew or ought reasonably to have known that Charles was in a special relationship. Charles is a financial analyst and Maggie might reasonably have concluded that he received the information from non-inside sources or had drawn the conclusion himself from non-confidential information. If Maggie was in a special relationship and traded on the basis of undisclosed material facts, she would be treated differently under the OSA and the CBCA or the OBCA with respect to the shares purchased for her father's account. Under the OSA, it is irrelevant that she effected a trade for the benefit of her father. However, under the CBCA or the OBCA, she is only liable if she traded to her own benefit or advantage. In neither case is it relevant that Maggie traded off the market. (Of course, in this case study, even if Splash was incorporated under the OBCA, the insider trading provisions of the OBCA would not apply since Splash is a reporting issuer.)

Owen
The information found by Owen contains undisclosed material facts. The issue is whether Owen received or learned of the information from a 'person' who was in a special relationship. Technically, Owen did not receive the information from anyone; he merely found it. Indirectly, the information came from a person, although it is not clear that that person was in a special relationship with Splash. For example, an assistant treasurer would not be in a special relationship unless the assistant treasurer in turn received the

information from someone who was in a special relationship. Certainly, if there are surrounding facts which suggest that Owen ought reasonably to have known that the figures came from a person in a special relationship (such as the wastepaper bin being the wastepaper bin in the president's office), it is possible that Owen would be held to be in a special relationship with Splash and liable for having traded with knowledge of the undisclosed material facts.

Mexico

Antje Zaldívar, Ritch,
Heather Y Mueller, SC, Mexico City

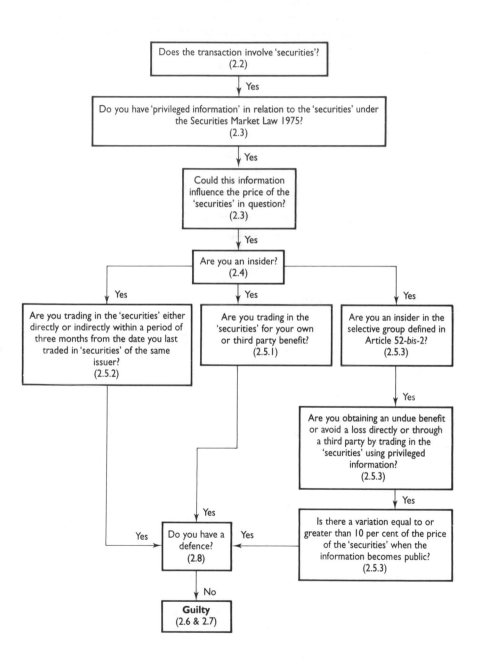

1 INTRODUCTION

The Mexican securities market legal framework consists of the Securities Market Law ('SML') (*Ley del Mercado de Valores*), which was enacted in January 1975, and administrative regulations or circulars (*circulares*), issued by the National Banking and Securities Commission (*Comision Nacional Bancaria y de Valores*) ('CNBV'), pursuant to the authority vested on such commission by the Securities Market Law and the National Banking and Securities Commission Law.

Contrary to many countries that have extensive regulation in securities matters, Mexico's legal framework is still embryonic. Aside from the statutory legislation and the circulars, the only additional piece of regulatory material are the internal regulations of the Mexican Stock Exchange (*Bolsa Mexicana de Valores, SA de CV*), the only stock exchange established in Mexico. The recent development of the Mexican financial market and consequent increased level of securities trading on the stock exchange has resulted in a need for more sophisticated regulation. While important amendments have been made to the securities market law, rather than enact primary legislation, circulars have been generally used as a means to introduce new securities legislation.

2 THE MEXICAN SECURITIES MARKET LAW

2.1 HISTORICAL BACKGROUND

Insider dealing was first made an offence in 1983 when an amendment to the Securities Market Law was passed by Congress. This amendment was very limited in its application since although it prohibited the use of 'privileged information' related to issuers to the prejudice of investors, the prohibition did not extend to persons who 'indirectly' acquired the information. Furthermore, the concept of 'privileged information' was limited to the information that the issuers had to submit to the former National Securities Commission (today, the National Banking and Securities Commission ('CNBV')) and the Mexican Stock Exchange; the nature of such information being determined by the National Securities Commission ('NSC').

Several amendments have been made to the insider dealing legislation, the latest of which was in 1993. The current prohibition on insider dealing is contained in art 16 to art 16-*bis*-8 of the SML.

The SML regulates the public offering of securities, brokerage activities, the National Securities and Brokers Registry and services related to the offering of securities in the securities market. It does not apply to transactions involving unlisted securities, which are regulated by other pieces of legislation, depending upon their characteristics, ie equity, debt, bank or government securities.

2.2 SECURITIES

The insider dealing provisions referred to in the articles of the SML, only apply to listed securities.

The SML defines securities as (i) 'shares, debentures and other credit instruments' (*titulos de crédito*) and other documents that grant their holders rights of credit, ownership or participation in the capital stock of entities, which documents are traded in the securities market and (ii) securities and other documents with the same characteristics as those set forth in para (i) that are issued abroad, but in respect of which provisions of the SML apply in respect of their trading and public offering.

Since futures and options are not traded on the Mexican Stock Exchange they are not within the ambit of the insider dealing legislation.

2.3 WHAT IS 'PRIVILEGED INFORMATION'?

Article 16 *bis* of the SML defines the concept of 'privileged information' as follows:

the knowledge of acts, facts or situations that may affect market prices of securities that are traded in the securities market, while such information has not been made public.

The definition implies that information, which has not been made available to the public relating to events that may result in either an increase or a decrease in the value of a security, will constitute privileged information.

Issuers are required to inform investors of privileged information on the business day following the day they became aware of it. Such information in order to be made public is required to be published in a major newspaper and filed with the CNBV and the Mexican Stock Exchange. The stock exchange, upon filing, will distribute it to the market (Circular No 11-25, issued by the NSC on 31 August 1993).

There is no definition nor precedent that clearly defines 'act, fact or situation'. It has, however, been construed as an objective situation that can be supported by evidence. For example, the entering into a letter of intent for a joint venture, merger, etc. Rumours about any such situation, would not fall under this category, even if they may, artificially, affect market prices.

2.4 WHO IS AN 'INSIDER'

The most recent amendment to the provisions of the SML included an article defining who shall be deemed to have access to privileged information, details of which are set out in Table (1).

TABLE (1)

Article 16-bis-1 of the Securities Market Law 1975.

The following shall be deemed to have access to privileged information of the relevant issuer:

- the members of the board of directors, directors, managers, commissioners, external auditors and secretaries of collective corporate bodies of corporations that have securities registered with the National Registry of Securities and Intermediaries ('relevant corporations') (such registration is necessary in order for a company to obtain a listing);
- shareholders of relevant corporations that control 10 per cent or more of the shares representing their capital stock;
- members of the board of directors, directors, managers and commissioners of corporations that control 10 per cent or more of the capital stock of relevant corporations;
- independent consultants of such corporations and their advisers in general, as well as commissioners (ie independent representatives or agents who have power to act on behalf of the company) of any corporation or business that has participated, advised or collaborated with an issuer, in relation to any matter that may be construed as privileged information;
- shareholders controlling 5 per cent or more of the share capital of credit institutions that maintain their securities registered with the National Registry of Securities and Intermediaries;
- shareholders controlling 5 per cent or more of the share capital of holding companies of a finance group or credit institution, as well as those controlling 10 per cent or more of share capital of other financial entities, when all of them are part of the same finance group and at least one of the corporations forming part of the group is an issuer of securities registered with the National Registry of Securities and Intermediaries;
- members of the board of directors of the holding companies and financial entities referred to in the foregoing paragraph.

For purposes of the SML, only the persons listed in art 16-*bis*-1 are presumed to be insiders. However, it is possible that other persons can be treated as insiders but, in such a case, it will be necessary to adduce evidence that they were in possession of privileged information. It should be noted that a person who received privileged information from an insider does not become an insider himself.

2.5 INSIDER DEALING OFFENCE

Article 16 *bis* and art 16-*bis*-2 provide for two offences:

2.5.1 Dealing in possession of privileged information

Persons who have access to privileged information and who carry out transactions for their own benefit or for the benefit of third parties in any class of securities whose price could be influenced by privileged information are guilty of an offence. Persons for the purpose of art 16 includes both individuals and corporations.

2.5.2 Dealing within a three-month period of last dealing

Persons who have access to privileged information who carry out, directly or through an intermediary, the acquisition of any class of securities issued by a company to which they are related by virtue of their position or relationship, during a period of three months from the date of the last sale carried out involving any class of securities issued by that same company are guilty of an offence. Similarly, if shares are sold and a later acquisition made within a three-month period, an offence will be committed.

This provision is intended to prevent insiders speculating in the shares of the companies to which they are connected. It is inspired by s 16(b) of the US Securities Exchange Act 1934 although less draconian in its application since the US provision has a six-month prohibition on dealing.

The following are exempt from this requirement:

- certain market professionals;
- dealings by credit institutions representing assets held by them;
- dealings authorised by CNBV relating to the restructuring or the re-organisation of listed companies.

2.5.3 Unlawful use of privileged information (art 52-*bis*-2)

The members of the board of directors, directors, managers and commissioners of issuers of securities, will be guilty of an offence if such persons:

- improperly use privileged information originating from the company with which they are linked; and
- directly or through a third party obtain an unlawful reward or avoid a loss by acquiring or selling those securities.

It should be noted that there is no express sanction for the third party who trades on the basis of inside information received from an insider although it might be possible to make such third party a party to any proceedings against the insider with a view to recovering damages.

However, the offence is only committed if the relevant sale or purchase is made at a 10 per cent premium, or as the case may be, discount, to the market price of the securities. For the purpose of calculating the market price, an average of the closing price on the stock exchange of the relevant securities is taken for ten days following the date of publication of the information.

2.6 SANCTIONS

The CNBV is the body authorised to ensure compliance with the provisions regarding insider trading and to investigate cases of suspected non-compliance. The CNBV may only impose a sanction within one year of the offence being committed.

2.6.1 Dealing while in the possession of privileged information (see 2.5.1)

A fine is determined by the CNBV of an amount up to two times the benefit obtained from the particular transaction plus an additional sum on such an amount equal to the average interest rate applied by the ten most profitable investment funds during the six months prior to the date of the transaction. For this purpose, the benefit of any particular transaction will be the difference between the cost and sale price of the shares. The dealing costs of the transaction would probably not be taken into account. It should also be noted that avoidance of a loss is not relevant to the calculation of any fine.

2.6.2 Dealing within a three-month period of last dealing (see 2.5.2)

A fine is determined by the CNBV, of an amount equal to the benefit obtained. If no benefit exists, the fine may be for an amount ranging between 400 to 5,000 times the minimum daily salary for the Federal District in Mexico being approximately M$18 (approximately £1.50 STG). The CNBV is entitled to determine the fine, depending upon the seriousness of the offence. If a single transaction involves a breach of both articles, then each of the fines may be separately applied.

2.6.3 Unlawful use of privileged information (see 2.5.3)

A prison sentence of between six months and five years and a fine of two to three times the benefit obtained or, unlike the penalties for the other offences, the loss avoided. Proceedings under art 52-*bis*-2 may only be brought by the Ministry of Finance and Public Credit, with the prior consent of the CNBV. Any fine can be imposed by the CNBV but a criminal prosecution will have to be commenced if a prison sentence is to be imposed.

2.7 OTHER SANCTIONS

The same penalties as are referred to in 2.6.1 will apply to these persons who have managerial functions, employment, commissions or positions with brokerage firms or other entities in relation to transactions involving the public offering of securities, if such persons deal in securities on the basis referred to in 2.5.3, 30 days before or after the public issue.

There have been very few prosecutions brought in the past five years (only one case was commenced). The reason for the lack of proceedings is the difficulty in obtaining the necessary proof for a successful prosecution.

2.8 DEFENCES AVAILABLE

The defence that an insider has, should it be sanctioned by the CNBV for insider trading, is the ability of claiming that the insider was not in possession of inside information when effecting the trade, or that he/she did not trade within the restricted time-frame set forth above. However, sufficient proof would have to be submitted to the competent court in order that it may stop the effects of a ruling imposing a penalty or sanction.

2.9 OBLIGATION OF ISSUERS TO DISCLOSE PRIVILEGED INFORMATION

The NSC issued in 1993, a circular setting out provisions that issuers have to comply with the disclosure of privileged information. Issuers who have the knowledge of acts, facts or situations that may be price sensitive, are obliged to disclose such information on the business day following the day on which it is obtained. Disclosure is by means of a publication in a major newspaper and the delivery of such information to the CNBV and the stock exchange. The stock exchange will, on receipt, release such information to its members and make it public to investors.

Information provided to the CNBV on behalf of the issuers and all other information that has to be made available is available for public inspection. As such, in the event of privileged information, these officers are liable if it is not disclosed on time. Sanctions are applied in terms of the SML. As stated in 2.3, Circular 11-25 requires that information pertaining to price-sensitive events, be disclosed. The CNBV is entitled to impose fines, to the extent such information is not filed. No specific provisions make reference to the size of the fine, it is at the discretion of the Commission.

3 CONCLUSION

Clearly, insider trading regulation in Mexico, is still relatively underdeveloped. Accordingly, there are a number of areas which need to be tightened if the insider trading regulation is to be effective in eliminating unfair market practices. In particular, the disclosure of privileged information or encouragement of third parties to deal while in the possession of such information should be prohibited, as should any dealing by the recipient of such information or encouragement. Further, it seems that too much power is vested in the CNBV. The Commission has power to oversee compliance, determine guilt and impose fines and sanctions. The determination of guilt or innocence which could lead to a fine should be a judicial function.

CASE STUDY

Splash Plc, a company listed on the Mexican Stock Exchange, manufactures rainwear and umbrellas. Alan, a weather forecaster, on discovering that there is an unseasonable amount of rain due in the next three months, instructs his broker to buy shares in Splash. Meanwhile, Charles, an analyst of the company's shares, is told in a conversation with Jeremy, one of the directors, that the Chairman is expected to be paid a salary of $500,000. Charles knows from his knowledge of the Chairman's service contract (which is available for public inspection) that this salary could only be paid if the company achieved profit in excess of $20 million. Charles revises his profit forecast for the company but before he publishes it he cancels instructions which he had previously given to his broker to sell his Splash shares. Charles also tells his girlfriend, Maggie, that 'things are looking up' for Splash. Maggie then buys shares in the name of her father from an old friend of hers who wanted to sell Splash shares off market to save the payment of brokers commission. In addition, Owen, an employee of the contracting firm which cleans Splash's offices, finds a draft of the latest management figures, which demonstrate Splash's high profitability, in a waste-paper bin. He immediately buys shares.

Alan
In order for Alan to be guilty of insider dealing it will be necessary for it to be shown: (1) Alan is in possession of inside information, (2) that he is an insider and (3) that he has dealt in the securities in a restricted period. The Mexican Securities Market Law ('SML') defines 'inside information' as 'the knowledge of acts, facts or situations that may affect market prices of securities that are traded in the securities market, while such information has not been made public'. The knowledge by a weather forecaster of information that could increase sales and affect market prices of an issuer in the rainwear industry, ie, unseasonal rain, could not be considered as 'inside information' that needs to be disclosed to securities authorities, as the second part of the definition of 'inside information' suggests. In addition, weather forecast information will not be considered as non-public information since such information could be obtained by the public if they wished to obtain it. Also, Alan does not belong to the category of insiders set out in the Mexican SML and no trading has been made in the restricted periods set forth therein. Alan will not be guilty of trading while in the possession of inside information.

Jeremy

Jeremy, as a director of Splash Plc, is considered by the Mexican SML as an insider. The information regarding the salary of the Chairman is also information that may fall under the definition of 'inside information', as referred to above, since it may impact market prices once it is made public. However, under the Mexican SML, there is no sanction contemplated for a person disclosing inside information to a third party and Jeremy cannot be convicted by reason of his disclosure, irrespective of the use thereof by the party to whom it was disclosed.

Charles

Charles is not considered an insider under the Mexican SML, since he is not within the definition of insider contained in the SML. The information about the salary of the Chairman is clearly inside information which, linked to the fact that such a salary would be payable only in the event that the profits of the company exceed a certain figure results in a fact that may affect market prices of the shares. However, the fact that he is only cancelling certain instructions to sell based on such information makes him not guilty of an offence. While the SML provides that avoiding a loss by acquiring or selling securities, provided certain requirements (percentage of loss/profit) are met, Charles did not sell or acquire securities based on such information and only avoided such a sale. In respect of Charles disclosing to Maggie that 'things are looking up' for Splash, it would be difficult to prove that such a statement and a trade by Maggie based on it, follows knowledge of inside information.

Maggie

Since Maggie is not an insider and, further, the information in her possession is not inside information, Maggie will not be guilty of an offence. While she is not an insider, it could in theory be proved that she dealt in possession of inside information.

Owen

Owen does not fall under the category of an insider, as provided by the SML. However, the information based on which he purchases shares is inside information and he had access to it by virtue of his employment. Pursuant to the provisions of the SML, Owen could be guilty of insider trading, however it would be difficult to prove that the information he based the trade on was inside information.

Brazil

Henrique da Silva Gordo Lang,
Pinheiro Neto-Advogados, São Paulo

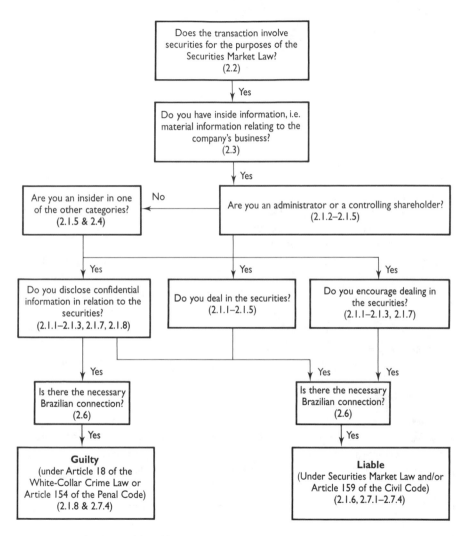

Note: There is also the possibility of being guilty of larcenous fraud although there is no precedent (1.5).

1 INTRODUCTION

1.1 DEVELOPMENT

The development of anti-insider dealing mechanisms in Brazil is closely linked to the reform of the capital market brought about by the Securities Market Law (Law No 6385 of 7 December 1976), which created the *Comissão de Valores Mobiliários* (the Brazilian Securities Commission ('CVM')), and the Corporation Law (Law No 6404 of 15 December 1976), which introduced profound modifications in the legislation that regulates publicly-held companies, as well as closely-held corporations.

1.2 CVM

CVM was based on the model of the US Securities and Exchange Commission with broadly similar regulatory responsibilities and powers. The creation of CVM was prompted by the Brazilian exchange crash of 1971, which had a particularly harsh impact on the economy given that it followed so soon after a period of great euphoria on the Brazilian stock exchanges.

1.3 KEY OBJECTIVES

One of the key objectives of the new legislation was to regain investors' confidence in the stock market, which had been badly damaged due to a number of financial scandals. The legislative framework which was set up in 1976 includes the Corporation Law, the Securities Market Law and regulations issued by CVM. The CVM's regulatory power derives from the Securities Market Law which provides for strict rules targeting protection of minority shareholders' rights and ensures the strict application of the Corporation Law.

1.4 PRINCIPAL MEASURES

The principal measures designed to ensure a fair market, including restrictions upon insider dealing are contained in the following regulations issued by CVM:

- CVM Instruction No 8 of 8 October 1979 which defines and prohibits the creation of artificial conditions of supply, demand or securities pricing, manipulation of prices, fraudulent transactions and use of inequitable practices;
- CVM Instruction No 31 of 8 February 1984 (the 'Insider Dealing Instruction'), which contains the main regulation regarding insider dealing, regulates disclosure and use of information on material acts or facts;
- CVM Instruction No 202 of 6 December 1993, which amends and consolidates the rules governing the registration with CVM of companies who

trade their securities on stock exchanges or on the over-the-counter market and provides for periodic and sporadic disclosure requirements with CVM for the updating of the company's registration.

1.5 INSIDER DEALING AS A CRIMINAL OFFENCE

Unlike other countries, insider dealing is not a specific criminal offence in Brazil, although in theory an insider trader could be indicted for the crime of larcenous fraud, under art 171 of the Penal Code. Whilst a broad interpretation of 'larcenous fraud' would encompass insider dealing, no criminal prosecution has, as yet, been made.

1.6 PROPOSED PENALTIES

Since 1988, Congress has been examining Bill No 1317, proposed by the government, which seeks to define and punish crimes involving the securities market. If enacted, this Bill will make insider dealing, and malpractices such as manipulation of prices and non-disclosure of material information to the public, a criminal offence. The proposed penalties are very severe: the latest draft of the Bill proposes, for example, that insider dealers be subject to imprisonment for a period of two to eight years, plus a fine. If a corporate entity deals in contravention of the insider dealing legislation, the fine will be levied on the corporate entity involved, based on the unlawful benefits gained.

2 THE REGULATIONS

2.1 INSIDER DEALING

2.1.1 Definition of insider dealing infractions

The Brazilian regulations do not provide for a clear and precise definition of the insider dealing infractions. However, the constituent elements of various infractions such as dealing, encouraging dealing and disclosure of confidential information may be extracted from the statutes of corporate, civil and even criminal law (see 1.5).

2.1.2 Principal prohibitions

The principal prohibitions on insider trading are contained in art 155, paras 1–3 of the Corporation Law, and Arts 9, 10 and 11 of the Insider Dealing Instruction. Article 155 provides:

> An administrator shall serve the company with loyalty, shall treat its affairs with confidence and shall not:
> 1   use any commercial opportunity which may come to his knowledge, by virtue of his position, for his benefit or that of a third party, whether or not harmful to the company;

II   fail to exercise or protect company rights or, in seeking to obtain advantages for himself
      or for a third party, fail to make use of a commercial opportunity of interest to the
      company;
III   acquire for resale at a profit property or rights which he knows the company needs or
      which the company intends to acquire.

Paragraph 1. An administrator of a publicly-held company shall also treat in confidence any
information not yet revealed to the public, which he obtained by virtue of his position and which
may significantly affect the quotation of securities, and shall not make use of such information
to obtain any advantages for himself or for third parties by purchasing or selling securities.

Paragraph 2. An administrator shall ensure that the provisions of paragraph 1 above are
not infringed by a subordinate or third party enjoying his confidence.

Paragraph 3. Any person detrimentally affected in a purchase or sale of securities contracted contrary to the provisions of paragraphs 1 and 2 above may demand indemnity from
the person responsible for the infringement for losses and damages, unless the person was
aware of the information at the time the contract was made.

2.1.3 Insider Dealing Instruction prohibitions

Articles 9 and 10 provide:

Administrators and controlling shareholders of publicly-held companies shall keep confidential any information relating to a material act or fact to which they have privileged access by
virtue of their office or position, until it is communicated and disclosed on the market.

Administrators and controlling shareholders of publicly-held companies shall not make use
of any information to which they have privileged access relating to a material act or fact not
yet disclosed to the market . . . in order to obtain advantages for themselves or others by
means of trading with securities.

Article 11 goes further, since it is not limited to administrators or controlling
shareholders, and provides:

Trading in securities is prohibited as an inequitable practice, when carried out by anyone who,
by virtue of his office, function or position, gained knowledge of information regarding a material act or fact before it is communicated and disclosed to the market.

2.1.4 Administrators

The term *administrators* includes not only the officers, which are vested with the
powers to represent the company, but also the members of the board of directors, which is the deliberative body responsible for the general strategy of the
company's business.

2.1.5 Controlling shareholder

The term *controlling shareholder* means an individual or legal entity, or a group of
individuals or legal entities contractually bound by a voting agreement or under
common control, which:

*   possesses rights which permanently assure him/it a majority of votes in
    resolutions of general meetings and the powers to elect the majority of
    the company administrators; and
*   effectively uses his/its power to direct the corporate activities and to guide
    the functioning of the bodies of the company.

2.1.6 Civil Liability

In addition to liability under the Corporation Law and/or the Insider Dealing Instruction, a person who is involved in insider dealing may incur civil liability pursuant to art 159 of the Civil Code, the guiding legal principle regulating civil liability in Brazil, which provides that: 'anyone who, by commission or voluntary omission, negligence or imprudence, violates a right or causes harm to another is obliged to make reparation for such damage'.

2.1.7 Insider held jointly liable

Even though the insider does not actually deal in the securities, but only encourages someone dealing in the securities or discloses confidential information in relation to the securities to a third person who uses the information to deal in the securities, the insider could be jointly liable for reparation for the damages caused to investors pursuant to art 1518 of the Civil Code, which provides that:

> The assets of the party responsible for the offence or the violation of another's rights shall be subject to make reparation for the damage caused; and if there is more than one perpetrator of such offence, all of them shall be held jointly liable for the reparation.
> Sole Paragraph—The accomplices and parties designated in Article 1.521 shall be held liable jointly with the perpetrators.

Under these circumstances, as the losses suffered by the investors would never be caused without the active participation of the insider who encouraged dealing or disclosed confidential information (see 2.7.4), the insider would be held jointly liable with the third person who dealt in the securities, as co-principal.

Likewise, art 1521, item III, provides for the joint liability of employers for damages arising out of acts performed by their employees when working:

> The following parties are also held liable for civil reparation:
> III—The employer, master or principal, for his/her employees, servants and agents in the exercise of the work which is their duty, due to such . . .

2.1.8 Violation of business secrets

Though insider dealing is not specifically considered a criminal offence in Brazil, depending on the circumstances of the case, certain crimes *may* be committed by the persons involved in the dealing, such as violation of business secrets pertaining to a financial institution (art 18 of the White-Collar Crime Law), or violation of professional secrecy (art 154 of the Penal Code), among others.

Problem Area 1

Sérgio, the chief executive officer of Target SA, a company listed on the São Paulo Stock Exchange, contracts Finance Bank SA to render financial advisory services to Target SA. After signature of the engagement letter, José, an officer of Finance Bank SA, receives from Sérgio confidential information on the serious financial difficulties faced by Target SA. Immediately after receiving this information, José instructs his broker to sell all his shares in Target SA. What consequences follow?

CVM would initiate an administrative investigation to determine liabilities. The investigation should result in the administrative conviction of José pursuant to art 11 of the Insider Dealing Instruction, who would be subject to the penalties provided for in the Securities Market Law (see 2.7.1 and 2.7.2). Neither Sérgio nor Target SA should be held liable for having disclosed inside information to José. Although the Corporation Law obliges Sérgio to ensure that anti-insider dealing provisions are not infringed by any third party enjoying his confidence, under the circumstances where a bank is contracted to render financial services, one might reasonably expect that the bank officers would refrain from using the information for illicit purposes.

As regards criminal liability, José would not be committing the crime of violation of business secrets pertaining to a financial institution (see 2.1.8), since he did not reveal the information to a third person, but merely used the information for trading with the securities issued by Target SA; statutes of criminal law must be interpreted strictly.

Under the Civil Code, not only José but also Finance Bank SA could be held liable (see 2.1.6 and 2.1.7) for reparation for damage caused to the investors who bought José's shares in Target SA and lost money after the harsh impact of disclosure of the information on the financial difficulties on the quotations of Target SA shares as employers are held jointly and severally liable for damages arising out of acts performed by their employees when working.

2.2 TO WHICH SECURITIES DOES THE LAW APPLY?

For the purposes of the Securities Market Law, the term *securities* currently means:

- shares;
- participation certificates and debentures, their respective coupons and subscription bonuses;
- securities deposit certificates;
- quotas of real estate investment funds;
- any other securities created or issued by corporations at the discretion of the Brazilian Monetary Council, such as commercial paper and options.

Generally, only shares and options are traded on the stock exchanges, with some rare exceptions (eg the certificates of deposit representing shares of the Argentinean oil company YPF Sociedad Anónima, the first foreign company listed in Brazil).

Therefore, although the scope of Brazilian anti-insider dealing regulations is to curb the misuse of inside information in the trading of any securities, in practice its application is limited to the trading of shares and options.

However, it should be noted that the rules under the Insider Dealing Instruction apply not only to transactions carried out on stock exchanges and the over-the-counter market, but also those carried out off-market.

2.3 WHAT IS INSIDE INFORMATION?

The Corporation Law requires administrators of publicly-held companies to disclose material information relating only to the company's own business (art 157, para 4), there being no requirement to provide information on matters beyond the scope of the company's business (ie market information).

2.3.1 Acts or facts that are material

Whether acts or facts are *material* is dependent on whether such information is price-sensitive, and applies to any resolution of the general meeting or administrative bodies of a publicly-held company, or any other act or fact occurring during the course of business that could appreciably influence:

- the quotation of securities issued by the company; or
- the investors' decision to trade in such securities; or
- the investors' decision to exercise certain rights as holders of such securities.

TABLE (1)

Examples of material acts or facts listed in art 1 of the Insider Dealing Instruction are:
- changes in control of the company;
- delisting of shares;
- merger, consolidation, spin-off, transformation or dissolution of the company;
- significant changes in the composition of the company's assets;
- revaluation of the company's assets;
- alteration in the rights and benefits of securities issued by the company;
- share splitting or granting of stock dividends;
- repurchase by a company of its shares;
- profit or loss ascertained in the financial statements of the company and granting of dividends;
- delay of payment of dividends or prospects of a change in dividend distributions;
- execution or termination of an agreement which is significant to the

company, or the failure to carry out such an agreement, the expectation of which was public knowledge;

- petition for *concordata* (court-approved composition with creditors) or bankruptcy, or filing of action against the company which, if judged valid, might affect its economic and financial situation;
- production on an industrial scale, sale or withdrawal from circulation of a product which might significantly affect the company's performance;
- any discovery, change or development in the technology or resources of the company which might significantly alter its results;
- any other relevant act or fact of a policy and administrative, technical, business, or economic and financial nature that might produce any of the effects provided for in 2.3.1 *above*.

2.3.2 Market information

Accordingly, market information is not covered, so that, for example:

- analysis of performance of company shares released by research departments of investment banks;
- new governmental policies or measures with general impact on the economic activity of the company;
- discovery of new technologies by competitors with possible impact on the distribution of market shares even if considered price-sensitive information for the securities of a publicly-held company;

are not considered to be material for the purpose of the Insider Dealing Instruction.

However, if the market information is in any way related to a company's own business, the information will be considered material. This was discussed by the courts during one of the rare cases of conviction of administrators of publicly-held companies in Brazil for the practice of insider dealing.

2.3.3 *Servix Engenharia* case

In 1978, Servix Engenharia SA, a contractor whose shares were traded on the São Paulo Stock Exchange, was regarded by the market as the favourite bidder in a governmental tender for the construction of a hydro-electric power station in Itaparica, an island off the Brazilian state of Bahia. The market's view was derived from the fact that Servix had acquired outstanding experience on a similar project in the same geographical area and which had been completed shortly before the tender. In addition, it was known that Servix already had machinery and personnel in the region. Immediately after having access to privileged information that the government had decided to cancel the tender, the chairman of the board of Servix sold a substantial number of shares on the stock exchange. A few days afterwards, the information was disclosed to the market, resulting in plummeting prices for the company shares. The CVM initiated an administrative investigation to determine the liability of the administrators resulting in a conviction of the defendant in the administrative sphere for insider dealing. This decision was annulled by the Brazilian Monetary Council. However, the investors who had bought the shares from the administrator brought a suit in the civil sphere to obtain reparation for the losses and damages suffered. The civil action was judged in favour of the plaintiffs, and was confirmed by the *Tribunal de Justiça do Estado de São Paulo* (Court of Appeals of the State of São Paulo) (see *Apelação Civel* No 12145–1, of 27.10.1981—TJSP *apud* EIZIRIK, Nelson and BASTOS, Aurélio Wander. *Mercado de Capitais e SA—Jurisprudência*, vol 2, p 725).

2.4 WHO IS AN INSIDER?

Under Brazilian legislation, insider dealing can be carried out by:

- administrators;
- members of the audit committee or any other technical or consulting body;
- controlling shareholders;
- any person who, in the performance of his/her duties, has access to material information, such as publicly-held company employees; and/or
- any person with access to material information, provided such person knows that it is a material act or fact that has not yet been disclosed to the market (ie inside information).

Therefore, any consultants, outside public accountants, attorneys, financial institution employees or others who, in the exercise of their professional duties, have access to inside information will be considered to be involved in insider dealing if they trade securities issued by the company in order to obtain any benefit for themselves or for any third party.

Problem Area 2

Roberto, a lawyer specialising in bankruptcies and *concordatas* (court-approved compositions with creditors), comments to his wife Suzana that he had spent all day working on the petition for withdrawal from *concordata* by one of his clients, Food SA, a listed company. On the following day, Suzana buys shares in Food SA, a short time before the information on the petition is disclosed to the market. What consequences arise?

CVM would initiate an administrative investigation to determine liabilities. Provided that it was proved that, pursuant to art 11 of the Insider Dealing Instruction, Suzana knew she had access to material information not yet disclosed to the market (see 2.3), the investigation should result with the administrative conviction of Suzana, who would be subject to the penalties provided for in the Securities Market Law (see 2.7.1 and 2.7.2).

Since he is married to Suzana, Roberto would probably be accused of using Suzana to deal on his behalf, but as the burden of proof rests on the plaintiff, he is likely to be absolved of the charge.

As a lawyer, Roberto is bound by a duty of professional secrecy, and therefore would be committing the crime of violation of professional secrecy (see 2.1.8). Under art 1518 of the Civil Code, both Roberto and Suzana would be held jointly and severally liable (see 2.1.7) for reparation for loss of profits caused to the investors who sold their shares in Food SA for a lower price than they could sell after the petition for withdrawal from *concordata* was disclosed to the market, as these losses result from the two illicit acts performed by Roberto (violation of professional secrecy) and Suzana (insider dealing).

2.5 WHAT ARE THE DEFENCES?

There is no specific regulation providing for defences to an accusation of insider dealing. The defences available will be specific for each case and will be based on general provisions of relevant laws.

An important point to consider is the burden of proof. Although legal scholars are of the view, which received support from the CVM in the *Servix* case, that the defendant, in the capacity of administrator of a publicly-held company, should be presumed guilty until proven innocent, the Court of Appeals of the State of São Paulo has held that the burden of proof rests on the plaintiff and that the defendant is presumed innocent until proven guilty.

2.6 WHAT IS THE TERRITORIAL SCOPE OF THE BRAZILIAN ANTI-INSIDER DEALING LAWS?

The internationalisation of the Brazilian securities market is a fairly recent phenomenon, initiated in the 1980s, and the issue of territoriality of the Insider Dealing Instruction has never been considered by either CVM or the Brazilian courts.

Brazilian civil and administrative laws are applicable to qualify and govern any obligations formed under the laws of Brazil. Apart from a few exceptions, the laws of Brazil neither authorise nor prohibit its extraterritorial application. The guiding principles regulating the extraterritorial Brazilian legislative authority are nearly the same as the guiding rules governing the jurisdiction of the courts of Brazil.

Brazilian courts have concurrent jurisdiction with foreign courts whenever the defendant is domiciled in Brazil (notwithstanding the defendant's nationality), or the obligation is to be performed in Brazil, or the suit results from a fact that occurred or an act that was performed in Brazil. This means that whenever one

of these three requirements exists, the limits of the Brazilian legislative authority
will be based on two criteria: convenience for the Brazilian State and the possibility of enforcement.

CVM has exclusive authority for the supervision and inspection of the Brazilian
securities market, but this authority could possibly be extended to facts that
occur overseas where CVM considers that they have a relevant impact on the
Brazilian securities market.

Problem Area 3

Technology SA is a Brazilian company with shares listed on the São Paulo
Stock Exchange and with ADRs listed on the New York Stock Exchange.
Luiz, the controlling shareholder, is concluding the negotiations for taking
over Challenge Ltda, the main competitor of Technology SA on the Brazilian
market, and uses his inside information to deal in ADRs, before the take-
over is disclosed to the public. What law and jurisdiction would apply?

Since the dealing was effected on the New York Stock Exchange (under
US law), the US anti-insider dealing provisions will apply. Notwithstanding
US jurisdiction, this trading could also possibly be subject to the concurrent jurisdiction of the Brazilian authorities due to the existing connection
between the fact under investigation and the Brazilian stock market.
Though the trading would be carried out overseas, the material information improperly used originated from Luiz, who was domiciled in Brazil and
linked to Technology SA.

In practice, one can say that the territorial scope of anti-insider dealing laws is
generally limited to Brazil, since it is probable that the Brazilian authorities will
not claim jurisdiction in respect to dealings abroad. It is more likely that CVM will
co-operate with the foreign authority in charge of the insider dealing investigation.

2.7 WHAT ARE THE PENALTIES AND CONSEQUENCES?

2.7.1 Penalties

The infringement of the provisions of the Insider Dealing Instruction constitutes
a serious violation for the purposes of the Securities Market Law. In accordance
with the Securities Market Law, CVM could impose the following penalties on vio-
lators:

- warning;
- fine;
- suspension from the position of administrator in a publicly-held company
  or an entity in the securities distribution system;

- disqualification for the positions referred to in the previous paragraph;
- suspension of authorisation or registration for the performance of the activities under the Securities Market Law, which includes all activities comprising the securities industry;
- annulment of the authorisation or registration referred to in the previous paragraph.

2.7.2 Fines

The fine imposed may be up to a limit of:

- 500 times the face value of the former *Obrigações Reajustáveis do Tesouro Nacional* (500 Readjustable National Treasure Bonds = approximately £2,000 STG); or
- 30 per cent of the amount of the irregular transaction;

whichever is highest.

Before imposing penalties for insider dealing, CVM start an administrative investigation to determine the liability of persons involved in the transaction. In accordance with data supplied by CVM (up to 7 June 1995) 17 administrative investigations were commenced to investigate the practice of insider dealing. As a result of these investigations, nine persons were fined, three warned, one disqualified, and 36 absolved.

The defendant is ensured full defence and the right of appeal to the Brazilian Monetary Council. In addition to this, the Federal Constitution ensures all persons the right of review by the judiciary of any violation of, or threat to, a right. Therefore, any penalty imposed on the defendant may be reviewed by the judiciary.

2.7.3 Reparation for losses and damages

The injured party may bring a suit against the insider dealer to obtain reparation for losses and damages suffered, based on art 159 of the Civil Code. Also in the civil sphere, in accordance with Law No 7913 of 7 December 1989, the Public Attorneys' Office, under its own authority or at the request of CVM and without prejudice to any indemnification action which may be brought by the injured party, is vested with the authority to adopt the necessary judicial measures to avoid losses or obtain a refund of the damages caused to the titleholders of securities and market investors. This is through a public civil action against the individuals involved in the practice of insider dealing, fraudulent transactions, manipulation or creation of artificial conditions on the securities market.

2.7.4 Indemnification for losses and damages

Unlike in the United States, there are no punitive damages in Brazil. In order to receive indemnification for losses and damages, the plaintiff (either the injured party or the Public Attorneys' Office) must prove:

(1) the misuse of inside information by the defendant,
(2) the existence of actual losses and damages to be indemnified, and
(3) the causation between the illicit action performed by the defendant and the losses and damages suffered.

In order to satisfy the burden of proof requirement, the plaintiff may make use of the results of any administrative investigation carried out by CVM, and any other kind of evidence admitted in court.

In addition, whenever an investigation concludes that a crime against the public has occurred, CVM is required to inform the Government Attorney's Office so that a criminal action may be filed (see 1.5 and 2.1.8).

2.8 PREVENTIVE REGULATIONS

Both the Corporation Law and the Insider Dealing Instruction contain a number of measures designed to prevent insider dealing.

2.8.1 Disclosure of material information

Disclosure of material information constitutes the main focus of preventive anti-insider dealing regulations in Brazil and reflects the principle that an administrator of a publicly-held company should base his/her conduct on compliance with the principle of full disclosure; that is, the wide, open and complete disclosure of material information to the market in order to provide total transparency for the trading of the company's shares. In addition, such information should be made accessible to everyone equally. Therefore, disclosure must not only be full, but also fair.

The administrators of a publicly-held company must immediately communicate to CVM and the stock exchange on which its securities are more commonly traded, and also in the press, any material act or fact that has occurred in the company's business.

Material acts or facts occurring in the business of a publicly-held company should be disclosed in the press, by means of a communication published in the same newspaper with wide circulation in which the company usually makes such publications as are required by the Corporation Law.

Any price-sensitive information received by the Brazilian stock exchanges is immediately transmitted to the market through their computer network, announcements at trading sessions and other vehicles of transmission of information.

The communication and disclosure must be accurate and complete. CVM or the stock exchanges may at any time request additional explanations on such communication and disclosure. In the event CVM considers that the information disclosed is inaccurate, incomplete or untrue, it may require the companies to republish it immediately with corrections or additions.

2.8.2 Administrators to provide information

In addition to the duty to disclose material information, administrators are under an obligation to provide the following information with respect to their dealings with securities issued by their companies:

- upon taking up office the administrator must state in the company books the number and relevant characteristics of any securities issued by the company, controlled companies or companies in the same group, in which he/she holds or over which he/she has a purchase option (art 13 of the Insider Dealing Instruction);
- details of dealing carried out, types of transactions and other information regarding the above mentioned securities owned by the administrator or his/her spouse, companion or any other dependant included on his/her income tax return (art 14 of the Insider Dealing Instruction);
- for the shareholders in annual general meeting, the number of securities issued by the company, controlled companies or companies in the same group, acquired or disposed of by the administrator either directly or through third parties, any options for the purchase and sale of shares contracted or exercised during the previous year, and any material acts or facts, when requested by shareholders representing at least 5 per cent of the share capital (art 157 of the Corporation Law).

The controlling shareholders of publicly-held companies must also provide the information mentioned in the first item above, upon acquisition of control of the company, and in the second item, within ten days of the end of the month in which the securities were traded.

2.8.3 Optional self-regulating procedures

Further to compulsory conduct requirements, the Insider Dealing Instruction provides for optional self-regulating procedures. Whenever the company adopts internal policy procedures including at least the measures below, the statements signed by the controlling shareholders, administrators and high level employees of publicly-held companies are presumed to be true, for the purpose of providing evidence to CVM (art 17 of the Insider Dealing Instruction):

- during the period of one month prior to the end of the fiscal year until publication of the public notice placing the company's financial statements at the disposal of the shareholders, the administrators, high level employees and controlling shareholders are prohibited to deal in their own securities issued by the company and its publicly-held controlling and controlled companies, and are prohibited to deal in such securities which are held by a spouse from whom they are not factually or legally separated, or by a companion, or by any dependant included in their annual income tax return;

- during the period between the decision taken by the competent corporate body to increase the share capital, to distribute dividends, stock dividends or splitting of shares, and publication of the respective public notices or announcements, the administrators, high level employees and controlling shareholders are obliged to refrain from trading in the securities mentioned in the preceding item;

- the officers, high level employees and controlling shareholders are obliged to keep in their possession for a minimum period of 180 days, prior to a new dealing, their securities or those belonging to the persons listed in the first item above, issued by the company itself and its publicly-held controlling and controlled companies;

- only in exceptional cases and provided details are submitted in writing in advance to the company, administrators, high level employees and controlling shareholders are authorised to trade the securities in a shorter period than that mentioned in the previous item, with due regard in any event of the provisions of the other two items above;

- the administrators and controlling shareholders are obliged to disclose their plans for periodic dealing with securities issued by the company, its publicly-held controlling and controlled companies, as a programmed investment of disposal of investment;

- the administrators and controlling shareholders are obliged to inform the company of non-compliance with the program provided for in the preceding item.

3 CONCLUSION

Brazilian law provides for a simple but comprehensive set of rules aimed at curbing insider dealing. Further measures could be introduced, for example, to improve the effectiveness of the protection of minority shareholders' rights, and also to provide better relief for losses and damages suffered from misuse of inside information by insiders.

One could maintain that insider dealing should be converted into a criminal offence, a policy adopted in many countries, in order to make the prohibition of misuse of inside information more effective.

However, it seems that the lack of greater effectiveness of anti-insider dealing laws in Brazil is not related to a deficiency in existing regulations, but a consequence of current financial difficulties faced by CVM. Due to budget constraints imposed by the federal government, CVM has been obliged to reduce its personnel over the years, while the securities market has grown in both size and complexity. Therefore, instead of creating new criminal offences, the Brazilian securities market needs a stronger and revitalised CVM, financially and functionally independent from the federal government, in order to be in a position to properly perform its important role in the supervision and inspection of the Brazilian market.

CASE STUDY

Splash SA a company listed on the São Paulo Stock Exchange, manufactures rainwear and umbrellas. Antonio, a weather forecaster, on discovering that there is an unseasonable amount of rain due in the next three months, instructs his broker to buy shares in Splash. Meanwhile, Carlos, an analyst of the company's shares, is told in a conversation with Andre, one of the directors, that the Chairman is expected to be paid a salary of $500,000. Carlos knows from his knowledge of the Chairman's service contract (which is available for public inspection) that this salary could only be paid if the company achieved profit in excess of $20 million. Carlos revises his profit forecast for the company but before he publishes it he cancels instructions which he had previously given to his broker to sell his Splash shares. Carlos also tells his girlfriend, Beatriz, that 'things are looking up' for Splash. Beatriz then buys shares in the name of her father from an old friend of hers who wanted to sell Splash shares off market to save the payment of brokers commission. In addition, Oscar, an employee of the contracting firm which cleans Splash's offices, finds a draft of the latest management figures, which demonstrate Splash's high profitability, in a waste-paper bin. He immediately buys shares in Splash.

Antonio
The issue is whether the information of an unseasonable amount of rain being due constitutes inside information. Though the disclosure of the information may have a significant impact on the sales of Splash, and possibly—but not necessarily—influence the quotation of Splash shares on the São Paulo Stock Exchange, the information cannot be considered material. It would actually be market information, since it is not related to Splash's own business and could be readily obtained by anyone who deals with Splash shares from other sources of weather forecasting. Therefore Antonio would not be committing an offence of insider dealing.

Andre
Since the information of the high salary expected to be paid to the Chairman is clearly material, if we consider that the market is sufficiently sophisticated to interpret its impact on the company's profitability, Andre would be in breach of the duty of loyalty under the insider dealing legislation. As Brazilian law places an obligation upon an administrator to ensure that this duty is observed by any third party in whom he confides, Andre could (a) be held liable for losses and damages, in the event that Carlos or Beatriz were convicted for insider dealing, which is unlikely to occur, or (b)

be subject to technical penalties imposed by the SML, which could result in his disqualification from holding the position of administrator of a publicly-held company.

Carlos

The mere act of using inside information to cancel instructions which had previously been given to Carlos' broker to sell his Splash shares does not constitute insider dealing, for the simple reason that no dealing was effected (in fact Carlos refrained from dealing). Likewise, the mere tip from an analyst of shares that 'things are looking up for Splash' is not enough to characterise it as inside information, unless other circumstances could lead to the conclusion that Beatriz knew that Carlos had inside information through indirect means. Proving this fact, however, would be very difficult, but if successful would result in Carlos being held jointly liable with Beatriz for reparation of damages caused as co-principal.

Beatriz

Only in the event that it can be proved that Beatriz, as a tippee, in fact had knowledge that Carlos possessed material information, not yet disclosed to the market, could Beatriz be held liable for insider dealing (Insider Dealing Instruction, art 11, Sole Paragraph). The fact that Beatriz is dealing on behalf of her father would not, in itself, negate her civil liability, but only make the investigation more difficult.

Oscar

The fact that Oscar is not an employee of Splash but an employee of the contracting firm which cleans Splash's offices, does not remove his liability, since the inside information was obtained by virtue of his function at Splash's offices. Therefore, Oscar would be held liable for insider dealing pursuant to art 11 of the Insider Dealing legislation.

PART 2

Europe/Africa

UNITED KINGDOM
GERMANY
FRANCE
SPAIN
SWITZERLAND
NETHERLANDS
ITALY
REPUBLIC OF SOUTH AFRICA

United Kingdom

Mark Stamp and Carson Welsh,
Linklaters & Paines, London

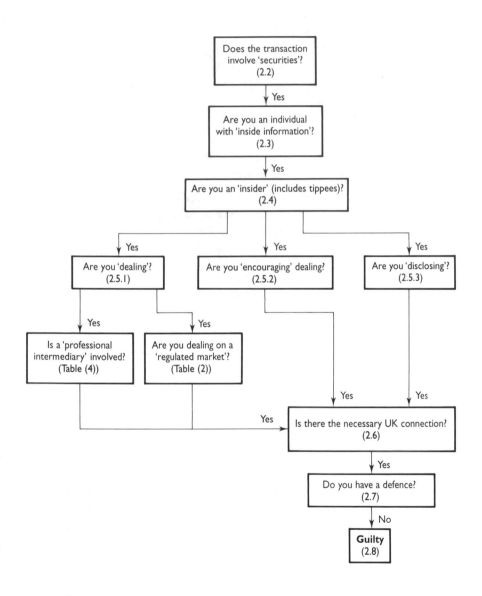

1 INTRODUCTION

The centrepiece of the anti-insider dealing regime in the United Kingdom is Part V of the Criminal Justice Act 1993 (the 'CJA'). The relevant provisions of the CJA came into effect on 1 March 1994 and represent the UK's implementation of the EC Directive on Insider Dealing (Dir 89/592 [1989] OJ L334/30) (the 'Directive').

The CJA superseded the Company Securities (Insider Dealing) Act 1985 and the equivalent legislation in Northern Ireland, the Company Securities (Insider dealing) (Northern Ireland) Order 1986 (together the '1985 Act') and replaced the 12 separate offences under the 1985 Act with three new offences:

- dealing while in possession of inside information;
- encouraging another to deal in such circumstances; and
- disclosing information other than in the proper performance of one's employment or professional duties.

The CJA continues the UK's historical commitment to the use of the criminal law as the principal weapon in combating insider dealing. It is fair to say that the previous legislation had only limited success: out of only 52 prosecutions which were made since insider dealing first became a criminal offence in 1980, only 23 had led to convictions as at January 1994. Despite this, the CJA merely tinkers with the framework established by the 1985 Act although in a number of important respects the scope of the CJA is wider than its predecessor.

Any offence which seeks to distinguish between the legitimate and illegitimate exploitation of market information has to be necessarily widely drafted. As a consequence, and to avoid prejudicing a number of accepted City practices, the three offences created by the CJA have a raft of rather technical defences. On the one hand this has tended to make professionals nervous about the full extent of the offences and, paradoxically, on the other hand, will make successful prosecutions difficult to secure.

During the CJA's passage through the UK parliament, calls were made by (amongst others) the Chairman of the London Stock Exchange for the introduction of civil penalties for insider dealing and also the establishment of an enforcement agency to monitor compliance with the law. However, these calls were rejected by the government, leaving as the only complements to the CJA, the Listing Rules of the London Stock Exchange, the City Code on Takeovers and Mergers and the rules of the various self-regulatory Organisations set up under the Financial Services Act 1986 to impose self-discipline on the financial services industry. In addition, there are a number of initiatives designed to limit the scope for insider dealing such as the London Stock Exchange's guidance on the dissemination of price sensitive information. To a much lesser extent the common law does provide a civil remedy for the determined shareholder to get an unscrupulous director to disgorge profits which have been obtained by abuse of that director's position.

2 THE CRIMINAL LAW

2.1 INTRODUCTION

Section 52 of the CJA creates three discrete offences: insider dealing; encouraging insider dealing; and disclosure. The offences, which are considered in detail *below* (see 2.5), are predicated on certain key definitions which are considered first. These definitions are essential to establishing the scope of each of the three offences. Generally speaking, an offence is only committed if it involves an insider exploiting inside information in relation to certain types of securities without the justification of a defence.

2.2 TO WHICH SECURITIES DOES THE CJA APPLY?

2.2.1 Types of security

The CJA is only capable of applying in the context of those types of securities set out in Schedule 2 to the CJA (as that schedule is amended by statutory instrument from time to time). Currently, these include the following.

2.2.1.1 Shares

Shares and stock in the share capital of a company, that is any incorporated or unincorporated body which is not a public sector body. This therefore includes shares in a building society, or in an open ended corporate fund (but not unit trusts) as well as shares in overseas and certain statutory companies. Public sector bodies include the governments, central banks and local authorities of any country (including the UK) as well as international organisations of which the UK or another member state of the European Union is a member.

2.2.1.2 Debt securities

Any instrument creating or acknowledging indebtedness which is issued by a company or public sector body (as both terms are described in 2.2.1.1 *above*). This potentially very wide definition includes debentures, debenture stock, loan stock, bonds, certificates of deposit, gilts and possibly also bills of exchange and promissory notes. The impact of this wide definition is, however, substantially reduced by the requirement discussed in 2.2.3 *below*.

2.2.1.3 Warrants

Any right to subscribe for shares or debt securities. This includes subscription warrants, certain convertible securities such as convertible debt securities where the debt element is released to subscribe new shares and, in the context of a rights issue, nil-paid rights once dealings in them have commenced.

2.2.1.4 Depositary receipts

Certificates or other records (whether or not in the form of documents) which are issued by or on behalf of a person who holds shares, debt securities or warrants of a particular issuer and which acknowledge that another person is entitled to rights in relation to such securities. As well as traditional depositary receipts, the definition also covers securities in global form but not receipts issued in respect of more than one security. ·

2.2.1.5 Options

Any option to acquire or dispose of any of the other securities described in 2.2. This therefore includes exchangeable bonds, warrants over securities and, if the shares in a take-over target satisfy the requirement discussed in the Insider Dealing Order 1994, an irrevocable undertaking which gives a bidder a discretion to bid. However, it does not include options over commodities, currencies or options over other options.

2.2.1.6 Futures

Rights under a contract for the acquisition or disposal of any of the other securities described in 2.2 under which delivery is to be made at a future date and at a price agreed when the contract is made, or at a price calculated by reference to an agreed formula.

2.2.1.7 Contracts for differences

Rights under a contract which does not provide for delivery of securities but whose purpose or pretended purpose is to secure a profit or avoid a loss by reference to fluctuations in either the price of any of the other securities described in 2.2 (or a basket of a number of such securities) or, alternatively, the interest rate offered on money placed on deposit. Interest rate swaps, index warrants and covered warrants relating to particular securities or a basket of securities are therefore covered. In contrast, currency swaps and contracts based on the price of a commodity (such as oil) are not covered.

2.2.2 Issuer of derivatives and depositary receipts

The CJA does not expressly recognise the fact that securities such as derivatives and depositary receipts may be issued not by the issuer of the relevant underlying security, but by another entity. However, price-sensitive inside information relating to the issuer of the underlying security will also be relevant (see 2.3.1 *below*) to the issuer of the derivative or depositary receipt in question.

2.2.3 Insider Dealing Order 1994

Section 54(1) of the CJA provides that the CJA only applies in the context of securities if they further satisfy conditions laid down in orders made by the government. The Insider Dealing (Securities and Regulated Markets) Order 1994 (SI 1994 No 187) (the '1994' Order') came into force on 1 March 1994 and provides that the provisions of the CJA only apply to securities which either are officially listed in a state within the European Economic Area (see Table (1)) or are admitted to dealing on, or have their price quoted on or under, the rules of those regulated markets listed in Table (2) *below*.

In the case of warrants, depositary receipts, options, futures and contracts for differences which are not themselves so listed or traded, the CJA will still apply if they relate to underlying securities which are. Accordingly, many over-the-counter derivatives fall within the ambit of the CJA.

It follows from the requirement in the 1994 Order for securities to be listed or traded on certain exchanges that grey-market trading is not subject to the CJA. It would also appear to follow, on a strict reading of the 1994 Order, that placees or underwriters of new issues of securities, whose obligations are conditional on listing, will also not be subject to the CJA. This on the face of it appears the case even though they may have assumed their responsibilities on the basis of inside information because the securities to which such information relates are not at the relevant time listed. The drafting of the 1994 Order does not, however, rule out an argument, which it is submitted is correct, that as the commitment of placees and underwriters contemplates an acquisition of securities only when those securities are listed, it follows that such placees and underwriters actually acquire warrants as defined in 2.2.1.3 *above*.

TABLE (1)

European Economic Area States:		
• United Kingdom	• Denmark	• Austria
• Germany	• Spain	• Finland
• France	• Greece	• Iceland
• Italy	• Portugal	• Norway
• The Netherlands	• Luxembourg	• Sweden
• Republic of Ireland	• Belgium	• Liechtenstein

TABLE (2)

Regulated Markets	
Any market established under the rules of:	
Amsterdam Stock Exchange	Bremen Stock Exchange
Antwerp Stock Exchange	Brussels Stock Exchange
Athens Stock Exchange	Copenhagen Stock Exchange
Barcelona Stock Exchange	Dusseldorf Stock Exchange
Bavarian Stock Exchange	Florence Stock Exchange
Berlin Stock Exchange	Frankfurt Stock Exchange
Bilbao Stock Exchange	Genoa Stock Exchange
Bologna Stock Exchange	Ghent Stock Exchange
Bordeaux Stock Exchange	Hamburg Stock Exchange

Hanover Stock Exchange	The exchange known as NASDAQ
Helsinki Stock Exchange	OMLX, the London Securities and
Irish Stock Exchange	Derivatives Exchange Limited
London Stock Exchange Ltd	Oporto Stock Exchange
Liege Stock Exchange	Oslo Stock Exchange
Lille Stock Exchange	Palermo Stock Exchange
Lisbon Stock Exchange	Paris Stock Exchange
LIFFE Administration & Management	Rome Stock Exchange
Luxembourg Stock Exchange	Securities Exchange of Iceland
Lyon Stock Exchange	Stockholm Stock Exchange
Madrid Stock Exchange	Stuttgart Stock Exchange
Marseille Stock Exchange	Trieste Stock Exchange
Milan Stock Exchange	Turin Stock Exchange
Nancy Stock Exchange	Valencia Stock Exchange
Nantes Stock Exchange	Venice Stock Exchange
Naples Stock Exchange	Vienna Stock Exchange

The range of securities to which the CJA applies is considerably wider than that to which the 1985 Act applied. In a UK context, it includes securities admitted to the Official List of the London Stock Exchange, but also those dealt in on the Unlisted Securities Market or quoted on SEAQ.

2.3 WHAT IS INSIDE INFORMATION?

Sections 56 and 60(4) of the CJA state that inside information must be information which:

- is relevant,
- is specific or precise,
- has not been made public; and
- is price-sensitive.

These features are considered in turn.

2.3.1 Relevant

Information will only be regarded as inside information if it relates to particular securities or to a particular issuer or issuers of securities and not to securities or issuers generally. Accordingly, it includes not only information relating to an individual issuer but also information relating to a particular sector of issuers. It will not include information which relates generally to the market such as information relating to the economic climate, although if the information has a disproportionate impact on a company or sector it may still constitute inside information. For example, and subject to the defence set out in 2.7.3 *below*, a proposed movement in interest rates may constitute inside information in relation to a bank even though it may be relevant to all companies. The ambit of the CJA is also wide enough to catch information on the business prospects of a company or companies. This may include, for example, information on the impending insolvency of an important customer, the development of a new production process, or details of an imminent regulatory decision for the sector in which a company operates. As the number and range of issues which can affect the business prospects of a company are so great, this part of the CJA was heavily criticised during its passage through Parliament.

2.3.2 Specific or precise

The Directive states that information can only be inside information if it is precise. The CJA goes further by stating that it may be 'specific or precise'. The full significance of this difference is not clear. Following the decision of the House of Lords in *Pepper (Inspector of Taxes) v Hart* [1993] 1 All ER 42 to allow debates in Parliament on legislation to be used in certain circumstances as an aid to interpreting the resulting legislation, it is helpful to look at the examples put forward in Parliament by the government minister introducing the legislation to explain the difference between 'specific' and 'precise'. It was suggested in Parliament that a decision by a company to make a bid for a target was 'specific' information, as was the disclosure by a company that its results would be much better than market expectations. However, neither would be 'precise' in the absence of the price at which the bid was to be made or some of the figures behind the good results. The inclusion of 'specific' is therefore designed to widen the scope of the definition. As a result, an individual may be regarded as having inside information about an event notwithstanding he is not in possession of all the surrounding details.

It follows therefore that the following additional examples of specific (but not precise) information may amount to inside information:

- knowledge (but not the details) of an imminent rights issue or other share issue by a company
- knowledge (but not the details) of substantial profits or losses made by a company or
- knowledge of interest in a company by potential predators.

In the final analysis, whether information is specific or precise is an objective question to be determined by the court. The uncertainties of the outcome have left many, particularly analysts, nervous. In *HM Advocate v Mackie* (unreported) one of the issues was whether the prosecution was able to establish that information passed by a company chairman to an analyst amounted to either a specific profits warning or less detailed information from which the analyst concluded a profits warning would be inevitable, but which itself was neither specific nor precise.

The difficulties for directors in conducting a relationship with their brokers and analysts and giving them a steer on the fortunes of their company without disclosing specific or precise information was thrown into sharp focus in May 1993 when the London Stock Exchange publicly censured a listed company for briefing analysts and certain institutional investors ahead of the rest of the market. Prompted in part by this, the London Stock Exchange published guidance on the dissemination of price-sensitive information in February 1994 (see 3.2.2 *below*).

Another issue is whether a person with knowledge of a specific or precise market rumour can be regarded as having inside information (see Problem Area 9). The CJA itself contains no express requirement that inside information be true and, when debating the legislation in parliament, one government spokesman said of inside information 'What matters is not whether it is true, but whether the market will believe it to be true'. He went on, however, to express the view that as inside information had to be specific, 'mere rumour' and 'untargeted information' were not intended to fall within the ambit of the CJA. In summary, it is likely that a rumour which, although untrue, is specific, will be held capable by the courts of constituting inside information. Of course, if a rumour is very widespread it may be that it is to be regarded as having been made public (see 2.3.3 *below*).

2.3.3 Made public

Information is not capable of being inside information if it has been made public. Again, this is a question of fact to be determined in each case by the jury. However, s 58 of the CJA sets out certain examples, which are not exhaustive, of when information will be treated by the law as having been made public.

Section 58(2) of the CJA provides that the following types if information will be regarded as having been made public:

- Information published in accordance with the rules of any of the regulated markets set out in Table (2) *above* for the purpose of informing investors and their professional advisers. In a UK context, this covers information required by the Listing Rules of the London Stock Exchange (the so-called 'Yellow Book') to be made public even if this is on a screen-based news information service to which there is limited access.
- Information contained in records which by virtue of any enactment are open to inspection by the public. It is not clear whether the enactments referred to must be those made within the UK (such as Acts of Parliament or Statutory Instruments) or whether the definition extends also to those made in the European Union or other overseas jurisdictions. Again, in a UK context, information filed at Companies House, for example, would be treated as having been made public.
- Information which can be readily acquired by those likely to deal in any securities about either those securities or their issuer. Accordingly, the test is whether a market professional rather than a member of the public would be able to discover the information. It is for the members of a jury to determine what information can and cannot be readily acquired, but in coming to their decision they are likely to be influenced by the guidance contained in s 58(3) of the CJA, which is described below.

- Information derived from information which has itself been made public. This covers the product of an analyst's research on a company based on public information such as, say, its published accounts.

Problem Area 1

Martin, an influential analyst with Wizzo Analysts Ltd and guest columnist in the Weekly Good Share Guide has been investigating Under-rated Plc and has drafted favourable research recommendations based on publicly available information. He plans to publish his recommendations in the widely read and respected Weekly Good Share Guide next week. He circulates his draft recommendations to a colleague, David, for comments. When the draft is settled it is sent to the printers where Malcolm prepares the typesetting. Before the Weekly Good Share Guide is published, Martin, David and Malcolm follow the recommendations and buy shares in Under-rated Plc.

Martin is not in breach of the CJA either by disclosing his draft recommendations to David or by dealing in Under-rated Plc's shares since his dealings are on the basis of information which is regarded as made public.

On the assumption that publication of a buy recommendation in the Weekly Good Share Guide is likely to have a significant effect on the price of the securities recommended, then both David and Malcolm arguably have inside information. The inside information is not that Under-rated Plc's shares are underpriced, but that Martin is about to make these recommendations.

The knowledge gained by directors and senior executives of listed companies can put them in a difficult position to the extent that that knowledge has not been made public. Although companies listed on the London Stock Exchange are obliged by the Listing Rules of the London Stock Exchange to make an official announcement regarding significant price-sensitive matters to the London Stock Exchange through its Company Announcements Office (see 3.2.2 *below*), most directors and senior executives have information on their company and the industry in which it operates which, although not sufficiently price-sensitive to require disclosure, is more detailed than the rest of the market will have access to from publicly available information.

Directors and executives in such circumstances must consider their actions carefully before dealing in the shares of their own company (or those of another company in the same industry) if they consider the market's valuation of such shares to be wrong.

The CJA also sets out, in s 58(3), factors which of themselves do not preclude information from being regarded as having been made public. These factors are intended to provide a degree of comfort to brokers and fund managers that, provided that the information does not have some other unusual quality about it, they will not necessarily be in breach of the CJA by acting with the benefit of this information. Accordingly, information *may*, but not necessarily *will*, be regarded as having been made public even though:

- it can be acquired only by persons exercising diligence and expertise;
- it is communicated to a section of the public and not to the public at large;
- it can be acquired only by observation;
- it is communicated only on payment of a fee; or
- it is published only outside the UK.

The decision whether such information has actually been made public rests with the courts. In reaching their conclusion it is not clear how much assistance the courts will derive from the provisions of s 58(3) of the CJA. That section may not do much more than illustrate just how uncertain the concept of 'made public' set out in the rest of s 58 of the CJA really is. For example, even though information does not have to be published within the UK for it to be made public, a court is likely to distinguish between its publication in, say, the *Tonga Evening News* and *The Wall Street Journal*. The burden of proof is, however, always on the prosecution to show that at the relevant time the information had not been made public.

The stated aim of the Directive is to afford an assurance to investors that they are placed on an equal footing and that they will be protected against the improper use of inside information. The inference to be drawn from this would seem to be that the market must be given time to absorb price-sensitive information and respond accordingly, before the information can be regarded as public. In contrast, however, the CJA regards information as 'made public' when published in any of the ways referred to above. It therefore follows that dealings may occur immediately after information has been made public and whether or not the market has had time to absorb and respond to the information.

2.3.4 Price-sensitive information

The final distinguishing feature of inside information is that it is price-sensitive—that is, if it were made public it would be likely to have a significant effect on the price of any securities. The CJA provides no guidance on what is to be considered a significant effect. In the absence of such guidance the requirement should be interpreted cautiously: for certain types of securities a movement of as little as 1–2 per cent may in all the circumstances of a case be regarded as significant. Although the test of significance refers to the prospective likely effect on the price of securities of releasing certain information, in practice how significant that information is, is likely to be measured retrospectively against the actual price movement recorded following disclosure of the information. With this in mind, it is usual for directors who are concerned about dealings in their company's shares to ask its brokers as to the likely effect on the market of the publication of a particular piece of information.

2.3.5 Knowledge

It is essential for the successful prosecution of each of the insider dealing offences under the CJA to show not only that the relevant information was inside information, but also that the accused knew (subjectively) that it was inside information. The immense difficulty in proving such subjective knowledge resulted in the collapse of a number of trials under the 1985 Act, which contained a similar provision.

2.4 WHO IS AN INSIDER?

The three insider dealing offences created by the CJA revolve around an individual having inside information as an insider. Section 57 of the CJA sets out the circumstances in which an individual is to be regarded as an insider. Not only must an insider know that he has inside information, but in addition he must know that he has it either:

- through being a director, employee or shareholder of an issuer of securities; or
- through having access to the information by virtue of his employment, office or profession; or
- by having it directly or indirectly from some such person.

Under the CJA not only directors but also employees (irrespective of their position) and shareholders of an issuer of securities (irrespective of the size of their shareholding) are deemed to be insiders if the inside information they have arises by virtue of their status as such. A person working in the post room of a company who discovers management accounts inadvertently caught up with some items of mail will be an insider—by virtue of his status as an employee.

Further, unlike the requirements of the 1985 Act, insiders do not have to have a connection with the issuer of the securities in relation to which they have inside information. Any person who, 'by virtue' of his employment, office or profession, obtains information which he knows to be inside information is deemed an insider. The definition would therefore cover a company's professional advisers such as solicitors, auditors, bankers, brokers and printers as well as investment analysts and public servants, such as officials of the Bank of England, the London Stock Exchange or the Take-Over Panel who come by such information in the course of their work. The requirement that the information is obtained by the insider 'by virtue' of his employment, office or profession raises a number of issues which are explored further below (see Problem Area 2).

Individuals who obtain information directly or indirectly from an insider are themselves regarded by the CJA as an insider. This would therefore apply to someone who has been given inside information by a company director, employee or shareholder, or by someone else who came by the information by virtue of his employment, office or profession.

It is not a requirement of the offence that the accused be shown to have actually sought the inside information. It is sufficient for him to have simply received it.

Problem Area 2

Tom, a barman at the local golf club, overhears inside information being exchanged by two directors of Big Plc, as he serves them at the bar. It could be argued that Tom has obtained that information by virtue of his profession as a barman. The CJA does not require Tom's employment or profession to be in some way connected with the company or securities to which the information relates. This leads to rather anomalous results. For example, if Tom had overheard the conversation of the directors after completing his duties for the day or whilst visiting the bar on his day off then he would not be treated as an insider. Similarly, why should Tom be in a worse position than any other person in the bar overhearing the conversation?

It should be noted that Tom will always be an insider if he knows that the two golfers are directors of Big Plc since he will have got the inside information indirectly from persons whom he knows to be insiders.

The anomalies illustrated in Problem Area 2 *above* could be reduced if the words 'through being' (in the case of directors, employees and shareholders of issues) and 'by virtue of' (in the case of an individual's employment, office or profession) were given an objective interpretation—that is, was it reasonably likely that inside information would be received by a person in the position of the alleged insider? It remains to be seen if the courts adopt this approach.

Under the 1985 Act it was frequently difficult for the prosecution to prove that the accused knew the information he had was unpublished price-sensitive information. Section 57(1) of the CJA makes it clear that the prosecution must prove that the accused knew not only that the information was inside information, but also that it was from an inside source. Proving actual knowledge is notoriously difficult and it is for this reason that many prosecutions are likely to fail under the CJA as they did in the past under the 1985 Act.

Problem Area 3

Fiona, a director of Go-ahead Plc reveals certain inside information about the company to Carol, her golfing partner. Carol passes it on to her husband Greg. Is Greg now an insider? To be such s 57(1)(*b*) of the CJA requires Greg to know that he has inside information from an inside source. The CJA does not make it clear whether Greg has to know that the source of the information is:

(1) one of his wife's golf partners, many of whom he knows are company directors; or

(2) his wife's golf partner whom he knows is a company director; or

(3) his wife's golf partner whom he knows is the finance director of Go-ahead Plc.

Article 4 of the Directive would treat Greg as an insider if the source of his information 'could not be other' than an insider. This suggests it is not necessary for Greg to know the precise identity and position of his source and it is likely that the CJA will also be interpreted in this manner.

2.5 WHAT ARE THE OFFENCES?

Section 52 of the CJA creates three discrete offences which are considered in turn below.

2.5.1 Dealing

It is an offence by virtue of s 52(1) of the CJA for an insider to deal in securities with information which if it were made public would be likely to have a significant effect on the price of the securities and if the insider deals as, or in reliance upon, a professional intermediary or the dealing involves an acquisition or disposal on one of the regulated markets set out in Table (2) *above*. It follows that the CJA does not apply to private off-market transactions without the involvement of a professional intermediary. Further, it is not necessary for the prosecution to show that the accused dealt *because* of the inside information he possessed.

TABLE (3)

Constituent elements for dealing offence:
- individual must possess inside information which he knows (subjectively) is inside information (see 2.3)
- individual must know (subjectively) that the inside information is from an inside source (see 2.4)
- the inside information must be likely to have a significant effect on the price of the securities dealt in (see 2.3.4)
- individual must deal (see 2.5.1) in securities (see 2.2) on a regulated market (see Table (2)) or rely on a professional intermediary or is himself acting as a professional intermediary

The CJA defines dealing in securities widely. In relation to a security it includes:

- acquiring or disposing or agreeing to acquire or dispose of the security as principal or agent;
- procuring directly or indirectly such an acquisition or disposal; or
- entering into or terminating the agreement creating the security.

The first limb of the definition makes it clear that the accused can be guilty of dealing simply by *agreeing to* acquire or dispose of securities without actually doing so. Taking a legal charge over the relevant securities would, for example, also constitute dealing. It follows that it is not necessary for property in the security to pass for an offence to be committed. Further, even if an individual acts as an agent for another and, therefore, does not take the economic benefit of the dealing, he can still be guilty of the offence (see Problem Area 4 *below*).

As many cases of insider dealing which have reached the courts show, the dealing in question is often committed through or facilitated by a nominee or agent. The CJA therefore includes in the definition of dealing the procurement, directly or indirectly of such dealing by the use of an agent, nominee, or some other third party who is acting at the accused's direction in relation to the relevant acquisition or disposal.

The offence of dealing is capable of being committed only by individuals. However, although the corporate entity of which an individual is a director or employee may be the actual purchaser or seller of the relevant securities, it is still possible that, say, the directors who authorised the deal may have committed an offence given the wide definition of dealing. Much will depend on the particular facts.

Problem Area 4

Helen, a director of Predator Ltd, has inside information that the directors of Target Plc, a London-listed company, are in talks with Rival Ltd about a possible take-over of Target Plc. She recommends to the board of Predator Ltd (without disclosing the inside information) that Predator Ltd should buy some shares in Target Plc. She votes in favour of the resolution at the board meeting to acquire those shares. John, Predator Ltd's stockbroker, is instructed to acquire 1,000 shares in Target Plc. Next day Helen learns that the talks between Target Plc and Rival Ltd have broken down. Again, without disclosing the inside information, Helen persuades the board of Predator Ltd to reverse its decision. Appropriate instructions are issued to John.

It is unlikely that Helen would be guilty of dealing, given that she alone would not be able to 'procure' the acquisition. If it were possible to show that Helen controlled the board, because, for example, she controlled a majority of the shares in Predator Ltd, or was such a charismatic individual that she invariably got her own way, then a prosecution under s 52(1) of the CJA would be possible. Similarly, 'shadow directors', that is, persons in accordance with whose directions or instructions the board is accustomed to act, will be caught if they procure their companies to deal. In any event, Helen would be guilty of encouraging dealing (see 2.5.2 *below*). It is important to note that, although John was instructed to reverse the trade before taking delivery of the 1,000 shares in Target Plc, his initial agreement to acquire the shares is an acquisition for the purpose of the CJA (see 2.5.1 *above*).

Predator Ltd had not committed any offence as the provisions of the CJA only apply to individuals. Even if Helen were found to have 'procured' Predator Ltd to issue dealing instructions to John, thereby making John an 'agent', John would not have committed any offence since, without knowing Helen's reasons for dealing, he was not in possession of any inside information—innocent agents are not guilty of any offence under the CJA.

Accordingly, while directors or employees of a body corporate may be guilty, their company will not. However, by virtue of s 1(1) of the Criminal Law Act 1977, their company may be guilty of statutory conspiracy, should at least two natural persons, one of whom may properly be regarded as 'the directing mind and will of the company', be a party to the conspiracy.

The Directive provides that member states may introduce measures covering all off-market transactions. However under the CJA, it is an essential constituent of the dealing offence that the dealing is conducted either on one of the regulated markets set out in Table (2) *above* or the insider has relied on a professional intermediary or was himself acting as a professional intermediary. A professional intermediary is defined in s 59 of the CJA (see Table (4)).

TABLE (4)

Professional intermediary
A person is a professional intermediary if either he is, or is employed by, a person who:
- carries on a business of acquiring or disposing of securities (whether as principal or agent) or of acting as an intermediary between persons taking part in any dealing in securities; and
- holds himself out to the public or any section of the public (including a section of the public constituted by persons such as himself) as willing to engage in any such business.

A person is *not* a professional intermediary if he conducts any of the activities referred to above either
- merely incidentally to some other activity; or
- merely occasionally.

The definition therefore covers stockbrokers and market-makers whose business it is to deal in securities but because of the exceptions for persons whose dealings are only occasional or are incidental to their main business, it excludes other professionals such as accountants and solicitors.

The definition however also includes anyone who is employed by a professional intermediary to carry out any of the activities referred to above. It is an open question whether such an employee is caught if he is acting in a personal capacity.

Problem Area 5

The directors of Blue Ink Plc, a London-listed manufacturer of inks, are contemplating a bid for their listed rival, Red Ink Plc. Based on confidential information relating to the inks industry, the directors value Red Ink Plc at £100 million. They plan to re-structure Red Ink Plc if the bid is successful to take advantage of this information and make the company more profitable. As a first step, Blue Ink Plc acquires a number of shares in Red Ink Plc from an individual known to Blue Ink Plc's Chairman.

Assuming, in the usual way, Blue Ink Plc engages a merchant bank to acquire shares in contemplation of an offer being made, then any dealing will be in reliance upon a professional intermediary.

Unlike industry information assembled from public sources, confidential information about ink manufacturing companies may constitute inside information (see 2.3.1 *above*) if it is specific or precise and would have a significant effect on the price of Red Ink Plc's shares if made public. Whilst the knowledge of the intention to make the bid would fall within the market information defence (see 2.7.2.2), the confidential information about the ink industry would not. The directors will be guilty of the dealing offence if, in such circumstances, Blue Ink Plc makes a bid, since they will have procured dealings.

The intention to restructure Red Ink Plc after the bid may itself be inside information, since information about a company's business prospects can be inside information. However, the no-profit defence considered below (see 2.7.1.1) may apply because, although the restructuring is presumably designed to increase the profits of Red Ink Plc, that restructuring and therefore those profits will only arise after the dealing. It is the bid that will result in a profit. In other words, the dealing will not itself result in a profit, it is subsequent events (ie, the restructuring) that will do so.

The dealing offence can be problematic for integrated banks with corporate finance and trading arms. If the staff of the corporate finance division obtain inside information about an issue of securities and a 'Chinese Wall' is not placed between them and those who give dealing instructions, the staff giving dealing instructions may be guilty of insider dealing. Such dealings may either occur on a regulated market or where the bank acts as a professional intermediary (see Table (4) *above*). The market-maker defence which is considered further below (see 2.7.2.1) may apply—but only if the insider has acted in good faith. The market information defence (see 2.7.2.2 *below*) will not apply.

2.5.2 Encouraging dealing

Section 52(2)(*a*) of the CJA also creates an offence of encouraging insider dealing. It makes it unlawful for an individual with inside information, which if it were made public would be likely to have a significant effect on the price of securities, to encourage another person to deal in such securities. Strictly speaking, the encouragement does not have to involve the disclosure of the relevant inside information: the CJA does not relate the encouragement to the inside information. The offence is also committed whether or not the party encouraged to deal does decide to deal at all. However, the offence is not committed unless the accused knew or had reasonable cause to believe that the relevant dealing would be conducted on a regulated market or by someone acting in the capacity of or in reliance upon a professional intermediary.

The CJA does not spell out any examples of what constitutes 'encouragement'. The Directive refers to 'recommending or procuring'. It is a question to be resolved by the jury in any case but the offence is obviously intended to have a wider scope than the 'procurement' offence discussed in 2.5.1 *above*. It may, for example, cover the position of a director briefing an analyst intending (or perhaps even merely knowing) that the information he is imparting will result in the analyst dealing in price-affected securities. (See also Problem Area 4 *above*.)

As with the offence of dealing, the offence of encouraging may only be committed by an individual, as opposed to a corporate entity. However, the actual dealing to which the encouragement relates may be conducted by either an individual or a corporate entity. The offence is not committed where an individual encourages another person to refrain from dealing in securities.

TABLE (5)

Constituent elements for encouraging offence: • individual must possess inside information which he knows (subjectively) is inside information (see 2.3) • individual must know (subjectively) that the inside information is from an inside source (see 2.4) • individual must encourage another person to deal in securities (see 2.5.2) • the inside information must be likely to have a significant effect on the price of securities the subject of the encouragement (see 2.3.4)

> • individual must know or have a reasonable cause to believe that a dealing would occur on a regulated market (see 2.2) or by or in reliance upon a professional intermediary (see Table (4))

Problem Area 6

Alexander, the Chairman of ABC Trading Co ('ABC') a London-listed company making an offer of warrants (ie, the right to subscribe for shares) attends a series of presentations with prospective investors. Also in attendance is John, a director of Global Bank, the underwriters of the offer. Both Alexander and John have negative inside information about ABC which, if it were made public, would be likely to have an adverse effect on the value of ABC's shares. Alexander is an insider because he has the information by virtue of his employment, as does John, following Global Bank's due diligence exercise on ABC. The inside information in question remains inside information because it relates to poor profit forecasts which, although specific, are too speculative to be included in the pathfinder prospectus since they are not capable of verification to the necessary standard. Are John and Alexander guilty of encouraging dealing, contrary to s 52(2)(*a*) of the CJA when they make the presentation to investors?

By stimulating investor demand rather than just presenting objective facts, John and Alexander may be guilty of encouraging dealing. If they disclose any of the inside information, they may be guilty of disclosing inside information (see 2.5.3 *below*) unless they were sanctioned to do it by ABC and Global Bank and are therefore acting in the proper performance of the functions of their employment.

As a defence to the charge of encouraging dealing they may contend they would have said what they said at the roadshow regardless of the inside information (see 2.7.1.3 *below*).

2.5.3 Disclosure

It is an offence by virtue of s 52(2)(*b*) of the CJA for any individual with information as an insider to disclose that information to another person otherwise than in the proper performance of the functions of his employment, office or profession.

The corollary of this is that the offence is not committed by someone who is properly performing their duties. As a result, the proper passage of information within and between banks, lawyers, accountants and other advisers will not result in the offence of disclosure being committed. Contrast the improper passage of such information such as information held on a confidential basis or information passed across a 'Chinese Wall' which may well result in an offence being committed. In deciding whether or not someone is properly performing their duties a court is likely to be influenced by factors such as whether the individual was acting in compliance with internal office procedures or, in the case of members of self-regulatory organisations, the rules of such organisations.

TABLE (6)

Constituent elements for disclosure offence:
- individual must possess inside information which he (subjectively) knows is inside information (see 2.3)
- individual must know (subjectively) that the inside information is from an inside source (see 2.4)
- individual discloses the information otherwise in the proper performance of the functions of his employment, office or profession to another person

Where an insider does act other than in the proper performance of his duties and is charged with the disclosure offence, (as with the offence of procuring dealing described at 2.5.1 *above*) the prosecution does not have to establish (as it does with the encouraging offence—see 2.5.2 *above*) that the insider knew or had reasonable cause to believe that dealing would result. It is sufficient for the prosecution to establish that the insider acted otherwise than in the proper performance of his duties. It is, however, open for the accused to overcome the burden of proof and raise a defence that on the balance of probabilities he did not expect dealing to occur (see 2.7.1.4 *below*).

2.6 WHAT IS THE TERRITORIAL SCOPE OF THE CJA?

Section 62 of the CJA sets out the territorial limits of the CJA. The position is summarised in Tables (7) and (8).

TABLE (7)

Dealing
An individual is not guilty of the dealing offence unless either:
- he was within the UK at the time he is alleged to have done any act constituting or forming part of the alleged dealing; or
- the dealing was alleged to have occurred on a UK regulated market— currently defined as being either the London Stock Exchange, LIFFE or OMLX, the London Securities and Derivatives Exchange Limited; or
- the professional intermediary was within the UK when he is alleged to have done anything by means of which the offence is alleged to have been committed.

TABLE (8)

> *Encouraging/disclosing*
> An individual is not guilty of the encouraging or disclosing offence unless either:
> - he was within the UK when he is alleged to have disclosed the information or encouraged the dealing; or
> - when receiving it, the recipient of the information or encouragement was within the UK.

Insider dealing falling outside the scope of the CJA because of the provisions of s 62 of the CJA may however be caught by overseas insider dealing legislation. In particular, other EU member states and the other members of the European Economic Area (see Table (1) *above*) are required to have legislation implementing the Directive.

Problem Area 7

Alan has inside information on Overseas Co, a company whose shares are listed on the London and New York stock exchanges. From his office in London he telephones a broker in New York and instructs him to acquire shares in Overseas Co.

Alan will be guilty of the dealing offence notwithstanding the dealing actually occurred outside the UK since the dealing was procured from within the UK.

2.7 WHAT ARE THE DEFENCES?

The wide scope of the offences in the CJA makes the statutory defences to such offences all the more important. Schedule 1 to the CJA creates a number of defences designed to cover specific circumstances and s 53 of the CJA creates a number of more general application. These are considered in turn below. In order for a person to take advantage of any defence it is necessary for a defendant to adduce evidence to establish the relevant defence on the balance of probabilities.

2.7.1 General defences

2.7.1.1 No profit/loss

It is a defence to each of the three offences—dealing, encouraging and disclosing—for an individual to show that he did not expect the relevant dealing in securities to result in a profit (or the avoidance of a loss) attributable to the fact that the information in question was price-sensitive information in relation to the securities. However to be an insider at all (see 2.3.5 and 2.4 *above*) an individual must know that he has inside information—that is information which he knows if it were made public would be likely to have a significant effect on the price of any securities. If he did not know or expect this why is there a need for a defence such as this? (See also Problem Area 5 *above*.)

The scope of this defence is therefore rather obscure. It would exonerate the rather unlikely insider who sold shares while in possession of inside information which was likely to receive a favourable reaction in the market and see the share price rise. It would not however assist, say, an analyst who decided on a course of dealing on the basis of conclusions drawn from publicly-available information and who subsequently continued the same course of dealing after gaining inside information which corroborated his conclusions. It may however be open for him to put forward the defence that he would have done what he did even if he had not had the inside information (see 2.7.1.3 *below*).

It might be open for an insider who bought shares in a company which he knew was involved in talks regarding its potential take-over, to argue that he *expected* those talks to fail and no profit to result.

2.7.1.2 Wide disclosure

It is a defence to the dealing and encouraging offences for an individual to show that at the time he believed on reasonable grounds that the information had been or alternatively, in the case of the encouraging offence, would be disclosed widely enough to ensure that none of those taking part in the dealing would be prejudiced by not having the information: in the language of the Directive—'equivalence of information'.

Again, the scope of this defence, and how it relates to the offences, is not clear. It contemplates that information may be disclosed widely enough to afford the accused a defence while at the same time not being 'made public' within the meaning of s 58 CJA (see 2.3.3).

During its passage through parliament a government spokesman suggested the defence applied where both parties to a transaction possess information which has not yet been made public—since the information will have been disclosed sufficiently widely to ensure that none of those taking part in the dealing would be prejudiced by not having it.

The drafting of the defence in the CJA suggests that both parties to such a dealing must have knowledge of the relevant information. The same government spokesman however seemed to suggest that the availability of the defence depended not on both parties having the same information but on neither party being prejudiced. He suggested this defence was therefore available to protect, for example, underwriters, who may possess inside information not made public in the relevant offer document. As they shared knowledge of that inside information with the issuer (or vendor shareholder in the case of a secondary offering), neither party to the underwriting arrangements would be prejudiced, and therefore could rely on this defence.

Problem Area 8

> Global Bank is underwriting an issue of warrants for ABC Trading Co
> ('ABC'), a London-listed company. The warrants are to acquire shares in
> ABC. As a result of due diligence at ABC, John a director of Global Bank
> obtains information that ABC's profitability is about to drop substantially
> due to the loss of an important customer. John none the less decides that
> Global Bank should proceed with the underwriting agreement accordingly.
>
> As John has acquired the inside information by virtue of his employment,
> he is an insider (see 2.4 *above*). Contrary to s 55(1) of the CJA he deals in
> securities as he procures a person (which includes a body corporate such
> as Global Bank) to agree to acquire the warrants. Global Bank is also a pro-
> fessional intermediary as described in 2.5.1 *above*.
>
> Although the underwriting relates, as it usually does on a primary issue,
> to unquoted securities (including securities to be, but not yet, listed on a
> regulated market) an offence will probably still be committed (see 2.2.3
> *above*). However, as this issue is one of warrants to acquire ABC's already
> listed shares it therefore is unquestionably subject to the CJA.
>
> As a defence John will have to contend that either there was equality of
> information between Global Bank and ABC (see 2.7.1.2) or, as the inside
> information is likely to depress the price of the warrants, no profit was
> expected to result. (See 2.7.1.1 *above*.)

2.7.1.3 Information irrelevant

It is also a defence to the dealing and encouraging offences for the accused to show
that he would have done what he did even if he had not had the information.

This defence is useful, for example, for trustees with inside information but
who act on the advice of an investment manager. Similarly, it may be open to a
debtor who is in urgent need of funds to argue that the reason for dealing was
the need for cash rather than because of possession of inside information. The
defence may also be availed of by others likely to have inside information, such as
liquidators or receivers if they can show they would have pursued the same
course of action regardless of their inside information.

In the context of the encouraging offence, it is important to note that the
accused must show that he would have so encouraged whether or not he had the
information. It is not a defence for him to show that the person whom he was
encouraging to deal would have so dealt whether he had the information or not.
(See Problem Area 6.)

2.7.1.4 Dealing not expected

It is a defence to the disclosure offence for the accused to show that he did not
expect at the time any person because of the disclosure to deal in securities on

a regulated market or in the capacity of or in reliance upon a professional intermediary.

This defence therefore covers the insider who confides information in, say, a trusted colleague, friend or family member and he can show, on the balance of probabilities, that he did not expect that person to deal.

2.7.2 Specific defences

In addition to the general defences, Schedule 1 to the CJA sets out three special defences which are tailored to various aspects of professional City life.

2.7.2.1 Market makers

An individual is not guilty of the dealing or encouraging offence if he proves on the balance of probabilities that he acted in good faith in the course of either his business as a market maker or his employment in the business of a market maker. A market maker is someone who holds himself out at all normal times, in compliance with the rules of one of the regulated markets listed in Table (2) or one of the international securities self-regulating organisations approved under the Financial Services Act 1986 as willing to acquire or dispose of securities and is recognised as doing so under those rules.

Accordingly, London Stock Exchange market makers are included in the definitions as are Eurobond market makers who are members of the International Securities Markets Association ('ISMA') by virtue of the reference to approved organisations. To take advantage of the defence a market maker must act in good faith in the course of his business or employment. Subject to the discussion in 2.3.2 *above* regarding specific rumours, market makers may react to market rumours and speculation but it is unlikely that they can, for example, breach internal rules, Chinese Walls or the rules of, say, the Securities and Futures Authority (see 3.4 *below*) and still claim the benefit of this defence.

Problem Area 9

> Elaine, a dealer at Intercontinental Bank (a market maker), picks up a rumour through her work that Panacea Plc, is about to announce excellent results of clinical trials it has been carrying out on its latest product, 'Wonderdrug'. She buys 1000 of Panacea Plc's London-listed shares on behalf of the Bank.
>
> As the rumour is specific, relates to a particular issuer and is price-sensitive it may well be inside information. Elaine could contend the rumour was so widely circulated within the City that the information had been 'made public'. This would be a question of fact. If the rumour turns out to be false there could be an argument that it was never 'information' at all and therefore cannot be inside information (but see 2.3.2 *above*). Alternatively,

the fact that a rumour is circulating may itself be inside information—whether or not the rumour proves to be true.

If the rumour is properly regarded as inside information and given Elaine dealt with the benefit of knowing the rumour, the good faith requirement in the market maker defence considered above (see 2.7.2.1) is likely to be difficult to satisfy.

2.7.2.2 Market information

It is a defence to a charge of dealing or encouraging for an individual to show that the information he had as an insider was market information and that it was reasonable for someone in his position to have acted as he did. Market information is information about any of the facts set out in Table (9) *below*.

TABLE (9)

> *Market information is information:*
> - that particular securities have (or have not) been or are (or are not) to be acquired or disposed of, or that their acquisition of disposal is being considered or negotiated; and/or
> - on the number of and price (or range of prices) at which securities have or will be acquired or disposed or at which their acquisition or disposal is being considered or negotiated; and/or
> - on the identity of persons involved or likely to be involved in any capacity in an acquisition or disposal.

Market information therefore is likely to cover information as to the demand for or supply of particular securities as well as information on the results of public offers of securities, such as the percentage take-up of rights in a rights issue.

In order to show that the insider has acted reasonably, the CJA states that a court should have regard to the content of the information he had obtained, the circumstances in which he first had the information and in what capacity, and the capacity in which he now acts. During the CJA's passage through parliament it was commented that regard should also be had to best market price in assessing the reasonableness of an insider's actions. This prompts the questions what happens if there is no market practice in a certain area or how bold should an innovative merchant bank be in changing market practice?

Problem Area 10

ABC Trading Co ('ABC'), a London-listed company, having invited several banks to submit proposals, offers a mandate to Global Bank to manage an issue of warrants it is proposing to make. The warrants are to acquire shares in ABC.

John, a director of Global Bank, has conducted the negotiations with ABC, and as a result has obtained inside information relating to ABC's warrant issue, release of which would be likely to affect their price significantly. Over lunch he reveals details to Sally, one of Global Bank's traders who that afternoon buys shares in ABC in the market on behalf of Global Bank.

As John has obtained the inside information by virtue of his employment, he is an insider (see 2.4 *above*). As such he may not deal, encourage others to deal or disclose information on the proposed warrant issue to Sally unless a defence is available.

Although inside information on the warrant issue may be market information (see Table (9) *above*) the market information defence (see 2.7.2.2 *above*) is only available for the reasonable use of such information—that probably means in accordance with normal market practice. It would not be normal market practice for John to use the information to encourage Sally to buy shares in ABC. Indeed the disclosure is likely also to be contrary to the proper performance of the functions of John's employment contrary to s 52(2)(*b*) of the CJA (see 2.5.3 *above*).

Sally's trading may not benefit from the market-making defence (see 2.7.2.1 *above*) as breaches of a 'Chinese Wall' are likely to undermine the requirement in that defence that Sally acts in good faith.

It is also a defence to a charge of dealing or encouraging for an insider to show that he acted in connection with one (or a series of) acquisition(s) or disposal(s) which were being negotiated or considered with a view to its (or their) being accomplished and the information he had was market information arising out of his involvement in the acquisition(s) or disposal(s). The defence does not require the insider to have acted reasonably and the defence extends to all market information arising out of his involvement in the transaction. It does not however cover other information, such as that emerging from a due diligence exercise, which is not market information. In practice the defence would apply to allow the directors of Company A to buy shares in Company B to facilitate a later take-over bid for Company B by Company A provided that the only inside information which the directors of Company A have is their knowledge of the intended take-over and the intended price at which their offer will be made.

2.7.2.3 Stabilisation

It is also a defence to a charge of dealing or encouraging for an insider to show that he acted in accordance with the price stabilisation rules contained within the Securities and Investments Board's Conduct of Business Rules.

Stabilisation of offers of new securities involves a stabilising manager buying back securities, thereby maintaining their price at a level other than that at which they would otherwise be, in order to provide a background of price stability to assist the marketing of the securities. The Conduct of Business Rules of the Securities and Investments Board strictly prescribe the extent, disclosure and timing of permitted stabilising activity.

2.7.3 Exemption

By virtue of s 63(1) of the CJA none of the offences created by the CJA are committed by an individual acting on behalf of a public sector body in pursuit of monetary policies or policies with respect to exchange rates or the management of public debt or foreign exchange reserves.

2.7.4 Summary

The table below summarises the defences available.

TABLE (10)

Defences	Dealing	Encouragement	Disclosure
1 no profit/loss expected	•	•	•
2 wide enough disclosure—no prejudice	•	•	
3 information irrelevant	•	•	
4 did not expect dealing to result			•
5 market maker	•	•	
6 market information	•	•	
7 stabilisation	•	•	
8* did not know/have cause to believe dealing would occur	•	•	
9* disclosure in proper performance of duties			•
* not defences—but elements of the offences.			

2.8 WHAT ARE THE PENALTIES AND CONSEQUENCES OF INSIDER DEALING?

The theoretical position on criminal penalties is contained in s 61 of the CJA. On summary conviction in the Magistrates Court the maximum penalty is a fine not exceeding the statutory maximum (currently £5,000) and/or imprisonment for a term not exceeding six months. On conviction on indictment in the crown court (before a jury) the maximum penalty is an unlimited fine and/or imprisonment for a term not exceeding seven years.

Section 61 of the CJA provides that proceedings for offences under the CJA shall not be instituted in England and Wales or Northern Ireland except by or with the consent of the Secretary of State or, in the case of England and Wales, the Director of Public Prosecutions or, in the case of Northern Ireland the Director of Public Prosecutions for Northern Ireland.

Historically however, since 1980 when insider dealing first became an offence in the UK, courts have convicted only a small number of individuals. In answer to a parliamentary question in January 1994 a government spokesman confirmed that as at that time there had been only 52 prosecutions which had led to 23 convictions. The vast majority of the cases that there have been, have involved very simple and somewhat amateur examples of insider dealing, usually involving sums under £10,000. There have, for example, been no complex or sophisticated insider dealing rings convicted. For those convicted of insider dealing the courts generally impose small fines—indeed not matching the profits made or losses avoided in a significant number of cases. In sentencing it is likely that the courts take account of the fact that the convicted individual's (often lucrative) employment prospects are prejudiced. Prison sentences are rare. Despite raising the statutory maximum imprisonment to seven years in 1988, prison sentences have been imposed on only a very small number of individuals and in all but one case those sentences have been suspended.

The court also has power to disqualify a director from acting as a company director pursuant to s 2 of the Company Directors Disqualification Act 1986. Such a disqualification has been made in only one reported case.

Breach of the CJA does not prejudice the validity of any relevant contract for buying or selling securities. Section 63(2) of the CJA provides that no contract shall be void or unenforceable by reason only of the breach of any of the three insider dealing offences contained in s 52 of the CJA. It should be noted that the counterparty to the contract has no right to claim damages from the insider.

Although a body corporate cannot be guilty of an offence under the CJA it can be guilty of conspiracy (R v ICR Haulage Ltd [1994] KB 551, CCA) provided at least two persons including a 'controlling officer' or the 'directing mind and will' of the company conspire. Under the Criminal Law Act 1977 there is no limit to the fine which can be imposed for statutory conspiracy.

3 NON-STATUTORY REGULATION

3.1 INTRODUCTION

In addition to the criminal sanctions imposed by the CJA, there are a number of other measures in place which are designed to prevent and regulate insider dealing. While a detailed consideration of all of these is outside the scope of this chapter, we shall look at three of the more significant areas: the role of the London Stock Exchange the ('LSE'), the UK take-over code and the regulation of the financial services industry in the UK.

3.2 LONDON STOCK EXCHANGE

3.2.1 Applying for a London listing

3.2.1.1 The Yellow Book

Many of the LSE's powers and duties stem from the requirement set out in ss 142–3 of the Financial Services Act 1986 ('FSA') that applications by issuers to list their securities on the London Stock Exchange should be made to and in compliance with rules drafted by the Council of the LSE. These rules known as the 'Listing Rules', or more colloquially as the 'Yellow Book', are intended to protect the integrity of the market by ensuring that all users of the market have timely and simultaneous access to information, thereby creating an orderly market and preventing insider dealing.

3.2.1.2 Listing particulars

When making an initial application for listing, the Yellow Book requires the relevant issuer to prepare listing particulars which contain all such information as investors and their professional advisers would reasonably require and reasonably expect to find there for the purposes of making an informed assessment of the assets and liabilities, financial position, profits and losses and prospects of the issuer of the securities.

3.2.2 Continuing obligations

The FSA also obliges the LSE to require issuers of investments dealt in on the exchange to comply with such obligations as will, so far as possible, afford to persons dealing in the investments proper information for determining their current value. Accordingly, having provided that initial information the Yellow Book, in order to preserve a level playing field with no parties having unfair access to inside information sets out 'Continuing Obligations' which the issuer must comply with and a code, known as the 'Model Code' regulating the manner in which the directors of listed companies—those most likely to have inside information—may deal in their company's securities.

The Yellow Book's continuing obligations go considerably further than the general legal duty on all persons set out in s 47 of the FSA not to create false or misleading impressions as to the market in or price of any securities. The main features of the continuing obligations relating to disclosure are set out in Table (11) *below.*

TABLE (11)

Continuing obligations
- A company must notify the Companies Announcement Office of the LSE (the 'CAO'):
  - (a) of any major new developments in its sphere of activity which are not public knowledge which may:

> (i) by virtue of the effect of those developments on its assets and liabilities or financial position or on the general course of its business, lead to substantial movement in the price of its listed securities; or
>
> (ii) in the case of a company with debt securities listed, by virtue of the effect of those developments on its assets and liabilities or financial position or on the general course of its business, lead to substantial movement in the price of its listed securities, or significantly affect its ability to meet its commitments; and
>
> (b) where to the knowledge of its directors there is such a change in the company's financial condition or in the performance of its business or in the company's expectations of its performance that knowledge of the change is likely to lead to substantial movement in the price of its listed securities.
>
> • Save in certain limited circumstances, information required to be notified to the CAO must not be given to a third party before it has been so notified.

Other sections of the Yellow Book require companies to publish, through the CAO, information on dividend announcements, board changes, profit warnings, share dealings by directors or substantial shareholders, acquisitions and disposals over a certain size or with related persons (such as directors and their families or substantial shareholders), annual and interim results, preliminary results and offers of securities—such as rights issues.

Information supplied to the CAO is validated and communicated to the market via the London Stock Exchange's electronic Regulatory News Service. This service supplies subscribers with details of all announcements made to the CAO within minutes of their receipt on business days between 7.00 am and 6.00 pm.

As discussed in 2.3.2 *above*, the continuing obligations of the LSE have not removed the anxiety over the relationship and flow of information which should exist between a listed company and its brokers and analysts. Prior to the LSE's public censuring of one such company in May 1993, it was virtually accepted practice that indications of good, or more especially, bad news were drip-fed to the market by companies thereby paving the way for a full but less shocking announcement later.

Prompted by cases such as this, the LSE published guidance on the dissemination of price-sensitive information in February 1994 (updated in February 1995). That guidance started from the twin propositions that stock markets need a flow of relevant and timely information to function efficiently and that the selective disclosure of price-sensitive information without a formal announcement to the CAO is never acceptable. Other key features of the guidance are set out in Table (12) *below.*

TABLE (12)

LSE guidance on price-sensitive information
- Information emanating from a company or its advisers must be given to the market as a whole and be sufficient, accurate and not misleading.
- Companies should correct widespread and serious misapprehensions in the market.
- No definition is given of what theoretical percentage movement in a share price resulting from the release of information will make that information price-sensitive—it depends on the circumstances.
- Companies should have internal procedures for determining what information is to be regarded as price-sensitive and therefore to be released to the market.
- Certain employees should be identified as being responsible for communications with analysts, investors and the press—all other employees should be prohibited from communicating with such people.
- Companies should have structured communication plans—for example quarterly announcements on trading position and immediate prospects.
- Companies should have procedures to ensure price-sensitive information is kept confidential until released to the market.
- Incorrect profit forecasts should be corrected.
- Records of analysts' meetings should be kept.

The emphasis of the guidance is that companies should develop policies for the identification, security and release of price-sensitive information. The authorisation of a limited number of people to release price-sensitive information should result in unauthorised disclosure being easier to identify and therefore less likely to occur.

On 1 March 1994 the Traded Securities (Disclosure) Regulations 1994 (SI 1994 No 188) came into force and implemented art 7 of the Directive which requires disclosure to the public to be made as soon as possible by any company or undertaking which is an issuer of a security admitted to trading on a regulated market (see Table (2)) of any major new developments in the issuer's sphere of activity which are not public knowledge and which may, by virtue of their effect on the issuer's assets and liabilities or financial position or on the general course of its business, lead to substantial movements in the price of that security.

3.2.3 Model Code

On top of the Continuing Obligations, the Yellow Book requires listed companies to adopt by board resolution and take all proper and reasonable steps to secure compliance with, a code of dealing in terms no less exacting than those of the Model Code by its directors and by employees of the company or directors and employees of a subsidiary or parent of the company who are likely to be in possession of unpublished price-sensitive information in relation to the company.

The main features of the Model Code are set out in Table (13) *below*.

TABLE (13)

Model Code
• A director with inside information must not deal.
• All dealings by directors must be approved by the Chairman or another director designated for the purpose.
• A director must not deal in his company's securities during the two-month period prior to the company announcing its half-yearly and preliminary annual results or the one-month period prior to the announcement of quarterly results.

Companies are obliged to keep records of all applications by (and approvals given to) directors for share dealings. Such information must be circulated to the board. During periods when directors are precluded from dealing because of the Model Code they must also seek to prohibit such dealings by persons connected with them—such as spouses and minor children. These requirements go further than the statutory obligations contained in s 324 of the Companies Act 1985 which requires directors simply to disclose their shareholdings in their own company or that of a subsidiary.

3.2.4 Sanctions

The LSE has powers to sanction listed companies for breach of the provisions of the Continuing Obligations in the Yellow Book. However, it is unlikely to be appropriate to sanction a listed company for insider dealing in its shares.

However, para 1.8 of the Yellow Book allows the LSE to sanction directors for breaches of the Listing Rules where those breaches are due to a failure by the directors to fulfil their obligations. Such directors may be censured publicly or privately. In extreme cases the London Stock Exchange may even suspend the relevant issuer's listing.

In October 1994, the LSE published a consultation document on the question of what sanctions and measures it should take to deal with suspicious dealings ahead of the disclosure of price-sensitive information. The document was prompted by several instances of substantial price movements which had occurred prior to the release of price-sensitive information about a company. Lack of any conclusive evidence of wrongdoing in these cases meant that there was, the LSE felt, 'a growing belief that the odds favour the "insiders" and "market manipulators" and that there is more frequent disorder in the market and therefore the danger of the market falling into long-term disrepute'.

As mentioned above, however, the Listing Rules cannot be used directly to take action against insider dealing activities. The LSE monitors substantial price movements. If the LSE's Surveillance Department is unable to conclude that there is an acceptable reason to justify the movements the matter is investigated further. These investigations may take time resulting in a significant volume of trading in a false market before the LSE decides to take further action.

In January 1995, following a consultation process, the LSE announced its intention to make increased use of its existing authority to declare the price of a specific security indicative (usually for a few hours at most) in cases where an announcement is pending and the underlying information has reached only a part of the market. This has the effect of removing from market makers the obligation to quote firm prices in the security. The indicative status will be removed once an announcement is made through the LSE's Regulatory News Service.

The LSE also announced that if after declaring a security indicative the company concerned feels unable to make an announcement, then it would impose a trading halt for up to 24 hours to prevent disorder in the trading of that security.

The recently more robust approach of the LSE was displayed very publicly in early 1995 when, following leaks of price-sensitive information which had caused considerable disorder in the market, the LSE forced what was then SG Warburg to disclose information on its subsequently abortive merger talks with Morgan Stanley.

3.3 THE TAKE-OVER CODE

The making of an offer to acquire public (and certain other) companies in the UK, necessitates compliance with the City Code on Takeovers and Mergers (the 'Code'). The Code is promulgated by a panel of City representatives including the Governor of the Bank of England known as the Panel on Takeovers and Mergers (the 'Panel') and has as its stated main aim the fair and equal treatment of all shareholders during a take-over bid. Although its decisions are subject to review by the courts neither the decisions of the Panel—nor for that matter, the Code itself— have the force of law. The real power of both the Panel and the Code stems from the fact that those City institutions not in compliance are likely to be reprimanded or sanctioned by their self-regulatory organisations (see 3.4.1 below) which they are required to be members of by the FSA.

The large movements in share values which can coincide with a take-over offer have made the Panel particularly sensitive to concerns over insider dealing. Public statements by the Panel have stressed the need for take-over offers to be made public as soon as possible and that prior to an announcement secrecy must be upheld.

The Code contains three levels of regulation: general principles, rules and more detailed notes to those rules. To retain flexibility the Panel is at pains to stress that it is not precedent-bound in its interpretation of the Code and that it expects and requires compliance with the spirit as well as the letter of the Code.   *it* Civil Action

At a general level the Code contains as General Principle 2 the statement that, 'during the course of an offer, or when an offer is in contemplation, neither an offeror, nor the offeree company, nor any of their respective advisers may furnish information to some shareholders which is not made available to all shareholders . . .'. The aim of ensuring equality of information for all is clearly aimed at removing the scope for inside information to exist. General Principle 2 is amplified by Rule 20.1 and the notes thereto. The Panel stresses that during an offer period information about the participants in an offer must be made equally available to all shareholders at the same time and in the same manner and thereafter no selective disclosure of new material information or significant opinions should be made to journalists, analysts or a section only of the shareholders by or on behalf of either the participants themselves or their financial advisers without, at the least, circulating that information or those opinions to all the shareholders.

As discussed above, the Panel is anxious to ensure the market is aware of a take-over offer as early as possible to prevent a window of opportunity being created for insider dealers to exploit. Rule 2.2 of the Code sets out the Panel's position on when it requires disclosure of an offer to be made. See Table (14) *below.*

TABLE (14)

Broadly speaking the Code requires an announcement:
- when a firm intention to make an offer is notified to the board of the offeree company from a serious source, irrespective of the attitude of the board to the offer;
- immediately upon an acquisition of shares which gives rise to an obligation to make a mandatory offer under the Code;
- when, following an approach to the offeree company, the offeree company is the subject of rumour and speculation or there is an untoward movement* in its share price;
- when, before an approach has been made, the offeree company is the subject of rumour and speculation or there is an untoward movement* in its share price and there are reasonable grounds for concluding that it is the potential offeror's actions (whether through inadequate security, purchasing of offeree company shares or otherwise) which have led to the situation;
- when negotiations or discussions are about to be extended to include more than a very restricted number of people (outside those who need to know in the companies concerned and their immediate advisers);

- when a purchaser is being sought for a holding, or aggregate holdings, of shares carrying 30 per cent or more of the voting rights of a company or when the board of a company is seeking potential offerors; and:
  (a) the company is the subject of rumour and speculation or there is an untoward movement* in its share price; or
  (b) the number of potential purchasers or offerors approached is about to be increased to include more than a very restricted number of people.
- * A movement of approximately 10 per cent should be regarded as untoward.

In the period prior to an announcement, Rule 2.1 provides that information of an offer must be kept secret. The Rule requires persons privy to confidential information concerning an actual or contemplated offer to treat that information as secret and then may only pass it to another person if it is necessary to do so and if that person is made aware of the need for secrecy.

In addition to their attempt to secure equality of information for all share-holders, the Panel, through the Code, seeks to prohibit certain types of securi-ties dealing. Rule 4 prohibits dealings of any kind in securities of the offeree company (or the making of recommendations to deal) by any person (other than the offeror) who is privy to confidential price-sensitive information concerning an offer or contemplated offer between the time when there is reason to suppose that an approach or an offer is contemplated and the announcement of that approach or offer or of the termination of the discussions.

Breaches of the Code have usually resulted in either private reprimands or public censures from the Panel for the individuals or organisations concerned. The Panel however can report its findings to the Department of Trade and Industry, the LSE or the relevant self-regulatory organisation (see 3.4 below).

3.4 OTHER NON-STATUTORY REGULATIONS

3.4.1 Regulation under the FSA

The FSA makes it a criminal offence for anyone to carry on investment business in the UK without either being an exempted person (such as the Bank of England) or more commonly by being authorised by the Securities and Investments Board ('SIB'), by membership of one of the self-regulatory organisations ('SROs') or by certification by one of the recognised professional bodies.

The SROs principally responsible for the securities industry are The Securities and Futures Authority. Members of SROs are obliged to comply with Principles and Core Conduct of Business Rules promulgated by SIB together with the supplementary rulebooks of their respective SROs. The key Core Conduct of Business Rule in this context is Rule 28 which provides that a firm (as opposed to an individual) must not effect (either in the UK or elsewhere) as own account transaction when it knows (that is, any of the relevant individuals involved on behalf of the firm knows) of circumstances which mean that it, its associate, or an employee of either, is prohibited from effecting that transaction by the statutory restrictions on insider dealing. In practice, compliance with the requirements of Rule 28, and in particular, ensuring successfully that relevant individuals within the firm do not possess the knowledge referred to above, has generally been measured by an after-the-event examination of adherence to a firm's internal compliance procedure, including especially the permeability of its Chinese Walls. Rule 28 does not however affect a firm's activities on a recognised market maker—an exemption analogous to that considered at 2.7.2.1 *above*. In addition to Rule 28, other Core Conduct of Business Rules restrict firms from dealing on their own account either ahead of the accounts of their customers or ahead of recommendations, research or analysis intended to be published to customers. The Core Conduct of Business Rules also place obligations on firms designed to ensure they use best endeavours not to effect transactions for customers whom they know are prohibited from so trading by the CJA and to ensure offices and employees conform with the CJA.

A firm's breach of the SIB's Principles or Core Conduct of Business Rules or SRO's rulebook can give rise to disciplinary action by, usually, the SRO or, on occasions, SIB itself. Both SIB and the SROs have extensive powers of investigation and can require member firms to answer inquiries and provide information, with failure to comply in itself constituting an offence. The SROs have similarly wide enforcement powers ranging from reprimands to expulsion from membership. They also have power to publish the results of their investigations. SIB has similar powers but in addition can by virtue of s 59 of the FSA disqualify individuals from being employed in connection with investment bankers, by virtue of s 60 of the FSA, make public statements as to a person's misconduct and in appropriate cases, by virtue of s 61 of the FSA, seek injunctions and restriction order.

3.4.2 Department of Trade and Industry

Section 177 of the FSA given powers, exercised by the Department of Trade and Industry ('DTI'), to appoint inspection if it appears there are circumstances suggesting that an offence under the CJA may have been committed to carry out such investigation as are requisite to establish whether or not any such offence has been committed. Such inspections have wide powers to require the disclosure of relevant information, the production of relevant documents and the examination under oath of relevant person. Failure to comply with such inspection is itself an offence under the FSA. It should be noted however that in recent years inspections have been appointed in very few cases.

4 CONCLUSION

The focus of the insider dealings debate in the UK has been towards ensuring that the market operates smoothly and that it is kept properly informed. The more successful one is in fulfilling these aims, it is argued, the fewer the opportunities there will be for insider dealing to occur. Correct though the attempts of the London Stock Exchange are to tackle issues such as preserving orderly markets and disseminating price-sensitive information, one will never (as recent examples clearly show) be able to remove the informational advantages of some in the market. Drawing a line between such advantages which are legitimate (for example *bona fide* research findings) and those which are not therefore remains one of the key tasks of the CJA. In meeting this task the CJA represents an improvement on the 1985 Act, but is not beyond criticism. As discussed above, the scope of concepts such as how and when information is 'made public', when an individual has information 'by virtue' of his employment and the 'wide disclosure' defence are all unclear.

Turning to detection and enforcement, it would be comforting to assume that the relatively few successful convictions in the UK are indicative of a low incidence of insider dealing and the success of initiatives aimed at ensuring market transparency. The harsh reality, however, is probably that although the improved surveillance mechanisms established by the London Stock Exchange means that examples of insider dealing are likely to be detected, only the least sophisticated examples of insider dealing are enforced and of those many fail to result in convictions due to the complexities of the legislation.

CASE STUDY

Splash Plc, a company listed on the London Stock Exchange, manufactures rainwear and umbrellas. Alan, a weather forecaster, on discovering that there is an unseasonable amount of rain due in the next three months, instructs his broker to buy shares in Splash. Meanwhile, Charles, an analyst of the company's shares, is told in a conversation with Jeremy, one of the directors, that the Chairman is expected to be paid a salary of £500,000. Charles knows from his knowledge of the Chairman's service contract (which is available for public inspection) that this salary could only be paid if the company achieved profit in excess of £20 million. Charles revises his profit forecast for the company but before he publishes it he cancels instructions which he had previously given to his broker to sell his Splash shares. Charles also tells his girlfriend, Maggie, that 'things are looking up' for Splash. Maggie then buys shares in the name of her father from an old friend of hers who wanted to sell Splash shares off market to save the payment of brokers commission. In addition, Owen, an employee of the contracting firm which cleans Splash's offices, finds a draft of the latest management figures, which demonstrate Splash's high profitability, in a waste-paper bin. He immediately buys shares.

Alan

Whether Alan is guilty of insider dealing under s 52(1) of the CJA will depend on whether the information on the rainfall constitutes inside information within s 56. This information does relate, albeit tangentially, to particular issuers of securities (ie companies whose sales are dependent on the weather) and is specific or precise. More difficult is whether it can be said that the information has already been made 'public'. It is probable that the information on rainfall could readily be acquired by those professionals who deal in securities of Splash. Even if this were not to be the case the court is able to treat information as public even though it can only be acquired by persons exercising diligence or expertise and it is difficult to believe in this situation that it would not exercise its discretion to treat the information as public. Accordingly, it is likely Alan will not be guilty of insider dealing.

Jeremy

The issue is whether Jeremy is guilty of disclosing inside information other than in the proper performance of the functions of his employment to another person contrary to s 52(2)(b). Clearly, the information appears to fall within the definition of 'inside information' since it is sufficiently related to Splash, is specific and not available to the public. Furthermore, although the company's brokers should be consulted, it is likely that the information about the Chairman's salary would, if made public, be likely to have a significant effect on Splash's market price since the market will probably be sufficiently sophisticated to interpret the implications that the level of the Chairman's salary meant the company's profitability was in excess of market expectation. Jeremy would be able to avoid conviction if he shows that he did not expect Charles to deal or that he did not expect any profit made to be attributable to the information disclosed. Jeremy may be able to establish on the balance of probabilities that since the rules of the Securities and Futures Authority apply to Charles and those rules precluded him from dealing on his own behalf whilst he was in possession of inside information, then it was reasonable to conclude that Charles would not deal. Finally, it is very unlikely that Jeremy by disclosing the level of the Chairman's salary could be said to be encouraging Charles to deal. Even if this were the case, for the reason mentioned above, it could not be said that he had reasonable cause to believe that Charles would deal.

Charles

Charles is not guilty of an offence under s 52(1) since he has not dealt in Splash's shares—merely omitting to deal where Charles would otherwise have done so is not an offence. Charles may have committed the offence of encouraging another to deal, if the prosecution can show that Charles knew or had reasonable cause to believe that Maggie would deal. In practice, this element of the offence would be very difficult to demonstrate especially given the equivocal nature of the encouragement.

Maggie

It is difficult to see how Maggie could be said to be in possession of insider information. The information is not sufficiently precise about Splash—Charles gave no indication as to why things are looking up or what impact this might have on Splash's share price. On the assumption that the information did constitute inside information, and since Maggie has not bought on market it is necessary to demonstrate that she has relied on a professional intermediary, which in this context, means that a person has acted as an intermediary between persons taking part in any dealing in securities. Accordingly, Maggie would not be treated as having dealt. It should be noted that the fact that Maggie is dealing on behalf of her father would not, in itself, have meant that she had not dealt since a person deals if he acquires or disposes of securities whether as principal or agent.

Owen

The only issue is whether Owen has information as an insider, which, in turn, requires a determination of whether the information is from an inside source. Owen can be said to have obtained this information by virtue of his employment. In any event, if the information is obtained indirectly from a director then the information is deemed to be received from an inside source. On the basis that the finance director prepared this information and Owen was aware of the source then it appears he would be guilty of insider dealing pursuant to s 52(1).

Germany

*Tony Hickinbotham, Linklaters & Paines, London
and Christoph Vaupel, Oppenhoff & Rädler, Frankfurt*

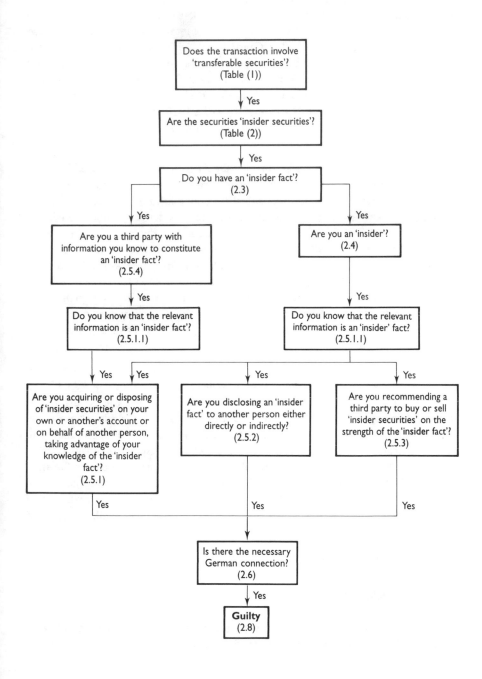

1 INTRODUCTION

Insider dealing was criminalised for the first time in Germany by the *Wertpapierhandelsgesetz* ('WpHG') or Securities Trading Act which was passed in 1994 as part of a comprehensive financial market reform package. Before the new law came into effect Germany had only a voluntary code against the misuse of inside information (the 'Insider Guidelines') which was sponsored by the German stock exchanges and the credit institutions and brokers constituting the main professional participants in the stock market. The Insider Guidelines were criticised for their voluntary status although they achieved some measure of success indirectly because they were used as the basis for disciplining of insider traders by their employers who incorporated the Guidelines into contracts of employment.

The WpHG introduces the EC Insider Dealing Directive (Dir 89/592 [1989] OJ L334/30) into German law. Four offences are created, the acquisition or disposal by an 'insider' of 'insider securities' by taking advantage of knowledge of 'insider facts', the unauthorised disclosure by an 'insider' of 'insider facts', the counselling by an 'insider' of a third party to acquire or dispose of 'insider securities' on the basis of knowledge of 'insider facts' and the acquisition or disposal of 'insider securities' as a third party (secondary insider) by taking advantage of knowledge of insider facts. Policing of insider trading is entrusted to a new body, the Federal Authority for the Supervision of Securities Trading (*Bundesaufsichtsamt für den Wertpapierhandel* or 'BAWe'), which, in addition, will oversee the complementary regime for *ad hoc* disclosure of price-sensitive information by companies listed on German stock exchanges.

So far, there has been no practical experience of the operation of the new law but preparatory materials leading up to new legislation such as the WpHG are frequently used by the courts as an aid to construction and the government's formal reasoning in support of the draft of the new law (the 'White Paper') will, no doubt, be similarly used by the courts. Additional help in understanding the views of the authorities on the scope of the duty to disclose price-sensitive information is to be gained from guidance published in October 1994 by the German Stock Exchange entitled *'Insiderhandelsverbote und Ad Hoc Publizität nach dem Wertpapierhandelsgesetz'*. The old Insider Guidelines, some of the structure of which has been adopted in the new law, and the EC Directive itself, will also aid construction.

2 THE CRIMINAL LAW

2.1 INTRODUCTION

Article 14 of the WpHG creates four separate offences which depend on the definitions of 'insider', 'insider securities' and 'insider fact'.

2.2 WHAT ARE 'INSIDER SECURITIES'?

In order for securities to constitute 'insider securities' for the purpose of art 12, they must be 'transferable securities' within art 2.

TABLE (1)

Definition of 'transferable securities':
- shares and certificates representing such shares, eg, depositary receipts;
- debt securities (*Schuldverschreibungen*)—these can be issued by any company, public body or state;
- profit participating bonds (*Genußscheine*)—these entitle their holders to participate in profits (they normally rank ahead of equity capital but behind all other liabilities);
- option certificates—eg warrants to buy or sell a transferable security;
- other securities which are similar to shares or debt securities—these would include for example instruments conferring some, but not all, normal shareholder rights eg a right to participate in profits and/or a surplus of assets on liquidation but with no right to vote.

The above categories of investment only fall within the definition of 'transferable securities' if they are *capable* of being dealt in (whether or not they are in fact dealt in) on a market which is regulated and supervised by a state recognised body and which operates regularly and is accessible directly or indirectly to the public. Such a market (described in art 2, para (1)) can be referred to as an 'organised market'. It corresponds to the definition in art 1 of the EC Directive.

TABLE (2)

Definition of 'insider securities':
- transferable securities which are admitted to trading [on a domestic German stock exchange] or included in the so-called free market (*Freiverkehr*) on a German stock exchange or admitted to dealing on an organised market in another EC state or EEA state;
- for this purpose a transferable security is deemed to be admitted to dealing on an organised market, or included in the German free market, when the application for admission or inclusion has been made or publicly announced;
- rights to subscribe for, acquire or dispose of transferable securities;
- rights to payment of a difference by reference to a change in the value of transferable securities;
- futures contracts on a share or bond index or interest rate futures agreements ('financial futures contracts') and rights to subscribe for acquisition or disposal of financial futures contracts in so far as their

> subject matter is transferable securities or relates to an index of which transferable securities form an element;
> - other futures contracts which give rise to a duty to acquire, or dispose of, transferable securities.

The rights or futures contracts referred to in the last four categories of Table (2) only fall within the definition of 'insider securities' if:

- they are themselves admitted to trading on an organised market in a member state of the EC or the EEA or included in the German free market;
- the securities referred to in those paragraphs are themselves so admitted or included in the free market. Once again, the making of an application for admission or the giving of public notice thereof is sufficient. Public notice would be given for example where a prospectus containing notice of intention to apply is distributed to the public.

It follows from the above that a necessary element in the definition of 'insider securities' is a listing (or application for a listing) on a European market and, where the insider security concerned is a derivative, the underlying securities must also be so listed. Thus, an over-the-counter derivative which is not included in the German free market and which is based on a listed security escapes the net as does a listed derivative based on a security which is only listed, for example, in the United States.

The German 'free market' used to include two distinct market segments, the so-called 'regulated free market' (*geregelter Freiverkehr*) and the telephone over-the-counter market. The reference in the WpHG refers to the regulated free market which is provided for in the Exchange Act (the '*Börsengesetz*'). This Act provides for an orderly market in securities which are not the subject of the price-fixing arrangements of the official market and the regulated market. Securities traded only on the regulated free market are not, however, within the definition of transferable securities in art 1 of the EC Directive and their inclusion there-fore represents a policy decision by the German government on the grounds that the public would not distinguish such securities from officially listed securities.

By contrast the entirely unregulated telephone over-the-counter market is not within the WpHG at all and, consequently, securities dealt in only in that way cannot be insider securities. It is presumably the case that similar dealing systems outside Germany such as, for example, the SEAQ system in the United Kingdom, will not be treated in Germany as satisfying the requirement of a listing.

2.3 WHAT IS AN 'INSIDER FACT'?

An insider fact, as defined in art 13(1) is:

- a fact which is not publicly known, which relates to one or more issuers of insider securities or to an insider security;

- which, if it becomes publicly known, is calculated significantly to affect the market price of the insider security concerned.

2.3.1 Fact or opinion

The White Paper contrasted the expression of an opinion of a subjective kind and a fact. The former were said to be incapable of being an insider fact. Article 13(2) goes on to stipulate, following the recitals to the EC Directive, that an evaluation based exclusively on publicly known facts cannot itself be an insider fact even if it is capable of significantly affecting market price. Thus, the analyst's opinion, if based on publicly-available information, cannot be an insider fact. However, the use of the word 'fact' (*Tatsache*) instead of the EC Directive's 'information . . . of a precise nature' may perhaps be unduly restrictive. It is possible to conceive of 'precise information' which would not necessarily be covered by the word 'fact'. Is a profit forecast to be treated as an opinion or a fact? Perhaps this difficulty will be resolved by treating the *making* of a profit forecast as a fact even if the content of the forecast is couched in terms of pure opinion.

Alternatively, on the other hand a detailed budget or forecast prepared by a company is likely to be based on all kinds of facts that are not publicly known. The market would react to such a forecast and it is perhaps irrelevant whether the making of such forecast itself constitutes the fact or whether the forecast is taken as a summary or analysis of all of the facts reflected in it, many of which will not be known to the public. It cannot be right that an insider who is aware of such a forecast should be permitted to act on it on the basis that it is an opinion rather than a fact.

2.3.2 Inter-relationship with Article 15

By contrast, publication of facts pursuant to art 15 WpHG (see 3 *below*) is only required for facts which are calculated significantly to influence the price because of their impact on the assets or on the financial or business condition. Clearly, a budget or forecast or even a fixed management plan cannot by itself have an impact on the assets, earnings or business—the budget or forecast only reflects the views of the likelihood of a development and the plan will have an impact only when steps are taken to implement it. Thus, the term insider fact has a broader meaning than facts requiring publication pursuant to art 15 of the WpHG.

2.3.3 Publicly known

As to precisely when something becomes publicly known it seems from the White Paper that access to the information concerned must be available to an indefinite number of market professionals generally. Thus, availability via a screen based information service or publication in a foreign, widely circulated newspaper such as the *Wall Street Journal* would, on this basis, suffice. It should, however, be noted that the courts are not necessarily bound by this interpretation. One could argue that the restricted dissemination of information merely increases the number of insiders. It is, however, generally accepted that the term 'public' can be interpreted in such restricted manner because if the relevant market participants have knowledge of the insider fact such fact is incorporated in the price almost immediately and further publication would not cause any price changes.

2.3.4 Significant effect on market price

The fact must, of course, be relevant to the price of the insider security concerned. It must, on becoming publicly known, be calculated to lead to a significant change in the price. The White Paper suggests that the likely effect on the price must go beyond normal market movements. The White Paper made reference to the regulation of the German stock exchanges pursuant to which the market participants themselves characterise certain price movements as significant. Thus, a broker is obliged to indicate expected price changes with a plus or minus if he executes a trade (or volume of trades) over a certain size on the market. Article 8 of the Terms of Dealing on the Frankfurt Stock Exchange ('*Bedingungen für Geschäfte an der Frankfurter Wertpapierbörse*'), which are similar to the terms of other German stock exchanges, provides that expected price changes of (i) 5–10 per cent, (ii) 10–20 per cent and (iii) more than 20 per cent must be indicated with a '+' or '–', '++' or '– –' and '+++' or '– – –' respectively.

The government seems to envisage that a price movement of such a hurdle of 5 per cent would be sufficient to constitute a significant change. However, in the legal literature a hurdle of 15 per cent has been suggested (Claussen ZBB 1992, 267, 278). Just how subjectively the volatility of individual stock prices can be taken account of is not clear. What is reasonably clear is that significance of potential price movements will, in practice, be judged retrospectively *ex post facto*. In theory, however, they must be judged in advance because the person considering a trade must be able to judge its legality at the time when he enters into it.

It may also be relevant to review the effect of the price movement in the context of the historic trading performance of the shares (see the discussion in 3.6 *below*).

The legal literature suggests that whether a trade was based on an insider fact must be analysed in three steps. First, the price movement caused by disclosure of the insider fact must be determined, second such movement must be qualified as significant or insignificant in comparison with similar securities and third, if it is significant, it must be determined whether, prior to the transaction, circumstances existed that would lead to the conclusion that the insider fact on which the insider traded could not cause such a price movement (Assman, ZGR 3/1994).

2.4 WHO IS AN INSIDER?

The definition of 'insider' in art 13 follows the EC Directive fairly closely. Thus, the definition confines itself to so-called primary insiders who have direct access to inside information. The three categories of such people are directors and supervisors, certain shareholders and employees, and advisers and contractors: in all cases the person concerned must be aware that the information he has is an insider fact or at least that it is not publicly known and is price-sensitive.

2.4.1 Directors and supervisors

This category includes members of the management board and supervisory board of the issuer of the insider securities or of connected companies. 'Connected companies' has a specific meaning under art 15 of the Stock Corporation Act.

TABLE (3)

Meaning of connected company:
- parent and subsidiary companies;
- members of the same group of companies;
- controlled and controlling companies (ie where a relationship of actual management control exists irrespective of shareholdings);
- companies with cross shareholdings in excess of 25 per cent; and
- companies which are parties to an enterprise agreement (these are agreements under which one company has the right to control the management of another and/or under which profits are transferred from one company to another or to pool profits).

It should be noted that whilst the issuer of insider securities which are shares in a German company is likely to be a stock corporation (*Aktiengesellschaft*), the connected companies could take any form including that of a GmbH or a limited partnership. Also included within this category of primary insider is the general partner of a limited partnership. It is irrelevant how this category of insider comes by his knowledge of an insider fact.

2.4.2 Shareholders

The second category of primary insider is a shareholder in the issuer or in a connected company. The extent of the shareholding is irrelevant but, surprisingly, the Stock Exchange Guidance suggests that the shareholding must be direct. Thus, a 10 per cent shareholder in an intermediate holding company which itself is a shareholder in the issuer will not be caught in this category. Such a structure is quite common in Germany to take advantage of the so-called *Schachtelprivileg* which allows the payment of dividends free of withholding tax to shareholders of a certain size. Such a shareholder may nevertheless be caught as a secondary insider (see *below*).

Persons in this category have to be in possession of the inside information 'on the basis of' their shareholding. The shareholding must, therefore, be the causal link between the person concerned and the possession of the information.

2.4.3 Advisers, employees, contractors

The third category of primary insider comprises professional advisers, employees and contractual counterparties of an undertaking. Advisers cover such people as accountants, lawyers, notaries and management consultants and their employees who come into possession of insider facts by virtue of their professional activity on behalf of a client undertaking. The contractual counterparty category covers any organisation (and its employees) which has access to insider information because of a contractual relationship with an undertaking. This can range from joint venture partners through major service providers such as banks to one-off contractors such as printers engaged to print a prospectus. According to the Stock Exchange Guidance it is an open question whether a financial journalist or analyst who is 'briefed' by an issuer might refrain from making recommendations if the 'briefing' contained an insider fact.

Once again the possession of the inside information must be 'on the basis of or by virtue of' the relationship of adviser, employee or contractual counterparty. For this category, however, there is an additional hurdle. The inside information must come into the possession of the person concerned within the scope of ('bes-timmungsgemäss') his activity as adviser, employee or contractual counterpart. The White Paper said that a purely chance acquisition of inside information would be insufficient to bring the person concerned within the definition. The Stock Exchange Guidance cites, as examples of employees who only hear things by chance, a secretary who 'listens in' to a confidential conversation and a chauffeur who learns of an insider fact by chance. The first example seems difficult to justify on policy grounds but apparently would not exclude from the definition the private secretary of a managing director whom, the Guidance suggests, would be caught. The principle seems to be that the knowledge of the insider fact has to come to the adviser, employee or contractor as part of the subject matter of his activity on behalf of the undertaking concerned.

The relationship of adviser, employee, etc does not have to be with the under-taking which is the issuer of the relevant insider securities, it can be more remote. The only requirement is that the insider fact is obtained by reason of and within the scope of the relevant relationship. Thus, for example, an employee of an investment bank advising a potential bidder can be an insider in relation to the insider securities of the bid target company.

2.5 WHAT ARE THE OFFENCES?

Article 14(1) creates three offences for insiders and art 14(2) a fourth offence for third parties who do not fall within the insider definition.

2.5.1 Dealing by an insider

It is an offence for an insider, by taking advantage of his knowledge of an insider fact, to acquire or dispose of insider securities for his own or another's account or on behalf of another.

TABLE (4)

Constituent elements for dealing offence:
- person must be an insider (see 2.4);
- person must have knowledge of an insider fact (see 2.3);
- person must subjectively know that the information constitutes an insider fact;
- person must acquire or dispose of insider securities (see 2.2) for his or another account or on behalf of another;
- person must intend to take advantage of his knowledge of an insider fact by dealing.

The elements of this offence, apart from those implicit in the definitions of insider, insider fact and insider securities, are the following.

2.5.1.1 Insider must know relevant information as insider fact

The insider must know that the relevant information of which he has possession is an insider fact. Whether or not the fact was likely to have a significant effect on market price is an objective matter to be judged, ultimately, by the court but the insider must have believed that the fact was price-sensitive. He also must believe that the information has not been made public.

2.5.1.2 Insider must take advantage of his knowledge

The insider must 'take advantage of' his knowledge. He takes advantage of his inside knowledge if he makes use of his perceived early knowledge of inside information (ie before it becomes public) in the hope and with the intention that he will achieve some commercial advantage. He must, so to speak, intend to 'steal a march' on the market or, as the Stock Exchange Guidance puts it, he must intend to obtain a special advantage by breaching the principle of equality of access to information by market participants. Actual achievement of a commercial advantage is not required.

Examples of activities which are said in the White Paper and Stock Exchange Guidance not to involve taking advantage of information are:

- The carrying out of a corporate objective which was decided upon without influence from any insider knowledge. The intending buyer of a large block of shares creates an insider fact by deciding to undertake the purchase. The putting into effect of this decision does not constitute taking advantage of the fact but only accomplishment of the corporate objective. The White Paper makes clear that this will be the case even where insider facts come to the knowledge of the intending buyer during negotiations for the acquisition of the block of shares from the intending seller. However, once that block has been acquired any further dealing, on or off exchange, would then constitute insider trading.

- Price stabilisation measures—Price stabilisation activities will not of themselves constitutes insider trading. Of course, if they are carried out on the basis of knowledge of some independent insider fact then they may constitute insider trading but it will be because of the knowledge of such insider fact.

- The activities of market makers—German price fixing brokers (*Kursmakler*) and other market makers necessarily have access to insider facts but their setting of a price and market making activities, provided they are carried out in conformity with the rules of the stock exchange, will not constitute insider trading.

- Non-discretionary dealings—Such dealings on behalf of a client will be alright so long as they are carried out strictly in accordance with the terms of the client's instructions. If an order is received by an insider to deal with any form of discretion left to him it will be very difficult for him to carry out the order without infringing the law. In those circumstances the White Paper suggests that the order should be passed to a non-insider for execution. The Stock Exchange Guidance lays some stress on the probability that the BAWe in pursuing insider trading is likely to take an objective view of whether the person under investigation has taken advantage of insider information and that, accordingly, it is best not to undertake any dealing in the securities concerned if it cannot clearly be shown that the dealing is lawful. This warning is given notwithstanding that the rule that an accused is innocent until proven guilty applies to insider trading as to any other offence.

It should be noted that Germany has not, in implementing the Directive, made it a condition of the dealing offence that the trade should be effected through a professional intermediary. Thus, even off market deals can fall within the offence. It has even been suggested that an off market deal between two persons who both have knowledge of the same insider fact might constitute an offence. A contrary view is that if both parties know about the insider fact then neither of them can be 'taking advantage of' the relevant information, at least not to the detriment of the other. On the other hand, it could nevertheless be said to be 'taking advantage of' the information as regards the rest of the investing public.

2.5.2 Unauthorised disclosure of insider facts by insiders

Disclosure can be direct or indirect. The White Paper cites as an example of indirect disclosure of information the disclosure to a third party of a password which enables him to access a databank containing insider facts.

TABLE (5)

Constituent elements for disclosure offence:
- person must be an insider (see 2.4);
- person must have knowledge of an insider fact (see 2.3);
- person must subjectively know that the information constitutes an insider fact;
- person must, without authorisation, inform another of, or make available to an insider fact.

It should be noted that the unauthorised disclosure of information within a single company can constitute this offence. If insider facts are disclosed within an organisation beyond the 'need to know' category of colleagues the offence will be committed. Companies must, where necessary, erect Chinese Walls to contain insider facts.

Mention was made above of the uncertainty as to whether a journalist or financial analyst can be an insider within the meaning of the WpHG. This difficulty is relevant as well to the disclosure offence. It used to be regarded in Germany as legitimate to provide price-sensitive information on a selective basis to journalists and analysts on the footing that the results of their work would be publicly available. Such 'drip feeding' of the market with price-sensitive information was until recently a feature of the relationship between leading German companies and the press and analyst community. It now seems that such activities will involve either the company representatives or the journalists or analysts, or perhaps both in potentially criminal activities.

The Stock Exchange Guidance recommends that prior to or at the same time as an interview with journalists or analysts the market must be informed and prior to an interview the stock exchange and the BAWe must be informed. Whether the provision of insider information to analysts or journalists is permissible as a means of making information public is an open question. The solution might be that the giving of access to such information would be acceptable if made *for the purpose* of publishing the relevant facts.

The Guidance raises the same issue with respect to shareholders meetings. In this situation, the board should issue a press release prior to the beginning of a shareholder meeting if the board intend to disclose price-sensitive insider facts.

2.5.3 Recommending others to deal

It is an offence for an insider to recommend a third party to deal in insider securities on the basis of insider facts. The recommendation need not mention the insider fact, it suffices if it is made on the basis of the recommender's knowledge of the insider fact. Of course, if the insider fact is mentioned, the third party recommended may himself commit the dealing offence in 2.5.4.

TABLE (6)

> *Constitutent elements for recommendation offence:*
> • person must be an insider (see 2.4);
> • person must have knowledge of an insider fact (see 2.3);
> • person must subjectively know that the information constitutes an insider fact;
> • person must recommend another to acquire or dispose of insider securities (see 2.2) on the basis of his knowledge of an insider fact.

2.5.4 Dealing by a third party

It is an offence for a third party (a secondary insider) to deal in an insider security for his own account or on behalf of or for the account of another by taking advantage of his knowledge of an insider fact. The source of the knowledge is irrelevant and no particular relationship is required between the third party and any other undertaking or person. This offence is thus widely formulated and may well catch many of the doubtful cases discussed in 2.5.1 *above*. In other respects this offence follows very closely the considerations outlined in 2.5.1 *above* regarding the 'taking advantage' element of the offence.

TABLE (7)

> *Constitutent elements for third party dealing offence:*
> • person must have knowledge of an insider fact;
> • person must subjectively know that it is an insider fact;
> • he must acquire or dispose of insider securities (see 2.2) for his own or another's account or on behalf of another;
> • he must intend to take advantage of his knowledge of an insider fact.

It should be noted that a third party who is not an insider but has knowledge of an insider fact can recommend the security concerned or disclose the insider fact to a fourth party without committing an offence. For instance, the wife of a board member overhears a telephone conversation of her husband thus learning of an insider fact. If she then makes a recommendation to her son no offence is committed by her. Nor does the son commit an offence unless it is proved that he was aware of the fact that the recommendation was based on an insider fact.

2.6 WHAT IS THE TERRITORIAL SCOPE OF THE WpHG?

The territorial scope of the criminal sanctions in the WpHG is governed by arts 3 and 7 of the Penal Guide. Accordingly, the criminal sanctions in art 38 apply to:

- violations committed within Germany;
- violations committed abroad against a German victim, provided that the act constitutes a criminal offence at the place where committed (in case

of insider trading it would be difficult to identify a German victim);

- violations committed in a foreign country if the act constitutes a criminal offence in that country too
  — by a German citizen or
  — by a foreigner, who is found in Germany and is not extradited.

As a German court will only apply German criminal law, art 38(2) of the WpHG provides that equivalent overseas offences to those contained in art 14 are to be treated in the same way as regards punishment. The purpose of this paragraph is said to be to get round the prohibition against extradition of German citizens contained in the German Constitution. It would thus permit equivalent offences perpetrated abroad by Germans or non-extraditable foreigners to be prosecuted and punished within Germany.

2.7 WHAT ARE THE DEFENCES?

There are no specific defences set out in the WpHG.

2.8 WHAT ARE THE PENALTIES?

Article 38 of the WpHG provides that each of the offences may be punished by imprisonment for a term of up to five years or by fine. The amount of the fine would depend in accordance with the Criminal Code on the personal and commercial circumstances of the accused but could extend up to DM 3.6 million. No distinction is made as regards limits on punishment between primary insiders and third parties (secondary insiders). However, the Stock Exchange Guidance suggests that the latter might be treated more leniently.

Although German law does hold companies responsible for the act of its officers, this principle is not applicable where the officer acts on his own, rather than the company's interest. Therefore, if a person commits insider trading it is safe to assume that he will generally act solely in his own interest and that, accordingly, the corporate body of which he is the legal representative will not be subject to a fine.

Suspected offences are to be reported by the BAWe to the relevant public prosecutor who decides whether or not a prosecution should be brought. Given the recent introduction of the WpHG no prosecutions have, as yet been brought.

3 *AD HOC* PUBLICITY PURSUANT TO ARTICLE 15 WpHG

3.1 ORIGINS

Article 15 of the new law builds significantly on the pre-existing s 44a of the Exchange Act. Both are based on the provision in the EC Council Directive (Dir

79/279 [1979] OJ L66/21) which required listed companies to inform the public of major new developments in its sphere of activity which might, by virtue of their effect on the company's assets and liabilities or financial position or on the general course of its business lead to substantial movements in its share price.

3.2 WHICH COMPANIES ARE COVERED?

Article 15 applies to companies any of whose transferable securities are admitted to official trading or regulated trading on a German stock exchange. In contrast to the insider dealing articles, the provision does not, therefore, apply to regulated free market trading or pure OTC trading nor does it apply to companies whose securities are only listed outside Germany.

The White Paper said that the regulated free market is not supervised by a state recognised authority and could therefore be excluded from the application of the disclosure requirements. It is debatable whether this is correct since inclusion within the regulated free market must be approved by the OTC committee ('*Freiverkehrsausschuss*') of the relevant exchange and the board of the exchange may suspend regulated free market trading in a security if it finds improper trading activities are taking place. One may also question the logic of not applying the *ad hoc* publicity regime to a category of securities which have expressly, for public interest reasons, been included in the insider dealing regime.

3.3 INFORMATION WHICH MUST BE PUBLISHED

The new provision applies to 'new facts' arising in the issuer's sphere of activity which are not publicly known and which, by reason of their effects on the assets, liabilities and financial position or on the general course of business of the issuer, are likely to lead to a significant movement in the stock exchange price of its listed securities. Where only debt securities are listed the disclosure requirement is further limited. In this case the 'new fact' must, instead of being likely to affect the stock exchange price, affect the ability of the issuer to comply with its obligations. This would include negative effects on specific security granted in support of the debt security.

Once again the concept of a new fact seems to exclude mere opinion (see 2.3.1 *above*). However, in relation to art 15, the White Paper suggests that an opinion could acquire factual characteristics by being associated with the dissemination of facts. The Stock Exchange Guidance draws attention to commentaries on art 186 of the Criminal Code which suggest that an opinion can acquire the status of fact if capable of objective verification.

3.4 TIMING OF DISCLOSURE

A particular problem for German Stock corporations is the dual board structure where certain decisions of the management board require the consent or approval of the supervisory board. The guidelines suggest that, in normal circumstances, such a decision does not become a new fact which might require disclosure until it has been approved by the supervisory board. In the meantime, it is clearly capable of being an insider fact. The guidance goes on to suggest, however, that a decision of the management board which still requires the consent of the supervisory board, can nevertheless be such a 'strong fact' that disclosure is required straight away. The example is cited of a friendly take-over agreed between the management boards of two companies subject to supervisory board approval. In such circumstances the condition of such approval must be clearly spelled out in any early announcement, and pre-sumably the eventual decision of the supervisory board must likewise be announced.

3.5 WHICH FACTS ARE RELEVANT?

Both the White Paper and the Stock Exchange Guidance distinguish *ad hoc* dis-closure from normal regular disclosure through the publication of annual results and interim reports. The two categories of disclosure are not, however, mutually exclusive. Facts which may fail to be included in the annual report might well give rise to an earlier duty of disclosure. As to the meaning of the requirement that the new fact must have an effect on assets and liabilities or the financial situation or the general course of business of the issuer, the report of the finance com-mittee of the German parliament suggests that new facts fall within the category if they should be reflected in accounts or in the annual report of the company. The Stock Exchange Guidance questions whether a change in the capital struc-ture of a company which does not result in an increase or reduction in assets or liabilities, for example conversion of preference shares into ordinary shares, falls within the category of facts requiring disclosure but, contradicting itself some-what, it says that a capitalisation issue of shares would have to be disclosed. Such a change would, in any event, require to be disclosed in any event by virtue of other disclosure obligations under, for example, the Stock Exchange Admission Regulation.

The White Paper states that press or news agency reports containing hard information, rather than mere speculation or rumour, relieve the issuer from its duty to disclose. It has been argued that it is irrelevant how the public is informed and that the publication procedure pursuant to s 15 of the WpHG is merely a safe harbour rule (Assmann, AG 1994, p 251). However, the Act clearly states that if the issuer learns of facts that are not publicly known it must follow the prescribed publication procedure.

Internal studies, analyses, plans, etc do not constitute facts within art 15 since they do not, by themselves, have any impact on the business of the issuer. Only if steps are taken to implement any such plan can any requirement to make an announcement arise.

Events, the consequences of which, cannot be determined because their effects could be offset by other circumstances or positive countermeasures are not, according to the White Paper, new facts within the meaning of the WpHG because they do not have the required effect on assets, liabilities or course of business.

3.6 WHEN DOES A NEW FACT AFFECT THE SHARE PRICE?

This is perhaps the most difficult question facing company boards. The White Paper suggests, naively, that management should, in cases of doubt, seek advice on this question from a bank or other suitable adviser. The difficulty, however, surely is that in practice, as with insider facts, price-sensitivity will be judged retro-spectively. If management itself is uncertain whether a disclosure obligation has arisen the prudent course must be either to disclose or, if there are good reasons why that might be damaging to the company's interests, to seek exemption from the requirement. Advice from an expert that no announcement is required might, however, help to establish that the board did not act recklessly in choosing not to announce or when to announce.

The judgment as to whether any likely price movement is to be regarded as significant is also particularly difficult. The White Paper suggests that a movement of 5 per cent in the price of a share is to be regarded as normal by virtue of the internal rules of the stock exchanges (see 2.3.4 *above*). On the other hand the Guidance suggests that it is difficult to generalise. A price movement may be sig-nificant in relation to a share whose market price changes only very modestly whilst a change of similar percentage size might be insignificant in relation to a more volatile share. However, it seems doubtful whether volatility should have an impact on the issuer's duty to disclose since volatility expresses the sensitivity of a security to market factors outside the sphere of the issuer. In contrast, the WpHG provides that the price change must be due to the impact of the fact on the issuer's business.

Another problem arises when the issuer can predict that the market will react strongly but considers such reaction is not justified by the impact of the new fact on its situation, ie, the market is expected to 'overreact'. The wording of the WpHG suggests that the issuer must disclose the fact even if it has only an insignificant impact on the issuer's business since 'significance' is relevant only in relation to the size of the expected price change of the security. However, the legal literature argues that an expected overreaction of market participants has no influence in determining whether a duty to disclose arises (Schwark, §44a BörsG Rn 6). This is because the fact by itself, ie its impact on the business of the issuer, would not be calculated or likely to cause a significant price change. The significance of the price change would rather be due to an incorrect analy-sis by the market participants, ie a market-related fact rather than an issuer-related fact.

3.7 EXEMPTION FROM DISCLOSURE

Upon application the BAWe may exempt the issuer from its duty to disclose facts if it can show that disclosure would be likely to damage its legitimate interests. The issuer will not be in breach of its duty to disclose if application for exemption is filed without delay upon occurrence of the relevant fact—which otherwise would have triggered immediate disclosure—and the BAWe later refuses to grant an exemption.

The Guidance suggests that an exemption should be granted if the board of directors would have the right to refuse to supply the relevant information in a shareholders' meeting, as set out in Table (8).

TABLE (8)

The board of directors has a right to refuse to supply information to shareholders under art 131 of the Stock Corporation Act: • to the extent that, according to sound business judgement, provision of the information would be likely to cause material damage to the issuer or a connected company; • if the information refers to valuations made for tax purposes or to the amount of individual taxes; • if the information refers to the difference between the book value and the fair market value of assets, unless it is the shareholders' meeting that approves the annual financial statements; • if the information refers to the accounting and valuation methods, provided that the notes to the annual financial statements provide sufficient information as to these methods to show a clear view of the financial position of the issuer, unless it is the shareholders' meeting that approves the annual financial statements; • if supplying the information would constitute a criminal offence; • in so far as, if the issuer is a bank, certain information about accounting and valuation methods or settlements of accounts need not be provided in the annual financial statements.

It is not sufficient for a board of directors to seek to justify non-disclosure with the unspecific assertion that a competitor should not obtain the relevant information. Further, exemption will not be granted solely on the ground of the subjective business judgement of the board of directors, the reason must be based on facts that can be verified.

The WpHG is silent as to whether the interests of potential investors or the public interest should be considered by the BAWe in deciding whether to grant an exemption. One may conclude, therefore, that only the interests of the company itself or those of its existing shareholders are to be taken into account.

3.8 METHOD OF DISCLOSURE

Prior to public announcement of the new fact the company concerned must first disclose it to the BAWe and to the management authority of the stock exchange or exchanges on which the relevant securities are listed. Disclosure is required to the '*Deutsche Terminbörse*', the German Options and Futures Exchange, if a derivative that relates to a security of the issuer, is listed thereon. The purpose of this provision is to enable the authorities to consider whether to suspend dealings in the securities concerned. The Stock Exchange Guidance suggests, however, that suspension of dealings is to be regarded as a last resort and avoided if at all possible. Accordingly, it suggests that announcement to the public should be made outside of the normal trading hours of the stock exchanges (floor trading 10.30 to 13.30, IBIS 8.30 to 17.00, DTB various between 8.00 and 17.00). The Guidance suggests that the prior notice required by the authorities will in normal cases be between 20 and 30 minutes.

Once prior notice has been given the issuer must cause the new fact to be published either in a stock exchange-approved national newspaper or via an electronic information system widely used by market participants. Hence, a press release prior to publication in the approved manner will be an offence under the WpHG.

The Guidance points out that it suffices that the information is available to market participants. By contrast, the EC Directive requires publication to the public. It has been argued that the WpHG has not properly enacted the EC Directive (Assman, AG 1994, pp 237, 252).

Since the board of an exchange may only make use of a new fact pre-notified to it in order to determine whether trading should be suspended, the issuer must forward the relevant information separately to the electronic information system provider of the exchange if the issuer wants to disseminate the fact via such electronic system.

A notice must be published in the federal gazette ('*Bundesanzeiger*') as to where the publication was made or from whom the publication can be obtained. Finally, the publication must be forwarded to the BAWe and the board of the exchange.

The publication must be in the German language, the issuer must be the author of the publication and a reader must be able to identify the issuer as the author. The issuer must publish all relevant facts. However, the BAWe may exempt the issuer from this requirement in suitable cases to the extent that the issuer may be allowed to publish a summary of the facts, provided complete information is available at the paying agents of the issuer and notice to that effect is given.

The Guidance states that the issuer need not describe what effect the fact could have on its business but the reader must be able to perceive that the fact is likely to influence the price of the security.

The announcement must be made without delay, ie it may not be negligently or intentionally delayed. The issuer has time to examine carefully the effects of an event in order to determine whether there is a duty to disclose. On the other hand, since the likelihood of an effect on the price is a crucial element, examination time is limited.

3.9 CONSEQUENCES OF FAILURE TO ANNOUNCE

Article 15(6) provides that no action for compensation will lie against a company by reason of its failure to comply with the announcement obligations. However, compensation on other legal grounds is not to be affected.

There are, however, criminal sanctions. A failure to pre-notify the authorities gives rise to a fine of up to DM500,000 (approximately £224,000 STG) while a failure to comply with the obligation to announce to the public can result in a fine of up to DM3 million (approximately £1,342,000 STG). The prosecution would have to prove that the failure was, in either case, intentional or reckless. Directors of the issuer may be personally liable.

Because violation of the duty to disclose can be punished by fine but exact prediction of market reaction seems to be impossible, it has been argued that the disclosure requirement imposed by the WpHG violates the German Constitution which provides that a criminal statute must be clear enough for a person to be able to judge in advance whether or not his conduct will be subject to sanctions (Pellens/Fülbier, DB 1994, p 1381 (1385); Peltzer, ZIP 1994, p 746 (749); Kallmeyer, Gastkommentar, DB 17/1994, p 1).

3.10 PRACTICAL EXAMPLES OF FACTS REQUIRING DISCLOSURE

The Guidance makes it clear that it is not possible to devise a generally binding catalogue of facts requiring disclosure. However, it has suggested some examples, listed in Table (9), where management should consider whether in the given conditions such facts call for disclosure.

TABLE (9)

Examples of situation where disclosure is required:
(1) changes to assets, liabilities and financial situation
• sale of a key activity
• merger contracts
• acquisitions, disposals, changes of corporate status, demergers and other important structural changes
• entry into a control and/or profit transfer contract (eg a contract between parent and subsidiary whereby the subsidiary agrees to transfer its profits and losses to the parent)

- acquisition or disposal of significant shareholdings
- take-over offers and offers of compensation arising from entry into profit transfer contracts
- capital changes (including capitalisation of reserves)
- change in dividend rate
- imminent suspension of payments/insolvency
- reporting of losses pursuant to art 92 of the Stock Corporation Act
- significant extraordinary measures (eg following serious damage or discovery of criminal activities) or significant extraordinary profits

(2) changes in the general course of business:
- withdrawal from or adoption of new corporate activities
- entry into, change or termination of particularly important contractual relationships (including co-operation agreements)
- important discoveries, filing of important patents and the grant (whether as grantor or grantee) of important licences
- significant product liability or environmental liability developments
- litigation and cartel proceedings of a special significance
- changes in key personnel in the undertaking.

CASE STUDY

Sonnenbrand AG, a company listed on the official market of the Frankfurt Stock Exchange, manufactures sun protection lotion. Ulrich, a professional meteorologist discovered upon analysing the latest weather data that the summer season will start this year six weeks earlier than in previous years. Since Ulrich knows that the public is aware of the dangers of extensive sun exposure he instructs his bank to buy shares in Sonnenbrand. Meanwhile, Berthold, an analyst of shares, is told by Georg, a member of the supervisory board of Sonnenbrand, that the company will retain Dieter as Chairman of the Management Board. Dieter has a reputation in the sun lotion industry as being highly successful in generating extraordinary profits. Berthold cancels instructions which he had previously given to his bank to sell his Sonnenbrand shares. Berthold also tells his friend Eva that Sonnenbrand 'is a great buy'. Eva subsequently buys shares in the name of her mother from an old friend of hers off the exchange markets. Thomas, Georg's private chauffeur, listens in on a telephone conversation Georg had in the back seat of the car, where he discussed the latest profits with another board member, overhearing Georg saying 'if this becomes known, our share price will go through the roof'. Thomas immediately buys shares in Sonnenbrand.

Ulrich
The first issue is whether knowledge of the early summer constitutes an insider fact. The statute provides that the fact must relate to the security

or the issuer. It is the common view expressed by the government and the legal literature that the fact must only relate to the security or the issuer in a sense that the information is likely to cause a significant change in the market price of the security. Thus, even market data of a general nature could be sufficiently specific if that data, if made public, could cause a significant price change in the relevant securities. Therefore, since insider facts do not need to be particularly related to the issuer other than that the information must be price-sensitive the issue is whether the information on the early summer is publicly known. The White Paper argues that a fact is publicly known when an undetermined number of persons could have obtained knowledge of the fact. The Act makes clear that conclusions arrived at by making use of publicly-available facts are not insider facts. If the facts on which Ulrich's conclusion is based were publicly available his knowledge of the early summer does not constitute an insider fact so that Ulrich will not be held guilty of insider dealing.

However, it remains unclear how the situation would be treated by the courts where the underlying facts on which Ulrich's conclusion was based could only be obtained by making use of a database available only to subscribers or specialist knowledge. Provided that the courts conclude that market data which can only be obtained by a limited number of persons by means of specialist knowledge or a subscription database, the issue is whether Ulrich would be a primary insider. Ulrich has received his knowledge by reason of his profession. The knowledge must further be 'specifically related to' his profession. This term is one of the most unclear elements of the offence. The government is of the opinion that 'specifically related' only meant to exclude cases where a person learned of insider information in the course of his profession occasionally or by chance. Further, the EC Directive does not provide for the information to be acquired in such a manner. A court could thus interpret the offence in a manner consistent with EC law so that any insider information received in the course of a person's profession would make such person a primary insider. However, it has also been argued that a person must have a special relationship to the issuer to fall into this category of primary insiders. If the court would accept this argument Ulrich may only be considered a secondary insider, provided of course, that the information of the early beginning of the summer constitutes an insider fact.

Georg

Georg as a member of the supervisory board is a primary insider. As an insider, Georg must refrain from disclosing insider facts to third parties without being authorised to do so. Whether Georg has committed an offence will depend on whether the fact that the company will retain Dieter as Chairman of the managing board will significantly influence the price of the Sonnenbrand shares if this information becomes publicly known. This question is a matter of fact and will, in practice, be judged retrospectively once it is announced that Dieter is to become Chairman. If the share price moves by more than 5 per cent it is probable that this will be sufficient to constitute a 'significant influence' on the price of the shares. It is irrelevant whether Georg expected Berthold to trade on the information. Disclosure of inside information to analysts and journalists is generally not considered to be authorised.

Georg may also be guilty of unauthorised disclosure with regard to Thomas. The utterance of a mere opinion does not constitute an insider fact. However, if an opinion is based on, or goes hand in hand with, hard facts it may be treated as a fact. If a member of the managing board makes a statement that the share price of his company will rise if some undisclosed facts become publicly known, such an opinion clearly is an insider fact. Whether the disclosure was unauthorised, again is an unresolved issue. Arguably, Thomas' occupation is driving and his hearing insider facts is not necessary to perform his duties so that Georg must be careful in what he is saying in his presence. On the other hand, a court may hold that it lies within the typical scope of a chauffeur's profession to hear such insider facts so that Georg was authorised to utter in his presence inside information. On the assumption that Georg made the inside information available to Thomas without authorisation, it will depend on Georg's state of mind whether he committed an insider offence. He must have intended to commit the offence, negligence is not sufficient. The distinction between negligence and intention is difficult to make when a person did not act with the intent to bring about a specific consequence. A court would apply the test whether Georg (1) knew of the possibility and (2) accepted that Thomas could hear what he was saying. It will depend thus on the specific circumstances of the case whether Georg would be considered to be acting intentionally. In any event, it is not required that Georg was certain that Thomas could hear him. It suffices that he perceived that it was possible that Thomas was listening. Georg, therefore, could be guilty of unauthorised making available of insider facts.

Berthold

As regards the cancellation of his order Berthold did not commit an insider dealing offence since only the execution of a sales or purchase transaction is prohibited. Where a person refrains from acquiring or disposing of insider securities, a crucial element of the offence is lacking. Similarly, where Berthold placed an order to buy, then learns of an insider fact and refrains from cancelling his order, Berthold would not be guilty of insider dealing for lack of taking advantage of his inside knowledge.

Berthold may, however, be guilty of recommending to Eva the purchase of the Sonnenbrand shares. Recommendation is any unilateral declaration with the intent to influence another person that expresses the advice that a certain conduct would be to the addressee's benefit. It suffices that an insider makes the recommendation based on his inside knowledge and it is irrelevant whether Eva knew that the recommendation was based thereon. However, only primary insiders must refrain from recommending while secondary insiders are merely prohibited from buying and selling. Whether Berthold is a primary insider depends again on whether he obtained his knowledge as specifically related to his profession. First, it should be noted that the fact that Georg's disclosure was not authorised does not lead necessarily to the conclusion that Berthold obtained the information not specifically related to his profession. If the court follows the argument that this element only excludes information obtained by chance or occasionally, Berthold is likely to be considered a primary insider.

Eva

Eva would be guilty of insider trading if Berthold's tip was insider information. Again, an opinion is only considered an insider fact when it is based on, or goes hand in hand, with hard facts. Therefore, if Eva knew that Berthold's tip was based on hard insider information, Eva is guilty of insider trading since the insider rules also apply in off market transactions. The German legislation refrained from implementing any exemptions in off market transactions. It is further irrelevant that Eva did not acquire the shares in her own name rather than in her mother's name since insider trading includes any dealings in the name or on behalf of third parties. In practice, however, it will not be easy to prove that Eva knew that the information was an insider fact where the tip is of such a general nature.

Thomas

As a chauffeur, the listening in on telephone conversations is not specifically related to Thomas' profession so that it is unlikely that he will be considered to be a primary insider. A court may, however, hold that Thomas is a primary insider if the element 'specifically related to' will be interpreted restrictively to conformity with the EC Directive. In any event, Thomas is guilty of insider dealing because any person who has knowledge of inside information, even if obtained occasionally or by chance, must refrain from acquiring and disposing of insider securities. Had Thomas merely recommended the inside information to another person or had he disclosed his inside knowledge to a third person, Thomas would not have committed insider dealing if he was only considered a secondary insider. In this case, however, he may be guilty for solicitation or aiding and abetting.

France

Patricia Peterson, Linklaters & Paines, Paris

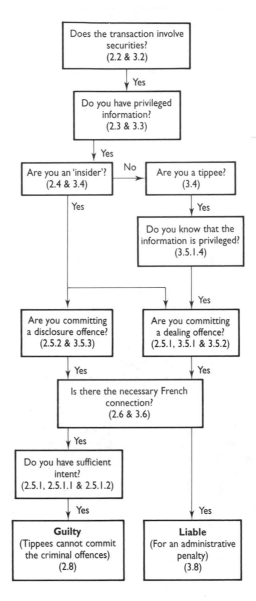

Note: Notwithstanding that there is no criminal offence to punish tippees who deal, there have been convictions of such tippees under the concept of *recel*, the equivalent of handling stolen property (2.1 & 2.5.3).

1 INTRODUCTION

Insider dealing has been a criminal offence in France since 1970. The original text of the criminal statute, art 10-1 of the *Ordonnance* of 28 September 1967 (the '*Ordonnance*'), was not dissimilar to the current provision. However, due to a fairly restrictive drafting style, the initial version of the insider dealing provision did not give rise to many convictions. As a consequence, the *Ordonnance* was amended in 1983, 1988 and 1989, each time with a view to extending its scope and to removing statutory language which presented obstacles for the prosecution in the context of enforcement proceedings before the French courts.

In the wake of certain well-publicised insider dealing scandals, such as the *Pechiney/Triangle* case, the French government decided in 1989 to endow the *Commission des Opérations de Bourse* ('COB') with the power to enforce its own regulations by means of a new system of administrative sanctions. Created in 1967 and modelled after the American Securities and Exchange Commission, the COB is the regulatory authority which is responsible for investor protection and law enforcement in France. Although, prior to 1989, the COB already possessed extensive investigatory powers, its enforcement powers in relation to insider dealing were limited to referring cases to the Public Prosecutor's Office, which took an independent view as to whether to commence proceedings under the *Ordonnance*. With the introduction of the COB's direct enforcement powers, a parallel insider dealing regime was put in place, over which the COB has complete control (subject to the possibility of an appeal to the *Cour d'Appel de Paris* ('Paris Court of Appeal')).

Shortly after the legislation providing for the COB's administrative sanctions was passed, the Minister of the Economy set up a commission, headed by Didier Pfeiffer, with a mandate of formulating principles of professional conduct in the financial services field which could serve as a basis for regulations to be enforced by the COB. In examining the issue of insider dealing, the Pfeiffer Commission took into consideration the requirements of the EC Insider Dealing Directive (Dir 89/592 [1989] OJ (334/30)) ('the Directive'). It formulated a series of five principles which have been faithfully incorporated in COB Regulation 90-08 on insider dealing (the 'Regulation'; see *Rapport au ministre d'Etat, ministre de l'économie, des finances et du budget de la Commission de déontologie boursière*, January 1990, the 'Pfeiffer Commission Report').

Now that there exist two insider dealing regimes in France, it is possible for parallel criminal and administrative proceedings to be commenced on the basis of the same set of facts. This was challenged before the *Conseil Constitutionnel* (the French tribunal that reviews constitutional law matters), which took the position that double prosecution in respect of insider dealing would not contravene any rule of French constitutional law, provided that the principle of proportionality was respected (decision no 89-260 DC of 28 July 1989, JO 1 August 1989,

p 9676). In this context, the *Conseil* considered that the application of the principle of proportionality would mean that the aggregate sanction imposed by the
COB and the criminal courts in a given case could not exceed the highest penalty
provided for in respect of either regime. At present the COB may impose fines
of precisely the same level as those which may be ordered by the criminal courts,
the only difference in the sanctions under the two regimes being that the COB
cannot impose a prison sentence. The two insider dealing regimes shall be considered separately below.

2 THE CRIMINAL STATUTE

2.1 INTRODUCTION

The *Ordonnance* creates two types of insider dealing offence: (i) dealing and (ii) disclosure of privileged information. As currently drafted, the *Ordonnance* dealing
offence is very broad indeed; on the face of the text, it is sufficient for one to be
an insider, in possession of privileged information, and to deal. Included in the
dealing offence is language which effectively creates a disclosure offence that
applies where an insider 'knowingly permits' a third party to deal before privileged
information becomes known to the public. A further disclosure offence, added in
1989, covers the communication of privileged information, acquired in a professional or work context, in a situation that falls outside that context. Not inappro-
priately, this disclosure offence is often referred to as the offence of *dîner en ville*.
The *Ordonnance* does not provide for sanctions in respect of trading carried out
by a secondary insider or 'tippee'; however, the French criminal concept of handling of stolen property (*recel*) has been used to punish secondary insider dealing.

Unlike the legislation in many other jurisdictions, there are no statutory
defences contained in the *Ordonnance*. As a consequence, defences are generally
constructed on the basis of a challenge to the adequacy of the evidence relating
to each element of the relevant offence.

2.2 TO WHICH INSTRUMENTS DOES THE *ORDONNANCE* APPLY?

The *Ordonnance* applies to transactions in quoted securities and negotiable futures
and option contracts (*contrats à terme négociables*). This would include all equity
and debt securities which are quoted on a French stock exchange. The
Ordonnance can also be applied to dealings in securities which are quoted on a
foreign regulated market (see 2.6 *below* regarding the territorial scope of the
Ordonnance). The reference to negotiable futures and options contracts was
added to the *Ordonnance* in 1988 following the creation of the French regulated
derivatives markets. This category would be limited to contracts traded on a regulated exchange such as MONEP (the traded options exchange) or MATIF (the
financial and commodity futures exchange).

The *Ordonnance* can be applied to negotiable rights which are linked to instruments that come within its scope. For example, in one case, proceedings were brought in respect of a sale of a shareholder's preferential subscription rights in the context of a rights issue (the accused was acquitted, but on other grounds; see the decision of the Paris Court of Appeal, 14 January 1992, *Gazette du Palais* ('Gaz Pal'), 28 May 1992, p 328, note Marchi). The *Ordonnance* will also be applied to transactions in the shares of an unquoted holding company where the objective is to carry out an indirect purchase or sale of shares in a quoted company (the shares of which are held by the holding company; see the decision of the Paris Court of Appeal, 15 March 1993, Dalloz ('D') 93, 611, note Ducouloux-Favard in a case referred to as *La Ruche Méridionale*; the two accused were acquitted on other grounds by the *Cour de Cassation, Ch Crim* in a decision of 26 June 1995, *Bulletin Joly Bourse et Produits Financiers* ('Bull Joly Bourse') July–August 1995, p 285, note Le Cannu).

2.3 WHAT IS PRIVILEGED INFORMATION?

2.3.1 Definitions

The *Ordonnance* provides that, to qualify as privileged information, the relevant information must relate to the prospects or financial situation of an issuer or to the prospects of future movement in the price of a security or negotiable futures or option contract. Apart from this requirement, there is no statutory definition.

Until very recently, the test applied with some consistency was one developed in the 1970s by the Paris Court of Appeal. This test required the information to be 'precise, specific and certain' (*précise, particulière et certaine*), in addition to being non-public (see *CA Paris*, 26 May 1977 and 30 March 1977, *Juris-classeur périodique (semaine juridique)* ('JCP') 78 II 18789, note Tunc). Although it was in some cases a factor considered indirectly, the Court of Appeal test did not place any emphasis upon the issue of price-sensitivity.

In a recent landmark decision relating to *La Ruche Méridionale*, the *Cour de Cassation* (the highest court in France) reversed a judgment of the Paris Court of Appeal, which had applied the old test, and reformulated the basic elements of the *Ordonnance* insider dealing offence (*Cass Crim*, 26 June 1995, *above*). According to the *Cour de Cassation*, to be privileged, information must be precise, confidential and of a nature that would influence the price of the relevant securities or instruments. This is essentially the definition of insider information that appears in the EC Directive which, as the *Cour de Cassation* noted, is not incompatible with the *Ordonnance*. Each element of the definition will be considered below.

2.3.1.1 Previous case law

To understand the significance of the decision of the *Cour de Cassation* in *La Ruche Méridionale*, it is helpful to examine briefly some of the earlier judgments of the lower courts.

As indicated, the case law in relation to insider dealing began to take shape with two 1977 decisions of the Paris Court of Appeal which defined privileged information as 'precise, specific and certain'. Athough neither judgment contained an analysis of the individual elements of this definition, it is clear that the Court of Appeal sought to distinguish privileged information from mere speculation or rumour.

The following are examples of information which has been held by the French courts to be privileged:

* a sudden revelation of significant and quantified losses to directors of a quoted company (CA Paris, 26 May 1977, JCP 78, II 18789, note Tunc);
* an announcement, at a board meeting of a quoted company, of profits which would result in an increase in dividends of 33 per cent over the previous year (Trib Corr Paris, 28 January 1985, D 85, 357, note Marchi);
* knowledge of negotiations concerning a take-over bid to be launched by a French company in respect of a company quoted in the United States (CA Paris, 6 July 1994, Les Petites Affiches ('Petites Affiches') No 137, 16 November 1994, p 17, note Ducouloux-Favard, referred to as the Pechiney case; Cass Crim, 26 October 1995);
* receipt by a stock broking firm of large purchase orders from various issuers in the context of the redemption of quoted bonds issued by them (Cass Crim, 18 February 1991, Revue de jurisprudence de droit des affaires ('RJDA') 5/91, No 412, p 360).

One element of the Court of Appeal definition of privileged information which has given rise to difficulties of interpretation has been the requirement of certainty. In some contexts, the certainty requirement has served to identify the commencement of the period during which an insider cannot trade, an issue which is particularly acute in the case of acquisitions or take-over bids. The dominant trend in the cases, to the extent that one could be extracted, was to consider that the test was met as long as there was a take-over proposal with a reasonable chance of success. This approach led to the conviction of a financial analyst with respect to a purchase of shares in a company about which he had prepared various studies and that he knew was the subject of take-over negotiations; the conviction was based upon a finding that the negotiations were sufficiently advanced so as to have a reasonable chance of succeeding (Trib Corr Paris, 18 April 1979, JCP 80, II 19306, note Tunc). A similar analysis was applied in respect of the negotiation of an exchange offer involving two quoted companies where an agreement in principle had been reached, but the exchange ratio had not been agreed. The court concluded that 'the proposal had such chances of succeeding, that the negotiations possessed the element of certainty required by the case law' (Trib Corr Paris, 3 December 1993, Gaz Pal 1994, 1, 28, referred to as the Delalande/Synthélabo case).

Nevertheless, the approach to this issue has not always been consistent. This is illustrated by a much criticised judgment of the Paris Court of Appeal in the

Thomson case. The accused, a high level civil servant, had been following negotiations between the French and Saudi Arabian governments concerning a contract which was to benefit the French company Thomson. Immediately after attending a meeting at which the matter was discussed, he purchased shares in Thomson. The meeting had taken place a few days after the relevant contract had been signed; however, the available evidence did not establish that the signature of the contract had been mentioned, nor that the accused knew that it had been signed. The court held that only knowledge of the actual signature of the contract would have been certain enough to have constituted privileged information. The accused's knowledge of the ongoing negotiations was therefore insufficient to support a conviction. The court disposed of the case by referring to the transactions as a 'troubling coincidence' (*CA Paris*, 11 February 1987; see also *Trib Corr Paris*, 13 May 1986, Gaz Pal 1986, 459, note Marchi).

A tendency to take a more relaxed view of the certainty issue has, however, been evident in certain recent decisions of the Paris Court of Appeal. In these cases, knowledge on the part of the accused that there might be a future demand for the relevant securities, with a corresponding movement in price, has sufficed in the absence of a specific transaction with reasonable chances of success.

Problem Area 1

> A bank ('BMI') had a mandate to advise a client who wished to take control of a company that had banking interests. Authorisation for the transaction was required from the French banking authorities. Following a refusal of the authorities to permit BMI's client to acquire more than 20 per cent of the capital of the target company, the Chairman of BMI purchased shares in that company on behalf of the bank. At trial it was argued that the accused's knowledge of the take-over project ceased to be privileged information once the authorities objected to the plan, at which point the Chairman considered the bank's mandate to have lapsed. The court rejected this argument, characterising as privileged information the knowledge on the part of the accused that his client was still interested in the project and that, in the coming months, there could be a significant number of shares acquired directly or indirectly on behalf of his client in a *ramassage* exercise (a gradual acquisition of shares). (See *CA Paris*, 14 January 1993, Gaz Pal 1993, 1, 14 note Marchi; *Cass Crim*, 14 June 1993, unreported; application dismissed as presenting no grounds for challenging the decision).

The decision of the Court of Appeal in the *La Ruche Méridionale* case was not dissimilar to the BMI case in its treatment of the element of certainty. In addition, however, it addressed the rather difficult issue as to whether the test for identifying privileged information was an objective or a subjective test. The facts of this case also merit review.

2.3.1.2 The La Ruche Méridionale case

The Paris Court of Appeal, in a controversial decision, dismissed an appeal from a judgment of a trial court convicting the Chairman and a senior manager of Banque de l'Union Européenne ('BUE') in connection with an acquisition of a block of shares (on behalf of BUE) in La Ruche Méridionale ('LRM'). Some shares were purchased on the stock exchange, but the majority were acquired from a client of BUE which had given it a mandate to find a purchaser for the holding (of approximately 10 per cent of LRM's capital, held through a holding company). At the time of these acquisitions, the two accused knew that two other companies, R and C, were interested in a shareholding in LRM and that at least one of them was in negotiations with LRM's management. In fulfilling BUE's mandate to find a purchaser for the block of LRM shares, the accused did not offer them to either R or C. Approximately six weeks later, R (advised by BUE) launched a take-over bid on LRM which was the subject of a competing bid by C. The latter eventually won the battle and purchased BUE's stake in this context, resulting in a very substantial profit for BUE.

The decision of the Court of Appeal in the LRM case was founded upon the proposition that, in determining whether or not information is sufficiently precise to be privileged, a court is entitled to take into consideration the particular knowledge and experience of the accused. The court did not find that the two accused knew anything about the future take-over bid at the time of the acquisition of LRM shares on behalf of BUE; however, it considered that, since they had expert knowledge of the relevant business sector, the two accused knew that there would be future transactions in LRM shares and a profit to be made in connection with a disposal of a strategic stake in the company. The Court of Appeal concluded that, in the minds of the two bankers, this information, which did not even reveal the nature of potential future transactions, was sufficiently precise to be privileged even if it would not have been for the average investor.

This subjective approach to determining whether information is privileged was rejected by the Cour de Cassation. The court specified that the privileged nature of a given piece of information could not result from an analysis of it carried out by a person receiving or using the information; the question as to whether information was privileged had to be examined in an objective manner, solely on the basis of the content of the information, and excluding any element of arbitrary judgement. In the circumstances of the LRM case, the Cour de Cassation found that the acquisition of shares by BUE prior to the announcement of the take-over bid on LRM had been based upon a long-standing financial analysis, arrived at from facts and circumstances that were known within the professional milieu. Critical to this decision were the findings of the lower courts that the two accused were not aware of a take-over bid proposal at the time of the acquisition of LRM shares. Evidence that the acquisition formed part of an investment strategy pre-dating the acquisition by at least six months was also of assistance to the defence.

A few brief observations should be made in relation to the decision of the *Cour de Cassation* in the *LRM* case. First, the decision establishes quite clearly that financial analysis cannot be the basis of an insider dealing conviction under the *Ordonnance*, at least in a situation where the accused is not in possession of confidential, price-sensitive information which the average person would be able to interpret as such. The adoption of an objective approach to the determination of whether or not information is privileged is consistent with the fundamental principle that criminal statutes are to be interpreted strictly.

Second, the definition of privileged information provided by the court ('precise, confidential and of a nature that would influence the price of a security') does not refer to a certainty requirement. This element of the definition of the Court of Appeal does not figure in the EC Directive definition of privileged information. Its apparent replacement with the more appropriate criterion of price sensitivity is to be welcomed and it is hoped that the certainty requirement, particularly as it was applied in the *Thomson* case, will not reappear in later decisions. Nevertheless, it must be recognised that, in some contexts, such as takeover bids, the concept of certainty could be enveloped in the precision criterion. One may continue, therefore, to see references to transactions having sufficient chances of succeeding as a measure of whether knowledge of the related negotiations constitutes information which is sufficiently precise to be privileged.

Finally, the exact meaning of each of the elements of the definition of privileged information adopted by the *Cour de Cassation* remains to be seen, since the facts of the *LRM* case are not of great assistance in understanding when information will be considered to be confidential or price sensitive. Even with respect to the meaning of 'precise', the judgment only sheds light on the situation where a longstanding strategy has been developed by a professional on the basis of facts known in professional circles (with some coverage in the press). One can probably only extract from this, that knowledge that a company is a potential target for a takeover and that certain companies have an interest in it is not sufficiently precise to be considered privileged information. This can be contrasted to inside knowledge of a proposed bid, which would probably suffice for a conviction.

2.3.2 Non-public

The *Ordonnance* does not provide any guidance on the issue of when information will be considered to be in the public domain. The text merely states that insiders must not deal whilst in possession of privileged information before the public has knowledge of the relevant information. As stated above, the decision of the *Cour de Cassation* in *La Ruche Méridionale* identified confidentiality as one of the elements of the definition of privileged information without giving any indication as to its meaning. Indeed, one might raise the question as to whether there is any significance in the *Cour de Cassation's* choice of the word 'confidential' rather than 'non-public', the terminology employed in the EC Directive. Although it could be argued that information can be non-confidential without being in the public domain, it is submitted that the focus should be on the concept of when information becomes known to the public, the language which appears in the *Ordonnance* itself.

Earlier decisions of the lower courts have never really attempted to provide a comprehensive definition of the word 'public' in this context. The matter has always been dealt with on a case-by-case basis. The following anouncements have failed, in the judgment of the French courts, to have rendered information public:

- an announcement of heavy losses made by the issuer (under 'embargo') at a meeting of approximately 100 journalists and financial analysts (*CA Paris*, 8 November 1993, Gaz Pal, 1–3 May 1994, 29);
- an announcement of an indemnity proposal given to shareholders at a general meeting, which the court described as a limited number of persons in comparison with all stock exchange 'partners' (*l'ensemble des partenaires du marché boursier*) (*Trib Corr Paris*, 30 March 1979, JCP 80, II 19306, note Tunc);
- the publication of an article, in a specialised periodical of limited circulation, referring to expected losses of a quoted company when the general and financial press in France carried more optimistic analyses regarding the company (*CA Paris*, 26 May 1977, D 78, 379, note Cosson).

One sees quite frequently in the cases defences advanced on the basis of press articles containing analyses which are compatible with the accused's decision to trade in the shares of the relevant company. Such a defence will not succeed unless the press articles contain the same specific information as that which is held to be privileged; the information must not be 'fragmentary' or 'incomplete' (see *CA Paris*, 26 May 1977, *above*). For example, in the case of an announcement to a company board of directors of an increase in dividends of 33 per cent, a publication which carried the prediction of a financial analyst of an increase in dividends of 10 to 15 per cent, together with a 'hold' recommendation, was not sufficient to place the specific information received by the directors in the public domain (see *Trib Corr Paris*, 28 January 1985, D 85, 357, note Marchi).

In contrast to the legislation in force in some jurisdictions, there is no exemption in France for information which is widely known to professional investors or 'market rumours'. The concern of French regulators and courts has traditionally been to ensure that small investors are put on an equal footing with professionals in terms of the information available to them to make their investment decisions. As a consequence, the court decisions on insider dealing often refer to the principle of equality among investors.

At present, the only situation in which one can be certain that information has reached the public domain, is where a communiqué has been published which provides complete information to the markets. In France, issuers of quoted securities have an obligation to advise the markets as soon as possible of any information which, if rendered public, could have a significant effect on the price of their securities or any linked products such as quoted derivatives (see COB Regulation No 90-02). The COB has observed that publication of a communiqué in the written press is not mandatory, but this is the method most frequently used (COB's *Vade-Mecum* in *Bulletin de la Commission des opérations de bourse* ('Bull COB'), September 1993). Any publication of an announcement of price-sensitive information should appear in newspapers with wide circulation. In the opinion of at least one author, publication of a communiqué by the issuer in the *Bulletin des Annonces Légales Obligatoires* ('BALO'—the official gazette in France) is necessary to render information public (see C Ducouloux-Favard, *JCL Banque et Crédit, fasc* 1040, para 44). Although publication of a notice in the BALO might be sufficient to render information public, more compelling arguments suggest that this should not be a necessary step if the information is available in newspapers of wide circulation, as these are more likely to reach the investing public. Information would probably not be considered to be in the public domain until the relevant publications are in circulation, since the COB has stated on several occasions that the communication of the information must be 'effective'. In this vein, the COB has indicated that the mere dispatch of a communiqué to press agencies will not be sufficient (COB's *Vade-Mecum*).

The question as to whether information is in the public domain arises frequently in the context of meetings between financial analysts and issuers. With the COB's approval, certain professional organisations, such as the *Société Française des Analystes Financiers* (the professional association of financial analysts—'SFAF') and the *Cercle de Liaison des Informateurs Financiers en France* (the equivalent organisation for issuers—'CLIFF'), have recently focused their attention upon the issue of contacts between analysts and issuers, the handling of privileged information and the manner in which analysts' research reports should be released to the public (see the joint recommendations of SFAF and CLIFF in Bull COB, February 1995).

Problem Area 2

A bank analyst specialising in the retail sector attended a private meeting with the finance director of a quoted company which ran a number of department stores. Two weeks prior to the meeting the company had announced in the French financial press that it was forecasting a substantial annual profit for that year (rounded figures were given). The analyst's research suggested that these figures were unrealistic, particularly in view of an economic recession which was depressing retail sales. With skilful questioning, the analyst managed to extract from the finance director that a large exceptional item, the expected proceeds from the sale of one of the company's subsidiaries, was included in the forecast. Two months previously an article had been published in the French financial press stating that the company intended to sell the subsidiary in question. However, the time-frame for the disposal had not been announced, nor the fact that a purchaser had been found.

Following the meeting, the analyst met with a colleague who was responsible for proprietary trading on behalf of the bank. He told his colleague about the meeting with the finance director. The analyst stated that, as a result of the exceptional item contained in the profit forecast, he intended to change his recommendation concerning the company from hold to sell, since the real profits arising from the company's operations would be quite unimpressive. That afternoon, the analyst's colleague sold, out of the bank's portfolio, a substantial number of shares in the company. At the same time, the analyst produced a report with a revised recommendation, which he distributed within the bank and subsequently sent out to his 'best clients' mid-afternoon the following day.

The information acquired by the analyst from the finance director was probably privileged information because the investing public had not been provided with a break-down of the profit forecast, nor the fact that the disposal of the subsidiary would actually be carried out before the end of the financial year. Prosecutions for disclosure of privileged information could be commenced in respect of the finance director and the analyst (see 2.5.2). A dealing offence would also have been committed by the proprietary trader, for which officers and/or managers responsible for supervising the trader could be pursued (see 2.5.1.4) in relation to trading carried out on behalf of a company).

As for the handling of the information itself, the company has failed to provide the market with complete information in breach of COB Regulation No 90-02 which defines an issuer's obligation to keep the public informed of matters which could affect its share price (this in itself could be the subject of administrative sanctions). The analyst has also failed to respect several of the SFAF/CLIFF guidelines which provide, notably, that research reports are to be distributed to clients in an equitable manner (at the same time and to all clients coming within a particular category) and in-house recipients should not receive them in advance of clients. Reports should also be distributed outside stock exchange trading hours and a copy should be addressed to the issuer. Although there are no direct sanctions for a breach of these rules, they have been endorsed by the COB as the recommended practice. A failure to respect them might lead to enforcement proceedings under art 6 of the COB insider dealing Regulation, where the practice contributes to the circulation or use of privileged information (see 3.5.4.2).

2.3.3 Price-sensitive

The third branch of the definition of privileged information was described by the *Cour de Cassation* in the *La Ruche Méridionale* case in the following terms: the information must be of a nature that would influence the price of the relevant security. The EC Directive was specifically cited by the court in its judgment as one of the sources of law that it had considered. The court also observed that the EC definition of privileged information was not incompatible with the text of the *Ordonnance*, which did not define these words. On the issue of price sensitivity, the EC Directive refers to information 'which, if it were made public, would be likely to have a significant effect on the price of . . . the securities in question'. The inclusion of the word 'significant' in that definition is of importance; without it, it can be argued that most events or information *could* have an effect on the quoted price of a security. As will be seen below, the definition of privileged information contained in the COB insider dealing Regulation has excluded the requirement that the relevant information have a 'significant' effect on the price of a given security. It is hoped that the French courts will follow more closely the European definition when interpreting the *Ordonnance*. In the absence of any further cases applying the new definition of privileged information, it is too early to predict how the matter will be resolved.

2.4 WHO IS AN INSIDER?

The *Ordonnance* creates two types of insider:

(1) persons who are considered to be insiders by statute as a result of their relationship to an issuer ('statutory insiders'); and
(2) persons who acquire privileged information in the exercise of their profession or in the performance of their duties. For ease of reference, these two categories of insider shall be referred to collectively as 'primary insiders'.

The first category consists of persons referred to in art 162-1 of the French Companies Law (Law No 66-537 of 24 July 1966). The list includes the chairman, directors (including the permanent representatives of any companies appointed as directors), general directors (*directeurs généraux*) and members of the *directoire* or *conseil de surveillance* in the case of companies which are organised with such bodies. It also extends to any minors of such persons and to their spouses, provided that they are not legally separated (*séparation de corps*). Persons coming within this category will automatically be deemed insiders and must take particular care not to deal in the shares of the issuer when in possession of privileged information. The tendency in the cases is to subject them to a fairly strict disclose or abstain principle (see 2.5.1.1 *below*).

The second category of primary insider, persons who acquire privileged information in a professional or work context, has been interpreted broadly. Perhaps the most famous illustration of this is provided by the *Carrefour* case (*Trib Corr Paris*, 15 October 1976, D 78, 381, note Guyenot).

Problem Area 3

Three persons were prosecuted for insider dealing, including an architect who had been hired in respect of a construction project by Carrefour (a company which ran a chain of supermarkets). From the vantage point of the waiting room of the Chairman of Carrefour, the architect had seen the latter emerge from his office with the Chairman of another company called Allobroge. He apparently linked this with a press article that he had read which indicated that Allobroge would benefit from the construction of a certain shopping centre. The following day the architect began purchasing a significant number of shares in Allobroge, which was quoted on the Paris Stock Exchange. It was subsequently announced that Carrefour and Allobroge would run a supermarket together and this caused the share price to increase. A finding that the architect's decision to deal in Allobroge shares had not been founded solely upon the article that he had read led to a conviction for insider dealing. The court held that the architect's conclusion that the two companies were about to enter into a joint venture had been inspired by his viewing of the two chairmen together and it therefore constituted privileged information. The judgment stressed that privileged information could be acquired in the context of a fortuitous event or as a result of a confidence; proceedings under the *Ordonnance* could be justified as long as the information was acquired in a professional or work context.

Of particular interest is the court's finding that the architect possessed privileged information at the time of dealing, even though he did not have knowledge of the nature of transaction being negotiated and the dealings were inspired by his analysis of a fact that may have had little significance for persons less familiar with the relevant business sector. In this sense, the judgment is reminiscent of the Court of Appeal decision in respect of *La Ruche Meridionnale*; however, unlike the defendants in the latter case, the architect in the *Carrefour* situation did receive a kind of 'tip', when he saw the two chairmen together, which gave him an advantage over other investors.

Other examples of this second category of primary insider have included the following:

- a financial journalist who acquired privileged information whilst interviewing officers of a quoted company (*Trib Corr Paris*, 12 May 1976, JCP 76, II 18496, note Tunc);
- a liquidator of a company who was given information regarding an indemnity scheme for shareholders of a related company (*Trib Corr Paris*, 30 March 1979, JCP 80, II 19306, note Tunc);
- a high level civil servant aware of take-over negotiations being discussed at the Ministry of the Economy (*CA Paris*, 6 July 1994, Petites Affiches, No

137, 16 November 1994, p 17, note Ducouloux-Favard; *Cass Crim* 26 October 1995—*Pechiney* case);

- an actuary and financial analyst aware of take-over negotiations involving a client (*Trib Corr Paris*, 18 April 1979, JCP 80, II 19306, note Tunc); and
- a pharmacist, head of the pharmaceutical division of a company, who became aware of a merger agreement involving the company that he worked for (*CA Paris*, 20 February 1984, unreported).

One of the most notable omissions from the *Ordonnance* is the fact that it does not cover secondary insiders, often referred to as 'tippees' . . . (persons who are not statutory insiders to whom privileged information is disclosed outside a work context). It is surprising, particularly in view of the requirements of the EC Directive, that the *Ordonnance* was not amended to cover secondary insiders during the last round of amendments in 1989 when the new disclosure offence was added. Although, in the past, secondary insiders were not pursued in the criminal courts, a successful attempt was made recently in the *Pechiney* case on the basis of the concept of *recel* (the rough equivalent of handling stolen goods—see 2.5.3).

One further category of insider not covered by the *Ordonnance* is persons who acquire privileged information by virtue of a shareholding in the relevant issuer. This too is included in the EC Directive, but has not been the subject of any amendments to the French criminal text (nor is it covered by the COB Regulation).

2.5 WHAT ARE THE OFFENCES?

2.5.1 Dealing

To be convicted of the dealing offence under the *Ordonnance* a person must be:

- an 'insider';
- in possession of 'privileged information';
- carry out, or knowingly permit to be carried out, either directly or through the interposition of a third party, one or more transactions on the market before the information is known to the public.

On the face of the text, the insider dealing provision is extremely broad and could, theoretically, catch anyone who is an insider and who trades whilst in possession of privileged information.

As in other jurisdictions, French criminal law requires proof of both the criminal act (*l'élément matériel*) and the will or intent to commit the relevant crime (*l'élément moral*; see art 121-3 of the New Criminal Code–*Nouveau Code Pénal*). As a general rule, the burden of proof lies with the Public Prosecutor who must convince the court that all elements of the offence are present in the evidence, thereby meeting a test of profound conviction (*intime conviction*) that the crime has been committed (see art 427 of the Criminal Procedure Code—*Code de Procédure Pénale*). One of the difficulties with insider dealing cases is that the only evidence available is usually circumstantial (eg the accused attended a meeting at which a price-sensitive matter was discussed and within a short period of time thereafter carried out trades in the relevant securities). In most cases it would be extremely difficult for the prosecution to provide hard evidence that the accused intended to take advantage of any privileged information in his or her possession. It is for this reason that the *Ordonnance* was amended in 1983 and again in 1988 so as to assist judges in drawing inferences from events and the positioning of persons in relation to them. The result is that there are various presumptions that operate in insider dealing cases under the *Ordonnance* and these presumptions effectively reverse the burden of proof in relation to certain issues.

2.5.1.1 The presumption of knowledge on the part of statutory insiders

Although there is no real basis for it in the text of the *Ordonnance*, the prevailing view among commentators is that there is a presumption of knowledge of privileged information on the part of statutory insiders (see E Gaillard, 'Le droit français des délits d'inités', JCP 1991, éd G, I, 3516; C Ducouloux-Favard, *JCL Banque et Crédit*, fasc 1640, para 32). This presumption is generally considered to be a companion to the principle that statutory insiders are subject to a strict duty to abstain from dealing during the 'suspect period' prior to disclosure of the relevant privileged information.

The presumption relating to statutory insiders is merely a presumption of knowledge and not a presumption of guilt. It basically permits the prosecution to suggest that, in view of the accused's position, he or she must have been aware of the privileged information. A review of the cases suggests, however, that evidence will still be adduced to demonstrate that the accused attended meetings or had other contacts where he or she would have become aware of the relevant privileged information.

This of course raises the question as to whether the presumption of knowledge on the part of statutory insiders is rebuttable. The better view, which is supported by several academics and by the Pfeiffer Commission Report, is that the presumption of knowledge can be rebutted by evidence that the accused officer or manager did not have actual knowledge of the relevant privileged information (see Gaillard, *above*, and Ducouloux-Favard *above*). Since the presumption would apply to directors of a company, who are often not truly involved in its management, this interpretation would prevent the unduly harsh result of persons coming within this category being convicted of insider dealing where they have disposed of or purchased shares in the relevant company without any actual knowledge of privileged information. This argument becomes even more compelling when one considers the fact that, along with persons holding strategic positions within the company such as the chairman and general directors, the category of statutory insider extends to cover the children of such persons who are minors and their wives (unless there has been a legal separation).

The decision of the *Cour de Cassation* in the *La Ruche Méridionale* case also lends support to the argument that the presumption of knowledge on the part of statutory insiders is rebuttable. The court stated that the offence was committed where the relevant privileged information constituted the motivating factor or determining reason (*déterminante*) in respect of the dealings giving rise to the proceedings. This statement suggests that there must be actual knowledge of the privileged information. It follows from this that the presumption of knowledge must be rebuttable.

The presumption of knowledge of privileged information on the part of statutory insiders is not considered to apply to persons who acquire privileged information through the exercise of their profession or the performance of their duties.

2.5.1.2 The élément moral

Once it has been established in a given case that the accused was an insider and in possession of privileged information, the current text of the *Ordonnance* appears to create a presumption that the accused based his or her decision to trade on that information. This presumption analysis arises out of amendments made to the *Ordonnance* in 1988. To understand the importance of these amendments it is helpful to review briefly the drafting history of this section of the insider dealing provision.

The original 1970 text provided that, to result in a conviction, the accused insider had to have traded whilst 'taking advantage of' (*en exploitant*) the relevant privileged information. This element of the offence raised evidentiary problems for the prosecution because it gave rise to arguments that a specific intent to commit the offence had to be proved. The *Ordonnance* was therefore amended in 1983 and these words were replaced with a requirement that the accused have traded 'on the basis of the said information' (*sur le fondement desdites informations*). Largely in response to the *Thomson* case (see 2.3.1.1), this language was deleted in 1988 in order to facilitate convictions on the basis of circumstantial evidence. As a result of the 1988 amendment, it is no longer necessary for the prosecution to prove the existence of a link between the privileged information and the trading.

The parliamentary studies and debates (*travaux préparatoires*) suggest that the 1988 revision of the text was intended to create, in respect of persons in possession of privileged information, a type of 'obligation to abstain' from dealing in the relevant securities (see *Assemblée Nationale* No 1073 *Rapport de M P Auberger* at p 109). This statement, of course, leads one to question whether the 1988 amendment effectively created a 'strict liability' offence, whereby it is sufficient for the prosecution to prove only that the accused was in possession of privileged information and traded (the nearest French equivalent to a strict liability offence being *infractions non intentionnelles*, which are only excusable in a case of *force majeure*). The analysis most consistent with the interpretation of other elements of the *Ordonnance*, would be that the removal of the necessity of proving a link between the trading and the privileged information in a given case creates a presumption that the relevant trades were carried out on the basis of the privileged information. Like the presumption of knowledge on the part of statutory insiders, this would effectively reverse the burden of proof (see 2.7 in relation to defences).

Although the decision of the *Cour de Cassation* in the *La Ruche Méridionale* case does not address the issue of the presumption of a link between the relevant trading and privileged information, it does confirm with reasonable clarity that there remains an element of intent to the insider dealing offence. In defining the main elements of the offence, the *Cour de Cassation* stated that the privileged information in a given case must be the motivating factor or determining reason behind the transactions carried out (*déterminantes des opérations réalisées*). Where the presumption operates, this would leave open the opportunity for the defence to demonstrate that the transactions in question were not motivated by the privileged information concerned.

It can be observed that the inclusion of such a condition in the *Ordonnance* insider dealing offence is quite in line with the text of the EC Directive, which requires member states to prohibit the taking advantage of insider information. The French text of the Directive uses the verb '*exploiter*', which was the terminology employed in the original 1970 text of the *Ordonnance*. Since the French Legislature removed this word from the *Ordonnance* in 1983, it was probably not open to the *Cour de Cassation* to effectively re-insert it. Instead the court chose the word '*déterminante*', which may be designed to achieve the same result.

Unfortunately the decision of the *Cour de Cassation* does not give any indication as to the precise meaning of this new condition. The choice of the word '*déterminante*' is more reminiscent of terminology and concepts found in French contract law than it is of principles of French criminal law. The classic use of this terminology in contract law is to refer to the determining reason for entering into a contract (*la cause impulsive et déterminante*). The term '*déterminante*' is employed in this context to mean that, in the absence of a particular reason or motive, the party in question would not have entered into the contract. Transposed to the insider dealing context, this would mean that, without the relevant privileged information, the accused would not have dealt. If this test were adopted in the application of the *Ordonnance*, difficulties could arise where the accused trades for a number of different reasons, one of which is related to privileged information. In such a case, there probably should be a conviction if all other elements of the offence are established; any other interpretation might be inconsistent with the EC Directive and, indeed, the principle expressed in the 1988 *travaux préparatoires* that insiders under the *Ordonnance* have a duty to abstain from trading until the relevant privileged information becomes public.

2.5.1.3 The élément matériel

Three points should be noted in relation to the act or élément matériel of the insider dealing offence. First, it is not necessary for the accused to have dealt in order for there to be a conviction. The offence is also committed where trading is carried out through the interposition of a third party (eg a company controlled by the accused) or where the accused has 'knowingly permitted a third party to trade' (which also covers a disclosure of privileged information to third parties— see 2.5.2).

Second, although still the subject of debate, the dealing offence will probably be committed where the relevant trades are carried out off the stock exchange. Prior to 1988, the Ordonnance insider dealing text referred to the carrying out of transactions on the stock market (sur le marché boursier). One of the amendments made to the Ordonnance in 1988 was the deletion of the word 'boursier' (a reference to the stock market) and the addition of quoted futures and options contracts to the list of instruments covered. There is some argument as to whether this deletion was only effected in connection with the extension of the insider dealing provision to cover derivative products, or whether it was intended to enlarge the scope of the provision to cover off-exchange transactions. It is submitted that, given the decision of the Cour de Cassation in the Pechiney case (discussed in 2.6), where the Ordonnance insider dealing offence was applied to transactions carried out on a foreign over-the-counter market (NASDAQ), the amended text should be considered to extend to off-exchange transactions. The objective behind the insider dealing provision which is most frequently identified by the courts is the promotion of equality amongst investors; investors are no less prejudiced by off-exchange trading in quoted instruments than they are by trading on an exchange. Furthermore, it would be all too easy to flout the Ordonnance if its application could be avoided by carrying out trades off-exchange.

Third, it is also unnecessary for the prosecution to prove that the suspect transactions resulted in a profit. The issue as to whether the accused realised a profit from the relevant transactions is only taken into consideration in determining the amount of any fine imposed (see 2.8).

2.5.1.4 Dealing on behalf of a company

In March 1994, the concept of direct liability of companies was introduced into French criminal law in the context of a general reform of the Criminal Code (Code Pénal). However, this liability only arises in respect of specific criminal offences and only where it has been expressly provided for. At present, the concept of criminal liability of companies has not been extended to apply to the Ordonnance insider dealing offence. Nevertheless, dealing on behalf of a company may result in the personal liability of its legal and de facto managers.

The *Ordonnance* states that, where transactions which breach the insider dealing provision are carried out by an entity with legal personality, its *de facto* and *de jure* managers will be criminally liable for the offences committed (see art 10-1, para 3). This provision was considered by the *Cour de Cassation* recently, which held that it created a presumption of involvement in, or responsibility for, the relevant transactions on the part of the officers or the *de facto* managers of the company (see the decision of the *Cour de Cassation* in a case referred to as *Société Générale de Fonderie* ('SGF'), 15 March 1993, D 93, 610, note Ducouloux-Favard). This presumption effectively reverses the burden of proof, requiring the officers and managers concerned to prove the contrary.

Problem Area 4

SGF, a French quoted company which had been in financial difficulty for some time, was the subject of certain misleading press communiqués suggesting that its situation was improving. This information inspired an increase in the price of SGF shares. Subsequently, however, very substantial losses for the financial year in progress were announced, causing the share price to fall by 40 per cent.

Prior to the announcement of the losses, OPFIP, a major corporate shareholder of SGF, disposed of a significant portion of its shareholding in the company. The disposal had been carried out progressively while the share price was at its highest level and at a time when certain of OPFIP's representatives were aware of SGF's real financial situation. At trial it was found that the decision to dispose of the shares was taken by the Deputy General Director of OPFIP ('C') and carried out by his assistant ('R'), a director of SGF who, together with C was responsible for monitoring the company's loans (SGF's principal banking institution was a company related to OPFIP).

The liability of C and R was easily justified in this case since they were directly involved in the disposal of SGF shares. However, the Public Prosecutor also sought to have the Chairman of OPFIP ('M') held liable under the *Ordonnance*. At the trial level, all three were convicted. The Paris Court of Appeal upheld the convictions against C and R but acquitted M on the basis that no precise facts had been proven which implied that he had been involved in the SGF disposal. The court's reasoning was that a manager or officer of a company could not be held liable under the *Ordonnance* unless evidence of all elements of the offence, including the *élément moral*, had been proven with respect to the relevant officer or manager. It was this aspect of the decision that was reversed by the *Cour de Cassation* so as to impose a presumption of liability on the part of the Chairman.

In the context of a re-trial before the Orléans Court of Appeal, M argued, in an effort to rebut the presumption of liability established by the

Cour de Cassation, that he should be exonerated because he had delegated his powers in respect of the SGF matter to C. The court held that the evidence did not establish either a written or verbal delegation of powers by M to C in respect of the SGF matter. This finding was based upon evidence that M had been copied in on memoranda reporting the SGF trades and an admission in a deposition given by M that he had been 'associated' with the decision. The court observed that, had M delegated his powers to C, the latter would have taken the disposal decision entirely alone.

The judgments in the *SGF* case do leave open the possibility of a defence based upon a delegation of powers. However, the Orléans Court decision suggests that evidence of a complete delegation of powers in respect of the specific subject matter to which the insider dealings are linked would be necessary to rebut the presumption. This would probably require an absence of reporting lines to the accused. Proof of a lack of knowledge of the transactions would clearly not be sufficient in respect of a person with responsibility, either on a factual level or as a matter of company law, for the subject matter concerned. (See *Trib Corr Paris*, 20 December 1990; Gaz Pal 4–6 August 1991, p 6, note J-P M; *CA Paris*, 15 January 1992, Gaz Pal 23 April 1992, p 293, note J-P M; *Cass Crim*, 15 March 1993, *above*; *CA Orléans*, 20 June 1994, D 95, 811 note Ducouloux-Favard).

Arguments for a defence based upon a delegation of powers can be found in a series of decisions in analogous cases, rendered by the *Cour de Cassation* shortly before the judgment in the *SGF* case, involving prosecutions of company officers for economic offences other than insider dealing. In one judgment, the *Cour de Cassation* held that, unless provided otherwise by law, the head of a business who has not personally taken part in the acts constituting the offence may be acquitted on the basis of evidence that he or she had delegated their powers to a person with 'sufficient competence, authority and the necessary means at their disposal'. A further decision in this series suggested that the nature and the size of the business of the company, which might make a delegation of powers necessary, could be taken into consideration (see the three decisions of the *Cour de Cassation* of 11 March 1993; only one of these decisions is reported: *Bulletin mensuel Joly d'information des sociétés* ('Bull Joly'), June 1993, §183, p 667, note Cartier).

This of course raises the question as to which persons within a company would be considered to have legal responsibility for acts constituting an insider dealing offence in the absence of any personal involvement. This is a matter which must be determined in accordance with the law under which the company was constituted. In a French *société anonyme* (the principal type of limited liability company in France), the obvious target is the Chairman (*Président du conseil d'administration*). Under art 113 of the French Companies Law, the holder of this office assumes responsibility for the general management of the company and is vested with very broad powers to represent the company in all circumstances. A complete delegation of the relevant powers to another person (preferably in writing) would therefore be necessary to absolve the Chairman of a French company.

2.5.2 Disclosure

There now exist two disclosure offences in the *Ordonnance*. The first one arises out of the language of the dealing offence which seeks to prevent primary insiders, in possession of privileged information, from 'knowingly permitting' (*sciemment permis de réaliser*) transactions in the relevant securities or instruments to be carried out before the information becomes known to the public. The language 'knowingly permitting' was added to the *Ordonnance* in the context of the initial amendments which were made to it in 1983. Inspired by the highly publicised *Pechiney* scandal of November 1988, a second disclosure offence, which covers communication of privileged information by an insider outside a work context, was added to the *Ordonnance* in 1989. The *Pechiney* case involved leaks of information, notably from the chief of staff of the Minister of the Economy, pertaining to the negotiation of a take-over by the French company *Pechiney* of a company quoted on the NASDAQ market in the United States (Triangle Industries). Commentators at the time of the investigation considered that the issue of disclosure of privileged information should be addressed in a more specific provision, since the existing language of the *Ordonnance* was viewed as difficult to interpret and the burden of proof thought to be extremely onerous due to the presence of the word 'knowingly' in the text (see *Travaux préparatoires*; *Sénat*, No 339, *Avis de M R Bourgine*). Notwithstanding concerns about the adequacy of the 1983 disclosure offence, this language served in the *Pechiney* trial as a basis for convictions of two persons for disclosure of privileged information and its terms were liberally applied (see decisions regarding A Boublil and S Traboulsi; *Cass Crim*, 26 October 1995; *CA Paris*, 6 July 1994, Petites Affiches, 16 Nov 1994, p 17, note Ducouloux-Favard).

In the *Pechiney* case privileged information had been disclosed by a primary insider ('B') to an individual ('P') who subsequently passed the information on to two further parties ('T' and 'R'). P, T and R each carried out transactions in Triangle shares, mainly through companies that they controlled. The *Cour de Cassation* upheld the conviction of B for disclosure of privileged information by having 'knowingly permitted' not only P to carry out transactions in the securities, but also T and R. The court held that, although it had to be established that the accused was a primary insider who had knowingly permitted third parties to trade (eg by communicating privileged information), it was not necessary for an accused to know the identities of persons who traded as a result of the disclosure, nor the terms of the transactions carried out. The court also ruled that the Paris Court of Appeal had provided sufficient justification for its finding that B had given privileged information to P for the sole purpose of permitting P to carry out transactions in Triangle shares; this had been deduced by the Court of Appeal from the mere fact that B had been the only person with inside knowledge of the transaction who had close personal relations with P (the latter, who was deceased at the time of the trial, had been identified by T as his own source for the information).

The Paris Court of Appeal had taken a similar approach to evidentiary requirements in respect of the second person convicted of the disclosure offence in the *Pechiney* case ('ST'), a prominent businessman who had acted as advisor to the target company. ST was found to have communicated privileged information to a friend and business associate ('G'), who carried out transactions, through a Swiss company that he controlled, on behalf of a company incorporated in Anguilla. The appellate court's conclusion, that ST had communicated privileged information to G in order to permit him to carry out transactions in Triangle shares, had been deduced from the timing of trades carried out by G, which seemed to track the progress of the take-over negotiations. This too was considered by the *Cour de Cassation* to constitute an adequate basis for a conviction (note: the approach taken to the evidence by the Court of Appeal in the *Pechiney* case is in striking contrast to the more restrictive approach that it took in the only other reported decision concerning this offence; see *CA Paris*, 27 December 1990, Gaz Pal 1991, p 157, note Marchi; accused acquitted).

The second disclosure offence, added in 1989, is committed where a person, who has acquired privileged information in the exercise of his or her profession or the performance of his or her duties, communicates that information to a third party outside the normal context of his or her profession or duties (see *Ordonnance*, art 10-1, para 2). At present, there are no reported cases involving the application of this offence. In the absence of any case law, it is difficult to predict precisely how the courts will view the *élément moral* of the offence. Although evidence that the accused communicated privileged information with the knowledge that it would be used by the 'tippee' will clearly not be required, it remains to be seen whether the courts will accept as a defence that the accused did not know that the information was privileged.

Although more focused than the 'knowingly permitting' language contained in the main dealing offence, the new disclosure offence clearly overlaps with it. However, the difference in the penalties is significant: the 'knowingly permitting' offence is punishable by a prison sentence of up to two years and/or fines of up to FF10 million (approximately £1,302,000 STG) or ten times the amount of any profit realised (by those who trade), while the new offence is punishable by only six months' imprisonment and a maximum fine of FF100,000 (approximately £13,000 STG). It may be that the 'knowingly permitted' offence will continue to be used in very serious cases of disclosure of privileged information outside a professional context (like the *Pechiney* case), with the separate disclosure offence reserved for cases of less gravity. The fact that the separate disclosure offence is restricted to disclosures made outside the normal context of a person's profession or duties may also leave scope for the application of the 'knowingly permitting' offence where the communication of privileged information takes place within a professional context. One example would be the case where a banker, analyst or stock broker communicates privileged information to clients while providing them with market information, a service which would probably come within the normal context of his or her profession or duties.

Finally, it should be noted that neither disclosure offence would cover communication of privileged information by a person who has not acquired the information in the exercise of their profession or the performance of their duties (or, in the case of the 'knowingly permitted' offence, a statutory insider; see 2.4). So, a 'tippee' who acquires privileged information in a social situation and passes it on to someone else, without dealing in the relevant instruments, cannot be pursued under the *Ordonnance* (although any primary insider who is the source of the information can be prosecuted in respect of trading carried out further down the line, as in the *Pechiney* case).

2.5.3 *Recel*

The *Ordonnance* does not contain any provisions directed at punishing secondary insider dealing. Nevertheless, in the *Pechiney* case, the *Cour de Cassation* held that the criminal law concept of *recel* (the rough equivalent of handling stolen property) could be used to address the problem (see reasons given by the Paris Court of Appeal in connection with the convictions of M Théret, J-P Emden, P Gruman, R Reiplinger and C Ghanem and the reasons given by the *Cour de Cassation* in relation to the latter two). According to the judgment of the *Cour de Cassation*, in order to obtain a conviction for *recel* in an insider dealing context, the Public Prosecutor need only prove:

(1)   that the accused knowingly 'benefited from the product of an insider dealing offence' (eg information communicated in the context of the commission of a disclosure offence); and

(2)   that the accused carried out transactions in the relevant instruments before the privileged information became known to the public.

The court specified that, unlike cases involving the handling of stolen property, there is no *recel* where a recipient of privileged information merely holds that information and does not deal. It will be noted that the facts which gave rise to the *Pechiney* prosecutions pre-dated the introduction of the New Criminal Code on 1 March 1994 and were therefore based upon the old *recel* provision, art 460 of the old Code. It is expected that the same analysis will be applied in respect of the new provision, art 321-1 of the New Criminal Code, which has reformulated the offence so that it specifically refers to the benefiting from the product of a crime (the previous offence only referred to 'things' obtained through the commission of a crime).

The requirement of knowledge on the part of the accused at the time of dealing that he had benefited from the product of an insider dealing offence may at first glance suggest that the offence would be difficult for the prosecution to prove. However, in the *Pechiney* case, the evidentiary burden was satisfied largely by process of deduction. For example, in the case of one person convicted of *recel* (referred to as 'R' in the discussion *above*), knowledge that the information he had received was privileged was deduced from the precipitation with which, after receiving the information, he entered into transactions in shares in a company that he had never invested in previously (see reasons of the Paris Court of Appeal and the *Cour de Cassation* in connection with the conviction of R Reiplinger).

Recel is an independent offence which can form the basis of a prosecution even if the perpetrator of the initial or principal crime is not pursued. The penalties for *recel* differ from those which may be imposed in respect of the *Ordonnance* dealing offence, which provides for shorter prison terms and higher fines that may result in confiscation of all profits realised (see 2.8.1). *Recel* is generally punishable by a prison sentence of up to five years and/or a fine of FF2.5 million (approximately £326,000 STG); however, in certain circumstances, notably where the offence is committed through the use of facilities available to the accused in the exercise of his profession, the sanctions can be increased to ten years' imprisonment and/or a fine of FF5 million. In either case, the fines can be increased to half the value of the goods which constitute the object of the offence; presumably in the insider dealing context this would correspond to the amount of any profits realised.

The use of the concept of *recel* in respect of secondary insider dealing constitutes a rather abstract application of a criminal offence that was clearly designed to deal with the handling of property procured in the commission of a crime. The addition of a specific secondary insider dealing offence to the *Ordonnance* (with penalties similar to those for the existing dealing offence) would be a more appropriate way of dealing with this issue and a welcome development in France.

2.6 WHAT IS THE TERRITORIAL SCOPE OF THE *ORDONNANCE*?

Prior to the *Pechiney* case, some observers were of the view that the *Ordonnance* insider dealing offence could only be applied in respect of transactions relating to securities or instruments quoted in France. The logic underlying this proposition is that the French insider dealing legislation exists to promote transparency of the French securities, futures and options markets and not the markets of other countries. This analysis was rejected in the *Pechiney* case.

The *Pechiney* case involved insider dealing on the NASDAQ carried out from France, in the sense that privileged information within the meaning of the *Ordonnance* was communicated in France and, in most cases, trade instructions were given from France. The connection with France was more tenuous in the case of one of the parties convicted of *recel* (previously referred to as G, since he was neither a French national nor resident in France and the transactions, which he carried out through a Swiss company, were for the account of a company incorporated in Anguilla. The jurisdictional issue was eventually considered by the *Cour de Cassation*, which enlarged considerably the reach of the French legislation by deciding that, where any elements of the offences contained in the *Ordonnance* are committed in France, the French courts have jurisdiction to apply its provisions regardless of whether the dealing has been carried out outside France. Even in the case of G, the court considered that the *recel* provision could be applied on the basis that the privileged information had been communicated to the accused (in Switzerland) by telephone from France (see preliminary decision of the *Cour de Cassation* on the jurisdictional issue, *Cass Crim*, 3 November 1992, D 93, 120, note Ducouloux-Favard; and *Cass Crim* 26 October 1995).

This decision was based upon the former art 693 of the Criminal Procedure Code which has now been replaced by art 113-2 of the New Criminal Code. The new provision is similar to the old one and essentially deems to have been committed in France any offence where one of its constituent elements has taken place or has been carried out in France. It then provides that French criminal law may be applied to any offence committed in France. It is expected, therefore, that under the new provision the *Ordonnance* will continue to be applied in respect of trading carried out from France on foreign stock exchanges. This provision would also justify the application of the *Ordonnance* in the reverse situation, where trading is carried out on the French exchanges from abroad. Certain articles of the French Criminal Procedure Code would enable the French courts to assume jurisdiction in respect of an accused who is resident outside France (see art 689 of the Criminal Procedure Code).

2.7 WHAT ARE THE DEFENCES?

In the absence of statutory defences, defences are usually constructed on the basis of a challenge to the adequacy of the Public Prosecutor's evidence in relation to each element of the relevant offence (the burden of proof being on the prosecution, except where it has been reversed as discussed above). The main area of debate in respect of defences to the dealing offence concerns the effectiveness of the argument that the accused dealt for reasons unrelated to the privileged information. As indicated, the decision of the *Cour de Cassation* in the *La Ruche Méridionale* case offers support for such a defence in that its reformulation of the offence requires the relevant privileged information to be the determining reason for the accused's dealings (see the discussion in 2.5.1.2). Although the precise meaning of that condition is yet to be defined by the *Cour de Cassation*, there is at least one example which can be drawn from the COB's investigation reports which would probably meet the test of the *Cour de Cassation*.

In the context of a well-publicised battle for control of the company *Louis Vuitton—Moët Hennessey* (*'LVMH'*), two series of trades were carried out by companies within the two rival camps and, in each case, at a time when the decision-makers were in possession of privileged information. In the first instance, shares were purchased on behalf of one rival company whilst the decision-makers were aware of an increase in half-yearly profits of 45 per cent as well as a restructuring of LVMH. The second set of trades consisted of purchases of *LVMH* shares on behalf of one of the rival companies and a sale of shares by another at a time when the parties had knowledge of an increase in annual profits of 50 per cent. It was determined by the COB that the purchases of shares were all part of a stake-building exercise and unrelated to the financial results. The disposal in the second series had been carried out at the insistence of the relevant company's bankers who were concerned about its level of indebtedness (the sincerity of this claim was borne out both by the fact that the privileged information was inconsistent with a sale strategy and the shares sold were purchased on the market by a company in the rival camp). In analysing these transactions, the COB concluded that there had been no insider dealing; even though the trades had been carried out by insiders in possession of privileged information, each had acted for legitimate reasons and did not seek to take advantage of the information (Bull COB No 225, May 1989, pp 4–6). The COB therefore accepted the argument that shareholders with strategic positions to defend in relation to a company must not be prevented from acting altogether because they are in possession of privileged information. However, since it appeared that, technically, all elements of the insider dealing offence were present, the COB referred the case to the Public Prosecutor's office which did not pursue the matter.

The COB's view in the *LVMH* case was consistent with that expressed by the Pfeiffer Commission in its 1990 Report on professional conduct rules. The Pfeiffer Commission distinguished between transactions which form part of a clearly established industrial or financial strategy and transactions related to the personal financial strategy of the insider. The Pfeiffer Commission considered that a defence should only be available in respect of the first category of transaction. The *Cour de Cassation* requirement, that any privileged information held by the accused should constitute the determining reason for the dealings, would, no doubt, exonerate an accused person who has traded on the basis of an established industrial or financial strategy. However, where trades are carried out as part of the personal financial strategy of the accused, it might not always accord with the Pfeiffer Commission's reasoning and, indeed, some of the previous case law.

One of the 1977 Paris Court of Appeal decisions (see 2.3 *above*) suggested that a director of a company in possession of privileged financial information could only be acquitted where he traded out of a pressing necessity ('*impérieuse nécessité*'—decision of 26 May 1977). Unless it is qualified by future decisions of the *Cour de Cassation*, the determining reason test might form the basis of a successful defence where the accused did pursue his own personal financial strategy which was unrelated to any privileged information in his possession. This could be the case where shares were sold in the context of a liquidation of assets at the insistence of the accused's bankers (eg the recall of a loan). However, there are no examples in the case law where such a defence has succeeded. Clearly, some guidance from the courts is needed in relation to this issue.

Problem Area 5

A bank which has acted as lead manager for an issue of bonds that are to be quoted on the Paris Stock Exchange has been responsible for the preparation of a prospectus for the issue. Whilst preparing the prospectus, certain members of its corporate finance team have attended due diligence sessions at which they have acquired privileged information about the issuer that has not been disclosed in the prospectus. The issuer has requested that the same bank also take responsibility for the stabilisation of the issue after its launch. This will involve the carrying out of transactions in the bonds on the Paris Stock Exchange in the weeks following the launch of the issue. The stabilisation activities will be carried out by the bond trading desk. A Chinese Wall within the bank separates the corporate finance team from the bond traders.

The issue of stabilisation has not yet been considered by the French courts in connection with the application of the *Ordonnance* insider dealing text. In the situation described above, the Chinese Wall between members of the corporate finance team who are in possession of privileged information and the bond trading team should be effective to prevent the privileged information from having any influence upon the decisions made by the traders in their efforts to stabilise the price of the bonds. As long as the bond traders respect the stabilisation guidelines established by the COB (Regulation No 90-04), and there are no leaks through the chinese wall, the bank should have a good defence to any allegations of insider dealing. However, the issue of multi-function institutions and chinese walls remains to be explored by the French courts, so the legal parameters for this type of activity are still uncertain.

2.8 WHAT ARE THE PENALTIES AND CONSEQUENCES OF A BREACH OF THE *ORDONNANCE*?

2.8.1 The penalties

The dealing offence under the *Ordonnance* is currently punishable by a sentence of two months' to two years' imprisonment and/or a fine of FF6,000 (approximately £800 STG) to FF10 million (approximately £1,302,000 STG) or ten times the amount of any profit made (but not less than the amount of any profit realised). The separate disclosure offence is punishable by a prison term of one to six months and/or a fine of FF10,000 (approximately £1,300 STG) to FF100,000 (approximately £13,000 STG). To date, the fines imposed have ranged from FF5,000 (approximately £700 STG) to FF20 million (approximately £2,604,000 STG), with the highest having been imposed in the *Pechiney* case for disclosure of privileged information ('knowingly permitting' third parties to deal; see 2.5.2 in respect of S Traboulsi, who did not deal, but assisted G, the person he informed, in the realisation of a profit of FF21 million (approximately £2,734,000 STG)). Until recently, prison sentences were rare and almost invariably accompanied by a suspended sentence (*sursis*). In the *Pechiney* case, several prison sentences were imposed, including sentences of two years with only one year of suspended sentence in the case of two of the accused (once again, these sentences were imposed for disclosure of privileged information in respect of A Boublil and S Traboulsi).

2.8.2 The effect of parallel administrative proceedings on sentencing

As indicated above, it is possible in the context of most insider dealing cases for there to be parallel criminal and administrative proceedings based upon the same set of facts (this would not occur where the facts fell outside the COB's territorial jurisdiction, but not that of the criminal courts). The COB has the power to impose fines of the same level as those which may be ordered by the criminal courts (FF10 million (approximately £1,302,000 STG) or up to ten times the amount of any profit realised; however, unlike the criminal courts the COB does not have an obligation to match the amount of any profit realised—see art 9-2 of the *Ordonnance* which defines the COB's powers of sanction). The only limitation imposed by French law on the accumulation of criminal and administrative sanctions is the principle of proportionality: the aggregate sanction must be in proportion to the offence committed.

At present, there is only one reported case where parallel proceedings have been conducted and decisions have been rendered by both the COB and the criminal courts. This case, referred to in 2.3.1.1 *above* as the *Delalande/Synthélabo* case, illustrates some of the difficulties that arise out of having parallel administrative and criminal proceedings and, notably, a difference in approach in the determination of the amount of any profit.

The *Delalande/Synthélabo* case involved a director of a company that was the subject of a negotiated take-over exchange bid. The accused had purchased a fairly substantial block of shares in the company of which he was a director (4.9 per cent of the capital of Delalande at a time when an agreement in principle had been reached in relation to the take-over, although the precise exchange ratio had not been agreed. Following the completion of its investigation of the matter, the COB commenced administrative sanction proceedings (applying its insider dealing Regulation) against the director, which resulted in the imposition of a fine of FF10 million (approximately £1,302,000 STG), the highest fine imposed by the COB to date. The level of the fine was justified on the basis that, under the COB Regulation, directors have a strict duty to abstain from trading whilst in possession of privileged information. An appeal to the Paris Court of Appeal was dismissed.

Although the respondent had exchanged his shares in Delalande for shares in Synthélabo, he did not receive any cash in the context of this transaction (and he subsequently retained the shares in Synthélabo). In its investigation report the COB had estimated the potential profit from the insider dealings at FF69.5 million (approximately £9,049,000 STG). This calculation was based upon a comparison of the market price of the shares in each company and the exchange ratio at the time that the Synthélabo shares were issued to the respondent. The Paris Court of Appeal approved this approach. Commentators on the COB decision expected that the criminal courts would be obliged to impose a fine of an amount that would, together with the COB's fine, be equal to the potential profit from the dealings because, under the *Ordonnance*, the fine imposed must not be less than the amount of the profit realised. In the event, the *Tribunal Correctionnel* found the accused to be guilty of the *Ordonnance* dealing offence, but it only ordered him to pay the administrative fees connected with the hearing of FF600 (approximately £80 STG); in other words, it effectively imposed no sanction after taking into consideration the amount of the fine ordered by the COB.

The *Tribunal Correctionnel* sought to justify its decision on the basis of the basic rule of statutory interpretation which requires a strict construction of criminal statutes. The *Ordonnance* refers to the 'amount of the profit realised, if any' (*le 'montant du profit éventuellement réalisé'*). The court interpreted those words as requiring 'the receipt of a sum exceeding the amount of the expenditure made'. This led to the conclusion that no profit had been realised by the accused, because he had retained the *Synthélabo* shares issued to him in the context of the exchange offer and had not received any cash. Resulting from a decision at first instance, this position could be reversed in future cases, as it effectively eliminates the possibility of a potential profit being taken into consideration in the context of an exchange offer.

The *Delalande/Synthélabo* case is probably indicative of a trend whereby most insider dealing cases will, in the future, be the subject of administrative proceedings prior to being heard by the criminal courts. Upon completion of an insider dealing investigation the COB is obliged, if of the view that there has been a breach of the *Ordonnance*, to refer the matter to the Public Prosecutor's office, which will take an independent view of the case (see art 40 of the Criminal Procedure Code). At the criminal justice level, a further investigation will be carried out by a magistrate (*juge d'instruction*), which will be followed by a trial if the *juge d'instruction* concludes that there is sufficient evidence to proceed. This process is quite lengthy and, by the time the matter comes before the criminal courts, the COB's administrative proceedings will have been concluded and there may even be sufficient time for an appeal of the COB decision to the Paris Court of Appeal. This could restrict the role of the criminal courts to imposing sanctions only in the more serious cases where a second penalty can be justified under the proportionality principle.

3 THE COB REGULATION

3.1 INTRODUCTION

The drafting style of the COB Regulation is more akin to that of a code of conduct than it is to a criminal statute which seeks to define the constituent elements of an offence. The Regulation establishes four categories of insider and sets out principles which must be respected by persons coming within them. These effectively create a dealing offence and a disclosure offence, since a failure to observe the principles may lead to sanctions (referred to as a *manquement d'inité*). Unlike the *Ordonnance*, the Regulation covers secondary insider dealing and therefore implements the EC Directive in this respect. In addition, it creates an obligation for French issuers, credit institutions (banks and *maisons de titres*) and stock-broking firms (*sociétés de bourse*) to take steps to prevent insider dealing.

The Regulation is enforced through sanctions imposed by the *Collège* of the COB (the decision making body within the COB; note: the structure and status of the COB may change in the context of the implementation of the EC Investment Services Directive in France). The COB's powers of administrative sanction are set out in the *Ordonnance* and may be applied where a breach of one of its regulations has had one of the following effects:

- it has interfered with the operation of the markets;
- it has procured for the respondent an unjustified advantage that he/it would not have obtained in a normal market context;
- it has contravened the principle of equality of information and treatment of investors; or
- it has permitted issuers and investors to benefit from a breach of professional conduct rules applicable to the respondent (see art 9-1 of the *Ordonnance*).

In most insider dealing cases, sanctions are justified on the basis of the second and third of these principles.

The *Ordonnance* also provides that the respondent(s) in any case must be given an opportunity to lead a defence, with representation by counsel if desired (see art 9-2; the rules of procedure which the COB must follow are set out in Decree No 90-263 of 23 March 1990). The *Collège* of the COB must provide reasons for any decision imposing sanctions and, as indicated, there is a right of appeal to the Paris Court of Appeal for a re-hearing of the case on the merits (see art 12 of the *Ordonnance* and the Decree of 23 March 1990).

3.2 TO WHICH SECURITIES DOES THE REGULATION APPLY?

The Regulation applies to quoted securities, negotiable futures and options contracts, quoted financial products and products linked to such instruments. Clearly

MONEP and MATIF products are covered and, with regard to securities, the Regulation specifies that it applies to securities traded on the Official List (*Cote Officielle*), the Unlisted Securities Market (*Second Marché*) and the over-the-counter market (*Marché Hors Cote*) of a French stock exchange.

3.3 WHAT IS PRIVILEGED INFORMATION?

In contrast to the *Ordonnance*, there is a definition of privileged information contained in the Regulation. Privileged information is defined as information relating to one or more issuers, or to one or more instruments of a type referred to in the preceding paragraph, that is (i) non-public, (ii) precise and (iii) which, if rendered public, could have an influence on the quoted price of such an instrument. This definition was inspired by the EC Directive. Each of these elements shall be considered below.

3.3.1 Non-public

Like the *Ordonnance*, the term 'non-public' is not defined in the Regulation. As indicated, the COB has quite consistently taken the position that the only way to ensure that information is in the public domain is to publish a press communiqué (see 2.3.2; see also the COB's *Vade-Mecum, above* and its *Rapport Annuel* 1990, p 96). Information would not be considered to be in the public domain until it has actually been published and publication must not be restricted to a highly specialised sector of the press. This was emphasised by the COB in a recent case where it was held that an announcement of price sensitive information by an issuer in the context of a meeting of 200 financial analysts was insufficient to render the information public (see the decision of the COB in the *Schneider* case, Bull COB, No 271, July–August 1993, p 88; see also discussion below in 3.5.4.1).

As with the *Ordonnance*, where a respondent seeks to rely upon press or journal articles containing references to matters which are found to constitute privileged information, the content of such publications must match that of the privileged information; the published information must therefore be specific and complete. An illustration of this principle can be found in the much publicised *Yves Saint Laurent* case, where one of its directors was fined under the Regulation (see the decision of the COB of 12 October 1993 regarding Mr P Bergé, Bull COB, No 277, February 1994, p 31 and decision of the Paris Court of Appeal, 16 March 1994, JCP éd E 94, II, 605, note Forschbach). The director in question sought to argue that the privileged information, which consisted of very substantial losses in the perfume division of the company (this division accounting for 80 per cent of the group's consolidated turn-over), had been the subject of comment in the financial press. Both the COB and the Court of Appeal rejected this defence because the relevant articles only identified weaknesses in the financial structure of the group and contained no references to the losses in the perfume division. These losses only became known to the public when the group's half yearly results where announced and this triggered a sharp decrease in the quoted price.

Similarly, the COB and the Paris Court of Appeal, in a case involving a substantial reduction of profits in the company *Lyonnaise des Eaux–Dumez* due to an increase in the level of provisions, refused to allow a defence based upon reports of financial analysts and press articles predicting a reduction in profits for the relevant financial year (see the decision of the COB of 13 September 1994, Bull COB, No 284, October 1994; decision of the Paris Court of Appeal, 15 March 1995, Bull Joly Bourse, May–June 1995, p 181, note Decoopman). Although some of the articles and reports did refer to the probability of increased provisions which would affect profits, the Paris Court of Appeal dismissed these as 'mere forecasts, which could not be viewed in the same light as information resulting from a communiqué emanating from the issuer'.

3.3.2 Precise

The requirement of precision in the Regulation is designed to distinguish privileged information from rumours and from information as to general market conditions (see COB *Rapport Annuel* 1990, p 96). To date, the cases where the Regulation has been applied have fallen into roughly two categories: (i) cases involving undisclosed financial results (where there has been little doubt as to their precise nature) and (ii) cases relating to take-overs. It is the latter category of cases which has been particularly instructive as to the import of the requirement of precision.

Essentially, these decisions have established that an agreement in principle concerning a take-over is sufficiently precise to constitute privileged information. The COB and the Paris Court of Appeal made such a finding in the *Delalande/Synthélabo* case where, it will be recalled, the parties had reached an agreement in principle regarding an exchange offer, but the exchange ratio had not been agreed (see 2.3.1.1 and 2.8.2). In another decision of the Paris Court of Appeal a take-over proposal was held to be privileged information from the point at which an agreement in principle had been reached between the bidding company and the target in relation to both the structure for the transaction and a price spread for the acquisition, in excess of the then quoted price (see the decision of the COB of 1 March 1994 in a case referred to as *Zodiac/Sicma*, Bull COB, No 279, p 25; decision of the Paris Court of Appeal, 15 Nov 1994, Bull Joly Bourse, January–February 1995, p 9, note Vauplane). The Paris Court of Appeal justified its decision on the basis that, at this stage, the proposal was 'sufficiently defined so that it had reasonable chances of being concluded, regardless of the existence of contingencies, inherent with respect to all transactions of this nature, concerning the actual carrying out of the project'. (See also *SA Compagnie Foncière de la Banque d'Arbitrage et de Crédit*, Bull COB, no 250, September 1991, p 7).

It will be noted that, although the language found in these cases is reminiscent of the old certainty test under the *Ordonnance*, the Paris Court of Appeal confirmed in its decision in the *Yves Saint Laurent* case that there is no requirement of certainty under the Regulation. These decisions do illustrate, however, that the degree to which a proposed transaction has become concrete is an element that can assist in determining whether or not knowledge of it is precise enough to constitute privileged information.

3.3.3 Price-sensitivity

Although the COB Regulation essentially adopts the EC Directive definition of privileged information, the drafting of the text of the Regulation is much broader on the issue of price sensitivity than the Directive. There is no requirement in the Regulation, as there is in the Directive definition, that the potential effect of the privileged information on the quoted price of the relevant securities or instruments be significant. It is sufficient that the information *could* influence the quoted price if it were rendered public (see the decision of the COB in the *Lyonnaise des Eaux–Dumez* case, *above*). The COB has taken the position that the price sensitivity requirement would still be met if information which *could* influence the price does not in fact cause a movement in the price of the relevant security or instrument once it is rendered public (see COB *Rapport Annuel* 1990, p 96). Since many financial transactions *could* influence the price of a quoted security, the scope for application of the Regulation is potentially very large indeed.

In commenting on the Regulation, the COB has specified that information which is not specific to a particular issuer, but which could affect the price of the securities of a group of issuers, could qualify as privileged information; for example, non-public information regarding the outcome of a court case, knowledge of a change in legislation which is about to be introduced or a change in a particular tax policy would qualify (see COB *Rapport Annuel* 1990, p 96). Similarly, market information, such as knowledge of a very large stock exchange order, would constitute privileged information if it was of a nature that could affect the quoted price of the relevant security or instrument.

Problem Area 6

A bank has been approached by a director of a company quoted on the Paris Stock Exchange and asked whether it would be prepared to enter into an over-the-counter put option contract with him. The option would permit the director to sell to the bank a block of shares in the company of which he is a director, representing 5 per cent of its capital. If the bank concludes the option contract with the director, it will want to enter into a series of transactions designed to hedge the put option. The bank considers that, if the existence of the option was known to the market, it could affect the price of the shares concerned.

The fact that the Regulation does not require privileged information to be capable of having a significant effect on the quoted price of the relevant securities does create a dilemma for the bank in this situation. If the bank's view is that knowledge of the existence of the put option *could* have an effect on the quoted price of the shares, it would be in possession of privileged information at the time that it entered into further transactions in the shares or purchased derivative contracts in order to hedge the put option. The current wording of the Regulation is clearly unsatisfactory in this regard and a judicial interpretation which qualifies it would be desirable.

3.4 WHO IS CONSIDERED TO BE AN INSIDER?

There are four categories of insider under the Regulation:

(1) persons in possession of privileged information by reason of their position in relation to an issuer (eg directors, officers and employees);
(2) persons in possession of privileged information by reason of their involvement in the preparation or the carrying out of a financial transaction (eg employees of an issuer, advisors and brokers involved in the transaction);
(3) persons to whom privileged information has been communicated in the context of the exercise of their profession or performance of duties (eg extending beyond category (2) to persons not directly involved in the preparation or the carrying out of a transaction but who have professional relations with an issuer); and
(4) persons who have knowingly received privileged information directly or indirectly from any of the above (eg secondary insiders).

For ease of reference, insiders coming within the first three categories will be referred to below as primary insiders.

3.5 WHAT ARE THE OFFENCES?

3.5.1 Dealing

It is an offence for persons coming within any of these four categories of insider to take advantage of privileged information (*exploiter*) on the market for their own account or for the account of another person.

3.5.1.1 Taking advantage of privileged information

When the Regulation was first introduced in 1990, the COB took the position in its annual report that the reference to the 'taking advantage of' privileged information implied that there must be a link between the information and the transactions carried out by the insider (see COB *Rapport Annuel* 1990, p 99). The COB stated further that these words also required the privileged information to have been the determining reason behind the dealings. It will be recalled from the discussion of the *La Ruche Méridionale* case above, that the *Cour de Cassation* has proposed the same analysis in relation to the *Ordonnance*, notwithstanding the fact that all language establishing the necessity of a link between the privileged information and the dealings has now been deleted from the text.

The Paris Court of Appeal, in a decision pre-dating the *La Ruche Méridionale* judgment of the *Cour de Cassation*, seems to have taken the opposite approach (see the *Lyonnaise des Eaux–Dumez* decision, *above*). After confirming that the word '*exploiter*' did not imply that speculative intent on the part of an insider was required, the appellate court held that the dealing offence under the Regulation could be established by the mere proximity in time between the receipt of the information and its being taken advantage of on the market; it was not necessary for a relationship of cause and effect between the privileged information and the dealings to be proven. Through this analysis, the Court of Appeal may be attempting to harmonise the position under the Regulation with that of the *Ordonnance*. It is submitted that, if this approach is to prevail in future decisions, the presence of the word '*exploiter*' in the Regulation should permit a defence based upon evidence that the respondent traded for reasons unrelated to the privileged information. This analysis would suggest that the Court of Appeal's remarks should be viewed, at best, as creating a rebuttable presumption, designed to assist the COB's prosecutor (referred to as the *rapporteur*) in proving a case, like that which seems to operate in connection with the *Ordonnance*. The issue, however, remains to be explored in future cases.

3.5.1.2 'Internal' insiders and the duty to abstain

Persons who have access to privileged information by virtue of their position in relation to the issuer, are subject to a duty to abstain from taking advantage of privileged information either directly or through the interposition of a third party by buying or selling shares in the relevant issuer or related financial products (referred to as first category insiders; see art 2 of the Regulation). In the case of company directors, the Paris Court of Appeal has interpreted this provision as imposing a strict duty upon directors to abstain from trading whilst in possession of privileged information (see the decision of the Paris Court of Appeal in the *Lyonnaise des Eaux–Dumez* case, *above*; see also the decision of the Paris Court of Appeal in the *Delalande/Synthélabo* case, and in the *Yves Saint Laurent* case, *above*). In the *Lyonnaise des Eaux–Dumez* case, the Court of Appeal described this duty to abstain as being of an 'absolute nature' and suggested that it applied to all persons coming within the first category of insider, not just directors and officers who would be in a position to arrange for disclosure of the information (this being the rationale behind the 'abstain or disclose' principle). The duty does not seem to apply to insiders within the other three categories, who would be external to the issuer.

This decision raises the question at to what if any defences exist for insiders in the first category. In the *Lyonnaise des Eaux–Dumez* judgment the court seems to eliminate imprudence or inadvertence as the basis for a defence. It is hoped that, as one author has suggested, defences founded upon the argument that the respondent traded for reasons unrelated to the privileged information, other than pursuing his own personal financial strategy, will be permitted (see the case comment by N Decoopman, Bull Joly Bourse, May–June 1995, p 185). An example of a defence which should be successful would be the circumstances of the *LVMH* case discussed above (see 2.7).

3.5.1.3 Indirect dealing

The dealing offence under the Regulation will be committed not only where the respondent has traded directly, but also where he has dealt indirectly in the relevant securities or instruments. An illustration of this principle can be found in the *Zodiac/Sicma* case where the respondent company, Zodiac, was fined by the COB in relation to an acquisition of shares through a 'warehousing' arrangement (*convention de portage*) which was entered into on behalf of the company at a time when its representative was in possession of privileged information (see the decisions of the COB and the Paris Court of Appeal, *above*). As indicated above in the discussion of the nature of privileged information, the insider information in this case consisted of an agreement in principle between Zodiac and the majority shareholder of Sicma that Zodiac would acquire its shareholding at a price per share falling within a certain spread. After reaching this agreement, but prior to filing a take-over bid with the Stock Exchange authorities, Zodiac entered into an agreement with its bank whereby the bank would acquire 5000 shares in Sicma. This agreement gave the bank a put option to sell those shares to Zodiac (with an undertaking not to sell the shares to anyone else) up to a certain date and at an agreed price (below the bid price). This warehousing arrangement was found to constitute an indirect acquisition of the shares by Zodiac coming within the scope of the dealing offence. Similarly, an acquisition or disposal of securities by a company controlled by a person in possession of privileged information could lead to sanctions under the Regulation dealing offence.

3.5.1.4 Secondary insider dealing

As indicated, in contrast to the *Ordonnance*, the Regulation dealing offence covers secondary insider dealing (see art 5 of the Regulation). The Regulation prohibits persons who knowingly (*en connaissance de cause*) possess privileged information, which has been acquired directly or indirectly from a primary insider (a person coming within one of the first three categories referred to above), from taking advantage of such information on the market for their own account or for the account of a third party. It should be emphasised that the Regulation requires a secondary insider to be aware that the information taken advantage of was privileged at the time of dealing. There have been no cases to date where this provision of the Regulation has been applied. It is therefore difficult to predict what proof will be required, if any, as to the fact that the respondent knew that the information was privileged at the time that it was taken advantage of. The approach taken by the Paris Court of Appeal in the *Lyonnaise des Eaux–Dumez* case would suggest that this issue may be examined on an objective rather than a subjective level.

3.5.1.5 Off-exchange dealing

Although the words 'on the market' may seem to suggest that the dealing offence only covers on-exchange trading, it has been established by the Paris Court of Appeal that it also applies to off-exchange transactions in instruments of a type described in 3.2 *above* (see the *Yves Saint Laurent* case). The rationale is that investors are still prejudiced where trading is carried out off-exchange.

3.5.2 Dealing on behalf of a company

Where transactions coming within the dealing offence have been carried out on behalf of a company, the Regulation permits the COB to prosecute the company itself and/or its managers (see arts 1 and 7 of the Regulation; note: the *Zodiac/Sicma* case, *above*, provides an example of a company being prosecuted directly). There is no textual basis in the Regulation for the presumption of liability of managers that is found in the *Ordonnance*. The Regulation merely provides that its provisions apply to 'the managers of the issuer or the legal entity concerned'. As a consequence, the position of a legal or *de facto* manager of a company who has not been personally implicated in transactions involving an insider dealing offence is probably not as unsatisfactory under the Regulation as it is under the *Ordonnance*. The fact that the COB can pursue the company itself does not require it to bring proceedings against such a person, whereas this may in some cases be the only way that the Public Prosecutor can proceed under the *Ordonnance*. Although there should be no reversal of the burden of proof (as there is under the *Ordonnance*), a defence based upon a complete delegation of powers might be available in the case of a manager who has not been personally involved in the relevant transactions.

3.5.3 The disclosure offence

All primary insiders have an obligation under the Regulation to refrain from disclosing privileged information for reasons other than those for which information is held (see arts 2, 3 and 4 of the Regulation). The Regulation does not extend this obligation to secondary insiders. At present, there are no decisions interpreting this provision of the Regulation; however, an example of a situation that might fall within the disclosure offence would be where a bank employee working on a corporate finance transaction mentions the deal to a trader within the same institution who is involved in proprietary trading for the bank. The Regulation would not prevent the same employee from discussing the transaction with other members of his corporate finance team (unless for some reason a Chinese Wall had been established between them). Obviously, the employee would also be prohibited under the Regulation from communicating the information to friends or family.

3.5.4 Prevention of insider dealing

The Regulation not only seeks to prevent insider dealing by establishing rules of conduct for insiders, but it also seeks to encourage institutions which frequently have access to privileged information to create a 'compliance' culture. Issuers, credit institutions (banks and *maisons de titres*) and *sociétés de bourse* have an obligation under the Regulation to take all necessary steps to prevent the circulation of, or the taking advantage of, privileged information (see art 6 of the Regulation). The COB has stated that this is a best endeavours obligation (*obligation de moyens*) as opposed to a strict obligation to achieve a certain result (*obligation de résultat*) (see COB *Rapport Annuel* 1990, p 100). However, no guidance has been provided as to the steps which must be taken in order to meet this obligation.

3.5.4.1 Issuers

In the case of issuers, compliance with the obligation to prevent the circulation and use of privileged information would encompass observance of guidelines concerning the disclosure of privileged information at the earliest opportunity (see COB Reg 90-02 relating to the obligation of issuers to inform the public of matters which may affect the price of their securities or linked instruments; see also the COB's *Vade Mecum*, *above* and the SFAF/CLIFF guidelines *above*). The link between an issuer's obligation to keep the public advised of price sensitive information and the obligation to prevent the circulation and use of privileged information was highlighted by the COB in a letter of reprimand addressed to the chairman of Schneider *SA* (Bull COB, no 266, February 1993, p 6).

In its letter the COB concluded that Schneider had breached its obligations under art 6 of the Regulation when it gave, during stock exchange trading hours, to approximately 200 financial analysts attending an information meeting, a forecast for its financial results that fell short of market expectations. Some analysts left the meeting and reported the forecast to their employers, which consisted of *sociétés de bourse*, institutional investors and portfolio managers. A significant volume of dealing, carried out in part by those institutions on proprietary accounts prior to the close of trading on the stock exchange, caused the quoted price of shares in Schneider to fall. The following day, different figures for the profit forecast were provided by Schneider to shareholders at a general meeting, which was followed by the publication of a press communiqué by the issuer. Proceedings only appear to have been commenced against a bank analyst who dealt in Schneider shares for his own account prior to the announcement of the forecast to the public. Although the COB did not commence enforcement proceedings against Schneider under the Regulation, it did remind its chairman that, by releasing incomplete and ultimately contradictory information about financial results during stock exchange trading hours, it had facilitated the circulation and abuse of privileged information in breach of art 6 of the Regulation.

An issuer's obligations under art 6 of the Regulation must also be considered at the internal level. The taking of all steps necessary to prevent the circulation and use of privileged information would probably include the establishment of staff rules requiring price sensitive transactions and unpublished financial results to be kept confidential, as well as the issue of guidelines on staff dealing.

3.5.4.2 Financial intermediaries

The prevention of insider dealing has received attention in various studies of professional conduct rules that have been carried out in France since the mid-1980s (see Brac de la Perrière *Rapport du groupe de travail sur la déontologie des activités financières*, March 1988; Report of the Pfeiffer Commission, *above*). However, efforts to define rules of conduct have not resulted in the propagation of detailed conduct of business rules in France as they have in other jurisdictions like the UK. In fact the French securities and banking regulators have produced very little in the way of regulations or policy statements which could serve to define the steps which must be taken by a credit institution or *société de bourse* in order to meet their obligations under art 6 of the Regulation. To the extent that they exist, the guidelines applicable to such institutions remain, at present, general statements of principle; it is therefore up to the individual bank or brokerage house to determine the manner in which they will be implemented (see for example, in the case of *sociétés de bourse*, art 2-6-1 of the *Règlement Général du Conseil des Bourses de Valeurs*).

Credit institutions and *sociétés de bourse* are required to have an internal regulation (*règlement intérieur*) which defines staff rules and circumstances in which disciplinary measures may be taken. The *règlement intérieur* of any such institution should contain staff dealing rules as well as prohibitions against the communication of privileged information and insider dealing. In addition, these institutions would be expected to establish Chinese Walls in order to stop the flow of privileged information to persons to whom it might be useful. Although there are at present no published decisions on the application of art 6 in this context, it is likely that the COB will take the position that it is insufficient for an institution to establish rules to prevent the circulation and use of privileged information without taking steps to ensure that they are actually put into practice by staff.

Finally, it will be observed that, since art 6 of the Regulation deals with issues of firm culture, the enforcement of this obligation could take the form of proceedings against the company and/or its managers who have responsibility for matters of firm practice in respect of professional conduct. There is also potential for the COB to proceed against an institution under art 6 in a case where several members of its staff have engaged in a practice which contravenes the principles set out in the Regulation. This could provide an alternative to commencement of enforcement proceedings against the individuals concerned, which might be justified in a situation where it can be said that the breach of the Regulation seemed to be a part of or at least acceptable within the firm's 'culture'.

3.6 WHAT IS THE TERRITORIAL SCOPE OF THE REGULATION?

The Regulation only applies to French securities and derivatives markets. As a consequence, the COB would not have jurisdiction to commence enforcement proceedings under the Regulation in respect of trading carried out from France on a foreign stock exchange, as was done in the *Pechiney* case under the *Ordonnance*. However, where transactions in instruments covered by the Regulation (as described in 3.2 *above*) are carried out by a French resident outside France, the COB has jurisdiction to exercise its powers of sanction (see the decision of the Paris Court of Appeal in the *Yves Saint Laurent* case, *above*). In the reverse situation, where a non-French resident carries out transactions from outside France on a French stock exchange (eg places orders for trades on the Paris Stock Exchange from London through a French broker), the Regulation should still apply. In contrast to prosecutions in the criminal courts under the *Ordonnance*, it is unclear in this situation whether the COB would be able to prosecute the persons concerned unless they were present in France. This is due to the fact that, as an administrative body, the COB may not rely on the cross-border judicial assistance measures which are available to the French criminal courts.

3.7 DEFENCES

Like the *Ordonnance*, there are no defences set out in the Regulation. In several cases defences have been advanced on the basis that the decision to trade was unrelated to the privileged information that was in the defendant's possession. These cases have fallen into roughly two categories:

(1) those where the defence has been founded upon the respondent's personal financial situation; and

(2) those where the respondent has sought to justify the trading on the basis that it was connected to a financial transaction such as a take-over bid.

There are no examples in the cases of a successful defence founded upon personal financial need. In the *Yves Saint Laurent* case, an attempt by M Bergé to argue that his trading was rendered necessary by repeated demands from his bankers that he reduce the level of his indebtedness (and that of M Saint Laurent) was rejected by the Paris Court of Appeal with the observation that it had not been demonstrated that the problem with his bank was 'insurmountable'. The court considered that, as a director, M Bergé was required to show particular reserve in managing his personal finances whilst in possession of privileged information. This element was, however, taken into consideration by the court when it reviewed the fine that had been ordered by the COB (see 3.8).

More recently, in the *Lyonnaise des Eaux–Dumez* case, the Paris Court of Appeal stated that, in respect of category one insiders (persons who become insiders by virtue of their position in relation to an issuer), only *force majeure* or a legitimate reason (*cause légitime*) could exonerate such a person. Unfortunately, the court did not explain what it meant by *cause légitime*. One would hope that the pursuit of an 'established industrial or financial strategy', to borrow the words of the Pfeiffer Commission, would qualify as a legitimate reason. For example, the facts of the *LVMH* case described above (see 2.7), where trading was carried out in the context of a battle for control of the company, should come within this category. This type of defence has been advanced unsuccessfully in two cases, but it has been rejected on the basis of findings in each case that the respondent's real objectives did not correspond to an alleged stake-building exercise.

In the *Zodiac/Sicma* case referred to above, the court suggested that gradual stake-building (*ramassage*) was possible prior to the launch of a take-over bid provided that the trading corresponded to the objective pursued, that is to acquire a significant holding in the capital of the target company or to reinforce one's position as against a future competing bid. In the circumstances of that particular case, the court did not find that the acquisition of Sicma shares by Zodiac, after it reached an agreement in principle to acquire a controlling block from Sicma's major shareholder, was carried out for any reason other than to economise on the price of the shares by purchasing them for a price which was lower than the public offer price. Similarly in the *Delalande/Synthélabo* case the court rejected, due to a lack of credibility, a defence based on the argument that the respondent had acquired shares in the target company because he was thinking of launching his own take-over bid. These two decisions should not prevent such a defence from succeeding where the respondent can demonstrate that his motives for dealing were in fact to build up a stake in the target company whilst seeking control.

The observations of the Paris Court of Appeal in the *Lyonnaise des Eaux–Dumez* case concerning the limited availability of defences appear to be confined to persons coming within the first category of insider. The COB has suggested that inadvertence or imprudence might be available as defences, but these were specifically excluded by the court in respect of 'internal' insiders in its *Lyonnaise des Eaux–Dumez* decision (see COB *Rapport Annuel* 1990, p 99). It remains to be seen whether other lines of defence, such as inadvertence, might develop in future decisions in respect of insiders coming within the remaining three categories.

3.8 SANCTIONS

The COB may impose fines of up to FF10 million (approximately £1,302,000 STG) or ten times the amount of any profit made. It is also empowered to publish its decisions and this has become its usual practice, although a respondent may request that the COB refrain from doing so. Compliance with such a request would be rare, since the publication of the COB's decisions is considered to serve as a deterrent.

The *Ordonnance*, which defines the COB's powers of sanction, states that the amount of any sanction imposed must be in proportion to the seriousness of the breach of the rules and the advantages and profits gained therefrom (see art 9-2, para 2 of the *Ordonnance*). This provision has inspired leniency on the part of the COB in certain cases. For example, a fine of only 1 franc was ordered in respect of the analyst who traded for his own account in the *Schneider* case (see 3.5.4.1 *above*). The mitigating factors identified by the COB in that case included the fact that the respondent had realised only a very modest profit in connection with the transaction and he had been fired by his employer as a result of the incident. The COB also mentioned that the breach of the Regulation by the journalist had been facilitated by the manner in which the issuer had released the information and the fact that his employer did not have adequate rules in place designed to prevent the circulation and abuse of privileged information (note: the employer bank does not seem to have been prosecuted under art 6 of the Regulation).

The realisation of substantial losses and personal financial difficulties have also been taken into consideration in determining the appropriate level of sanction. In proceedings brought against Friedland Investissements in connection with a disposal of shares in Métrologie International, whilst its representatives were in possession of unpublished information as to losses incurred by the issuer, a fine of FF100,000 (approximately £13,000 STG) ordered by the COB was eliminated altogether by the Paris Court of Appeal (see *CA Paris*, 12 January 1994, Gaz Pal 27/28 May 1994, p 13, note J-P M). In vacating the fine (but not the finding that the respondent had breached the Regulation), the court was sensitive to arguments that the respondent had only sold 10 per cent of its holding in Métrologie International and, due to the steadily descending share price, it had nevertheless incurred a capital loss in the amount of FF664,500 (approximately £87,000 STG). The avoidance of a loss was, however, viewed by the COB and the court as an advantage justifying the imposition of a fine in several other decisions rendered in the *Métrologie* matter involving disposals of shares by directors of the company (see the decisions of the COB relating to M Blaise, M Fraiberger, M Moulin, M Schwartzman and M Haddad in Bull COB, no 269, May 1993, p 25 *et seq*; appeals to the Paris Court of Appeal on behalf of M Fraiberger, M Haddad and M Schwartzman were dismissed).

As was indicated above in the discussion of defences, in the *Yves Saint Laurent* case, the court rejected as a defence the argument that the respondent, M Bergé, had disposed of shares in the company whilst under pressure from his bank to reduce the level of his indebtedness (see 3.7 *above*). Although this argument did not form the basis of a successful defence, it was taken into consideration by the Paris Court of Appeal in connection with the penalty and led to a reduction of the fine imposed against M Bergé from FF3 million (approximately £390,000 STG) to FF1 million (approximately £130,000 STG). This decision provides an interesting contrast to the judgment of the court in the *Delalande/Synthélabo* case, where it approved the fine of FF10 million (approximately £1,302,000 STG) imposed by the COB on the basis of the respondent's duty as a director to abstain from trading. There were no extenuating personal circumstances in that case.

3.9 CONCLUSION

Since the *Ordonnance* insider dealing text was introduced in 1970, the regulatory environment in France has changed quite considerably from one which attacked insider dealing with a certain degree of reticence to one which favours enforcement. Not only has the criminal text been amended several times in order to facilitate the prosecution of insider dealing cases, but the COB has been given the power to define its own insider dealing rules and to enforce them directly. Now that the French regulatory authorities are equipped with two very broadly drafted texts, which contain no specific defences, the task for the French courts will be to define with greater precision the parameters within which persons exposed to privileged information must work. The long awaited decision of the *Cour de Cassation* in the *La Ruche Méridionale* case provides a good starting point, but it will take several further judgments before each element of the criminal offence, as reformulated by the court, will be understood. Future decisions will also determine whether parallel criminal and regulatory regimes in this area can be complementary, rather than duplicative, and whether each set of rules can serve a useful purpose.

Note:

At the time of publication of this book, the French parliament was proposing to make further amendments to the Ordonnance in the context of a general reform of the financial markets undertaken in connection with the implementation in France of the EC Investment Services Directive. The new legislation, which is expected to be passed in late May or early June 1996, will make the following amendments to the Ordonnance: (1) the criminal liability of companies will be introduced in connection with the criminal insider dealing offence (see 2.5.1.4 above); (2) the words 'on the market' will be removed from the text so as to make it clear that the dealing offence applies to off-exchange transactions (see 2.5.1.3 above); (3) the instruments to which the Ordonnance applies will be expanded to include all securities and 'financial instruments' that are traded on a regulated market; although still being debated, language may also be added to the text which states that the offence will apply to securities of issuers which are traded on the *Marché hors cote* (the over-the counter-market) (see 2.2 above); and (4) specific language authorising criminal judges to order penalties which shall accumulate with fines ordered by the COB in respect of the same case will be added (see 2.8.2 above).

Also, in reference to the Haddad case on p 193, please note that the Haddad decision is subject to an application to the Cour de Cassation to have it set aside.

COMPARISON OF THE ORDONNANCE AND THE REGULATION

	Ordonnance 67-833 of 28 September 1967	Regulation No 90-08 of the COB
Definition of insider	i) Primary insiders: a) Internal insiders: —the chairman, general directors (*directeurs généraux*), directors and members of the *directoire* or *conseil desurveillance* (including the permanent representatives of any companies appointed as director or member of the *conseil de surveillance*); —spouses provided that they are not legally separated (*séparation de corps*). b) External insiders: —all persons who acquire privileged information in the exercise of their profession or in the performance of their duties. ii) Secondary insiders: —the *Ordonnance* contains no provisions directed at punishing secondary insider dealing. The concept of *recel* (the rough equivalent of possession or use of stolen property) has been applied in one case.	i) Primary insiders: a) Internal insiders: —internal to the issuer: persons in possession of privileged information by reason of their position in relation to an issuer (eg directors, officers and employees); —internal to a transaction: persons in possession of privileged information by reason of their involvement in the preparation or the carrying out of a financial transaction. b) External insiders: —persons to whom privileged information has been communicated in the context of the exercise of their profession or performance of duties. ii) Secondary insiders: —persons who have knowingly received privileged information directly or indirectly from any of the above.

	Ordonnance 67-833 of 28 September 1967	Regulation No 90-08 of the COB
Definition of privileged information	i) precise; ii) confidential; and iii) of a nature that would have an influence on the quoted price of an instrument. The issue as to whether information is privileged should be addressed in an objective manner, solely on the basis of the content of the information and excluding any element of arbitrary judgment.	i) precise; ii) non-public; and iii) which, if rendered public, *could* have an influence on the quoted price of an instrument.
Transactions covered	Any transaction in quoted securities or derivatives contracts (whether carried out on- or off-exchange). Can be applied to transactions carried out on a foreign regulated market.	Any transaction in instruments traded on a French stock exchange or regulated derivatives market (whether carried out on or off exchange).
Offences	i) To carry out, whilst in possession of privileged information, either directly or through the interposition of a third party, one or more transactions on the market. The privileged information must be the determining reason for the dealing (*déterminante des opérations réalisées*) ii) To permit knowingly one or more transactions to be carried out on the market (eg disclosure of privileged information). iii) To communicate privileged information to a third party outside the normal context of one's profession or duties.	i) To take advantage of (*exploiter*) privileged information, either directly or indirectly, on the market for one's own account or for the account of another person. ii) To communicate privileged information for reasons other than those for which such information is held or has been communicated.
Dealing on behalf of a company	The company's legal and *de facto* managers will be liable (presumption of liability). The company itself may not be prosecuted.	Both the company and its officers or managers may be subject to enforcement proceedings.

	Ordonnance 67-833 of 28 September 1967	Regulation No 90-08 of the COB
Sanctions	i) Dealing offence: —fine of FF6,000 (approximately £800 STG) to FF10 million (approximately £1,302,000 STG) or ten times the amount of any profit made (but not less than the relevant profit); —sentence of two months to two years. ii) Separate disclosure offence: —fine of FF10,000 (approximately £1,300 STG) to FF100,000 (approximately £13,000 STG); —sentence of one to six months.	i) Fine of up to FF10 million (approximately £1,302,000 STG) or ten times the amount of any profit made. Any fine imposed must be in proportion to the seriousness of the offence committed and any profits realised. ii) Publication of the COB's decision.

CASE STUDY

Splash Plc, a company listed on the French stock exchanges, manufactures rainwear and umbrellas. Alan, a weather forecaster, on discovering that there is an unseasonable amount of rain due in the next three months, instructs his broker to buy shares in Splash. Meanwhile, Charles, an analyst of the company's shares, is told in a conversation with Jeremy, one of the directors, that the Chairman is expected to be paid a salary of FF500,000. Charles knows from his knowledge of the Chairman's service contract (which is available for public inspection) that this salary could only be paid if the company achieved profit in excess of FF20 million. Charles revises his profit forecast for the company but before he publishes it he cancels instructions which he had previously given to his broker to sell his Splash shares. Charles also tells his girlfriend, Maggie, that 'things are looking up' for Splash. Maggie then buys shares in the name of her father from an old friend of hers who wanted to sell Splash shares off-market to save the payment of a broker's commission. In addition, Owen, an employee of the contracting firm which cleans Splash's offices, finds a draft of the latest management figures, which demonstrate Splash's high profitability, in a wastepaper bin. He immediately buys shares.

Alan
The principal issue to be considered in respect of Alan's potential liability for insider dealing is whether the information in his possession, that there is an unseasonable amount of rain due in the next three months, constituted privileged information. Under the *Ordonnance*, this would raise two issues in connection with the definition of privileged information: (1) whether the information relates to 'the prospects or financial situation of *an issuer* or to the prospects for future movement in the price of *a security* . . .' and (2) whether the information was non-public. On the first point, the restrictive wording of the *Ordonnance*, which refers to issuers in the singular, seems to exclude from the category of privileged information a piece of general information that might affect a whole industrial sector. The forecast of heavy rainfall therefore falls outside the definition. Assuming that the weather predictions were publicly available, this information would probably be disqualified on the basis of the second requirement as well. In fact, Alan's decision to deal seems to have been based solely upon his own analysis of publicly available information, which, in accordance with the decision of the *Cour de Cassation* in the *La Ruche Méridionale* case, could not form the basis of a conviction for insider dealing. The analysis would be similar under the Regulation, except that the first issue raised above would be resolved differently. The Regulation specifically provides that the relevant information can relate to 'one or more issuers' and the COB has interpreted this language as including information which would affect a whole industrial sector (see art 1).

Jeremy

The information disclosed by Jeremy about the Chairman's salary would probably qualify as privileged information under both the *Ordonnance* and the Regulation because it is precise and would probably be interpreted by the market in a way that would make it price sensitive. The question as to whether the separate disclosure offence contained in the *Ordonnance* was committed by Jeremy would turn on whether or not he disclosed the information to Charles in a work context (eg in the latter's capacity as financial analyst) or outside that context (eg during a social occasion). If it was the latter, the offence was committed. The other disclosure offence contained in the *Ordonnance* (knowingly permitting a third party to deal) can be eliminated from the analysis on the basis that Charles did not actually deal in the securities (he cancelled a dealing order). If Jeremy communicated the information to Charles for reasons other than those for which he held the information, which appears to be the case, he would also be guilty of the Regulation communication offence (as a director of Splash, Jeremy is a category one insider under the Regulation and is therefore to observe the strictest standards of discretion; see art 2).

Charles

The cancellation by Charles of a sell order, following the receipt of privileged information from Jeremy, highlights a gap in the *Ordonnance*. The *Ordonnance* insider dealing offence requires one or more 'transactions' (*opérations*) to be carried out. The cancellation of a dealing order would probably not qualify as a transaction. The position would be less clear under the Regulation since it requires the 'taking advantage of' (*exploiter*) privileged information 'on the market' (*sur le marché*; see art 4). This issue has not been considered in any of the cases to date, but the language of the Regulation may be broad enough to cover the cancellation of an order as a result of the taking advantage of privileged information.

The question also arises as to whether Charles committed a disclosure offence when he advised Maggie that 'things are looking up' for Splash. Under the *Ordonnance* there would be two possible disclosure offences; (1) knowingly permitting a third party to trade and (2) the separate offence of disclosing information acquired in a work context to a third party outside the work context; however, these would only apply if Charles' statement qualified as privileged information. It is doubtful that Charles' statement would be considered by a French court to be precise enough to constitute privileged information since he did not indicate why things were looking up and only presented his analysis of the situation. A similar conclusion would be reached in relation to the Regulation definition of privileged information.

Maggie

As indicated above, the information received by Maggie would probably not meet the test for privileged information under either the *Ordonnance* or the

Regulation. Even if Maggie had been given privileged information, as a secondary insider (or 'tippee') she could not be prosecuted under the *Ordonnance*. She could, however, be prosecuted for *recel* if it could be demonstrated that (1) she knowingly benefited from the product of an insider dealing offence (eg disclosure of privileged information) and (2) carried out transactions before the information became public. As demonstrated in the *Pechiney* case, there can be a conviction for *recel* even where trades are carried out for the benefit of a third party. If the information had been privileged she could also be pursued under the Regulation, which prohibits secondary insiders from taking advantage of, for their own account or for the account of another, information which they know is privileged (art 5). The fact that she dealt for her father would not be an issue because the Regulation covers trading for the account of another. That the trade was carried out off-market is also of no consequence, since the Regulation has been interpreted as covering off-exchange trading in securities that are quoted in France.

Owen

Since Owen has come across the document containing the latest management figures whilst in the performance of his duties, he could probably be prosecuted under the *Ordonnance*. The unpublished management figures would undoubtedly come within the definition of privileged information; therefore, Owen has probably committed the *Ordonnance* dealing offence. In addition, Owen could be pursued under the Regulation secondary insider dealing provision (art 5). This provision is aimed at all persons who knowingly possess privileged information which has been obtained either directly or indirectly from an insider in one of the other categories (eg a director, officer, employee or advisor). Although we do not know exactly where Owen found the document in Splash's premises, it seems likely that it was tossed in the bin by an insider and could therefore be considered to have been obtained indirectly from an insider.

Spain

Iñigo D Berrícano,
Uría & Menéndez, Madrid

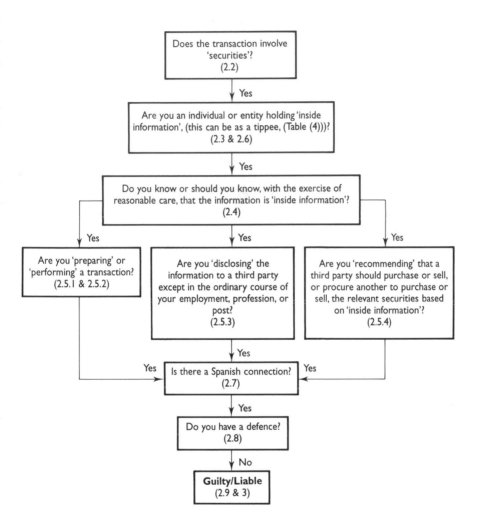

1 INTRODUCTION

The Spanish provisions regarding insider dealing are principally contained in art 81 of the Securities Market Act 1988 ('*Ley 24/1988, de 28 de julio, del Mercado de Valores*', the 'Act') as amended by Law 9/1991 of 22 March, and represent the implementation in Spain of the European Union Directive on Insider Dealing (Dir 89/592 [1989] OJ L334/30) (the 'Directive').

The Act enacted on 28 July 1988, represented the first effort in Spain to regulate, on a general basis, the securities markets, market professionals and their activities. It created a regulatory body called the National Securities Market Commission ('*Comisión Nacional del Mercado de Valores*' or 'CNMV') which mirrored the United States' Securities and Exchange Commission and which was entrusted with the supervision, inspection and control of members and activities performed in the securities markets. In addition, the Act created new legal entities with special capacity to intermediate in the securities markets and set up a code of conduct to be complied with by all market players.

Law 9/1991 of 22 March amended the Act so as to conform to the Directive and imposed higher administrative sanctions on the legal entities and their administrators for a breach of the insider dealing rules.

Insider dealing in contravention of the Act is not a criminal offence although fines and other sanctions may be imposed by the CNMV. However, civil servants who unlawfully use insider information gained in the course of the performance of their public duties may be subject to criminal prosecution in accordance with the existing Penal Code.

Notwithstanding the above, a new Penal Code was enacted on 23 November 1995 ('Ley Organica 10/1995, de 23 de noviembre del Codigo Penal') coming into force on 24 May 1996 which introduces in Spain a criminal offence for the use of inside information, provided the benefit obtained from such conduct exceeds 75 million pesetas (approximately £38,000 STG).

Finally, before reviewing in detail the insider dealing provisions contained in art 81 three considerations must be borne in mind:

(1) since the introduction of the Act no case law exists interpreting the general and widely-drafted provisions contained in it; in fact, until the end of 1994 only six proceedings had been opened by the appropriate regulatory authorities in relation to insider dealing;

(2) a general principle of administrative law precludes an administrative offence from being interpreted widely through analogy so as to cover conduct not falling strictly within the prohibition contained in the law;

(3) the existence of a criminal offence should preclude the imposition of an administrative sanction by the regulator of the securities market based on the same facts. In addition, conduct and fact established in a criminal court may not be challenged or re-interpreted in administrative proceedings.

2 ADMINISTRATIVE LAW

2.1 INTRODUCTION

Article 81 contains the following general prohibition concerning the use of inside information:

> Any party having inside information is precluded from carrying out the following activities, directly or indirectly, and whether acting on its own behalf or on behalf of a third party:
> (i) to prepare or enter into any transaction in the market regarding the securities to which the information refers;
> (ii) to communicate such information to third parties except in the ordinary course of their employment, profession, post or duties;
> (iii) to recommend to a third party to purchase or assign such securities, or to procure that any other third party purchases or assigns such securities based on such information.

In addition, 'inside information' is defined as 'all specific information which refers to one or various issuers of securities or one or various securities, is not public and, had it been made public, it would or could have influenced substantially the quoted price of such security or securities'.

2.2 TO WHICH SECURITIES DOES THE ACT APPLY?

2.2.1 Negotiable securities

The Act applies to negotiable securities represented by physical instruments or through book entry. The Act lacks any precise definition of 'security' although in its preamble it does recognise that the Spanish securities markets now deal in 'securities', where a physical instrument is no longer required and which are capable of being negotiated in a market where their economic terms have prominence over the identity of the parties dealing in them.

Secondary legislation has developed the term 'negotiable security' in the context of public offers and issues of securities subject to prospectus requirements, so that the term will include:

- shares in a limited liability company, participations in savings banks, preemption rights, warrants, or other similar rights that directly or indirectly grant a right of subscription or purchase;
- bonds and similar instruments representing a participation in a loan or debt, issued by public or private entities, with an explicit or implicit return, including those granting a right for their purchase either directly or indirectly and those granting a right over interest or principal payments;
- letters of credit, commercial paper, certificates of deposit or analogous instruments except for those issued singularly in a commercial transaction and which do not imply funds are being obtained from the public;
- mortgage bonds and certificates and mortgage participations;
- participations in investment funds;
- any other right of an economic nature whatever the name given to it

which, due to its legal nature and transferability, is capable of negotiation on a general and impersonal manner in a financial market.

In addition, 'negotiable security' has been defined so as to expressly *exclude* the following:

* participations in private limited liability companies ('*sociedades de responsabilidad limitada*');
* participations in partnerships;
* capital contributions in co-operatives;
* quotas in the capital of mutual guarantee companies;
* shares in the regulatory bodies of the securities markets and of the relevant settlement and clearing institutions.

No reference is made in the legislation to other instruments such as futures, options, SWAPs and forward rate agreements which are closely linked to the securities markets in general. It would seem that the concept of 'negotiable security' is not capable of including instruments which by definition are only contracts (not securities) and lack an identified issuer who undertakes to comply with certain terms and conditions in exchange for some consideration. Furthermore, these 'securities' are not, generally, negotiable, since transfer of title is never passed between investors, the normal 'sale' of any such instrument taking place by entering into an opposite transaction, so that the economic terms of the previous 'purchase' are cancelled.

Accordingly, it would appear that a person is not capable of insider dealing if the insider deals in derivatives, at least, not until securities are transferred pursuant to the derivative instrument (see 2.5.2). Notwithstanding this, the existing futures and options markets in Spain have been created under the regulatory framework of the Act and its rules for the organisation of secondary official markets of negotiable securities. Thus, the CNMV, which exercises its supervision over the futures and options markets, would probably interpret that transactions in futures and options being 'negotiated' in the official futures and options markets should be capable of falling within the prohibition of art 81.

In addition, it should be noted that a Bill presented before Parliament on 26 December 1995 amending the Act in order to implement the Investment Services Directive (03/02/EEC) purports to widen its scope to cover not only 'negotiable securities' but also other 'financial instruments' traded on authorised markets in Spain, thus making transactions in futures, options, forward rate agreements, SWAPS etc traded on an authorised market subject to the insider dealing provisions of the Act.

2.2.2 Listed security

The information concerning the security, securities or the issuer itself must be capable of having an impact on its quoted price and, therefore, by implication the security has to be listed. The Act does not contain any reference as to whether the relevant securities must be listed on a Spanish market.

In principle, the Act regulates the primary and authorised secondary markets in Spain and applies (see 2.7 *below*) to any security issued, negotiated or marketed in Spain. Therefore, art 81 would seem to apply to the following types of listed securities:

- securities listed on an organised market in Spain, official or otherwise. There are three organised official markets: (a) the Spanish stock exchanges (there are four: Madrid, Barcelona, Bilbao and Valencia linked in their trading through the computerised trading system); (b) the futures and options market; and (c) the public debt market. There is also an organised non-official market: the wholesale private debt AIAF market;
- securities listed in foreign markets provided the negotiation or transaction in breach of the insider dealing prohibition is performed in Spain.

Article 81, will not, however, apply to securities where listing has been sought but not yet granted. In Spain, listing of newly issued securities is not obtained until after their subscription and payment. Consequently, transactions which occur in respect of those securities will not fall within the prohibition of the Act until after listing. Accordingly, grey market-trading stabilisation which takes place before listing will not be covered although it will be if the stabilisation takes place in respect of a secondary offer.

2.3 WHAT IS INSIDE INFORMATION?

Article 81 states that inside information must be information which:

- is relevant,
- specific,
- has not been made public; and
- is price-sensitive.

2.3.1 Relevant

Information will only be regarded as inside information if it relates to an issuer or issuers of securities or the listed securities themselves. Therefore, the following would fall within the definition of relevant information under art 81:

- information which relates to a number of related issuers and affects the quotation of one or all of the issuers' listed securities. This could be the case if the information related to an economic sector, a specific trading organisation or group of controlled companies;
- information regarding a special bonus payable on a particular bond issue listed in the market even though the issuer's share capital remains unlisted.

However, the following examples would fall outside the scope of the Act because the relevant circumstances would not relate to a listed issuer or its quoted securities:

- Information regarding a particular issuer without any listed securities of its own but which has an effect on the quoted price of its listed subsidiaries. In Spain some listed companies are controlled by the state, its agencies or regional authorities or indirectly through unlisted holding companies. In these circumstances, it has not yet been tested whether the CNMV or the courts would use the far-reaching concept of group of companies of 'relevant information' to include that relating to the unlisted parent company of a listed company.

- Adverse information regarding an issuer, (say, for example, a default in interest payments on a bond issue, or a reduction in nominal value to compensate losses) having an effect on the quoted price of the shares of a competitor in the market in this case, the information is not relevant in so far as it relates to the competitor in the market, even if the information has the effect of moving its share price.

2.3.2 Specific

It is interesting to note that the Act, prior to its amendment in 1991 to implement the Directive, already incorporated the term 'specific' as opposed to the term 'precise' used in the Directive and such term was not incorporated to Spanish law. This is probably because the phrases have a similar meaning in Spanish.

The term 'specific' would cover any information that is self-standing, sufficient in its terms and determined enough to be capable of having a significant effect on the quoted price of the relevant securities. The information, therefore, will meet the following requirements if it is to fall within the provisions of art 81;

- the information must not need to be interpreted or assessed by the recipient of the information in order to be capable of affecting the listed price of a particular security or securities;
- the information must not be vague so as to constitute mere expectations or opinions;
- the information must not need to be put in the context of other information or otherwise combined with any other data, whether public or not, to be susceptible of affecting the listed price of a particular security.

Therefore, and in normal circumstances, notice that a significant joint venture agreement is to be reached with a major competitor may not be 'precise' (in the English sense of the word) because it does not include any reference as to the contents of the proposed agreement, but it would probably fall within the scope of a 'specific' information.

An example of information not being sufficiently specific would be the disclosure by an issuer that it was able to obtain raw material at a particular price, if such information, for the purposes of being specific, needed to be put in the context, say, of an excessive increase in the prices of raw materials not affecting the particular issuer because of the existence of a long-term contract with a supplier at cheaper rates.

2.3.3 Made public

Information is not capable of being inside information if it has been made public. This is a question that will need to be assessed on a case-by-case basis by the CNMV at the time of investigating an alleged breach of the prohibition and ultimately, by the courts.

No guidelines are included in the Act or its secondary legislation to determine when the information is deemed to be 'public' and therefore incapable of being rendered as inside information. Specifically, the Act does not consider whether the term 'public' will cover members of the public or just the professional participants in the securities market.

One of the objectives of the Act is to encourage transparent price fixing in the securities markets, whilst ensuring that information regarding issuers and securities was available without restriction to the market. For these purposes, the Act entrusted the CNMV with the obligation of receiving and publishing information mandatorily delivered by listed issuers of securities, in the following ways:

- distributing the information to all market participants through computerised systems; and/or
- registering the original document used to deliver the information to the CNMV and making it accessible to the public.

Accordingly, information mandatorily delivered to the CNMV by listed issuers and subsequently released to market participants and the public by the CNMV will not constitute inside information. The information which is required to be delivered will cover:

- information disclosed in the context of a public offer of securities in the form of a prospectus registered with the CNMV;
- information contained in the quarterly and half-yearly reports filed by listed issuers with the CNMV;
- certain off-market transactions in listed securities publicly disclosed in the market;
- significant participations held in listed securities;
- events and circumstances that may have a 'sensitive effect' (as defined) in the quoted price of a security.

Although disclosure to the CNMV is the principal manner in which information can be made public, other general principles of Spanish law still apply. For example, information which is contained in public registries such as the *property and commercial registries* will in all cases be deemed public.

It can be concluded that for the purposes of information to be considered public under art 81, it will need to be accessible to the public in general either directly or indirectly through the CNMV. Information which is disclosed to a limited number of participants, even if those participants constitute all the relevant market professionals, will not be treated as public and may, therefore, be treated as inside information.

2.3.4 Price-sensitive information

If information is to be treated as inside information it must, if made public, be capable of influencing significantly the listed price of the relevant security or securities.

A 5 per cent movement in the price of a security would probably be treated as 'significant' for the purpose of the Act. The Act, as developed by secondary legislation, allows for certain off-market transactions to be carried out outside normal trading hours provided certain conditions of volume of the relevant trade and price are complied with. Specifically, regulations only allow in limited circumstances, and provided an authorisation is previously obtained from the regulatory authorities, trades to be completed off-market when the price exceeds or is less than the closing price on that session and the average price of that session by 5 per cent or more.

In addition to the above, the CNMV may consider that any decision or event triggering the obligation of a particular issuer to make a public announcement (see 2.3.3) may, itself, be treated as producing a significant effect in the quoted price of the relevant securities, whatever the actual movement in the share price.

It is worth noting that the Spanish legislator has, in the context of defining issuers' disclosure obligations, determined events that, in our opinion, should be rendered as price-sensitive information for the purposes of art 81. According to art 82, issuers are obliged to inform the public of any event or decision that may have a 'sensitive influence' in the quoted price of the listed securities. This general principle has been developed by Circular 2/1993 of 3 March of the Madrid Stock Exchange and covers the following events and decisions that need to be disclosed to the regulatory bodies of the securities markets and are considered to be susceptible of affecting the price of a listed security:

- rights issues, increases and reductions in share capital;
- dissolution, liquidation, winding up;
- mergers, acquisitions, public take-overs;
- changes in the articles of association;
- changes in the members of the board of directors;
- suspension of payments, bankruptcy;
- dividend payments;
- strategic agreements with third parties;
- litigation that may have a significant effect on the financial position of the issuer;
- change in the accounting principles of the issuer.

2.4 WHO IS AN INSIDER?

According to art 81, anyone holding inside information is precluded from dealing, encouraging dealing or disclosing the information to a third party. Spanish law, unlike the Directive, does not define an insider by reference to the manner in which the information has been obtained. Accordingly, it is not necessary for the CNMV to show in any proceedings that the information was obtained by virtue of the insider's position within the company, or, in the case of secondary insiders, that the source of the information was an insider. All that is required is to show that the person was 'in possession of' inside information.

However, as a general principle of Spanish administrative law for an individual or entity to be sanctioned for an alleged breach of a prohibitory rule, he must have acted knowingly or without due care.

Therefore, if the alleged insider did not know and would not have known if he had exercised reasonable care that the relevant information was inside information then he will not be liable under art 81.

Whether an individual should have known that information was inside information capable of affecting the quoted price of a particular security, will be related to a person's business acumen and experience. Accordingly, the duty of care will be higher if the alleged insider is a market professional and lower if the individual is not so experienced.

Problem Area 1

A neighbour of a professional broker employed as a financial executive by a listed company overhears a telephone conversation in the next door garden relating to the financial difficulties of that company. The neighbour, because he knows or should reasonably have known that the information was price-sensitive is an insider.

A taxi driver overhears a conversation of two passengers in the taxi relating to the same financial difficulties faced by the same issuer and which will appear in the next half-yearly report to be submitted to the CNMV. That night the taxi driver tells his friends about the conversation. The taxi driver would probably not be considered as an insider since, if he did not know the identity of his passengers, his duty of care should not oblige him to check that the information is publicly available and that it can affect the quoted price of the security.

2.5 WHAT ARE THE OFFENCES?

Article 81 of the Act creates three different offences which are considered in turn.

2.5.1 Prepare a deal

It is an offence by virtue of art 81 for an insider to prepare or perform a transaction on the market in relation to the securities to which the inside information relates.

The offence covers preparatory actions to a subsequent deal based on inside information. This would cover the following transactions:

- any contact made by the insider to his broker with the aim of giving the necessary instructions so as to implement a particular transaction to which the inside information relates;
- carrying out a transaction in the market with the objective of preparing for a deal in respect of the securities affected by the inside information (eg purchasing the securities at market price when they are to be the target of a take-over);
- obtaining financial assistance (eg a loan) necessary to carry out the deal in relation to the affected securities.

It is fair to say, however, that only in exceptional circumstances, will preparatory activities for a subsequent deal be, in practice, investigated and sanctioned. Usually, preparatory conduct will not be revealed as falling within the prohibition unless the subsequent deal is carried out, since it is only that subsequent transaction which will trigger the supervisory mechanisms of the market in the hands of the CNMV. Nevertheless, the fact that preparatory conduct falls within the offence will serve as the basis for *bona fide* third parties involved in the preparatory dealings to claim the nullity of any such dealings and the compensation for any damages incurred (see 2.9 *below*).

It is worth noting that the offence relating to the preparation of transactions in respect of the affected securities is not included in the Directive and is therefore a further example of the widened scope of the prohibition introduced by the legislator.

TABLE (1)

Constituent elements for preparatory conduct offence:
- The offender has information which he knew or ought to have known was inside information;
- The information must be likely to have a significant effect on the price of the securities;
- The offender has carried out preparatory actions for a deal in the securities (as defined) to be performed; it is irrelevant whether such transaction takes place or not.

Note: The source of the information obtained by the offender is not relevant.

2.5.2 Dealing in the relevant securities

Article 81 precludes an insider carrying out a transaction in the market in respect of the securities to which the inside information relates.

The Act regulates transactions carried out in the authorised Spanish markets referred to in 2.2.2. For these purposes, a transaction is defined by art 36, as a sale and purchase in an authorised market. The Act requires the mandatory intervention of a market member for any sale and purchase on the market to be valid and enforceable; failure to do so will mean the transaction is null and void. The Act does allow, with certain restrictions, off-market transactions to be carried out provided a market member is ultimately involved or informed of any such transaction taking place. Accordingly, the prohibition contained in the Act as regards dealing with securities to which inside information refers would seem to cover all sale and purchase transactions carried out in the Spanish authorised markets (whether official or not), including off-market sales and purchases, which, in accordance with current regulations, need to be ultimately notified and transacted through a member of the market. Arguably, the Act would not seem to cover other dealings in the market such as stock lending and pledging of securities.

TABLE (2)

Constituent elements of the dealing offence: • the offender has information which he knows or ought to have known is inside information; • the inside information must be likely to have a significant effect on the price of the securities dealt in; • the offender must have carried out a sale and purchase transaction which is required to be carried out through a market member. **Note:** The source of the information obtained by the offender is not relevant.

Examples of transactions that would be caught within the prohibition would include:

* private sale and purchase agreements in respect of securities entered into off-market and which will need to be transacted through a market member in order to be valid and enforceable by the parties;
* the entry into an option or futures agreement over the counter will not involve a transaction since there will be no purchase or sale of a security in an authorised market (such as the futures and options market) (see 2.2.2). However, the exercise of options giving the right to the physical delivery of the underlying security will give rise to a dealing at the time of carrying out the relevant sale and purchase.

However, derivative transactions which do not involve, at the time of exercise, the transfer of title over the relevant securities, including contracts for differences, would not be so covered. Nor would gifts of securities be covered.

2.5.3 Disclosure of information

The Act makes it an offence of anyone to release inside information to any third party save in the normal course of their employment, profession or post.

In principle, any act of transmitting inside information will be caught within the prohibition and therefore it will be irrelevant:

(1) whether the information is released to a single individual or a group of people;
(2) if there is some form of connection (family ties, professional, etc), save as described below, between the alleged offender and the recipient of the information;
(3) the means through which the information is disclosed (in writing or orally); and
(4) whether the information is used or not for the purposes of carrying out a transaction in the market in respect of the affected securities, although in this case and as explained in 2.5.1 *above*, the offender will in practice hardly ever be prosecuted.

TABLE (3)

> *Duty of confidentiality*
> In addition to the disclosure offence, art 81(1) imposes specific obligations (ie not necessarily inside information) regarding the treatment of information of the securities markets by the following individuals or entities; (1) those operating in the securities markets or carrying out activities in respect thereof, and (2) individuals that due to their employment, profession or post have had access to such information. Anyone falling within the above is obliged to:
> • keep confidential all information and prevent it being disclosed to third parties save in the context of an administrative or judicial proceeding;
> • prevent the unlawful use of such data or information;
> • notify any such use it becomes aware of; and
> • take immediate steps to avoid, prevent and eventually correct the consequences of any such actions.

The duty imposed on issuers, market participants and individuals having access to information due to their employment or post, forms part of the implementation in Spain of the Directive. On the one hand, the Spanish legislator has limited the use of inside information regardless of its source, and on the other, it has imposed on those sources of information covered by the Directive an all-embracing duty of confidentiality. The scope of the prohibition on disclosing inside information is wider than the obligation of confidentiality since it is imposed on anyone holding such information irrespective of the activities carried out by the entity in question or the source of the information. However, the duty of confidentiality under art 81(1) is wider than the insider dealing offence in that *all* information regarding the securities markets, irrespective of its specificness or relevance is caught within the duty of secrecy.

The offence of disclosure of inside information will not be committed if the disclosure is made in the normal course of employment and, accordingly, no offence will be committed where:

- any disclosure is made in the context of assisting any administrative or judicial proceeding initiated by a court or regulatory authority of the securities markets;
- any disclosure made within the organisation in which the individual operates carried out in compliance with its particular code of conduct or that imposed by the regulators of the market (for example, the Madrid Stock Exchange by virtue of Circular 7/1993 of 30 November imposes on its members the obligation to make internal disclosure of the inside information (whether such information relates to that particular company or another) gathered in the exercise of their duties to an appropriate member of senior management) with the aim of precluding the information being improperly used. The prohibition on the disclosure of information also applies when breaching 'Chinese Walls' within an organisation.

TABLE (4)

Constituent elements for the disclosure offence: • the offender has information which he knows or should have known in the circumstances that it is inside information; • the information must be likely to have a significant effect on the listed price of the security; • the alleged offender must have disclosed in whatever manner to any third party the inside information, other than in the context of a profession, employment or post. The disclosure of inside information to a third party converts it into an insider and thus subject to the prohibitions contained in art 81.

2.5.4 Encourage dealing

The Act prohibits a person with inside information recommending a third party to purchase or sell or to procure another third party to acquire or sell the relevant securities based on such information.

The offence is committed irrespective of whether or not the third party actually deals in the listed securities. As explained above, it will be evidentially difficult to establish that an offence has been committed if no actual transaction is carried out.

The offence will have its principal application in circumstances upon which the inside information is not disclosed directly to the third party, but rather such party is persuaded to enter into a particular transaction (or, in turn, procures a third party enter into it) based on the existence of the information known to the insider.

TABLE (5)

Constituent elements of the encouragement offence:
- the alleged offender has information which he knows or should have known in the circumstances that it is inside information;
- the inside information must be likely to have a significant effect on the quoted price of the security;
- the offender recommends a third party, in light of the inside information gathered, either to carry out a particular transaction or to make another party carry out such sale and purchase in respect of the affected securities.

Examples of situations that would fall within the prohibition would include:
- a broker holding inside information regarding poor forecasts of a listed company obtained through an informal meeting with that company recommends certain of its best clients to disinvest in the company without disclosing the reason for such recommendation;
- a director in a listed company holding information about an important alliance agreement with a competitor not yet made public in the market, recommends a stock broker to induce clients to buy shares in the company.

In this case, as opposed to the provisions in 2.5.3 *above*, the third party receiving the recommendations may not become an insider if such recommendation did not include the disclosure of the inside information and thus, the transaction performed by the recipient of the recommendation will not be in breach of art 81.

2.6 WHO CAN BE PROSECUTED?

The legal position can be summarised as follows:

- An individual who commits an offence in contravention of the Act will be personally liable.
- As an exception to the principle set out in the point above, if the individual carries out the activity in breach of the Act in the course of his employ-

ment with a legal entity acting in its name and on its behalf, the legal entity will be rendered responsible for the actions of its employee. Conversely, if the employee carried out the prohibited conduct not in the course of its employment but rather in his own name and behalf, no such liability will arise against the employer.

- Similarly, if an individual is acting as an agent or representative on behalf of a legal entity, the entity will be liable for the conduct of its agent. It is irrelevant whether the individual is acting as nominee for the legal entity, that is, in his own name but on behalf of the represented entity, or in the name and on behalf of the entity itself.

- When a legal entity is held liable for the alleged conduct in breach of art 81, it is possible that such liability may also be extended to the following:
  —board members;
  —managing directors;
  —director generals holding full powers in the entity only subject to the instructions and decisions of the board;

  provided the breach of art 81 may be imputed to some wilful conduct or act of negligence taken by them.

- The liability of board members will be joint and several unless any one of them may prove that (1) he did not attend the meeting that took the decision in breach, for a justifiable reason; (2) he voted against the relevant resolution; or (3) he did not vote stressing his opposition in respect of the resolution that led to the conduct in breach of art 81.

2.7 WHAT IS THE TERRITORIAL SCOPE OF THE ACT?

Article 81 does not include any reference to its territorial scope. However, this may be inferred from the general principles contained in the Act regarding its scope, namely:

(1) The Act regulates the primary market (issue) of negotiable securities and the secondary authorised markets (see 2.2 *above*) in Spain. In addition, under art 3 of the Act, the negotiation and marketing of securities in the Spanish territory is subject to the provisions of the Act. Therefore, (a) actions and conduct relating to securities listed in an authorised market in Spain will be capable of falling within art 81 and the supervisory role of the CNMV; and (b) transactions and negotiations carried out in Spain in respect of securities listed in a foreign market will also be capable of falling within art 81.

(2) Article 81 entrusts the CNMV with the overall supervision of investment services firms, namely, securities companies ('*sociedades de valores*') and securities agencies ('*agencias de valores*'). Although not yet tested by the CNMV or the courts, it could be argued that all activities carried out by such entities irrespective of their place of performance will be subject to art 81 and the supervisory role of the CNMV. That conclusion is supported by the

extra-territorial scope of the rules of conduct imposed on such entities by virtue of Royal Decree 629/1993 of 3 May.

In relation to the possible extra-territorial effect of the prohibition contained in art 81, it is necessary to remember the ability of CNMV to enter into co-operative arrangements with other regulatory authorities that may allow it to investigate conduct carried out abroad but with relevance to the Spanish securities markets. Although most of such agreements do not qualify as international treaties and are not binding on the parties to them, they may prove, in the future, to be a successful measure to control international transactions.

2.8 WHAT ARE THE DEFENCES?

Notwithstanding the wide scope of the offences contained in art 81, no defence to such offences are expressly included. It is interesting to note that the Directive does include certain exemptions to the prohibition to deal or disclose inside information. Those would include, transactions by market makers in the ordinary course of their activities, stabilisation transactions and transactions carried out by central or regional governments in respect of their public debt.

The Spanish legislation has not incorporated any of those defences or exemptions in its regulation of the insider dealing offence, and has thus taken advantage of art 6 of the Directive which allows member states to include a stricter regime to that envisaged under the Directive.

2.9 WHAT ARE THE PENALTIES AND CONSEQUENCES OF INSIDER DEALING?

Article 99 of the Act defines any breach of the prohibition contained in art 81 as regards the unlawful use of inside information as a 'very serious offence'. In addition, art 102 et seq of the Act, as modified by Law 3/1994 of 14 April provides for the following sanctions for those who act in breach of art 81:

(1) a fine of not less than the profit obtained from the prohibited conduct, and up to five times that profit, or, in the event that such criteria may not be applicable, the highest of the following:
(a) 5 per cent of the funds of the offender;
(b) 5 per cent of the funds used to commit the offence;
(c) 50 million pesetas (approximately £250,000 STG);
such a fine being, in all cases, not less than 5 million pesetas (approximately £25,000 STG); and one or more of the following depending upon the particular circumstances of the offender;
(2) suspension or limitation in the type or volume of transactions that the offender may be entitled to transact in the Spanish securities market for a term of up to five years;

(3) suspension as a member of an official secondary market for a term of up to five years;

(4) withdrawal of the authorisation as a securities company ('*sociedad de valores*'), securities agency ('*agencia de valores*'), portfolio management company ('*sociedad gestora de cartera*') or member of the public debt market ('*entidad gestora del Mercado de Deuda Pública en Anotaciones*').

TABLE (6)

Factors taken into account by the court in determining the amount of any sanction pursuant to Law 26/1988 of 29 July of Discipline and Intervention of Credit Entities and Law 30/1992 of 26 November on the Legal Regime of the Public Administration:

• the nature and entity of the offence;

• the degree of danger or damage caused by the offender;

• the profits obtained by the offender;

• the financial credibility of the offender taking into account its balance sheet;

• the negative impact of the prohibited conduct for the financial system and the national economy;

• the fact that measures were taken to correct the prohibited conduct;

• the previous conduct of the offender with regard to the rules of conduct in the securities market, taking into account final sanctions imposed on the offender during the last five years;

• the existence of knowledge or willingness in the commission of the offence (in our case, knowledge of the nature of the inside information);

• the fact that the offender has committed similar offences in the last year;

• the nature of the damage caused.

In addition to the above, and when the offence is committed by a legal entity rather than an individual, art 105 provides that the following sanctions may be imposed on the administrators, members of the board of directors or similar managing body, or Directors General or associates (including within such definition an individual carrying out management functions under the direct control of the relevant administrator, board of directors, executive committee or managing directors) responsible for the offence:

• a fine equal to the higher of; (a) 5 per cent of the funds used to carry out the offence or (b) 50 million pesetas (approximately £250,000 STG). and one of the following sanctions:

• suspension from office for a term not exceeding three years;

• removal from office and disqualification from holding managerial or executive office in the relevant entity for a period not exceeding five years;

• removal from office and disqualification from holding managerial or executive office in any financial institution of a similar nature for a term not exceeding ten years.

TABLE (7)

Factors taken into account for the purposes of determining the sanction to be imposed on the relevant administrator, member of the board or director pursuant to Law 26/1988 on Discipline and Intervention of Credit Entities and Law 30/1992 on the Legal Regime of the Public Administration: • the individual's degree of responsibility in the committal of the offence; • the individual's previous conduct in the same or another entity in relation to compliance with 'market rules', taking into consideration final sanctions imposed during the past five years; • the nature of the office that the offender holds; • those matters referred to in Table (6).

Finally, and as regards securities companies ('*sociedades de valores*'), securities agencies ('*agencias de valores*') and member of any of the Spanish official secondary markets, if due to the number of sanctions imposed or the identity of the administrators, members of the board or directors sanctioned, the continuation of the administration of the legal entity is prejudiced, the Ministry of Economy and Finance is entitled to name provisional administrators, members of the board, or directors, as the case may be. The legal entity would still be entitled to replace such provisional administrators as soon as the relevant body could pass the necessary resolutions to appoint new officers in accordance with the law and its statutes.

The Act does not consider any legal consequence for the transaction carried out by the insider in breach of the prohibition contained in art 81 and therefore the general principles of civil law will apply. Accordingly, under art 6 of the Civil Code, the transaction entered into in breach of a prohibitory provision like art 81 will be rendered null, void and with no effect. As a consequence, the *bona fide* party to the transaction will be entitled to request the return of any consideration given to the offender and claim for any damage incurred.

3 CRIMINAL LAW

Organic Law 9/1991 of 22 March which came into force on 28 March 1991 amended the existing Spanish Penal Code and incorporated for the first time in Spain a criminal offence for the unlawful use of inside information.

According to art 368 of the Penal Code, the civil servant who through the use of confidential information obtained in the course of this employment or inside information, obtained a profit for his own benefit or that of a third party, will be punished with disqualification and a fine equal the amount of the profit obtained. If the damage caused to the public or a third party was serious in nature, the offender can be punished with disqualification and imprisonment from six months and one day up to six years.

4 NEW CRIMINAL CODE

On 23 November 1995 a new Penal Code was enacted by the Spanish Parliament which comes into effect on 24 May 1996 covering for the first time in Spanish law the offence of insider dealing. Article 285 of the new Penal Code prohibits any individual with information relevant for the quoted price of negotiable securities or instruments listed on an organised market whether official or recognised, obtained confidentially in the course of his professional activities or business, from:

- using the information himself or through a third party;
- disclosing the information;

in either case with the intention of obtaining a benefit or causing a loss to another party of at least 75 million pesetas (approximately £375,000 STG).

The offence is punished with imprisonment of one to four years and a fine equal to or up to three times the benefit obtained.

Article 286 of the new Penal Code contemplates a higher penalty including imprisonment of four to six years and a fine of up to 36 million pesetas (approximately £180,000 STG) if:

- the individual carries out such activities habitually; or
- the profit obtained is of special relevance; or
- substantial damage is caused to the general interest.

The other main features of the new Penal Code are:

(1) the new Penal Code covers information relating not only to negotiable securities but also to other negotiable instruments listed in the organised or official markets, consistent with the proposed amendment of the Act following the implementation of the Investment Services Directive;

(2) no definition is included as to what 'relevant information' for the quoted price of the security or instrument means. The term is drafted extremely widely since almost all information may be relevant for the quoted price of a security or instrument. A similar qualification to that contained in art 81 and the Directive should have been introduced so that only information which is relevant, specific and may significantly affect the quoted price would be caught within its scope;

(3) there are no exemptions available such as the relevant information being already in the public domain or having been released to the relevant regulatory authorities;

(4) only information to which the offender has had confidential access due to his profession or business is caught within the prohibition, and so is more restrictive than art 81;

(5) all transactions concerning the affected securities or instruments as well as 'any use' made of such information by the offender will be caught;

(6) the offence is drafted in a manner that allows only wilful conduct (ie knowledge of the nature of the information) to be punishable. Negligent conduct capable of falling within the provisions of art 81 may not be caught under the terms of the new Penal Code;

(7) due to the different definitions of inside and relevant information in the Act and the new Penal Code, and the different types of offences, it is possible that:

    (a) in certain circumstances an offence that falls within the definition of the criminal offence but not reaching the 75 million pesetas threshold may not be punishable under art 81: information/transactions related to financial instruments not being negotiable securities (until the amendment of the Act) or any transaction over the securities carried on off-market (eg over the counter options/futures); and

    (b) vice versa, certain conduct punishable under the Act will not be regarded as a criminal offence even if the 75 million pesetas threshold is exceeded: prohibited actions performed pursuant to inside information not obtained confidentially in the course of professional activities or business.

(8) the incorporation of a new criminal offence regarding the unlawful use of reserved as opposed to inside information by individuals or legal entities, opens the way to third parties not directly involved in the prohibited conduct to be rendered responsible (collaborators and accomplices) and for tentative and frustrated criminal activities to fall within the prohibition.

The existing Spanish Penal Code and the new Penal Code in general terms, consider responsible for a particular conduct; (1) that individual or legal entity which takes part directly in the execution or performance of the relevant conduct; (2) the individual or entity which procures or induces a third party to perform the prohibited conduct; (3) those who co-operate in the performance of the transaction without whom no offence would have been committed.

Finally, it is worth noting that under the new Penal Code directors or representatives/policyholders of individuals or legal entities will be personally liable for a criminal offence, notwithstanding the fact that they do not personally fulfil the criteria to be an offender under the terms of the Code, if all such criteria have been fulfilled by the individual or legal entity on whose behalf they have committed an offence.

5 CONCLUSION

Since the enactment of the Act in 1988, the CNMV has proved an efficient regulator entrusted with the supervision of the Spanish securities market. It supervises the newly created market members (securities companies and agencies) and has designed a complete set of rules of conduct for market participants. However, it is true that since 1988, few administrative proceedings have been commenced by the CNMV dealing with the alleged committal of insider dealing offences. The CNMV face difficulties in obtaining evidence necessary to establish that an offence has been committed.

Notwithstanding this, recent financial scandals have focused public opinion on the issue of insider dealing which has led to the 1994 amendment of the Act imposing higher penalties and fines on offenders of the securities markets rules of conduct. This has also influenced the new Penal Code to come into force shortly which for the first time has included, although in excessively wide terms, insider dealing as a criminal offence. The future will tell whether the criminalisation of the insider dealing offence will increase the number of investigations and proceedings commenced, or even more relevant, the number of prosecutions achieved.

CASE STUDY

Splash España SA, a company listed on the Spanish stock exchanges, manufactures rainwear and umbrellas. Alan, a weather forecaster, on discovering that there is an unseasonable amount of rain due in the next three months, instructs his broker to buy shares in Splash. Meanwhile, Charles an analyst of the company's shares, is told in a conversation with Jeremy, one of the directors, that a new contract has been signed with a customer to produce umbrellas for it over the next two years which will absorb the production of the London factory. Charles revises his profit forecast for the company but before he publishes it he cancels instructions which he had previously given to his broker to sell his Splash shares. Charles also tells his girlfriend, Maggie, that 'things are looking up' for Splash and that she 'should buy shares in Splash'. Maggie then buys shares in the name of her father from an old friend of theirs who wanted to sell Splash shares and advises Peter, her brother, that he should buy shares in Splash España SA. In addition, Owen, a employee of the contracting firm which cleans Splash's offices, finds a draft of the latest management figures, to be incorporated in the next quarterly report to be presented to the CNMV, which demonstrate Splash's high profitability, in a wastepaper bin. He immediately buys shares.

Alan
Alan would not be made an insider under art 81 of the Act and would not therefore break the insider dealing prohibition by purchasing shares in Splash. The meteorological information he has gathered does not refer to particular listed securities or their issuers, and even if a connection with umbrella manufacturers was deemed to exist, the information may not be rendered specific if interpreted as being scientific expectations lacking the necessary degree of certainty. In addition, the information could very well be rendered as not capable of affecting significantly the price of the shares of Splash in the Spanish stock exchanges.

Charles

Charles is an insider under art 81 of the Act. He holds information which is relevant to Splash, specific, price sensitive and, in principle, not public. However, the information may have been disclosed by the management of Splash to the CNMV in compliance with its duty to disclose any event that may affect considerably the quoted price of Splash's shares and, in particular, any strategic alliance, as provided by Circular 2/1993 of the Madrid Stock Exchange. In that case, and notwithstanding the fact that such information may not have reached the public, the information would not be considered to be inside information.

Assuming that Charles is an insider, he would not have committed an offence under the Act by cancelling the instruction previously rendered to his broker to sell his shares in Splash.

Notwithstanding the above, Charles would have breached the prohibition of encouraging dealings in the securities affected by the inside information by advising his girlfriend to buy shares in Splash. No such offence would have occurred if he had limited himself to state that 'things are looking up' for Splash since he would not be disclosing inside information, preparing a deal, dealing or encouraging to deal.

Jeremy

Jeremy is an insider under art 81 of the Act holding information that is relevant to Splash, specific, price sensitive and not in the public domain, unless already disclosed to the CNMV as provided for under the previous paragraph. Jeremy has breached the insider dealing provisions by disclosing the information to Charles. He knew or ought to have known that the information was specific, price-sensitive, and not in the public domain.

Maggie

Maggie cannot be rendered as an insider since she has not received any inside information regarding Splash. She has only benefited from a recommendation to buy shares in Splash. Therefore, any other subsequent actions, whether buying shares in Splash or encouraging her brother Peter to buy shares in the company do not constitute a breach of the insider dealing offence under art 81 of the Act.

Owen

Owen is an insider since he is holding specific, price-sensitive information regarding Splash, which is not available to the public since it has not yet been delivered to the CNMV. In addition, he has committed an offence by purchasing shares in Splash. He could argue that he did not know and was under no duty to know that the information was inside information. However, his subsequent action, purchasing immediately the shares and the nature of the information, limit the strength of his argument.

Switzerland

Dr Michel Haymann, Haymann & Baldi, Zurich

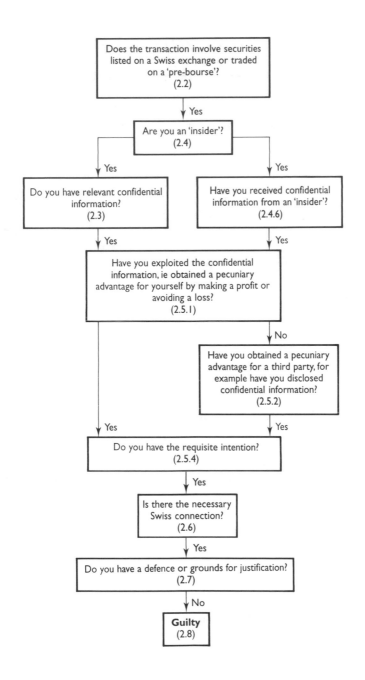

1 INTRODUCTION

Insider dealing was made a criminal offence in Switzerland with effect from 1 July 1988, by the introduction of art 161 to the Penal Code ('PC'). During the course of the discussions surrounding enactment of the article, the question was raised whether the issue of insider dealing could be addressed in a satisfactory manner without adequate legislation on the supervision of stock exchange transactions. To date, there is no stock exchange law which governs Switzerland as a whole. The stock exchanges and trading with securities are governed by cantonal laws, of which the most important are those of Zurich, Geneva and Basle. This cantonal legislation does not contain any rules on insider dealing that would complement the provisions introduced in the PC. A Federal Stock Exchange Act is at present in the process of being enacted and expected to come into effect in the course of 1996. Consequently, the criminal legislation enacted in 1988 to combat insider dealing is incomplete.

Furthermore, the insider dealing law is not ultimately based on a Swiss tradition of law. This legislation was introduced as a result of pressure from the United States—the Stock Exchange Commission ('SEC') had become frustrated that it was unable to seek judicial assistance from Switzerland in respect of cases of alleged insider dealing since there was no comparable offence in Switzerland. Direct economic pressure was brought to bear by the SEC, taking out injunctive relief against assets held by the Swiss banks concerned in the United States and imposing coercive measures against such banks in order to compel them to disclose information relating to the banks' clients under investigation, which would have amounted to a breach of Swiss secrecy rules.

Swiss insider dealing legislation, therefore, primarily served the purpose of enabling the Swiss authorities to grant judicial assistance in connection with insider dealing transactions investigated by the SEC. It was developed in connection with foreign securities transactions and therefore bears the mark of a *lex americana*. It has no basis in the domestic legal tradition. The often repeated criticism voiced during the legislative process of art 161 of the PC that the acts banned by the proposed legislation should not be criminal offences because neither the company concerned nor the 'innocent' third parties are financially harmed, is still widely held.

2 THE CRIMINAL LAW

2.1 INTRODUCTION

The offences caught by art 161 of the PC are described in the marginal title of the law as 'exploitation of the knowledge of confidential information'.

The provision is subdivided into two paragraphs, with the first dealing with the actual insider, the second with a third party who obtains confidential information caught by the provision, ie the tippee. The common denominator for the offence is the obtaining of a pecuniary advantage by the exploitation of confidential information relating to securities. The striking feature of this provision is its brevity and abundant use of undefined general terms. This gives it a potentially wide application, the boundaries of which will have to be determined by case law. No defences are specified in the law. The general principles of criminal law may apply which will allow a defendant to claim, for example, justification as a defence to an insider dealing charge (see 2.7.2).

2.2 TO WHICH SECURITIES DOES ARTICLE 161 OF THE PC APPLY?

2.2.1 Securities listed on an exchange

Swiss insider legislation is only applicable to securities listed on a Swiss exchange or traded on what is called a 'pre-bourse'. The latter is a semi-official market of secondary securities for which requirements for admission to trading are considerably lower than for securities listed on the main market. Insider dealing in Switzerland with securities listed on a foreign exchange is not an offence within the meaning of art 161 of the PC. However, an offence committed abroad may indirectly be caught by art 161 if foreign prosecuting authorities request judicial assistance in criminal matters from the Swiss authorities in respect of elements of the alleged offence which takes place wholly or partly in Switzerland. In order for judicial assistance to be given it is necessary for the principle of 'double incrimination' to be established, ie the offence is punishable both in Switzerland and the relevant overseas jurisdiction.

2.2.2 Categories of securities

The law does not define securities, but lists the following categories:

- shares;
- other negotiable instruments;
- ledger securities of a company;
- options over the above securities.

There is general agreement that the instruments described below fall under the following terms used in art 161 of the PC:

(1) Shares
  (a) *Shares within the meaning of Swiss company law*
      The shares in a company limited by shares within the meaning of company law, ie negotiable instruments with a nominal value representing a part of the share capital of a privately organised company whether in the form of bearer shares of registered shares. Swiss company law has no concept of public companies.
  (b) *Participation and bonus certificates*
      Participation certificates are negotiable instruments with a nominal value

representing part of the equity of a company without conferring voting rights, but giving the owner rights to dividends and to share in any liquidation proceeds. Bonus certificates entitle the holder to certain rights, eg of profits, liquidation proceeds or subscription rights in respect of newly issued shares within the meaning described under para (1) *above*.

(2) *Other negotiable instruments*

    (a) *Debt securities*

The law catches any negotiable instruments representing an acknowledgment of indebtedness to the owner, such as traditional bonds, whether or not combined with options or warrants to subscribe for shares or for negotiable instruments conveying rights to other pecuniary advantages and irrespective of whether or not they are expressed to be interest bearing or issued on a discount basis.

The term 'note' is used in Swiss banking practices and refers to debt instruments placed privately within the banking system and which are not listed. They are, therefore, not subject to the insider dealing legislation.

    (b) *Social parts*

The social parts that may qualify as falling under the law are the social parts of a co-operative. The only practical example are the parts of the Swiss Popular Bank which is organised in the form of a co-operative and listed on the Swiss stock exchanges despite the fact that they are not technically negotiable instruments. Section V of art 161 of the PC therefore expressly includes these securities as falling within the legislation on insider dealing.

    (c) *Participation certificates of funds*

These participation certificates are negotiable instruments without nominal value representing a part of a fund or investment trust that exists as an unincorporated collective investment instrument managed by a depository bank. The term participation certificates of funds includes parts or shares in foreign investment trusts, even if organised in corporate form, provided they are open-ended. The decisive criterion is that the fund management is committed to repurchasing parts at any time.

    (d) *Other securities in general*

The general wording is intended to include any kind of negotiable instrument or social parts that may be developed in future, whether in Switzerland or abroad, that is fit to be listed on an exchange in Switzerland and that represents either a share in the equity of a company or indebtedness.

(3) *Ledger securities*

The term covers any kind of entitlement to securities within the meaning of the law for which no physical document has been issued, but where the entitlement is recorded in ledger form in the register of the issuer and accounted for through a clearing agent or depositary agent.

(4) *Options*

Article 161 of the PC covers any right to purchase, subscribe, sell or convert securities, irrespective of whether such options are issued by the issuer of the securities to which they relate or by a third party, for example, covered warrants. The form of the option is irrelevant. It may exist as an independent right or be linked or attaching to debt securities in the form of warrants. Options as defined in this section must relate to securities. The law therefore does not apply to commodities, currencies or interest rates or indices. However, since the law expressly includes options in the term 'securities', it will apply to options over other options, always provided the latter relate to securities within the meaning of art 161 of the PC.

(5) *Depositary receipts*

The traditional depositary receipts, as commonly used for securities of foreign issues listed on a Swiss exchange, are treated as securities for the purpose of art 161 of the PC.

(6) *Forward and short transactions, derivatives*

Forward and short transactions relating to securities within the meaning of art 161 of the PC are treated like spot sales or purchases of securities and are therefore subject to the law.

However, futures or other contracts for differences relating to securities are not listed on Swiss exchanges and therefore do not fall within art 161 of the PC. The same applies to an increasing number of derivative products relating to combinations of listed securities and commodities (eg precious metals) or currencies, but which themselves are not listed on an exchange in Switzerland, but offered through the banking system. Depending on how the derivatives are structured, they may qualify as options.

2.2.3 Securities within the meaning of article 161

The following securities or financial instruments, even if in the form of negotiable instruments, are not securities within the meaning of art 161 of the PC:

- cash bonds, ie short or medium-term debt instruments issued by a Swiss bank for the purpose of refinance among their clients which are sold by the banks directly to the client and are not listed;
- notes, commercial paper, certificates of deposit, bills of exchange—all of which are normally not listed on a Swiss exchange;
- financial futures;
- warrants (relating to goods in warehouses).

2.3 WHAT IS INSIDE INFORMATION?

Article 161 of the PC requires that for inside information to be relevant the persons to which it applies must have knowledge of:

- confidential facts;

- which facts, if disclosed, will considerably influence the quoted price of securities listed in Switzerland; and
- this effect is foreseeable.

The law does not contain any guidance as to how the general terms used in the law are to be interpreted.

2.3.1 Knowledge of a fact

The knowledge of the insider must relate to a fact which may have already occurred or may in the future occur, such as that relating to anticipated future conduct of the affairs of the company concerned. The relevant fact is not necessarily limited to events relating to internal matters of the relevant enterprise, but may relate to any fact occurring in the environment within which the enterprise operates and which is likely to influence its business prospects and thus, the appreciation of the value of its shares to the public. In addition, the facts to which the information relates must be sufficiently precise and concrete so as to rule out reliance on pure rumour.

The facts must relate to securities of the enterprise with which the potential offender is related. This is a result of the definition of the persons that qualify as insiders within the meaning of art 161, s 1 of the PC which will be dealt within in greater detail in 2.4 *below*.

2.3.2 Facts consisting of an imminent issue of new participation rights, a combination of enterprises or a similar set of facts of comparable importance

Where a fact relates to a planned amalgamation of two enterprises the wording of art 161, s 1 would only allow prosecution of a director of one of the participants if he exploited the knowledge of facts relating to his company, but not if he engaged in insider dealing with securities of the other company. To prohibit such activity, s 3 of art 161 of the PC now defines as 'facts' within the meaning of ss 1 and 2 an imminent issue of new participation rights, a combination of enterprises or a similar set of facts of comparable importance in order to catch the dealing in securities with the stock of either of the companies involved in a planned amalgamation. A fact relating to a joint venture plan is also covered under s 1 provided that the other requirements of s 3 are met. Article 164, s 4 provides that ss 1 to 3 of art 164 are applicable to both companies.

It should be noted that the wording of the law excludes the imminent issue of debt instruments. Facts relevant for the purposes of art 161, s 3 of the PC are limited to securities giving the owner a right to a participation, ie shares, participation certificates and bonus certificates. The issues that qualify as relevant must therefore directly affect the equity of the issuer. However, convertible bonds or bonds linked with options or warrants are likely to also qualify. It is also not inconceivable that a massive bond issue may be interpreted to be indicative of an imminent take-over and possibly be caught by the general clause added to s 3 and characterised as 'a similar set of facts of comparable importance'.

The term combination of enterprises is used in an untechnical sense. It certainly encompasses mergers as well as acquisitions irrespective of how they are legally effected. The French and Italian text of the law uses the term 'a regrouping of enterprises', thus allowing this element of the offence to be interpreted so as to encompass sales and divestitures.

The general term 'similar set of facts of comparable importance' has generally been held by authorities and other commentators to encompass any circumstances which aim at or result in fundamental changes in the structure of an enterprise or which relates to a material change of control or matters which affect its profitability. To date, this section has not been interpreted by the Swiss courts. However, within the context of a decision of the Federal Court of Switzerland relating to proceedings for judicial assistance in criminal matters under the Swiss-American Treaty, the Swiss Supreme Court has narrowed the scope of applicability of this section to sets of facts similar to the issue of new participation rights and combinations of enterprises. Structural changes and material influence on the control of profitability of an enterprise will therefore only be caught by art 161, s 3 of the PC relating to the combination of enterprises or the issue of participation rights.

2.3.3 Confidential nature of the relevant fact

Any fact that is publicly known cannot constitute confidential information. The confidential nature of the fact is a central element of the offence. This is also illustrated by the circle of persons that are characterised as insiders in art 161, s 1 of the PC which all hold a privileged position within or in relation to the company concerned (see 2.4 *below*). Again, the law does not define or indicate how confidentiality is to be interpreted.

It is generally understood that any kind of published or publicly accessible information is not confidential for the purposes of insider dealing. Thus, the portfolio manager employed by a bank that by experience is able to predict the price of a stock by charting its historical price movement does not have confidential information, when his analysis tells him a large price movement is expected, but is only familiar with certain patterns of behaviour on the markets. Similarly, the financial analyst who uses his expert knowledge of the market to draw conclusions from publicly available information, will not be guilty of insider dealing. The situation would be different if the information obtained by a financial analyst was not readily available, but restricted to top management and given in confidence to him prior to being made public.

Expectations as to future developments of a company expressed by an executive or director are unlikely to be regarded as a fact. Precise indication of an event of material importance for the business revealed prior to its being made officially public, however, will be treated as inside information.

Problem Area 1

Hans, a securities dealer employed by Credit Suisse and Fritz, a securities dealer employed by BZ-Bank, agree to jointly purchase a significant number of Credit Suisse shares. The day after, Credit Suisse publicly announce an important restructuring of the CS Group which results in a sharp increase of the quoted price of their stock. The planned restructuring of the CS Group had been discussed at an internal employees meeting of the bank CS Group organised for persons that were not insiders. Simultaneously, recommendations to buy CS stock had been given by the chief options dealer of the BZ-Bank to fellow employees on the basis of his observations of the market. Hans and Fritz, were acquitted from the charge of insider dealing on grounds that the analysis of the developments on the stock exchange by the chief options dealer of the bank did not constitute knowledge of confidential facts. They were found to have based their dealings on recommendations of a person that had drawn the right conclusions. [24 March 1993, Federal Court of Switzerland, March 1993].

Directors and executives of a company are in a particularly delicate situation. The vague wording of the insider dealing provision exposes them to considerable risk of prosecution if dealing in the stock of their company.

When the insider dealing provision was discussed in parliament, the opinion was voiced that the directors of a company that plan a transaction likely to affect the quoted price of their company's stock have an obligation to take measures against preventing possible exploitation by employees of confidential information relating to the planned transaction.

Problem Area 2

The Chairman of the board and representative of the family controlled majority of a chocolate manufacturer quoted on the Zurich pre-bourse and its general manager have conducted secret negotiations with a large food concern to sell control of the company. After having received a formal indicative offer, they instruct Kurt, the chief financial officer, to prepare the necessary documentation for the company's accountants in order to initiate the due diligence investigation. The contemplated sales intention which is likely to substantially influence the quoted price of the company stock causes Kurt to buy shares of the company on the pre-bourse markets in anticipation of the realisation of a profit.

Should the Chairman of the board and the managing director have taken measures to prevent Kurt from engaging in dealing in the firm's shares? No court cases on this issue in the field of insider dealing exist. However, precedents on general principles of criminal law suggest that the board's omission to take protective measures does not expose it to the risk of criminal prosecution.

The decisive criteria for a reprehensible failure to act in order for a board of the management to prevent punishable offences by employees or by other dependents of a company are that:

- there is either an express obligation to take preventive measures provided for by law; or
- the offence to be prevented is clearly foreseeable; and
- the offence is imputable to the company, not the individual committing it.

The ultimate test is that the director's or management's failure to act is prompted by a realisation that this omission will result in some benefit to the company. Accordingly, in practice, companies have a very limited duty to take protective measures against the insider dealing of employees since the employees' principal motivation in insider dealing will be personal gain. Although it is certainly prudent of a board to enact internal regulations and provide for checks aimed at preventing employees from exploiting confidential information that they may obtain in the course of their professional activity, failing to do so would not normally result in criminal liability of management or members of the board in the light of current court practice.

In order to be relevant, confidential information must originate from within the company the shares of which are the subject of the insider dealing. This may raise delicate problems in a take-over situation.

Problem Area 3

Paul plans a take-over of ABC Company, a leading manufacturer of turbines, through his company Absorba Holdings, which is listed on the Geneva Stock Exchange. With the absence of disclosure rules of Swiss exchanges on participations held, he is able to secretly purchase a substantial number of shares on the stock exchange. The continuous demand that he creates causes the price of the ABC shares to rise sharply. In anticipation of a take-over bid which he will procure through Absorba Holdings, he personally purchases call-options on ABC shares which he plans to sell to Absorba Holdings at a profit.

The question whether Paul is to be considered as an insider is controversial. A widely-held belief of a number of writers is that the raider cannot be guilty of insider dealing in his relationship to the target company, because he cannot be an insider in respect of his own intentions. The issue may be viewed with more equivocation by the courts, depending on the particular circumstances of each case.

The basic tenet that a person cannot become an insider in respect of his own intentions is certainly correct. However, the take-over plan affects two companies. The issue may therefore become critical as soon as the raider controls, albeit secretly, a substantial part of the shares of the target company, because this situation may result in his being considered an insider by virtue of art 161, s 4 of the PC which provides thaty where there is an anticipated combination of two companies, the insider dealing provisions apply to both companies. Problems comparable to that of the raider arise in connection with the repurchase of own shares on the stock exchange by a listed company, the nursing of stocks (see 2.7.4.2) and management buy-outs that are not publicly announced.

2.3.4 Price-sensitive information

The relevant information must, if made public, be of a nature to have a foreseeably significant effect on the price of securities. Both the drafting of the statute and the history of the legislative process show that the legislator's intention was to catch material circumstances in the business life of the relevant enterprise. Minor fluctuations are intended to be excluded. To date, no guidance as to the materiality criteria can be drawn from decided cases. However, materiality is not measured by the size of the transaction conducted by the insider, but by the materiality of the effect on the development of quoted prices of a security. The critical moment is when the confidential information is exploited, irrespective of whether or not the expected effect, ie realisation of a profit or avoidance of a loss, occurs.

2.4 WHO IS AN INSIDER?

The circle of persons qualifying as insiders is defined in art 161, s 1 of the PC which expressly refers:

(1) members of the board;
* members of the management;
* members of the auditing body; or
* agents
of a company limited by shares or of any company controlling or controlled by it;
(2) members of an authority or civil servants;
(3) auxiliaries of the above.

2.4.1 Board members

The inclusion of members of the board as insiders shows that the law is primarily intended to be limited to persons that, on account of their responsibilities within the company concerned, have access to privileged information. Although no decided cases exist on this issue, it is likely that the law would include as insiders persons that are not formally elected as members of a board, but de facto exercise decision-making powers that are normally reserved to board members or chief executives. The term 'management' is used loosely and designates persons effectively in charge of the executive powers within a company. This distinguishes them clearly from normal employees.

The term 'auditing body' comprises both the statutory auditors as well as external auditors appointed *ad hoc* as may be provided for by Swiss banking law and the law on investment trusts. The term 'agent' includes any person carrying a mandate of the company, for instance as adviser such as lawyers, tax advisers, investment advisers or advisers retained for the purposes of preparing an issue of securities, a restructuring or an acquisition.

It is difficult to determine how the judiciary will draw the line between those who carry a mandate of the company and who are deemed to be insiders and contractual partners of the company concerned which are not caught by the law. The classic example given for a borderline case is the printer of a prospectus for a company's securities.

Only individuals are capable of being insiders within the meaning of the Act. The offence cannot be committed by a corporate entity. The above definition of insiders is by reference to companies limited by shares. This would narrow the circle of persons qualifying as insiders to persons holding such privileged position in respect of a company limited by shares registered in Switzerland. However, art 161, s 5 of the PC extends the applicability to securities issued by a co-operative and foreign corporations.

2.4.2 Members of an authority or civil servants

The second category of persons qualifying as insider are members of an authority or civil servants.

The term 'members of an authority' intends to cover, in particular, the members of supervisory authorities eg banks, investment funds, stock exchanges and other regulators of financial markets. It therefore applies without limitation to the members of the Federal Banking Commission, the Swiss National Bank, the cantonal authorities supervising the stock exchanges, including the Swiss Admission Board and the boards of the cantonal stock exchanges even though such boards are organised as private associations. The decisive test is whether these bodies exercise supervisory or regulatory functions and are ultimately answerable to state authorities (if they are organised in private form) and whether they have access, as a result of the duties they perform, to confidential information.

The term 'civil servants' applies to persons who exercise an official function as employees of government or public administration or the judiciary or otherwise as employees of any other body created by the public authority of the state. Although the law does not expressly state it, it follows from the purpose of the insider dealing provision that the capacity as a civil servant must give them access to confidential information. It would therefore be applicable to members of secretariats of regulatory authorities such as of the Banking Commission and Stock Exchange Supervision in the cantons as well as to civil servants in a leading function of the Federal Fiscal Administration concerned with stamp duty in connection with restructurings, mergers or issues of securities.

2.4.3 Auxiliaries

The term 'auxiliaries', finally, is designed to catch persons that, without being insiders, work in close co-operation with an insider and in this capacity and function acquire knowledge of confidential information.

Problem Area 4

Jean-Philippe is a major shareholder of Immo-Swiss, a company listed on the Geneva Stock Exchange owning chalet settlements for sale and rental in Swiss mountain resorts. He intends to sell a substantial part of his holdings on the market. In order to provide against a drop of the price in respect of the shares that he intends to realise, he purchases put options on the shares of the company so as to secure a certain price level.

Although Jean-Philippe is related to the company, he is not so in any of the capacities enumerated in art 161, s 1 of the PC. Even as a major shareholder, he does not qualify as an insider.

The situation would be different if, as a result of the level of his shareholding, he would *de facto* exercise influence on the decision-making of the company. He could then be qualified as a *de facto* director or executive and thus as an insider within the meaning of art 161 of the PC.

2.4.4 Persons in a relationship with a listed enterprise

Except if qualifying as insiders for other reasons, eg as a tippee, the persons not falling within art 161, s 1 of the PC are not deemed to be insiders as a result of their relationship to a listed enterprise, even if their position puts them in a position to acquire confidential information about that company.

Thus, the director of a private company engaging in quality control that purchases a division of a conglomerate public company that is in need of cash, is not an insider, even if the disposal is likely to influence the price of the company's securities on the stock exchange, because it results in an improvement of its liquidity situation. Depending on the size of the transaction, however, it may fall under art 161, s 3 of the PC as a partial demerger. Where the line is to be drawn can only be determined after consideration by the courts. Conversely, the printer that is commissioned to print the prospectus for an issue of shares will become an insider as a 'mandatary' (ie a person who has a mandate from the issuer), even though his contractual relationship does not relate directly to the preparation of the issue.

2.4.5 Exploitation by a third party

The third party that obtains and exploits confidential information is dealt with separately in art 161, s 2 of the PC. Before the insider provision was enacted in the Penal Code, the disclosure of confidential information and its exploitation by the tippee could be caught under art 162 of the PC which prohibits the disclosure of manufacturing or business secrets or their exploitation by a third party. Nevertheless, not one example of a prosecution in a domestic case exists since the offence is not prosecuted at the discretion of the public authorities, but only if a complaint is lodged by an injured party. Since the company to which the information refers is not injured by the transactions in its securities, no complaint was ever filed. However, the provision was relied upon by the Swiss authorities in order to construe double incrimination so as to be able to grant judicial assistance in criminal matters to the United States in a number of insider dealing cases.

2.4.6 Obligation on a third party

The insider dealing provision of PC art 161, s 2 imposes an obligation on a third party to abstain from certain acts, ie dealing in securities. The actual disclosure of facts is not punishable, however the exploitation of any information disclosed is against the law.

In order to qualify as a tippee, the following requirements must be met:

- the information must be confidential;
- the information must be obtained from an insider;
- the information must relate to 'securities'.

The manner in which the information is made accessible by the insider must in itself be a punishable offence, irrespective of whether the insider can be prosecuted or not (eg because the insider resides outside the country).

Problem Area 5

Hansueli, a messenger in the M&A Department of Bellerive Bank, overhears a discussion relating to an imminent take-over bid of Tally International SA by the shareholders of Kinderschuhe AG and which is prepared by Bellerive Bank. Article 162, s 2 of the PC does not cover confidential information obtained through an unintentional leak or by chance. It presupposes an intentional passing on of confidential infromation by the insider to the tippee. Hansueli will not be chargeable with insider dealing if he exploits the knowledge he has acquired fortuitously.

The law covers information passed on through a chain of insiders, since art 161, s 2 of the PC refers to information obtained directly or indirectly from an insider. The secondary tippee may be prosecuted even though the information is not passed on by an insider to that tippee. However, prosecution must prove that the secondary tippee was aware of the fact that the original information could only be supplied by an insider.

2.5 WHAT ARE THE OFFENCES?

2.5.1 Obtaining a pecuniary advantage

The constituent element at the core of the offence consists in exploiting relevant information. To exploit relevant information means obtaining a pecuniary advantage. This may either be the making of profit or by avoiding a loss. The advantage may be exploited by the insider or, equally punishable, the insider may commit the offence by procuring the pecuniary advantage to a third party. This is dealt with in 2.5.2 *below*.

TABLE (1)

Constituent elements of the insider dealing offence
Person must be:
(1) a director, manager, auditor or agent of a company limited by shares, a co-operative or foreign company or of a company controlling or controlled by such company; or
(2) any member of an authority or civil servant; or
(3) (a) a person who assists any person referred to in (1) or (2) *above*
     (b) person must obtain a pecuniary advantage to himself or for another through the misuse of a confidential fact, or through passing such information to a third party;
     (c) publication of such information will foreseeably have a significant effect on the price of 'securities' traded on a Swiss stock exchange or pre-bourse market;
     (d) person intends to commit the offence as set out in 2.5.4.

The reprehensible act may be committed by engaging in dealings with 'securities' whether or not the dealing is done on an exchange or by a direct transaction. Accordingly, although the legislation only covers listed securities, it will apply where the transaction takes place off-market. For the insider, the advantage must not necessarily result from the transaction with sensitive securities. An offence is committed if, for instance, the insider sells confidential information and thus makes a paid tip to a third party. Similarly, confidential information gifted to a third party in order to put the tippee in a position to obtain a pecuniary advantage is equally punishable.

2.5.2 Procuring a pecuniary advantage to a third party

Article 161, s 1 is directed against the disclosure of confidential information to third parties, but only if it relates to price-sensitive information relating to certain securities.

TABLE (2)

Constituent elements of 'tippee' offence
* A person who obtains confidential information from a person referred to in the first paragraph of Table (1) and who, by misuse of such information, obtains a pecuniary advantage for himself or another person guilty of an offence.
* The tippee must have the intention set out in 2.5.4.
* The decisive criterion is that the insider passes on his knowledge of privileged information in order to procure a pecuniary advantage to a third party.

Problem Area 6

As secretary to the Chairman of the board of Emmentaler Handelsbank, Heidi learns of substantial losses incurred by this important regional bank in the wake of the collapse of a large building concern in the area. She knows that her mother has invested part of her savings in the bank's shares. Without giving any clear-cut recommendation, she manages to convince her that she should sell them.

Although Heidi does not reveal confidential information to her mother, there is a likelihood that she may be prosecuted for having exploited her own knowledge of confidential facts and thus procured a third party, her mother, a pecuniary advantage. Her mother, however, does not exploit confidential information relating to a certain stock, even if she follows Heidi's advice. The result is that she probably cannot be prosecuted.

2.5.3 Realising the pecuniary advantage

It is a constituent element of the offence that the pecuniary advantage that was intended to be achieved by the offender has in fact been obtained, either by the insider or the tippee. If the result sought by the perpetration of the offence is not achieved, the offence is not completed. Accordingly, if an insider having obtained confidential information buys shares which subsequently, and unexpectedly, fall in value the offence will not have been completed. The offender may still, however, be prosecuted for the attempt.

It should be noted that the offence is committed even if the advantage is not realised. For instance, if the insider who has purchased sensitive stock sees the stock rise as he expected, the pecuniary advantage has been achieved, although it may not be realised. If the offender hesitates to realise the profit and the price of the shares subsequently drops, the offender has failed to realise a pecuniary advantage which he has in fact obtained by committing the offence.

Problem Area 7

The investment banker's Kathrin and Karl-Johann are involved in the acquisition process of Pharmafin SA by Allschwiler Chemiewerke. They build up a position of shares and call options of the target company in anticipation of an increase of the stock's price on publication of the take-over.

In the course of the due diligence investigation, the stocks start to move as a result of rumours on the market. Kathrin and Karl-Johann hold on to their positions. The due diligence investigation reveals material adverse facts that leads to the withdrawal of Allschwiler Chemiewerke. The take-over is not consummated and the shares of Pharmafin experience a severe drop.

Two problems arise: In respect of the positions in Pharmafin shares, the anticipated result has been obtained, because the share price rose, albeit not owing to the take-over, but to rumours circulating in the market. Even though not realised, a pecuniary advantage was obtained. The question is whether its cause is the exploitation of confidential information by Kathrin and Karl-Johann or the rumours. If the rise was due to the rumours, they would be prosecuted for the attempted offence. Otherwise, the offence has been completed.

As regards the options, the anticipated result has not been achieved and the offence is not committed, however, Kathrin and Karl-Johann have done all that was necessary to achieve the reprehensible result and will be prosecuted for an attempt of the offence.

2.5.4 Intention

The offence is only capable of being committed intentionally. The offender must be aware of all the constituent elements of the offence, ie confidentiality of the information, the price sensitivity of the information, exploitation of the information, aptitude to lead to a pecuniary advantage. As regards the tippee in particular, the intention must relate to the same constituent elements of the offence, with the added requirement that the tippee must be aware of the fact that the insider was in breach of his duties of confidentiality by disclosing information with the intention to procure the tippee a pecuniary advantage. In order to be prosecuted, the tippee must exploit the advice he has received from the insider. If he does not, the insider remains punishable for the attempt to commit the offence.

2.6 WHAT IS THE TERRITORIAL SCOPE OF ARTICLE 161 OF THE PC?

The issue is governed by the general principles of the Swiss Penal Code. The offence is punishable in Switzerland if it is committed in or takes effect in Switzerland.

TABLE (3)

Acts done in Switzerland
In order to be deemed to be committed in Switzerland, the offender must do such acts or parts of acts aimed at obtaining or procuring a pecuniary advantage by the exploitation of confidential information, such as:
— within Switzerland, giving an order to deal in sensitive securities, either in writing or by telephone or by any other means of communication; or
— within Switzerland, passing on confidential information to a third party; or
— outside Switzerland, giving an order to deal in sensitive securities that is intended to be implemented in Switzerland, irrespective of whether the pecuniary advantage is obtained in Switzerland or abroad.
However, the general principles of Swiss penal law consider an offence to be within the territorial scope of Switzerland's jurisdiction if the effects take place in Switzerland. This is normally the case, if the sensitive securities are kept or cleared in Switzerland. This is as a result of the narrow definition of 'securities' within the meaning of art 161 of the PC which applies only to securities listed on a Swiss exchange.

Problem Area 8

While in London, Roger orders his Geneva bank to purchase sensitive stock of a company listed on the New York Stock Exchange. Since the transaction is implemented through a Swiss bank as an intermediary, the offence would be deemed to have been committed in Switzerland. The relevant shares, however, do not qualify as securities within the meaning of art 161 of the PC and, therefore, the Swiss insider dealing rules do not apply. Roger is likely to be involved in a SEC investigation that would qualify for judicial assistance in criminal matters in Switzerland so that the Swiss bank, if requested to disclose the name of its client, must do so to the Swiss authorities acting on the request of the SEC.

The situation could be different if the company was also listed on a Swiss exchange in the form of Swiss depositary receipts as is often the case with shares of a US issuer. It is uncertain how courts would determine the case if Roger had given express order to deal in the actual shares of the company on the New York Stock Exchange rather than with Swiss depositary receipts relating to those shares on a Swiss stock exchange, because he may find the Swiss market too limited. The law will not equate the Swiss depositary receipts listed in Switzerland and the shares of the company listed in New York so that Roger could not be prosecuted in Switzerland.

2.7 WHAT ARE THE DEFENCES?

2.7.1 General considerations

The Swiss provision prohibiting insider dealing does not contain any specific defences available under it as may be the case in other jurisdictions. Committing the offences defined in art 161 of the PC will result in prosecution and punishment of the offender, unless the offender is able to establish on the basis of the facts of each individual case that the act was justified in accordance with the general principles applicable to the Swiss Penal Code. The grounds of justification are essentially limited to the exercise of a duty imposed by law or a professional or official duty within art 32 and self-defence within art 34 of the PC (see Problem Area 10). The latter provision states that an act or an omission committed in order to save, among other things, one's own interests from imminent danger that cannot be averted other than by committing what is to be characterised objectively as an offence, is not punishable. The same applies if the offence is done in order to protect another person's interests.

These defences should be distinguished from borderline cases that cannot be prosecuted, because the constituent elements of the offence have not been fulfilled. Thus, objections raised against a prosecution on grounds that the critical information was widely disclosed and therefore not confidential or that it could not be expected that dealing in the critical securities would result in a pecuniary advantage in the form of a profit or the avoidance of a loss, relate to constituent elements of the offence.

Problem Area 9

Felix is a securities lawyer with a large Zurich law firm and engaged in the preparation of an issue of an innovative debt instrument for a large corporate client that is designed to favour existing shareholders of the issuer. He tells his wife Susi, because he must work late hours and is also excited about the innovative features of the issue. Susi buys stock of the issuer. In the ensuing investigation, Felix argues forcefully that he never expected that his wife would exploit the information given to her in confidence.

What Felix is pleading is the lack of intention to procure Susi as a tippee a pecuniary advantage by revealing confidential information. He does not seek to justify an offence, but denies that the subjective constituent element of the offence is being fulfilled.

2.7.2 Grounds for justification of acts done following a duty imposed by law, a profession or office

The most common duty imposed by law is the duty to testify in respect of a fact that may be confidential. In the unlikely event that an insider were to be compelled to testify on confidential information within the usually short time-span before the information is publicly disclosed, the witness would have grounds for justification from any insider dealing offence based on art 32 of the PC. Suffice to say that a banker that has confidential information would be able to rely on the banking secrecy which can only be lifted by a judge after proceeding to a balance of conflicting interests. By the time such a decision would be enforceable, it is highly improbable that the information would still be confidential within the meaning of art 161 of the PC. Unlike this rather theoretical example, the issue of justification is likely to be more practical in connection with the situations akin to that described in Problem Area 10. They are likely to be of particular interest to bankers, portfolio managers or investment advisers.

Problem Area 10

George heads the private banking department of the Geneva subsidiary of a large foreign bank with worldwide activities in all segments of banking. Geneva is one of the places where its portfolio management is centred within the group. It is the group's policy that part of the fixed interest investments for clients that have given discretionary powers for the administration of their assets to the bank are invested in bonds issued by the parent bank abroad. George obtains confidential information to the effect that the parent bank is in very serious difficulties as a result of speculative engagements in derivatives of its Singapore branch and that there is a likelihood that the parent bank will have to be declared bankrupt. He takes a decision and, relying on his power to manage the clients' assets, liquidates as many as possible of the bond positions held by his clients.

There can be no doubt that the offence has been committed. Can George rely on justifiable grounds? It is submitted that he can. George has a legal and contractual duty to act in his clients' best interests. He would likely be found in breach of these obligations if he failed to act as he did. In a situation of conflicting duties, a court will have to proceed to a balance of interests and it is thought that he would not be held liable for insider dealing.

No decided cases exist on the issue of justification. It is difficult to forecast how courts will balance the conflicting interests, in particular having regard to the very limited number of cases that ever reach the courts. One decisive fact, however, may prove to be the relative indifference of the Swiss legal community to the offence of insider dealing which is reflected in the fact the offence has no tradition in Swiss law. This may cause the courts to exercise their discretion, in cases of doubt, in favour of justifiable grounds in cases comparable to that described in Problem Area 10.

2.7.3 Self-defence

Conflicting duties will often overlap with the more general justification of self-defence of art 34 of the PC. In order for the latter to apply, the following conditions must be met:

- A legally-protected interest, ie patrimony, must be exposed to imminent danger.
- The danger must not have been caused to occur by a fault of the offender.
- Under the particular circumstances of the case, the offender may not reasonably be expected to accept the loss of the endangered interest.

These principles also apply to the situation where the offender acts in order to protect a third party's patrimony.

The somewhat vague criteria defined by the law indicate that a justification will probably not exist in a situation as that in Problem Area 10, if done to achieve a profit in the best interest of the client, rather than in order to avoid a loss.

2.7.4 Other defences

These defences which may be of a practical importance in particular for banks and financial advisers are not defences in the technical sense, but directed at showing that the constituent elements of the insider dealing offence have not been fulfilled.

2.7.4.1 Information irrelevant

The objection raised by an insider within the course of an investigation to the effect that the act under prosecution would have been done even without the inside information in essence aims at establishing that there is no causal link between the inside information and the intention to exploit it. Once it is established that the insider has confidential information at the time of dealing, this defence will be very difficult to sustain. It nevertheless may be of considerable practical importance for members of a board of a target company in a take-over situation.

Problem Area 11

Allfinanz AG, a publicly-quoted financial corporation, is the target of Banque Publique that has acquired 20 per cent of its shares on the stock exchange. Prior to making a public offer, negotiations between the top management take place to enable the prospective bidder to better assess the target. The management of Allfinanz benefits from a management stock option plan, and various managers exercise options on the shares of Allfinanz in the period prior to the public announcement of the bid.

The members of the management that were informed of the planned transaction will have to prove that the information they had was irrelevant to their decision to exercise the options. The defence will be successful if they can establish that the options under the plan can be exercised after the critical period and that the exercise price at which the option could be exercised was unaltered. This demonstrates that the exercise of the option is not, itself, linked to the possession of the inside information, since the option can be exercised at a fixed price, unrelated to the current market price of the shares. The exercise could also have occurred after the inside information became public thus ensuring the holder of the option could have, in any event, benefited from the rise in market price. The other directors will merely have to establish that they did not have privileged information.

2.7.4.2 Nursing of stocks

Swiss public companies frequently buy back their own stocks in order to avoid what may be considered an excessive drop of their share prices. This type of intervention is generally held to be irrelevant under insider dealing rules in Switzerland relying on the maxim that a person cannot be an insider because of his own intentions, that the fall in the price of shares on the stock exchange is not privileged information, but public, and that share purchases on the markets designed to avoid a fall in one's own securities do not result in a profit, but rather in an unrealised capital loss.

The situation is potentially different when a public company's treasurer holds important positions of his company's own stocks in its nostro portfolio. If he exploits inside information in this particular situation, it is doubtful whether the maxim that one cannot be one's own insider can really be upheld. The treasurer that exploits such confidential information in order to procure a pecuniary advantage to his company may expose himself to prosecution.

2.8 WHAT ARE THE PENALTIES AND CONSEQUENCES OF INSIDER DEALING?

2.8.1 Imprisonment or fine

The Penal Code provides for insider dealing offences to be punished by imprisonment or fine. The fine is likely to be the more frequent sanction. The maximum amount of the fine is SFr40,000 (approximately £22,000 STG), except where the offender has acted with 'greediness', in which case the courts are not bound by the maximum amount. 'Greediness' is interpreted by Swiss courts as 'an unscrupulous or particularly developed addictive striving for profit'. Imprisonment means a detention of a minimum of three days up to a maximum of three years.

A corporation is not capable of committing the offence of insider dealing. However, persons acting on behalf of a corporation may be found guilty of insider trading if the pecuniary advantage benefits the corporation.

To this date, no convictions have been made under the insider dealing provision of the Swiss Penal Code. All ancillary sanctions provided by the Penal Code can be applied to an offender guilty of an insider dealing offence such as being declared unable to hold office, the prohibition to exercise certain professions for which a concession of permit from the state is required or, if committed by a foreigner, expulsion from Switzerland. Article 58 of the Swiss Penal Code provides for the possibility that the proceeds resulting from the offence may be confiscated and forfeited in favour of the state.

2.8.2 Sanctions

Sanctions available independently from the Penal Code may be imposed by regulators. At present, this is the case if the offence has been committed by somebody subject to the supervision of the Federal Banking Commission, ie as the member of the management of a bank or an investment fund. The Federal Banking Commission may require that the person be removed from his position within the bank, because it is unable to warrant the impeccable conduct of the bank's affairs.

At present, on the level of cantonal laws, certain sanctions may be taken against securities' dealings within the meaning of the cantonal securities' dealing laws. Thus, the concession given to a securities' dealer may be withdrawn or a member of a stock exchange excluded.

2.8.3 Statistics on conviction for insider dealing

Since its coming into effect on 1 July 1988, not one single sentence or penalty has been pronounced for breach of Swiss insider dealing legislation. The overwhelming majority of cases that reached the courts concerned judicial assistance in criminal matters following requests of foreign states, predominantly from the United States.

No federal statistics exist on the number of preliminary or full-scale investigations conducted in the various cantons or on the number of prosecutions initiated and subsequently abandoned on the level of the prosecuting authorities.

In the canton of Zurich, the banking centre of Switzerland, until January 1996, 30 preliminary investigations were initiated of the District Attorney's own motion which have led to twelve formal investigations being conducted. Of these, two led to an indictment and subsequent acquittals. In all other cases, the charges were dropped by the District Attorney's Office. This information has been supplied by the District Attorney's Office of Zurich.

CASE STUDY

Splash Plc, a company listed on the Zurich Stock Exchange, manufactures rainwear and umbrellas. Alan, a weather forecaster, on discovering that there is an unseasonable amount of rain due in the next three months, instructs his broker to buy shares in Regenass AG. Meanwhile, Charles, an analyst of the company's shares, is told in a conversation with Jeremy, one of the directors, that the Chairman is expected to be paid a salary of SFr500,000. Charles knows from his knowledge of the Chairman's service contract (which is available for public inspection) that this salary could only be paid if the company achieved profit in excess of SFr20 million. Charles revises his profit forecast for the company but before he publishes it he cancels instructions which he had previously given to his broker to sell his Regenass AG shares. Charles also tells his girlfriend, Maggie, that 'things are looking up' for Regenass AG. Maggie then buys shares in the name of her father from an old friend of hers who wanted to sell Regenass AG shares off-market to save the payment of brokers commission. In addition, Owen, an employee of the contracting firm which cleans Regenass AG's offices, finds a draft of the latest management figures, which demonstrate Regenass AG's high profitability, in a wastepaper bin. He immediately buys shares.

Alan
Two questions need to be answered: The first is whether Alan is an insider within the meaning of art 161, s 1 of the PC. The second is whether the results of the work of an expert for a company, which may influence the price of its stock, constitutes confidential information within the meaning of the insider dealing provisions.

In reading the text of the legislation it becomes clear that Alan is not an insider, as he is not: (a) a member of the board of management, (b) a member of the auditing body, (c) an agent of Regenass AG, (d) a member of an authority, (e) a civil servant or (f) an auxiliary of any of the categories of persons expressly named in PC art 161, s 1. Even if he was, and assuming that weather forecasting is his hobby, an accurate weather forecast would not be characterised as confidential information. Rather, it is the result of a correct analysis based on particular skills. It is also questionable whether a Swiss court would find the forecast of excessive rainfall to be liable to influence the price of Regenass AG stock. It may result in an increased turnover, but this may also be influenced by other factors in the rainwear and umbrellas market, such as its degree of saturation. An increased turnover would not necessarily increase the profitability of Regenass AG as this also depends on Regenass AG's cost structure and unexpected events such as difficulties with suppliers, industrial disputes, a disruption of production owing to an accident and suchlike.

Jeremy
Jeremy qualifies as an insider in his capacity as a director of Regenass AG. The information disclosed to the company's analyst, Charles, directly relates to the company's performance and is confidential. In his capacity as analyst of Regenass AG employed by an independent broker, Charles does not qualify as an insider, but as a third party. He is a tippee within the

meaning of PC art 161, s 1. If the profit forecast for Regenass AG that can be deduced from the information disclosed by Jeremy was to be made public, it would be likely to have a significant effect on the price of its stock. Even if the information passed on by Jeremy is conveyed by way of gossipping, ie without the intention to enable Charles to take advantage of confidential information, Jeremy may be liable to be prosecuted. The prosecution would have to establish that the information was passed on with the intention to financially benefit Charles or at least accepting that he may exploit information known to be confidential. Under the particular circumstances, taking into account that Jeremy is a director of Regenass AG and necessarily aware of the relevance of the information disclosed and of the professional capacity of Charles, there is a strong likelihood that a court would conclude that Jeremy is deemed to have intended to provide Charles with an opportunity to take advantage of confidential information. The burden to prove the absence of intention to this effect would be on Jeremy.

Charles

The Swiss insider dealing provisions catch the exploitation of confidential information either for profit or for the avoidance of loss. As an analyst employed by an independent firm of stockbrokers, Charles is not an insider. However, the information received from Jeremy, under the particular circumstances of the case, is likely to be viewed by a Swiss court to be confidential. Charles would therefore qualify as a tippee within the meaning of art 161, s 2 of the PC. By cancelling the sales order prior to the publication of confidential information, Charles undoubtedly exploits confidential information and avoids making a loss. The issue that remains is whether the insider dealing provisions can be breached by way of failure to act rather than actually having to take positive action. Disregarding the fact that a prosecutor will hardly be able to support the burden of proof that Charles had an intention to sell which he subsequently changed upon receipt of confidential information, it is submitted that PC art 161 requires active dealing. On the other hand, passing on information and encouraging Maggie to deal, even if the information is imprecise, but coming from a professional, is likely to be sufficient to be guilty of insider dealing if done with the intention of financially benefiting Maggie.

Maggie

Maggie is a typical tippee as in art 161, s 2 of the PC. The offence presupposes a punishable offence of the actual insider Charles. The knowledge of the confidential information must be precise in respect of the knowledge of the insider. The tip may be passed on in any form apt to encourage the tippee to deal. It is not necessary that this information be precise. The recommendation to purchase a certain stock, in particular, if from a person professionally concerned with stocks and who makes it understood that he has confidential information, is sufficient. Under the circumstances, a Swiss court may find Maggie guilty of exploiting confidential information if she procured a pecuniary advantage for her father by purchasing the shares in his name, because, in the circumstances, she may be found to have had reason to believe that Charles' remark was an encouragement to buy Splash shares. The fact that the purchase is made directly, and not through the stock exchange, does not influence liability as the decisive test is that the shares are listed on a Swiss exchange.

Owen

The question whether Owen qualifies as an insider depends on whether he falls within the categories of people listed in PC art 161, s 1. The cleaning firm that employs him is not an agent of Splash within the meaning of the insider dealing provision, because the nature of the work to be performed does not imply the disclosure of confidential information. The situation would be different for an employee at a printing firm who is retained to print a prospectus for a new issue. On the other hand, the confidential information obtained by Owen does not make him a tippee, because he was not given the information by an insider that intended to give him a financial advantage. Owen would therefore not be guilty of exploiting confidential information under the Swiss insider dealing provisions.

Netherlands

Paul Storm, Arjen Tillema and Robert Fibbe,
Nauta Dutilh, Rotterdam and Amsterdam

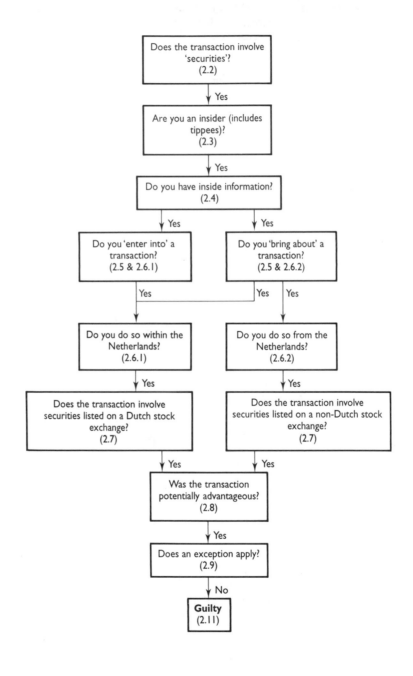

1 INTRODUCTION

The Dutch anti-insider dealing regime is based on a single statutory provision, art 46 of the Act on the Supervision of the Trade in Securities 1995 (*Wet toezicht effectenverkeer*, 1995 or 'WTE') and represents the Dutch implementation of the EC Directive on Insider Dealing (Dir 89/592 [1989] OJ L334/30) ('the Directive'). Prior to 1989, the Netherlands did not have any legislation on insider dealing. Certain non-statutory regulations designed to prevent and regulate insider dealing, which will be discussed in 3 *below*, had been in place prior to 1989.

On 16 February 1989 the Act against the abuse of inside information came into effect ('the 1989 Act'). The 1989 Act introduced a new provision, art 336a of the Criminal Code ('CC'), as a result of which the abuse of inside information became a criminal offence. Article 336a of the CC was introduced after elaborate discussions in and outside parliament extending over a period of approximately 20 years as to whether the use of inside information should be criminalised.

By an Act of 1 July 1992 the substance of CC art 336a was transferred to the version of the Act on the Supervision of the Trade in Securities which was in force at the time (art 31a). The wording remained virtually the same, even though it now had to comply with the Directive. However, the wording deviates from the Directive in several respects. This is permitted only to the extent that the Dutch provision is more stringent than the Directive (see art 6 of the Directive). On 1 January 1996 the Act on the Supervision of the Trade in Securities 1995 came into effect. Its art 46 is identical to the previous art 31a.

Until 1 January 1996, only one case had been decided by a criminal court. This was a case decided under the old CC art 336a, the *Van den Nieuwenhuyzen* case (see *below* at 2.4.2). In *Van den Nieuwenhuyzen*, the Supreme Court (*Hoge Raad*) interpreted certain elements of CC art 336a which are also incorporated in WTE art 46. According to the Dutch Minister of Finance, the Supreme Court's narrow construction of the widely drafted terms of CC art 336a/WTE art 46 was contrary to the intention of the legislator. In July 1995 the Minister indicated that he would propose amendments to WTE art 46 in parliament in order to clarify the broad intentions of the legislator.

In January 1996, the District Attorney's Office was investigating several other cases where a violation of WTE art 46 was suspected. It appeared to be lacking manpower, drive and conviction.

Practice has so far shown that it has been extremely difficult to apply any Dutch provision on insider dealing. To some extent this is due to the rather ambiguous way in which these provisions have been drafted. The unfortunate consequence is that it is very difficult to make any positive statement about the state of the law in this field.

It should be noted that the final authority on the interpretation of the Directive is the Court of Justice of the EC. Where a Dutch court is in doubt as to whether certain facts fall within the terms of WTE art 46, it will have to interpret those terms in the light of the Directive. Where it is in doubt about the interpretation of the Directive it can (and if it is the Supreme Court it must) ask the Court of Justice of the EC for a preliminary ruling under art 177 of the EC Treaty. However, given the fact that it takes about two years to obtain a preliminary ruling, asking for such a ruling in criminal proceedings may be even more problematic than in civil proceedings.

2 THE WTE

2.1 ARTICLE 46

The text of WTE art 46 reads as follows:

(1) Any person in possession of advance knowledge is prohibited from entering into or bringing about in the Netherlands any transaction in securities listed on a securities exchange authorised under Article 22 (of the WTE), if any advantage may result from that transaction.

(2) Any person in possession of advance knowledge is prohibited from bringing about from the Netherlands any transaction in securities listed on a securities exchange outside the Netherlands, if any advantage may result from that transaction.

(3) Advance knowledge means knowledge of any particular circumstance concerning the legal entity, company or institution to which the securities relate or concerning the trade in the securities:
   (a) of which the person who is aware of such circumstance knows or should reasonably suspect that it is not in the public domain and cannot come or has not come outside the circle of persons bound by a duty of secrecy without violation of a secret; and
   (b) publication of which may reasonably be expected to affect the price of the securities.

(4) The prohibition laid down in the first and second paragraphs shall not apply to the intermediary who, in possession of advance knowledge with respect to the trade only, acts on an exchange in accordance with the rules of good faith to serve principals.

(5) With respect to criminal offences as referred to in the first paragraph, the District Court of Amsterdam shall have exclusive jurisdiction in first instance.

Accordingly, WTE art 46 distinguishes two criminal offences, one consisting of either entering into or bringing about a transaction *in* the Netherlands in securities listed on a Dutch securities exchange, and the other of bringing about a transaction *from* the Netherlands in securities listed on a securities exchange outside the Netherlands. The rather mysterious distinction between 'entering into' (*verrichten*) and 'bringing about' (*bewerkstelligen*) a transaction will be briefly discussed below (see 2.5.1). In this chapter the term 'inside information' is used instead of 'advance knowledge' (*voorwetenschap*).

2.2 TO WHICH SECURITIES DO THE PROHIBITIONS APPLY?

For the purpose of the WTE 'securities' include:

(1) shares, debt certificates, profit and founders' shares, option certificates, warrants and similar negotiable instruments;
(2) rights of joint ownership, options, futures, entries in share and debt registers, and similar rights, whether or not conditional;
(3) depository receipts representing securities as referred to above;
(4) scrips for securities as referred to above.

Article 46 of the WTE only applies to listed securities. It is unclear whether this refers to officially listed (ie admitted) securities only, or also to the trade in unofficially listed securities, such as the so-called 'as, if, and when issued' ('AIW') trade in securities for which an application for listing has been made. The Explanatory Memorandum to the 1989 Act (*Memorie van Toelichting*—a document accompanying the Bill submitted by the government to Parliament) seems to indicate that only officially listed securities are covered by art 46.

It is equally uncertain whether the AIW trade is covered by the Directive. It has been argued by one legal commentator that art 1(2)(b) of the Directive could indeed be read as including the AIW trade. If this is correct WTE art 46 should be interpreted in line with the Directive in this respect.

Problem Area 1

> Global Bank is underwriting an issue of warrants for ABC Trading NV ('ABC'), an Amsterdam-listed company. The warrants are to acquire shares in ABC. As a result of due diligence at ABC, John, a director of Global Bank, obtains information that ABC's profitability is about to substantially drop due to the loss of an important customer. John none the less decides that Global Bank should proceed with the underwriting agreement and Global Bank acts accordingly.
>
> At the time the underwriting agreement is concluded the warrants are unlikely to be listed. Consequently, we submit that WTE art 46 has not been breached. Compare, however, Problem Area 9 for the situation where the warrants have already been listed. Also compare that Problem Area for a possible violation of WTE art 47 by Global Bank.

2.3 TO WHOM DO THE PROHIBITIONS APPLY?

The circle of persons to whom the prohibitions apply is wider under the WTE than under the Directive (arts 2 and 4). The WTE prohibition is applicable to *anyone* who possesses inside information.

It should be noted that under Dutch law a criminal offence may be committed not only by individuals, but also by legal entities. Normally, acts of natural persons may be attributed to the legal entity if such acts are part of, or a logical consequence of, transactions which the legal entity enters into in the ordinary course of its business. The Dutch provisions seem to be broad enough to comply with art 2(2) of the Directive.

In case a criminal offence has been committed by a legal entity, sanctions may not only be imposed upon that legal entity itself, but also upon the individuals who have ordered, or who were actually in charge of, the actions which constitute the criminal offence (CC art 51(2)). It has been correctly pointed out that second or third echelon corporate employees as well as directors and senior officers may be subject to sanctions (*V de Serrière* in *Insider Trading in Western Europe* (Graham & Trotman and IBA, London, 1994)).

A different question is to what extent the *knowledge* of a natural person employed by a legal entity may be considered to be the knowledge of the legal entity. The answer to this question may depend on the position of the person within the hierarchy of the company, his/her powers of representation and the nature of the business of the company, etc. This question may also involve the role of so-called Chinese Walls established by securities houses and banks, a topical discussion at present. It is not clear whether knowledge 'on the other side of the wall' must be imputed to the bank where the trading department of the bank enters into a transaction without having this knowledge because the 'Chinese Walls' were respected. To what extent knowledge of an individual may actually be imputed to the company is therefore a question to which no clear answer is available; much will depend on the circumstances of each case. Compare also Problem Areas 2 and 8.

Problem Area 2

ABC Trading NV ('ABC'), an Amsterdam-listed company, having invited several banks to submit proposals, offers a mandate to Global Bank to manage an issue of warrants it is proposing to make. The warrants are to acquire shares in ABC.

Stephen, a director of Global Bank, has during the negotiations with ABC, obtained inside information relating to ABC's shares, release of which is likely to affect their price significantly. Over lunch he reveals details to Sally, one of Global Bank's traders, who that afternoon buys shares in ABC in the market on behalf of Global Bank.

Global Bank is likely to have violated WTE art 46 since Sally, acting on its behalf, was entering into a transaction Global Bank regularly entered into and her knowledge of the inside information would probably be imputed to Global Bank.

Sally is also likely to be liable to prosecution under WTE art 46 since she ordered the transaction (see *above*).

Stephen seems to have violated regulations on Chinese Walls (see 3.2.3). If he has encouraged Sally to enter into the transaction he would be guilty of bringing about the transaction (WTE art 46(1)).

2.4 WHAT IS INSIDE INFORMATION?

A definition of the term 'advance knowledge' is provided by para 3 of WTE art 46. The main elements are:

(1) Inside information is knowledge of any 'particular circumstance' (*bijzonderheid*) concerning:
    (a) the legal entity, company or institution to which the securities relate; or
    (b) the trade in securities.
(2) Inside information must be understood to be:
    (a) not in the public domain; and
    (b) subject to a duty of secrecy; and
    (c) price-sensitive.

Before considering each of the elements of the definition of inside information, it should be noted that the elements are cumulative. It is evident that the cumulative nature of the definition does not improve the chances of a conviction.

2.4.1 The elements of the definition

2.4.1.1 *Particular circumstance*

A 'particular circumstance' refers to specific information. According to the Explanatory Memorandum to CC art 336a—the legislator has used the term 'particular circumstance' in order to distinguish it from a general development and rumours that cannot be substantiated. The term 'particular circumstance' does not seem exactly to cover the term 'information . . . of a precise nature' used in art 1(1) of the Directive, but it is difficult to indicate what in practice the difference would be.

Problem Area 3

Elaine, a dealer at Intercontinental Bank (a market-maker), picks up a rumour through her work that Panacea NV is about to announce excellent results of clinical trials it has been carrying out on its latest product, 'Wonderdrug'. She buys 1,000 of Panacea NV's Amsterdam-listed shares.

It is not clear whether this rumour is a 'particular circumstance' within the meaning of art 46(3). It may well be a rumour that cannot be substantiated. However, if it can be substantiated and if it is also specific (which seems to be the case) it is a 'particular circumstance'. Since it relates to Panacea NV, could come from a source which should have kept it secret and is price sensitive, it may well be inside information. This would be a question of fact. If the rumour turns out to be false, it could be argued that it had never been a 'particular circumstance' at all and therefore cannot be inside information.

> Elaine could contend the rumour was so widely circulated within finan-
> cial circles in Amsterdam that the information 'was in the public domain'.
> The fact that a rumour is circulating is very unlikely in itself to be regarded
> as inside information since that information neither relates to the company
> nor to the trade in its shares.
>
> Since the information relates to the issuer, not the trade, art 46(4) would
> not help Elaine (see 2.9.1).

2.4.1.2 The subject matter of inside information

2.4.1.2.1 Legal entity, company or institution

In the Explanatory Memorandum to CC art 336a it was noted that knowledge of
a future amendment to certain legislation important to a company, or a familiarity with upcoming regulations regarding subsidies which will particularly affect a
company, may constitute inside information concerning that company.
Information about the future bankruptcy of a competitor could also be regarded
to be inside information.

The institution to which the securities relate need not be the issuer of the
securities eg a foundation or trust company may issue depository receipts for
shares in a listed company.

It is doubtful whether the mere advice to buy or to sell certain securities given
by a well-informed insider to a tippee constitutes inside information if the advice
has been given without any further details. Such advice would presumably not
contain any 'particular circumstance' with respect to either the company concerned or the trade in securities. The insider giving such advice might, however,
be 'bringing about' a transaction by the tippee (see 2.5.1 *below*).

2.4.1.2.2 The trade

A particular circumstance may also relate to 'the trade in the securities'. It has
been pointed out that the term used here is vague and may expand the application of the prohibition considerably. However, the Explanatory Memorandum to
the 1989 Act specifies as follows:

> Inside information may also involve the trade in securities; advance knowledge of personnel of
> banks, brokers and institutional investors with respect to sizeable orders to be spread out over
> a period of time and which are expected to have an influence on the market price, may be
> used for personal gain.

The type of inside information discussed here would therefore seem to be
limited to the professional trade and would not normally be available to persons
other than those referred to above.

2.4.1.3 Information not in public domain

The definition of 'advance knowledge' in WTE art 46 provides that the person concerned 'knows or should reasonably suspect' that the particular circumstance concerned is not in the public domain (and is secret). The requirement of knowledge on the part of the person concerned is mitigated by the alternative that s/he should reasonably suspect that the particular circumstance is not in the public domain, thus enabling the court to impute knowledge which a person in such a position should reasonably be deemed to have.

It would seem that information will not be considered to be in the public domain as soon as it has been published but only after it may reasonably be expected to have reached the public.

The requirement concerning the information being not in the public domain is in line with art 1(1) of the Directive. The additional requirement of WTE art 46 concerning the information being secret might, if permitted under the Directive, render that requirement meaningless since what is secret is certainly not in the public domain. This additional requirement will be discussed below.

Problem Area 4

Anthony, an influential analyst with Wizzo Analysts BV and a guest columnist in the weekly Good Share Guide has been investigating Underrated NV and has drafted favourable research recommendations based on publicly available information. He plans to publish his recommendations in the widely read and respected weekly Good Share Guide next week. He circulates his draft recommendations to a colleague, Belinda, for comments. When the draft is settled it is sent to the printers where Christoffer prepares the typesetting. Before the weekly Good Share Guide is published, Anthony, Belinda and Christoffer follow the recommendations and buy shares in Underrated NV.

It is submitted that this case does not involve any inside information with respect to Underrated NV. The information upon which the publication is based is publicly available. The requirement of 'in the public domain' does not entail that everybody actually knows all available information, but that everybody *could* know if an effort is made.

The only object of inside information relevant to WTE art 46 is the trade in Underrated's securities. It is, however, doubtful whether information about an impending publication can be considered to be information about the trade in securities (see 2.4.1.2.2).

Even if the information were held to relate to Underrated NV or the trade in its securities it would be doubtful whether it is secret. No statutory regulations prevent Anthony, Belinda or Christoffer from disclosing the information. It is unclear whether they should be considered to have reached an implicit agreement to keep the information secret.

One could also argue that it is evident that the impending publication of

Anthony's article in the weekly Good Share Guide should be top secret until publication and that this should have been clear to all involved. This example illustrates that the Supreme Court's decision in *Van den Nieuwenhuyzen* on 'secret' makes it difficult to anticipate the legality of any transaction.

Rules adopted by the Amsterdam Stock Exchange ('the ASE') will, however, prohibit Anthony from 'scalping' (see 3.2.4).

2.4.1.4 Secret information

A controversial element of the definition of inside information is that the person concerned 'knows or should reasonably suspect' that the particular circumstance 'cannot come or has not come outside the circle of persons bound by a duty of secrecy without violation of a secret'.

The element of secrecy was incorporated in the definition of inside information in 1989 (before the final version of the Directive was known). A major objection against this element is that it is not in line with the Directive and consequently WTE art 46 would be less stringent than the Directive.

On the occasion of the inclusion of art 31a in the previous version of the WTE the government was not impressed by the argument. In its opinion, abuse of inside information is in particular objectionable if a duty to maintain secrecy protected by criminal law is violated. Meanwhile, doubts remain as to whether this additional element is reconcilable with the Directive.

In *Van den Nieuwenhuyzen*, the Supreme Court has adopted a broad interpretation of the concept of secrecy. According to the Supreme Court, a duty to keep secret may be inferred not only from statutory rules but also for instance from a corporate decision, an agreement or a customary practice. The circumstances of each particular case will be decisive. By taking this non-formalistic approach, the Supreme Court has narrowed the gap between WTE art 46 and the Directive (see 2.4.2 *below*).

The Supreme Court implicitly accepted the Court of Appeal's view that one of the objectives of WTE art 46 was to ensure an orderly trade on the stock exchange, ie to create a level playing field for all investors. Trading should take place on the basis of information which is equally accessible to all parties participating in the trade. This objective would not be met if WTE art 46 were interpreted to mean that inside information is exclusively information of which the secrecy is protected by law.

It should be noted that under WTE art 46(3)(a) the test of information being 'secret' is not only met if the person concerned knew or should reasonably have suspected that the information actually had not without violation of a secret come outside the circle of persons bound by a duty of secrecy, but also if that person knew or should reasonably have known that this could not otherwise have happened. The nature of the information and the circumstances of the case are, therefore, decisive.

Problem Area 5

Tom, a barman at the local golfclub, overhears inside information being exchanged by two directors of Big NV as he serves them at the bar.

If Tom knows or should reasonably suspect that the information he overheard is subject to a duty of secrecy—which implies that it is not in the public domain—and if that information may reasonably be expected to be price-sensitive he must be held to possess inside information within the meaning of WTE art 46.

If Tom does not know and should not reasonably suspect that the two golfers are directors of Big NV it would seem unlikely that he should suspect the information to be secret.

Problem Area 6

Fiona, a director of Go Ahead NV (listed on the ASE), reveals certain inside information about the company to Carol, her golfing partner. Carol passes it on to her husband Greg. Is Greg now an insider? To be an insider, WTE art 46 requires Greg to know or at least suspect that he has inside information.

The chances that Greg should know or reasonably suspect that the information Carol passed to him was secret are progressively greater in the case that Greg knows that the source of the information is:

(1) one of his wife's golf partners many of whom he knows are company directors; or
(2) his wife's golf partner whom he knows is a company director; or
(3) his wife's golf partner whom he knows is finance director of Go Ahead NV.

However, not only the source of the information but also its nature may be decisive. Greg became an insider if he knew or should have suspected that Fiona's information was secret. This may be evident from the nature of the information and may be independent of Greg's knowledge of the source thereof.

2.4.1.5 Price-sensitive information

Article 46 of the WTE provides that inside information is information which, when published, may reasonably be expected to affect the price of the securities in question. The Explanatory Memorandum to CC art 336a emphasises that the wording of the provision indicates a kind of information the publication of which has been shown by experience—ie objectively—to have a 'clearly appreciable effect' on the price. In this respect, the Dutch provision seems to be somewhat more stringent than art 1(1) of the Directive which requires a 'significant effect' on the price.

In the event of a prosecution, an expert witness may opine on the question of whether or not certain information was price-sensitive. The court may also rely on the opinion of the Stock Exchange Association (*Vereniging voor de Effectenhandel*, 'the Association'), the administrator and supervisor of the ASE.

2.4.1.6 Knowledge of direction of price movement necessary

In *Van den Nieuwenhuyzen*, one of the main issues was whether at the time of the transaction one could not only reasonably have expected that publication of the information would have affected the price of the relevant securities but also in which direction the price would move, even if the defendant himself did not have this insight.

The Supreme Court held that it is a necessary requirement under CC art 336a/WTE art 46 that at the time of the transaction insight into the direction in which the price of securities would develop 'could exist'. It is not necessary that the accused himself had such insight. In so holding, the Supreme Court was citing legislative history where it is indicated that CC art 336a is designed to prevent anyone from taking advantage of inside information by buying prior to a price increase or selling prior to a price decrease.

The holding of the Supreme Court has met with approval in literature. It is, however, not entirely clear whether the Supreme Court's holding is in line with the Directive. The Directive merely requires that publication 'would be likely to have a significant effect on the price'.

2.4.1.7 No intentional use of inside information required

It is important to note that WTE art 46 does not require that someone is intentionally using inside information when entering into a transaction. The mere fact that someone is trading while possessing inside information constitutes a criminal offence. One of the reasons for this approach is that it would otherwise be too difficult for the public prosecutor to prove that someone decided to enter into or bring about a transaction because s/he possessed inside information.

It is not only in order to avoid problems for the public prosecutor that the WTE is rather broad regarding evidence. The legislator also intended to provide certainty for all participants on the stock exchange that trading takes place in a fair and honest manner. No doubt should therefore exist whether one is, or may be, trading with someone who possesses inside information but is claiming not to be trading on the basis thereof. In the Explanatory Memorandum to CC art 336a it was made clear that anyone who possesses inside information should avoid the stock market and refrain from encouraging others to enter into transactions.

It would seem that in this respect the WTE is more stringent than the Directive which provides in art 2(1) that member states shall prohibit insiders from taking advantage of inside information 'with full knowledge of the facts by acquiring or disposing of . . . securities'.

2.4.2 The *Van den Nieuwenhuyzen* case

So far, the only case decided by any Netherlands court on insider dealing is *Van den Nieuwenhuyzen* (*Hoge Raad*, 27 June 1995, published in extract in NJB 1995, pp 374–7). In this case, the Supreme Court reversed the decision of the Amsterdam Court of Appeals. The case has now been referred to the Court of Appeals at The Hague. The Supreme Court has clarified certain of the elements of CC art 336a (and the almost identical WTE art 46). Over a period of several years the *Van den Nieuwenhuyzen* case has been one of the major issues in the financial press in the Netherlands and the subject of dozens of publications in legal literature. It should be kept in mind, though, that this is not a typical case of insider dealing. It has often been called a case of 'market orchestration' and its atypical nature may have influenced the outcome so far.

2.4.2.1 The facts

In the evening and night of 30–31 July 1991 a meeting took place in Amsterdam at which members of the managing and the supervisory boards of HCS Technology NV ('HCS'), representatives of HCS's banks and three major share-holders (including Van den Nieuwenhuyzen ('VdN')) were present. The purpose of the meeting was to discuss whether and on what conditions the participants in the meeting would be prepared to participate in a final rescue plan for the ailing HCS. It was agreed that HCS would be provided with new capital, *inter alia*, by an issue in which the major shareholders guaranteed to participate for NLG60 million. By 2 August 1991 it would be decided whether the issue would be public or private and what the price of the shares would be. The banks strongly favoured a private offering at a substantially lower price than the market price at 30 July.

On 31 July 1991 HCS issued a press release in which it was announced that the capital of HCS would be increased by NLG185 million, among others by a guaranteed issue of new shares yielding NLG127.5 million. VdN guaranteed to participate in the issue for NLG25 million. The press release noted that further announcements would follow regarding the particulars of the issue. The next day a large amount of HCS shares (4.1 million) were sold by order of VdN, with the specific intent to lower the market price of the HCS shares.

Van den Nieuwenhuyzen was summoned in criminal court for violation of CC art 336a in that he had been in possession of non-public, secret information regarding HCS (ie certain details about the agreement reached between HCS, its major shareholders and the banks) while trading in HCS shares.

2.4.2.2 The Amsterdam District Court

The Amsterdam District Court acquitted VdN of the charges. The court held that some of the information of which VdN had knowledge included 'particular circumstances' regarding HCS which were not in the public domain. The court concluded, however, that no duty of secrecy had been imposed at the meeting regarding this information, neither explicitly nor implicitly. The court furthermore held that, although the alleged inside information could reasonably have been expected to affect the market price of the securities involved, it was not clear in which direction the price would have been affected.

2.4.2.3 The Amsterdam Court of Appeals

Van den Nieuwenhuyzen was subsequently convicted by the Amsterdam Court of Appeals. The court held that VdN had knowledge of 'particular circumstances' regarding HCS, ie:

(1) that HCS's bankruptcy was inevitable if no funds were made available;
(2) that it had been determined that by 2 August 1991 the type of issue would be decided;
(3) that a private issue would be chosen if the price of the shares were to fall from NLG4.00 to no more than NLG2.50; and
(4) that the price of the issue would be determined on the basis of the price development of HCS shares from 31 July to 2 August.

All this information was not (explicitly) part of the press release. The court rejected VdN's argument that the element of duty of secrecy in CC art 336a is limited to a duty the violation of which is a criminal offence, and held that it had to be determined according to the circumstances of each case whether a duty of secrecy existed. In this instance, VdN and the other participants in the meeting, all experienced in their fields, could have understood that the information discussed had to be kept secret.

With respect to the influence on the market price, the court held that CC art 336a does not require that VdN had to know in which direction the prices would have been affected if the secret information had become public. The court held that the mere knowledge that the market price would have been affected was sufficient.

Van den Nieuwenhuyzen also claimed that the requirement 'any advantage may result from that transaction' had not been met since he actually lost money on the sale of the HCS shares (which was below the price for which he had originally bought the shares). The court rejected this argument stating that the intended purpose of the transaction was to reduce the price of the HCS shares. The court held that it would most certainly have been possible that after the subsequent issue the price of the shares would have soared as a result of which VdN's (increased) shareholding would have increased in value. In the event of a public issue VdN might have had the advantage that he would not have been called upon under his guarantee if the issue had been a success.

The court sentenced VdN to six months in prison (three months suspended) and to a penalty of NLG100,000 (approximately £40,000 STG).

2.4.2.4 The Supreme Court

In the Supreme Court VdN claimed that the Court of Appeals had adopted an incorrect interpretation of 'the duty of secrecy' in CC art 336a. The Supreme Court disagreed. It held that a duty of secrecy may be inferred from the circumstances of each case if the duty to keep the specific information secret has expressly or implicitly been imposed on the person having the knowledge (for example through a statutory regulation, an agreement, a corporate decision or a customary practice). The approach of the Court of Appeals to this matter was therefore not held to be incorrect.

With respect to the influence on the market price, the Supreme Court agreed with the District Court. The Supreme Court held, *inter alia*, on the basis of the rationale and the legislative history, that CC art 336a required that at the time of the transaction it could by objective standards reasonably be expected not only that publication of the secret 'particular circumstance' would affect the price of the shares but also in which direction the price would move. The legal standard applied by the Court of Appeals was therefore held to be incorrect.

As to the element of possible advantage, the Supreme Court, again partly on the basis of the legislative history, held that the causal relationship between the transaction and the advantage which may result from the transaction must be sufficiently direct in order to establish that the (possible) advantage can be deemed to stem from the transaction as such. This will not be the case if the advantage is dependent upon uncertain, new developments which may occur after the transaction has been concluded. The Supreme Court held that the Court of Appeals had interpreted this element of CC art 336a too broadly.

The Supreme Court quashed the decision of the Court of Appeals and referred the case to the Court of Appeals at The Hague to decide it on the basis of the Supreme Court's holdings. In January 1996 it was not yet known when the Court of Appeals would pass sentence.

2.4.3 Trading

2.4.3.1 Trading in own securities

The question has been raised whether knowledge of a company of its own plans to acquire and/or sell shares in its own share capital may constitute inside information. The same question could be raised with respect to depository receipts issued by a third party (trust company) in exchange for the company's shares and to debentures issued by the company itself. If the answer is affirmative, a company trading in its own securities or depository receipts would almost by definition be guilty of an abuse of inside information. The opinions on this issue are divided.

It has been pointed out that the Dutch Civil Code allows a company to acquire shares in its own capital up to a maximum of 10 per cent (art 2:98(2)). It would therefore be contrary to the system of the Civil Code to prohibit a company from trading in its own securities. The Second EC Directive on company law also permits a company to acquire its own securities. In addition, some authors have argued that information with respect to a company's decision to trade in its own securities is not inside information since such information is not subject to a duty to maintain secrecy.

It seems, however, that a majority of commentators are of the opinion that a company trading in its own securities will violate WTE art 46. Article 46 of the WTE does not contain an exception to the effect that anyone intending to sell or purchase shares held by himself, or a company intending to sell or purchase shares in its own share capital, will not be considered to be in possession of inside information.

The Minister of Justice offered a somewhat surprising solution to this problem in parliament. According to the Minister, the mere knowledge by a company of its own intention to sell or purchase its own securities does not in itself constitute inside information. Abuse of inside information does, however, take place where inside information constitutes the reason for the company's decision to buy or sell its own securities. However, where a company decides to purchase or sell its own securities on the basis of publicly available information there would, according to the Minister, be no abuse of inside information.

It is not certain whether the opinion offered by the Minister will be accepted by the courts. Arguably, the fact that a company decides to allocate part of its assets to the acquisition of its own share capital instead of using the assets for its normal business activities would by itself be information relevant to its shareholders. Information about such a decision by the company may well influence the price of securities if the information becomes public knowledge.

In addition, one could perhaps argue that a decision by a company to buy or sell its own securities constitutes information regarding the trade in securities and would therefore fall within the definition of inside information even if the decision had been taken on the basis of publicly available information.

The Minister of Justice has also stated that a company might purchase its own shares with impunity if it does so by way of defence against an unfriendly take-over bid. The impunity would in that event be based on the general rules of criminal law under which *force majeure* may remove the punishability of an act. Again, it is not certain whether the courts will accept this opinion.

Finally, in this context reference must be made to the preamble to the Directive where it is stated:

... whereas likewise the fact of carrying out transactions with the aim of stabilizing the price of new issues or secondary offers of transferable securities should not in itself be deemed to constitute use of inside information.

It is not clear whether this refers to transactions by the subscribing syndicate or other intermediaries only or also to transactions by the issuing company itself. In the latter event it would mean that at least certain transactions by a company in its own shares are permitted.

In conclusion, it would seem that a company trading in its own securities would run a considerable risk of violating WTE art 46. The public prosecutor has been reported to have been investigating a case where a company had been trading in its own securities, allegedly while having inside information. In July 1995 this case was settled. The company agreed to pay by way of a fine the profit it had made on the transaction (see also 2.4.3.3 *below*).

2.4.3.2 Trading in anticipation of own public offer

It is unclear whether the purchase of a target company's shares in anticipation of one's own public offer for such shares is an offence under WTE art 46. Reference is made to the Directive which states in its preamble:

Whereas, since the acquisition or disposal of transferable securities necessarily involves a prior decision to acquire or dispose taken by the person who undertakes one or other of these operations, the carrying-out of this acquisition or disposal does not constitute in itself the use of inside information.

It could be argued that this quotation does not refer to a purchase prior to the intended public offer, but this is not the view taken by Prof Klaus Hopt ('The European Insider Dealing Directive' [1990] CMLR 51–82).

It would, however, seem that the fact that a public offer will or is likely to be made (or even that talks to that purpose are being held) satisfies all the conditions of 'inside information' where third parties are making use of that information. It is difficult, then, to maintain why the offeror himself should be free to deal.

Problem Area 7

The directors of Blue Ink NV, an Amsterdam-listed manufacturer of inks, are contemplating a bid for their other listed rival, Red Ink NV. Based on confidential information relating to the inks industry, the directors value Red Ink NV at NLG100 million. They plan to restructure Red Ink NV if the bid is successful, to take advantage of this information and make the company more profitable. As a first step, Blue Ink NV acquires a number of shares in Red Ink NV from an individual known to its Chairman.

Unlike industry information assembled from public sources, confidential information about ink manufacturing companies may constitute inside information about Red Ink NV if it concerns a 'particular circumstance' of which the directors know or should reasonably suspect that it is not in the public domain, and which is price-sensitive (see 2.4). Consequently, Blue Ink NV may well have committed the dealing offence by acquiring shares in Red Ink NV while in possession of this information.

In addition, Blue Ink NV may have committed the dealing offence by acquiring shares in Red Ink NV while contemplating a bid for Red Ink NV (see 2.4.3.2).

If the intention to restructure Red Ink NV were nevertheless held to be inside information about Red Ink NV, Blue Ink NV would be likely to be found guilty of the dealing offence since its entire board, and therefore the company (see 2.3), were aware of inside information while acquiring shares of Red Ink NV.

In that event, the directors would be guilty of ordering or directing the criminal offence committed by Blue Ink NV.

It would seem doubtful that the intention of Blue Ink NV to restructure Red Ink NV after the take-over is inside information about Red Ink NV since it will only become relevant after the take-over (when further trading is unlikely to occur to any significant extent) and only in the event that that intention is realised. These eventualities seem to be too remote to be a basis for inside information.

2.4.3.3 Customary practice

The Minister of Justice has indicated in Parliament that there may be no abuse of inside information where a transaction by a company in its own securities, falling within the definition provided by the WTE, is 'customary practice and acceptable' in the securities trade. It is, however, not evident why a transaction which is contrary to WTE 46 would not constitute a criminal offence if it is 'customary practice and acceptable'.

The argument that a transaction which is 'customary practice and acceptable' does not violate WTE art 46 was raised by the defence in *Van den Nieuwenhuyzen*. It was claimed that a sale/purchase of shares designed to orchestrate the market price of the relevant shares constitutes such a practice. The Amsterdam Court of Appeals rejected the argument, holding that CC art 336a had been specifically designed to redress certain practices of the market. However, in his conclusion before the Supreme Court decision, the Attorney-General supported the argument and concluded that the Court of Appeals should have addressed this issue more carefully in light of the legislative history of CC art 336a. The Supreme Court did not rule on this issue, which is therefore still open to debate.

2.4.4 Trading among insiders

Given the legislator's position that one should avoid the stock market if one possesses inside information, a criminal offence may be committed if an insider is trading with another insider even though both are possessing identical (inside) information, eg because the buyer has informed the seller fully of all the (inside) information he possessed.

2.5 WHAT ACTION IS PROHIBITED?

2.5.1 'Entering into' or 'bringing about' a transaction

As mentioned above, WTE art 46 distinguishes 'entering into' a transaction from 'bringing about' a transaction. The 'Note in Response to the Final Report' ('the Note') to the 1989 Bill states that 'entering into' refers to a situation where the person concerned effects the transaction himself, whereas 'bringing about' includes all cases where one person induces another to enter into the transaction, regardless of whether that other person also possesses inside information. According to the Note, these latter cases include procuring (*doen plegen*), inciting (*uitlokken*) as well as commissioning (*opdracht geven*) and tipping.

However, during the discussions in Parliament the relationship between the special provision on insider dealing and the system of the Criminal Code has not been considered at all. We do, however, not see how the government's definition of 'bringing about' a transaction can be reconciled with general legal doctrine on procuring (*doen plegen*), inciting (*uitlokken*) and participating (*medeplegen*) in criminal offences as well as complicity (*medeplichtigheid*) thereto, as laid down in CC arts 47 and 48. If, as the Note suggests, 'bringing about' comprised all of the offences referred to in CC arts 47 and 48, then, for instance, procuring the procuring of a transaction would constitute an offence.

The interpretation given by the Note seems even more difficult to apply when CC art 46a is considered. Under this provision, even an attempt at inciting someone (eg by gifts or promises or by providing him with the opportunity, means or information) to commit a crime (*misdrijf*, which includes insider dealing) is a criminal offence. This would mean that attempting to procure someone else to procure a transaction is a criminal offence.

Problem Area 8

Helen, a director of Predator NV, has information that the directors of Target NV, an Amsterdam-listed company, are in talks with Rival NV about a possible take-over of Target NV.

She recommends to the Board of Predator NV (without disclosing the inside information) that Predator NV should buy some shares in Target NV. She votes in favour of the resolution at the Board Meeting to acquire those shares. John, Predator NV's stockbroker, is instructed to acquire 1,000 shares in Target NV. The next day Helen learns that the talks between Target NV and Rival NV have broken down. Again, without disclosing the inside information, Helen persuades the Board of Predator NV to reverse its decision. Appropriate instructions are issued to John.

Helen did not enter into any transaction in shares of Target NV. If John had already entered into a transaction to acquire shares in Target NV, Helen is guilty of bringing about this transaction while having inside information.

If John had not yet entered into such transaction, Helen may be guilty of a criminal attempt to cause a transaction in securities with respect to which she had inside information (CC art 45).

Predator NV does not seem to have committed any offence since the company did not have any inside information at the time John was instructed to acquire shares in Target NV. If Helen is only one of a number of directors her knowledge would be unlikely to be imputed to Predator NV (see 2.3 *above*). John, who did not possess Helen's inside information, does not seem to have committed any offence either. If he was in possession of any inside information it could only be information relating to the trade in Target's shares and WTE art 46(4) would apply to him (see 2.9.1).

All the same, the distinction between 'entering into' and 'bringing about' is vital for the application of the second paragraph of WTE art 46. This provision deliberately does not include 'entering into' a transaction from the Netherlands in securities listed on a foreign securities exchange. According to the Member of Parliament who proposed the amendment introducing this provision its scope was limited, in line with the Note. Where, as indicated, the Note is hardly helpful in understanding the provision, we have even more difficulty understanding the intention of the MP.

Apparently, 'bringing about' was intended to be interpreted broadly. This raises the question of what meaning should be attributed to the term 'entering into' in the first paragraph of art 46. Given the fact that almost any transaction in listed securities is effected through intermediaries it would appear that 'entering into' includes not only the rare case where the person concerned concludes a transaction with another outside the stock exchange but also the normal case where he instructs a broker to conclude a transaction on the stock exchange and the broker subsequently concludes the transaction. This interpretation is in line with common parlance and, it would seem, not in conflict with the above explanation in the Note.

Problem Area 9

Alexander, the Chairman of ABC Trading NV ('ABC'), an Amsterdam-listed company making an offer of warrants attends a series of presentations with prospective investors. Also in attendance is John, a director of Global Bank, the underwriters of the offer. Both Alexander and John have damaging inside information about ABC which if it were made public would be likely to have an adverse effect on the price of ABC's shares. The inside information in question relates to poor profit forecasts which are too speculative to be included in the pathfinder prospectus since they are not capable of verification to the necessary standard. The information is not disclosed.

By stimulating investor demand rather than just presenting objective facts, are ABC, Global Bank, Alexander or John guilty of bringing about transactions in ABC's shares while they are aware of inside information with respect thereto? We assume that the warrants are already listed at the time they are purchased by the investors.

The wording of WTE art 46 is broad enough to conclude that ABC would be guilty of bringing about, as an insider, transactions in securities. The same would most likely apply to Global Bank, depending on its precise involvement in making the offer (see 2.5.1 *above*). Alexander and John may be guilty of ordering the (forbidden) activities of their companies (see 2.3 *above*).

It is, however, not entirely clear whether art 46 would be applicable here. Article 47 of the WTE may be regarded as a *lex specialis* taking priority over art 46. Article 47 reads as follows:

> Any person who issues securities or assumes a commitment to issue or co-operate in the issue of securities is prohibited from attempting to induce the public to subscribe to such issue or to participate therein by wilfully withholding information or distorting true facts or deluding the public with false facts or circumstances.

In addition, CC art 334, providing for a general prohibition on price manipulation by disseminating false information, may possibly be applicable. The relation between WTE arts 46 and 47 and CC art 334 has not been tested in practice. Consequently, no clear answers can be given.

2.5.2 The term 'transaction'

It should be noted that WTE art 46 relates to transactions with or without the involvement of a professional intermediary and on or outside a securities exchange (see art 2(3) of the Directive).

Articles 46 of the WTE and 336a of the CC are different from the text originally proposed to parliament. The original wording prohibited insiders from taking advantage from acquiring or disposing of securities. As noted above, the WTE now prohibits insiders from entering into or bringing about 'any transaction' in securities. The change in wording was made to eliminate the central position of 'taking advantage' and had nothing to do with the words 'acquiring or disposing'. Nevertheless, it has been pointed out that in Dutch 'entering into or bringing about any transaction' may be narrower than 'acquiring or disposing of'.

Thus, the current wording of the WTE does not seem to prohibit a person who possesses inside information from accepting an inheritance which includes the relevant securities. Also, it is not certain whether it is a criminal offence for a former spouse to accept securities in a division of matrimonial property belonging to both spouses, where he or she possesses inside information relating to those securities.

On this interpretation, the wording of the WTE would be narrower than that of art 2(1) of the Directive which prohibits insiders from taking advantage of inside information by 'acquiring or disposing of' securities.

Dutch courts might be inclined to interpret the WTE extensively to mean that 'transaction' shall be deemed to include any acquisition or disposal of securities. However, too broad an interpretation of the criminal provision may be difficult in light of the principle of *nulla poena sine praevia lege* (no penalty without prior law).

A question has arisen with respect to the acquisition of a right (not being an option which is listed on a securities exchange) pursuant to which one may purchase or sell certain listed securities. Such an unlisted right is of course not a listed security within the meaning of art 46(1) and (2). However, it has been argued that the term 'transaction' in WTE art 46 should be interpreted broadly, so as to include any agreement in connection with the acquisition or disposal of listed securities. So far, this question remains unresolved.

2.5.3 Refraining from action

The WTE prohibits entering into or bringing about a transaction. It is not a criminal offence for an insider to refrain from doing so, even if any advantage may result from such inactivity.

2.6 TERRITORIAL MATTERS

The original Bill restricted the offence to 'securities listed on a Dutch securities exchange and acquired or disposed of in the Netherlands, even though the order thereto may originate from abroad' (Explanatory Memorandum to the 1989 Act). 'The provision aims at protecting a regulated trade in securities on Dutch exchanges. The protection of the trade in securities on foreign exchanges is a matter for the foreign legislator' (Second Chamber, Document 19 935, nr 8). The Dutch government was extremely reluctant to give its legislation any extraterritorial effect.

This very limited view was, however, not acceptable to a majority in the Second Chamber who supported an amendment introducing what is now WTE art 46(2). This occurred prior to the adoption of the Directive.

The Directive, in art 5, is ambiguous. The first sentence of art 5 requires each member state to apply the prohibitions 'at least to actions undertaken within its territory to the extent that the transferable securities concerned are admitted to trading on a market of a Member State'. This would cover, eg an order given in Amsterdam to a Paris broker to buy shares on the Paris Bourse.

However, the second sentence takes back a large part of what the first sentence has given: 'In any event, each member state shall regard a transaction as carried out within its territory if it is carried out on a market . . . situated or operating within that territory'. This second sentence effectively reduces the obligation of the member states to prohibiting transactions on their own markets. Of course, the member states are free to go beyond this minimum requirement.

2.6.1 Entering into or bringing about in the Netherlands

The first paragraph of WTE art 46, which is in this respect similar to the first paragraph of CC art 336a reflects the original intention of the government referred to at 2.6 *above*.

It should be noted that the offence of WTE art 46(1) consists of 'entering into or bringing about in the Netherlands any transaction . . .' *not* of 'entering into or bringing about any transaction in the Netherlands . . .'. Nevertheless, the competent Ministers stated in parliament that they wished to maintain the requirement that the offence involves the entering into or bringing about of a transaction 'which takes place in the Netherlands' (see 2.6 *above*). In our view, however, the *wording* of a provision of criminal law must prevail.

2.6.2 Bringing about from the Netherlands

As mentioned above, the second paragraph of WTE art 46 is limited to bringing about from the Netherlands any transaction in securities listed on a foreign securities exchange. As long as the meaning of 'bringing about' is uncertain the scope of this paragraph remains in doubt.

Article 46(2) of the WTE does not seem to claim any extraterritorial effect. It only refers to action 'from the Netherlands' ie committed inside the Netherlands. Whatever the meaning of 'bringing about', the scope of this paragraph would seem to be limited. One would not expect extensive insider dealing activity from the Netherlands with respect to securities listed on foreign exchanges, but it may occur.

The combined effect of paras 1 and 2 of WTE art 46 would seem to be that at least the following actions meeting all other requirements of insider dealing do not constitute criminal offences under Netherlands law:

- entering in or from the Netherlands into a transaction in securities listed on a non-Dutch securities exchange; and
- entering into or bringing about outside the Netherlands a transaction in securities listed on a non-Dutch securities exchange.

It would seem that Dutch law leaves plenty of scope to international opera-tors in the field of insider dealing. It should, however, be noted that the Netherlands has ratified the Council of Europe Convention and Protocol on Insider Trading (Strasbourg, 20 April and 11 September 1989). The Convention provides for exchange of information and mutual assistance among the parties thereto. As between EU member states, the Convention is superseded by art 10 of the Directive which provides for exchange of information and co-operation among the competent authorities in the member states. The Netherlands is also a party to the European Treaty on Mutual Assistance in Criminal Matters (Strasbourg, 20 April 1959) and the Additional Protocol thereto (Strasbourg, 17 March 1978). In addition, the Netherlands has a Treaty with the USA (dated 12 June 1981) on mutual assistance in criminal matters.

In 1994, the WTE, the Act on the Supervision of the Credit System, the Act on the Supervision of the Insurance Industry and the Act on the Supervision of Investment Institutions were amended to include provisions enabling Dutch supervising authorities to provide other national and foreign supervising author-ities information obtained in the exercise of their duties as well as to obtain infor-mation from, and make enquiries with, anyone at the request of a foreign supervising authority (WTE arts 33, 34, 36 and 37).

Problem Area 10

Stephen has inside information on Overseas Inc, a company whose shares are listed on the Amsterdam and New York exchanges. From his office in The Hague he telephones a broker in New York and instructs him to acquire shares in Overseas Inc.

Various approaches to this problem are possible, depending on the inter-pretation of the terms 'entering into' and 'bringing about'. The simplest approach is as follows: since Stephen acted in the Netherlands in respect of securities listed on the ASE he has committed the offence of WTE art 46(1), whatever the exact interpretation of the above-mentioned two terms may be. Such action is in any event intended to be caught by either one or the other term. Under the ASE Securities Regulations a listing on the ASE means that *all* the shares of the kind listed are included in the listing, includ-ing any shares that may be traded on other stock exchanges.

However, we tend to believe that in most situations (see 2.5.1 *above*) 'entering into' consists of two elements: the giving of an order and the car-rying out of an order by a broker. If that is correct one could argue that only if both elements take place in the Netherlands can it be said that the transaction is 'entered into' in the Netherlands, as art 46(1) requires. In this case only one element (the giving of the order) took place in the Netherlands. The order was executed in New York.

Of course, one could argue that the decisive element is the giving of the order. But where the stated aim of the Dutch provision is to protect trading on the Amsterdam Stock Exchange while avoiding the regulation of any dealing on foreign stock exchanges (see 2.6 *above*) it could also be argued that the execution of the order is the decisive element. In that event, Stephen would not have committed a criminal offence under art 46(1) since the decisive element of 'entering into' took place in New York. He would not have committed an offence under art 46(2) either, since that paragraph does not refer to 'entering into'.

This would be a rather unsatisfactory solution to the problem, unless one had to conclude that the giving of the order was in fact a form of 'bringing about' the transaction. In that event, Stephen would be caught by art 46(2) ('bringing about from the Netherlands'). If this were so, it would be very difficult to give any meaningful interpretation to the term 'entering into' (see 2.5.1 *above*).

What if the shares were listed on the New York Stock Exchange only? In that event the only question would be whether WTE art 46(2) applied. If Stephen should be held to have 'entered into' the transaction in New York he could not have 'brought it about' as art 46(2) requires. In the event that he was found to have 'brought about' the transaction the above would apply.

It is of course possible that Stephen has committed insider dealing pursuant to the laws of the United States.

TABLE (1)

Constituent elements for insider dealing in securities listed in the Netherlands:
- Individual or legal entity must possess inside information (see 2.4).
- Individual or legal entity must act in the Netherlands (see 2.6.1).
- Transaction must concern securities listed on a Netherlands securities exchange (see 2.7).
- Transaction must be potentially advantageous (see 2.8).

2.7 TO WHICH SECURITIES EXCHANGE DO THE PROHIBITIONS APPLY?

The reader is reminded that WTE art 46 relates to transactions both on and outside a securities exchange. Article 46(1) applies to securities quoted on the following securities exchanges, all of which are authorised under art 22 of the WTE:

- The Amsterdam Stock Exchange (*Amsterdamse Effectenbeurs*);
- The European Options Exchange;
- The Financial Futures Exchange (*Financiële Termijnmarkt*);
- The Agricultural Futures Exchange Amsterdam (*Agrarische Termijnmarkt Amsterdam*).

The foreign securities exchanges referred to in para 2 of WTE art 46 are not defined. Even though the relevant wording of that paragraph dates from prior to the Directive one may expect the courts to interpret this wording in accordance with art 1(2) of the Directive. This refers to 'a market which is regulated and supervised by authorities recognised by public bodies, operates regularly and is accessible directly or indirectly to the public'.

2.8 POTENTIAL ADVANTAGE

According to WTE art 46 insider trading is an offence only if any advantage may result from the transaction. The element of a potential advantage was a major issue in *Van den Nieuwenhuyzen*. The Supreme Court held that the causal relationship between the transaction and the advantage which may result therefrom must be sufficiently direct in order to establish that the potential advantage may be deemed to stem from the transaction as such. No dependency on uncertain new developments after the transaction should exist.

The Supreme Court's holding on this issue is sharply in contrast with literature on the subject. Prior to the decision, it was generally held that the element of potential advantage would not add to the public prosecutor's burden of proof.

The fact that the Supreme Court has taken a direction not quite in line with previous commentaries may actually be a warning not to rely too heavily on any commentary on elements of WTE art 46 of which the Supreme Court has not yet provided an interpretation.

The Directive contains the requirement that the insider has the intention of 'taking advantage of that information' (art 2(1)). It is not clear whether the decision of the Supreme Court is in line with the text of the Directive.

TABLE (2)

Constituent elements for insider dealing in securities listed outside the Netherlands
• Individual or legal entity must possess inside information (see 2.4).
• Individual or legal entity must 'bring about' from the Netherlands a transaction (see 2.5.1 and 2.6.2).
• Transaction must concern securities listed on a stock exchange outside the Netherlands (see 2.7).
• Transactions must be potentially advantageous (see 2.8).

2.9 EXCEPTIONS

2.9.1 Intermediaries

Article 46, para (4) of the WTE contains an exception on behalf of brokers, and in particular jobbers and market-makers who act on an exchange in good faith to serve principals. According to the Explanatory Memorandum to the 1989 Act, such action need not always be on the direct instructions of principals. In performing their task of furthering the liquidity of the market they may take positions for their own account. This forms part of their service to their principals. In doing so, however, they are in possession of inside information on the trade in the securities concerned since they know they will have to liquidate their positions in the near future. Article 46(4) is designed to protect them from criminal liability, provided they act 'in accordance with the rules of good faith'. It is not quite clear what this means, but it may be taken to mean in any event that they must observe the relevant rules of the ASE.

From the wording of WTE art 46 it follows that it applies exclusively to intermediaries if and when they are trading on the exchange. Consequently, where they are trading on the ASE they must be subject to the non-statutory regulations issued by the ASE.

The exception contained in art 46(4) is not contrary to the Directive since the definition of 'inside information' in art 1(1) of the Directive only includes information relating to issuers and securities, not to the trade in securities.

2.9.2 Other

The Dutch legislator has not incorporated in the insider dealing legislation the exception laid down in art 2(4) of the Directive relating to transactions carried out in pursuit of monetary, exchange-rate or public debt-management by public authorities.

2.10 DISCLOSURE

Article 46 of the WTE does not prohibit a person or legal entity from disclosing inside information to another person or legal entity. However, the disclosure of inside information may nevertheless constitute a criminal offence. Article 273 of the CC provides that it is a criminal offence for anyone who is or has been working for a commercial enterprise to disclose particular circumstances regarding the enterprise, if a duty to maintain secrecy with respect to such circumstances has been imposed on him. It is generally accepted that this provision is limited to persons or legal entities who have entered into a contractual relationship with the enterprise.

Since it is not a criminal offence to disclose information if no duty to maintain secrecy has been imposed, the scope of CC art 273 is rather limited. The provision may, however, be more effective if it is interpreted in connection with art 2.3 of the Model Code of the ASE (see *below* at 3.2.2) which provides that a managing director or supervisory director of a listed company shall not disclose price-sensitive information to a third party. In principle, this provision is binding only on the listed company and not on directors of the listed company. Listed companies, however, are under a duty pursuant to the Model Code to impose on their directors a duty to maintain secrecy with respect to price-sensitive information. This would mean that where such a duty has been imposed the disclosure of such information would constitute a violation of CC art 273.

It should be noted that on the basis of CC art 273 the disclosure of inside information exclusively with respect to the *trade* in securities (and not regarding the enterprise) is not a criminal offence. However, it is conceivable that important information relating to the trade in securities may also relate to the issuer itself. In that event it may also be information regarding the enterprise.

Furthermore, it should be borne in mind that the disclosure of inside information in order to bring about a transaction in listed securities may be regarded as a dealing offence (see 2.5.1).

2.11 PENALTIES

Under art 1(3°) of the Act on Economic Offences (*Wet Economische Delicten*, hereinafter 'WED'), violation of WTE art 46 is an economic offence. In Dutch criminal law offences are distinguished into crimes (*misdrijven*) and infringements (*overtredingen*). Crimes are the more serious offences. According to the WTE and the WED, violation of WTE art 46 is a crime.

2.11.1 Individuals

Article 6(1)(2°) of the WED provides for imprisonment for up to two years or a fine of up to NLG25,000 (approximately £10,000 STG) for individuals. Where the profit arising from the offence exceeds one quarter of the maximum fine the maximum is increased to NLG100,000 (approximately £40,000 STG).

In addition, the court may order that the insider pay to the state an amount equal to the advantage which the insider obtained as a result of his offence (WED art 8a and CC art 36e).

2.11.2 Legal entities

As discussed above (see 2.3) legal entities as well as individuals may commit criminal offences. Where the maximum fine for an individual is NLG25,000 (approximately £10,000 STG) a legal entity may be sentenced to a maximum fine of NLG100,000 (approximately £40,000 STG). The maximum fine for a legal entity is NLG1 million (approximately £400,000 STG) where an individual may be sentenced to a maximum fine of NLG100,000 (approximately £40,000 STG). The same rules apply with respect to orders to pay to the state an amount equal to the advantage obtained.

Where a criminal offence has been committed by a legal entity the individuals who ordered the offence, or who were actually in charge thereof, may also be prosecuted (see 2.3 *above*). In such cases, the maximum fines which may be imposed on individuals are also applicable to the individuals mentioned here.

2.12 SUPERVISION AND PROSECUTION

Article 8 of the Directive requires the member states to designate one or more administrative authorities to ensure the application of the provisions adopted pursuant to the Directive. This provision has not (yet) been formally implemented. However, most of the powers of the Minister of Finance under the WTE have been delegated to the Securities Board (*Stichting Toezicht Effectenverkeer*, the 'STE'). As part of its supervisory task, the STE may require (pursuant to WTE art 29) any relevant information from, *inter alia*, any stock exchange authority, broker, portfolio manager, issuer of securities (outside a restricted circle) and even holders of an interest of not less than five per cent in any enterprise or institution.

Normally, the supervisory department of the ASE, the Control Bureau (*Controlebureau*) will have warned the STE that a possible violation of the insider dealing rules may have occurred. The Control Bureau will have been notified of a suspicion of insider trading by a subdivision of the Exchange Trading Supervision Department (*Afdeling Toezicht Effectenhandel*) of the ASE, the so-called Stockwatch (see further on the Stockwatch *below* at 3.2.1 and 3.2.2). Since the powers of the Control Bureau are limited (the most far-reaching power is laid down in art 12 of the Model Code, see 3.2.2 *below*), the STE may need to be involved in the matter at an early stage. In practice, the STE will have the Control Bureau conduct its investigation (see *V de Serrière* in *Insider Trading in Western Europe*, pp 118–120, 125).

Where the STE, in co-operation with the Control Bureau, finds that a well-founded suspicion of a violation of WTE art 46 exists, it will inform the judicial authorities (*aangifte*). Subsequently, the Economic Surveillance Department (*Economische Controle Dienst*, the 'ECD') will be authorised to further investigate the matter. The powers of the ECD are based on the ordinary investigative powers laid down in the Code of Criminal Procedure, as well as on special, more extensive, powers laid down in the WED. Pursuant to WED arts 18–20, investigative officers are authorised, *inter alia*, to:

(1) at all times impound, or require the surrender of any materials;
(2) require inspection of all documents which they reasonably consider necessary to fulfil their duty; and
(3) compel access to any place to the extent that such access is reasonably necessary for the fulfilment of their duty.

The ECD activities will take place under supervision of the public prosecutor who will eventually decide whether or not to prosecute.

As can be seen, many authorities are involved in any investigation of a violation of WTE art 46: Stockwatch, Control Bureau, STE, ECD, the public prosecutor. Some of the investigation may be duplicated or repeated and inevitably it will take a long time before the decision of whether or not to prosecute may be reached. This is why recently discussions have been initiated between authorities involved to see how these investigations can be better and more efficiently co-ordinated.

3 NON-STATUTORY REGULATION

3.1 INTRODUCTION

In addition to the criminal sanctions imposed by WTE art 46, there are a number of other rules in place designed to prevent and regulate insider dealing. Most of these rules emanate from the ASE and belong to the ASE's extensive body of self-regulation. Some rules have been made by other authorities, as will be briefly set out below. A detailed consideration of all of these rules is outside the scope of this book.

3.2 AMSTERDAM STOCK EXCHANGE

3.2.1 The Listing Rules

In order to be listed on the ASE, a company has to enter into a listing agreement (*noteringsovereenkomst*, 'the Agreement') with the Association. Under the Agreement, parties agree to observe the rules laid down in the Rules Relating to the Requirements for Listing on the ASE (*Fondsenreglement*, the 'Listing Rules'). Article 28 of the Listing Rules deals with information to be provided by the issuer to the investing public. Pursuant to art 28(h) the issuer of listed securities is obliged to notify the public forthwith of, *inter alia*, any fact or event concerning the issuer which is likely to considerably (*aanmerkelijk*) affect the price of the securities. The Association may grant an exemption if publication of the information could prejudice the legitimate interests of the issuer.

On the basis of art 28 the ASE may require the issuer to publish specific information if this is necessary for the protection of the investor or for an orderly operation of the market.

The Listing Rules (in particular art 28(h)) are designed to prevent the abuse of inside information by providing for a duty to make public the relevant information as soon as possible. It should be noted that the test applied by the Listing Rules is a '*considerable* effect on the price', as opposed to a mere effect on the price as required by WTE art 46. It may, in other words, not be sufficient to merely comply with art 28(h) of the Listing Rules and forthwith publish any price-sensitive information that may have a *considerable* effect on the price, in order to avoid violation of WTE art 46.

Implementation of the rule laid down in art 28(h) of the Listing Rules is the primary responsibility of the issuer. However, in order to monitor possible deviations from regular trading patterns (which may be the result of a failure to notify under art 28(h) of the Listing Rules) the Association set up in 1985 a 'Stockwatch'. The Stockwatch regularly reports to the Listing Officer (*Commissaris voor de Notering*), who is the official within the Association in charge of an orderly operation of the market. The Listing Officer may on the basis of the information provided to him inquire with the listed company whether a reason exists to make a public announcement. Depending on the outcome of the inquiry, the Listing Officer may decide to take certain trade measures (*handelsmaatregelen*), ie may suspend trading for a few hours or prohibit trading for a period not exceeding two days. Where a suspicion of insider trading exists, the Listing Officer may also combine a prohibition to trade with cancellation of the market prices and therewith of any transactions entered into during a certain period prior to the suspension or prohibition of trade (art 10 of the Quotations Rules, *Reglement voor de Notering*).

In addition to these trade measures, failure to comply with the provisions of the Listing Rules or the Listing Agreement may also lead to suspension or cancellation of the official listing under art 65 of the Listing Rules.

3.2.2 The Model Code

Following the example of the London Stock Exchange, the ASE has adopted a Model Code to Prevent Insider Dealing (*Modelcode voorkoming misbruik van voorwetenschap*, 'the Model Code'), effective from 1 January 1987. The Model Code is attached as Annex IX to the Listing Rules and each company listed on the ASE has to file a declaration with the ASE that it has adopted an internal code to prevent insider trading applying, as a minimum requirement, the rules of the Model Code. In practice, companies tend to adopt the integral text of the Model Code as their internal code.

The requirements of the Model Code apply to:

(1) managing directors; and
(2) supervisory directors of the issuer; and
(3) certain persons (to be designated by the issuer) who by virtue of their position within the issuer (or a subsidiary thereof within the Netherlands) have access to price-sensitive information

(the above persons in this section collectively referred to as 'insiders').

The requirements of the Model Code do not apply to the issuer itself.

The fact that the issuer *itself* may determine the application of the Model Code with respect to the persons referred to at (3) above, has elicited the obvious criticism that 'diligent' issuers could as a result more easily violate the Model Code. It may also be noted that the scope of possible 'insiders' under the Model Code is less broadly defined than 'insiders' as defined in art 2 of the Directive.

In general terms, the requirements of the Model Code amount to the following:

(1) A *general* prohibition to directly or indirectly purchase or sell securities of the issuer for one's own account or for the account of a third party, when the insider is in possession of price-sensitive information in relation to such securities. This prohibition also applies to securities in other companies listed on the ASE when by virtue of his position the insider possesses price-sensitive information in relation to such securities.

(2) A *specific* prohibition to purchase or sell securities of the issuer during certain time periods, ie:

   (a) for two months immediately preceding a first publication of the issuer's annual results;

   (b) for 21 days immediately preceding an announcement of the issuer's semi-annual or quarterly results or the announcement of a dividend or interim dividend; and

   (c) for (in principle) one month immediately preceding the preliminary publication of a prospectus for a share issue.

In exceptional cases and on special grounds, the issuer may grant dispensation from a prohibition mentioned under (2).

(3) A prohibition to take short-term positions in securities of the issuer, ie a prohibition to sell and purchase, or vice versa, within six months. This prohibition is designed to prevent short-swing profits.

(4) A prohibition to disclose price-sensitive information to a third party, save where this is done in order to comply with a statutory obligation or in the performance of one's duties.

(5) In the absence of knowledge of price-sensitive information and provided that the time-based restrictions mentioned above are duly observed, an insider of an issuer is free to purchase or sell securities of the issuer. Nevertheless, such transactions remain subject to a notification and registration duty. Managing and supervisory directors are required to give prior written notice of their dealing intentions to the 'central officer', who is someone especially appointed for this purpose by the issuer.

The insiders are only permitted to effect the projected trade for a period of 20 days after receiving acknowledgement of the notification from the central officer. Once the securities have been purchased or sold, the central officer must be immediately notified that the transaction has been completed. The central officer will then record the transaction in a register maintained for this purpose. Other designated persons, ie those specified by the issuer as having access to price-sensitive information, are only required to notify the central officer on a quarterly basis of trade in securities of the issuer.

It should be noted that 'price-sensitive information' is defined in the Model Code as:

... an unpublished matter publication of which may reasonably be expected to have a *consid-erable effect* on the market price of such class of security (emphasis added).

The definition is less strict than the definition in WTE art 46, which merely requires the possibility of 'an effect' on the price. The definition seems to be in line with the definition in the Directive, which reads 'significant effect'.

Whenever an investigation is carried out in connection with suspected abuse of inside information by the Association's Stockwatch into dealings in certain securities, the issuer, if so requested, is obliged to produce the register prepared by its central officer for inspection by the Control Bureau of the Association (art 12).

The Model Code makes no specific mention of sanctions for non-compliance with any of its provisions. Enforcement of the requirements set forth in the Model Code is primarily the responsibility of the issuer itself. It is expected to take disciplinary measures against the wrongdoer.

In the event of a violation of the Model Code, the Association may make a public announcement (after giving the issuer the possibility to issue a formal response) which may or may not include the name of the wrongdoer. The issuer will then be under a duty to take appropriate measures. In the event of a serious violation of the Model Code, the Association may censure the issuer involved. If the issuer is unwilling to take measures against the wrongdoer, the Association could eventually force it to do so by threatening to suspend or cancel the listing pursuant to art 65 of the Listing Rules. However, in practice the Association resorts very rarely to these sanctions. The Association has no authority to take direct measures against the wrongdoer.

Apparently, the Association considers the effect of the Model Code to be insufficient. In January 1996 it published a consultation document containing a draft of a new Model Code with an extended scope including, *inter alia*, transactions entered into by the issuer with respect to its own securities.

An interesting discussion relating to the Model Code involves the question of whether a violation of the provisions of the Model Code would constitute a tort against investors who claim damages as a result of a failure of the issuer to timely inform the investors of certain inside developments. Some commentators have held that investors may indeed claim that a tort has been committed against them where an issuer violates provisions in the Listing Rules designed to protect the interests of the investors. An ancillary question is whether investors may require from the issuer that it observe the provisions of the Agreement (including, indirectly, the Model Code) which the issuer has entered into with the ASE. Case law on these issues seems to indicate that courts do not hold at present that a violation of the insider dealing rules in the Model Code in itself constitutes a tort.

Problem Area 11

David, the director, and Allan, a senior executive of Make Money NV, an Amsterdam listed company, are obliged by virtue of the Model Code to keep confidential significant price-sensitive matters until they have become public or are announced pursuant to the Listing Rules of the ASE.

Although there is an obligation to disclose such matters, David and Allan, like most directors and senior executives, have information on their company and the industry in which it operates which, although not sufficiently price-sensitive to require disclosure, is more detailed than the rest of the market will have access to from publicly available information.

Directors are subject to a general prohibition (imposed by the Model Code) to deal in the shares of their own company if they are aware of information which may have a material effect on the price of those shares. A similar prohibition may apply to certain employees of the company designated by the company.

Where the information that David and Allan possess will not *considerably* affect the price of the shares of their own company, the Model Code does not in a general manner (compare, however, 3.2.2(2)) prohibit David and Allan from dealing in shares of their company. However, WTE art 46 is more stringent than the Model Code. If secret information may reasonably be expected to simply affect the price of the shares, it constitutes inside information. Allan and David should therefore abstain from dealing, if such expectation exists.

They are in danger of committing the offence of bringing about insider dealing if they alert, for example, brokers or journalists of the information (see *above* at 2.5.1).

3.2.3 ASE Membership Rules

Chapter 2 of the ASE Membership Rules (*Ledenreglement*) contains some rules regarding the prevention of the abuse of inside information. Article 10 of the Membership Rules provides that any corporate member (*bedrijfslid*, which can be a partnership) of the ASE has the duty to adopt an adequate internal code on the confidential treatment of price-sensitive information and has to monitor its implementation. In addition, art 10(b) provides that any corporate member has to take adequate measures to ensure a separate treatment of confidential price-sensitive information relating to the businesses of credits, issues, and trade brokerage, ie each corporate member has to establish so-called 'Chinese Walls'.

In implementation of art 10(b) of the Membership Rules, the Netherlands Association of Banks (*Nederlandse Vereniging van Banken*) has issued a Code for the separate treatment of price-sensitive information (*Gedragscode ter bevordering van een gescheiden behandeling van koersgevoelige informatie*); this Code has been made mandatory for most corporate members of the ASE by the Association's Circular 91-43.

The Membership Rules provide in arts 11 and 12 that:

(1) any member of the ASE—both corporate members and stock exchange members—(*beursleden*, ie managing directors and managing partners of a corporate member); and
(2) any supervisory director of a corporate member; and
(3) any person designated by the member to have access to price-sensitive information,

shall abstain from trading in securities (listed or unlisted) for his own account, when such person has inside price-sensitive information relating to these securities. Such person shall also refrain from inducing a third person to trade or abstain from trading on the basis of confidential price sensitive information. The definition of price-sensitive information is the same as the definition contained in the Model Code.

The Control Bureau is authorised to investigate any breach of the Membership Rules. Depending on the outcome of the investigation, various disciplinary measures against the member concerned may be taken.

3.2.4 Financial reporters and employees of the ASE

Without going into any detail, two more regulations by the ASE should be mentioned. Firstly, the Regulation applying to financial reporters. In order to obtain access to the ASE, financial reporters will need to submit to a regulation especially designed for them. The regulation contains a general prohibition to trade when the reporter has knowledge of price-sensitive information. Financial reporters are also under a duty not to disclose price-sensitive information to third parties. Interesting to note is that price-sensitive information for financial reporters includes 'information relating to a projected publication on a listing company until release of the publication'. This extension of the definition of price-sensitive information is designed to prevent 'scalping', ie a situation where the financial reporter trades prior to releasing the price-sensitive publication.

Secondly, a separate regulation applies to employees of the Association. This regulation also contains a general prohibition to trade, as well as a tipping prohibition and applies to both listed and soon-to-be-listed securities.

The Control Bureau is again authorised to investigate any violation of the regulations discussed above. Disciplinary measures may be taken in case of violations.

3.2.5 regulations on private portfolio investment transactions

The Central Bank of the Netherlands ('DNB') has issued effective from 12 January 1994 a Regulation containing directives concerning private portfolio investment transactions by insiders and members of Supervisory Boards and

comparable bodies, and a recommendation concerning private portfolio investment transactions by bank employees who are not insiders (*Regeling Privé-beleg-
gingstransacties*), which is applicable to persons working with a credit institution
supervised by DNB. Since the Regulation is issued by DNB under art 22 of the
Act on Supervision of the Credit System 1992 (*Wet toezicht kredietwezen 1992*),
it cannot properly be considered 'non-statutory'. The Regulation seeks to
prevent any (semblance of) insider trading and any intermingling of private and
business interests in private portfolio investment transactions. It provides for
in-house supervision of compliance with the prescribed standards by a 'compliance officer'. If the standards are violated, the credit institution may impose
sanctions. The Regulation consists of three sections: a general section, directives as to insiders and a recommendation with respect to bank employees not
being insiders.

The Association has, in co-operation with DNB, issued its sequel to the DNB
Regulation, the Minimum Regulation Private Portfolio Investment Transactions for
Managing Directors and Employees of Corporate Members (*Minimumregeling
privé-effectentransacties voor directieleden en medewerkers van bedrijfsleden/Circulaire
R94-002*), also effective from 12 January 1994. The main characteristics of both
DNB's and the Association's Regulation are summarised in the table below.

TABLE (3)

- An insider is anyone who by virtue of his function or position has or
  may have regular access to price-sensitive information.
- Duty to keep secret price-sensitive information (ie any non-public
  datum regarding any legal entity, company or institution the disclosure
  of which may reasonably be expected to influence the price of the
  securities of that legal entity, company or institution).
- Prohibition against (inducing) insider trading.
- Avoiding the semblance of (induced) insider trading.
- Prohibition of intra-day trading.
- Prohibition of front-running.
- Prohibition against (inducing) trade with knowledge of undisclosed
  stock exchange analysis.
- Prohibition to subscribe to an issuance of stock when involved.
- Prohibition of evasion of rules through third parties.
- Duty to bind agents and portfolio managers to the same rules.
- Securities transactions in principle only through own bank or through
  discretionary manager.
- Duty to report (intended) transaction to compliance officer for check
  on compliance with regulation.
- Duty to supply information to compliance officer.
- Rules on termination of insidership.

Supervision of the implementation of the Association's regulation again takes place through the Control Bureau.

3.3 FURTHER REGULATION ON THE SUPERVISION OF THE SECURITIES TRADE 1995 (*NADERE REGELING TOEZICHT EFFECTENVERKEER 1995*)

Implementing the Decree of 8 December 1995 on the Supervision of the Securities Trade 1995, the STE has issued the Further Regulation on the Supervision of the Securities Trade of 18 December 1995 (*Nadere regeling toezicht effectenverkeer 1995*, the 'Further Regulation'). This relates mainly to securities brokers and portfolio managers who operate outside the regulated securities exchanges.

The Further Regulation provides, *inter alia*, for transparency (by way of a duty to report) of private transactions by brokers and portfolio managers. Since it is based on the WTE it cannot be classified as 'non-statutory'. Violation of its rules constitutes an economic offence.

Under the Further Regulation, securities institutions must draw up a list of all persons who, by virtue of their function or position within the institution, have regular access to confidential price-sensitive information. Such persons are prohibited from purchasing or selling securities, in whatever capacity, either directly or indirectly, for their own account, when they have knowledge of confidential price-sensitive information relating to those securities. They are also prohibited, *inter alia*, from inducing third parties to purchase or sell securities on the basis of such information.

3.4 THE MERGER CODE

Finally, it should be noted that the Rules relating to Mergers 1975 (*SER Fusiegedragsregels*, the 'Merger Code', a non-statutory code of conduct adopted by the Social and Economic Council) contain certain provisions which are more or less specifically designed to prevent the abuse of inside information. These provisions require public announcement of an intended public offer at an early stage as well as disclosure of dealings in the securities concerned by the offeror and the offeree, the members of their managing and supervisory boards as well as their family members.

3.5 SUMMATION

The above has provided a short introduction to the various non-statutory and semi-statutory regulations relevant to the issue of insider dealing. Since the different regulations were set up *ad hoc* over the last ten years and since they apply to different persons and entities, they do not form a coherent system providing for an identical set of definitions, sanctions, etc. To trace the legal framework for any particular set of circumstances will therefore require a thorough consideration of the full text of all the applicable rules.

The ASE regulations discussed apply by definition only to persons or entities with which the ASE has a certain legal relationship. The regulations are preventive in nature and possible sanctions are repressive: a public announcement, a censure or listing measures with respect to issuers; disciplinary measures with respect to members; exclusion from the trade floor for journalists; and labour sanctions for ASE employees. The private nature of the sanctions has made commentators query whether these sanctions may at all be effective. The Chairman of the Association, Baron van Ittersum, has in addition observed that the private nature of the regulations may hamper any investigation into a suspected abuse of inside information. Enforcement measures as for instance laid down in the Code of Criminal Procedure (including the hearing under oath of witnesses or accused) are not available to the Association (see 2.12 *above*). In addition, persons or entities with which the ASE has no legal relationship will not be subject to its rules, ie private investors—the largest group of potential insiders—are not bound by the detailed ASE rules.

4 CONCLUSION

In the Netherlands, the (criminal) law on insider dealing is at an early stage of development. Article 46 of the WTE which makes insider dealing a criminal offence, is hard to interpret and apply. So far, only one case has been brought to trial—and the trial is not yet over. Many questions are still to be resolved in court or by new legislation before it will be possible to give clear legal advice in specific cases.

In the meantime, in almost any case which might possibly concern the abuse of inside information the existing uncertainties will lead to the advice that the risk of a criminal offence may arise or exists.

In view of the difficulties of interpreting WTE art 46 it is also difficult to determine whether Netherlands law is entirely in line with the Directive. It may well turn out to be necessary to amend WTE art 46.

In addition to the provision of WTE art 46, a series of non-statutory or semi-statutory regulations are relevant with respect to insider dealing. Those regulations do not form a coherent system with each other or with WTE art 46.

It seems that patience and reaching a very old age will be necessary to witness a mature set of rules regulating the (ab)use of inside information in the Netherlands.

CASE STUDY

Splash NV, a company listed on the Amsterdam Stock Exchange manufactures rainwear and umbrellas. Alan, a weather forecaster, on discovering that there is an unseasonable amount of rain due in the next three months, instructs his broker to buy shares in Splash. Meanwhile, Charles, an analyst of the company's shares, is told in a conversation with Jeremy, one of the directors, that the Chairman is expected to be paid a salary of NLG 500,000. Charles knows from his knowledge of the Chairman's service contract (which is available for public inspection) that this salary could only be paid if the company achieved a profit in excess of NLG 20,000,000. (Under Dutch law, directors' service contracts are not available for public inspection. However, we have decided not to change the facts of the UK case study in order to facilitate comparison.) Charles revises his profit forecast for the company, but before he publishes it he cancels instructions which he had previously given to his broker to sell his Splash shares. Charles also tells his girlfriend, Maggie, that 'things are looking up' for Splash. Maggie then buys shares in the name of her father from an old friend of hers who wanted to sell Splash shares off market to save the payment of brokers commission. In addition, Owen, an employee of the contracting firm which cleans Splash's offices, finds a draft of the latest management figures which demonstrate Splash's high profitability, in a wastepaper bin. He immediately buys shares.

Alan
Whether Alan is guilty of insider dealing under WTE art 46 will depend on whether the information on the rainfall constitutes inside information within WTE art 46(3). It could be argued that this information can be regarded as a particular circumstance concerning Splash NV (whose sales depend on the weather) to which the securities relate. Also, the information is price-sensitive.

It seems, however, rather doubtful that this information meets the other requirements for being 'inside information'. Probably the information on rainfall is neither 'in the public domain' (see WTE art 46(3)(a)) nor 'not publicly available' (see penultimate paragraph of preamble to the Directive). And, in case the Dutch requirement of 'secrecy' as an element of 'inside information' is permitted under the Directive, it is even more doubtful that Alan was under a duty to maintain secrecy with respect to the weather forecast for the next three months (see WTE art 46(3)(a) and 2.4.1.4 and 2.4.2).

Accordingly, one may conclude that Alan does not possess inside information.

Jeremy

The disclosure of inside information is not in itself a criminal offence. The issue is whether Jeremy is guilty of infringing a contractual obligation to maintain secrecy with respect to information concerning his company. This would constitute a criminal offence (CC art 273; see also 2.10).

Since the shares of Splash are listed on the Amsterdam Stock Exchange, Splash is under a duty to prohibit its directors from disclosing price-sensitive information as referred to in the Model Code, which defines price-sensitive information as information which may reasonably be expected to have a considerable effect on the price of shares (see 3.2.2).

Consequently, Jeremy would commit the offence of CC art 273 if the information disclosed by him related to Splash and was price-sensitive and if Splash had prohibited him from disclosing that information. There can be no doubt that the information related to Splash. Furthermore, the information about the Chairman's salary might, if made public, be expected to have a considerable effect on the price of Splash's shares given the fact that the chairman's service contract was available for public inspection.

Since Charles did not enter into a transaction in Splash shares, Jeremy did not, by disclosing to Charles the level of the Chairman's salary, bring about any transaction in those shares (see 2.5.1).

Charles

Refraining from entering into or bringing about a transaction is not an offence under WTE art 46 (see 2.5.3).

Maggie

It is difficult to see how Maggie could be said to be in possession of inside information even if Charles is in possession of inside information. The information is not sufficiently precise about Splash—Charles gave no indication as to why things are looking up for Splash or what impact this might have on Splash's share price. Accordingly, Maggie is not guilty of the dealing offence. It should be noted that neither the fact that Maggie acted in the name of her father nor that she did so outside the stock exchange and without any intermediary would have detracted from the applicability of WTE art 46.

Owen

The issue is whether Owen has inside information. This is obviously the case. The information relates to a 'particular circumstance' of the company. Given the circumstances in which Owen acquired his information he must have been aware that the information was not in the public domain and could not without violation of a secret come outside the circle of persons bound by a duty of secrecy. Given his eagerness to buy Splash's shares he must also have been aware of the price-sensitive nature of the information. Finally, it is clear that 'any advantage' might result from his purchase of the shares (see 2.8). He would be found guilty of insider dealing under WTE art 46(1).

Italy

Francesco Ago and Lee Unterhalter,
Chiomenti e Associati, Rome

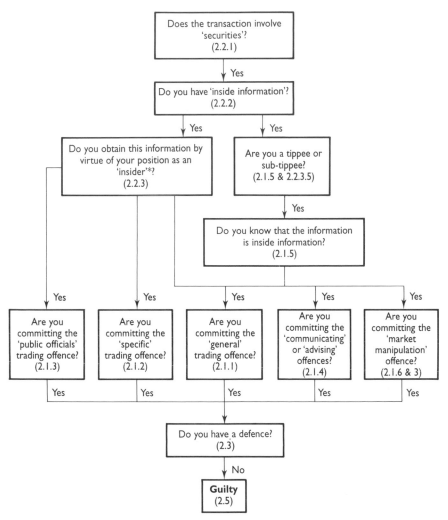

*Note: Care should be exercised in deciding what category of insider a person is in because not all categories can be guilty of all of the offences, for example only 'specified insiders' can commit the 'specific' trading offence (2.2.3.3)

1 INTRODUCTION

1.1 SOURCES OF LAW

Italy's insider trading law (Law no 157 of 17 May 1991) ('Law 157') became effective on 21 May 1991. Shortly thereafter the National Commission for Securities and the Stock Exchange ('CONSOB') issued a regulation implementing arts 6 and 7 of Law 157 (CONSOB Resolution No 5553 of 14 November 1991 ('Regulation 5553')) concerning certain reporting requirements and related penalties for non-compliance (discussed in 4 and Case Study *below*).

CONSOB has not issued any significant interpretations of Law 157 since its enactment, but it has commenced a number of investigations in exercise of its investigative and prosecution powers under art 8 of Law 157 discussed in the Case Study *below*. Since 1992 only approximately 20 insider dealing investigations have been conducted. To date, no actual prosecutions have been commenced and, as a result, no court decisions have been issued. In fact, there is only one court decision interpreting Law 157 and that decision deals with fraudulent market manipulation (also regulated by Law 157) and not insider dealing. Under Law 157 (art 8(3)) CONSOB does not itself determine whether to proceed with a prosecution. Rather, CONSOB submits the file, with a reasoned report thereon, to the competent public prosecutor, who determines whether or not to pursue the case.

Due to its recent introduction and the fact that CONSOB's investigations, prior to the commencement of actual prosecutions, are confidential and therefore no information regarding enforcement of Law 157 by CONSOB is available, interpretations of Law 157 are primarily based on the writings of Italian legal scholars* who in turn base their arguments on the drawing of analogies to other Italian laws, the EC directive on insider dealing (Dir [1989] OJ C 334/30) 89/592 the 'Directive') and the insider dealing laws of other jurisdictions.

1.2 OTHER PROVISIONS OF LAW

Given that insider dealing was only made an offence in 1991, it is worth noting that prior to the adoption of Law 157, a certain degree of market transparency was achieved by other legislation. For example, Law No 216 of 7 June 1974 ('Law 216') (the legislative basis for Italy's securities offering regulation) contains a number of provisions requiring certain corporate 'insiders' to report their share

---

* In preparing this chapter, the authors referred primarily to the commentated version of Law 157 by Prof Paolo Carbone, Università di Torino, 'Norme Relative all Uso di Informazione Riservate nelle Operazioni in Valori Mobiliari e alla Commissione Nazionale per le Società e La Borsa' in *Le Nuove Leggi Civili Commentati*, 1992, vol II, pp 963 *et seq* and Andrea Bastalena, 'Insider Trading' in *Digesto delle Discipline Privatistiche—Sezione Commerciale* VII, UTET, pp 399 *et seq.*

ownership to CONSOB. First, owners (whether directly or indirectly) of more than 2 per cent of the issued voting share capital of a listed company are required to report their share ownership to the company and to CONSOB within 48 hours of their exceeding the 2 per cent threshold and, thereafter, within 30 days of any greater than 1 per cent change in such ownership. CONSOB, in turn, is required to give immediate public notice of any such notifications it receives (Law 216, art 5). In addition, although only since early 1992, ownership levels exceeding each of the thresholds of 10, 20, 33, 50 and 75 per cent are also required to be reported to CONSOB within two days of the shareholder obtaining knowledge of the transaction which will result in the exceeding of such thresholds (Law 216, art 5 *bis*). Second, directors, internal auditors and general managers of listed companies are required to notify the company and CONSOB, within 30 days of their acceptance of any such position in the company or from the date they acquire shares thereof, of their direct and indirect ownership of shares in such company and its subsidiaries. Failure to file such reports is punishable by a prison term of up to three months and a fine ranging from 2 million to 40 million lire (approximately £800 to £17,000 STG). The late filing of such reports by not more than 30 days is punishable by a fine ranging from 1 million to 20 million lire (approximately £400 to £8,000 STG). The filing of notices containing false information is punishable by a prison term of up to three years.

In addition to the foregoing transparency protection provisions of law, art 2628 of the Italian Civil Code provides that the publicising of false information or the use of other fraudulent means by company directors, general managers, internal auditors and liquidators aimed at creating in the public market or on commercial exchanges an increase or decrease in the price of shares of their company or other securities belonging to it, is punishable by imprisonment for a term of one to five years and a fine of not less than 600,000 lire (approximately £200 STG). Where such activity results in serious damage to the company, the punishment may be increased by up to one half.

Finally, the Italian Criminal Code (art 640) contains a general anti-fraud provision. Its application in the area of insider dealing, however, has been limited in that the elements required to prove criminal fraud are not readily present in insider dealing cases. These are:

(1) the use of artifice or deceit to accomplish the fraud;
(2) inducement into error; and
(3) a causal connection between the fraud and the damage suffered (ie in the case of insider dealing, between the use of privileged information to trade in the market and the damage to the counterparty).

1.3 LEGISLATIVE BACKGROUND

The preparatory legislative reports submitted to the Italian Parliament in connection with its analysis of Law 157 indicate that the primary purpose of Law 157 was considered to be the guaranteeing of a 'level playing field' to all those with access to the securities markets. Thus, by prohibiting the participation of certain 'insiders' in the market, other market participants who do not have privileged access to information are able to participate in the market on, at least initially, equal terms. Italian legal scholars, however, have criticised the 'level playing field' purpose of Law 157 using the arguments that:

- equality in bargaining position is impossible to establish in that the market is unable to absorb and reflect all information immediately and therefore, for a period of time, no matter how brief, market participants will not have access to equal information;
- the capacity (economic or otherwise) of different market participants to acquire information varies and thus excluding insiders from participating in the market would only result in the transfer of the informational advantage from such insiders to professional market participants;
- a requirement of immediate publication of information would result in a disincentive to information gathering;
- the enactment of a law which might induce individual market participants to believe that they are adequately protected and do not need professional investment advice is, in reality, dangerous to such market participants.

On the basis of the above arguments, Italian legal scholars have argued that the express purpose of Law 157 should rather have been expressed in a manner which reflects its contents (ie the elimination or limitation of market activities of certain participants in the market who obtain information on the basis of which to make trades in the market by virtue of their position as corporate 'insiders' (as specifically defined)). In fact, a 'level playing field' may sometimes be a byproduct of Law 157 but it cannot be said to be the aim or even a consistent result thereof.

2 LAW 157

2.1 THE OFFENCES

Law 157 added several defined criminal offences to the Italian legal system:

- the general trading offence;
- the specific trading offence;
- the public officials trading offence;
- the communicating offence;
- the advising offence;
- the market manipulation offence.

2.1.1 The general trading offence

Law 157 prohibits the purchase or sale of, or conclusion of other transactions in securities, including related option rights, either directly or indirectly, by anyone while in possession of inside information obtained by virtue of his ownership of capital in a company or by reason of his employment, including public employment, profession or office (art 2(1)). The elements of the general trading offence are therefore:

*   a transaction in securities (see 2.2.1);
*   possession of inside information (see 2.2.2);
*   the obtaining of such information as a result of one's ownership of capital in a company or one's employment, profession or office.

2.1.2 The specific trading offence

Law 157 also prohibits the purchase or sale of, or the conclusion of other transactions in securities, either directly or indirectly, after the calling of a board of directors meeting or meeting of any equivalent corporate body which will deliberate on any transaction which might have a significant effect on the price of the security itself, prior to the resolution taken at that meeting being made public, by:

(1)   controlling shareholders of the company (control to be determined in accordance with art 2359 of the Civil Code); and
(2)   the company's directors, liquidators, general managers, management level employees, internal auditors and accountants (art 2(3)).

The elements of the specific trading offence are therefore:

*   a transaction in securities (see 2.2.1);
*   occurring during the period after the calling of a meeting of a corporate body for the purpose of adopting resolutions which might have a significant effect on the price of the security and prior to such resolutions being made public,
*   by the persons specified in (1) and (2) above.

2.1.3 Public officials trading offence

Law 157 prohibits government ministers and under-secretaries of state from purchasing or selling or concluding other transactions in securities, either directly or indirectly, after the calling of a Council of Ministers or an interministerial committee meeting for the adoption of measures which might have a significant effect on market trends, prior to such measures being made public (art 2(7)). The elements of the public officials trading offence are therefore:

*   a transaction in securities (see 2.2.1);
*   occurring during the time period after the calling of a Council of Ministers or an interministerial committee meeting for the purpose of adopting measures which might have a significant effect on market trends and prior to such resolutions being made public;
*   by a public official.

2.1.4 The communicating and advising offences

Persons who are covered by the general trading offence are also prohibited from communicating, without just cause, inside information to third parties and from advising, on the basis of inside information, third parties to purchase or sell or conclude other transactions in securities, including related option rights (art 2(2)). The elements of the communicating and advising offences are therefore:

- possession of inside information (see 2.2.2);
- by a person who obtained such information through his ownership of securities of a company or employment, profession or office; and
- communication of the inside information to third parties without just cause or advising, on the basis of inside information, third parties to effect transactions in securities.

2.1.5 Tippee offences

Each of the foregoing prohibited activities (other than the public officials' trading offence and, although not specified in Law 157 commentators agree, the specific trading offence) is also prohibited by those who, directly or indirectly, obtain inside information from persons who possess such information by reason of their employment, profession or office and who are aware of the fact that the information obtained is inside information (art 2(4)). The elements of the tippee offences are therefore:

- a transaction in securities (see 2.2.1);
- the obtaining of inside information (see 2.2.2) from a person who obtained such information through his employment, profession or office; and
- knowledge that the information obtained is inside information.

2.1.6 Market manipulation

In addition to the above-mentioned, Law 157 prohibits the publication of false or exaggerated or otherwise misleading information and the concluding of simulated transactions and other artificial transactions which might have a significant effect on the price of securities (art 5). This provision of Law 157 is discussed in 3 *below*.

2.2 DEFINED TERMS

The above-described offences are based on a series of defined terms which must be closely analysed in order to determine whether any given activity is sanctioned by Law 157.

2.2.1 'Security'

Law 157 does not contain an explicit definition of 'security' but it states that 'security' as used in Law 157 means 'securities which are admitted to trading on

Italian regulated markets or on the regulated markets of other EU jurisdictions' (art 1).

Regulation 5553 defines 'listed security' to be 'any security or uniform forward contract on financial instruments related to securities admitted to trading on a regulated market, interest rates or currency exchange rates, including those which have as their object indices on such securities, interest rates or currency exchange rates, admitted to trading in a regulated market' (collectively 'Uniform Forward Contracts') (reg 5553, art 2(1)(c)). 'Regulated market', in turn, is defined as 'the stock exchange, the restricted market ("*mercato ristretto*"), on which certain securities which do not qualify for admission to the stock exchange are traded, and the markets referred to in art 20(4) and (8) and art 23 of Law No 1 of 2 January 1991 (the "SIM Law") (reg 5553, art 2(1)(b))'.

The markets referred to in the SIM Law are:

(1) any markets instituted by CONSOB regulation for the trading of securities which are neither listed nor traded in the restricted market;
(2) any foreign regulated markets which are specifically recognised by CONSOB, and
(3) any market for the trading of Uniform Forward Contracts authorised by CONSOB.

By resolution No 8469 of 30 September 1994, CONSOB adopted general regulations regarding the institution of national markets for the trading of securities not listed on the stock exchange or traded in the restricted market. No such markets have yet been instituted. In addition, by resolution No 8625 of 2 November 1994, CONSOB issued regulations for the trading of Uniform Forward Contracts on the electronic stock exchange system ('*mercato telematico*').

In addition, case decisions under Italy's public offering law have defined security to include 'any document or certificate which directly or indirectly represents a right in a company or which represents a credit or a negotiable or non-negotiable interest or confers the right to acquire one of the foregoing securities'. For purposes of the public offering legislation, court decisions have maintained that the critical element in determining whether any given instrument may be classified as a security is that 'it is capable of valuation in the financial markets in such a way as to render it the subject of trading independent of the underlying interest which it represents' (Pretura di Roma, VII, 26 January 1984).

While there are no case decisions on point in the insider dealing area, based on:

(1) the definition of 'listed security' in reg 5553;
(2) the similar definition contained in the SIM Law; and
(3) the fact that the EC Directive defines 'security' so as to include options,

contracts and forward financial instruments related to such securities, so long as they are admitted to trading on a regulated market (EC Directive, art 1(2)(b), (c) and (d)).

Italian legal scholars have argued that 'security' as used in Law 157 should be interpreted broadly. In fact, the operative part of art 1 of Law 157 is 'traded on a regulated market' and 'security' is deemed to include any instrument (other than foreign currency instruments) which is traded on a regulated market. Italian law therefore does not contain an exhaustive list of instruments which will be considered to be securities for purposes of the insider dealing law but rather qualifies securities for such purposes as any instrument (other than foreign currency instruments) now or hereafter traded on regulated markets.

2.2.2 'Inside information'

'Inside information' is defined by art 3 of Law 157 as information which:

- is specific information having determined content;
- has not been made public;
- concerns one or more issuers of securities or one or more securities;
- if made public, might have a significant effect on the price.

The Italian word used in Law 157 to describe such information is 'riservata' which is generally translated into English as 'confidential'. Commentators agree, however, that the term confidential is inappropriate in this context in that the information concerned is not confidential as a result of its intrinsic nature but is, rather, destined to become public at some stage. In addition, the insider dealing offences do not concern the breach of confidentiality by disclosure of information but rather the exploitation of such information as a result of one's knowledge thereof prior to the relevant general public obtaining or being able to obtain knowledge of such information.

2.2.2.1 'Specific information having determined content'

The EU Directive requires that inside information be 'precise'. Law 157, on the other hand, requires that it be 'specific having determined content'. Certain Italian commentators have argued that the differences between 'specific' and 'of determined content' are merely linguistic as opposed to substantive. Others have argued that as Law 157 uses both terms, each should be attributed significance. In this case, it is argued that the concept 'determined' expresses a degree of certainty, while the concept 'specific' describes the subject to which the information relates. The foregoing interpretation of 'specific', however, could lead to the imposition of a requirement that, in order to be considered inside information, information must relate to a specific company or security. However, as indicated below, this is generally accepted not to be the case. While the ultimate determination of whether the information at issue is sufficiently specific and of determined content to be considered inside information is left up to case by case analysis by the courts, it is fair to say that inside information must be characterised by a degree of certainty (ie it should be more than mere rumour, uncorroborated by objective evidence).

2.2.2.2 'Not public'

Law 157 states that for information to be considered inside information it must not be public information. Law 157 does not further develop this concept either in terms of the methods which must be used for publicising information, the relevant 'public' among whom the information must be diffused or the amount of time which must lapse in order to presume sufficient diffusion among the public. These issues remain to be fine-tuned by application in the courts. However, commentators agree that at one extreme it can be assumed that if a company has fulfilled its obligations to report company information to CONSOB as required by reg 5553 (see 4 *below*) such information would cease to be inside information and become public information. Of course, such company information may become public information at an earlier date if it is published elsewhere before it is provided to CONSOB. It therefore remains unclear whether information will be considered to be public when it becomes available to market professionals or whether, in order to be considered public, the information must be diffused to the general investing public.

2.2.2.3 'One or more issuers of securities or one or more securities'

While a number of legal commentators disagree, the prevailing view in Italy is that the requirement in the definition of 'inside information' that it relate to one or more issuers of securities or one or more securities, confirms that inside information may be specific to a single issuer or security or may relate to more than one security or issuer and therefore have the character of market information.

2.2.2.4 'Significant effect on price'

This requirement is generally taken to mean that, in order to be considered inside information, information must be such that, if it were disclosed, it would influence the investment decisions of market participants either causing them not to effect a trade which, in the absence of the information, they did effect, or causing them to effect a trade on different terms and conditions than those on which, in the absence of such information, they traded. It is important to note that inside information is not required to have an effect on the intrinsic value of the securities but merely on their market value.

The most problematic aspect of the classification of information as inside information is the degree to which it is required to affect the market if it were disclosed. While this can only be determined by a judge based on an evaluation of the facts after the event, according to Italian commentators, it is clear that in order to determine the presence of sanctionable conduct, the evaluation of the likelihood of the information having an affect on price were it disclosed must be made at the time the insider makes his trade in the market. Secondly, it is also clear that the price-sensitivity of the information must be evaluated on objective grounds. The importance attributed to the information by the insider is not relevant. Rather, a reasonable investor test should be applied.

2.2.3 'Insider'

As indicated above in defining the insider dealing crimes, Law 157 defines the following categories of insiders:

(1) those who, by virtue of the fact that they hold shares in a company or as a result of their employment, including public employment, or their exercise of a profession or holding of an office possess inside information (art 2.1) (these insiders are collectively referred to herein as 'general insiders');

(2) shareholders who have or exercise, even de facto, control over the company (the meaning of control is determined by reference to art 2359 of the Civil Code which is discussed below) (such shareholders are referred to herein as 'significant shareholders'), directors, liquidators, general managers, management level employees and internal auditors of a company and accountants (art 2.3) (these insiders, together with significant shareholders, are collectively referred to herein as 'specified insiders');

(3) government ministers and under-secretaries of state (art 2.7) (referred to herein as 'public officials');

(4) those who, directly or indirectly, obtain information, with the knowledge that such information is 'inside information' from persons who come into possession of such information by reason of their exercise of a profession or holding of an office (art 2(4)) (referred to herein as 'tippees').

Only individuals may be considered to be insiders and are subject to the insider dealing crimes. This does not, however, exclude the possibility that an individual, acting exclusively in the interests of a company, or other entity, will be subject to Law 157.

2.2.3.1 Shareholders

For purposes of the general trading offence, Law 157 applies to all shareholders to the extent that they hold even a single share in a company. No importance is given to the number of shares owned. This position is clear from the text of Law 157 but has been criticised by Italian legal commenators because it results in subjecting small shareholders to the same treatment as significant shareholders in an area where they are in a significantly different factual position. While the legal entitlement to receipt of company information is the same for all shareholders regardless of the number of shares held, as a matter of fact, significant shareholders have greater access to members of the company's management body and, therefore, to information which is likely to affect the price of the company's securities prior to its being made public. Small shareholders, on the other hand, cannot be expected to come into contact with such information as a result of their status as a shareholder. Certain commentators have argued, therefore, that the general trading offence need not extend to shareholders at all in that adequate protection would be achieved by the tippee provisions of Law 157.

In addition, legal commentators have criticised the reference in Law 157 to *ownership* of shares rather than to *possession* of shares. This is important in that Italian law recognises certain legal forms in which shares may be owned by one party while the rights of the shareholder are exercised by another (eg usufruct and pledge). In such cases it is the usufruct holder or the pledgee who is more likely than the shareowner to come into the possession of inside information and yet, under the terms of the law, such persons would not be considered insiders. Law 157 requires that the insider be a shareholder of any company and does not require the shareholding to be in the company the shares of which are traded on the basis of the inside information.

Significant shareholders are defined with reference to the concept of 'control' as defined in the Italian Civil Code. Article 2359 of the Civil Code provides that a party will be considered to control a company when such party, directly or indirectly:

(1) controls the majority of the votes exercisable in the company's ordinary shareholders meeting;
(2) controls enough votes in order to exercise a dominant influence in the ordinary shareholders meeting of the company; or
(3) benefits from contractual ties which permit it to exert a dominant influence on the company.

Only significant shareholders may commit the specific trading offence. Pursuant to a strict reading of Law 157, therefore, the presence of contractual ties which permit the exertion of a dominant influence in the absence of even a minimum shareholding or other requisites for qualification as a specified insider, would mean that the person would not qualify as a specified insider.

2.2.3.2 General insiders (other than shareholders)

As indicated above, the general trading offence can be committed by all persons who by reason of their position or activity, including public position, profession or office have preferential access to information. Commentators agree that the term professional, as used in Law 157 above, should be interpreted broadly so as to include not only the traditional professions but also all those who render services to a company on an indepndent basis or, who, on the basis of contract, continuously render services to the company. On this basis, the definition of insider requires a working relationship with the company and certain persons, regardless of their access to information (eg the spouse of an insider) would not be considered insiders and would be subject only to the tippee provisions of Law 157.

Law 157 does not specify a causal connection between one's status as an employee, professional or officeholder and the information acquired, however it does imply that the information should be obtained by reasons of such status and not merely fortuitously during the conduct of one's activities. In addition, the information need not concern the company by which one is employed or in which one holds an office or conducts a profession.

2.2.3.3 Specified insiders

Italian legal commentators agree that the specific trading offence applies only to the specific insiders specifically mentioned in Law 157 and that such list is to be considered exhaustive. Once it is determined that a given person holds one of the positions included in the list, Law 157 does not require that there be a functional connection between the position held and privileged access to inside information. To this extent, certain commentators have argued that persons who do not actually have direct privileged access to information are caught by the parameters of the specific trading offence and are therefore subject to the increased penalties which are provided in Law 157 in respect of such offence when it would seem that they should be considered mere tippees not subject to such increased penalties.

2.2.3.4 Public officials

As indicated above, Law 157 has created a specific offence applicable to public officials which prevents their trading after the calling of a Council of Ministers or interministerial committee meeting at which matters which could significantly influence market trends will be decided and before the decisions taken at such meetings regarding such matters are rendered public. The penalties otherwise applicable to offences under Law 157 are doubled in respect of this offence. It remains unclear why the foregoing provision has been included in Law 157, in that public officials would be covered in any event by the general provisions of Law 157 to the extent that they obtain inside information by virtue of their holding of a particular office. Moreover, the specific provision of Law 157 relating to public officials contains only a prohibition on trading by such persons and does not specifically limit their right to communicate information to third parties or to advise third parties to conclude transactions in the market. As a result, such communicating or advising activities by public officials would not be subject to the increased penalty provisions.

The purpose of the public officials' trading offence seems to be to extend the period of time during which trading would otherwise be restricted by the general provisions of Law 157. The public officials' trading offence would be superfluous if the fact of the calling of a meeting could be considered inside information and therefore otherwise covered by Law 157. Commentators agree, however, that it would be difficult to argue, on the basis of the definition of inside information contained in Law 157, that the mere calling of a meeting would constitute inside information. The public officials trading offence removes this doubt and prohibits trading by public officials from the time of the calling of such a meeting.

2.2.3.5 Tippees

As drafted, Law 157 subjects not only tippees but also sub-tippees to the tippees' offence. It is consistent with this provision that tippees themselves are prohibited from disclosing inside information to third parties. It is arguable that third parties who obtain a trading tip based on inside information rather than the inside information itself would not be prevented by Law 157 from passing along such trading tip to other third parties.

In order to qualify as a tippee, one must obtain inside information with the knowledge that the information is inside information. The means in which the information is obtained would seem to be unimportant and the punishment of the primary insider who passes along a tip is detached from the punishment of the tippee who may be held liable even if the primary insider is not liable because he has a valid defence.

Finally, it has been argued (although this is a minority view) that in order to be considered a tippee, one must take positive action in order to obtain the inside information and that persons who obtain such information passively should not be covered by the offence. An objective limit which does apply to the tippee offence, however, is that under Law 157 a person is only considered a tippee to the extent that the inside information is obtained, directly or indirectly, from primary insiders who are such by reason of their function, profession or office. Shareholders are not specifically included and it would therefore seem that tips received from shareholders may be acted upon by third parties with impunity.

2.3 DEFENCES

2.3.1 Specific exclusions

Law 157 specifically provides that the insider dealing offences do not apply to transactions effected by the Italian State, the Bank of Italy, the Italian Exchange Office or by any person acting for the account of the foregoing for reasons of monetary policy, exchange control or management of the public debt or official reserves (Law 157, art 4).

2.3.2 No intent

In the insider dealing offences, under Italian law, the presence of a subjective intent ('dolo') on the part of the actor is required to be proven in order to establish the offence. Under Italian criminal law, intent may either be specific or general. In the absence of a specific requirement of specific intent in Law 157, commentators generally agree that the general intent of the actor is sufficient in order to establish the crimes of insider dealing. Unlike the EC Directive which requires the knowing exploitation of inside information, Law 157 requires only that the actor has knowledge of the insider character of the information at the time of the trade or other sanctioned behaviour and the intent to exploit such information for profit is not required to be established. In Italy, there is therefore no defence based on the fact that the dealing activity was conducted for reasons other than the exploitation for profit of inside information and the only defence is that the actor, at the time of the dealing activity, was not aware, nor should have been aware, of the inside nature of the information in his possession.

2.3.3 Just cause

A defence to the communicating to third parties offence is that the disclosure of information involved was effected for just cause (Law 157, art 2(2)). The communicating offence does not require that the tippee actually deal in securities on the basis thereof but is independent of the subsequent behaviour of the tippee. Therefore, if one has a justified motive for disclosing information (eg a company executive disclosing information to the company's legal or financial advisers), the elements of the communicating offence may not be present. However, the third parties to whom the information is communicated, even with just cause (eg the company's advisers), would nevertheless be considered to be tippees and therefore would not be able to trade on the basis of the information received by them to the extent that the other elements of the tippee offences are present.

2.3.4 Stabilisation activities in accordance with law

Stabilisation activities which are conducted in accordance with law are exempt from the insider dealing offences. In Italy, trading activities by selling shareholders, the issuer and members of an underwriting syndicate on an Italian stock exchange before, during and after a public offering of securities are governed by CONSOB reg No 6237 of 3 June 1992 and, more generally by CONSOB release No 92005334 of 23 July 1992 each aimed at ensuring that stabilisation transactions are transparent and not manipulative.

Stabilisation activities are regulated during the period of an offering and for the 30 day period following the beginning of trading of the securities on a stock exchange. During this period, the persons specified above may purchase or sell the offered securities for their own account only on a stock exchange, only through a company that has been specifically designated in writing and subject to certain volume limitations, price restrictions and notice requirements.

The offering prospectus must indicate whether stabilisation activities are intended to be conducted. Also, the entity through which trading is conducted must notify CONSOB on a daily basis of trades effected during an offering and in the 30 days thereafter and, at the end of such period, summarise such trading in a notice to CONSOB, also released to at least two press agencies.

2.4 CONSOB'S POWERS

Under Law 157, CONSOB has specific powers of investigation in order to establish whether or not any of the activities prohibited thereby have been conducted including the power to request information from insiders and from securities intermediaries (Law 157, art 8(1)). In performing its investigative and supervisory functions CONSOB may utilise the infrastructure of the public administration.

Persons subject to Law 157 who do not comply with CONSOB's requests for information or otherwise do not co-operate or who hinder CONSOB's investigative operations are subject to imprisonment for up to three months or a fine of between 2 million and 40 million lire (approximately £820 STG and £16,400 STG). CONSOB is also authorised to exchange information with the competent authorities of other European Union member states and, if based on reciprocity, with the competent authorities of non-European Union states (Law 157, art 9(1)).

When CONSOB has determined that there exist elements indicating violation of the provisions of Law 157, it submits the relevant documentation and a reasoned report thereon to the public prosecutor (Law 157, art 8(3)). The competent court is that which has its seat in the principal city of the Court of Appeals district in which the crime was committed (Law 157, art 8(4)). In the criminal proceedings, CONSOB assumes the role of the offended party.

2.5 PENALTIES

Law 157 specifically provides that the penalties available in the Law apply to acts in violation of the law which are committed outside of Italy, as long as such acts involve securities traded in Italian regulated markets (Law 157, art 2(6)).

Violations of all insider trading offences (including direct dealing, communication of information to third parties and advising third parties to deal) are subject to punishment by up to one year's imprisonment and a fine of between 10 million and 300 million lire (approximately £4,000 STG and £120,000 STG). In addition to the foregoing, penalties such as prohibition on the holding of public office or the performance of a profession or the ability to contract with the public administration for a period of between six months and two years may be applied. The judge has discretion to increase the fine up to three times depending on the gravity of the offence. Finally, any conviction will be published in two daily newspapers of national circulation one of which must be a financial newspaper. As already indicated, for certain insiders (ie specified insiders and public officials), the foregoing penalties are doubled. As yet, no prosecutions have been brought.

It is interesting to note, that the first draft versions of Law 157 contained provision for penalties up to three times the amount of the profit realised from the prohibited dealing activity. As indicated above, however, Law 157, as enacted, permits increases in the applicable fines and other penalties but such increases are always relative to the basic penalty established by law. This position has been criticised by legal commentators in that it would permit the penalties provided by Law 157 to be calculated as a mere cost of dealing.

3 MARKET MANIPULATION

Unlike the EC Directive, Law 157 contains a specific provision regarding market manipulation. It provides that the disclosure of false, exaggerated or otherwise misleading information or the implementation of other schemes which might affect the price of securities is punishable by imprisonment of up to six months and a fine between 1 million and 30 million lire (approximately £400 STG and £12,000 STG) (Law 157, art 5(1)). If such disclosure or scheme is performed with intent to move the price of a security or to create the appearance of an active market therein, penalties of imprisonment of up to three years and a fine between 1 and 30 million lire apply (Law 157, art 5(2)). In addition, the amount of the fine is subject to increase to the extent that the price of securities actually moves or an appearance of an active market in securities actually results (Law 157, art 5(3)). Additionally, as provided by the Criminal Code, the penalties may be doubled if an Italian citizen manipulates the market as described above in order to favour foreign interests or if a devaluation of the Italian lire or state securities results. Similarly, the penalties are doubled if the market manipulation is effected by any of the specified insiders or by issuers of securities that conduct securities dealing activities, stockbrokers or members or employees of CONSOB or the supervisory authorities of local stock exchanges or if the disclosed information involves publication in the press or other means of mass communication (Law 157, art 5(5)).

Market manipulation therefore differs from insider dealing in two primary respects:

(1) market manipulation involves false, exaggerated or otherwise misleading information while insider dealing is based on true information; and

(2) market manipulation requires a specific intent while insider dealing requires only general intent. A full discussion of market manipulation is not provided herein as it is beyond the scope of this chapter.

4 PUBLICATION

Law 157 contains provisions which required CONSOB to issue regulations concerning the reporting and publication of certain information. Regulation 5553 was issued by CONSOB under Law 157. In summary, Regulation 5553 contains provisions regarding the recording of all securities transactions indexed by security and by intermediary and the recording by all intermediaries of transactions in securities effected by them indexed by security and client. In addition, reg 5553 contains the terms and conditions for the disclosure to the public of information, facts, statistics and studies concerning listed companies and their controlled, controlling or otherwise affiliated companies (even if not listed), which would be of interest to shareholders, the public and enables the proper functioning of the securities market. Regulation 5553 also addresses the means by which authorised intermediaries are required to report off-market trades concerning listed securities effected by them.

Regulation 5553 includes provisions which permit a company's directors, upon reasonable grounds, to object to the disclosure of information required by CONSOB if such disclosure would seriously damage the company. CONSOB may approve the non-disclosure of such information or a delay in its disclosure provided that such non-disclosure does not mislead the public regarding important facts and circumstances. Violations of CONSOB's regulations are punishable by fines of between 10 million and 250 million lire (approximately £4,000 STG and £100,000 STG). Application of such fines will also be published, at the expense of the person or entity against whom they are applied, in the manner determined by CONSOB.

In addition, any voting syndicate or shareholders' agreement, in respect of a listed company or a company whose shares are traded on the restricted market, which limits or regulates voting rights, requires prior consultation for the exercise of voting rights, limits the transfer of shares or regulates the purchase of shares in concert is required to be notified to CONSOB within five days of its being entered into and publicised, in abstract, in at least three national newspapers of which two must be economic newspapers. (Law No 149 of 18 February 1992, as amended). If not so notified such agreements are null and the voting rights in respect of shares purportedly subject to such agreements may not be exercised.

Failure to so notify and publish such voting syndicates and shareholders' agreements is subject to administrative fines of between 25 million and 100 million lire (approximately £10,000 STG and £40,000 STG).

CASE STUDY

As indicated in the introduction to this chapter, there have been no case decisions which provide guidance in interpreting Italy's insider dealing law and regulations. The following discussion is therefore based only on our best interpretation of Law 157 in the light of general Italian legal principles.

Splash Plc, a company listed on the Milan Stock Exhcnage, manufactures rainwear and umbrellas. Alan, a weather forecaster, on discovering that there is an unseasonable amount of rain due in the next three months, instructs his broker to buy shares in Splash. Meanwhile, Charles, an analyst of the company's shares, is told in a conversation with Jeremy, one of the directors, that the Chairman is expected to be paid a salary of $500,000. Charles knows from his knowledge of the Chairman's service contract (which is available for public inspection) that this salary could only be paid if the company achieved profit in excess of $20 million. Charles revises his profit forecast for the company but before he publishes it he cancels instructions which he had previously given to his broker to sell his Splash shares. Charles also tells his girlfriend, Maggie, that 'things are looking up' for Splash. Maggie then buys shares in the name of her father from an old friend of hers who wanted to sell Splash shares off market to save the payment of a broker's commission. In addition, Owen, an employee of the contracting firm which cleans Splash's offices, finds a draft of the latest management figures, which demonstrate Splash's high profitability in a wastepaper bin. He immediately buys shares.

Alan

Whether or not Alan would be found guilty of insider dealing under Law 157 depends upon whether he is caught by the general trading offence. If we assume that Alan obtained the information in the course of his job, the issue becomes whether the information on the rainfall is 'inside information' as defined in art 3 of Law 157. It could be argued that the information is specific and of determined content and, if made public, might have a significant effect on the price of securities relating to companies in the rainwear business. It could also be argued that the estimate relates to issuers of securities whose business is weather sensitive, and therefore may be considered to be market information. In our view, however, while strict interpretation of the defenition of 'inside information' would result in a classification of rainfall information as 'inside information', an Italian court would be more likely to take a broader view and find that the information, as it is not directly related to one or more issuers of securities, would not be considered 'inside information'. In addition, as the information is generally obtainable with reasonable diligence, the court is unlikely to find Alan guilty of insider dealing.

Jeremy

Jeremy has communicated information concerning Splash which is specific, of determined content and not publicly available. The issue, therefore, is whether, if the information concerning the Chairman's salary were made public, the market would likely be able to infer that the increased salary was due to Splash's increased profitability and therefore have a significant effect on the price of Splash's securities. In Italy, such an inference by the market cannot be taken for granted. If, however, a court did determine that the information disclosed by Jeremy is inside information, Jeremy would be guilty of the communicating offence if he did not have just cause for communicating the information regarding the Chairman's salary to Charles.

Charles

Charles would not be guilty of insider dealing because he has not traded securities. However, he might be considered guilty of the advising offence if his statement to Maggie is considered to be advice to Maggie to trade in Splash securities. It would be more difficult to establish that Charles has communicated inside information to Maggie. While his statement to Maggie is formulated on the basis of inside information he has received, in itself it is not specific and of determined content.

Maggie

Maggie's information (that things are looking up for Splash) is likely not to be considered to be inside information as it is neither specific nor of determined content and has the character of mere rumour. If Maggie knew, however, that Charles was advising her to trade on the basis of inside information, there might be a case to be made that Maggie should be guilty of the tippee offence. Law 157 does not contain a requirement that trades be made on a market and therefore Maggie is not saved by the fact that her trade is off market. In addition, as the general trading offence prohibits trading, either directly or indirectly, the fact that Maggie trades in her father's name would not be a valid defence.

Owen

It might be argued, based on a strict interpretation of Law 157, that Owen has obtained specific and determined non-public information by virtue of his employment. In our view, however, as Owen's employment is peripheral to the information acquired, it is more likely that he will not be subject to the general trading offence but rather to the tippee offence in that he obtained inside information from a person who obtained such information through his employment and, due to the circumstances in which he obtained the information, it could be argued that he should have had knowledge that the information was inside information.

Republic of South Africa

Jeff Feldman and Stephen Logan,
Bowman Gilfillan Hayman Godfrey Inc, Sandton

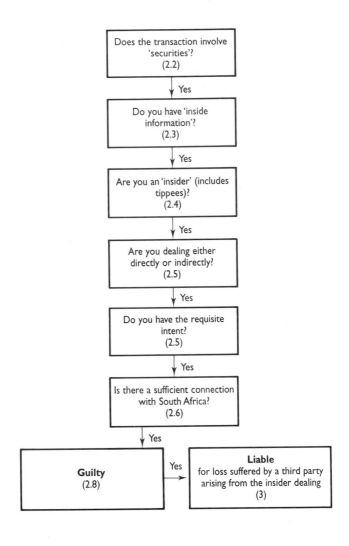

1 INTRODUCTION

Dealing in securities on the basis of unpublished price-sensitive information is an offence. The prohibition on insider dealing in South Africa is based on the view:

(1) that it amounts to a misappropriation to deal in securities on the basis of price-sensitive information obtained in an unlawful manner, and

(2) that it amounts to a breach of a fiduciary duty to deal in securities contrary to a relationship of trust.

Chapter XVA of the Companies Act 63 of 1973 incorporates provisions aimed at prohibiting insider dealing. Section 440F(1) makes insider dealing a criminal offence and ss 440C and D empower the Securities Regulation Panel ('SRP') to investigate and regulate insider dealing. The SRP has broad powers and can *inter alia* subpoena, interrogate and oblige certain persons to disclose information to the panel relating to their holdings of securities. It is also charged with supervising dealings in securities and with receiving and dealing with representations regarding alleged instances of insider dealing.

2 THE CRIMINAL LAW

2.1 INTRODUCTION

The various elements necessary for the successful prosecution of the offence of insider dealing are governed by s 440F of the Companies Act and are dealt with below.

2.2 TO WHICH SECURITIES DO THE PROVISIONS OF s 440F APPLY?

The provisions apply to shares, stock or debentures convertible into shares and any rights or interests in a company or in respect of any such shares, stock or debentures, as well as any 'financial instrument' which is defined in the Financial Markets Control Act 1989 as a futures contract, an option contract, loan stock and any other instrument so declared from time to time.

2.2.1 Shares

Shares, stock and debentures in a company include any rights or interests in a company, its shares or debentures, and irrespective of whether the company falls within the definition of a company under the Act.

2.2.2 Futures contract

A futures contract is a standardised contract whereby either:

(1) a person agrees to deliver or receive from another a certain quantity of things before or on a future date at a pre-arranged price; or

(2) a person agrees to pay to or receive from another an amount of money before or on a future date depending on whether the pre-arranged value or price of the asset, index, currency, rate of interest or any other factor is higher or lower before or on that future date than the actual price or value.

2.2.3 Option contract

An option contract is a standardised contract whereby a person acquires an option to buy from or sell to another a certain quantity of things before or on a future date at a pre-arranged price.

2.2.4 Loan stock

Loan stock is an instrument creating or acknowledging indebtedness and issued by the Government of South Africa, a provincial or local government, various state controlled institutions, and other institutions designated by the Minister of Finance from time to time. Depository receipts are not covered by the provisions of s 440F.

Problem Area 1

> Loan stock is defined as an instrument creating or acknowledging indebtedness issued by the Government of South Africa, a provincial administration or any other state controlled institution as well as other entities specified from time to time by the Minister and published in the Government Gazette.
>
> Section 440F(2)(a)(i) requires that price-sensitive information must relate to a 'company'. Should persons deal in loan stock (gilts) on the basis of unpublished price-sensitive information, they cannot be convicted of the offence of insider dealing as the information does not relate to a company.

The problem referred to in Problem Area 1 also relates to derivative instruments such as futures and options, for although they are included in the definition of securities they are not covered by the offence in s 440F(1) as the definition of 'unpublished price-sensitive information' only refers to information in respect of a company. As a result, trading in derivatives such as index derivatives, commodity derivatives and loan stock derivatives cannot amount to an offence in terms of the Companies Act as it presently stands.

The SRP has made various submissions to the Minister of Trade and Industry pointing out that the definition of unpublished price-sensitive information is flawed as it has to relate to a company. The SRP has recommended that the definition be amended to include price-sensitive information relating to loan stock, options and futures contracts.

The scope of the Act is sufficiently broad to encompass dealing in securities in any company, including an external company (ie one incorporated outside of the Republic of South Africa) or any other body corporate.

The SRP Code which regulates dealings in shares applies to all public companies, whether listed on the Johannesburg Stock Exchange or not, and to companies which are or are deemed to be resident in the republic. A company is deemed to be resident in the republic if it is incorporated or registered, or if it has a head office or a place of central management in the republic. The Code also applies to private companies, but only where the shareholders' interests in the company exceed R5 million (approximately £842,000 STG) and there are more than ten beneficial shareholders.

2.3 WHAT IS INSIDE INFORMATION?

The Act specifically lists what is considered to be price-sensitive information. These are matters which are internal to the affairs of a company . . .

> 'Unpublished price-sensitive information', in respect of a security, means information which—
> (i)   relates to matters in respect of the internal affairs of a company or its operations, assets, earning power or involvement as offeror or offeree company in an affected transaction or proposed affected transaction;
> (ii) is not generally available to the reasonable investor in the relevant markets for that security; and
> (iii) would reasonably be expected to affect materially the price of such security if it were generally available . . .

Although of a general nature, each category listed is distinct and could individually and materially impact upon the price of the security.

Any information which at a given moment relates to the internal workings of a company, which is not generally available to the reasonable investor, and which could materially affect the price of the company's shares if it were available, is unpublished price-sensitive information.

The Act does not cover regulatory decisions emanating from the government affecting a whole industry as opposed to information specific to a company. Accordingly, the information must relate to the internal affairs of a company.

Information that the government plans to re-open trade links with a country which will significantly increase the market for a particular company's product might be held to relate to matters in respect of the earning power of a company. This information may not be generally available to the market and could reasonably be expected to materially affect the price of the company's shares. If market information of this type were covered by s 440F, this would increase the scope of the offence of insider dealing.

Whether market information amounts to unpublished price-sensitive information is subject to judicial interpretation. As yet this issue has not been presented for consideration before the courts.

The information must not be generally available to the investing market. 'Generally available' means that steps have been taken to publicise the information and sufficient time has elapsed in order for the investing market to digest and act on the information. The steps to be taken are not defined, and will differ from one case to the next, but it is submitted that the test to be applied in a court is whether the reasonable investor would or ought to have been aware of the information.

The Act requires that the information be reasonably expected to materially affect the price of a share. No guidance is given as to what 'materially' is considered to be.

Rumours and speculation which are not factually based on the internal affairs of the company and turn out to be false are not considered inside information. Trading on the basis of rumours does not fall within the jurisdiction of the SRP. However, trading on this basis may be an offence under the common law crime of fraud for 'rigging the market'.

2.4 WHO IS AN INSIDER?

A person must have dealt 'on the basis of unpublished price-sensitive information' as defined in s 440F(2)(a). A person can be an individual, a governmental authority, a company registered as such under any law, or any body of persons corporate or unincorporate.

It is immaterial whether the person who deals is a primary or a secondary inside trader. Previous South African legislation provided that the only persons capable of committing the offence of insider dealing were directors, past directors, and officers of the company. The new amendments cover any persons who deal in securities on the basis of unpublished price-sensitive information.

Section 440F(1) of the Act now caters for three categories of insider trader:

(1) the primary insider who 'by virtue of a relationship of trust or any other contractual relationship' has access to inside information;
(2) the secondary inside trader—'whether or not the person concerned is a party to that relationship'—who obtains information from either a primary insider or another secondary insider; and
(3) any person who obtains inside information unlawfully 'through espionage, theft, bribery, fraud, misrepresentation or any other wrongful method, irrespective of the nature thereof'

Problem Area 2

Information passed on quite innocently or inadvertently can lead to the recipient of the information committing an offence.

A and B are directors of a company. After a round of golf they discuss a pending take-over. C overhears the conversation and buys the shares on the strength of that information. The directors are unaware that C over-heard them. For the offence to be committed there must be dealing on the basis of the information, with the knowledge that the information is unpub-lished and price-sensitive and that its origin is as contemplated in the Act. Even so it is possible that C may be guilty of the offence, as the state of mind of the person who imparts the inside information is not relevant.

The passing on or receipt of inside information by itself is not an offence. This distinguishes the situation from the position in the UK where mere disclosure amounts to an offence. So if a person, whether a primary or a secondary insider passes on information to another who deals on the basis of the information, but the first person does not deal himself, he is not guilty of the offence. However should the other party deal on behalf of the party who imparted the inside infor-mation the latter would be guilty of dealing indirectly within the meaning of the Act. In South Africa a 'pointed hint' or a 'recommendation' does not amount to an offence.

Problem Area 3

Director A tells his friend B to buy shares in his company, without giving a reason why. Subsequently, information is published which materially affects the share price, and upon which A based his recommendation. B has dealt in the shares, but not on the basis of the unpublished price-sensitive infor-mation. B was not aware of the information itself. Although it seems unlikely that B could be guilty of an offence, this has not been tested before the courts. However, should B be convicted of an offence, A could be guilty under the common law as an accomplice.

2.5 WHAT ARE THE OFFENCES?

Only one offence is contemplated in terms of s 440F, that of knowingly dealing in securities on the basis of unpublished price-sensitive information. The law in South Africa differs from that in the UK in that neither the encouraging of insider dealing nor disclosure of price-sensitive information constitute offences in themselves. The elements of the offence in South Africa are dealt with briefly below:

- *Knowledge*
  As in most criminal offences (other than offences for which strict liability is imposed) *mens rea* is a necessary element in the offence of insider dealing. In the words of the Act a person must 'knowingly' deal in a security on the basis of unpublished price-sensitive information. *Mens rea* in the form of intention to deal, knowing that the information is unpublished and price-sensitive, is therefore essential for a conviction of the offence.
- *Dealing*
  The offence only occurs when a person knowingly 'deals' in a security 'directly or indirectly' on the strength of unpublished price-sensitive information. As the Act covers listed and unlisted public companies as well as private companies it is immaterial whether the dealing concerned occurs on or off market.

  Section 440F(3) creates certain rebuttable inferences, *inter alia* that once the prosecution has proved that an accused was 'knowingly' in possession of unpublished price-sensitive information, he is deemed to have dealt, in any dealings, on the basis of such information.

2.6 WHAT IS THE TERRITORIAL SCOPE OF s 440F?

The provisions of this section of the Companies Act which criminalise insider dealing only apply within the borders of the Republic of South Africa. There is no provision either in the Companies Act or in the Stock Exchange Control Act which allows the provisions of s 440F to apply to trading on stock exchanges other than those within the borders of the republic.

With the advent of screen trading in South Africa, and consequently the decentralisation of trading, the definition of a stock exchange will have to be amended to include screen traders who do not operate from a central stock exchange. In accordance with the theory of intra-territoriality of statutes, the Act only applies to the area within the borders of the republic.

Problem Area 4

Company A is listed on the Johannesburg Stock Exchange and the London Stock Exchange. It is involved in a take-over which will materially affect the share price, but the information is still confidential. B, who lives in South Africa, has knowledge of this take-over. B deals in the shares on the London Stock Exchange. Is he guilty of the offence of insider dealing in South Africa?

B has not committed an offence in South Africa. As the laws of a country only apply intra-territorially, B cannot be prosecuted in South Africa. Under certain circumstances B could be prosecuted in the UK under the Criminal Justice Act. Even if the SRP was aware of B's dealings in the UK s 440(1) of the Act prohibits it from disclosing this information to the UK authorities.

The SRP has pressed for reform in regard to international co-operation but no amendments have been effected yet. However legislation is being tabled which will permit international co-operation between bodies regulating insider dealing.

2.7 WHAT ARE THE DEFENCES?

There are no statutory defences created by the Act. However, one provision of the Act that has sparked debate is s 440F(6) which provides that the Minister may, on the advice of the panel, exempt any class of persons from the provisions of s 440F.

2.8 WHAT ARE THE PENALTIES AND CONSEQUENCES OF INSIDER DEALING?

The penalty capable of being imposed upon conviction is a fine not exceeding R500,000 (approximately £84,000 STG) or imprisonment not exceeding ten years or both. Severe criticism has been levied on the imposition of a maximum penalty, which has been viewed as not sufficient to provide the necessary deterrent.

3 CIVIL REMEDIES

Section 440F(4) has made provision for a civil remedy whereby a person who contravenes the criminal provisions of s 440F is made liable to any other person who has suffered loss or damage by the contravention. Due to the faceless nature of dealing in listed securities through an intermediary the wording of the section has taken the remedy provided out of the law of contract and placed it firmly within the law of delict (torts), however the elements of the criminal offence must be met before delictual liability can be imposed. An action based on delict (tort), must, in order to succeed, establish:

(1) *Wrongfulness*
Section 440F(1) criminalises the act of insider dealing, and therefore this element of the civil claim simply needs to be alleged as the court will accept the wrongfulness of insider dealing due the criminalisation of this activity.

(2) *Intention*
Section 440F(4)(b) specifically provides that a plaintiff need not prove either intention or negligence towards him in any delictual action, and does not distinguish between the two.

(3) *Causation*
The wrongful action (commission of the offence) must be the direct cause of the loss or damage suffered. In addition, South African law provides that no

new intervening event must interrupt the chain of events linking the wrongful action and the loss or damage suffered.

(4) *Damage or loss (patrimonial)*
    Actual patrimonial/financial loss arising out of the wrongful action must be
    proved.

A delictual action resulting from the course of insider dealing only requires
proof of insider dealing, causation and damage. The Act specifically provides that
a plaintiff need not prove intention where the dealing has occurred on a stock
exchange or a financial market. The remaining elements of the delict must be
proved on a balance of probabilities and not beyond reasonable doubt as is
required in criminal proceedings.

The South African Law Commission has proposed a draft bill which caters for
public interest and class actions. Should this Bill be enacted the SRP would be entitled to bring actions in the public interest or on behalf of investors.

4 NON-STATUTORY REGULATION

4.1 INTRODUCTION

The Companies Act provides the enabling legislation for the creation of the SRP,
which is the watchdog over insider dealing and situations in which there is a
change of control in a company which may affect minority shareholders.

Other bodies which perform similar functions are the Johannesburg Stock
Exchange ('JSE') and the Financial Services Board (FSB). The three entities operate
in different spheres of the financial industry, while also working in conjunction
with one another.

The JSE regulates the actions of its members and ensures that its business is
carried on with due regard to the public interest. The FSB keeps a watchful eye
over dealings in the country's financial markets, while the SRP ensures that dealings in securities where there is a change in control are conducted in a fashion
that is commercially and legally acceptable.

4.2 THE JOHANNESBURG STOCK EXCHANGE

One of the functions of the JSE is to provide an orderly market place for trading
in securities. As such it has developed general principles and listing requirements
for both the listing of companies of the stock exchange and for listed companies.
Although the JSE has the structure, it does not have any specific regulations
regarding insider trading. Instead, the JSE requires the timely disclosure of information that would have an influence on the price of shares if it were to be published.

Accordingly, before a company is granted a listing, it has to comply with the JSE's listing requirements. Once listed, the company is still obliged to honour its continuing obligations of disclosure of all matters that may affect the price of its securities, thereby ensuring that all market investors have equal access to information.

Interested parties may initiate inquiries concerning a suspected illegal transaction. The Surveillance Department of the JSE having received such an inquiry concerning share or gilt transactions investigates the allegations. The Surveillance Department, having isolated the individual trades concerned endeavours to ascertain whether any illegality or reasonable grounds to suspect illegality exist—and if so refers transactions relating to shares to the SRP, and transactions relating to gilts to the FSB for further investigation. At present the JSE's policing powers extend only to its licensed brokers and to the companies listed on it.

Where insider dealing is suspected in relation to an exchange other than the JSE, the rules of the exchange may well prohibit insider dealing and where grounds exist to suspect such trading an in-house investigation will be carried out: the results of which would be reported to the FSB or SRP. Once a thorough investigation has been carried out by either body, and where grounds exist, the matter is referred to the Attorney-General for prosecution. A working group has been constituted by the Minister of Finance which aims to investigate the possibility of insider dealing in futures and other newer markets and provide for the regulation thereof.

4.3 THE SECURITIES REGULATION PANEL

Unlike the JSE and the FSB, which fall under the Department of Finance, the SRP falls under the Department of Trade and Industry. The Companies Act establishes the panel, sets out its functions, and its powers. The members of the panel are the principal constituents of the securities industry.

The Act states that one of the functions of the panel is to supervise dealings in securities as contemplated in Chapter XVA of the Act. In order to do this s 440D grants to the panel the power to summon any person before it, to disclose any documents the panel deams necessary, and to interrogate that person. The person so summoned is not ordinarily entitled to legal representation, but the panel may permit representation at its discretion.

Since the enactment of the South African Constitution, numerous questions regarding the rights of individuals have been placed before the Constitutional Court. Of fundamental importance to the SRP's powers of interrogation is whether an individual is entitled to refuse to answer a question on the basis that the answer may tend to incriminate him/her. The Constitutional Court is presently deliberating over the issue and should the judgment confirm this right the SRP will be unable to conduct interrogations in its current manner.

One difficulty experienced by the SRP is that once it has concluded its investigation the matter is referred to the Attorney-General for prosecution. The Attorney-General's Office is conscious of the difficulties in proving a case of insider dealing due to the onerous burden of proving that it was the unpublished price-sensitive information which in fact affected the share price materially or at all. Furthermore, due the shortage of qualified personnel, prosecutions are generally not proceeded with.

4.4 THE SECURITIES REGULATION PANEL CODE ON TAKE-OVERS AND MERGERS

The Securities Regulation Panel has drawn up a Code which carries the force of law, directed specifically at take-overs and mergers and lays down the manner in which parties are to conduct themselves in such situations, and the disclosures they are obliged to make. The Code is based to a large extent on the City Code on Take-overs and Mergers.

The purpose of the Code is to ensure the fair and equal treatment of all holders of securities in situations where there is a change in control of a company. It also sets out the procedure to be followed in implementing a transaction which results in a change of control. Any person who contravenes the Code is liable to any other person for any loss or damage suffered by them as a result of the contravention (s 440M(4)).

The Code sets out general principles to be observed which are purely standards of commercially acceptable behaviour, and a series of Rules to be adhered to. The SRP has the flexibility to relax the Rules in circumstances where their application would result in undue hardship to the parties concerned.

The Rules contemplate two distinct stages in a transaction and require announcements to be made which are designed to keep the holders of securities informed of matters which may affect the share price. Secrecy is required of all parties concerned before the announcement of a firm intention to make an offer. This is designed to ensure information is made available to all shareholders at the same time, thereby reducing the circumstances in which insider dealing could occur.

(1) The Rules require that before or during negotiations, but before any firm offer is made, a cautionary announcement is required—
  (a) when the offeree company is the subject of rumours and speculation or there is an abnormal movement in the price of its shares, or in the volume of its shares traded on the stock exchange; or
  (b) when negotiations or discussions are about to be extended to include persons other than those in the companies concerned who need to know and their advisers.
(2) An announcement of a firm intention to offer is required to be made—

(a) when the board of the offeree company has been notified in writing of a firm intention to make an offer from a serious source, irrespective of the attitude of the board to the offer; or

(b) immediately upon an acquisition of securities which gives rise to an obligation to make a mandatory offer in terms of the Code.

In order to ensure that all shareholders are treated equally no delays in the announcement are permitted while full information is being gathered. Additional information may be made available in a further announcement.

During the offer period the offeror and any persons acting in concert with it are precluded from selling any securities in the offeree company unless there is compliance with the Rules and the prior consent of the Panel obtained.

5 CONCLUSION

The regulation of insider dealing has not yet been extended so as to include instruments such as futures, options and loan stock but has already been proposed. A working group has been constituted to investigate this proposal as well as various other aspects relating to the regulation of insider dealing. In this regard new legislation is expected to be enacted in 1996.

To date there have been no recorded prosecutions for the offence of insider dealing. The difficulties experienced in prosecuting offenders in terms of the Companies Act lead one to believe that insider dealing could be better regulated by giving the SRP the power to investigate and prosecute allegations itself.

Should persons refuse to answer questions put to them regarding allegations of insider trading on the basis that the answer may intend to incriminate them, new avenues of investigation may have to be sought, depending on the deliberations of the constitutional court in order to prevent regulation by the SRP being rendered ineffectual.

CASE STUDY

Splash Ltd, a company listed on the Johannesburg Stock Exchange, manufactures rainwear and umbrellas. Alan, a weather forecaster, on discovering that there is an unseasonable amount of rain due in the next three months, instructs his broker to buy shares in Splash. Meanwhile Charles, an analyst of the company's shares is told in a conversation with Jeremy, one of the directors, that the Chairman is expected to be paid a salary of R500,000. Charles knows from his knowledge of the Chairman's service contract that his salary could only be paid if the company achieved profit in excess of R20 million. Charles revises his profit forecast for the company but before he publishes it he cancels instructions which he had previously given to his broker to sell his Splash shares. Charles also tells his girlfriend Maggie, that 'things are looking up' for Splash. Maggie then buys shares in the name of her father from an old friend of hers who wanted to sell Splash shares off market to save the payment of a broker's commission. In addition, Owen, an employee of the contracting firm which cleans Splash's offices, finds a draft of the latest management figures, which demonstrate Splash's high profitability, in a wastepaper bin. He immediately buys shares.

Alan

Whether Alan is guilty of insider dealing in terms of s 440F(1) will depend on whether the information on the rainfall constitutes unpublished price-sensitive information within the meaning of s 440F(2). Clearly, it does not fall within the definition which requires knowledge of the internal affairs of the company. It is therefore immaterial whether the information is published or not. Alan will not be guilty of the offence of insider dealing.

Jeremy

Jeremy has disclosed unpublished price-sensitive information, but has not dealt on the strength of it. Consequently, he has not committed the statutory offence of insider dealing; but may be guilty of the common law offence of being an accomplice to Charles, should Charles deal in the shares, as a reasonable person in Jeremy's position would have foreseen that Charles, being an analyst, would deal on the strength of the information.

Charles

Charles is not guilty of an offence under s 440F(1) since he has not dealt in Splash's shares. Merely omitting to deal where Charles would otherwise have done so is not an offence.

He is also not guilty of an offence when he suggests to Maggie that Splash was performing well, as a pointed hint or recommendation is not an offence in terms of the Act. However, he may be guilty under the common law as an accomplice (if Maggie is guilty of the offence of insider dealing).

Maggie

It is immaterial whether one deals directly or indirectly, as the dealer commits the offence in both instances. It is unclear whether Maggie will be guilty of the offence as she has not dealt on the basis of unpublished price-sensitive information. It could perhaps be argued that she is dealing 'indirectly' on the strength of the information forming the basis of the hint or recommendation, however s 440F does not allow for dealing on the basis of 'indirect information'.

Owen

Owen has obtained unpublished price-sensitive information. It is immaterial whether or not he obtained this information by virtue of his employment. He falls squarely within the definition contained in s 440F as the information relates to the internal affairs of the company. It is unpublished, price-sensitive and he has dealt on the basis of it. He is therefore guilty of the offence.

PART 3

Asia/Pacific Region

JAPAN
HONG KONG
TAIWAN
MALAYSIA
REPUBLIC OF KOREA
SINGAPORE
AUSTRALIA
THAILAND

Japan

Toshio Kobayashi, Hidetaka Mihara and Fumihide Sugimoto, Tsunematsu Yanase & Sekine, Tokyo

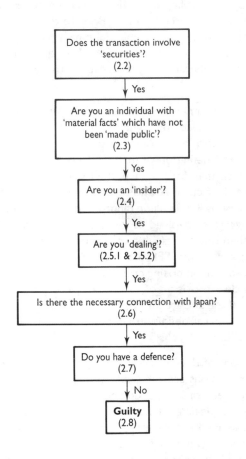

1 INTRODUCTION

The principal prohibition in Japan against insider dealing is set out in a 1988 amendment (the 'Amendment') to the Securities and Exchange Law of Japan (the 'SEL') which prohibits the selling or buying of certain types of securities by an insider in certain prescribed circumstances. Prior to the Amendment a provision in the SEL had prohibited the use of unlawful means, contrivances or manipulation in relation to transactions in securities. The language of this provision, however, proved too general and ineffective, with virtually no cases being reported under it.

In contrast, the Amendment, which sets out offences with criminal liability attached, is both very detailed and highly technical. This is illustrated by the fact that it is an essential feature of the offences that they involve the use of 'material facts' by an insider. The definition of material facts is set out with considerable precision in the SEL so that, for instance, the issue of new shares by a company may constitute material facts in relation to that company if the aggregate of the issue price of the shares is ¥500 million (approximately £3,095,000 STG) or more, whereas if the aggregate involved is only, say, ¥400 million (approximately £2,476,000 STG) then it is not capable of constituting material facts. This highly technical characteristic of the SEL has particular significance as the Japanese courts are prohibited from imposing criminal liability other than where there has been a breach of a clear provision of a law enacted by the Diet. Accordingly, the criminal provisions of the SEL are strictly interpreted. As such, dealing which falls outside the strict technical definition of insider dealing will not constitute an offence under the SEL.

Since the provisions of the SEL create criminal offences, the principal organs to implement the provisions are the public prosecutor's offices and the courts. Following the enactment of the Amendment, however, there were few cases reported where insider dealing offences were prosecuted successfully. Following a number of scandals involving securities companies, banks and other financial institutions, a further amendment to the SEL was enacted in 1992, creating an independent Securities Surveillance Committee within the Ministry of Finance (the 'Committee') to deal with improper securities transactions. The Committee is empowered, among other things, to investigate cases suspected to involve insider dealing. Their investigative powers include the right to conduct search and seizure operations, pursuant to a warrant issued by a judge. Since its creation, a few cases have been reported where the Committee has officially requested the public prosecutor's office to commence proceedings.

In addition to the creation of criminal offences of insider dealing in securities, the SEL contains other provisions designed to reduce the incidence of insider dealing. These are also considered at 2.9 *below*.

2 THE CRIMINAL LAW

2.1 INTRODUCTION

Articles 166 and 167 of the SEL make it an offence for insiders to buy or sell certain specified types of securities with knowledge of material facts, unless and until such information has been made public in a manner recognised by the SEL.

2.2 TO WHICH SECURITIES DOES THE SEL APPLY?

The SEL is only capable of applying when certain types of securities issued by certain types of entity are involved. These entities are corporations (*kabushiki, kaisha*) and certain co-operative financial institutions which are capable of issuing preferred capital contributions ('Preferred Capital Contributions') under a special law. Such entities must be issuing bonds, such Preferred Capital Contributions, shares, warrants or rights to subscribe for shares such securities being listed on one of Japan's eight stock exchanges set out in Table (1) *below* or traded in the over-the-counter market in Japan. Foreign entities are included if they are issuing the above securities so long as such securities are listed on one of Japan's stock exchanges or traded in the Japanese over-the-counter market.

TABLE (1)

Japanese stock exchanges	
• Tokyo Stock Exchange	• Hiroshima Stock Exchange
• Osaka Securities Exchange	• Fukuoka Stock Exchange
• Nagoya Stock Exchange	• Niigata Stock Exchange
• Kyoto Stock Exchange	• Sapporo Stock Exchange

Currently, the securities to which the SEL apply are:

2.2.1 Shares

Only shares in corporations and Preferred Capital Contributions in certain co-operative financial institutions are included in the definition. Interests in limited liability companies (*yugen kaisha*) are excluded.

2.2.2 Debt securities

There are three types of relevant debt securities: straight bonds, convertible bonds and bonds with warrants issued by corporations (which may be secured or unsecured). Unlike other securities, dealing in straight bonds is subject to only limited regulation under the SEL. It is an offence for an insider to deal in straight bonds if he has knowledge of only limited categories of inside information. These categories are those set out in 2.3.1.7, 2.3.1.16, 2.3.2.8 and 2.3.2.9 *below*. Dealing in debt securities is not relevant to the offence set out in 2.5.2 *below*.

2.2.3 Warrants

These are rights allotted to shareholders to subscribe for shares (other than those issued with bonds), or warrants issued with bonds.

2.2.4 Options

This definition covers any option to acquire any of the securities described in 2.2.1 to 2.2.3 *above*. Interestingly, an option to dispose of such securities is not covered.

2.2.5 Foreign securities

Securities issued by foreign entities having a nature similar to those set out at 2.2.1 to 2.2.3 *above* and which are listed on a Japanese stock exchange (see Table (1)), or traded in the over-the-counter market in Japan. It should be noted that derivatives (other than options), depositary receipts and government (treasury) instruments are not covered by the SEL.

2.3 WHAT IS INSIDE INFORMATION?

Article 166 SEL sets out four categories of 'material facts' which are capable of constituting inside information. These are:

(1) facts based on a corporate decision;
(2) facts based on the happening of certain events;
(3) facts based on forecasts;
(4) other facts having a material effect on an investor's investment decision.

These are considered in turn below. As will be seen, each category is highly technical and seeks to set out in detail an exhaustive list of all the types of information capable of constituting inside information. It should be noted, however, that a rumour, which only after any relevant dealing occurs proves to be false (and at the time of the dealing was believed to be true), cannot constitute inside information.

2.3.1 Material facts based on a corporate decision

A corporate decision constitutes a material fact if it is arrived at by an executive organ of the company concerned, relates to one of the matters set out in 2.3.1.1 to 2.3.1.19 *below* and either involves implementing one of those matters or reversing an earlier corporate decision (pubicly announced) to implement one of such matters. The relevant 'executive organ' depends on the actual division of power within the company and the nature of the decision in question, but is usually the board of directors, or a committee of directors (or a sole director) to whom authority has been delegated by the board. It should be noted that, in the context of dealings in straight bonds, only those categories of information based on a corporate decision set out in 2.3.1.7 and 2.3.1.16 *below* are relevant.

2.3.1.1 Issues of equity or equity-related securities

This covers a decision to issue shares (including convertible bonds, bonds with warrants and Preferred Capital Contributions) by way of a public offering or a private placement, either in the domestic or foreign markets. It does not, however, cover an issue which is either designed to raise less than ¥500 million (approximately £3,095,000 STG), or which involves the issue of new shares to existing holders on a pre-emptive basis and which will result in an allotment of fewer than one share for every ten already held.

2.3.1.2 Reduction of capital

This covers a decision to reduce, by whatever amount, the size of the company's issued share capital, irrespective of the manner of implementing that reduction.

2.3.1.3 Purchase of own or parent's shares

This refers to a decision by a company to acquire its own shares or those of its parent corporation in the exceptional circumstances permitted under the Commercial Code of Japan.

2.3.1.4 Stock split

This covers any decision to effect a stock split other than one resulting in fewer than 11 new shares being issued for every ten existing shares.

2.3.1.5 Dividends

This means a decision to pay a dividend (or an interim dividend) of an amount less than 80 per cent or more than 120 per cent of the most recent dividend (or interim dividend as the case may be).

2.3.1.6 Merger/consolidation

This refers to a decision to effect a merger or consolidation other than one with a wholly owned subsidiary, or following which the expected increase in both net sales and the book value of total assets will be less than certain levels specified in the SEL.

2.3.1.7 Acquisition/disposal of business

This means a company's decision to dispose of, or acquire from a third party, the whole or part of its business or enterprise, if such transaction is expected to result in an increase (in the case of an acquisition) or decrease (in the case of a disposal) in the net sales and total assets of the company above certain levels specified in the SEL.

2.3.1.8 Dissolution

This covers a company's decision to dissolve itself, other than as a result of a merger or consolidation (but see also 2.3.1.6).

2.3.1.9 New product or technology

This refers to a decision to develop and market a new product or to introduce a new technology, unless the total net sales expected to result from and the costs of developing the new product or technology, are below certain levels specified in the SEL.

2.3.1.10 Business tie-up

This includes any decision to establish a new, or dissolve an existing business tie-up, of whatever nature, with another entity. It generally does not, however, include such a decision if net sales are not expected to increase (or decrease, as the case may be) as a result in excess of certain levels specified in the SEL.

2.3.1.11 Acquisition/disposal of shares in a subsidiary

This refers to a decision to acquire or dispose of all the shares in a company whose levels of net sales and the book value of its total assets, as compared with those of the parent, are above certain levels specified in the SEL.

2.3.1.12 Acquisition/disposal of fixed assets

This refers to a decision relating to the acquisition or disposal of land, buildings and other assets, prescribed by the Corporate Tax Law as fixed assets, if the book value of such assets, as compared with the level of total fixed assets, is above a certain level specified in the SEL.

2.3.1.13 Business ceases

This refers to a company's decision to cease temporarily or to terminate completely all or part of its business, if such cessation is expected to result in a reduction in net sales above a certain level specified in the SEL.

2.3.1.14 Delisting of shares

This refers to an application to the Minister of Finance or any relevant stock exchange to delist the company's shares and would include, in the case of a company whose shares are listed on two or more stock exchanges, an application for delisting on one of those exchanges.

2.3.1.15 De-registering of shares

This means a decision to apply to the Minister of Finance or the Japan Securities Dealers Association to de-register shares from the over-the-counter market.

2.3.1.16 Insolvency

This includes an application for bankruptcy, or the commencement of an arrangement or a corporate re-organisation.

2.3.1.17 New business

This covers a company's decision to commence a new business which is expected either to involve the company incurring expenditure above a certain level (specified in the SEL) as compared with the book value of its fixed assets, or to result in an increase in the net sales above certain specified levels.

2.3.1.18 Tender offer defence

This refers to a decision by a company, the target of a tender offer, to request a friendly third party to acquire its shares.

2.3.1.19 Tender offer

This includes a decision to make a (or withdraw an already publicly announced) tender offer. A tender offer is defined in the SEL and includes, for example, the purchase of more than one third of the total issued share capital of a target corporation. The target corporation must either be a corporation subject to the periodic disclosure requirements of the SEL (such as a corporation whose shares are traded on any Japanese stock exchange (see Table (1)) or in the over-the-counter market), or alternatively a foreign corporation subject to similar disclosure obligations in Japan. Unlike in the case of the material facts set out in 2.3.1.1 to 2.3.1.17, the shares subject to regulation are those of the target company, not the company making (or withdrawing) the offer.

2.3.2 Material facts based on the happening of certain events

It should be noted that, in the context of dealing in straight bonds, only those categories of information based on the happening of certain events set out in 2.3.2.8 and 2.3.2.9 are relevant.

2.3.2.1 Damage caused by a calamity or arising out of business

This refers to losses which are in excess of a certain level specified in the SEL as compared with the book value of the corporation's total assets and which arise out of either a disaster or business operations.

2.3.2.2 Change in principal shareholder

This covers a change in the identity of a shareholder who either before, or as a result of the change, beneficially owns 10 per cent or more of the total outstanding share capital of the company.

2.3.2.3 Delisting or deregistering

This refers to an event which will give rise to a delisting of shares of common stock or a deregistering of such shares from the over-the-counter market.

2.3.2.4 Material litigation

This covers the commencement of proceedings before a Japanese or foreign court, the delivery of a judgment in such proceedings, or the abandonment or settlement of such proceedings before judgment (unless the claim made in the proceedings is immaterial). The claim will be regarded as immaterial in each case if, as compared with the book value of the total assets of the company, it is below a certain level specified in the SEL and the effect on net sales, if the claim were to succeed, is also expected to be below a certain specified level.

2.3.2.5 Injunctions, etc

Similar to 2.3.2.4 *above*, this covers the filing of a petition seeking injunctive relief against the company in respect of its business operations provided the expected consequence, if the petition were granted, is a decrease in net sales in excess of a certain level specified in the SEL.

2.3.2.6 Regulation

This covers the cancellation of a licence necessary to operate all or part of the business of the company, or an order (but not merely administrative guidance) to cease operating duly issued by an administrative agency in Japan or elsewhere, provided the expected impact on net sales is in excess of a level specified in the SEL.

2.3.2.7 Change of control

This refers to any change in ownership of the entity (Japanese or foreign) which beneficially owns more than 50 per cent of the voting share capital in a company.

2.3.2.8 Insolvency

This covers a petition by a creditor or other third party for the commencement of bankruptcy or corporate re-organisation procedures, or for an adjustment to, or foreclosure of, an enterprise mortgage.

2.3.2.9 Bank facilities

This covers the refusal of a bank or other financial institution to honour a cheque, promissory note or bill of exchange due to a lack of funds in the company's account or a decision by a clearing house to withdraw its facilities to the corporation (*torihiki teishi shobun*).

2.3.2.10 Related party insolvency

This refers to the matters set out in 2.3.2.8 *above* being commenced against the company's parent or a majority-owned subsidiary, irrespective of the size of that subsidiary.

2.3.2.11 Debtors

This refers to the occurrence of a likelihood that sums due from a debtor (including a party whose obligations to third parties the corporation has settled under the terms of a guarantee) will not be honoured by that debtor for whatever reason including, for example, bankruptcy. It does not refer to immaterial claims against a debtor, that is, claims below a level specified in the SEL as compared with the total book value of the company's assets.

2.3.2.12 Customer/supplier difficulties

This refers to the cancellation of contracts with principal trading partners who account for 10 per cent or more of either the company's sales or purchases and which will result in a reduction in net sales below a level specified in the SEL.

2.3.2.13 Waiver of obligations

This covers a decision by a creditor of a company to waive obligations over a specified value owed to it by that company, or the decision of a third party to assume such obligations.

2.3.2.14 Discovery of new natural resources

This covers the discovery of new natural resources which are expected to result in an increase in net sales above a certain level specified in the SEL.

2.3.3 Material facts based on forecasts

This covers information on a company's non-consolidated financial results or newly calculated projections which show material variations from the corresponding figures set out in either the most recent projections made public or, if none, the published results for the previous financial year/semi-annual period. The financial results or projections and the relevant material variations from the earlier figures are set out below:

net sales	10 per cent
income before income taxes	
and extraordinary profits or losses	30 per cent
net income	30 per cent

2.3.4 Material facts which affect an investor's investment decision

This catch-all category is designed to cover facts relating to the management, business or assets of the company concerned, which will have a material effect on the investment decision of investors but which do not fall specifically within any of the other categories listed in 2.3.1 to 2.3.3.

The scope of this category is not entirely clear. However, this category was relied on in a Tokyo District Court judgment dated 25 September 1992 where a director of a listed company was found guilty of insider dealing, following the disposal of his shareholding in the company. The material facts he had were that the company's published forecast of net sales was based on fictitious raw data. The court held that this information did not fall within any of the specific categories set out in the SEL (including that one referred to in 2.3.3) but did fall within the catch-all provision described in this paragraph 2.3.4.

If items of information fall within any of the categories set out above, the SEL will regard them as material facts whether or not they are particularly material or price-sensitive. The categories apply equally to Japanese and non-Japanese corporations. As only securities issued by foreign entities which are similar in nature to the securities issued by Japanese corporate issuers are the subject of the SEL's provisions (see 2.2.5) it follows that foreign non-corporate issuers (such as sovereign issuers) are not subject to insider dealing regulations in Japan.

The categories of material facts which are prescribed in the SEL can be amended or supplemented from time to time by cabinet order or ministerial ordinance. To be guilty of an offence an insider must be aware that the items of information he possesses are material facts, although it is not necessary for the prosecution to prove that he knew which specific category they fell into or even the existence of any law prohibiting insider dealing.

2.3.5 Material facts made public

Information which has been 'made public' will not be regarded as constituting 'material facts'. Article 166 SEL deems information to be made public when either:

(1) twelve hours have elapsed after a director or some other duly authorised person on behalf of the relevant company has made it public to at least two members of the media. Such members are set out in a Cabinet Order and currently include papers of general circulation in Japan, news agencies and radio and television stations. In the case of news agencies these may be foreign. So, for example, information disclosed to Reuters in London would be regarded as having been made public, whereas disclosure to the European edition of the *Financial Times* or the US edition of the *Wall Street Journal* would not; or

(2) it is set out in certain disclosure documents, such as securities registration statements, annual or semi-annual securities reports and extra-ordinary reports filed with the Minister of Finance and available for public inspection.

2.4 WHO IS AN INSIDER?

Each of the two insider dealing offences created by arts 166 and 167 of the SEL (see 2.5) revolve around an individual dealing, while knowing material facts as an insider. Articles 166 and 167 of the SEL set out slightly different definitions of who is to be regarded as an insider for the purposes of their respective offences.

2.4.1 'Company insiders'—SEL, Article 166

For the purposes of the offence under SEL, art 166, an insider includes any of the persons referred to in Table (2) *below* but only when their knowledge of the relevant material facts is acquired in the manner which is also set out there.

TABLE (2)

Company insiders:

Person

		When
(1)	Any director, statutory auditor, attorney-in-fact or employee (full or part-time) (the 'Officers') who is engaged in the business of the company.	When such persons acquire the knowledge in connection with the performance of his duties.
(2)	Any shareholder (or his agent or employee) who by virtue of a shareholding of 3 per cent or more in the company is entitled under arts 293–6 of the Commercial Code of Japan to inspect certain accounting records of the company; or any ordinary investor (or his agent or employee) as defined in the SEL including, in either case, the Officers of any such shareholder or ordinary investor which is itself a company.	When such persons acquire the knowledge in connection with the exercise of such power.
(3)	Any person who possesses statutory power over the company, for example, a public servant who has authority to licence or regulate the business of the company.	When such persons acquire the knowledge in connection with the exercise of such power.
(4)	Any person (including the Officers of a corporate person or the agents or employees of a non-corporate person) who has a contractual relationship with the corporation, other than the Officers of the corporation itself—this would include the corporation's lawyers, accountants, bankers and joint-venture partners.	When such persons acquire the knowledge in connection with the entering into or performing of the contract.
(5)	The Officers of the corporate persons referred to in (2) and (4) *above*.	When such persons acquire the knowledge in connection with the performance of their duties.

It should be emphasised that the persons set out in Table (2) shall be regarded as company insiders only if they obtain their knowledge in the manner which is also set out in Table (2). This point is illustrated by Problem Area 1.

Problem Area 1

Ken, a director of Takeshita Corp Ltd, an office furniture manufacturing company listed on the Tokyo Stock Exchange, is enjoying his regular Saturday morning game of golf with his life-long personal friend Hideki. Hideki mentions he has had a stressful week, as his company has had difficulty obtaining payment for outstanding bills from their main customer, No Cash Ltd, and they had reluctantly filed a petition on Friday afternoon to have No Cash Ltd declared insolvent. Ken is horrified, as Takeshita Corp Ltd, coincidentally, have recently fitted-out No Cash Ltd's plush new offices and have unpaid bills outstanding for over ¥150 million which is about one-tenth of the book value amount of Takeshita Corp Ltd's total assets. Ken, feeling unwell, abandons the game of golf and telephones Mr Sato, Takeshita Corp Ltd's corporate driver, to call at the golf club urgently, pick him up and take him home. While in the car, Ken tells Mr Sato the terrible news.

The information constitutes 'material facts' (see 2.3.2.11) but are Ken (a director), and Mr Sato (an employee), of Takeshita Corp Ltd both company insiders?

One has to consider if Ken obtained knowledge of material facts 'in connection with the performance of his duties'. This depends on the scope of his duties as a director. If Ken is responsible for the sales department or pursuing Takeshita Corp Ltd's debtors, then Ken is likely to be regarded as having come by this knowledge in connection with the performance of his duties. Although it would be open to Ken to argue that the knowledge he obtained was acquired in a personal context, in practice it will be difficult for him to claim that the conversation is not relevant to his duties as a director.

Since Sato's duties are to drive and not to handle sensitive or confidential information he is not likely to be a primary insider, but assuming Ken is an insider, Sato will be an insider too, by virtue of being a tippee (see *below*).

The definition of company insider also includes two other categories of person. These are:

(1) any person who has ceased to be a company insider (as defined in Table (2)) for less than one year; and

(2) any person ('a tippee') to whom any company insider (other than another tippee) has communicated the material facts directly.

To be guilty, a tippee must know (subjectively) that the person he has obtained the relevant material facts from is a primary insider. The definitions of company insider are applied *mutatis mutandis* by the courts in the context of foreign companies and a non-corporate issuer.

2.4.2 'Related persons in a tender offer'—Article 167 of the SEL

For the purposes of the offence under art 167 of the SEL, which concerns dealing in the context of a tender offer (see 2.5), an insider is referred to as a 'related person'. To be a 'related person' one firstly has to have knowledge of the making of a tender offer by a person (the 'tender offeror') (or following the public announcement of such a tender offer, its withdrawal) with respect to the shares of a foreign or domestic company which is subject to periodic disclosure requirements under the SEL. Secondly, one is only a 'related person' where, in addition to having the knowledge referred to above, one is in the same relationship with respect to the tender offeror as a company insider with respect to his company (see 2.4.1). In other words, a related person must fall within one of the categories of persons set out in Table (2) as if references in that table to 'company' were to 'tender offeror'.

As with the definition of 'company insider' (see 2.4.1) the definition of 'related person' is deemed to include those persons who have ceased to be related persons for less than one year and those persons ('tippees') to whom any related person (other than another tippee) has communicated knowledge of the tender offer (or, following its public announcement, its withdrawal).

2.5 WHAT ARE THE OFFENCES?

Articles 166 and 167 of the SEL create two criminal offences of insider dealing. Article 166 of the SEL makes it an offence for a company insider (see 2.4.1) to deal in securities (see 2.2) while in possession of material facts (see 2.3) which have not been made public (see 2.3.5). Article 167 of the SEL makes it an offence for a related person (see 2.4.2) to deal in the securities of a foreign or domestic company which is subject to periodic disclosure requirements under the SEL in circumstances where a tender offeror decides either to make a tender offer for the company or, having announced such a tender offer publicly, decides to withdraw it. These two offences are described more fully below.

2.5.1 Dealing by a company insider under SEL Article 166

It is an offence by virtue of art 166(1) and (3) of the SEL for a company insider to deal in securities while in possession of inside information which has not been made public and which has been acquired by him in one of the ways set out in Table (2).

'Dealing' in securities is given a wide meaning. It includes any purchase, sale, disposition or transfer of title for value. The dealing can occur on or off exchange, either within Japan or overseas. In addition, 'dealing' includes an agreement to deal. This would cover, for example, placing an order with brokers to purchase or sell securities. The granting or purchase of an option over other securities is also covered. An agent who deals, but does not derive any economic benefit from the dealing may none the less be guilty (under general principles of Japanese criminal law), of the offence of aiding his principal and if the dealing is done in the name of a company, the directors of that company may be guilty.

As it is a requirement that the dealing be 'for value', the making of a gift of securities does not constitute dealing. However, this rule does not exonerate a tippee who, say, makes a gift of securities to his wife who then deals, safe in the knowledge that as a tippee's tippee she is not an insider. In such circumstances the tippee is guilty if the whole scheme is pre-ordained.

TABLE (3)

> *Constituent elements for offence in SEL, art 166:*
> * individual must be an insider and have acquired material facts in one of the prescribed ways (see Table (2));
> * individual must deal (see 2.5.1) in securities;
> * it should be noted that it is *not* an element of the offence that the individual must realise that under the SEL he is an insider but he must be aware that the information he has constitutes material facts (see 2.3).

This offence affects the activities of integrated securities houses which have both corporate finance and trading arms. Traders who deal can be guilty of an offence if they have inside information from their corporate finance colleagues and so Chinese Walls are erected between those who are entitled to such information and those who are not.

2.5.2 Dealing by a related person under SEL Article 167

It is an offence for a related person (which includes someone who was a related person within a year of the relevant dealing, or the direct 'tippee' of a related person, as discussed in 2.4.2) to sell, purchase, or otherwise acquire for value, shares, convertible bonds or warrants to subscribe for shares or options over such securities (but not straight bonds) issued by the subject of a tender offer in circumstances where the related person has knowledge of the material fact that a tender offeror has decided to make a tender offer. Conversely, it is an offence for a relevant person to sell or otherwise dispose of such securities in circumstances where he has knowledge of the withdrawal of a previously publicly announced tender offer.

2.5.3 Encouraging dealing

The SEL does not set out a specific offence of encouraging insider dealing, but as Problem Area 2 *below* illustrates, those who encourage insider dealing may themselves be guilty of the offence.

Problem Area 2

> Mr Sato (a director of Alpha Corporation) is offered finance by Mr Yamada (who is not connected with Alpha Corporation) to deal in the listed shares of Alpha on the understanding that any resulting profits will be shared. Mr Sato deals at a time when he has knowledge of material facts.
>
> Mr Sato is clearly guilty of an offence, but so too is Mr Yamada. Assuming Mr Yamada knew Mr Sato had knowledge of material facts, they co-operated with each other to bring about an unlawful result in accordance with a pre-determined arrangement made between them.

In addition, if a person (who may or may not be a company insider) discloses material facts to a company insider subjectively knowing that such disclosure will encourage that company insider to deal in securities and such dealing does in fact occur in violation of the SEL, then the person concerned is guilty of the offence of instigating insider dealing, under a general principle of the Japanese Criminal Code. Under that Code the 'encourager' can be punished to the same extent as the 'dealer'.

2.5.4 Disclosure

It is not in itself a criminal offence for a company insider to disclose inside information to others. However, those lawyers, medical doctors and accountants who breach their duties of confidentiality in respect of information which they obtain in connection with the performance of their duties, commit a criminal offence under the Japanese Criminal Code. See also 2.5.3 *above*.

2.6 WHAT IS THE TERRITORIAL SCOPE OF THE SEL?

In general the offences under the SEL will apply in circumstances where at least part of the act of dealing is conducted within the territory of Japan.

Problem Area 3

> Mr Tanaka, a director of X Corp, obtains material facts in connection with the performance of his duties. He places an order by telephone from his office in Osaka with his brokers in (i) Tokyo and (ii) London, to purchase shares in X Corp. Both orders are executed on the London Stock Exchange. A week later, while on a business trip to New York, Mr Tanaka again telephones his brokers in (iii) Tokyo and (iv) London to purchase further shares in X Corp. Again, these trades are executed on the London Stock Exchange.

> Parts (i), (ii) and (iii) of Mr Tanaka's activities are conducted within Japan and are, therefore, an offence under the SEL. In contrast, transaction (iv) has insufficient connection with Japan and therefore, no offence has been committed.

It is not a requirement of the SEL that an insider or a tippee be within Japan when he learns of the relevant material facts.

Problem Area 4

> Mr Suzuki, an employee of Y Corp, learns of material facts in relation to his company while on a business trip to Zurich. At the airport, waiting for the flight back to Osaka, Mr Suzuki meets Mr Sakuma. They start chatting and Mr Suzuki discloses the material facts to Mr Sakuma. On arrival at Osaka, both Mr Suzuki (an insider) and Mr Sakuma (now a tippee), purchase shares in Y Corp. Both have committed an offence.

2.7 WHAT ARE THE DEFENCES?

In additon to the general defences applicable to all criminal charges, such as infancy and insanity, the SEL recognises a number of other specific defences. These are considered in turn below. It should be noted at the outset, however, that unlike some jurisdictions, such as the UK, it is not a defence for the accused to contend that he did not expect the relevant insider dealing to result in a profit or the avoidance of a loss.

2.7.1 Defences to a charge under Article 166 of the SEL

2.7.1.1 Exercise of share subscription rights

The exercise of share subscription rights (including the subscription rights to a preferred capital contribution under the Preferred Capital Contribution Law) by an insider will not render that insider guilty of an offence.

2.7.1.2 Conversion of convertible bonds

An insider, in possession of inside information, who exercises his conversion rights is not guilty of an offence.

2.7.1.3 Mandatory purchase of shares

In those circumstances where a company becomes obliged under the Commercial Code of Japan to purchase its shares mandatorily, no offence is committed.

2.7.1.4 Purchase of shares or certain other securities at the request of directors of a target company

A person who, at the request of the board of directors of a company which is the subject of a tender offer, purchases or otherwise acquires any shares or certain other securities, or an option over such shares or securities with a view to resisting the tender offer, does not commit an offence.

2.7.1.5 Stabilisation

The insider dealing offence does not apply to dealings carried out in compliance with the SEL's stabilisation rules.

2.7.1.6 Straight bonds

The offence does not apply to dealings in straight bonds unless the 'material facts' concerned fall within those categories of material facts referred to at 2.2.2 *above*.

2.7.1.7 Dealings between company insiders

The offence does not apply to private deals between two or more corporate insiders. This covers deals where both the purchaser and seller know the relevant inside information and trade outside the stock exchanges set out in Table (1) (in the case of securities listed on such exchanges), or outside the over-the-counter market (in the case of securities registered for trading over-the-counter). This defence does not, however, apply where both purchaser and seller know the securities in question will be later transferred in breach of the insider dealing provisions of the SEL.

2.7.1.8 Information irrelevant

An offence is not committed by an insider who is either:

(1) merely dealing in securities in a manner required to perform obligations under an agreement which was entered into prior to the insider obtaining inside information; or
(2) pursuing a pre-determined scheme of dealing.

2.7.2 Defences to a charge under Article 167 of the SEL

The defences set out in 2.7.1 apply with minor amendments to the offence under SEL, art 167 also.

2.8 WHAT ARE THE PENALTIES AND CONSEQUENCES OF INSIDER DEALING?

By international standards, the criminal sanctions for breach of the SEL are very light. The maximum sentence is a fine not exceeding ¥500,000 (approximately £3,000 STG), and/or imprisonment for a term not exceeding six months. However, unlike many jurisdictions, in Japan where the convicted insider is an employee, his representative or agent may also be fined to the same extent as the insider himself. Directors who are convicted of insider dealing and sentenced to be imprisoned without compulsory labour are prevented from holding office during the period of such imprisonment.

2.9 'SHORT-SWING' PROFITS

In addition to the criminal offences created by the SEL, the SEL also contains provisions in respect of so called 'short-swing profits'. A company whose shares or certain other securities are listed on one of the stock exchanges in Table (1), or are traded on the over-the-counter market in Japan, may demand that any of its directors or principal shareholders (as defined in 2.3.2.2 *above*), return to the company the profits realised by purchasing such securities within six months of selling them (or selling them within six months of purchasing them). This is regardless of whether or not it can be shown that the person concerned had purchased or sold such securities with the benefit of knowing material facts. Directors and principal shareholders are obliged to file reports with the Minister of Finance setting out details of such purchases or sales by the fifteenth day of the month, immediately following the month in which such purchases or sales took place.

3 NON-STATUTORY REGULATION

3.1 INTRODUCTION

In addition to the provisions of the SEL, several self-regulatory organisations, such as the Japan Securities Dealers Association, the Federation of Bankers Associations of Japan, the Trust Companies Association of Japan and each of the stock exchanges set out in Table (1), have established internal regulations, guidelines or model codes intended to be adopted by their members and which are designed to prevent and regulate insider dealing in various financial businesses. What follows is a discussion of some of the more important of these.

3.2 THE JAPAN SECURITIES DEALERS ASSOCIATION ('JSDA')

Articles 13 and 19 of the JSDA's Regulations on Investment Solicitation and Client Relations provide that each member shall use its best efforts to prevent insider dealing and shall take reasonable measures to achieve this, such as the establishment of internal insider dealing prevention rules. In 1988, the JSDA also published guidelines on the prevention of insider dealing, as well as a model insider dealing prevention code of internal rules suggested for use by members. The following is a summary of this Model Code.

3.2.1 General provisions

3.2.1.1 Purpose

The purpose of the Model Code is to provide for:

- the standard treatment of information which officers or employees (together 'personnel'), of a member have acquired while conducting their business and which has not been made public;
- the handling of clients;
- the control of selling and buying;
- the regulation of personnel and related matters for the prevention of insider dealing; and
- the proper operation of the business activities of the member.

3.2.1.2 Compliance with laws and regulations, etc

The Model Code requires the personnel of a member to conduct their business in a fair manner and in compliance with the SEL, other related laws and regulations thereunder, and internal regulations and rules provided for by the JSDA, stock exchanges, etc. The model code also requires the personnel of a member to remind the personnel of issuers of securities, with whom they are in daily contact, of the need for compliance with these laws and regulations.

3.2.2 Treatment of confidential information relating to an issuer

3.2.2.1 Confidential information relating to an issuer

The Model Code sets out specific requirements governing the treatment of 'confidential information relating to issuers'. This is information which:

- the personnel of a member may acquire while conducting their business;
- has not been made public;
- relates to certain matters with respect to the operation, business and assets of a corporation whose shares are listed on one of the stock exchanges set out in Table (1), or are traded on the Japanese over-the-counter market (an 'issuer'); and
- has a substantial influence on the investment decisions of investors with respect to shares, convertible bonds, bonds with warrants to subscribe for new shares (or certificates representing such warrants and straight bonds of the issuer), or on the decision to make or withdraw a tender offer (or any purchase similar to a tender offer), of such securities of the issuer.

3.2.2.2 Report

The Model Code requires that the personnel of a member who has acquired confidential information relating to an issuer, while conducting their business, immediately make a report of the fact to their relevant section or branch manager who, in turn, shall promptly give such personnel the appropriate instructions with respect to the treatment of the information. A section or branch manager who receives such a report or who has himself acquired confidential information relating to an issuer while conducting his business shall without delay notify his supervisor or a compliance officer of such information.

3.2.2.3 Requests to issuers for the making public of information

The Model Code also requires that a member shall (when it deems it necessary that any confidential information relating to an issuer shall be made public) request that the relevant issuer take appropriate measures, for instance making public disclosure of such information.

3.2.2.4 Manner of custody of information

With respect to documents containing confidential information relating to an issuer which is a client corporation, and documents with information concerning important transactions (for example, a consolidation or merger, an acquisition, a tender offer, an issue of new shares, etc or a material change in the business operations of the issuer) in which the member is engaged, the Model Code requires that that member shall cause such documents to be kept in the custody of the division in charge of such matter and shall keep such documents physically apart from other divisions.

3.2.2.5 Control of investment information materials

The Model Code requires that if a division within a member is preparing investment information materials or analysts' reports such division, together with the compliance division, shall examine whether or not any confidential information relating to an issuer is contained therein and shall use its best efforts to cause investment information to be disclosed simultaneously to all divisions within the member.

3.2.3 Prohibited activities

The Model Code also sets out the following prohibitions:

- The member shall not carry out any selling or buying transactions for its own account which makes use of confidential information relating to an issuer.
- The personnel of a member shall not make use of confidential information relating to an issuer when conducting brokerage business.
- The personnel of a member shall not carry out their own account transactions making use of confidential information relating to an issuer.
- The personnel of a member in charge of corporate finance, underwriting or compliance matters shall not carry out any selling or buying transactions of securities for their own accounts (other than straight bonds), of a client issuer for whom they are personally responsible.

- The personnel of a member shall not disclose to any other person any confidential information relating to an issuer which they have acquired or on which they have received a report, unless the relevant compliance officer authorises the disclosure thereof.
- The personnel of a member shall not solicit customers for transactions in securities which have been designated by the compliance division following receipt of relevant confidential information relating to the issuer.

3.2.4 Handling of clients

The Model Code requires members to take reasonable care to confirm whether or not any of their clients is an officer or a principal shareholder (as defined in 2.3.2.2) of an issuer or is a person who has access to inside information relating to the issuer (an 'insider'). If such client is an insider, the member shall prepare an insider registration card containing the client's name, title and any other matters prescribed by the member.

When an insider, with respect to an issuer, sells or buys securities of the issuer the Model Code requires personnel of the member immediately to make a report to the relevant section or branch manager, of the contents of such transaction. He, in turn, shall without delay make a report to the relevant compliance officer of the contents of such transaction and confirm whether or not the securities have been traded in by the insider within the prior six months' period. The section or branch manager shall re-examine the report every month and make a further report to the relevant compliance officer.

3.2.5 Limitation on acceptance of orders

The Model Code requires the personnel of a member, when accepting orders from clients for selling or buying transactions in securities, to consider the price, quantity and terms of such transactions and the prevailing market conditions with a view to establishing the fairness of the price and promoting smooth trading. If such orders clearly seem to be made upon the basis of confidential information relating to an issuer, then personnel shall not accept these orders.

If an order in respect of the securities of an issuer clearly seems to be made by an officer, or a principal shareholder of such issuer for the purpose of gaining profits by selling (or buying) the securities within six months after buying (or selling) the same, the Model Code prohibits as a matter of principle the personnel of the member from accepting such order.

3.2.6 Control of selling and buying transactions

Where a member has confidential information relating to an issuer and a transaction is proposed in relation to securities of that issuer, the Model Code requires the member's compliance division (if it deems it necessary) to give the division responsible for the transaction any of the following instructions, specifying the securities to which such instructions relate:

- as a matter of principle a transaction for the personnel's own account shall not be carried out;
- such securities shall not be especially recommended; and
- if necessary, enquiry shall be made of the relevant client as to the reasons for placing an order.

The Model Code requires the compliance division of a member to monitor the volume, frequency and other relevant matters of selling and buying transactions in securities of an issuer carried out by insiders of such issuer in accordance with the following procedures:

- it shall receive and examine the insider registration cards from section or branch managers (see 3.2.4);
- when a report that an insider has dealt in shares of the relevant issuer is received from a section or branch manager, it shall examine the contents of such transactions and, if necessary, inspect whether or not confidential information relating to the issuer is involved;
- when a report is made by personnel of the member that confidential information relating to an issuer has been received, it shall determine whether or not any extraordinary movements have taken place in the recent trends of selling or buying such securities and monitor closely these trends daily until the relevant confidential information relating to the issuer is made public; and
- where it decides that there are extraordinary movements and the member is involved in such movements, it shall make an immediate investigation to clarify all the surrounding circumstances from the office handling the relevant transactions and shall supervise the office to prevent unfair transactions.

The Model Code states that where a member establishes that an insider has made profits by buying and selling securities of the relevant issuer within a six month interval, it shall recommend that insider to return such profits to the issuer.

If the section or branch manager deems an order from a client for selling or buying securities not proper because of, for instance, the size of, or price at which, the transaction is to be effected then the section or branch manager shall ask for an explanation of the reasons and circumstances for the order from the client.

3.3 TOKYO STOCK EXCHANGE ('TSE')

The TSE monitors transactions effected on the TSE daily and, if any unusual transactions are found, may give a warning to the member which has effected such transactions, or require such member to report on the transactions to the TSE. The TSE may, if it deems necessary, stop the relevant transactions and take other related measures.

When listed companies disclose material facts (as defined in 2.3) or other information prescribed by the TSE which affects investors' investment decisions, such companies must submit reports containing such information and other related materials to the TSE and the TSE will make them available to the public (the 'filing system'). The purpose of the filing system is to provide for timely disclosure of 'material facts' and to prevent insider dealing.

3.4 FEDERATION OF BANKERS ASSOCIATIONS OF JAPAN ('FBA')

In 1988 the FBA established guidelines designed to prevent banks (and some other banking institutions) which regularly lend funds to issuers of securities, from exploiting inside information obtained from that lender-borrower relationship when those banks invest their own funds in securities of such issuers. The following is a summary of those guidelines.

3.4.1 Control of important information relating to clients

*   When the personnel of a bank acquire important information relating to clients while conducting their business, such personnel shall immediately make a report to the relevant section or branch manager who, in turn, shall give to them necessary instructions with respect to the control of such important information.
*   The personnel who obtain important information relating to clients or receive a report with respect thereto shall, unless the section or branch manager approves otherwise, keep it confidential.
*   The section or branch manager shall keep all documents containing important information relating to clients physically apart from other divisions and shall take other appropriate measures so that such divisions which do not need this information for their business shall not receive it.

3.4.2 Restrictions on activities of equity investment division

*   Unless otherwise permitted under laws and regulations, each bank shall not buy or sell shares, etc while it has important information relating to client-issuers.
*   Each bank shall take necessary organisational measures, such as the establishment of Chinese Walls between the securities investment division (which invests the bank's own funds) and those which handle transactions with client-issuers, in order that the securities investment division shall not use any information relating to such client-issuers for insider dealing.
*   The personnel of each bank shall not give important information relating to clients to the securities investment division.
*   The division which handles investments in securities of issuers with which the bank has transactional relationships ('client-issuers') shall examine whether or not its investment decisions are based on any important

information relating to the client-issuer, so that this information shall not be used for any such decision and if so, it shall not engage in any buying or selling transaction.

3.4.3 Restrictions on own account transactions by the personnel of banks

*   Bank personnel shall not, unless permitted by laws and regulations, effect a buying or selling transaction in securities while they have knowledge of important information relating to the client-issuer.
*   The personnel of corporate divisions of banks shall not trade for their own account in securities of client-issuers for which they are responsible.

'Important information relating to clients' or 'important information relating to client-issuers' means information relating to non-public facts or events ('important facts') relating to issuers and which has a substantial influence on the investment decisions of investors. The guidelines provide for certain concrete facts and events (many of which are similar to those set out in 2.3) which constitute such important facts.

In February 1995, the Securities Surveillance Committee requested the Tokyo District Public Prosecutor's Office ('TDP') to indict The Shimizu Bank Ltd (a regional bank) as well as several officers of the bank, for insider dealing and TDP started investigating this case. It was alleged that the bank sold shares in its client, based upon confidential information which related to a 'stop payment' (*shiharai teishi*), indicating the client's insolvency and issued by the client to the bank's lending division (*Nihon Keizai Shinbun*, 11 February 1995). This is the first case in which a bank has been investigated and prosecuted. On 24 March 1995 the Tokyo Summary Court fined The Shimizu Bank Ltd ¥500,000 (approximately £3,000 STG).

3.5 TRUST COMPANIES ASSOCIATION OF JAPAN

On the same day as the FBA introduced the guidelines which are discussed in 3.4, the Trust Companies Association of Japan promulgated regulations which provide, in addition to the matters regulated under the FBA's guidelines, the following matters which are particular to the trust banking business.

3.5.1 Regulations on agency business by clients' written orders

Each trust bank, when it effects a buying or selling transaction of securities on behalf of and for the account of a client in accordance with such client's written order ('Agency Business'), shall not accept a selling or buying order which seems to be based on important information relating to the relevant issuer.

If an order is obviously made by an officer or principal shareholder of an issuer for the purpose of gaining profits by selling the securities within six months after buying the same, or by buying the securities within six months after selling the same, the trust bank shall not accept such order.

If, when doing Agency Business, each trust bank realises that an officer (or his/her spouse, parent, child, grandchild, sister or brother), or principal shareholder, affiliate or high-ranking employee of the issuer effected a selling or buying transaction of such issuer's securities, such trust bank shall investigate the details of the transaction and shall prepare a 'card relating to transactions of the issuer's officer, etc' which includes the items prescribed by the trust bank.

Where a trust bank finds out that an officer or a principal shareholder of an issuer has made profits from buying and selling (or selling and buying) transactions within a six month period, the trust bank shall recommend such officer or principal shareholder to submit such profits to the issuer.

3.5.2 Regulations on investment advisory business

Each trust bank shall not advise any investors based upon 'important information relating to clients'.

3.6 OTHERS

Most other publicly traded companies have established their own insider trading rules, which are broadly similar to those of financial institutions. It is, however, doubtful that such rules are closely complied with or enforced. In November 1994, the Securities Surveillance Committee requested the Osaka District Public Prosecutors' Office to indict approximately 30 people on charges of insider trading. In this case, when a pharmaceutical company received reports of deadly side-effects of a new medicine which the company had recently introduced onto the market, some employees of the company and their tippees sold their shares in the company before information regarding the side-effects was made available to the public (*The Nohon Shoji* case, *Nihon Keizai Shinbun*, 6, 14, 15, 16, 27, 28 and 31 October and 2, 7 and 8 November 1994).

Although in this case the pharmaceutical company had established internal regulations designed to prevent insider dealing, such as a requirement that employees wishing to buy or sell shares in the company notify it in advance and a reporting system for recording important facts (see 3.4.1) and any restrictions on dealing by its employees which arise as a result of the important facts. Such regulations and reporting system did not work because apparently, it was very difficult for employees and other relevant parties to decide whether or not information regarding side-effects fell within the 'material fact' definition.

How to prevent similar trading in other industries is an open question, as discussion of this subject has only just started in Japan.

4 CONCLUSION

By virtue of the 1988 amendment to the Securities and Exchange Law of Japan, the legal framework to suppress insider dealing has been established. Since the adoption of the amendment, however, it has been pointed out that it will be difficult to implement effectively the provisions of the amendment because of the clandestine and technical nature of insider dealing. The establishment of the Securities Surveillance Committee was expected to cope with the situation and, to a limited extent, it seems to be working well. The future success of the anti-insider dealing regime in Japan will largely depend on the effectiveness of the Committee's activities.

CASE STUDY

Suzuki Co Ltd, a company listed on the Tokyo Stock Exchange, manufactures rainwear and umbrellas. Yamada, a weather forecaster, on discovering that there is an unseasonable amount of rain due in the next three months, instructs his broker to buy shares in Suzuki Co Ltd. Meanwhile, Tanaka, an analyst of the company's shares, is told in a conversation with Sato, one of the directors of Suzuki Co Ltd, that the president is expected to be paid a salary of ¥100 million. Tanaka knows from his knowledge of the president's service contract (which is available for public inspection) that this salary could only be paid if the company achieved profit in excess of ¥4 billion. Tanaka revises his profit forecast for the company but before he publishes it he cancels instructions which he had previously given to his broker to sell his Suzuki shares. Yamada also tells his girlfriend, Takahashi, that 'things are looking up' for Suzuki Co Ltd. Takahashi then buys shares in the name of her father from an old friend of hers who wanted to sell Suzuki Co Ltd shares off-market to save the payment of brokers' commission. In addition, Watanabe, an employee of the contracting firm which cleans Suzuki Co Ltd's offices, finds a draft of the latest management figures in a wastepaper bin, which demonstrates Suzuki Co Ltd's high profitability. He immediately buys shares.

Yamada
Whether Yamada is guilty of insider dealing under the law will depend on whether the information on the rainfall constitutes a material fact under the SEL. Although the information on the rainfall can be categorised by its nature as a 'material fact based on the happening of certain events' (see 2.3.2), information on the rainfall does not fall under any of the events specifically enumerated in the SEL. It must be considered, however, whether the information on the rainfall falls under the catch-all provision described in 2.3.4.

Although there is a scarcity of court precedents and scholars' views on the point, under the circumstances such information will almost certainly not constitute a material fact, since the provisions of the SEL must be interpreted narrowly as they create a criminal offence. Although the company's business is dependent on the weather, the weather forecast is very contingent and it will probably not have a material effect on an investor's investment decision.

Sato

The issue is whether the information Sato disclosed is a material fact. The fact that the company achieved a certain profit will constitute a material fact under the 'material fact based on forecasts' category (see 2.3.3), if such fact is related to (i) an increase (in excess of a specified percentage) in the ordinary profit or net income of the company, as compared with the most recent estimate which was made public and (ii) an increase in absolute terms above a specified level in the net assets or stated capital of the company.

Assuming then, that the forecast is a material fact, the next question is whether Sato is an 'insider', by obtaining the inside information in the performance of his duty. As Sato is a director of the company, he can be an insider if he obtains the inside information in performing his duty. If Sato is the director in charge of accounting, he would be an insider. If he is not, he would not necessarily be an insider, since accounting may not be within the scope of his duty. In practice it is often difficult to determine the scope of a director's duty.

However, as Sato did not purchase or sell shares in Suzuki Co Ltd, nor encourage Tanaka to commit an offence, he would not himself, be guilty of an offence.

Tanaka

Assuming that the information Sato disclosed to Tanaka is a material fact, Tanaka will be a tippee. As such, Tanaka is prohibited from selling or buying the shares in question. If the broker had not executed Tanaka's order to buy the shares yet, his cancelling the order will not constitute selling or buying the shares knowing a material fact. If the order had already been executed and the broker agreed to purchase the shares, then he may be held liable since he dealt in the shares knowing the material fact.

Takahashi

Takahashi is not guilty of an offence. First of all, the information she received will not, as is discussed above, be a material fact even if the full details of Yamada's forecast are communicated to her. In this case, what Takahashi is told is a rather ambiguous suggestion, which will make the possibility of her being held guilty even more remote. Second, neither Yamada nor Takahashi will be an insider since they have no connection with the company.

Watanabe

Assuming the information Watanabe happened to obtain is inside information, the crucial issue is whether he received it in the course of performing his duty as an employee of the contracting firm.

A person with a contractual link with the company concerned will only be guilty if the contract has some connection with the inside information in question. For instance, a chauffeur would not be an insider if he overheard a highly confidential conversation between the company's executives, since his duty is to drive, not to deal with confidential information. In this case, the contractual duty of the contracting firm is, arguably, just to clean Suzuki's offices. As such, neither the contracting firm nor Watanabe as its employee would be an insider. Thus, Watanabe could not be guilty of insider dealing.

Hong Kong

Raymond Cohen, Linklaters & Paines, Hong Kong

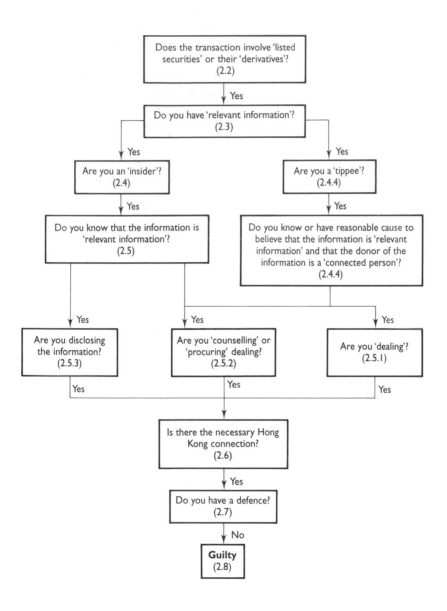

1 INTRODUCTION

The Securities (Insider Dealing) Ordinance 1990 (the 'Insider Dealing Ordinance') came into force on 1 September 1991. This amended the law relating to insider dealing which had previously been dealt with in the Securities Ordinance. The previous legislation empowered the Financial Secretary to require the Insider Dealing Tribunal (the 'Tribunal') to investigate alleged cases of insider dealing with a view to preparing a report on whether insider dealing had taken place, the identity of those involved and the extent of their culpability. It provided neither criminal sanction nor civil remedy against those found to be insider dealers, its sanctions being limited to the publication of a public report identifying a particular person as an insider dealer.

In short, the two main changes to the law on insider dealing introduced by the Insider Dealing Ordinance were: first, a more comprehensive definition of insider dealing and, second, new powers granted to the Tribunal to impose sanctions on those identified as having been involved in insider dealing. Whilst the roots of the Hong Kong legislation can be traced to Part V of The Companies Act 1980 and the Company Securities (Insider Dealing) Act 1985 of the United Kingdom (both now repealed), there are a number of differences, the most important of which is the omission to make insider dealing a criminal offence.

In addition to the statutory regulations, insider dealing may give rise to breaches of self-regulatory codes of conduct such as the Hong Kong Codes on Take-Overs and Mergers and Share Repurchases and the Listing Rules of the Stock Exchange of Hong Kong.

2 THE INSIDER DEALING ORDINANCE

2.1 INTRODUCTION

Section 9(1) of the Insider Dealing Ordinance stipulates when insider dealing is deemed to take place. These are discussed fully below (see 2.5), though at this stage it is worth considering the constituent elements of insider dealing (see flow-chart *above*).

2.2 TO WHICH SECURITIES DOES THE INSIDER DEALING ORDINANCE APPLY?

2.2.1 Listed securities

The Insider Dealing Ordinance applies to the 'listed securities', or their 'derivatives', of a 'listed corporation'. A 'listed corporation' is defined as a corporation which has securities listed on The Stock Exchange of Hong Kong Limited (the 'SEHK') at the time of any insider dealing. A 'corporation' comprises any company (or other body corporate) or unincorporated body, regardless of whether or not it is incorporated or formed in Hong Kong. The Insider Dealing Ordinance, therefore, applies to overseas entities provided they have securities listed on the SEHK. 'Listed securities' refers to those securities that are listed on the SEHK at the time of any insider dealing in relation to the listed corporation that has issued those securities. It should be noted that the securities are treated as listed regardless of whether dealing in them has been suspended.

2.2.2 Derivatives

The derivatives of a listed corporation do not have to be listed themselves but are caught by the Insider Dealing Ordinance if the underlying securities to which they relate are listed.

2.2.3 Related companies

It should be noted that insider dealing can take place by a person who is connected with a company dealing (or carrying out other acts prohibited by s 9(1)—see 2.5) in the listed securities of that company or a related company. Derivatives of a related corporation are likewise included. A 'related corporation' means any corporation which is a listed corporation's subsidiary or holding company, or where both the listed corporation and related corporation have a common holding company or the same 'controller'. A 'controller' is any person who customarily directs or instructs the directors of that corporation or its holding company to act in accordance with its wishes, or who either individually or with an associate, controls 33 per cent of the votes at a general meeting of the corporation or its holding company.

2.2.4 Meaning of securities

The term 'securities' is defined widely by the Insider Dealing Ordinance to mean any shares, stocks, debentures, loan stocks, funds, bonds, or notes of, or issued by, any incorporated or unincorporated body. The definition specifically includes such instruments issued by Hong Kong and overseas public sector bodies. It also includes:

*   rights, options, or interests in, or in respect of, any of these instruments;
*   certificates of interest or participation in, or temporary or interim certificates for, receipts for, or warrants to subscribe to or purchase any of these instruments; and
*   any instruments commonly known as securities.

2.2.5 Meaning of derivatives

In respect of the listed securities of a listed corporation or a related corporation, derivatives are defined in the Insider Dealing Ordinance as:

*   certificates of interest or participation;
*   temporary or interim certificates;

- receipts, including depositary receipts; and
- warrants to subscribe or purchase.

The definition also includes rights, options or interests and contracts whose purpose, or pretended purpose, is to make a profit or avoid a loss by reference to the price, or change in price, of these instruments or the underlying listed securities. The Insider Dealing Ordinance applies to derivatives whether or not they are issued or made by the listed corporation or a related corporation and as such they include those instruments issued by third party financial institutions known as 'call warrants' or 'covered warrants'.

2.3 WHAT IS RELEVANT INFORMATION?

'Relevant information' is the term employed by the Insider Dealing Ordinance for what is commonly called inside information. There is no precise guidance as to what constitutes relevant information; reliance is placed instead on the vague definition that it is information about a corporation which is:

- specific;
- not generally known to those persons who are accustomed, or would be likely to deal in the listed securities of that corporation; and
- which would, if it were generally known to such persons, be likely materially to affect the price of those securities.

2.3.1 Specific

The requirement of specificity is not clearly defined in the Insider Dealing Ordinance with the result that it is not possible to say conclusively whether the specificity refers to the information itself, or to its relevance to the particular corporation in question. However, the better view is that it is the information itself which must be specific. What 'specific information' actually means in practice is a question of fact to be decided in each case, though the essence of the definition is the distinction between the particular and the general. In the Singapore case of *Public Prosecutor v GCK Choudhury* [1981] 2 Co Law 141 the information in question concerned knowledge that a certain company was facing a financial crisis. This was deemed to be specific by the Court of Appeal on the grounds that it was capable of being pointed to, identified and unequivocally expressed.

While vague or woolly rumours are not likely to amount to relevant information given the lack of specificity, 'concrete' rumours (which turn out to be false) may amount to relevant information if the conditions as to specificity, not generally known to the market, and materiality to price are met. However, the test as to who an insider is (ie a person connected with a corporation or a 'tippee' of such person), would effectively exclude a person acting on market rumours alone, since such person would be unlikely to have the requisite connections or inside information satisfying the criteria of an insider.

Problem Area 1

> Christopher comes into possession of a leaked first draft board paper containing proposals for a possible share repurchase offer. Whether this constitutes relevant information is not determined so much by the fact that the document relates to a contemplated transaction, but rather by the question whether the contemplation of the board is sufficiently advanced so that the proposals have become specific information. Hence, much would depend on the degree of detail of the information contained in the document and whether it gives any indication as to likelihood of the transaction taking place.

2.3.2 Information not generally known

The information must not be generally known to those persons who are accustomed, or would be likely to deal in, the securities of the corporation in question. However, no guidance is given in the Insider Dealing Ordinance as to what criteria would be used to establish whether an investor is accustomed or would be likely to deal in the securities of a particular corporation. Clearly professional dealers would be included within this category, as would many institutional investors (and any other investors who could reasonably be expected to be familiar with financial market information).

It is a question of fact as to what is deemed to be a wide enough dissemination of information to constitute being 'generally known'. It does not have to be widely disseminated amongst the investing public, as in many other jurisdictions, but only among those accustomed or likely to deal in the securities concerned. What is clear is that it is not sufficient to be able to show that the information, while not actually known by those accustomed or likely to deal, was available to them on request. However, the availability of such information on request is likely to give rise to a rebuttable presumption that the information was generally known to this class of person.

Problem Area 2

> The board of directors of Raw Materials Ltd, authorises the release of a statement to a number of chosen institutional investors announcing the discovery of a major new mineral deposit.
>
> Disclosure of this information to such a select group accustomed or likely to deal is unlikely to be sufficient for the purposes of the Insider Dealing Ordinance. Consequently, both the board and the institutional investors should not deal in Raw Materials' securities until the information has been disseminated to market professionals generally. However, the directors do not have to wait until the entire market has had time to act on the information, nor for the market to absorb the implications of the information before dealing.

2.3.3 Materiality

The information must be such that if it were generally known to persons who are accustomed, or would be likely to deal in those securities, it would be liable materially to affect the price of them. Accordingly, it is not enough to be able to show that the information would be likely to influence most investors in arriving at a decision whether to sell or buy the relevant securities, if it would not also be likely to affect the market price to a material degree (though obviously there is often a correlation between the two).

Whether the information will materially affect the price of the securities clearly depends on the particular circumstances of the case in question. However, general examples of information which may have this ability include the announcement of a take-over bid, a substantial increase or decrease in profits or losses and a senior management shake-up.

The materiality aspect is a convenient starting point for an investigation into suspected insider dealing by the Tribunal (see 2.8), since it is a straightforward exercise to establish whether or not the price materially moved and if not, the Tribunal can avoid a potentially complex investigation as to whether the information is relevant information in other respects.

2.4 WHO IS AN INSIDER?

There are four categories of 'insider' identified in the Insider Dealing Ordinance:

- persons connected with a corporation;
- persons contemplating take-overs;
- persons in a privileged capacity; and
- 'tippees' of each of the above.

2.4.1 A person connected with a corporation

A 'person connected with a corporation' is someone who has access to information about a corporation by reason of being a director or substantial shareholder of that corporation, or by virtue of some other relationship with it. The rules defining when a person is connected with a corporation are set out in considerable detail in s 4 of the Ordinance. It is not necessary for the person to be aware that he is connected with a corporation since the test is purely objective.

The definition of a connected person is couched in terms of individuals, though s 4(2) provides that a corporation will be considered to be a person connected with a corporation if any of its directors or employees is a person connected with that other corporation within the meaning of 2.4.1.1 to 2.4.1.4 *below*.

The individual must be currently connected with a corporation, or have been so connected at any time within the six months preceding any insider dealing in relation to it. This six month period is entirely arbitrary. An individual will not be an insider dealer if the utilisation of the relevant information is delayed for one day over the six month deadline. However, in practice, given the definition of relevant information in s 8 (see 2.3) this is rarely going to be an issue. Six months should normally be sufficient time for any relevant information to have become public knowledge or, if not, to render it outdated and unlikely materially to affect the price of the securities. An individual, is deemed to be connected with a corporation if he satisfies any of the criteria set out in 2.4.1.1 to 2.4.1.4 *below*.

2.4.1.1 A director or employee of the corporation or a related corporation (see 2.2.3)

There is no requirement that either the directors or employees occupy positions which in fact give them access to relevant information: all are included on the basis that by the very nature of their positions they are likely to have relevant information. 'Director' is defined to include any person occupying the position of director regardless of whether he is actually called a director, and any person in accordance with whose directions or instructions the directors of the corporation are accustomed to act. As such, the Insider Dealing Ordinance draws no distinction between executive, non-executive, and shadow directors.

The term 'employee' is left undefined by the Insider Dealing Ordinance, though it is clear that it encompasses all employees and is not restricted to those occupying the more senior positions in a corporation. For these purposes, individuals employed under a contract of service may be considered employees, while those retained under a contract for services might not. However, this distinction may be of little consequence since any individual in a position involving a professional or business relationship between himself and a corporation is deemed to be connected in any case (see 2.4.1.3 *below*).

2.4.1.2 A substantial shareholder in the corporation or a related corporation

A substantial shareholder is defined as someone who has an interest in voting shares equal to, or more than, 10 per cent of the nominal value of issued shares carrying the right to vote. This brings into the ambit of the legislation the large holdings held by institutional investors who, although are not strictly entitled to any more information than other shareholders, are likely to have access to relevant information given the close nature of their relationship with a corporation (see 2.2.3). In addition, s 4(1)(c)(ii) extends the concept of a connected person to include an individual in a position which may reasonably be expected to give him access to relevant information, by virtue of his being a director, employee or partner of a substantial shareholder in the corporation or a related corporation.

2.4.1.3 A professional or business relationship

An individual will be deemed to be connected if he occupies a position which may reasonably be expected to give him access to relevant information concerning the corporation by virtue of any professional or business relationship with it.

The professional or business relationship need not be strictly contractual, although it should have a commercial element at least to the extent of an expectation of payment and the receipt of professional fees. It could be said that the relationship should be such that a corporation could restrain the unauthorised disclosure of confidential information that comprises the relevant information in question. Table (1) sets out the range of potential parties in a professional or business relationship.

TABLE (1)

The relationship can be between:
- an individual; or
- an individual's employer; or
- a corporation of which the individual is a director; or
- a firm of which the individual is a partner;

on the one side, and on the other side:
- the corporation in question; or
- a related corporation of the corporation in question; or
- an officer of the corporation in question or a corporation related to it; or
- a substantial shareholder in the corporation in question or a corporation related to it.

Therefore, the scope of the provision includes professional advisers such as solicitors, auditors, brokers and bankers, as well as major suppliers, customers and major creditors, all of whom potentially have access to relevant information but whose professional or business relationship may not be directly with the corporation in question. It would not, however, catch analysts or journalists, who may be better informed about a corporation than many of these and have a greater likelihood of possessing relevant information.

Problem Area 3

Sally, a trainee solicitor, is engaged on a matter for Countdown 1997 Ltd, a client of the firm which employs her. As a result, she is privy to 'relevant information' regarding Sino Products Ltd. Unknown to Sally, Red Star Ltd owns a 50 per cent stake in the share capital of both Countdown 1997 Ltd and Sino Products Ltd.

By virtue of her employers' professional relationship with Countdown 1997, Sally is deemed to be connected with Sino Products since Countdown 1997 is a related corporation by virtue of Red Star Ltd being the common controller of the two corporations, and because she occupies a position which may reasonably be expected to give her access to relevant information in Sino Products.

2.4.1.4 A transaction involving another corporation

If an individual is connected (within the meaning of 2.4.1.1 to 2.4.1.3) with a corporation involved in a transaction with another corporation, he will be deemed to be connected with the other corporation if he has access to relevant information which specifically relates to:

- any transaction (actual or contemplated) involving both corporations; or
- any transaction (actual or contemplated) involving one of the corporations and the listed securities or their derivatives of the other; or
- the fact that a transaction is no longer contemplated.

The concept of a 'contemplated' transaction causes problems in application. It gives rise to a difficulty in establishing precisely when the required degree of contemplation is reached. However, the requirements that the information be specific and materially affect the price in order to be relevant information, gives an indication of how far advanced the contemplation of the transaction must be.

2.4.2 Persons contemplating take-overs

A person who is contemplating, or has contemplated making a take-over offer for a corporation, is a potential insider. The legislation specifically prevents such persons from utilising any relevant information about the take-over offer other than for the purpose of facilitating the take-over itself (subss 9(1)(b) and 9(1)(d)).

Problem Area 4

> Ken, an analyst at Hong Kong Insurance Ltd, is aware of relevant information in respect of a take-over bid to be made by Asia Ltd for Yang Ltd by virtue of his employer being a substantial shareholder in Asia Ltd.
>
> Ken is not personally contemplating making the take-over offer and therefore he is not insider dealing by virtue of subs 9(1)(b). He is, however, deemed to be connected with Asia Ltd by virtue of being an employee of a substantial shareholder in it and it may be reasonable to expect that such a position would give him access to relevant information. Ken would, therefore, be precluded from dealing in the listed securities or derivatives of Asia Ltd on the basis of this information. Nor would Ken be able to deal in the securities or derivatives of Yang since he is deemed connected with that company by virtue of subs 4(1)(d) (see 2.4.1.4 above).

A 'take-over offer' is defined in s 7 as an offer made to all the holders (or all the holders other than the person making the offer and his nominees) of the shares, or a particular class of shares, in a corporation to acquire those shares or a specified proportion of them. Hence, where a person's contemplated acquisitions do not amount to a take-over as defined, but merely a substantial acquisition, there can be no insider dealing under subss 9(1)(b) and 9(1)(d).

2.4.3 A person in a privileged capacity

Section 5 of the Insider Dealing Ordinance provides that persons who receive relevant information about a corporation by virtue of a privileged capacity are considered to be connected with that corporation. A privileged capacity exists where a person occupies a position as a public officer, or a member or employee of certain specified bodies. The bodies specified in the Insider Dealing Ordinance are listed in Table (2) *below*.

TABLE (2)

- the Executive Council;
- the Legislative Council;
- the Futures Exchange, SEHK and any clearing house;
- any body appointed by the Governor or the Governor in Council under any Ordinance;
- any corporate body established by Ordinance; and
- any corporate body specified by the Financial Secretary by notice in the Gazette.

Such persons are deemed to be insiders since they are public officers in sensitive positions which provide access to relevant information despite the fact that they have no direct links with any particular corporation. The apparent width of the provision is qualified by the fact that such persons must come across the relevant information by virtue of their capacity as a person in a privileged capacity. Furthermore, such persons can utilise any relevant information in their possession immediately on ceasing to occupy a privileged capacity since there is no six month quarantine period.

2.4.4 'Tippees'

The three categories of insiders which have been considered so far are commonly known as primary insiders. Secondary insiders are not themselves connected with a corporation, nor contemplating making a take-over offer, but are persons who receive relevant information from a primary insider. Primary insiders in such circumstances are commonly known as 'tippers' and secondary insiders as 'tippees'.

'Tippee' trading is covered by subss 9(1)(e) and 9(1)(f). Table (3) outlines the requirements that have to be established to identify a person as an insider dealer under subs 9(1)(e).

TABLE (3)

Meaning of 'tippee'
A person who has received, either directly or indirectly, relevant information about a corporation:

- knowing it to be relevant information;
- knowing it came from a person who is connected with that corporation or has been so connected within the previous six months; and
- knowing or having reasonable cause to believe that the connected person held the information by reason of being so connected.

Subsection 9(1)(*f*) is broadly similar to subs 9(1)(*e*) except that the tippee receives the information, knowing that it is relevant information, directly or indirectly from a person whom the tippee knows or has reasonable cause to believe is contemplating or is no longer contemplating a take-over offer for a corporation.

It should be noted that a tippee is someone who 'receives' relevant information. Consequently, as soon as the tippee comes into possession of the information he becomes a secondary insider regardless of whether he actively procured the information from the primary insider or came by it without any positive action on his part. An unwilling recipient is offered no protection but does not become an insider dealer provided he refrains from utilising the information.

The tippee can receive the information either directly or indirectly from the tipper. Whilst there is little difficulty with direct communication, it is questionable how far the scope of indirectly received information extends. Whilst information can be passed indirectly to the ultimate tippee through a chain of people, the further down the chain he is, the harder it is likely to be to establish that he knew the source of the information to be connected with the corporation and that the informant obtained the information by virtue of this connection. In such situations, consideration also has to be given as to whether the information is still relevant since the more information changes hands the more imprecise and unreliable it becomes.

Under subs 9(1)(*e*) the tippee's awareness is subjective in that he must know that he has received relevant information and that it originated from a connected person. Although subs 9(1)(*f*) incorporates a subjective test as to the insider's appreciation of relevant information, there is also an objective test in respect of the tippee's knowledge, which gives the Tribunal scope to find it sufficient that the tippee had factual knowledge which would put a reasonable man on inquiry that a take-over bid was to be made.

In addition, subs 9(1)(*e*) includes the requirement that the tippee must have known or had reasonable cause to believe that his informant held relevant information by virtue of being connected with the corporation in question, which means that constructive knowledge is enough to identify him as an insider dealer. It should be noted that a recipient of information from a person in a privileged capacity will also be regarded as a tippee by virtue of s 5, which deems such privileged persons to be a person connected with a corporation for the purpose of subs 9(1)(e).

Finally, it is irrelevant to the tippee's liability that the tipper knew or did not know that he was supplying relevant information to the tippee. Nonetheless, the circumstances surrounding the transmission of the information are likely to be relevant in establishing the tippee's awareness.

2.5 WHEN DOES INSIDER DEALING OCCUR?

Subsection 9(1) of the Insider Dealing Ordinance details dealing, counselling or procuring, and disclosing as being the three separate instances when insider dealing is deemed to occur.

2.5.1 Dealing

All four categories of insider (see 2.4) will breach the Insider Dealing Ordinance if they deal in certain circumstances. Section 6 of the Insider Dealing Ordinance gives a fairly wide definition of dealing to the extent that a person deals if he buys, sells, exchanges or subscribes for, acquires or disposes of, the right to buy, sell, exchange or subscribe for, any listed securities or their derivatives, or agrees to do any of these things whether as principal or agent. Accordingly, the Insider Dealing Ordinance applies both to off-market as well as on-market dealing.

TABLE (4)

Constituent elements for dealing offence pursuant to s 9(1)(a)
• the dealer must be connected with the company whose securities or derivatives are dealt in;
• the dealer must be in possession of relevant information in relation to that company;
• the dealer must know the information is relevant information in relation to that company;
• the dealer must deal in any listed securities or derivatives of that corporation or in the securities of a related corporation.

In similar circumstances, a public servant should not deal by virtue of s 5 and subs 9(1)(a), and a tippee by virtue of subss 9(1)(e) and 9(1)(f). In addition, it is a breach of subs 9(1)(b) for a person to deal who is contemplating, or has contemplated, making a take-over offer for a corporation and who knows that such information about the offer or the fact that it is no longer contemplated is relevant information, otherwise than for the purpose of the take-over.

It should be noted that the provisions are extended to prevent dealing in the listed securities or derivatives of a corporation related to the one with which the insider is connected, or about which he has relevant information.

Problem Area 5

Julian is a director of Foodco Ltd and knows that Foodco is about to enter into a significant contract for the sale of biscuits to a major customer. Foodco owns 51 per cent of Drinkco which, like Foodco, is listed on the HKSE.

Not only is Julian precluded from dealing in Foodco shares but he is not able to deal in the listed securities or derivatives of Drinkco, being a related company of Foodco (ie its subsidiary company—see 2.2.3), even though the relevant information related to Foodco and not Drinkco. Similarly, if the relevant information related to Drinkco then Julian is deemed to be connected with Drinkco by virtue of s 4 which connects a director to any related company and, on the assumption Julian knows about the relevant information, he would be precluded from dealing in shares of Foodco or Drinkco.

2.5.2 Counselling or procuring

Section 9 provides that all categories of insider (see 2.4) should refrain from counselling or procuring another person to deal. This aims to prevent the transmission of recommendations and subtle hints, rather than the direct and obvious unauthorised communication of relevant information, which is known as disclosing (see 2.5.3 *below*). To 'counsel or procure' is not defined in the Insider Dealing Ordinance. To counsel (in its broad sense) means, in the words of Parker LJ in *R v Calhaem* [1985] 1 QB 808 CA 'to advise, solicit or something of that sort'. The trial judge in that case described it as to 'put somebody up to something'.

TABLE (5)

Constituent elements for the counselling and procuring offence pursuant to s 9(1)(a):
• the offender must be connected with the company whose securities or derivatives he counsels or procures another to buy;
• the offender must be in possession of relevant information;
• the offender must know that the information is relevant information;
• the offender must counsel or procure another person to deal in the securities or derivatives of the company or a related company, knowing or having reasonable cause to believe that such person would deal in them.

To procure something means, broadly, to see that a certain state of affairs prevails, whereas to establish an act of counselling it is not necessary to prove a strict causal connection. Thus, the counselling of an act is established if it can be shown that there was counselling and that the act was committed, regardless of whether a causal link between the two can be demonstrated.

Similarly, a person who is precluded from dealing by virtue of either contemplating a take-over pursuant to subs 9(1)(a) or being a tippee pursuant to subs 9(1)(e) or (f) is precluded from counselling or procuring another to deal and in such cases it is not necessary to establish that the offender knew, or had reasonable cause to believe that the recipient of the information would deal.

Problem Area 6

Daniel, an office junior employed by Rothwell Gaunt, reads a confidential report containing relevant information about its proposed take-over of Shopwell Supermarkets Ltd. He jokingly suggests to his impecunious friend Edward that he should invest some money in the shares of Shopwell Supermarkets. Subsequently, Edward comes into an inheritance and acquires a holding in the company.

Since Daniel was aware that Edward had no money at the time he counselled him to deal he is not an insider dealer, since he reasonably believed Edward would not deal in the shares.

2.5.3 Disclosing

Subsections 9(1)(c) and 9(1)(d) provide that a person who should not deal by virtue of subss 9(1)(a) and 9(1)(b), due to his possession of relevant information (see 2.5.1 *above*) should not disclose that information, either directly or indirectly, to any person if he knows or has reasonable cause to believe that the person or some other person will make use of the information to deal or will counsel or procure another person to deal.

TABLE (6)

Constituent elements for the disclosure offence pursuant to subs 9(1)(a):
• the offender must be connected with the company whose information he discloses;
• the offender must disclose directly or indirectly relevant information to another person;
• the offender must know the information is relevant information;
• the offender must know or have reasonable cause for believing that the other person will make use of the information for the purpose of dealing, or counselling or procuring another to deal, on the listed securities or derivatives of the relevant corporation or a related corporation.

These subsections are designed to cover the insider who deliberately leaks relevant information with a view to someone else using that information to deal.

There are two things in particular to note: first, the insider's awareness is to be measured against both subjective and objective criteria and second, it would seem that the insider who communicates relevant information without giving any thought to the consequences of his actions will not be covered by these provisions.

Problem Area 7

> Malcolm, a director of Rag Trade Ltd, is told by his son that Alun, an old college friend of his, has requested some investment advice. Malcolm informs his son that he should tell Alun to buy shares in Rag Trade Ltd since though it has not been publicly announced yet, this year's profits will well exceed market expectations. Malcolm's son informs Alun to buy the shares, but Alun has already invested the money elsewhere and so does not acquire any.
>
> Despite the fact that no dealing in the company's shares actually takes place, Malcolm is still liable for disclosing the relevant information since actual disclosure, together with a reasonable belief that the information will be used to counsel or procure another to deal, is sufficient in itself to found liability. Malcolm's son may also be liable under s 9(1)(e) as a tippee since he is aware of the source of the relevant information and would be aware that this information was obtained by his father by virtue of his position as a director of Rag Trade.

2.6 WHAT IS THE TERRITORIAL SCOPE OF THE INSIDER DEALING ORDINANCE?

The prohibition on insider dealing in subs 9(1) is limited to those securities listed and those corporations with securities listed, on the SEHK. However, subs 9(2) extends the territorial scope of the Insider Dealing Ordinance to prevent relevant information being passed to third parties outside the jurisdiction and then dealing taking place in those securities which have a listing on an overseas stock exchange, in addition to a listing on the SEHK. Under this subsection insider dealing takes place when a person who is knowingly (subjective) in possession of relevant information about a corporation with securities listed on the SEHK and obtained it in any of the circumstances described in 2.5 *above*:

- counsels or procures any other person to deal in the listed securities (or their derivatives) of that, or a related corporation knowing or having reasonable cause to believe that he would deal in them on any stock exchange outside Hong Kong; or
- discloses that relevant information to another person knowing or with reasonable cause to believe that he or some other person will use it to

deal or counsel, or procure another to deal in the listed securities or derivatives of that or a related corporation, on a stock exchange outside Hong Kong.

2.7 WHAT ARE THE DEFENCES?

Sections 10, 11 and 12 of the Insider Dealing Ordinance set out certain types of transaction which are technically 'insider dealing' but which will not be held to be such if certain 'defences' can be established. Once a person has been identified as an insider dealer the burden of proof is reversed so that the onus is on him to establish the balance of probabilities that he can utilise one of the defences.

2.7.1 Qualifying shareholding, underwriting agreements and liquidations

Subsection 10(1) provides that a person who enters into a transaction which would normally constitute insider dealing will not be held to be an insider dealer if he entered into the transaction:

*   as a director solely to acquire a qualifying shareholding;
*   in the *bona fide* performance of an underwriting agreement. It is unclear whether the performance of an underwriting agreement would include sub-underwriting (since strictly speaking, sub-underwriting is a process of risk sharing arising from, but is not in itself a part of, the underwriting obligation), but arguably it should be interpreted as including sub-under-writing, to accord with the 'spirit' of the legislation; or
*   *bona fide* as a liquidator, receiver or trustee in bankruptcy.

2.7.2 Chinese Walls

A corporation will not be held out as an insider dealer if it can establish that 'Chinese Wall' arrangements were in place and operated properly to segregate functions (subs 10(2)). Such a defence is necessary from a commercial per-spective. If one director of a merchant bank knowingly has relevant information about another listed corporation, at a time when another director on the dealing side, who knows nothing about that information, enters into a dealing on behalf of the bank in the listed securities (or their derivatives) of the other it may be argued that insider dealing has occurred because the bank dealt (through the agency of one director) at a time when (through the knowledge of another direc-tor) it could be said to be knowingly in possession of relevant information. This defence provides that the corporation will not be liable as an insider dealer provided it can demonstrate that the director who made the deal was not aware of the information and that a Chinese Wall was in place to ensure that he received neither the information nor advice from anyone in possession of the information.

2.7.3 Dealing otherwise than for profit or avoiding a loss

A further defence is found in subs 10(3) for a person who enters into a transaction for some reason other than with a view to making a profit or avoiding a loss (whether for himself or someone else) by the use of the relevant information. In general, this defence will be difficult to establish since the insider will be dealing, procuring, counselling or disclosing whilst in the possession of price-sensitive information. The defence will be available where, for example, an insider with relevant information which will result in the share price increasing, sells shares (see the comparable position in the UK (see 2.7.1.1 of that chapter)).

2.7.4 Acting as agent

Protection is provided under subs 10(4) for those persons who are in possession of relevant information but act as agent for another person and as such do not select or advise on the choice of securities which are dealt. This would, for example, protect market professionals, such as brokers, who may possess relevant information but act simply as intermediaries to facilitate a transaction for the principal who instructs them.

2.7.5 Equality of information

Subsection 10(5) provides that it is not insider dealing if:

- the other party to the transaction knew, or ought reasonably to have known, of the relevant information in question before entering into the transaction; and
- the transaction was neither recorded on the SEHK nor required to be notified to it under its rules.

The first limb employs the objective, in addition to the subjective, test of *mens rea* and requires the other party to know the contents of the relevant information. It is effectively limited to other insiders. The second limb requires that the transaction was effected off-market.

2.7.6 Knowledge of connection

Additionally, protection is provided under subs 10(6) for a person who enters into a transaction which is an insider dealing in relation to a listed corporation if he can establish that the other party to the transaction knew, or ought reasonably to have known, that he was a person connected with that corporation. This will not, however, absolve liability for such person as an insider dealer in respect of his having counselled or procured another person to deal. It is none the less a useful defence since there is no requirement that the other party to the transaction be aware that the connected person is in possession of relevant information—the fact that he is connected is sufficient in itself. In addition, the inclusion of the objective test of awareness ensures that this defence would be applicable if the other party ought reasonably to have known that he was so connected.

2.7.7 Market contracts

Subsection 10(7) provides a defence to an insider dealing if the offender can establish that the transaction is a market contract. A market contract is a contract which complies with the rules of a recognised clearing house, the purpose of which is the clearing and settlement of securities transactions on the SEHK.

2.7.8 Trustees and personal representatives

A defence is available under s 11 to those trustees and personal representatives who enter into a transaction, which is technically an insider dealing, if they can establish that they acted on advice obtained *bona fide* from a person who appeared to be an appropriate person from whom to seek such advice and did not appear to be a person who would be held to be an insider dealer if such a transaction were entered into. Note that a trustee's and personal representative's perception of the person on whose advice they act is purely subjective.

2.7.9 Exercise of options

Finally, a person who exercises a right to subscribe for or otherwise acquire securities (eg an executive share option or a listed subscription or call warrant), can avoid liability for insider dealing by virtue of s 12, provided he can show that the grant of the right predated, or was derived from securities held by him prior to, his coming into possession of relevant information. This is a wide defence and capable of abuse, since it allows the insider the ability to time the exercise of the option to take the maximum advantage of the relevant information.

2.8 THE INSIDER DEALING TRIBUNAL

2.8.1 Constitution, objects and procedure

The Tribunal established under the Securities Ordinance continues to operate under Part III of the Insider Dealing Ordinance. The Financial Secretary may order the Tribunal to conduct an inquiry into any suspected insider dealing to determine:

- whether insider dealing has taken place;
- the identity of every insider dealer; and
- the amount of any profit gained or loss avoided as a result of the insider dealing.

2.8.2 Powers of the Tribunal

The powers of the Tribunal in making any inquiry are extensive and are set out in Table (7) *below*.

TABLE (7)

The Tribunal, *inter alia*, may:
* take oral, written and documentary evidence, whether or not that evidence would be admissible in a court of law;
* require any person to attend before it to give evidence on oath or affirmation and to produce any documentary evidence;
* cross-examine any person; and
* forbid further disclosure of any material received by it.

The Tribunal can also authorise the Securities and Futures Commission, *inter alia*, to:
* inspect and take copies of any book or other document of any person where the Tribunal has reason to believe it contains information relevant to the inquiry; and
* order any person within a specified time to give information as to whether or not there exists any book or other document which may contain relevant information and if so where that book or other document is situated.

The Insider Dealing Ordinance interprets the phrase 'book or other document' widely to include bankers' books and records, and also cheques, other negotiable instruments and securities in the possession of a banker. A 'document' includes any register, book, record, tape recording, any form of computer input or output and any other document or similar material (whether produced mechanically, electrically or manually or by any other means whatsoever).

Any person who fails to disclose or produce any information, gives false or misleading information, obstructs the Securities and Futures Commission in its investigation or destroys, falsifies, conceals or otherwise disposes of any evidence with the intention of concealing information from the Commission or the Tribunal commits a criminal offence and may be liable to a fine of HK$100,000 (approximately £8,000 STG) and six months' imprisonment. In addition, s 20 of the Ordinance prescribes a penalty of up to a HK$100,000 fine and six months' imprisonment for failure to comply with various requirements of the Tribunal or for disrupting the Tribunal. There is also a list of further offences in subs 20(2) which amount to contempt of the Tribunal, for which the maximum penalty is a fine of HK$200,000 (approximately £16,000 STG) and one year's imprisonment.

2.8.3 Privileged information

Under s 21 certain information and documents are privileged and are not required to be given to the Tribunal. An authorised banking institution acting as the banker or financial adviser of a person whose conduct is the subject of an inquiry, cannot be compelled to disclose to the Tribunal confidential information relating to the affairs of its customers except the customer who is himself the subject of the insider dealing inquiry. Privilege is also extended to any information (other than the name and address of a client) which would be covered by legal professional privilege in an action in the High Court.

2.8.4 Report of the Tribunal

Under s 22, on conclusion of its inquiry the Tribunal must issue a report to the Financial Secretary and, unless any part of the inquiry was held in private, also publish the report to the public and supply copies to any person whose conduct was directly in question in the inquiry, the Securities and Futures Commission and any professional body of which the insider was a member. Even where part or all of the inquiry was held in private the Financial Secretary can order the whole or any part of the report to be made public if he thinks it is in the public interest to do so.

2.8.5 Orders of the Tribunal

Under s 23 of the Ordinance the Tribunal may, in respect of any insider dealer, make any or all of the orders described in Table (8) *below*.

TABLE (8)

The insider dealer shall:
- not be a director or a liquidator or a receiver or manager of the property of a company or in any way, whether directly or indirectly, be concerned or take part in the management of a company for such period (not exceeding five years) as may be specified, without the leave of the High Court;
- pay to the government an amount not exceeding the amount of any profit gained or loss avoided by that person as a result of the insider dealing;
- be fined an amount not exceeding three times the amount of any profit gained or loss avoided by that person as a result of the insider dealing; and
- bear the expenses of the inquiry.

By virtue of s 25 the extent of an insider dealer's total liability is limited to a maximum of three times the profit gained or loss avoided by all persons as a result of the insider dealing. It should be noted that s 14 expressly provides that insider dealing does not make the transaction either void or voidable.

Section 34 provides that where a corporation or a partner in a partnership is identified as an insider dealer any director, manager, secretary of that corporation, or other partner in the partnership, who has consented to, connived in, or been negligent in respect of, the insider dealing is also guilty of insider dealing and liable to punishment. Furthermore, under s 24 where a corporation has been identified as an insider dealer and the insider dealing is directly or indirectly attributable to a failure by an officer of that corporation to take measures to ensure safeguards are in place to prevent the corporation from insider dealing, that officer is liable to disqualification and/or a fine regardless of whether he is identified as an insider dealer in the Tribunal's report.

Under s 30, any person who contravenes a disqualification order may be liable to a maximum of two years' imprisonment and a fine of HK$1 million (approximately £84,000 STG). Note that the disqualification order will relate to the directorship not of a 'corporation' but of a 'company'. The definition of a 'company' is limited to a company incorporated under the Hong Kong Companies Ordinance.

2.8.6 Appeal

Any person who is dissatisfied with a report about him or an order made against him by the Tribunal may appeal to the Court of Appeal but only in respect of a point of law or, with leave of the Court of Appeal, on a question of fact or in respect of an Order made under ss 23, 24 or 27 (expenses of the inquiry).

2.9 CONCLUSION—EFFECTIVENESS OF THE ORDINANCE

To date, there have been two cases of insider dealing assessed by the Tribunal. In the first case (concluded in July 1994) concerning insider dealing in the securities of Success Holdings Limited, the maximum penalty of three times the profit gained as assessed by the Tribunal was imposed. In the second case concerning insider dealing in the securities of Public International Investments Ltd (concluded in September 1995), the insider dealers were again fined substantially and banned from participating in the management of listed companies for three years.

It is probably too early to gauge the success of the Ordinance but the following points may be of interest as to the practical application of the Ordinance:

(1) Difficulty in settling the composition of the Tribunal. In the Public International Investments Ltd case, the selection of the Tribunal panel was not a straightforward process as a number of panel candidates had to withdraw for reasons of potential conflicts of interest. The hearings in the case had to be suspended for some time while impartial panel members were found. In the relatively small Hong Kong corporate finance community, there is a possibility that this sort of problem may recur.

(2) Coping with the workload. The Success Holdings Ltd hearing took the Tribunal six months to conclude, and the Public International Investments Ltd case over a year. In the meantime, a backlog of six or so cases has built up. While the findings and penalties levied in the two concluded cases so far have been praised in the Hong Kong financial circles as having a sufficiently deterrent effect, nevertheless, the slow pace with which the cases have been handled has been the cause for some criticism.

The Hong Kong authorities apparently had under-estimated the time required for each hearing by, and the likely caseload for, the Tribunal. In order to expedite Tribunal hearings, amendments to the Ordinance have been made this year to allow the establishment of 'concurrent' Tribunals, ie to allow for the establishment of two or more divisions of the Tribunal so as to accommodate concurrent hearings of more than one case in times of greater workload. The establishment of a second division of the Tribunal is expected before the end of 1995.

(3) Burden of proof. By making the insider dealing prohibition a civil, as opposed to a criminal matter, a lower burden of proof is required to be in enforcement, thus avoiding the difficulties of proof encountered in jurisdictions where insider dealing constitutes a criminal offence. The omission to make insider dealing a criminal offence in Hong Kong may therefore have some practical advantages for the enforcement agencies.

3 NON-STATUTORY REGULATION

3.1 INTRODUCTION

While the Insider Dealing Ordinance is the centrepiece of the regulatory regime aimed at preventing insider dealing, the more general regulatory environment of Hong Kong's financial sector comprises several non-statutory sets of rules and regulations which impact on the issue of insider dealing in the wider sense. In particular, the Rules Governing the Listing of Securities on The Stock Exchange of Hong Kong Limited ('Listing Rules'), and the Hong Kong Codes on Take-Overs and Mergers and Share Repurchases, though principally concerned with disclosure requirements to facilitate dissemination of information to the market, also contain certain restrictions on dealings in the securities of listed companies by insiders.

3.2 LISTING

3.2.1 Continuing obligations

A prerequisite to an issuer listing on the SEHK is the requirement that it enters into a Listing Agreement in which it covenants to adhere to a number of continuing obligations regarding, among other things, the prompt disclosure of any information which might reasonably be expected to have a material effect on market activity in, and the prices of, listed securities. One objective of this provision is to prevent insiders having an unfair access to relevant information.

3.2.2 An issuer is required to:

(1) Keep the SEHK and holders of any of its listed securities informed as soon as reasonably practicable of any information which:
 (a) is necessary to enable them and the public to appraise the position of the issuer;

    (b) is necessary to avoid the establishment of a false market in its securities; and

    (c) might be reasonably expected materially to affect market activity in and the price of its securities;

(2) Ensure that, if the securities are also listed on other stock exchanges, the SEHK is simultaneously informed of any information released to any other exchanges and that such information is released to the market in Hong Kong at the same time as it is released to the other markets;

(3) Ensure that the prescribed information is contained in the directors' report and annual accounts;

(4) Prepare an interim report every six months and publish a preliminary announcement annually, detailing:

    (a) certain accounting information;

    (b) the share interests of each director and the chief executive; and

    (c) any other information necessary for a reasonable appreciation of the results; and

(5) Provide notification of:

    (a) acquisitions and realisations of assets insofar as they constitute notifiable transactions;

    (b) dividend announcements and preliminary announcements of profits or losses;

    (c) changes in the directorate; and

    (d) changes in rights attaching to a particular class of security.

3.2.3 The Model Code

In addition to these disclosure requirements a listed issuer is also required to covenant to adopt rules regulating dealings by directors in the listed securities of the issuer no less exacting than those of the Model Code issued by the SEHK. The Model Code establishes notification procedures required to be implemented by a listed issuer in respect of dealings by any of its directors and details instances when a director is prohibited from dealing entirely. It applies to companies listed on the SEHK, whether they are incorporated or established in or outside Hong Kong. The main features are set out in Table (9) *below*.

TABLE (9) MODEL CODE

Absolute prohibitions on dealing
- A director should not deal when he possesses unpublished price-sensitive information.
- A director should not deal in the securities of any other listed issuer when by virtue of his position as a director of his own company, he possesses unpublished price-sensitive information in relation to those securities.
- Other than in exceptional circumstances, a director should not deal in

the month preceding the preliminary announcement of annual results and publication of the interim report.
- The restrictions on dealing also apply to dealings by the director's spouse or infant child or corporations which the director controls, or any other dealings in which he is or is treated to be interested for the purposes of the Securities (Disclosure of Interests) Ordinance.

Notification of dealing
- Prior to any dealing in the securities of his own company a director should notify the chairman (or such other director specified) and receive a dated acknowledgement of the notification.
- A written record should be kept by the company of such notifications.

In addition, the Model Code provides that the directors should endeavour to ensure that employees of the company or a subsidiary who, because of their employment are likely to obtain insider information, face similar constraints on dealing as if they were directors.

3.2.4 Sanctions

Any failure to comply with the obligations imposed by the Listing Agreement or with any requirement for further information may lead to the suspension of dealings in, or the cancellation of the listing of the issuer's securities. Guidance Note 1 to the Listing Rules makes it clear that the SEHK will not hesitate to suspend dealings where it considers that improper use is being made of price-sensitive information, whether by persons connected with the company or otherwise. Furthermore, the SEHK may require a detailed explanation from an issuer as to who may have had access to unpublished information and why security had not been properly maintained, and may publish the findings of its inquiries if appropriate. Where the SEHK believes that a listed issuer or its advisers have permitted price-sensitive information regarding the issue of new securities to leak prior to its proper publication, it will not normally consider an application for the listing of those securities.

3.3 THE HONG KONG CODES ON TAKE-OVERS AND MERGERS AND SHARE REPURCHASES

The Codes on Take-Overs and Mergers and Share Repurchases require timely and adequate disclosure of information to ensure that there is a fair and informed market in the shares of companies affected by take-overs, mergers and share repurchases, and thereby minimising the risk of insider dealing. The Codes do not have the force of law but represent a consensus of opinion of those who participate in Hong Kong's financial markets and the Securities and Futures Commission regarding acceptable standards of conduct. It should be emphasised that they apply only to transactions affecting public companies in Hong Kong.

In addition to these disclosure requirements, the Code on Take-Overs and Mergers restricts dealings by any person who has confidential price-sensitive information concerning a take-over offer between the contemplation of the offer and either its announcement or its termination other than for the purpose of facilitating the takeover itself (Rule 21.1). Furthermore, Rule 21.2 restricts the selling of securities during an offer period by the bidder in the target company, while Rule 21.4 restricts dealings after the decision not to proceed with the offer has been taken but before this has been announced. Finally, Rule 22 and the Notes accompanying it set out disclosure requirements in respect of dealings in relevant securities during the offer period.

CASE STUDY

Splash Ltd, a company listed on the SEHK, manufactures rainwear and umbrellas. Alan, a weather forecaster, on discovering that there is an unseasonable amount of rain due in the next three months, instructs his broker to buy shares in Splash. Meanwhile, Charles, an analyst of the company's shares, is told in a conversation with Jeremy, one of the directors, that the Chairman is expected to be paid a salary of HK$5 million. Charles knows from his knowledge of the Chairman's service contract (which is available for public inspection) that this salary could only be paid if the company achieved profit in excess of HK$200 million. Charles revises his profit forecast for the company but before he publishes it he cancels instructions which he had previously given to his broker to sell his Splash shares. Charles also tells his girlfriend, Maggie, that 'things are looking up' for Splash. Maggie then buys shares in the name of her father from an old friend of hers who wanted to sell Splash shares off-market to save the payment of a broker's commission. In addition, Owen, an employee of the contracting firm which cleans Splash's offices, finds a draft of the latest management figures, which demonstrate Splash's high profitability, in a wastepaper bin. He immediately buys shares.

Alan
Alan is not an insider dealer by virtue of his acquisition of shares, since he is not connected with Splash. Also, the information is not relevant information as it is not 'specific information about' Splash.

Jeremy
Whether Jeremy is an insider dealer depends on whether he can be said to have disclosed relevant information under subs 9(1)(c). The information appears to constitute relevant information. It is specific since it is sufficiently detailed and unambiguous. It would seem that the particular information in respect of the Chairman's salary is not generally known to the market since it appears to be confidential. However, the fact that the Chairman's service contract is available for public inspection raises a rebuttable presumption

that this knowledge is known to the market. If the market were then told of the particular information about his proposed salary, it would be likely to affect materially the price of the securities.

As a director Jeremy is automatically deemed to be connected with Splash. It is a question of fact whether or not he is aware that the information is relevant information, though this does seem likely given his position as a director. Finally, since Charles is an analyst, Jeremy should have reasonable cause to believe that he would utilise the information to deal himself, or counsel or procure others to do so.

Charles
Charles is not guilty of an offence under subs 9(1)(a) as he is not connected with Splash and also he did not deal in Splash shares. The definition of dealing does not encompass omitting to deal where a person would otherwise do so. However, he is an insider dealer by virtue of subs 9(1)(e) due to his counselling Maggie to deal in them. Charles does possess relevant information about Splash which he received from Jeremy, whom he should know, by virtue of his occupation as an analyst of the company's shares, is a director and therefore connected with Splash. He is also likely to have reasonable cause to believe that Jeremy held the information by virtue of being connected with Splash. In order for Charles to be guilty of an offence under subs 9(1)(e) it is not necessary to demonstrate that he had a reasonable expectation that Maggie would deal.

Maggie
Maggie is not an insider dealer since she does not possess relevant information. The most that can be said is that she is probably counselled to deal but this does not give rise to liability on her part. On the assumption that the information received by Maggie did constitute relevant information, then Maggie could be liable under subs 9(1)(a) since dealing incorporates dealing as an agent and off-market deals in listed securities fall within the ambit of the subsection.

Owen
Owen is not an insider dealer since he is not connected with Splash. Despite the fact that he comes across the relevant information by virtue of his employee's business relationship with Splash, Owen does not occupy a position which might reasonably be expected to give him access to relevant information and this would not fall within subs 4(1)(c).

Taiwan

Lawrence S Liu, Lee and Li, Taipei

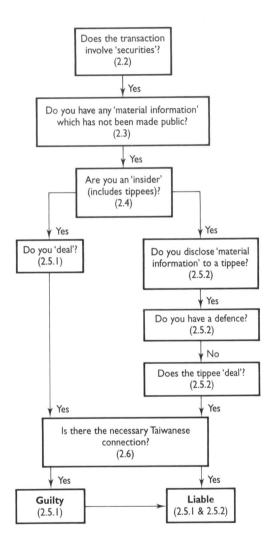

1 INTRODUCTION

The current anti-insider dealing legislation in the Republic of China ('Taiwan') is primarily contained in art 157-1 of the Securities and Exchange Law (the 'SEL'), which was added as an amendment to the SEL in 1988. Before 1988, there were only two articles regulating insider dealing, both of which were seen as ineffectual in combatting the widespread incidence of insider dealing on the Taiwan Stock Market. Article 20 of the SEL punishes any fraudulent market behaviour and art 157 SEL prohibits any issuing company's directors or major shareholders from making profits out of selling their company's stock within six months of its acquisition. Article 157-1 of the SEL was enacted to further safeguard the sound development of the stock market.

Any person who violates art 157-1 of the SEL is subject to the criminal penalties stipulated in art 175 SEL and to civil liabilities which include triple damages compensation. These sanctions are considered further at 2.5 *below*.

2 THE CRIMINAL LAW

2.1 INTRODUCTION

The activity prohibited by art 157-1 of the SEL is insider dealing—that is both the selling and buying of certain kinds of stock certificates. However, unlike legal regimes in some other jurisdictions, the act of merely disclosing inside information by an insider does not constitute a criminal offence under the SEL. An insider may however, be subject to civil liabilities if the person receiving such information subsequently buys or sells stocks in the market.

2.2 TO WHICH SECURITIES DOES ARTICLE 157-1 SEL APPLY?

Article 157-1 of the SEL covers only two types of securities, namely, stock certificates traded on a centralised securities exchange market and those traded on the over-the-counter market. Like all other penal regulations in Taiwan, SEL art 157-1 is subject to the provisions of the Criminal Codes of Taiwan which provide that an act is punishable only if it is expressly so prohibited by the law in force at the time of its commission. It follows therefore from the wording of SEL art 157-1 that since debt securities, warrants, depositary receipts, options, futures, contracts for differences and unlisted stock certificates are not expressly referred to, that these securities are not covered by SEL art 157-1. In any event, warrants, depositary receipts, options, futures and contracts for differences are not currently traded on the Taiwan Stock Market.

2.2.1 Stock certificates traded on a centralised securities exchange

This category covers 90 per cent of the securities listed and traded on the Taiwan Stock Exchange, the only centralised securities exchange in Taiwan. The other types of listed securities which are not included in this category are corporate bonds, government bonds and beneficiary certificates issued by closed-ended mutual funds.

2.2.2 Stock certificates traded in the over-the-counter market

This market was formed by the Taipei Association of Securities Firms. The stock certificates traded in this market are the stocks of certain public companies. Such public companies must have a minimum paid-in capital of NT$50 million (£1,181,000 STG) two years of corporate existence, profit after tax equal to at least 2 per cent of their paid-in capital and have met a stock diversification test.

2.3 WHAT IS INSIDE INFORMATION?

Article 157-1 of the SEL does not specifically provide a definition of what inside information is. However, the SEL prohibits insiders from taking advantage of information which:

- influences the price of stock certificates significantly; and
- has not been made public.

These features are considered in turn.

2.3.1 Material information

Paragraph 4 of art 157-1 of the SEL defines, in a somewhat circular way, information which influences the price of stock certificates significantly ('material information') as either:

- any information concerning an issuing company's financial condition and operations; or
- any information with respect to the demand for and supply of the relevant stock certificate on the stock market involved;
- and which, in either case, can affect the price of stock certificates or the investment decision of normal investors significantly.

In the absence of any guidance from the courts as to what amounts to material information, art 7 of the Enforcement Rules of SEL provides some assistance. Article 7 defines incidents which can substantially affect the interests of shareholders or prices of the stock certificates significantly, and these are set out in Table (1) *below*.

TABLE (1)

The following are examples of material information:
- A decision by an issuer's bankers not to honour a cheque or to refuse permanently to accept the issuer as a client or any other major incidents which would damage the credit of the issuer.

- An issuer's involvement in any litigation, legal proceedings or administrative act or proceedings which, in any such case, would affect the issuer's finances or operations significantly.
- Any substantial reduction in an issuer's production or any stoppage of all or part of an issuer's business or any leasing of plant or major facilities or granting of a pledge or mortgage on all or part of an issuer's assets which, in any such case, could affect the operations of the issuer.
- The execution, amendment or termination of any contract for the lease of all the business of an issuer, or for entrusting others to operate all the issuer's business or the regular joint operation of such business with others, and which has a material bearing on the operation of the issuer.
- The transfer of all or any major part of the business or assets of an issuer which has a material bearing on the operation of the issuer.
- The transfer of the whole business or assets of another entity to an issuer and which has a material bearing on the operation of the issuer.
- Stock certificates of an issuer being foreclosed by the court in accordance with Item 5, Para 1, art 289 of the Company Law.
- The removal of the Chairman of the board, president or more than one third of the Directors of an issuer.
- The replacement of an issuer's auditors.
- The signing of a material contract by an issuer, the material alteration of an issuer's business plan, the completion of the development of new products or the acquisition of other companies.
- Any other material act which may affect an issuer's continuous operation.

The above items are exemplary illustrations and therefore not exhaustive. It follows that the courts have considerable discretion in determining what is properly to be regarded as material information. It should be noted that rumours about an issuer which significantly affect the stock price of the issuer, but which later prove to be false, do not constitute inside information. There is no statutory or judicial guidance as to what sort of price-movement information would have to cause if made public in order for it to be regarded as material information. Inside information in relation to Company A can also be inside information in relation to Company B if both companies are in the same business and both likely to be affected by the information in the same way.

2.3.2 Non-public information

Article 157-1 of the SEL provides that an insider shall not buy or sell any stock certificate prior to the inside information which the insider possesses being made public. The SEL does not however provide any guidance as to when information will be treated by the law as having been made public. In other contexts the courts

have frequently applied the concept of what is public, in the light of a binding interpretation handed down by Judicial Yuan, the former authority to interpret the
constitution of Taiwan who declared that a 'public' event was one 'where an indefinite number of people or most people can hear or see the event'. Applied to the
present context, it would follow that inside information is information not having
been seen or heard by an indefinite number of people or most people.

As a result, it would seem likely that publication of inside information by means
of any public medium, (such as in a newspaper or on television) would result in
that information ceasing to be inside information because it would have reached
an 'indefinite number of people'. The same may even be true if publication is made
in a foreign country, depending on the effect such publication has within Taiwan.
Once published, the SEL does not require there to be a delay for the market to
absorb and react to the information before trading can begin.

In order to be guilty, the prosecution does not have to prove that the accused
knew that the information he possessed was inside information.

2.4 WHO IS AN INSIDER?

The SEL defines an insider as any one of those individuals or entities set out in
Table (2) *below*.

TABLE (2)

Insiders with respect to an issuer are:
(1) directors, supervisors and managers of the issuer;
(2) shareholders holding more than 10 per cent of the equity share capital of the issuer;
(3) any person who possesses inside information due to an occupational or controlling relationship with the issuer, such as lawyers, accountants or public officials;
(4) any person who possesses inside information from any of the persons referred to above (a 'tippee').

Pursuant to para 5 of art 157-1 of the SEL, stock certificates held by those
insiders referred to in items (1) and (2) of Table (2) *above* are deemed to include
those stock certificates held in the names of such insiders' spouses, minor children and nominees. Thus, for the purposes of making the calculation stipulated
in item (2) of Table (2) as to whether a shareholder has a 10 per cent shareholding, the stock certificates held by such shareholders' spouses, minor children and
nominees are taken into account. Furthermore, insiders are not only prohibited
from trading in their own stocks while in possession of inside information but also
the stocks of their minor children, spouses and nominees. It should be noted that
an insider can be a company or other entity as opposed to just individuals.

2.5 WHAT ARE THE OFFENCES AND THEIR RESPECTIVE CONSEQUENCES?

The SEL creates two different offences which are considered in turn below.

2.5.1 Buying or selling stock certificates

It is an offence for an insider to buy or sell the stock certificates of a company with respect to which such insider has inside information. Pursuant to SEL art 175, any insider who violates such restrictions shall be subject to imprisonment for a period not exceeding two years and/or a fine of not more than NT$450,000 (approximately £11,000 STG). In addition, pursuant to SEL art 157-1, para 2, such insider shall also be liable to pay civil damages to those who were the *bona fide* counterparts to the transactions constituting the insider dealing. Such damages, in the case of listed securities, are calculated based on the difference between the insider's buying or selling price prior to the relevant inside information being made public and the average of the closing prices for the ten consecutive business days after the information is made public. If the violation is egregious, the court may even impose an award of triple damages.

In an attempt to reduce the incidence of insider dealing, art 36, para 2, item 2 of the SEL, requires issuers to disclose details of any material development which will affect shareholders' interests or the price of stock certificates, within two days after of such development occurs. Persons in control of an issuer not complying with this requirement shall be subject to a fine of not more than NT$300,000 (approximately £7,000 STG) and not less than NT$60,000 (approximately £1,000 STG).

Problem Area

> Mr Wang, a director of XYZ Co claimed that he sold the stock certificates of XYZ when he learned that XYZ would make a profit out of the sale of land owned by XYZ. The Taipei High Court (the appellate court of Taipei District Council) ruled that Mr Wang did not violate the insider dealing provisions of SEL because he had sold (but not bought) XYZ stock certificates when he received this favourable inside information.

The problem area above indicates that although the text of the SEL does not draw any express distinction between inside information likely to lead to an increase in an issuer's stock price as opposed to a decrease, the courts in Taiwan, in common with those in many other jurisdictions, recognise that it is a defence for the accused to show that no profit would result from the relevant insider dealing.

2.5.2 Disclosure of inside information

In addition to the criminal offence of dealing, the SEL makes it a civil offence for primary insiders (those insiders referred to in items (1), (2) and (3) of Table (2)) to disclose inside information to tippees in certain circumstances. If such a primary insider discloses inside information and as a result the relevant tippee buys or sells stock certificates, then, pursuant to SEL art 157-1, the primary insider and tippee involved shall be subject to those civil liabilities set out in art 157-1, para 3 of the SEL.

The SEL does however in these circumstances provide a defence to civil liability for primary insiders if it can be shown that they had justifiable reasons to believe that the inside information had already been made public.

2.6 WHAT IS THE TERRITORIAL SCOPE OF SEL?

Generally speaking, the laws of Taiwan do not have extra-territorial application to acts done outside the territory of Taiwan. However, under the Criminal Codes of Taiwan, offences committed outside of Taiwan but which give rise to consequences in Taiwan shall be deemed to be offences committed within Taiwan. Therefore any insider who buys or sells share certificates from abroad by giving telephone or fax instructions to a broker, for example, in Taiwan can be liable under SEL art 175.

3 CONCLUSION

The promulgation of SEL art 157-1 and the continuing efforts of the Securities Exchange Commission ('SEC') demonstrate that the Government of Taiwan is determined to combat insider dealing and to provide a sound environment for investors to invest in the Taiwanese capital markets. However, this policy seems less well received by the judiciary. The courts have, on occasions, interpreted SEL art 157-1 more narrowly than the SEC, which has resulted in some perpetrators going unpunished. Moreover, even where insiders have been convicted, the courts have often shown considerable leniency by declining, in most cases, to impose custodial sentences or serious civil liabilities. The courts' lenient policy towards insider dealing reduced the deterrence value of SEL art 175. Since SEL art 157-1 was only promulgated in 1988, not many directives from the SEC or decisions from the courts have been delivered. As a result, it is fair to say the jurisprudence of anti-insider dealing law is still evolving. It will take a few more years and a change in the judiciary's approach for SEL art 157-1 to achieve its stated aims.

CASE STUDY

Splash Co Ltd, a company listed on the Taiwan Stock Exchange, manufactures rainwear and umbrellas. Alan, a weather forecaster, on discovering that there is an unseasonable amount of rain due in the next three months, instructs his broker to buy shares in Splash. Meanwhile, Charles, an analyst of the company's shares, it told in a conversation with Jeremy, one of the directors, that the Chairman is expected to be paid a salary of NT$500,000. Charles knows from his knowledge of the Chairman's service contract (which is available for public inspection) that this salary could only be paid if the company achieved profit in excess of NT$20 million. Charles revises his profit forecast for the company but before he publishes it he cancels instructions which he had previously given to his broker to sell his Splash shares. Charles also tells his girlfriend, Maggie, that 'things are looking up' for Splash. Maggie then buys shares in the name of her father from an old friend of hers who wanted to sell Splash shares off market to save the payment of a broker's commission. In addition, Owen, an employee of the contracting firm which cleans Splash's offices, finds a draft of the latest management figures, which demonstrate Splash's high profitability, in a waste-paper bin. He immediately buys shares.

Alan

The weather forecast can be characterised as material information since such a forecast will strengthen the sales figures of Splash and increase the demand for Splash's stock certificates. However, Alan is not an insider for the purposes of art 157-1, para 1 of the SEL. As a result, although he dealt in Splash's stock certificates, he is not guilty of any criminal offences nor liable for any civil offences.

Jeremy

Since Jeremy did not deal in Splash's stock certificates, he is not guilty of any criminal offences as described in art 175 of the SEL. The issue of whether Jeremy is liable for civil offences, as described in art 157-1, para 3 of the SEL, depends on whether he was only discharging his employment duties or was intentionally disclosing inside information to Charles. However, even if Jeremy was intentionally disclosing the Chairman's salary to Charles, and wished Charles to deal in Splash's stock certificates, since Charles cancelled his instruction and refrained from dealing in Splash's stock certificates, Jeremy is not liable for any civil offences.

Charles

Charles is not guilty of insider dealing because he did not actively deal in Splash's stock and refrained from dealing in Splash's stock certificates.

Maggie

Maggie is not guilty of insider dealing since Charles gave no indication as to why 'things were looking up' or what impact this might have on Splash's stock price. This information is too general and vague to constitute inside information. In Taiwan, except in special circumstances, all trading of shares in listed companies must be conducted on the Taiwan Security Exchange ('TSE'). However, the offence of insider dealing can be committed irrespective of whether the relevant transaction is made on- or off-TSE.

Owen

Since Owen is an employee of the contracting firm which cleans Splash's offices, it is clear as a matter of Taiwanese law that he obtained the inside information by virtue of his occupation. According to arts 175 and 157-1 of the SEL, he is guilty of criminal charges and is liable for civil offences.

Malaysia

Andrew Phang, Kuala Lumpur

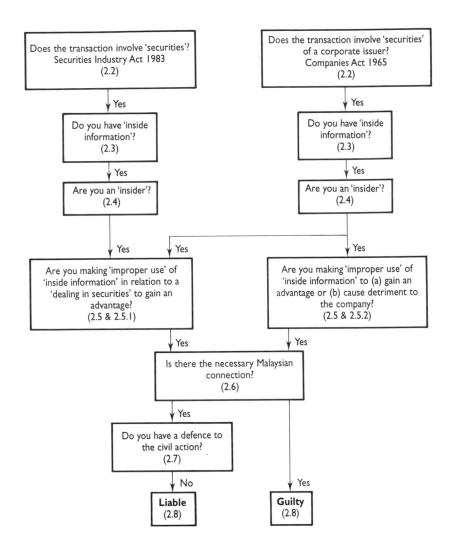

1 INTRODUCTION

In Malaysia, insider dealing is primarily regulated by the Malaysian Securities Industry Act 1983 ('SIA') and the Companies Act 1965 ('CA'). These statutes are based on the former Australian legislation, the Australian Securities Industry Act 1980 and the Australian Uniform Companies Acts of 1961, and 1962, respectively and create offences which give rise to both civil and criminal liabilities. Given the complexity and overlapping nature of the legislation, appropriate extracts are set out in the appendix to this chapter.

The listing requirements of the Kuala Lumpur Stock Exchange ('KLSE') and the Malaysian Code on Take-overs and Mergers supplement the prohibitions contained in the SIA and CA. The prohibitions set out in the listing requirements and the code are dealt with at 3.2 and 3.3 below. The elements of s 405 of the Penal Code, which creates the offence of criminal breach of trust, are also described at 3.5.

The Malaysian regulatory framework also attempts to control insider dealing through various indirect means. These include the disclosure requirements prescribed by the CA, and the regulation of various unfair market practices for example, market manipulation, market rigging and other fraudulent conduct. These are outside the scope of this chapter.

2 PRIMARY REGULATION

2.1 INTRODUCTION

Sections 89 and 90 of the SIA and ss 132(2), 132A and 132B of the CA (the 'insider dealing provisions') each create separate offences of insider dealing. In order to establish that these offences have been committed, certain key elements must be proven. Many of these elements, which are considered below, are common to each of the offences. Broadly speaking, an offence is committed if it involves an insider making improper use of inside information in relation to certain types of securities to gain an advantage or, in the case of CA s 132(2), to cause detriment to the relevant company.

2.2 TO WHICH SECURITIES DO THE SIA AND CA APPLY?

2.2.1 Types of securities under the SIA

The SIA applies to the types of securities set out in s 2(1) of the SIA and described in Table (1). These are:

TABLE (1)

> (a) debentures, stocks and shares in a public company or corporation;
> (b) bonds of any government or of any body corporate or unincorporate; although not specifically stated in the CA, this type of

security is probably narrower than 'debenture' which is referred to in
(a);

(c)   any interest in a unit trust scheme; and

(d)   any right or option in respect of any of the securities in (a) or (b)
      above.

Nothing in the definition suggests that the right or option must be
granted by the entity itself. Arguably, therefore, options granted by third
parties (eg covered warrants) would fall within the definition.

2.2.2 Types of securities under the CA

The CA does not define 'securities'. However, s 132A(4) of the CA contains a
definition of 'dealing in securities in relation to a corporation'. In relation to that
corporation, the definition includes those securities described in Table (2):

TABLE (2)

(1)   shares in the corporation (which may be either a foreign or Malaysian
      corporation);

(2)   debentures of the corporation (including debenture stock, bonds,
      notes or any other security, whether constituting a charge on the
      corporation's assets or not);

(3)   any right to participate in, or interest in, any profit sharing scheme or
      undertaking;

(4)   rights or options in respect of the acquisition or disposal of any of
      the securities in (1) to (3) *above*.

For the purposes of s 132A, a 'corporation' includes its holding company and
any subsidiary or sister company. By implication, therefore, a 'security' for the
purposes of CA s 132A includes only those types of securities mentioned in the
definition in s 132A(4). Although there is no corresponding definition in CA
s 132B, a 'security' for the purposes of that section would arguably be given the
same meaning as in CA s 132A.

2.2.3 Stock Exchange

Sections 89 and 90 of the SIA and ss 132A and 132B of the CA (but not CA
s 132(2)) are limited in their application to dealings in securities which are listed
for quotation on the KLSE. This conclusion follows from the fact that the sections
are expressed to apply only to information which 'if generally known might reasonably be expected to affect materially the price of the subject matter of the
dealing on a stock exchange'. Although the CA does not contain a definition of
'stock exchange', a stock exchange for the purposes of the SIA means a stock
exchange approved as such under the SIA. Currently, only the KLSE has been
approved as a stock exchange under the SIA. Arguably, a stock exchange for the
purposes of CA ss 132A and 132B should have the same meaning.

In contrast, the offence under CA s 132(2) is much broader in scope (see 2.5.2). It relates to insiders making improper use of inside information in any way. To the extent that the offence can be committed by dealing in securities, it does not matter whether those securities are listed or not.

2.2.4 Futures

Prohibitions similar to those set out in CA and SIA apply to futures contracts by virtue of the Futures Industry Act 1993. This is considered in more detail at 3.4 *below*.

2.3 WHAT IS INSIDE INFORMATION?

2.3.1 Definition

The definition of inside information varies depending on which of the insider dealing provisions is being considered. Table (3) *below* summarises the constituent features of each definition.

TABLE (3)

Inside information	SIA s89 & CA s132A	SIA s90 & CA s132B	CA s132(2)
Unpublished price-sensitive information		•	
Any information			•
Is specific confidential information	•		
Acquired or held by insider by virtue of his position	•		•
If generally known might reasonably be expected to affect materially the price of the relevant securities	•	•	
It would be reasonable to expect insider would not disclose except in official capacity		•	

2.3.2 SIA s 89 and CA s 132A

The elements of 'inside information' for the offences under SIA s 89 and CA s 132A are the same and are considered in turn below. An insider must have:

- specific confidential information;
- it must be acquired by virtue of his position; and
- it must have a material effect on price.

2.3.2.1 Specific confidential information

Inside information must be specific confidential information. Whether or not any information satisfies this criterion is a question of fact (*Public Prosecutor v G Choudhury* [1981] 1 MLJ 76). The following general principles assist in determining this question.

(1) 'Information' is the knowledge of a particular event or situation such as advice, communication, intelligence, news or notification (see *Public Prosecutor v G Choudhury*).

(2) 'Specific' information must not simply be the product of a process of deduction. Instead, it must have an existence of its own, be capable of being pointed to and identified and of being expressed unequivocally. The fact that a person is discussing a proposed purchase of shares in a corporation may lead to the deduction that that person is prepared to purchase shares in the corporation. Such a deduction, however, is not specific information (*Ryan v Triguboff* (1974–76) 1 ACLR 337). On the other hand, information that a company is facing a financial crisis is specific (see *Public Prosecutor v G Choudhury*).

(3) 'Confidential' information must not be generally known or available. Whether or not information is generally known is a question of fact. Information which is published in a newspaper may be generally known depending on the extent of circulation and level of detail contained in the publication. Publication of the information in substantial detail in a newspaper coupled with disclosure to a stock exchange would most probably mean that the information is generally known and no longer confidential (see for example *Kinwat Holdings Pty Ltd v Platform Pty Ltd* (1982) 6 ACLR 398).

This section, unlike s 340 of the KLSE Listing particulars (see 3.2), does not require any time delay between inside information being made public and the commencement of legitimate dealing.

2.3.2.2 Acquired by virtue of position

Inside information must be acquired by the insider by virtue of his position as opposed to what is known in the public domain. It is sufficient if a director of a company acquires such information at a meeting of directors of the company. If he does, it is irrelevant that that information is supplemented by information acquired as a matter of common knowledge or by reference to outside sources (see *Waldron v Green* (1977) 3 ACLR 289).

2.3.2.3 Material effect on price

Inside information must be information which 'if generally known might reasonably be expected to affect materially the price' of the relevant securities. The standard by which materiality is to be judged is whether the information on those securities is such that it would influence the ordinary reasonable investor in deciding whether or not to buy or sell those securities (see *Public Prosecutor v Allan Ng Poh Meng* [1990] 1 MLJ). In other words, it is the impact of the information on the ordinary reasonable investor and thus, on price, which must be considered.

There are no precedents, however, to provide guidance as to the sort of price movement which will be considered material.

2.3.3 SIA s 90 and CA s 132B

These offences require the inside information to be such that if it were generally known it might reasonably be expected to affect materially the price of the relevant securities (see 2.3.2.3 *above*). The information must also be information which the accused knows to be unpublished price-sensitive information.

It should be noted that, unlike the offences under s 89 of the SIA or s 132A of the CA, there is no requirement that the information be specific or confidential. Hence a hint may suggest information or may enable an inference to be drawn as to information (see *Waldron v Green* (1977) 3 ACLR 289). Information may also include a rumour (see *Hooker Investments Pty Ltd v Baring Bros Halkerston* (1986) 10 ACLR 462).

2.3.4 CA s 132(2)

Inside information for the purposes of CA s 132(2) need not be specific or confidential. Instead, CA s 132(2) applies to any information acquired by an insider by virtue of his position.

2.4 WHO IS AN INSIDER?

Only 'insiders' are prohibited from engaging in insider dealing. For the purposes of SIA s 89 and CA s 132A, the persons set out in Table (4) *below* are insiders.

TABLE (4)

SIA s 89 and CA s 132A insiders are:
(1) Any officer of the corporation the securities of which are the subject of insider dealing.
(2) Any person who was an officer of that corporation within the 12 months preceding the dealing.
(3) Any agent of that corporation (including a banker, advocate and solicitor, auditor, accountant and stock broker of that corporation).
(4) Any person who is, or at any time in the six months preceding the dealing has been:
   —knowingly connected with that corporation; and
   —has information which he holds by virtue of being so connected and it would be reasonable to expect him not to disclose (except for the proper performance of his functions) and which he knows is unpublished price-sensitive information.
(5) Any employee of that corporation.
(6) Any officer of the KLSE.

Reference in Table (4) to 'officers' includes a director, shadow director, secretary, any liquidator appointed by the members in a voluntary winding up, or a receiver and manager appointed under a power contained in any instrument but not one appointed by a court.

Section 90 of the SIA and s 132B of the CA are not limited in their application to the categories of persons described above. Instead, any person holding information by virtue of his official capacity or former official capacity could be an insider for the purposes of s 90 of the SIA and s 132B of the CA.

Section 132(2) of the CA applies to the same categories of persons mentioned in parts (1), (3), (4) and (6) of Table (4). Past officers are also included within the definition of an 'officer' for the purposes of s 132(2) of the CA.

The legislation and jurisprudence in Malaysia has not yet established who is an insider in the context of a non-corporate issuer, who is to be considered as being 'knowingly connected' with an issuer or whether insiders can include either tippees or corporations (as well as individuals).

2.5 WHAT ARE THE OFFENCES?

Broadly, the insider dealing provisions create the following offences:

(1) *Dealing.* It is an offence under SIA ss 89 and 90 and CA ss 132A and 132B for an insider to make improper use of inside information in relation to a dealing in securities to gain, directly or indirectly, an advantage for himself or another person.
(2) *Causing detriment.* It is an offence under CA s 132(2) for an insider to make improper use of any information to gain, directly or indirectly, an advantage for himself or another person or to cause detriment to the company of which he is an officer or agent.

These offences are considered in turn below.

2.5.1 Dealing in securities

The SIA and CA define 'dealing' in significantly different ways. The SIA defines 'dealing in securities' to mean, whether as principal or agent, making or offering to make with any person, or inducing or attempting to induce any person to enter into or to offer to enter into:

(1) any agreement for or with a view to acquiring, disposing of, subscribing for, or underwriting securities; or
(2) any agreement the purpose or avowed purpose of which is to secure a profit to any of the parties from the yield of securities or by reference to fluctuation in the value of securities.

In order to fall within the definition, it is not necessary for there to be a concluded agreement of the kind mentioned in the definition. A person may be dealing in securities simply by offering to make such an agreement, or by inducing or attempting to induce another to enter into or offer to enter into such an agreement.

In contrast to the wide definition of 'dealing in securities' in the SIA, s 132A(4) of the CA is considerably narrower and defines a 'dealing in securities in relation to a corporation' to mean a transaction in relation to any of the securities referred to in Table (2) *above*.

Curiously, the phrase 'dealing in securities *in relation* to a corporation' is not actually used in the offences set out in ss 132A and 132B of the CA, which refer instead to a 'dealing in securities *of* a corporation'. This appears to be an oversight by the legislative draftsman. However, assuming that the definition does apply to ss 132A and 132B despite this drafting defect, a dealing for the purposes of ss 132A and 132B is limited to a 'transaction' of the kind mentioned in s 132A(4). Arguably, some form of binding agreement must exist before there can be a transaction. Presumably, the act of inducement by itself would not be a 'transaction'.

In order to commit any of the offences, the insider must make 'improper' use of insider information. What is improper must be determined by reference to the particular duties, obligations and responsibilities of the insider having regard to his position (see *Grove v Flavel* (1986) 11 ACLR 161). Hence, for example, in determining what is improper conduct for a director, a court will consider the duties of a director including the duty to act for the benefit of the company and to consider the interests of creditors of the company (see *McNamara v Flavel* (1988) 13 ACLR 619). A purpose may be improper even if it is not illegal and even if the officers of the corporation authorising the act believe it to be in the overall interest of the corporation (see *Jeffree v NCSC* (1990) 15 ACLR 217).

In addition, the insider must make use of inside information for the purpose of gaining an advantage. The difficulties for a prosecutor in establishing this subjective purpose to the standard required are considerable. The prosecutor must show something more than the mere sequence of events from the gaining of the information to the dealing (see *Waldron v Green*). This is likely to require the prosecutor to adduce direct evidence of the insider's subjective purpose.

2.5.2 Causing detriment, etc

Section 132(2) of the CA makes it an offence for an insider to gain an advantage for himself or to cause detriment to his company, whether by dealing or otherwise. The discussions in 2.5.1 *above* regarding improper use of information and gaining an advantage are equally applicable to the offence under CA s 132(2). However, one element of the offence which is absent from the other insider dealing provisions is the causing of detriment to the relevant company. What would amount to causing detriment is again a question of fact. The transfer of the benefit of the business name of a company would, for example, cause detriment to the company because it would deny the company the use of that business name (see *McNamara v Flavel*).

2.6 WHAT IS THE TERRITORIAL SCOPE OF THE CA AND SIA?

The insider dealing provisions are not expressed to be limited in their application to Malaysian securities or activities in Malaysia although ss 89 and 90 of the SIA and ss 132A and 132B of the CA only apply to securities listed on the KLSE. In theory, therefore, they could apply to trading by a non-Malaysian on a foreign stock market in securities of a Malaysian company which are also listed on the KLSE.

It is likely, however, that the insider dealing provisions are limited in their application to dealings occurring within Malaysia. Whether or not this is the case will depend on the extent to which a Malaysian court gives effect to the general principle of statutory interpretation that a criminal law does not have extra-ter-ritorial application unless expressly provided in that law. It will also depend on the extent of jurisdiction conferred on the relevant court by statute. The Courts of Judicature Act 1964, for example, confers on the High Court in Malaya very limited jurisdiction to hear criminal matters involving acts committed outside Malaysia.

2.7 WHAT ARE THE DEFENCES?

Section 89(2) of the SIA and s 132A(2) of the CA exclude civil liability (see 2.8.1) of an insider for any loss suffered by a counterparty if that person knew or ought reasonably to have known of the inside information before entering into the rel-evant transaction. It is unclear what an insider has to show in order to establish this defence. By definition inside information is information which is confidential. If that information is known to the person who suffered the loss, or is informa-tion which that person ought reasonably to have known, the information can hardly be said to be confidential.

There is also a two-year limit for commencing any action for the recovery of the amount of the loss.

2.8 WHAT ARE THE PENALTIES AND CONSEQUENCES OF INSIDER DEALING?

2.8.1 Civil liability

Section 89 of the SIA and s 132A of the CA make the insider liable to any person for loss suffered by that person by reason of the relevant dealing. The sections appear to contemplate actual loss. Hence, for example, an insider will not be liable if his dealing deprives the other party of a potential gain.

2.8.2 Criminal liability

In addition to the civil liability described above, a contravention of the insider dealing provisions is punishable by a fine and imprisonment. These sanctions are summarised in Table (5) *below*.

TABLE (5)

Offence	Penalty
SIA ss 89 and 90	Fine Ringgit 1 million (approximately £250,000 STG) (minimum) and imprisonment ten years
CA ss 132A and 132B	Fine Ringgit 30,000 (approximately £8,000 STG) imprisonment five years or both
CA s 132(2)	Fine Ringgit 30,000 or imprisonment five years

Under s 130(1) of the CA a person convicted of an offence under CA ss 132(2) or 132A is prohibited from taking part in the management (whether as a director or otherwise) of a corporation in Malaysia for a period of five years.

3 SECONDARY REGULATION

3.1 INTRODUCTION

There are a number of other measures designed to supplement the insider dealing legislation and prevent or regulate insider dealing. We will look at four areas: the role of the Kuala Lumpur Stock Exchange, the Malaysian Code on Take-overs and Mergers, the Futures Industry Act 1993 and s 405 of the Penal Code.

3.2 KUALA LUMPUR STOCK EXCHANGE LISTING REQUIREMENTS

A corporation desiring to have its shares listed for quotation on the KLSE must comply with the listing requirements issued by the KLSE (the 'Listing Requirements'). In addition, the corporation must comply with the continuing obligations imposed by the Listing Requirements. Under SIA s 11, the KLSE may impose a maximum fine of Ringgit 100,000 (approximately £26,500 STG) on a listed corporation which fails to comply with the Listing Requirements.

The obligations imposed by the Listing Requirements include s 340, which sets out the KLSE's policy on insider dealing:

> Insider[s] should not trade on the basis of material information which is not known to the investing public. Moreover, insiders should refrain from trading, even after material information has been released to the press and other media, for a period sufficient to permit thorough public dissemination and evaluation of the information.

Section 340 sets out detailed provisions on the KLSE's view of persons who are insiders and what constitutes inside information and insider dealing. Many of the limitations contained in the legislation mentioned above do not apply to s 340. Hence, for example:

(1) There is no restriction on the categories of persons who may be regarded as insiders. Instead, all persons who come into possession of material inside

information before its public release are considered insiders for the purposes of the KLSE's disclosure policies.

(2) Importantly, the KLSE regards tippees as insiders.

(3) Tipping itself is considered a form of insider dealing.

(4) Insider dealing extends beyond dealings in securities to dealings in puts, calls and other options with respect to securities.

(5) The KLSE sets out guidelines on when an insider may trade. Essentially, an insider may not trade until the inside information has been publicly released and the public has had an opportunity to thoroughly evaluate that information. As a general guide, the KLSE recommends a 24-hour waiting period if dissemination of the information is made in accordance with the policies of the KLSE through general publication in a national medium. Otherwise, a 48-hour waiting period is recommended.

3.3 THE MALAYSIAN CODE ON TAKE-OVERS AND MERGERS

The Malaysian Code on Take-overs and Mergers (the 'Take-overs Code') is issued by the Malaysian Securities Commission pursuant to powers conferred on it by s 33 of the Malaysian Securities Commission Act 1993. The Take-overs Code sets out general principles and rules applicable to take-overs and mergers of Malaysian companies.

The Take-overs Code expressly prohibits dealings of any kind in the securities of the target company by any person who is privy to confidential price-sensitive information concerning a take-over offer. Dealings in the securities of the offeror are also prohibited if the take-over offer is price-sensitive in relation to such securities.

The prohibitions contained in the Take-overs Code supplement s 89(5)(a) of the SIA and s 132A(5)(a) of the CA.

Section 33(9) of the Securities Commission Act provides that a failure by any person to observe any of the general principles and rules in the Take-overs Code does not of itself render that person liable to criminal proceedings. However, the failure may be relied upon by any party to any civil or criminal proceedings to establish or negate any liability which is in question in those proceedings.

In addition to s 33(9), the Malaysian Securities Commission may impose various sanctions for failure to observe the Take-overs Code. These include private reprimand, public censure and deprivation of the enjoyment of the facilities of the KLSE.

3.4 FUTURES INDUSTRY ACT 1993

Section 86 of the Malaysian Future Industry Act 1993 ('FIA') contains a prohibition similar to s 90 of the SIA and s 132B of the CA except that it relates to futures contracts. Section 86 prohibits a person from making improper use of inside information to gain an advantage for himself or another person. For the purposes of FIA s 86, 'inside information' is information which:

(a) is information which the insider holds by virtue of his official capacity or former official capacity;

(b) the insider in his official capacity or former official capacity would reasonably be expected not to disclose (except for the proper performance of the functions attached to that official capacity); and

(c) the insider knows is unpublished price-sensitive information in relation to an underlying instrument which is the subject of a futures contract or in relation to trading in a futures contract.

Briefly, futures contracts include contracts which are settled by physical delivery and contracts for differences and options. Currency swaps and forward contracts, interest rate swaps and forward contracts and commodity futures contracts are expressly excluded.

3.5 CRIMINAL BREACH OF TRUST

In addition to the specific insider dealing offences mentioned above, it is conceivable that an insider may also be prosecuted for criminal breach of trust under s 405 of the Malaysian Penal Code. Under that section, the offence of criminal breach of trust is committed if a person:

- dishonestly misappropriates, or converts to his own use, property which is entrusted to him or over which he had dominion; or
- dishonestly uses or disposes of such property in violation of any direction of law, or any legal contract, relating to the discharge of such property.

It is also an offence if that person wilfully forces any other person to do those things.

The punishment for committing such an offence is imprisonment for a term of one to ten years and a fine. If, however, the offence is committed by a person in his capacity as a public servant or an agent (for example, an officer of a company), it is punishable by imprisonment for a term of two to 20 years, whipping and a fine.

In order for a prosecution to succeed, a court would have to conclude that inside information used by the insider is property for the purposes of s 405. Whether or not a Malaysian court will form this conclusion is unclear.

It is also essential that the prosecution prove that the insider was actuated by dishonest intention (see *Chang Lee Swee v Public Prosecutor* [1985] 1 MLJ 75). Where a person fails to account for money received or gives a false account of its use, it is relatively easy to establish dishonest intention. However, it is much more difficult to do so where the 'property' which is misappropriated is comprised of information. The fact that the person to whom the information belongs may not have suffered any loss (other than potential loss) adds to the problem.

4 CONCLUSION

The insider dealing legislation in Malaysia is still developing with many important questions of law still to be resolved. The Malaysian courts have not had occasion to consider many of the provisions of the relevant legislation and in the absence of such judicial precedent it is difficult to be certain how particular provisions of the legislation are likely to be applied by the courts. As of January 1996 no successful prosecutions had been secured in the Malaysian courts for insider dealing. In an effort to improve on this record, the Malaysian Securities Commission are understood currently to be conducting a review of the existing legislation.

CASE STUDY

Growbig Berhad is a Malaysian public company whose shares are listed on the Kuala Lumpur Stock Exchange. Mr Big is the chief executive officer of Growbig. Growbig is waiting for approval from the Malaysian Securities Commission for a proposed issue of new shares. The proposed issue will affect materially the price of existing Growbig shares.

Mr Big
While on their way to a fund raising dinner, Mr Big discusses the proposed issue and the effect it will have on Growbig's share price with Mrs Big. Their driver, Mr Small, overhears their conversation. The next day, Mr Small instructs his stockbroker to buy Growbig shares. Mrs Big, who is an employee of the Securities Commission, does the same.

As a director of Growbig, Mr Big is an insider. However, he has not himself traded in Growbig shares or otherwise made use of the information he has about the proposed issue. Accordingly, he is not guilty of any offence under any of the insider dealing provisions.

Mrs Big has bought Growbig shares based on the information she obtained from her husband. However, as she is not an insider for the purposes of the insider dealing provisions, she is not guilty of insider dealing. Mrs Big must be careful, however, that she is not in breach of her obligation of secrecy under the Malaysian Securities Commission Act 1993. Under that Act, it is an offence for Mrs Big to disclose any information obtained by her in the course of her duties. Mrs Big also runs the risk of being charged for criminal breach of trust under s 405 of the Penal Code. Mr Big himself could fall foul of s 405 if he permitted or condoned Mrs Big's trading.

Mr Small is not guilty of insider dealing because he is not an insider for the purposes of the insider dealing provisions. However, both Mrs Big and Mr Small are insiders for the purposes of the listing requirements of the Kuala Lumpur Stock Exchange and have engaged in insider dealing for the purposes of the listing requirements. However, neither Mrs Big nor Mr Small are under any obligation to comply with the listing requirements and therefore the Kuala Lumpur Stock Exchange does not have any jurisdiction over either of them.

Mr Solicitor

One week before the issue date, Mr Solicitor, an advocate and solicitor with Solicitors & Co, and Mrs Cleaner, a cleaner employed by Cleaning Services Company Ltd, enter a lift in Growbig Towers. In it, they find copies of a document setting out details of the proposed issue. Mr Solicitor and Mrs Cleaner each take a copy of the document.

From time to time, Mr Solicitor is asked by Growbig to provide legal advice on general corporate matters (unrelated to the proposed issue). On this particular day, Mr Solicitor is on his way to visit his stockbroker. He intends to sell his shares in Growbig (which he purchased five years ago while a law student) to raise funds for the purchase of a house. He instructs his stockbroker accordingly and the shares are sold. Mr Solicitor is an insider. However, as he has not acquired the inside information by virtue of his position as Growbig's solicitor, SIA s 89 and CA ss 132(2) and 132A do not apply. Whether or not he is guilty of insider dealing under SIA s 90 and CA s 132B will depend on whether the prosecution can establish that Mr Solicitor made use of the inside information to gain an advantage. In his defence, Mr Solicitor would argue that the purpose of selling his shares was to raise finance for his purchase of the house. In addition, his decision to sell the shares had been made before he acquired the inside information.

Mrs Cleaner regularly trades in shares listed for quotation on the Kuala Lumpur Stock Exchange. She reads the draft prospectus and subsequently instructs her stockbroker to buy Growbig shares. Mrs Cleaner is not guilty of insider dealing under any of the insider dealing provisions as she is not an insider for the purposes of those provisions.

Philip

Philip, a Malaysian citizen residing in Hong Kong, hears rumours about the proposed issue. He contacts his broker in Singapore and instructs him to acquire Growbig shares (which are also listed on the Singapore Stock Market). If the insider dealing provisions are construed literally, Philip could be guilty of insider dealing despite the fact the dealing occurred outside Malaysia. However, Philip would argue that those provisions should be limited in their application to acts within Malaysia because they do not expressly purport to have extra-territorial application.

Even if the insider dealing provisions apply, the information which Philip has may not be sufficiently specific for purposes of SIA s 89 or CA s 132A (although a rumour may be sufficient for purposes of SIA s 90 and CA ss 132(2) and 132B). In addition, Philip is not an insider for the purposes of the insider dealing provisions, nor has he acquired the inside information by virtue of his position as an insider.

APPENDIX: EXTRACTS FROM THE LEGISLATION

SECURITIES INDUSTRY ACT 1983

SECTION 89 DEALINGS BY OFFICERS IN SECURITIES

89(1) [Improper use of confidential information]

An officer, agent or employee of a corporation or officer of a stock exchange who is or in relation to a dealing in securities of the corporation by himself or any other person makes improper use to gain, directly or indirectly an advantage for himself or any other person of specific confidential information acquired by virtue of his position as such officer, agent or employee or officer of the stock exchange which if generally known might reasonably be expected to affect materially the price of the subject-matter of the dealing on a stock exchange shall, in addition to any penalty imposed under s 91, be liable to a person for loss suffered by the person by reason of the payment by him or to him of a consideration in respect of the securities greater or lesser, as the case may be than the consideration that would have been reasonable if the information had been generally known at the time of the dealing.

89(2) [Where officer, etc., not liable under subs (1)]

An officer, agent or employee of a corporation or officer of a stock exchange shall not be liable under subs (1) to a person for any loss suffered by that person if that person knew or ought reasonably to have known of the information referred to in subs (1) before entering into the transaction relating to the dealing in securities of the corporation.

89(3) [Action for recovery of loss]

An action for the recovery of the amount of a loss referred to in subs (1) shall not be commenced after the expiration of two years after the date of the completion of the dealing in securities in respect of which the loss was suffered.

89(4) [Interpretation]

In this section—

'agent' includes a banker, advocate and solicitor, auditor, accountant or stock broker of the corporation and any person who is or at any time in the preceding six months has been knowingly connected with the body corporate and has information which:

(a) he holds by virtue of being connected with the corporation;
(b) it would be reasonable to expect a person so connected and in the position by virtue he is so connected not to disclose except for the proper performance of the functions attaching to that position; and
(c) he knows is unpublished price-sensitive information in relation to the securities of the corporation;

'officer' includes a person who at any time within the preceding twelve months was an officer of the corporation.

89(5) [Information regarding take-over offers, etc]

This section shall be extended to apply to an officer, agent or employee of a corporation or officer of the stock exchange who makes improper use to gain, directly or indirectly, an advantage for himself or any other person, by means of specific confidential information acquired by virtue of his position as such officer, agent or employee of the corporation or officer of the stock exchange, regarding:

(a) the possibility of a take-over offer or bid being made to another corporation by the corporation to which he belongs; or
(b) the possibility of his corporation entering into a substantial commercial transaction with another corporation;

to deal in the securities of that corporation in the expectation that, if this information becomes generally known the price of the securities of that other corporation on a stock exchange might be materially affected.

SECTION 90 PROHIBITION ON ABUSE OF INFORMATION OBTAINED IN OFFICIAL CAPACITY

Any person, who is or in relation to dealing in securities of a corporation, has any information which if generally known might reasonably be expected to affect materially the price of the subject-matter of the dealing on a stock exchange and which:

(a) he holds by virtue of his official capacity or former official capacity;
(b) it would be reasonable to expect a person in his official capacity or former official capacity not to disclose except for the proper performance of the functions attaching to that official capacity; and
(c) he knows is unpublished price-sensitive information in relation to securities of the corporation,

shall not make improper use of such information to gain, directly or indirectly, an advantage for himself or for any other person and any person who contravenes or fails to comply with the provisions of this section commits an offence.

COMPANIES ACT 1965

SECTION 132(2) IMPROPER USE OF INFORMATION

An officer or agent of a company or officer of the Stock Exchange shall not make improper use of any information acquired by virtue of his position as an officer or agent of the company or officer of the Stock Exchange to gain directly or indirectly an advantage for himself or for any other person or to cause detriment to the company.

SECTION 132A DEALINGS BY OFFICERS IN SECURITIES

132A(1) [Improper use of specific confidential information]

An officer, agent or employee of a corporation or officer of the Stock Exchange who in or in relation to a dealing in securities of the corporation by himself or any other person makes improper use to gain, directly or indirectly, an advantage for himself or any other person of specific confidential information acquired by virtue of his position as such officer, agent or employee or officer of the Stock Exchange which if generally known might reasonably be expected to affect materially the price of the subject matter of the dealing on a stock exchange shall, in addition to any penalty imposed under subs (6), be liable to any person for loss suffered by that person by reason of the payment by him or to him of a consideration in respect of the securities greater or lesser, as the case may be, than the consideration that would have been reasonable if the information had been generally known at the time of the dealing.

132A(2) [Limited liability]

An officer, agent or employee of a corporation or officer of the Stock Exchange shall not be liable under subs (1) to a person for any loss suffered by that person if that person knew or ought reasonably to have known of the information referred to in subs (1) before entering into the transaction relating to the dealing in securities of the corporation.

132A(3) [Time limit on action to recover loss]

Notwithstanding the provisions of the Limitation Act 1953, an action for the recovery of the amount of a loss referred to in subs (1) shall not be commenced after the expiration of two years after the date of the completion of the dealing in securities in respect of which the loss was suffered.

132A(4) [Interpretation]

In this section;

    'agent' includes a banker, advocate and solicitor, auditor, accountant or stockbroker of the corporation and any person who is or at any time in the preceding six months has been knowingly connected with the corporation and has information which;

(a) he holds by virtue of being connected with the corporation;

(b) it would be reasonable to expect a person so connected and in the position by virtue he is so connected not to disclose except for the proper performance of the functions attaching to that position; and

(c) he knows is unpublished price sensitive information in relation to the securities of the corporation;

'corporation' includes a corporation that is related to a corporation under s 6;

'dealing in securities in relation to a corporation' means a transaction relating to;

(a) shares in or debentures of the corporation or interests within the meaning of s 84 made available by the corporation or by a related corporation; or

(b) rights or options in respect of the acquisition or disposal of such shares, debentures or interests;

'officer' includes a person who at any time within the preceding 12 months was an officer of the corporation.

132A(5) [Improper use of information concerning takeovers]

This section shall be extended to apply to an officer, agent or employee of a corporation or officer of the Stock Exchange who makes improper use to gain, directly or indirectly, an advantage for himself or any other person, by means of specific confidential information acquired by virtue of his position as such officer, agent or employee of the corporation or officer of the Stock Exchange, regarding;

(a) the possibility of a takeover offer or bid being made to another corporation by the corporation to which he belongs; or

(b) the possibility of his corporation entering into a substantial commercial transaction with another corporation,

to deal in the securities of that corporation in the expectation that, if this information becomes generally known, the price of the securities of that other corporation on a Stock Exchange might be materially affected.

132A(6) [Offence]

An officer, agent or employee of a corporation or officer of the Stock Exchange who commits a breach of the provisions of this section shall be guilty of an offence against this Act.

Penalty: Imprisonment for five years or thirty thousand ringgit or both.

SECTION 132B PROHIBITION ON ABUSE OF INFORMATION OBTAINED IN OFFICIAL CAPACITY

Any person, who in or in relation to a dealing in securities of a corporation, has any information which if generally known might reasonably be expected to affect materially the price of the subject matter of the dealing on a Stock Exchange and which;

(a) he holds by virtue of his official capacity or former official capacity;
(b) it would be reasonable to expect a person in his official capacity or former official capacity not to disclose except for the proper performance of the functions attaching to that official capacity; and
(c) he knows is unpublished price sensitive information in relation to securities of the corporation,

shall not make improper use of such information to gain, directly or indirectly, an advantage for himself or for any other person and any person who contravenes the provision of this section shall be guilty of an offence against this Act.

Penalty: Imprisonment for five years or thirty thousand ringgit or both.

'securities' means debentures, stocks and shares in a public company or corporation, or bonds of any government or of any body, corporate or unincorporate, and includes any right or option in respect thereof and any interest in unit trust schemes.

'dealing in securities' means, whether as principal or agent, making or offering to make with any person, or inducing or attempting to induce any person to enter into or to offer to enter into;

(a) any agreement for or with a view to acquiring, disposing of, subscribing for, or underwriting securities; or
(b) any agreement the purpose or avowed purpose of which is to secure a profit to any of the parties from the yield of securities or by reference to fluctuations in the value of securities;

'stock exchange' means any body corporate which has been approved by the Minister under subs (2) of s 8.

Republic of Korea

Kye Sung Chung, Kim & Chang, Seoul

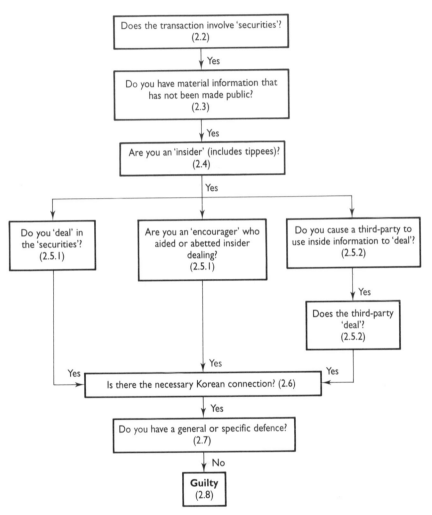

Note: There may also be civil liability for damages caused by any loss to those whom the 'insider' transacted with (2.8.2)

1 INTRODUCTION

In Korea, insider dealing is regulated by the Securities and Exchange Law ('SEL') (including its enforcement regulations) together with rules promulgated by the Securities and Exchange Commission of Korea ('KSEC'), the Ministry of Finance and Economy ('MOFE') and the Korea Stock Exchange ('KSE'). This chapter considers the criminal offences that may be committed by insider dealers, disclosure requirements under the SEL and civil actions that may be available against insider dealers.

2 CRIMINAL SANCTIONS

2.1 INTRODUCTION

Article 188-2 of the SEL is the main statutory provision in Korea governing insider dealing. It defines the key terms of the insider dealing offence: 'inside information' and 'insider'. Article 208, Item 6 SEL provides for criminal sanctions against those persons who violate art 188-2 of the SEL.

2.2 TO WHICH SECURITIES DOES THE SEL APPLY?

In order to be subject to criminal sanctions under the SEL, the alleged offence must involve a dealing in 'securities'. Unlike the US securities laws for instance, the SEL defines the term 'securities' narrowly.

The categories of instruments, dealings in which may subject a person to criminal sanctions and that are considered as 'securities' are set out in Table (1) *below*.

TABLE (1)

Securities:
(1) bonds/debentures (including convertible or exchangeable bonds) issued by companies;
(2) bonds/certificates of capital contribution issued by statutory juridical entities;
(3) stock certificates/instruments giving pre-emptive right to subscribe for new shares;
(4) certificates/instruments issued by a foreign corporation which are similar to (1), (2) or (3) *above* and which are designated by MOFE;
(5) other certificates/instruments similar or related to (1) to (4) and which are designated by the Presidential Enforcement Decree 1962 (as amended)—eg beneficial certificate issued pursuant to the Securities Investment Trust Business Law.

It should be noted that currently 'stock index' is within the definition of 'securities' under the SEL. There is currently only one stock index in Korea, the Korea Stock Price Index 200 ('KOSPI 200') whose value is based on the market capitalisation of 200 listed companies. However, in December 1995, the Futures Trading Law ('FTL') which will become effective 1 July 1996, was enacted. Under the FTL, the provisions relating to stock index will not become effective until the date stipulated in the Presidential Decree on the FTL ('Presidential Decree'). Although the Presidential Decree will be issued in the near future, it is uncertain whether the Presidential Decree will specify the date on which the provisions relating to stock index will become effective. If the provisions relating to stock index under the FTL become effective however, stock index will no longer be within the definition of 'securities' under the SEL. In such case, rather than being governed by the SEL, stock index will be governed by the FTL which has insider dealing provisions similar to those contained in the SEL. Furthermore, it is expected that stock options, stock futures and stock index options will also be governed by the FTL.

The insider dealing provisions of the SEL only apply to listed securities and securities issued by registered corporations. In the case of exchangeable bonds, information regarding either the issuer of the bonds or the issuer of the shares into which the bonds are exchangeable can constitute inside information.

2.3 WHAT IS INSIDE INFORMATION?

Article 188-2 of the SEL defines inside information as 'any material information that has not been made public'. Accordingly, for information to be inside information, it must be (1) material and (2) non-public.

2.3.1 Materiality

Under the SEL, information may be deemed inside information if it has the potential to influence materially an investor's decision to trade in the specific securities involved. This supports the views of scholars in Korea who believe that in order for information to be inside information, it must relate to specific securities. In other words, information relating generally to the market (eg information about fluctuations in foreign exchange rates or interest rates) is considered to be market information and not inside information. However, inside information relating to Company A may also constitute inside information with respect to Company B, if both companies are in the same business and likely to be affected by that information in the same way. Table (2) *below*, provides examples of information which are likely to be considered as material information regarding a company under the SEL.

TABLE (2)

Material information regarding a company:
  (1) when one of the company's issued bills or cheques is not honoured,
       or when its transactions with banks are suspended or prohibited;
  (2) when the company's business operations are suspended in whole or
       in part;
  (3) when the company petitions for, or commences actual, re-
       organisation;
  (4) when the company changes its business objective;
  (5) when the company suffers enormous damage due to fire;
  (6) when a lawsuit that may greatly affect the company's listed securities
       is brought against it;
  (7) when the company effects a merger or sells all or a substantial part
       of its assets;
  (8) when there is a legal ground for dissolution of the company;
  (9) when the board of directors passes a resolution to increase or
       reduce the company's stated capital;
 (10) when the company suspends or is unable to continue its business;
 (11) when a creditor bank takes over the company's management;
 (12) when the company acquires its own shares; or
 (13) when an event that may have a significant effect on the company's
       management occurs.

The price-sensitivity of information is a factor in considering whether the information is material but the courts, who ultimately decide what factors will be considered in determining whether information is inside information, have never ruled that price-sensitivity is a separate factor that needs to be considered on its own merits.

There has been no clear judicial guidance, but information is likely to be regarded as material if upon its release to the market it would lead to some price movement in the relevant security. The precise degree of price movement required is unclear. There has been no academic consideration on the point. The courts, however, presently impose no threshold levels and consequently it would in theory seem that any price movement could be sufficient.

2.3.2 Information made public

Information which has been made public is not inside information. Under the SEL, information is deemed to be public information after it has been made available to the general public through one of the methods prescribed by regulations pro-mulgated by MOFE and following the lapse of a certain period of time.

Table (3) gives details of these methods and time periods. However, Table (3) is not an exhaustive list of the ways in which information may be made public.

TABLE (3)

Information is considered public if it is:
- contained in reports and other documents submitted to the Securities Supervisory Board or the KSE—one day after the submission of the reports or documents;
- published in at least two national newspapers—one day after the publication;
- broadcast by a national broadcasting company—12 hours after the broadcast;
- reported to the KSE and publicly broadcasted—24 hours after the broadcast.

2.3.3 Tender offers

Under the SEL, with the exception of those shareholders who own 10 per cent or more of the total outstanding shares of a corporation at the time of listing of the shares, no other person may acquire more than 10 per cent of the shares of a corporation. However, this 10 per cent limitation does not apply in the case of a tender offer.

In Korea, the concept of tender offers is relatively new and none were made until the end of 1994. Since the last quarter of 1994 however, a small number of friendly and hostile tender offers have been reported. Paragraph 3 of art 188-2 of the SEL expressly makes any information regarding the making or withdrawal of a tender offer, inside information.

2.3.4 Knowledge

It is essential for the successful prosecution of an insider dealing offence to show not only that the relevant information was inside information, but also that the accused knew (subjectively) that it was inside information.

2.4 WHO IS AN INSIDER?

'Insider' is defined as any one of the persons set out in Table (4) who obtains inside information by virtue of his office or position.

TABLE (4)

(1) Officers, employees or agents of a corporation;
(2) Major shareholders of a corporation (ie owning more than 10 per cent of issued share capital);
(3) A person who has administrative or supervisory authority over a corporation under applicable laws;
(4) A person who is entering into a contract with a corporation;

> (5) Agents or employees of the persons mentioned in (2) or (4) *above*;
> (6) Persons falling within any of the categories (1) to (5) during the previous period of one year.

In addition, persons ('tippees') who have received inside information from one of the persons mentioned in Table (4) are also deemed to be insiders. However, those who have received inside information from tippees are not deemed to be insiders. Accordingly, if inside information has been communicated through many persons, only the person who originally obtained the inside information and the first recipient may be subject to criminal sanctions, provided that, subsequent recipients are not aiders, abettors or inducers.

Problem Area

> Dong Woo is employed by Office Cleaners Co and is working late one evening, tidying up the office of the Chairman of one of his employer's clients, Bright Spark Electric Co. On the Chairman's desk is a memorandum giving details of a major new contract about to be signed by Bright Spark with a customer and which could lead to Bright Spark's sales increasing by 50 per cent.
>
> It is not clear whether Dong Woo would be regarded by Korean law as a primary insider because he was an employee of a corporation who has come by inside information relating to another corporation by virtue of his employment. No case on this point has yet been considered by the Korean courts. He may however be regarded as a tippee.

It should be noted that as the definition of insider includes, for example, major shareholders, insider dealing can therefore be committed by not just individuals but also, for example, corporate shareholders.

2.5 WHAT ARE THE OFFENCES?

2.5.1 Dealing

Under the SEL, it is unlawful for an insider to use inside information to deal or transact in securities, whether on-market or in a private off-market transaction. It should also be noted that property in the securities does not have to pass—the execution of an agreement to deliver securities in the future may constitute 'dealing'. Most of the cases on insider dealing reported to date concern major shareholders or representative directors selling their shareholdings immediately before their company files for bankruptcy. The SEL does not provide for a separate offence of encouraging insider dealing. However, if the 'encourager' is found to have aided or abetted the unlawful insider dealing, then the 'encourager' may himself be found guilty of insider dealing. In addition, one should note that where a corporation uses insider information and deals in securities, then both that corporation and the officers of that corporation may be liable.

2.5.2 Disclosure

Under art 188-2 of the SEL, an insider is prohibited from causing others to use inside information to deal or transact in securities. If a tippee (being someone who has received inside information from an insider) were to pass inside information on to a third party and that third party were to use it to deal in securities, then both the third party and the tippee may be guilty of insider dealing offences. It must be noted that the third party is not an insider as defined in 2.4 but may still be guilty of insider dealing offences as, theoretically, the third party may be an aider, abettor or inducer.

It is unlikely that an insider or tippee will be found guilty simply because he improperly communicated inside information to a third party. It is an essential element of the offence that the third party must have unlawfully used this inside information to deal in securities. Consequently, no offence would be committed where the insider or tippee did not know that the third party would use the inside information communicated to him to deal in securities.

2.6 WHAT IS THE TERRITORIAL SCOPE OF THE SEL?

The insider dealing provisions of the SEL are applicable in the following cases:

- if the act of insider dealing or results thereof (eg receiving profits) occur within the Republic of Korea; or
- if a Korean national is involved in the insider dealing, wherever in the world that dealing occurs.

2.7 WHAT ARE THE DEFENCES?

2.7.1 General defences

The SEL does not set out any particular statutory defences. However, the courts do have a discretion to consider and recognise certain defences.

2.7.1.1 No profit/loss

Although there is no precedent, it is highly unlikely that criminal liability will be imposed in insider dealing cases where no profits were made or losses avoided.

2.7.1.2 Wide disclosure

Again, although no precedent exists, it may be possible to argue that non-public information known by both parties to the transaction is not inside information.

2.7.1.3 Information irrelevant

Although not specifically stated in the SEL, it may be a defence to the insider dealing offence for the defendant to show that he would have dealt in the securities concerned even if he did not have the inside information.

2.7.2 Specific defences—Market makers

It may be possible for an underwriting securities firm to argue that because of its obligation to create and stabilise the market for the securities concerned (ie act as a market maker), it cannot be found guilty of violating the insider dealing provision of the SEL as long as it acts in good faith. Unfortunately, however, under the SEL, it is not entirely clear who may be deemed a market maker.

2.8 WHAT ARE THE PENALTIES AND CONSEQUENCES OF INSIDER DEALING?

2.8.1 Criminal consequences

Persons who are found guilty of insider dealing are subject to the following criminal sanctions:

(1) imprisonment for up to three years; or
(2) a fine of up to 20 million Won (approximately £17,000 STG) or three times the amount of profits made or losses avoided, whichever is greater.

2.8.2 Civil consequences

An insider who is guilty of insider dealing will be liable in damages to those whom he transacted with. In the case of on-market transactions, a successful plaintiff would have to show that he suffered losses from trading securities at the same time as the insider traded securities on the market.

Civil actions against an insider must be brought within one year from the discovery of the insider dealing or two years after the actual occurrence of the insider dealing. The measure of damages is, in the absence of any guidelines in the SEL, often difficult to predict.

To date only a small number of civil cases have been tried. In one such case, the measure of damages was calculated by taking the difference between the actual price paid for the securities and the price at which such securities were sold after the relevant insider information was made public and absorbed by the market.

3 PUBLIC DISCLOSURE REQUIREMENTS AND CIVIL LIABILITY

3.1 INTRODUCTION

In addition to the threat of criminal sanctions, the SEL seeks to deter and prevent insider dealing by requiring public disclosure of certain information.

This section will consider the public disclosure requirements under the SEL and the civil remedies that may be available against those who breach the requirements.

3.2 DISCLOSURE REQUIREMENTS FOR PUBLIC OFFERINGS

Under the SEL, before making a public offering of securities (as defined in 2.2 *above*) in Korea, an issuer must file a registration statement and a prospectus. The prospectus must be made available for public inspection at the issuer's head office, branch offices, the KSEC, the KSE and the offices of the securities companies managing the offering.

Any of the persons set out in Table (5) *below* may be subject to civil liability for any untrue statement or omission of any material fact in a registration statement or prospectus.

TABLE (5)

> *Civil liability may be imposed on:*
> * the issuer or the directors of the issuer;
> * a certified public accountant who vouched for the truthfulness of the statements made in the registration statement or prospectus;
> * an underwriter of the securities involved;
> * any person who has prepared the prospectus.

However, the persons referred to in Table (5) may avoid civil liability if they can successfully raise and prove one of the two defences available to them: first, that the purchaser of the securities knew of the untrue statements or omission at the time the securities were offered to the purchaser; or secondly, that they could not have known of any untrue statement or omission even upon exercise of due care. Under the SEL, civil actions must be brought within either one year from the discovery of the untrue statement or omission or, if longer, three years from the effective date of the registration statement.

If a person is found liable, damages will be determined based on the difference between the price the purchaser paid for the securities and the market price of the securities (or the price at which the securities were sold).

3.3 CONTINUING DISCLOSURE REQUIREMENTS

After filing the registration statement, the SEL requires listed corporations and certain other issuers to file annual and semi-annual interim reports with the KSEC and KSE. All such reports are made available for public inspection by the KSEC and the KSE for two years. Interestingly, the securities laws of Korea do not provide for civil liability for any untrue statement or omission of any material fact in such reports.

3.4 SHORT-SWING PROFITS

Under the SEL, any officer, employee or major shareholder of a listed corporation or a corporation which registers with the KSEC who has realised a profit
from purchasing and then selling (or from selling and then purchasing) the corporation's shares within a period of six months can be required by his company
or the KSEC to return such profit to the corporation. A major shareholder of a
corporation is defined as any shareholder or a contributor of capital who owns
more than 10 per cent of the total outstanding number of shares or contribution
certificates issued by the corporation.

CASE STUDY

Splash Co Ltd, a company listed on the Korean Stock Exchange, manufactures rainwear and umbrellas. Alan, a weather forecaster, on discovering
that there is an unseasonable amount of rain due in the next three months,
instructs his broker to buy shares in Splash. Meanwhile, Charles, an analyst
of the company's shares, is told in a conversation with Jeremy, one of the
directors, that the Chairman is expected to be paid a salary of 500,000
Won. Charles knows from his knowledge of the Chairman's service contract (which is available for public inspection) that this salary could only be
paid if the company achieved profit in excess of 20 million Won. Charles
revises his profit forecast for the company but before he publishes it he
cancels instructions which he had previously given to his broker to sell his
Splash shares. Charles also tells his girlfriend, Maggie, that 'things are
looking up' for Splash. Maggie then buys shares in the name of her father
from an old friend of hers who wanted to sell Splash shares off market to
save the payment of a broker's commission. In addition, Owen, an employee
of the contracting firm which cleans Splash's office, finds a draft of the latest
management figures, which demonstrate Splash's high profitability, in a
wastepaper bin. He immediately buys shares.

Alan
Whether Alan is guilty of insider dealing under the SEL will turn on the issue
of whether Alan, as a weather forecaster, is really an 'insider' with respect
to Splash Co Ltd (the 'company'), which does not seem likely. Though the
information he has obtained probably is 'material' with respect to having the
potential of materially influencing an investor's decision to trade in the
shares of the company, there is no prohibition under Korean securities laws
for a person diligently to seek out information (other than from an 'insider'
as defined under the SEL) that may have the effect of potentially influencing
an investor's decision to trade in specific securities. Assuming Alan was an
'insider', whether Alan is guilty of insider dealing would then depend on
whether the information he obtained was 'public' information.

Jeremy

Under Korean securities laws, it appears that Jeremy, as a director of the company (an insider), did improperly communicate material non-public information (eg the Chairman's salary) to Charles, a potential 'tippee', that would likely have the potential of materially influencing an investor's decision to trade in the shares of the company (given that the Chairman's salary is directly tied to the performance of the company). However, whether Jeremy is guilty of disclosing inside information is dependent upon whether Charles' intent in not selling his shares in the company was based on the inside information he had received. This issue would be decided by the Korean courts. If the Korean prosecutor could prove that Charles' intent in not selling his shares was based on the inside information he had received from Jeremy, then Jeremy, under art 188-2 of the SEL, would likely be found guilty of disclosing inside information.

Jeremy may seek to raise the defence that the rules governing broker/dealers in Korea gave him every expectation that Charles would not use the inside information he had received from him to deal in the company's securities, but this is not likely to be viewed favourably by the Korean courts.

Charles

As indicated above, whether Charles is found guilty of insider dealing would be dependent upon a showing by the Korean prosecutor that Charles' intent in not selling his shares was based on the inside information he had received from Jeremy. If proven, a person's forbearance in the sale of shares of a listed or registered corporation in Korea in order to make a profit based on inside information would constitute insider dealing under Korean securities laws.

Maggie

It would be unlikely that Maggie would be found guilty of insider dealing under Korean securities laws. First, it does not appear that the information that Charles communicated to her was non-public material information about the company. Charles simply indicated that 'things are looking up' for the company. Second, even if the Korean courts deemed this statement to be non-public material information with respect to the company, it would be unlikely Maggie would be found guilty of insider dealing if she traded on this information since inside information received from a 'tippee' and used to trade shares by such a recipient would not constitute insider dealing under Korean securities laws. It should be noted that if Maggie had been found guilty of insider dealing, there is no requirement in Korea that she rely on a professional intermediary in her purchase of the shares in order to be found guilty of insider dealing. Also, the fact that she is dealing on behalf of her father would not reduce any liability she might have for insider dealing.

Owen

Under Korean securities law, Owen's guilt or innocence is dependent upon whether Owen is an 'insider'. The information he used to purchase his shares was non-public material information that would have the potential of materially influencing an investor's decision to trade in the shares of the company. Theoretically, Owen, as an employee of a person contracted by the company to clean its offices, probably would be found guilty of insider dealing pursuant to Korean securities laws. However, in practice, it is likely that the Korean courts would employ a threshold test as to the amount of money Owen made in purchasing shares in the company in determining how serious a crime he should be charged with and whether Owen is guilty of insider dealing.

Singapore

**Indranee Rajah and Gary Pryke,
Drew & Napier, Singapore**

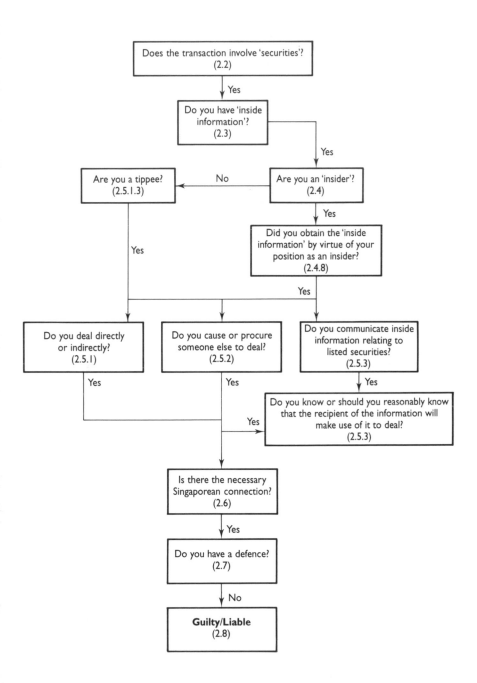

1 INTRODUCTION

'The overall object of insider dealing laws, shortly stated, is to protect corporate confidences and to prevent insiders privy to such confidences from benefiting from an unfair advantage when they deal in the market. When they do deal in those circumstances, they abuse their position and the confidences reposed in them which, in turn undermines the integrity of the market' (*per* Senior District Judge Foenander in *PP v Allan Ng Poh Meng* [1990] 1 MLJ v).

Insider dealing in Singapore is regulated by three statutory provisions. First, s 103 of the Securities Industry Act (Cap 289) (the 'SIA'), which is directly targeted at insider dealing. Second, s 102 of the SIA, which is a more general provision aimed at controlling manipulative and deceptive devices in connection with securities transactions (s 102 of the SIA is similar to Rule 10b-5 made under s 10(*b*) of the Securities Exchange Act 1934 in the United States and insider dealing has been held to be caught by the parent provision in the United States). Third, s 157(2) of the Companies Act (Cap 50) (the 'Companies Act') makes it an offence for an officer or agent of a company to make use of any information acquired by virtue of his position to gain directly or indirectly an advantage for himself or any other persons, or to cause detriment to the company.

The ensuing discussion will focus on SIA s 103 as it is the primary provision that deals directly with insider trading in Singapore.

The SIA came into force on 15 August 1986. It repealed the old insider dealing provision, s 158 of the Companies Act, and replaced it with the present SIA s 103. Section 103 of the SIA was based on s 128 of the Australian Securities Industry Act 1980 (the 'Australian SIA'). Hence, Australian cases interpreting s 128 of the Australian SIA would be persuasive in Singapore.

It is interesting to note however that in 1991, the Australian insider dealing laws were completely redrafted in order to overcome the shortcomings of s 128 of the Australian SIA and to enhance regulation of insider dealing.

Other rules dealing with insider dealing are found in the Special Policies on Insider Trading in the Listing Manual of the Stock Exchange of Singapore ('SES'), the SES Guidelines on Securities Transactions by Directors, and the Singapore Code on Take-Overs and Mergers. Common law also provides some civil remedies to victims of insider dealing in certain circumstances.

2 THE CRIMINAL LAW

2.1 INTRODUCTION

Section 103 of the SIA creates three offences relating to insider dealing, namely:

- dealing while in possession of insider information;

- causing or procuring another person to deal in such circumstances; and
- communicating inside information relating to listed securities to another person when the informant knows or ought reasonably to know that the recipient of the inside information will make use of the inside information by dealing in the securities or will procure or cause another person to deal in those securities.

2.2 TO WHICH SECURITIES DOES THE SIA APPLY?

The SIA applies to both listed and non-listed securities of a company incorporated in Singapore or elsewhere. However with regard to the offence of tipping under SIA s 103(5), the securities must be listed (see 2.5.3). The SIA applies only in the context of issuers which are bodies corporate.

Section 2 SIA defines 'securities' as any of those items set out in Table (1) *below*:

TABLE (1)

Securities are:
(1) debentures, stocks or bonds issued or proposed to be issued by a government;
(2) debentures, stocks, shares, bonds or notes issued or proposed to be issued by a body corporate or unincorporate;
(3) any right or option in respect of any such debentures, stocks, shares, bonds or notes; or
(4) any right to participate or interest whether enforceable or not and whether actual, prospective or contingent:
  - in any profits, assets or realisation of any financial or business undertaking or scheme, whether in Singapore or elsewhere;
  - in any common enterprise, whether in Singapore or elsewhere, in which the holder of the right or interest is led to expect profits, rent or interest from the efforts of the promoter of the enterprise or a third party; or
  - in any investment contract (which is defined to mean any contract, scheme or arrangement which in substance and irrespective of the form thereof involves the investment of money in or under such circumstances that the investor acquires or may acquire an interest in or right in respect of property which under or in accordance with the terms of investment will, or may at the option of the investor, be used or employed in common with any other interest in or right in respect of property acquired in or under like circumstances),
  whether or not the right or interest is evidenced by a formal document and whether or not the right or interest relates to a

> physical asset. The most common example of such an 'interest' would be a unit in a unit trust, but the definition is a wide one which could include many other types of investment scheme.

It should be noted from the foregoing that those items set out in Table (2) are not securities for the purposes of the SIA.

TABLE (2)

Securities do not include:
- futures contracts that are governed by any written law regulating trading in futures contracts;
- bills of exchange;
- promissory notes; or
- certificates of deposit issued by a bank.

2.3 WHAT IS INSIDE INFORMATION?

Inside information with respect to securities is 'information that is not generally available, but, if it were, would be likely to affect materially the price of those securities'. In other words, for the relevant data to constitute 'inside information', the prosecution must show the following three elements:

- it is information;
- that is not generally available; and
- it is price-sensitive in nature.

2.3.1 Information

Under the old insider dealing provision, s 158 of the Companies Act, it was necessary for the prosecution to show that the inside information was 'specific' and 'confidential' in nature.

In *Ryan v Triguboff* [1976] 1 NSWLR 588, an Australian case, it was held that 'specific' information meant information which had an existence of its own quite apart from the operation of any process of deduction, hence a conclusion based on deduction was not information at all. In *PP v Choudhury* [1981] 1 MLJ 76, a case decided by the Singapore Court of Criminal Appeal it was held that what constitutes 'specific confidential information' is a question of fact in each case to be resolved on the evidence adduced at the hearing of the case.

'Information' if widely defined may encompass more than just facts and may include other data such as intention, opinion and any inference drawn from such data. In *PP v Choudhury*, the judge defined 'information' as 'knowledge of a particular event or situation such as advice, communication, intelligence, news, notification and the like'.

A broad definition of 'information' has also been accepted in Australia. The Supreme Court of Victoria in *Commissioner for Corporate Affairs v Green* [1978] VR 505 held that information is not limited to factual knowledge of a concrete kind and in many cases a hint may suggest information or may enable an inference to be drawn as to information. This case was decided under s 128 of the Australian SIA and therefore would be persuasive in Singapore.

Unlike the former Companies Act s 158, s 103 of the SIA no longer requires the inside information to be specific or confidential in nature. Nevertheless, it is still necessary for the prosecution to show that the offence involves some sort of 'information'. The cases referred to above would therefore remain relevant in interpreting what constitutes 'information' under the SIA. How specific or vague the information is may also be relevant in determining whether or not it is price-sensitive.

2.3.2 Not generally available

The words 'not generally available' are not defined under the SIA but they have been interpreted by courts in other jurisdictions.

In *Kinwat Holdings Pty Ltd v Platform Pty Ltd* (1982) ACLC 398, the Supreme Court of Queensland held that because of a story published in the newspapers, coupled with the filing of an affidavit in a legal action and a letter written to the stock exchange regarding certain price-sensitive information, the information had become generally available and would therefore not constitute inside informatin.

In *SEC v Texas Gulf Sulphur Co*, 401 F 2d 833 (1968), the US Court of Appeals held that immediately after a public announcement of the price-sensitive information, the information would still remain 'not generally available' until a reasonable time had lapsed so as to enable a thorough dissemination of the information to the investing public.

What constitutes a reasonable period of time should be determined by reference to the particular circumstances of each case, such as the complexity of the information, the nature of the market for the security and the nature of the disclosure itself.

The new Australian legislation, the Australian Corporations Law, now defines information to be 'generally available' if it is made known in a manner that would or would be likely to bring it to the attention of the investing public and that a reasonable period has since elapsed for it to be disseminated among the investing public. Courts in Singapore are likely to be persuaded by this.

It is recommended by the Singapore Stock Exchange Corporate Disclosure Policy that insiders should wait for at least 24 hours after the general publication of a press release, and 48 hours if the publication is not so widespread, before dealing in the securities. An insider runs the risk of being prosecuted under SIA s 103 if he deals in the securities before the information is made generally available to the public.

The Model Code on Securities Transactions by Directors and Associated Companies of Listed Companies provides that any dealings by a director in his company's securities should be carried out only during the period commencing one week after the release of the company's annual or half-yearly results, and not within one month of the expiry of the financial year or of the half-year.

2.3.3 Price-sensitive information

Section 103 of the SIA requires the information to be of a nature that 'if generally available, would be likely materially to affect the price of securities'. This phrase was interpreted in the *Allan Ng* case. The judge said:

> What has to be decided is whether the information would be 'likely materially to affect the price'. Information that is *likely* materially to affect the price, is information which *may well* materially affect the price. Put in another way, it is more likely than less likely that the price will be affected materially.
>
> The further element of the statutory test concerns 'materiality'. The section provides that the information may well *materially* affect the price. It may be that what is a material price increase in one case may not necessarily be a material price increase in another case. It all depends on the share and the circumstances obtaining at the time.
>
> However, the standard by which materiality is to be judged is whether the information on the particular share is such as would influence the ordinary reasonable investor in deciding whether or not to buy or whether or not to sell that share. A movement in price which would not influence such an investor, may be termed immaterial. Price is, after all, to a large extent determined by what investors do. If generally available, it is the impact of the information on the *ordinary reasonable investor*, and thus on price, which has to be judged in an insider dealing case . . . [T]he true test of price-sensitivity in the [SIA] . . . is an objective one.

(Emphasis added.)

Hence, in determining the price-sensitivity of the relevant information, an objective test should be applied. The subjective opinion of the insider is not relevant.

Although the most objective evidence of price-sensitivity in the majority of cases is probably the effect of the information on the actual price of the security when it is disclosed, nevertheless the *Allan Ng* case showed that the mere fact that the price of the securities was not significantly affected by the release of the inside information would not prevent the court from finding that the information was of a price-sensitive nature.

In the absence of judicial guidance it is difficult to suggest what magnitude of price movement is likely to be considered price-sensitive.

2.4 WHO IS AN INSIDER?

2.4.1 Definition of an insider

An insider is a person who is or has been in the preceding six months 'connected' with a corporation. A person who falls within the ambit of SIA s 103 will still be barred from dealing in the securities for a period of six months, notwithstanding the ending of his connection with the company. A director therefore may not simply resign from his office so as to enable himself to deal in the securities of his company.

The six months' period imposes an arbitrary limit and upon its expiry the person who used to be connected with the company would no longer be caught by the section. Nevertheless, a director who had resigned from his office may still be barred from using the inside information he possesses to obtain any personal gain by reason of the continuing fiduciary duty he owes to the company, even after his resignation.

A person who is connected with a company incorporated outside Singapore may still be an 'insider' for the purposes of the SIA.

An insider can be a natural or an artificial person. In the *Allan Ng* case, a case decided in the Singapore District Court, the judge observed that s 103(1), (2) and (3) of the SIA should be applicable to both natural and artificial persons.

2.4.2 Connected with a body corporate

A person can be 'connected' with an issuer in any of the ways set out in Table (3) *below*.

TABLE (3)

Section 103(9) of the SIA provides that for the purposes of s 103 of the SIA, a natural person is 'connected' with a body corporate if:
(1) he is an officer of the body corporate or of a related body corporate (see 2.4.6);
(2) he is a substantial shareholder (see 2.4.5) of the body corporate or in a related body corporate;
(3) he occupies a position that may reasonably be expected to give him access to inside information by virtue of any professional or business relationship (see 2.4.3) existing between himself (or his employer or a body corporate of which he is an officer) and that body corporate or a related body corporate; or
(4) he occupies a position that may reasonably be expected to give him access to inside information by virtue of his being an officer of a substantial shareholder in that body corporate or in a related body corporate.

Items (3) and (4) in Table (3) *above* do not specifically refer to bankers, auditors, accountants and stockbrokers of the corporation, but nevertheless such persons may well be regarded as insiders under one or both of such items.

It should be noted that an indirect relationship between a person and a corporation may be sufficient to render a person liable as an insider under SIA s 103. For instance a business relationship between a person's employer and another corporation may be sufficient to render the employee a 'connected person' under SIA s 103. See also 2.5.1.3 *below* for the position of tippees.

2.4.3 Business or professional relationship

A person may also be deemed to be connected with a corporation by virtue of the business relationship established between himself and the corporation. The expression 'business or professional relationship' has not been defined in the SIA but it may conceivably include situations where negotiations regarding a business transaction are carried on between a person and a corporation. In such a case, even if the negotiations are aborted, the insider will not be permitted to use or disclose any inside information he obtained from the corporation by virtue of his position as an insider for a period of six months or longer if the information is of a confidential nature.

2.4.4 Officer in relation to body corporate

Section 103(12) further provides that for the purpose of s 103(8) (several writers have contended that this was a drafting error and it should have referred to s 103(9) instead) 'officer' in relation to a body corporate, includes:

- a director, secretary, executive officer or employee of the body corporate;
- a receiver, or receiver and manager, of property of the body corporate;
- a judicial manager of the body corporate;
- a liquidator of the body corporate; and
- a trustee or other person administering a compromise or arrangement made between the body corporate and another person or other persons.

An 'executive officer' is defined in SIA s 2 to mean, in relation to a body corporate, any person, by whatever name called, who is concerned or takes part in the management of the corporation. Hence a person who is involved in the day-to-day management of the company is an executive officer within the definition in the SIA, notwithstanding that he does not hold any formal title such as a manager or a director.

An insider with respect to Company A who has inside information about Company A's business is not, in the absence of any other connection with Company B, regarded by the SIA as an insider with respect to Company B, even though he knows that Company B is likely to be affected by the relevant inside information in the same manner as Company A.

2.4.5 Substantial shareholder

A person is deemed to be a 'substantial shareholder' of a company if he has an interest or interests in voting shares in the company amounting to not less than 5 per cent of the nominal amount of all voting shares in the company.

2.4.6 Related company

There is no definition of 'related body corporate' under the SIA but under the Companies Act, two corporations are deemed to be related to each other where one of them is the holding company or a subsidiary of the other or where both corporations are subsidiaries of the same holding company.

2.4.7 Corporations as insiders

As mentioned above, a corporation may also be an insider by virtue of its substantial shareholdings in another corporation or its business relationship with the corporation. Section 103(6) of the SIA also provides that a body corporate is precluded from dealing in securities where any of its officers is prohibited by SIA s 103 from dealing in those securities. This is however subject to the 'Chinese Wall defence' which is discussed below (see 2.7.1).

2.4.8 Inside information acquired by virtue of position

For an insider to be convicted under SIA s 103, it is also necessary to show that he obtained the inside information by virtue of his position as an insider. In an unreported decision by the Singapore District Court in 1979, *PP v Yong Teck Liam*, the court acquitted the accused as the prosecution did not prove that the accused was possessed of the inside information by virtue of his position as an insider.

2.5 WHAT ARE THE OFFENCES?

As mentioned above (see 2.1), SIA s 103 creates three offences relating to insider dealing, namely:

(1) dealing in securities;
(2) causing or procuring another person to deal; and
(3) communicating inside information in certain circumstances.

2.5.1 Dealing in securities—s 103(1)–(3) of the SIA

Section 103 of the SIA prohibits three forms of dealing in securities; first, SIA s 103(1) prohibits an insider from dealing in the securities of the corporation with which he is connected ('direct' insider dealing); second, SIA s 103(2) prohibits an insider of one corporation dealing in the securities of another corporation if he has inside information which he obtained by virtue of his position in the first mentioned corporation ('indirect' insider dealing); and third, SIA s 103(3) prohibits dealing in securities by a tippee.

2.5.1.1 Direct insider dealer—s 103(1)

There are four elements to the offence of direct insider dealing:

- the person in question was an insider at the material time;
- he was in possession of inside information;

- he obtained the inside information by virtue of his position as an insider; and
- he dealt in the securities of the corporation.

Both natural and artificial persons are prohibited from direct insider dealing.

An insider is prohibited from dealing in the securities by the mere fact that he possesses such inside information as an insider. Under the former s 158 of the Companies Act, an insider would only be liable for insider trading if it could be shown that he had made use of the inside information. This is to say that the inside information must have been a factor in the decision of the insider to trade (see *Green v Charterhouse Group Canada Ltd* [1976] 68 DLR (3d) 592). However, it appears from a literal reading of subss 103(1) and (2) that under the new provision it is no longer necessary for the prosecution to prove that the insider himself knew that the information he received was in fact 'inside information' or that he had 'made use of' the inside information in any way.

However, rules of statutory interpretations require a provision imposing criminal liability to be construed strictly in favour of the accused. It has been argued that in the absence of clear and express language to the contrary, *mens rea* should continue to be a necessary element of the various offences under SIA s 103. It has been argued that if this is correct, the prosecution would therefore still be required to prove that the inside information had been 'made use of' by the insider (see Walter Woon, 'Insider Trading and the Abuse of Corporate Information' [1987] 2 MLJ). Such an interpretation does not appear to be supported by the literal wording of the section. Even if *mens rea* is required that does not necessarily mean that the prosecutor must show that the inside information was made use of. Reading in such a requirement would significantly increase the difficulty of securing a conviction under the section. In Canada, although the requirement that the accused must have 'made use of' the inside information was read into its insider dealing provision, the courts reversed the burden of proving this requirement. Once the prosecution proved that the accused traded in the securities while in possession of inside information, the burden would shift to the accused to show that the information was not a factor in his decision to trade in the securities.

Alternatively, the court may require the prosecution to prove a lesser *mens rea* requirement. The following are the various other possible *mens rea* requirements that could be imposed:

(1) the accused must know the content of the information;
(2) the accused must know the source of the information; and/or
(3) the accused must know that the information is not generally available and is of a price-sensitive nature.

Section 103 prohibits an insider from 'dealing in securities'. Under the SIA, 'dealing in securities' means:

- making or offering to make any agreement for acquiring, disposing of, subscribing for or underwriting securities;
- inducing or attempting to induce any person to enter into any agreement for acquiring, disposing of, subscribing for or underwriting securities;
- making or offering to make any agreement the purpose of which is to secure a profit from the yield of securities or from speculation;
- inducing or attempting to induce any person to enter into any agreement the purpose of which is to secure a profit from the yield of securities or from speculation.

2.5.1.2 Indirect insider dealing—s 103(2)

There are five elements (see Table (4) *below*) in this offence and they are largely similar to the offence of direct insider dealing.

TABLE (4)

Constituent elements of indirect insider dealing offence:
• the person in question was an insider at the material time;
• he was in possession of inside information;
• he obtained the information by virtue of his position as an insider—case law suggests that such an insider must be in a position which is likely to give him access to inside information;
• the information related to transactions (actual or proposed) between his corporation and another corporation, or to dealings by his corporation in another corporation's securities; and
• he dealt in the securities of the other corporation.

Section 103(2) of the SIA is therefore applicable where an officer of an offeror company, which has proposed a take-over bid, deals in the securities of the offeree company using the inside information he has acquired by virtue of his position in the offeror company.

2.5.1.3 Dealing by tippee—s 103(3)

Four things must be shown for a tippee to be guilty under s 103(3) of the SIA:

- he obtained inside information directly or indirectly from an informant;
- he is aware or ought to be aware that the informant is an insider who is prohibited by SIA s 103(1), or s 103(2) of the SIA from dealing in the securities concerned;
- he was associated with the informant or had with the informant an arrangement for the communication of inside information with a view to dealing in securities by himself and the informant or either of them;
- he dealt in the securities of the corporation to which the information related.

Hence, a person who was not subjectively aware of the fact that the informant (a term which is not defined in the SIA) was an insider but 'ought reasonably to know' of that fact may nevertheless be guilty of dealing as a tippee under the SIA.

As can be seen under SIA s 103(3), a tippee is prohibited from dealing in securities only when, at the time the inside information is received, there is some association or arrangement between the tippee and the informant.

2.5.1.3.1 Associated persons

Section 3 of the SIA, which is summarised in Table (5) *below*, defines when a person is deemed to be associated with another person.

TABLE (5)

Section 3 of the SIA provides that:
(1) a director or secretary of a corporation is associated with that corporation;
(2) two related corporations (see 2.4.6 *above*) are also associated with each other;
(3) a director or secretary of a corporation is associated with that corporation's related corporation(s);
(4) two persons are associated with each other if they act, or propose to act, in concert with each other;
(5) two persons may be regarded as associated with each other by virtue of any regulation that may be introduced (to date, none have been);
(6) a person who is, or proposes to become, associated whether formally or informally with another person, or in any other way in respect of the matter to which the reference relates is associated with that other person; and
(7) two persons are associated with each other where one of them has entered into or proposes to enter into a transaction or has done or proposes to do any other act or thing with a view to becoming associated with the other person as mentioned in the other items above.

For the purposes of items (4), (5) and (6) in Table (5) a person shall not be taken to be associated with another person by reason only of the fact that one of the persons furnished advice to, or acts on behalf of, that other person in the proper performance of the functions attaching to his professional capacity or to his business relationship with the other person.

2.5.1.3.2 Arrangement between the tippee and the informant

The *Allan Ng* case held that as long as there was sufficient unity of purpose and the object was clear, there would be no less an arrangement even though there was no prior agreement as to every detail of the arrangement. The District Court also held that it was not necessary to show that the arrangement was for an improper or illegitimate purpose.

Where the prosecution cannot establish a nexus between the tippee and the informant, the tippee cannot be convicted under the SIA s 103(3). Hence, an eavesdropper who overheard the communication of inside information or a spy who obtained inside information through industrial espionage would not be prohibited by the section from dealing in the securities.

In Australia, the Griffiths Committee stated that 'the existing tippee provision [ie s 128 of the Australian SIA] is inadequate. The need to demonstrate an association or arrangement is an unnecessary and complicating factor. It detracts from the objective of the provision, which is to prohibit persons from using inside information received from insiders to trade in or subscribe for the securities of the company which is the subject of the information.' (Griffiths Committee Report 1989: see para 4.7.8).

A 'sub-tippee' is a person who receives inside information from a tippee. Such a person may still be caught by s 103(3) of the SIA as he could be said to have received information indirectly from the insider. However, to convict as sub-tippee under the section, the prosecution must prove that the requisite nexus between the sub-tippee and the original informant is satisfied. This may be extremely difficult to prove in practice.

An informant may be guilty under s 103(4) of the SIA (see 2.5.2 *below*) or s 103(5) of the SIA (see 2.5.3 *below*).

2.5.2 Causing or procuring another person to deal—s 103(4) of the SIA

Where an insider or a tippee is prohibited by the SIA from dealing in securities, he is not permitted to cause or procure any other person to deal in those securities. The words 'cause or procure' are not defined in the SIA.

2.5.3 Communicating inside information in certain circumstances—s 103(5) of the SIA

Section 103(5) of the SIA prohibits an insider or a tippee from communicating any inside information regarding any securities which are listed on a securities exchange whether in or outside Singapore to any other person, if he knows or ought reasonably to know that the other person will make use of the information to deal in those securities. Communication of information regarding securities which are not listed is not covered by this subsection.

A tipper may be guilty of the offence under SIA s 130(5) even though the tippee (or any sub-tippee) does not in fact trade in the securities (either on- or off-exchange).

On the face of it, a Singaporean informant who communicates inside information to another person regarding securities listed on an overseas securities exchange could be guilty of an offence under the SIA, even though no offence has been committed in the overseas country concerned. However, the SIA defines 'securities exchange' to mean a stock exchange or a securities organisation, in each case which has been approved by the Minister under the SIA. To date, only the Singapore Stock Exchange and no foreign stock exchange or securities organisation has been approved by the Minister for the purpose.

2.6 WHAT IS THE TERRITORIAL SCOPE OF THE SIA?

The SIA is silent as to the exact territorial scope of its operation. Section 15 of the Supreme Court of Judicature Act (Cap 322) provides that the High Court shall have jurisdiction to try all offences committed: within Singapore or in any place or by any person if it is provided in any written law that the offence is triable in Singapore.

Hence in the absence of any specific provision limiting or extending the criminal jurisdiction of the High Court, the High Court shall only have criminal jurisdiction to try an offence relating to insider dealing under the SIA if it was committed within Singapore.

In *PP v Loh Ah Hoo* [1974] 2 MLJ 216, it was held that if a person's criminal act or responsibility for the criminal act runs from outside the jurisdiction to within the jurisdiction then he is liable to be tried within the jurisdiction. Hence in a situation where an alleged insider dealing offence was partly performed in Singapore and partly outside Singapore, it would appear that the Singapore courts will have jurisdiction over the offence provided that all the acts constituting the elements of the offence form part of a continuous criminal act and not several separate criminal acts.

2.7 WHAT ARE THE DEFENCES AND EXCEPTIONS?

2.7.1 'Chinese Wall defence'—s 103(7)

The 'Chinese Wall' is a procedural device designed to ensure that a corporation's investment trading staff do not have access to insider information obtained by its other departments, for example its corporate finance or banking department. The Chinese Wall may consist of a physical separation of the various departments in the corporation or adopted practices or procedures directed at the dissemination of information within the organisation so as to prevent any leakage of information. The 'Chinese Wall defence' is especially important in banks and multi-service financial institutions.

The SIA precludes a body corporate from dealing in certain securities when any of its officers, being an insider or a tippee, is prohibited from dealing in those securities (s 103(6) of the SIA). The 'Chinese Wall defence' under SIA s 103(7) states that notwithstanding SIA s 103(6) a body corporate may still deal in securities if:

(1) the decision to enter into the transaction was taken on behalf of the corporation by a person other than the officer prohibited from dealing;
(2) the corporation had in operation at that time arrangements to ensure that the inside information was not communicated to that person and that no advice relating to the transaction was given to him by a person in possession of that inside information; and
(3) the inside information was not so communicated and such advice was not so given.

The success of the 'Chinese Wall' ultimately depends on the integrity of the employees of the firm. For the defence to be invoked successfully, the accused must adduce evidence to show that rigorous compliance programmes are in place to detect any leakage of information. This defence is only available to a body corporate. It is not enough that there is a Chinese Wall in place. The corporation will also have to show that as a matter of fact no inside information was given to the officer who did the dealing.

2.7.2 Knowledge of certain inside information by an officer of the corporation—s 103(8) of the SIA

Section 103(8) of the SIA provides that a corporation is not precluded from dealing in the securities of another corporation merely because:

(1) one of the officers of the first mentioned corporation has information relating to the proposed dealing in such securities; and
(2) such information was acquired by the said officer in the course of performing his duties as an officer of the corporation.

This may apply, for example, where an offeror company intends to make a takeover bid at a premium above market price. This may itself constitute inside information. Section 103(6) of the SIA would then preclude the offeror and its officers who possess the inside information from making any pre-bid purchases of securities of the offeree company.

The exemption afforded by SIA s 103(8), although somewhat obscurely worded, would appear to allow the offeror company itself to make pre-bid purchases (see also Rule 29 of the Singapore Code on Take-Overs and Mergers; discussed at 3.4 *below*). This exemption however does not extend to officers of the offeror company.

Similarly, information regarding intended purchases or sales of a substantial number of securities by a large institutional investor may also amount to 'inside information'. Section 103(8) of the SIA would also appear to allow such an investor to deal in the securities before the release of the inside information concerning the investor's purchases or sales.

Section 103(8) however does not apply to every proposed business dealing between two corporations. For instance, information that Company A is about to award a large building contract to Company B may affect the price of the securities in Company B when it is finally released to the public. However, Company A is not permitted to trade in the securities of Company B under s 103(8) of the SIA as the inside information in this case does not relate to any proposed dealing in relation to the securities in Company B.

2.7.3 Exception for holder of a dealer licence—s 103(10) of the SIA

Section 103(10) of the SIA provides that an insider who is also the holder of a dealer's licence will be allowed to deal in securities when:

(1) the holder of the licence enters into the transaction concerned as agent for another person pursuant to a specific instruction by that other person to effect the transaction;
(2) the holder of the licence has not given advice to his principal; and
(3) the principal is not associated with the holder of the licence.

Under s 2 of the SIA, a 'dealer' is a person who carries on a business of dealing in securities as a body corporate. An individual cannot be a 'dealer' under the SIA. In Singapore, dealer's licences are issued to bodies corporate only. Individuals who perform the function of a dealer on its behalf are licensed as dealer's representatives.

While s 103(10) of the SIA provides an exception for a dealer who acted merely as agent in effecting the transaction, it does not appear to exempt the individual dealer's representative who effected the transaction on behalf of the broking firm he works for.

Even though an individual dealer's representative who acts as a mere agent for an insider investor is technically caught by SIA s 103, it is very unlikely that any prosecution will be commenced against an individual dealer's representative who effected a transaction in circumstances in which the broking firm he works for is exempted under SIA s 103(10) and where he himself has complied with the requirements of the exemption.

2.7.4 Where the other party to the transaction knew or ought reasonably to have known of the inside information— s 103(11) of the SIA

Section 103(11) of the SIA provides that it is a defence for an insider or a tippee who is prosecuted under SIA s 103(11) to show that the other party to the transaction knew, or ought reasonably to have known, of the inside information before entering into the transaction.

This defence to a criminal prosecution is only available to parties to a transaction. It appears that an insider who has disclosed information to an executive officer or a director of a corporation before entering into a contract with the corporation will not be able to resort to this defence if the insider could not show that the other party to the transaction (ie the corporation) knew or ought reasonably to have known of the inside information. The knowledge of the executive officer or the director will not be imputed to the corporation. On the other hand, where the disclosure is made to the board of directors of the corporation, the insider may then be able to rely on this exemption.

Under s 103(10) of the SIA an insider who discloses relevant inside information to the other party to a transaction will not be guilty of insider dealing, assuming of course that by disclosing such information an offence under SIA s 103(5) is not committed (see 2.5.3).

Where such information is confidential in nature, the insider may also be restrained from disclosing it by the corporation concerned under common law. To succeed in an action under the law of confidence, the plaintiff must show that the information has a quality of confidence (ie it is not common knowledge within the public domain), a relationship of confidence exists between the plaintiff and the defendant (such a relationship exists when a reasonable person who had received the information would realise that an obligation to maintain confidentiality was imposed on him or it may arise by virtue of an office held for example, that of director) and the defendant must have used or intends to use the confidential information to the detriment of the plaintiff (*Coco v Clark* [1968] FSR 415; *X v CDE* [1992] 2 SLR 996). Where the insider had already disclosed the confidential information and caused detriment to the owner of the information, he may be liable for damages under an action for breach of confidence.

2.7.5 Exceptions provided by the Securities Industry Regulations 1986

Regulations 51 and 52 of the Securities Industry Regulations 1986 provide for exceptions to the insider dealing laws in certain circumstances.

Regulation 51 sets out five exceptions to s 103(1) (see 2.5.1.1), (3) (see 2.5.1.3) and (6) (see 2.7.1) of the SIA, whereas Regulation 52 sets out four exceptions to s 103(1) (see 2.5.1.1), (2) (see 2.5.1.2), (3) (see 2.5.1.3) and (6) of the SIA. These are summarised in Table (6).

TABLE (6)

The five exceptions provided for by Regulation 51 are:
- the obtaining by a director of a share qualification in accordance with s 147 of the Companies Act;
- the subscription for and acquisition pursuant to the subscription of securities of a corporation by, or by a trustee for, employees of the corporation, or of a corporation that is deemed to be related to the first-mentioned corporation by reason of s 6 of the Companies Act,

under a superannuation scheme, pension fund or other scheme
established solely or primarily for the benefit of such employees;
- a transaction entered into by a person in accordance with his
  obligations under an underwriting agreement;
- a transaction entered into by a manager of an issue of securities in
  accordance with his obligations solely as such under an agreement
  with the issuer or corporation; or
- a transaction entered into by a person as a market maker in securities
  to which that transaction relates.

TABLE (7)

The four exceptions set out under Regulation 52 are:
- a personal representative of a deceased person, a liquidator or a
  person holding the office of Official Assignee under the Bankruptcy
  Act in respect of any transaction entered into by him in good faith in
  the performance of the functions of his office as such a representative,
  liquidator or Official Assignee;
- a transaction by way of, or arising out of, a mortgage or charge of
  securities of a mortgage, charge, pledge or lien of documents of title to
  securities;
- the acquisition of securities by a person under a will or on the
  intestacy of another person; or
- if dealing in securities which consists only of the transfer of the legal
  estate in those securities from one trustee to another trustee.

In the above four situations the transactions are effected by the 'insider' on
behalf of another person. The 'insider' does not derive any real benefit from the
transactions even though the transactions fall technically within the prohibitions
laid down by SIA s 103.

2.8 WHAT ARE THE PENALTIES AND CONSEQUENCES OF INSIDER DEALING?

A person who is guilty of insider dealing faces both criminal and civil liabilities.

2.8.1 Criminal penalties

Section 104 of the SIA provides that a natural person who is found guilty under
SIA s 103 shall be liable on conviction to a fine not exceeding $50,000 (approxi-
mately £23,000 STG) or to imprisonment for a term not exceeding seven years.

A corporate insider is liable on conviction to a fine not exceeding $100,000
(approximately £46,000 STG). However, SIA s 111 further provides that where
a corporation is guilty of an offence under the SIA, any director, executive

officer, secretary or employee of the corporation who was knowingly concerned in or party to the commission of the offence shall also be guilty of that offence and therefore liable to a fine not exceeding $50,000 or seven years' imprisonment.

2.8.2 Civil liabilities

An insider may face potential civil suits initiated by:

(1) the corporation affected by the insider dealing; and
(2) any person who bought (or sold) securities at a higher (or lower) price than they would have done had they been aware of the inside information (ie the victims of the insider dealing).

2.8.2.1 Civil suit brought by the corporation

An affected corporation may have the following remedies against the insider:

2.8.2.1.1 Injunction
In a case where the insider dealing transaction is not yet completed, a corporation may apply for an injunction under SIA s 114 to restrain the insider from dealing with the securities in a manner contrary to SIA s 103.

Under common law, the law of confidence also enables the corporation to obtain an injunction against a director or employee of the corporation so as to prevent the use or disclosure of confidential information obtained by the director or employee by virtue of their position in the corporation (see 2.7.4).

2.8.2.1.2 An account for profit
Under common law, a director of a company, being a fiduciary of the company, must account to his company for any benefits he enjoyed or obtained as a result of a breach of the fiduciary duty he owes to the company (*Boardman v Phipps* [1966] 3 All ER 721). The liability to account is a strict one.

Section 157(3)(a) of the Companies Act provides that an officer or agent who makes a profit from the improper use of information obtained by virtue of his position is accountable to the company for all the profits made.

2.8.2.1.3 Damages
Section 157(3)(a) of the Companies Act gives a Singaporean company a right to recover damages from an officer or agent who profited from the improper use of information obtained by virtue of his position in the company.

2.8.2.2 Civil suit brought by victim of insider dealing

Section 105(1) of the SIA provides that a victim of insider dealing may sue the guilty insider or tippee for civil remedies if:

(1) the offender has been convicted under the SIA; and

(2) the civil action was brought within the limitation period laid down by the SIA (ie two years after the date of completion of the transaction on which the loss occurred).

The two years' limitation period appears to be unduly restrictive considering the fact that it may take more than two years for the prosecution to secure a conviction of an insider under SIA s 103.

2.8.3 Compensation orders

Section 401 of the Criminal Procedure Code (Cap 68) empowers the court, before which a person is convicted of an offence, to order the offender to pay compensation to any person injured by the offence. In practice, however, the court's power under s 401 is rarely exercised.

Where the compensation ordered by the court is inadequate, it will not prevent the victim from seeking further redress under civil law.

2.8.4 Common law and equitable remedies

Section 105(4) of the SIA preserves the victim's rights to seek redress under the common law. Causes of action which may be available to a victim of insider dealing would include breach of statutory duty and tortious or contractual misrepresentation.

In equity, a constructive trust may be imposed in certain circumstances where the justice of the case requires it to make a person accountable for property inequitably obtained. Equitable remedies are available to a victim of insider dealing under causes of action such as breach of confidence or fiduciary duties, knowing receipt, knowing assistance and unjust enrichment.

3 NON-STATUTORY REGULATION

3.1 INTRODUCTION

The insider dealing legislation in Singapore is supplemented by non-statutory regulations.

3.2 SINGAPORE STOCK EXCHANGE ('SES') LISTING MANUAL

Clause 1207 of the SES Listing Manual sets out certain specific policies on insider dealing. It states, *inter alia*, that the husbands, wives, other immediate family members and those under the control of insiders may also be regarded as insiders. Where a listed issuer is involved in the negotiation on an acquisition or other transaction, the other parties to the negotiation would also be regarded as insiders. Clause 1207 also encourages listed issuers to establish and enforce effective procedures for transactions by insiders in their securities so as to prevent improper trading and to avoid any question of the propriety of insider purchases and sales.

3.3 SES GUIDELINES ON DIRECTORS' DEALING

The SES Listing Manual requires listed companies to have rules governing directors' dealing in securities which are no less stringent than the Model Code issued by the SES ('the Model Code').

The Model Code applies to dealings by a director (and his spouse) in the securities of the company in which he holds office, or subsidiaries of such a company. The Model Code is also extended to dealings by associated companies of a listed company. Its application is however limited to companies that are incorporated in Singapore and not to foreign corporations.

The three main guiding principles governing all dealings covered by the Model Code are:

(1) A director should not deal in his company's securities on considerations of a short-term nature.
(2) Dealings should not take place prior to the announcement of a matter that involves material unpublished price-sensitive information in relation to the securities of the company (or, where relevant, any other listed company).
(3) Unless the circumstances are exceptional, a director should not deal in the company's securities during the period commencing one month before the expiry of the financial year or half-year, as the case may be, to the announcement of the company's annual or half-yearly results and/or of any dividends and distributions to be paid or passed.

The Model Code also provides that in the event where a dealing is effected, the director is required to notify the company secretary or other authorised person within 24 hours of a dealing, stating the date of the transaction, the transaction price and the amount of securities acquired or disposed of.

3.4 SINGAPORE CODE ON TAKE-OVER AND MERGERS

Rule 29(1) of the Singapore Code on Take-Over and Mergers (the 'Code') states that all persons privy to confidential price-sensitive information concerning an offer or contemplated offer, must treat that information relating to the potential offer as secret and must not pass it to any other person unless it is necessary to do so. Such persons should not make any recommendation to any other person as to dealing in the relevant securities and must conduct themselves so as to minimise the chance of an accidental leak of information.

Rule 29(2) further provides that no dealings in the securities of the offeree company by any person, not being the offeror, who is privy to the preliminary take-over and merger discussions or to an intention to make an offer, may take place between the time when there is reason to suppose that an approach or an offer is contemplated and the announcement of the approach or offer or the termination of the discussion.

The Code also provides that no such dealings shall take place in the securities of the offeror except where the proposed offer is not deemed price sensitive in relation to such securities.

4 CONCLUSION

There have only been three reported prosecutions for insider dealing in Singapore to date. In two of the three cases, the accused persons eventually pleaded guilty to the charges and in the other case, the accused was acquitted. There are no known proposals for any reforms of the SIA to be made.

CASE STUDY

Splash Co, a company listed on the Singapore Stock Exchange, manufactures rainwear and umbrellas. Alan, a weather forecaster, on discovering that there is an unseasonable amount of rain due in the next three months, instructs his broker to buy shares in Splash. Meanwhile, Charles, an analyst of the company's shares, is told in a conversation with Jeremy, one of the directors, that the Chairman is expected to be paid a salary of $500,000. Charles knows from his knowledge of the Chairman's service contract (which is available for public inspection) that this salary could only be paid if the company achieved profit in excess of $20 million. Charles revises his profit forecast for the company but before he publishes it he cancels instructions which he had previously given to his broker to sell his Splash shares. Charles also tells his girlfriend, Maggie, that 'things are looking up' for Splash. Maggie then buys shares in the name of her father from an old friend of hers who wanted to sell Splash shares off market to save the payment of a broker's commission. In addition, Owen, an employee of the contracting firm which cleans Splash's offices, finds a draft of the latest management figures, which demonstrate Splash's high profitability, in a wastepaper bin. He immediately buys shares.

Alan
Alan is not a person 'connected' to Splash nor a 'tippee' under s 103 and is therefore not liable for insider dealing. Furthermore it is also questionable whether the relevant information could amount to inside information (ie information which is not generally available and if it were, would be likely to

materially affect the price of those securities). The information in this case, even if not generally available to the investing public, does not appear to be information which would be more likely than less likely to influence the ordinary reasonable investor in deciding whether or not to buy or sell shares in Splash. Even if it may amount to inside information, as mentioned above, Alan would still not be liable because he is not an insider nor a tippee.

Jeremy

For Jeremy, who is clearly an insider, to be guilty of the offence of communicating inside information in certain circumstances under SIA s 103(5), it must first be shown that such information amounts to inside information. It appears that the information in question is not generally available.

The courts have held that an objective test is to be applied in determining whether such information, *if* generally available to the investing public, would be more likely than less likely to materially affect the price of the securities. Hence, the price-sensitivity of the information would depend on the particular facts of each case.

In this case, as the Chairman's service contract is available for public inspection and as that contract presumably contains a salary formula based on the company's performance, it is likely that, information relating to the Chairman's salary could amount to inside information as the investing public may reasonably deduce from such information that Splash has made substantial profits and would therefore be more likely to buy Splash's shares at a higher price.

For Jeremy to be convicted under s 103(5), it must be shown that Jeremy knew or ought reasonably to have known that Charles (bearing in mind that Charles is an analyst of Splash's shares) would make use of the information for the purpose of dealing in the securities of Splash. It would depend on the facts whether or not it could be established that Jeremy had the requisite knowledge. But on the face of it, it is perhaps unlikely that Jeremy knew or ought reasonably to have known that Charles would make use of the information regarding the Chairman's salary for the purpose of dealing in Splash's shares.

Charles

Charles is not guilty of 'dealing in securities' as the term does not include refraining from dealing in securities. Charles is also not a 'connected' person (for the purposes of s 103(1) and (2)) nor is he 'associated' and nor does he have any 'arrangement' with Jeremy for the purpose of s 103(3), hence it appears that he would not be guilty of 'communicating' inside information to Maggie under s 103(5). Furthermore, Charles may also lack the necessary knowledge for the purposes of s 103(5). It must be shown that he knew or ought reasonably to have known that Maggie would make use of the information to deal in Splash's shares.

Maggie

To constitute inside information under the SIA, it is not necessary to prove that the information is specific. However, the information in this case may not be sufficiently detailed to be 'likely materially to affect the price' of Splash's shares.

Even if such information amounts to inside information, Maggie would still not be liable as a tippee dealing in securities under s 103(3) because as stated above, Charles is not a person prohibited from dealing in securities under s 103(1), (2) or (3) and also because Maggie was not associated with, and had no arrangement with Charles with a view to dealing in securities.

Owen

To determine whether Owen is a person connected to Splash for the purposes of s 103(1), it is necessary to first determine whether an employee of Splash's contracting cleaning company is in a position that may *reasonably be expected to give him access to price-sensitive information* in Splash.

If the answer to that is yes, then it would follow that any inside information received by Owen in doing his job as a cleaner would be obtained *by virtue* of his position as an employee of the cleaning company and Owen would be prohibited by s 103(1) from dealing in the securities of Splash.

On the other hand, if the answer to that is no, then Owen would not be guilty of dealing in securities under s 103(1) or (3) (see *PP v Yong Teck Lian*). The offence of 'communicating' inside information under s 103(3) requires the inside information to be communicated by a person who is either 'associated' with Owen or has an 'arrangement' with Owen with a view to dealing in securities. The section therefore does not apply to the inadvertently 'leaked' inside information in this case as the requisite nexus cannot be established.

Australia

Marie McDonald,
Blake Dawson Waldron, Melbourne

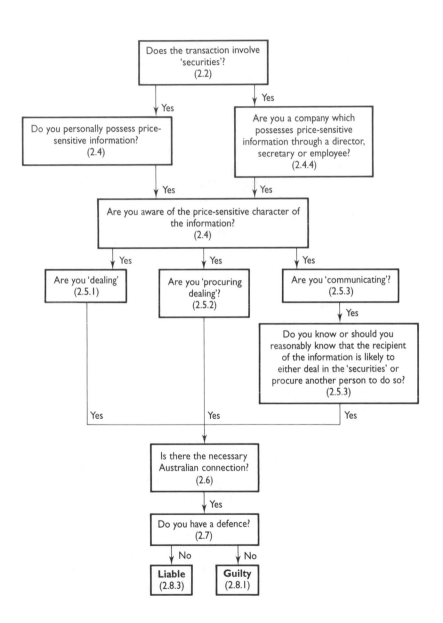

1 INTRODUCTION

The principal Australian legislation relating to insider trading is contained in Division 2A of Part 7.11 of the Corporations Law. The Corporations Law came into effect on 1 January 1991. It combined the Companies Codes, Companies (Acquisition of Shares) Codes, Securities Industries Codes and Futures Industries Codes of each Australian jurisdiction into one piece of comprehensive corporate legislation. Each state and territory of Australia has adopted the Corporations Law and the Australian Securities Commission ('ASC') is the single regulatory authority administering this legislation.

The current insider trading provisions contained in Division 2A of Part 7.11 came into force on 1 August 1991 and replaced provisions which were essentially the same as those contained in the predecessor Securities Industries Codes. The August 1991 amendments were introduced and enacted in an attempt to correct deficiencies in the previous legislation (there had never been a successful insider trading prosecution). The impetus for the change was a heightened public concern in the late 1980s about improper securities practices and a desire on the part of the government to promote investor confidence.

In large part, the new laws reflect the recommendations of an enquiry by the House of Representatives Standing Committee on Legal and Constitutional Affairs (known as the 'Griffiths Committee'). The report was entitled 'Fair Shares for All: Insider Trading in Australia'. Although these laws are drafted much more widely than the previous legislation, the Australian record of successful prosecutions has not improved and there has still not been a successful prosecution under the Corporations Law.

The Australian insider trading laws govern trading in securities by both corporations and natural persons. The laws impose criminal and civil liability and it is not necessary, as a matter of law, that a criminal conviction be secured before civil liability can be established.

The discussion which follows below relates to insider trading in securities other than futures. Insider trading in futures is governed by Division 1 of Part 8.7 of the Corporations Law. These provisions are largely the same as those previously contained in the Futures Industries Codes.

In addition to these specific provisions of the Corporations Law, there are more general provisions in s 232 which prohibit officers or employees of a corporation making improper use of information acquired by virtue of their positions or making improper use of their positions to gain an advantage for themselves or another person. Contravention of these provisions can attract civil and criminal liability. Further, s 232 expressly preserves the operation of the common law (which could render a person liable to a company in respect of insider trading if the person had breached a fiduciary or contractual duty to the company).

2 THE CRIMINAL LAW

2.1 INTRODUCTION

Section 1002G creates three offences which can be committed by an insider: trading, procuring another person to trade and communicating price sensitive information to another person. These offences, which are considered in detail below (see 2.5), rely upon a number of definitions which are considered first.

2.2 TO WHICH SECURITIES DOES PART 7.11 APPLY?

2.2.1 Kinds of securities

Section 1002A(1) lists the kinds of securities to which the regime set out in Division 2A of Part 7.11 applies. They are:

(1) Shares in a body corporate. It has recently been held that the Division does not apply to unissued shares (*Exicom Pty Ltd v Futuris Corporation Ltd* (1995) 18 ACSR 404).

(2) Debentures (including notes convertible into shares issued by the body corporate).

(3) Prescribed interests made available by the body corporate. 'Prescribed interests' are widely defined and involve the type of security that an investor would receive where he contributes funds to a venture in reliance on the managerial or investment skill of others to produce a return on his investment. New kinds of prescribed interests often evolve as a result of a change in income tax law. Examples of prescribed interests include various kinds of property trusts, equity trusts, cash management trusts and other collective investments. Time sharing schemes are also prescribed interests, although interests in retirement village schemes are excluded.

(4) Units of shares or of prescribed interests. A 'unit' of a share or a prescribed interest is a right or interest, whether legal or equitable, in the share or prescribed interest and includes an option to acquire such a right or interest (s 9). The drafting of this definition pre-supposes that the share or prescribed interest exists already. The ASC has expressed the view, in the context of the prospectus laws, that renounceable rights to subscribe for securities and options to subscribe for securities are not 'units'. As mentioned below, it appears that such rights are not 'option contracts' and, accordingly, that the insider trading laws do not apply to rights or options to subscribe for shares and prescribed interests.

(5) An option contract under which a party acquires from another party an option or right, exercisable at or before a specified time, to buy from or sell to that other party a number of shares, debentures, prescribed interests or units of shares at a price specified in, or to be determined in accordance with, the contract. This definition includes exchange traded options as well as

options created by private contract. It includes both put and call options. Special definitions of 'purchase' and 'sell' have been included to encompass the arrangements by which an existing position is closed out (s 1002A(1)).

The kinds of securities to which these laws apply also include any securities issued by a government, unincorporated body or any other person (s 1002A(2)). The insider trading laws apply in relation to such securities in the same way, as nearly as practicable, as if the issuing body were a body corporate.

Futures contracts are expressly excluded from the operation of Division 2A, Part 7.11. As mentioned in the introduction, however, they are governed by Division 1 of Part 8.7 of the Corporations Law. The relevant insider trading laws are discussed at 4 *below*.

2.2.2 Prohibitions on securities

The prohibitions in s 1002G(2) on insider trading and procuring another person to trade apply to both listed and unlisted securities. The prohibition on communication of price-sensitive information (the 'tipping' offence) applies only where trading in the securities is permitted on the stock market of one of the securities exchanges listed in Table (1) *below*, even though such trading may be temporarily suspended (s 1002D(1)).

TABLE (1)

Australian Stock Exchange Ltd
Australian Stock Exchange (Adelaide) Ltd
Australian Stock Exchange (Brisbane) Ltd
Australian Stock Exchange (Hobart) Ltd
Australian Stock Exchange (Melbourne) Ltd
Australian Stock Exchange (Perth) Ltd
Australian Stock Exchange (Sydney) Ltd
The Stock Exchange of Bendigo Ltd
The Stock Exchange of Ballarat Ltd
The Stock Exchange of Newcastle Ltd
Any other body approved by the Minister as a stock exchange or securities organisation. To date, the only approved securities organisation is the Australasian Bloodstock Exchange Ltd.

2.3 WHAT IS INSIDER INFORMATION?

The major difference between the insider trading laws in force prior to 1 August 1991 and those presently contained in Part 7.11 is their approach to the identification of an 'insider'. It was previously the case that the insider must be 'connected' with the body corporate in some way (eg a director). Under the new regime, a person is an insider solely by reason of possessing price-sensitive information and being aware of the character of the information.

2.4 WHO IS AN INSIDER?

2.4.1 The definition

A person is an insider if:

(1) he possesses information that is not generally available but, if the information were generally available, a reasonable person would expect it to have a material effect on the price or value of securities of a body corporate; and
(2) the person knows, or ought reasonably to know, that:
   (a) the information is not generally available; and
   (b) if it were generally available, it might have a material effect on the price or value of those securities.

It can be seen that the determination of whether or not a person is an insider involves both an objective assessment of the price-sensitivity of the information (item (1)) and a subjective assessment of the person's state of knowledge (item (2)).

In relation to the first objective test, s 1002C provides some guidance. It provides that a reasonable person would be taken to expect information to have a material effect on the price or value of securities if the information would, or would be likely to, influence persons who commonly invest in securities in deciding whether or not to subscribe for, buy or sell the securities. A criticism of this definition is that it involves a shift from the test of 'materiality' to a test of whether the information has *influence* or not. For example, information that the government is reviewing taxation concessions available for research and development might cause a potential investor in a technology company to 'wait and see' (ie it could affect his decision whether or not to buy those securities at that time), even though the information may not affect the price of the technology company's securities in a significant way.

The 'influence' test set out in s 1002C does not apply to the subjective limb of the 'insider' definition. In order to satisfy that definition it must be shown that the person knew or ought reasonably to have known that the information was not generally available and, if it were generally available, it *might* have had a material effect on the price or value of those securities. A criticism of this limb of the test is that the use of the expression 'might' rather than 'would' lowers the threshold of knowledge which must exist.

2.4.2 What is information?

Section 1002A(1) sets out an inclusive definition of 'information'. Information includes:

(1) matters of supposition and other matters that are insufficiently definite to warrant being made known to the public; and
(2) matters relating to the intentions, or likely intentions, of a person.

This is a very wide definition. Unlike the recommendations of the Griffiths Committee, there is no requirement that the information be derived from within a company. Nor is there any requirement that the information be precise or specific.

It has been held that knowledge that directors of a company had given consideration to making a call on contributing shares and had resolved not to make a decision for the time being constituted information (*Commissioner for Corporate Affairs v Green* [1978] VR 505). It has also been said that a person possesses information if he has been informed of something the truth of which he neither knows nor cares about (*Hooker Investments Pty Ltd v Baring Bros Halkerston & Partners Securities Ltd* (1986) 10 ACLR 462). It seems that hints and rumours, even those of apparently little foundation, may constitute 'information' (*ICAL Ltd v County Natwest Securities Aust Ltd* (1988) 13 ACLR 129).

Knowledge that a major shareholder intends to retain his shares for one year may constitute 'information'. On the other hand, the knowledge that a person proposes to enter into, or has previously entered into, transactions in relation to securities of a particular company does not preclude that person subsequently dealing in those securities (ss 1002P–R, discussed at 2.7.6 *below*). Likewise, a generalised deduction based on the facts may constitute 'information' even though it is not regarded as specific information (*Ryan v Triguboff* [1976] 1 NSWLR 588).

Although the definition of 'information' is surprisingly wide, its impact is lessened to some extent by the requirement in s 1002G that the information have, or be reasonably expected to have, a material effect on the price of securities.

2.4.3 When is information generally available?

Section 1002B(2) provides that information is generally available if any of items (1), (2) or (3) *below* apply:

(1) the information consists of readily observable matter. The legislation does not provide any guidance on what constitutes 'readily observable matter', although the Explanatory Memorandum which accompanied the relevant Bill referred to it as being 'facts directly observable in the public arena'. (Regard may be had to the Explanatory Memorandum in construing the legislation by virtue of s 109J of the Corporations Law);

(2) each of the following conditions apply:

   (a) it has been made known in a manner that would, or would be likely to, bring it to the attention of persons who commonly invest in securities of bodies corporate of a kind whose price or value might be affected by the information (ie the professional investor); and

   (b) since it was so made known, a reasonable period for it to be disseminated among such persons has elapsed.

   This definition would encompass releases to the Australian Stock Exchange Ltd ('ASX'). It could be expected that such information would be absorbed rapidly and a short period only for dissemination would be required. In the case of closely held and unlisted companies, the Explanatory Memorandum stated that information must be made known to a cross section of persons who commonly invest in such securities and it is not sufficient to release it to a small section of such investors; or

(3) the information consists of deductions, conclusions or inferences made or drawn from any of the information referred to in items (1) or (2).

Problem Area 1

Conglomerate Ltd is a diversified listed company which announced at its previous annual general meeting that it was considering disposing of a major asset, its poorly performing retail food division. Jessica, an employee of Conglomerate, is aware that Conglomerate has nearly concluded confidential negotiations with Hungry Ltd for the possible sale of the food division to Hungry at a price which another employee informs her, is substantially in excess of market expectations. She is not aware of the actual price, nor the likely outcome. She instructs her broker to purchase more shares in Conglomerate, before any announcement of the sale is made.

She also tells Tom about the negotiations and the favourable price. Tom tells his broker to purchase more shares in Conglomerate immediately an announcement concerning the sale is made.

Xenia is aware from Conglomerate's annual report that Conglomerate wishes to dispose of its food division. She is also aware from public reports that Hungry has sufficient cash on hand to make a significant acquisition. She sees that Hungry has significant unused floor space in its own retail food division. She instructs her broker to purchase more shares in Conglomerate.

The knowledge that Conglomerate and Hungry are having negotiations and the favourable sale price constitute 'information', even though the outcome of the negotiations and actual sale price are not known. It seems likely that the information possessed by Jessica would be likely to materially affect the price of shares in Conglomerate and that she should be aware of the price-sensitive nature of the information (see 2.4.2). As the information was not generally available at the time Jessica instructed her broker to buy more shares (see 2.4.3), Jessica is guilty of insider trading.

Although Tom waited for a public announcement of the information to be made before he purchased shares, he may be guilty of insider trading if it can be said that he did not allow a sufficient period to elapse for the information to be disseminated among professional investors (see 2.4.3). On the other hand, the information possessed by Xenia was generally available. It involved a deduction by her based on, first, information which had been publicly known for some time and, secondly, her observation of Hungry's premises.

2.4.4 When does a person 'possess' information?

Sections 1002E and 1002F are relevant to determining whether a body corporate or a member of a partnership should be regarded as an 'insider' by reason of an officer of the body corporate or a member or an employee of the partnership being in possession of certain information. These sections contain presumptions which relate back to the first and second limbs of the test of whether or not a person is an insider under s 1002G(1) (see 2.4.1).

Section 1002E(a) provides that a body corporate is taken to possess any information which an officer of the body corporate possesses and which came into his possession in the course of his performance of duties as such an officer. The use of the word 'taken' indicates that this is an irrebuttable presumption. It is relevant to determining whether the body corporate possesses information for the purposes of the first limb of the test in s 1002G (see 2.5).

Section 1002E(b) provides that if an officer of a body corporate knows or ought reasonably to know any matter or thing because he is an officer of a body corporate, it is to be presumed that the body corporate knows or ought reasonably to know that matter or thing. This presumption appears to be rebuttable (although it is not clear what evidence would be necessary to achieve this) and is relevant to the second limb of the test in s 1002G (see 2.5).

An officer is defined in s 9 to include a director, secretary or employee of a body corporate.

These provisions raise interesting questions in the case of nominee directors. The information learned by a director who has been nominated to the board of a particular company would normally be regarded as being acquired by him in the course of performance of his duties as a director of that company, rather than the company which nominated him to the board. It may be, however, that the circumstances of his appointment require a different conclusion. For example, the Articles of Association of the company may make it clear that he is to act in the interests of his appointor, or the circumstances surrounding his appointment (eg as representative of a joint venturer on the board of directors of an incorporated joint venture) may indicate that information is learned by him in his capacity as officer of the appointor company.

Section 1002F deals with the possession of information by a member of a partnership in circumstances where another member or an employee of the partnership possesses information. It mirrors the provisions of s 1002E.

It is possible for a body corporate or a partnership to avoid the operation of these deeming provisions by establishing a 'Chinese Wall'. The requirements for such a Wall are discussed at 2.7.5.

2.5 WHAT ARE THE OFFENCES?

Section 1002G of the Corporations Law creates three offences which are described separately below.

2.5.1 Dealing

A person who is an 'insider' in relation to certain securities must not (whether as principal or agent) subscribe for, purchase or sell those securities or enter into an agreement to do any of those things (s 1002G(2)).

The prohibition on a person dealing as a 'principal' makes it clear that he cannot avoid liability by giving instructions to a nominee. Conversely, the reference to 'agent' makes it possible for a person who is aware of price-sensitive information and acts as an agent for another to be guilty of an offence, even though his principal may not be aware of the information and may have given the agent no discretion in relation to the dealing. (An exception for stockbrokers who have established appropriate Chinese Walls is discussed at 2.7.7.)

The prohibition on insider trading applies to 'persons'. The definition of 'person' in s 9 of the Corporations Law includes a body corporate and, as mentioned, in 2.4.4, s 1002E sets out various presumptions to be applied in determining whether the body corporate is an 'insider' or not. As mentioned above, this prohibition on insider trading applies to both listed and unlisted securities.

The dealing offence cannot be committed by a failure to deal. Accordingly, a person who had issued instructions to his stockbroker to sell securities at a particular price and then learned information which would substantially increase the price of those securities may cancel the unexecuted order without contravening s 1002G(2).

TABLE (2)

> *Constituent elements for dealing offence:*
> - The person (individual or body corporate) must possess information which would be likely to influence dealing by investors (objective test) (see 2.4).
> - The person should reasonably know that the information is not generally available and might have a material effect on the price of securities (subjective test) (see 2.4).
> - The person must as principal or agent subscribe for, purchase or sell the securities or enter into an agreement to do so (see 2.5.1).

2.5.2 Procuring dealing

Section 1002G(2)(b) prohibits an insider (whether as principal or agent) procuring another person to subscribe for, purchase or sell the relevant securities or to enter into an agreement to do these things.

The normal meaning of 'procure' would involve some concept of a person intentionally causing another to do an act. Section 1002D(2) considerably expands this meaning. It provides that, in addition to its normal meaning, a person 'procures' an act if he 'incites, induces or encourages the act'.

A person may be guilty of the 'procurement' offence even though his actions do not cause another to deal in securities, but he has merely encouraged an action. Similarly, he could be guilty of the procurement offence if he is aware of inside information and encourages another to purchase securities even though he has not been motivated by the inside information (eg he may believe that irrespective of the inside information, the securities would form part of a balanced portfolio).

The procurement offence does not require that the insider disclose the inside information to the other person or that he indicate that he is aware of any price-sensitive information. A wink may be enough. As with the offence of insider trading, the offence of 'procuring' may be committed by bodies corporate. It also relates to both listed and unlisted securities.

TABLE (3)

> *Constituent elements for procuring offence:*
> - The person (individual or body corporate) must possess information which would be likely to influence dealing by investors (objective test) (see 2.4).
> - The person should reasonably know that the information is not generally available and might have a material effect on the price of securities (subjective test) (see 2.4).
> - The person must incite, induce or encourage another person to subscribe for, purchase or sell securities or to enter into agreement to do so (see 2.5.2).

2.5.3 Communication

The communication ('tipping') offence applies to listed securities only. The rationale for this is contained in the Griffiths Committee Report. It expressed the view that shareholders in proprietary companies were generally better informed and had easier access to information than shareholders of listed companies, and that restrictions are generally placed on the transfer of shares in proprietary companies. In view of the increased disclosure requirements now imposed on listed companies this distinction no longer seems appropriate.

The 'communication' offence is committed where an insider communicates price-sensitive information to another and knows or ought reasonably to know that the other person would be likely to deal in the securities or procure another person to do so (s 1002G(3)). The offence is not committed by the mere communication of price-sensitive information. It is an essential element of the offence that the insider know that the recipient of the information is likely to deal in the securities.

The offence does not require that the 'tippee' purchase shares from a third party. The offence may be committed where the recipient intends to purchase shares from the 'tipper' himself. It may seem an unfair result that an insider who makes full disclosure to the other parties to the proposed dealing would be guilty of the 'communication' offence, even though he would avoid the 'trading' offence by reason of all parties being fully informed (see 2.7.8). If s 1002G(3) does apply in this manner, the justification for its operation may lie in the view that no person should be allowed to deal at a time when investors at large do not have access to the information (even if the parties to the particular transaction are not disadvantaged in any way).

The 'communication' offence may also prevent a company disclosing price-sensitive information to a potential subscriber for shares (although there is an exemption for disclosure to underwriters discussed at 2.7.2 *below*). It may also prevent a company which is subject to a take-over bid disclosing price-sensitive information to a potential rival bidder for the purpose of eliciting a higher offer for its shares. In these situations, there is a conflict between the insider trading laws and the fiduciary duties of company directors. In one case where this conflict was considered (*ICAL v County Natwest Securities Aust Ltd* (1988) 13 ACLR 129) the court refused to grant an injunction to restrain target company directors disclosing price-sensitive information for the purpose of promoting interest in the company's shares.

In *Exicom v Futuris* the court held however, that the company itself cannot be an insider. It is unclear whether this view will prevail. It would be advisable for a target company which is proposing to disclose information to a potential bidder to obtain an undertaking from that bidder that it will not deal in the relevant shares until the information has become public. The target company can then argue that it ought not reasonably have known that the recipient of the information would be likely to deal in the securities.

TABLE (4)

Constituent elements for communication offence:
• The person (individual or body corporate) must possess information which would be likely to influence dealing by investors (objective test) (see 2.4).
• The person should reasonably know that the information is not generally available and might have a material effect on the price of securities (subjective test) (see 2.4).

> • The person must know or ought reasonably to know that the recipient
>   of the information is likely to either deal in securities or procure
>   another person to do so (see 2.5.3).

Problem Area 2

> Hector is an employee of an accountancy firm. He needs cash in order
> to buy a house and resolves to sell all of his shares and instructs his
> broker accordingly. His portfolio includes shares in Shaky Ltd, a listed
> public company. Before the sales are executed, Hector learns, in the
> course of his duties, that a receiver is about to be appointed to Shaky.
> He advises his friend Ingrid, who also holds shares in Shaky, that she
> should dispose of those shares although he does not provide any details.
> He tells another friend Callum, who was considering buying shares in
> Shaky, not to do so and, when Callum asks for an explanation, tells him
> the reason.
>
> Hector is guilty of insider trading because he sold shares in Shaky at a
> time when he was an 'insider' (ie in possession of price-sensitive infor-
> mation and aware of the character of the information), even though he
> had already decided on that course prior to learning the information
> (see 2.5.1). He is also guilty of procuring Ingrid to deal in those securities
> (see 2.5.2). He is not guilty of the communication offence, because
> although he has provided full details to Callum, he has not encouraged
> Callum to deal in the securities (rather he has encouraged him not to deal)
> (see 2.5.3).

2.6 WHAT IS THE TERRITORIAL SCOPE OF THE INSIDER TRADING PROVISIONS?

Section 1002 sets out the territorial limits of the application of Division 2A, Part
7.11 of the Corporations Law.

TABLE (5)

> *The insider trading laws apply to:*
> • Acts within Australia in relation to securities of any body
>   corporate, whether formed or carrying on business in Australia or
>   not.
> • Acts outside Australia in relation to securities of a body corporate
>   that is formed or carries on business in Australia.

Problem Area 3

> Athena, a resident of Greece, has price-sensitive information in relation to Multi-national Plc, a company incorporated in United Kingdom and whose shares are listed on the London Stock Exchange. Multi-national Plc carries on business in Australia and is registered as a foreign company in Australia. Athena instructs her London stockbroker to acquire more shares in Multi-national Plc on her behalf in contravention of the Corporations Law.
>
> Athena will be guilty of the insider trading offence, notwithstanding that the relevant actions all occurred outside Australia. It is sufficient that Multi-national Plc carried on business in Australia for Athena's actions to fall within the ambit of the Australian insider trading laws (see 2.6).

2.7 WHAT ARE THE DEFENCES?

It will be apparent from the above that the Australian insider trading laws are drafted very widely. In particular, the deeming provisions with respect to bodies corporate and partnerships could produce unfair and unintended results. Part 7.11 contains a number of exceptions and defences to ameliorate these possible effects.

Each of these exceptions and defences is discussed below. It should be noted that although a number of the exceptions appear to operate as a qualification on whether or not a contravention has occurred, they are in fact defences (s 1002T(1)). In other words, it is not necessary for the prosecution to prove the non-existence of the circumstances to be discussed below, but it is a defence if the court is satisfied that those circumstances existed.

2.7.1 Redemption under a buy-back covenant

A trustee who re-purchases prescribed interests in accordance with a buy-back covenant contained in the relevant deed does not contravene the prohibitions on insider trading or procuring, provided that the price to be paid is calculated, so far as reasonably practicable, by reference to the underlying assets of the enterprise (s 1002H). The reference to 'so far as reasonably practicable' is intended to allow for the lags which may occur where the buy-back price is adjusted on a periodic basis.

2.7.2 Underwriters

This is an unusual exception and appears to run counter to the spirit of the entire insider trading legislation. Section 1002J provides that an underwriter or sub-underwriter does not contravene the prohibitions on insider trading or procuring if he subscribes for securities, or has entered an agreement to do so, pursuant to an underwriting agreement or sub-underwriting agreement. The sale of securities subscribed for under such an agreement is also exempted. Although there may be some justification for permitting underwriters and sub-underwriters to subscribe for shares while they are in possession of price-sensitive information, it is difficult to devise any justification for permitting those underwriters and sub-underwriters to engage in insider trading by on-selling those shares.

Section 1002J(2) also contains exceptions from the communication offence in the context of an underwriting agreement. It provides that the communication offence is not committed where:

(1)   Information is communicated solely for the purpose of procuring the recipient to enter into an underwriting agreement in relation to the relevant securities. This would apply to disclosure of price-sensitive information by the company to an underwriter; or

(2)   The information is communicated by a person who may be required under an underwriting agreement to subscribe for the relevant securities and the communication is made solely for the purpose of procuring another person to either enter into an underwriting agreement in relation to the securities or to subscribe for the securities. This leaves in a difficult position a person who is not an underwriter or sub-underwriter but who has subscribed for securities after hearing the price-sensitive information. That person will not be able to dispose of the securities until the information has become generally available.

The government has acknowledged that these underwriting exceptions are unusual and has stated that it will maintain a 'watching brief' in relation to their operation.

Problem Area 4

Expansive Ltd is a listed public company which wishes to raise more capital. It decides to make an issue of shares to the public, to be underwritten by Gamble Ltd. During due diligence, Gamble becomes aware that an important government licence granted to Expansive may not be renewed. Gamble decides to proceed with the underwriting and also enters into a sub-underwriting agreement with Risky Ltd, after informing it of the information. Risky sells the shares allocated to it under the sub-underwriting agreement, before the information becomes public.

Gamble also recommends to one of its clients, Claire, that Claire subscribe for securities in Expansive and informs Claire of the possible non-renewal of the government licence.

Gamble's conduct in communicating the information to Risky and Claire is not a contravention of the communication offence, by virtue of the defence in s 1002J(2). Nor does the sale of shares by Risky constitute insider trading, by virtue of the defence in s 1002J(1). On the other hand, Claire cannot sell her shares in Expansive until the information has either become public or unless the potential purchaser already knows the relevant information (see 2.7.2).

(There would also be significant issues about the adequacy of Expansive's prospectus.)

2.7.3 Purchase pursuant to a legal requirement

The prohibitions on insider trading and procuring do not apply in respect of the purchase of securities pursuant to a requirement imposed by the Corporations Law (s 1002K). The Explanatory Memorandum stated that this is intended to apply to schemes of arrangement, reconstructions and take-overs where dissenting shareholders may compel a body corporate to acquire their shares.

2.7.4 Information communicated pursuant to a legal requirement

Section 1002L provides that the communication offence does not apply in respect of the communication of information pursuant to a requirement imposed by the Commonwealth, a state or a territory or any regulatory authority. The Explanatory Memorandum indicated that communication pursuant to a legal requirement to the ASC or the ASX would be exempted by this section.

2.7.5 Chinese Walls

As mentioned at 2.4.4, the erection of a Chinese Wall by a body corporate or a member of partnership may provide a defence to the insider trading and procuring offences.

TABLE (6)

Constituent elements of a Chinese Wall for bodies corporate (s1002M):
• The decision to enter into the transaction must be taken by a person other than the officer who possesses the inside information.
• The body corporate must have in operation arrangements that could reasonably be expected to ensure the information was not communicated to the persons who made the decision and that no advice with respect to the transaction was given by the insider officer.
• The information was not communicated and no advice was given.

Section 1002N contains a mirror provision in respect of members of a partnership. In addition, s 1002N(2) provides that a partner who is deemed to possess inside information, by reason of another partner or an employee possessing that information, does not contravene the prohibitions on insider trading or procuring if he enters into a transaction otherwise than on behalf of the partnership. This prevents an inadvertent contravention of the insider trading laws by a partner who trades on his own account and is not aware of the inside information.

Problem Area 5

Battery Ltd is a listed public company which makes car batteries. It has two major shareholders, Investor Ltd and Consultant Ltd. A director of Investor, Charles, is also director of Battery. Consultant provides environmental advisory services to Battery through one of Consultant's senior employees, George.

At a Board meeting of Battery, Charles learns that Battery has been served with an unexpected environmental clean-up notice which will require expenditure of significant sums of money. George learns the same information in the course of Consultant providing services to Battery. Neither Charles nor George informs Investor or Consultant of the information.

Could Investor or Consultant sell their shares in Battery prior to the information becoming public?

Because Charles learned the relevant information in his capacity as a director of Battery, Investor should not be deemed by s 1002E to possess the information. Accordingly, Investor may sell its shares (see 2.4.4).

On the other hand, George learned the information in the course of performance of his duties as an employee of Consultant. If Consultant wishes to sell its shares, it must ensure that the decision to sell is taken by persons who do not include George and must have in place arrangements to ensure that George cannot communicate the price-sensitive information to those who take the decision (see 2.7.5).

2.7.6 Knowledge of one's own intentions

A natural person is not precluded from dealing in securities of a body corporate by reason only that he is aware that he proposes to enter into, or has previously entered into, a transaction in relation to securities of the same body corporate (s 1002P). This exception is confined to knowledge about one's own intentions and past activities in relation to *securities* of the body corporate. A person who has entered into or proposes to enter into a transaction involving other assets of the body corporate (eg a person who proposes to acquire a major asset from the body corporate) may be regarded as having price-sensitive information and precluded from dealing in that body corporate's securities.

There is a similar exemption in s 1002Q for knowledge by a body corporate of its own intentions. Officers and agents who enter into transactions on behalf of a body corporate are likewise protected under s 1002R.

Problem Area 6

Construction Ltd is a supplier of building products and a listed public company. Some time ago it was granted an option by Cement Ltd to acquire Cement's cement division on terms which now appear favourable to Construction and unfavourable to Cement. Construction's board has resolved to exercise the option, but before Construction notifies Cement of this decision, Construction sells its shareholding in Cement. Construction also intends to make a take-over bid for one of its competitors, Developer Ltd, and commences purchasing small parcels of shares in Developer with a view to establishing a 'platform' to stage a bid.

Construction is guilty of insider trading in relation to the disposal of shares in Cement. Although the knowledge possessed by Construction related only to its own intention to exercise its option to buy the cement business, that intention did not relate to securities of Cement. On the other hand, Construction's purchase of a platform of shares in Developer does not constitute insider trading because Construction's intention to make a take-over bid for Developer relates to securities of Developer and the defence in s 1002Q applies (see 2.7.6).

2.7.7 Chinese Walls for dealers

As mentioned at 2.5.1, the prohibition on insider trading extends to persons acting as agents. The deeming provisions in ss 1002E and 1002F (relating to possession of information by bodies corporate and partnerships) could therefore expose innocent brokers acting on client's instructions to liability for insider trading. This is a particular problem for stockbroking firms with advisory arms which may have access to price-sensitive information.

Section 1002S contains a defence where a Chinese Wall has been erected by the holder of a dealer's licence. The exception applies where the holder of a dealer's licence or one of its representatives ('broker') has entered into a transaction on the specific instructions of its principal and a Chinese Wall was in place at that time which ensured that the price-sensitive information was not communicated to the agent. It must also be shown that the principal was not an associate of the licence holder or any of its representatives.

In addition, Rule 3.5(2) of the Business Rules of the ASX provides that a broker which is in possession of price-sensitive information as a result of its relationship to a client must not give any advice to any other client of a nature that would prejudice the interests of either of those clients. Rule 3.5(3) provides that a broker is not regarded as being in possession of information if a Chinese Wall has been established and the person giving the advice is not in possession of the information. In order to rely on this Business Rule, the broker must not only establish a Chinese Wall in accordance with the ASX's guidelines, but notify the ASX that it has done so and require the ASX to place its name on a public register of brokers maintaining such walls.

2.7.8 Knowledge of other party

Subsections 1002T(2) and (3) contain defences to the insider trading, procuring and communication offences where the other party to the transaction was already aware of the information. The defences apply where:

(1) The recipient was already aware of the information as a result of it being made known in a manner that would, or would be likely to, bring it to the attention of persons who commonly invest in the relevant securities. This would apply, for example, to a person who becomes aware of information as a result of its release to the ASX. There is no requirement that a reasonable period elapse for the information to be disseminated. The defence would not be applicable, however, to a person who was aware of the information prior to its public announcement and who sought to exploit it by trading immediately after the information was announced. The defence is intended to protect the diligent investor who relies on publicly available information.

(2) The other party to the transaction or communication knew, or ought reasonably to have known, the information.

Problem Area 7

Trader Ltd and Investor Ltd each hold 30 per cent of the shares in Blue Chip Ltd, a listed public company. Trader and Investor decide that they will dispose of their shareholdings to a single purchaser. A director of Trader, Sandy, tells his brother, John, that Trader and Investor are intending to sell their shares. Sandy is not aware that John holds any shares in Blue Chip. John immediately instructs his stockbroker to sell his shares on market (and before any public announcement of the proposed joint sale is made).

The information that each of Trader and Investor intends to sell its shares is price-sensitive. Although Trader is aware that Investor intends to sell its shares, and vice versa, neither will commit the insider trading offence because the other party to the transaction, the purchaser, is also aware of the information (see 2.7.8).

Although Sandy communicated price-sensitive information to John, he would not be guilty of the communication offence unless he knew, or ought reasonably to have known, that John would deal in Blue Chip shares. This does not appear to be the case. John, however, would be guilty of insider trading because he sold his shares prior to the information becoming generally available (see 2.5.1).

(Sandy's conduct is probably a breach of his fiduciary duty to Trader and actionable separately.)

2.7.9 Other exemptions

Regulation 7.11.01 of the Corporations Regulations contains exemptions to the insider trading and procuring offences for certain 'justifiable' transactions. These include a director obtaining a share qualification, acquisitions of shares in a company by trustees of an employee pension or superannuation fund, transactions that are entered into by a personal representative or liquidator or a sale of securities under a mortgage.

TABLE (7)

Defences	Dealing	Procuring	Communication
1. Buy-back covenant	•	•	
2. Underwriters	•	•	•
3. Legal requirement	•	•	•
4. Chinese Wall	•	•	
5. Knowledge of own intentions	•	•	
6. Information made known in a manner likely to bring it to professional investor's attention	•	•	•
7. Information known, or ought reasonably to be known, by other party	•	•	•
8. Justifiable transactions	•	•	

2.8 WHAT ARE THE PENALTIES AND CONSEQUENCES OF INSIDER TRADING?

2.8.1 Criminal liability

A natural person who contravenes insider trading laws is liable to a penalty of $200,000 (approximately £98,000 STG) or imprisonment for five years or both (Sched 3 of the Corporations Law). A body corporate is liable to a fine of five times the maximum amount which may be imposed on a natural person (ie $1 million (approximately £490,000 STG)). At the time these penalty levels were introduced, the government indicated that it was conscious that they were high but stated that it was necessary to send a very clear signal to the market that insider trading would not be tolerated. As there have not been any successful convictions under these insider trading provisions, it is not possible to predict how courts will approach sentencing issues.

2.8.2 ENFORCEABILITY OF TRANSACTIONS INVOLVING A CONTRAVENTION

It appears that transactions entered into in contravention of the insider trading laws are not void from the beginning, but may be voidable at the option of the purchaser (*Singh v Crafter* (1992) 10 ACLC 1,365).

Under the Corporations Law, the court also has wide powers to make orders in proceedings relating to a contravention of insider trading laws. Such orders may include a declaration that a contract for purchase or sale of securities is void or voidable (ss 1114 and 1325).

2.8.3 Civil liability

Section 1005 affords a civil right of action to a person who has suffered loss or damage by reason of conduct in contravention of the insider trading laws. It is not necessary, as a matter of law, that the insider trader be first convicted before the innocent party can exercise his civil rights. It is sufficient for the innocent party to show on the balance of probabilities that a contravention has occurred (s 1332). Any such action must be commenced within six years after the date that the cause of action arose.

Section 1013 appears to set out a statutory formula for calculating the damages which an innocent party can recover in respect of the insider trading or procuring offences (except in the case of option contracts). Subsections 1013(2) and (4) provide that the innocent party who was not aware of the inside information may recover from the insider trader as a loss suffered by him the difference between the price at which the securities were bought or sold and the price at which they would have been likely to be bought or sold had the information been generally available. Recovery by the innocent party under these provisions does not require that he suffer any actual loss. An innocent party who purchased shares from an insider trader could theoretically recover the statutory loss even though he decided to retain his shares and ultimately made a profit on their sale. An innocent party may encounter significant practical difficulties in identifying the insider trader in an on-market transaction in an actively traded stock (because, for example, the Business Rules of the ASX allow brokers a discretion in the allocation of securities to clients).

In addition to the innocent party's right of action, the body corporate may institute an action and recover the amount of the statutory loss from the insider (s 1013(5)). Section 1015(1) sets out a 'first come first served' principle which is intended to avoid the insider being liable for the same amount to various persons under these provisions.

In the case of a subscription for securities by an insider, the body corporate may recover as a loss the deficiency between the price at which the securities were subscribed for and the price at which they would have been likely to have been sold in a sale made at the time of the subscription if the information had been generally available (s 1013(2)). Accordingly, the company could recover the statutory loss from the insider in circumstances where the company was aware of the price-sensitive information but other investors were not.

The ASC is also empowered, if it considers that it is in the public interest to do so, to bring an action in the name of the body corporate to recover amounts which the body corporate is entitled to recover under these provisions (s 1013(6)).

It is a defence to civil liability under s 1013 if the insider trader establishes that he became aware of the relevant information solely as a result of it being made known in a manner that would be likely to bring it to the attention of professional investors (s 1013(7)).

Section 1013 does not prescribe the amounts recoverable in respect of insider trading in relation to option contracts (possibly because of difficulties in quantification) or in respect of the 'communication' offence. Accordingly, the innocent party must prove his actual loss or damage in respect of insider trading in such securities in an action under s 1005 (s 1013(9)).

2.8.4 Court orders

In addition to the criminal and civil liabilities which may be attracted by a contravention of the Corporations Law, various additional orders may be made by a Supreme Court or Federal Court. These include orders restraining the exercise of various rights attached to the securities (for example, voting rights) or restraining the acquisition or disposal of securities or vesting the securities in the ASC (s 1002U).

Further, the Corporations Law sets out a variety of orders which may be made in relation to securities offences generally. These include injunctions and orders for compensation, as well as orders varying a contract or refusing to enforce any or all of its provisions (ss 1324 and 1325).

3 OTHER REGULATION

3.1 INTRODUCTION

Insider trading is only possible where the market has not been kept fully informed. There has been considerable discussion in Australia in recent years about the extent of disclosure obligations which should be imposed on companies and whether the ASX or ASC is the appropriate body to administer and enforce such obligations. The end result is that the principle of continuous disclosure continues to be embodied in the Listing Rules of the ASX. These obligations are backed up by sanctions in the Corporations Law for companies which have intentionally or recklessly failed to comply with these obligations. In addition, s 776(2A) requires the ASX to inform the ASC if it believes that a person is committing or about to commit a serious contravention of the ASX's Business Rules or Listing Rules.

The ASC and ASX have also executed a Memorandum of Understanding relating to surveillance of listed companies and compliance with the disclosure requirements of the Listing Rules. The Memorandum also sets out a mechanism for exchange of information between the two organisations.

In addition to the continuous disclosure obligations, there are various specific obligations in the Listing Rules and Corporations Law which apply in certain circumstances. A number of these are discussed below.

3.2 AUSTRALIAN STOCK EXCHANGE LTD

3.2.1 Applying for an Australian Listing

The ASX is an incorporated body which operates nationally. Its subsidiaries are Australian Stock Exchange (Adelaide) Ltd, Australian Stock Exchange (Brisbane) Ltd, Australian Stock Exchange (Hobart) Ltd, Australian Stock Exchange (Melbourne) Ltd, Australian Stock Exchange (Perth) Ltd and Australian Stock Exchange (Sydney) Ltd.

Companies may be listed on the ASX and applications for admission are considered by its National Listing Committee. A company which is listed is required to comply with the continuous disclosure requirements and must provide any releases or explanations to its home exchange (being one of the local subsidiaries) designated by the ASX.

Admission to the Official List of the ASX is at the ASX's discretion. The application for admission requires that certain information concerning the company's previous financial results and capital structure be disclosed. There is no general requirement that price-sensitive information be disclosed as part of the application for listing. Most companies, however, will be listed as a result of shares being issued pursuant to a prospectus which is lodged or registered under the Corporations Law. Section 1022 of that law requires that the prospectus contain all such information as investors and their professional advisers would reasonably require, or reasonably expect to find in the prospectus, for the purpose of making an informed assessment of:

- the assets and liabilities, financial position, profits and losses, and prospects of the corporation; and
- the rights attaching to the securities.

3.2.2 Continuing obligations

The most fundamental rule to the operation of the ASX is Listing Rule 3A(1) which forms the basis of the continuous disclosure regime. It places the onus on the company and those managing it to determine what information should be released to the market and to ensure its timely release. A listed company must immediately notify the exchange of any information concerning the company of which it becomes aware and which a reasonable person would expect to have a material effect on the price or value of securities of the company. The company is deemed to be aware of information if a director or executive officer has, or ought reasonably to have, come into the possession of information in the course of performance of his duties as a director or executive officer.

It may of course be commercially prejudicial to a company to be required to make an immediate announcement of price-sensitive information (for example, a mining company which has discovered a very promising prospect but not yet applied for the necessary tenement). Accordingly, there are some exceptions to the disclosure requirement.

TABLE (8)

The disclosure requirement does not apply for so long as each of the following conditions remains satisfied:
(1) A reasonable person would not expect the information to be disclosed.
(2) The information is confidential.
(3) One or more of the following conditions apply:
    (a) it would be breach of a law to disclose the information;
    (b) the information is, or is part of, an incomplete proposal or negotiation;
    (c) the information comprises matters of supposition or is insufficiently definite to warrant disclosure;
    (d) the information is generated for the internal management purposes of the company; or
    (e) the information is a trade secret.

In addition to this general disclosure obligation, there are specific disclosure obligations in relation to significant transactions, dividend announcements, communications from the Commissioner of Taxation disallowing deductions, options to acquire mining tenements, winding-up applications or appointments of receivers and so on. Listed companies must also provide a half-yearly report to the exchange and a preliminary final statement after the end of each financial year and immediately figures are available. Mining companies are also required to provide quarterly reports.

There are several procedures in the Business Rules of the ASX which enable the company to warn the market that an announcement is pending. A company may notify the market that an announcement is imminent. A Notice Pending (NP) tag is then placed against the company's securities and the market is placed in the Pre-Opening Phase for a period of ten minutes. During this period, transactions cannot be effected, although bids and offers for the company's securities may be entered or cancelled. After this period of ten minutes, normal trading resumes.

A related, although different, procedure is a trading halt. Under Business Rule 2.6(9) a company may request a temporary trading halt in its securities and, if the ASX agrees, the securities will be placed in the Pre-Opening Phase (allowing bids and offers to be entered or cancelled).

A trading halt may last for up to 24 hours or such longer period as the ASX agrees. The ASX has stated that it is appropriate to seek a trading halt in circumstances where:

- there is sufficient speculation about the company to warrant a response by it to the market but the company considers that it is not able to make the information available immediately;
- the company is about to make an announcement but is not able to make it immediately; or
- share price or trading enquiries have been made by the ASX and the company is unable to reply in the time specified.

A request for a trading halt must explain the reasons why it is made and the request will be released to the market unless the company is able to convince the ASX otherwise. If the request for a trading halt is not granted, the company may wish to consider seeking a suspension of the quotation of its securities. This results in all bids and offers in place being removed and no new bids or offers being made during the period of suspension.

The operation of the Listing Rules is underpinned by various provisions of the Corporations Law. In particular, s 1001A provides that it is an offence for a company to intentionally or recklessly contravene a Listing Rule which imposes disclosure obligations on it.

In addition, s 777 empowers a court to make an order compelling compliance with the Listing Rules in certain circumstances and s 1114 empowers the court to make a wide variety of orders where a person has contravened the Listing Rules.

3.2.3 Sanctions

Under the contract constituted by acceptance of a company's application for admission to the Official List of the ASX, the ASX may remove a company from the Official List or suspend its securities from Official Quotation if the company fails to comply with the Listing Rules. Suspension of a company's securities from Official Quotation is the usual sanction where the ASX believes that the market is not fully informed. Suspension usually occurs after a period of some communication and correspondence between the company and the exchange.

3.3 TAKE-OVER LAWS

The making of take-over offers for public (and some other) companies is governed by Chapter 6 of the Corporations Law. The philosophy behind the legislation is to be found in a report published in 1969 by the Company Law Advisory Committee (known as 'the Eggleston Committee'). That Committee identified four principles which were necessary to safeguard shareholders. One of these principles was that the offeror be 'required to give such information as is necessary to enable the shareholders to form a judgment on the merits of the proposal and, in particular, where the offeror offers shares or interests in a corporation, that the kind of information which would ordinarily be provided in a prospectus is furnished to the offeree shareholders'.

The other principles required equality of opportunity among shareholders, that shareholders and directors have a reasonable time in which to consider the proposal and that the identity of the offeror be known to shareholders and directors.

These themes recur throughout Chapter 6. For example, both the offeror and the target company directors are required to provide statements to shareholders setting out, among other things, all information material to a decision whether or not to accept the offer being information which is known to them and has not previously been disclosed to shareholders. In addition, s 731 requires the ASC to consider the Eggleston principles in deciding whether or not to grant an exception from or a modification of the operation of the take-over laws in a particular case.

A potentially significant, but rarely used, means of enforcing these principles rests with the Corporations and Securities Panel. The Panel is constituted pursuant to the Australian Securities Commission Act and its members are to be appointed by virtue of their experience in relevant areas of business, law, accounting and so on. The Panel has jurisdiction, on application of the ASC, to make a declaration that unacceptable circumstances have occurred in relation to an acquisition of shares and to then make a wide variety of orders. Unacceptable circumstances are deemed to have occurred only where there has been a failure to comply with one of the Eggleston principles. Although the Panel has had such jurisdiction for a number of years, there has only been one referral to it by the ASC. One of the difficuties with this regime is that referral can only be made by the ASC, a body with limited resources. In general, a person involved in a hostile take-over would prefer to allege that a specific provision of the Corporations Law (rather than the general Eggleston principles) has been contravened and seek to litigate the matter more speedily in the courts.

In addition to the Corporations Law, the Listing Rules require that directors of a company maintain secrecy while discussions are being conducted which may lead to an offer being made. Once the company receives a notice of intention to make a take-over bid, the company must immediately give copies of the notice to the ASX (Listing Rule 3R).

4 FUTURES

The law governing insider trading in futures is set out in Division I of Part 8.7 of the Corporations Law. The lack of uniformity between the insider trading laws governing futures and those governing other securities does not appear to be intentional. It is a result of the amalgamation of the Futures Industry Codes governing futures, and Securities Industries Codes (governing other securities) into the Corporations Law in 1991. Although it was suggested in the Explanatory Memorandum which introduced the new Part 7.11 into the Corporations Law that the futures insider trading provisions would be reviewed with a view to enacting uniform laws, no amendments have yet been made.

Part 8.7 applies to a futures contract which 'concerns' securities of a body corporate only. This is a futures contract which is:

- a commodity agreement and a commodity to which it relates is securities of a body corporate; or
- an adjustment agreement and a state of affairs to which it relates concerns the price of securities of a body corporate, or the prices of a class of securities that includes the securities of the body corporate, at a particular time.

The Sydney Futures Exchange Ltd presently offers futures contracts over shares in several leading Australian companies.

The ASX has also developed a new derivative product called a 'Share Ratio Contract'. This product compares the performance of individual shares to the All Ordinaries index. Although the product would normally fall within the definition of a 'futures contract', the Corporations Regulations prescribe that Division 2A of Part 7.11 governs insider trading in such products.

Part 8.7 operates by prohibiting a natural person from dealing in a futures contract concerning a body corporate if by virtue of being, or having been at any time during the previous six months, connected with a body corporate, the person has inside information in relation to the relevant futures contract. A person is regarded as 'connected' with the body corporate if he:

(1) is an officer (which includes director, secretary or employee) of the body corporate or of a related body corporate;
(2) is a substantial shareholder (ie entitled to more than 5 per cent of the voting shares) in the relevant body corporate or a related body corporate;
(3) occupies a position that may reasonably expect to give him access to inside information by virtue of:
    (a) a professional or business relationship existing between him and the relevant body corporate or a related body corporate;
    (b) his being an officer of a body corporate that is a substantial shareholder in the relevant body corporate or in a related body corporate.

Sections 1253 and 1256 prohibit a natural person from dealing in a futures contract concerning a body corporate if:

(1) by virtue of being, or having been at any time during the previous six months, connected with the body corporate he has inside information in relation to

that futures contract (being information which is not generally available but, if it were generally available, would be likely to affect materially the price for dealing in that futures contract or a futures contract of the same kind);

(2) by virtue of being, or having been at any time during the previous six months, connected with another body corporate he has inside information in relation to that futures contract and the information relates to any transaction (actual or expected) involving both bodies corporate or involving one of them and securities of the other; or

(3) he has inside information in relation to that futures contract which is obtained directly or indirectly for another person in circumstances where he is aware or ought reasonably to be aware that the other person was precluded from dealing. It must also be shown that when the information was obtained from the other person, he was an associate of that other person and had an arrangement in place for the communication of information of this kind with a view to a dealing by one of them in that futures contract or futures contracts of that kind.

In addition, s 1256(2) provides that where the insider is precluded from dealing in a futures contract, he must not communicate that information to another person if he knows, or ought reasonably to know, that the other person will make use of the information for the purpose of dealing in that futures contract.

Although the primary prohibition applies to natural persons, a body corporate is precluded from dealing in a futures contract if one of its officers is precluded by ss 1253 and 1256 from dealing (s 1254(1)). There is an exception, however, where a Chinese Wall has been established (s 1254(2)).

There is also an exception for a licensed futures broker who deals on his client's specific instructions. The broker must not give any advice in relation to the dealing to the client and the client must not be an associate of the licensee in relation to the dealing (s 1255).

It can be seen that in a number of ways the restriction on insider trading in futures is more limited than that in relation to other securities. The requirement that the 'insider' be connected with the body corporate significantly reduces the scope of these provisions.

Problem Area 8

Edward is a budding investor and arranges to meet a friend in Predator Ltd's foyer. While he is waiting, he overhears two directors of Predator (whom he recognises) discussing a take-over bid for Target Ltd which is to be announced the next day. Edward immediately purchases shares in Target and Target Share Futures contracts.

Because Edward is in possession of price-sensitive information (and ought reasonably be aware that the information might have that character (see 2.4)) his purchase of shares is a contravention of Part 7.11. On the other hand, the purchase of share futures by him does not contravene Part 8.7, because he is not 'connected' with either Predator or Target. Further, he did not learn the information from an 'associate' of from a person with whom he had a 'tipping' arrangement.

Section 1257 provides that it is a defence to prosecution for insider trading in futures if it is proved that the other party to the dealing knew, or ought reasonably to have known, the information before entering into the transaction.

5 CONCLUSION

The insider trading laws in Australia are very widely drafted. They potentially apply to any person who possesses price-sensitive information and is aware of the significance of that information. Notwithstanding this broadening of the 'net', not one insider trader has yet been successfully prosecuted. This appears to be due to difficulties in detection, a reluctance to convict on the basis of circumstantial evidence and some poorly conducted prosecutions. These factors may change and the width of these provisions and the significant penalties which may be imposed should be matters of concern for the culpable insider trader.

The width of the insider trading laws means, however, that these issues often need to be considered in transactions involving corporate purchasers and vendors. Such issues often arise unexpectedly (and in circumstances which may not be intended by the legislature). These issues are also often aired during contested take-overs and may provide a basis for tactical litigation.

CASE STUDY

Splash Plc, a company listed on the Sydney Stock Exchange, manufactures rainwear and umbrellas. Alan, a weather forecaster, on discovering that there is an unseasonable amount of rain due in the next three months, instructs his broker to buy shares in Splash. Meanwhile, Charles, an analyst of the company's shares, is told in a conversation with Jeremy, one of the directors, that the Chairman is expected to be paid a salary of Aus$500,000. Charles knows from his knowledge of the Chairman's service contract (which is available for public inspection) that this salary could only be paid if the company achieved profit in excess of Aus$20 million. Charles revises his profit forecast for the company but before he publishes it he cancels instructions which he had previously given to his broker to sell his Splash shares. Charles also tells his girlfriend, Maggie, that 'things are looking up' for Splash. Maggie then buys shares in the name of her father from an old friend of hers who wanted to sell Splash shares off market to save the payment of a broker's commission. In addition, Owen, an employee of the contracting firm which cleans Splash's offices, finds a draft of the latest management figures, which demonstrate Splash's high profitability, in a wastepaper bin. He immediately buys shares.

Alan
The information possessed by Alan is 'information' within the meaning of s 1002A(1); there is no requirement that the information be specific or precise (see 2.4.2). Whether Alan is guilty of insider trading or not will depend on whether the information is 'generally available' within the meaning of s 1002B(2) (see 2.4.3). This will involve determining whether the information has been made known in a manner which would be likely to bring it to the attention of professional investors and also whether sufficient time has elapsed for the information to be disseminated among such persons. On the assumption that such professional investors would be likely to have access to the information, Alan should not be guilty of insider trading.

Jeremy
It seems fairly clear that the information possessed by Jeremy is price-sensitive and that Jeremy could reasonably be expected to know this. Jeremy will not be guilty of the communication offence unless it can be shown that he knew or ought reasonably to have known that Charles would or would be likely to deal in shares in Splash (see 2.5.3). As Charles has not dealt in the shares (rather he has cancelled an order to do so), it is unlikely that Jeremy would be convicted.

Even if Charles had instructed his broker to buy more shares in Splash, Jeremy might still argue that he provided the information to Charles in his capacity as an analyst of Splash's shares and that Jeremy did not have any knowledge or expectation that Charles would deal in the shares.

Charles
Charles is not guilty of insider trading because he has not dealt in Splash's shares (see 2.5.1).

Charles may be guilty of the 'procuring' offence if he has encouraged Maggie to buy shares (see 2.5.2). Having regard to the relatively innocuous nature of Charles's statement, it is difficult to say that the statement alone would constitute an encouragement to buy the shares. The position might be different if the statement had been accompanied by other gestures or signs.

Maggie
It seems unlikely that the information possessed by Maggie would result in her being regarded as an 'insider' (see 2.4). First, the information (Charles's remark) would not be expected to have a material effect on the price of shares in Splash and, secondly, it seems unreasonable to expect Maggie to

know that the information might have a material effect on the price of Splash's shares. If Maggie is not an 'insider' she is not precluded from dealing in Splash securities.

If the information had constituted price-sensitive information, Maggie would be guilty of insider trading because she purchased shares as an agent for her father. Section 1002G(2) prohibits insider trading as principal or agent (see 2.5.1).

Owen

The information discovered by Owen is price-sensitive. If it can be shown that Owen knew, or ought reasonably to have known, that the information was not generally available and that, if it were generally available, it might have a material effect on the price of securities, Owen would be prohibited from dealing in shares in Splash (see 2.4).

Owen's relationship to Splash, and the circumstances in which he discovered the information, are not relevant to the prohibition in s 1002G(2).

Thailand

Orawan Tejapaibul,
International Legal Counsellors Thailand Ltd, Bangkok

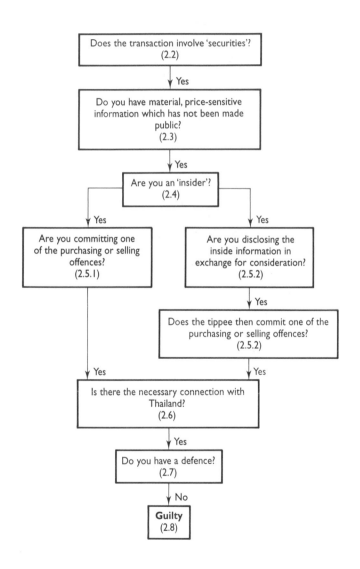

1 INTRODUCTION

The principal legislative prohibition on insider dealing in Thailand is currently set out in the Securities and Exchange Act (the 'SEC Act'), which came into force in May 1992. Under the SEC Act, a new supervisory body, the Securities and Exchange Commission (the 'SEC'), was established to oversee the development and supervision of the securities markets generally, including two aspects of unfair securities dealing practices; insider dealing and market manipulation. As of December 1994, no prosecutions for insider dealing had been brought by the SEC although one ultimately unsuccessful prosecution for market manipulation was brought in 1993. In October 1994, the SEC issued new regulations prohibiting employees of finance and securities companies from investing in their companies' shares. The SEC Act imposes both civil and criminal sanctions for the offence of insider dealing.

2 THE LAW

2.1 INTRODUCTION

The SEC Act creates two offences of insider dealing with regard to securities which are listed on the Stock Exchange of Thailand (the 'SET') or traded at an over-the-counter centre ('OTC'). The offences, which are considered in detail below (see 2.5), are insider dealing and disclosure.

2.2 TO WHICH SECURITIES DOES THE SEC ACT APPLY?

The offences set out in the SEC Act relate only to dealings in 'securities', as defined in s 4 of the SEC Act and summarised in Table (1) *below*.

TABLE (1)

Securities are:
- Treasury bills.
- Government bonds.
- Bills. Any bill issued for raising funds from the public as specified in any notification issued by the SEC (as of November 1995 no such notification had been issued).
- Shares. The SEC Act contains no indication as to whether this relates only to shares of Thai companies or whether it also includes those of foreign companies.
- Debentures. Any debt instrument of whatever name, excluding bills, divided into units, each with equal value and a predetermined rate of return, issued by any company to a lender or purchaser, representing the right of the holder of such instrument to receive money or other benefits.

- Investment units which are instruments or evidence representing rights to the property of a mutual fund.
- Certificates representing the right to purchase shares: that is, warrants to acquire shares in the issuer of the warrants.
- Certificates representing the right to purchase debentures.
- Certificates representing the right to purchase investment units.
- Any other instruments as may be specified by the SEC in the future (as of November 1995 no such instruments had been so specified).

In addition, the insider dealing offence relates only to those securities set out in Table (1) if they are listed on the SET or traded at an OTC. First OTC, the Bangkok Stock Dealing Centre (the 'BSDC') opened for business on 14 November 1995. The BSDC is expected to create a new market for trading second tier securities while the SET will accept only 'blue-chip' companies for trading.

2.3 WHAT IS INSIDE INFORMATION?

Section 241 of the SEC Act states that inside information must be information which:

- is material;
- is price-sensitive; and
- has not been made public.

These factors are not further described in the SEC Act and while they may have been judicially considered no case notes are apparently available.

2.4 WHO IS AN INSIDER?

An insider can be anyone who has access to inside information by virtue of his office or position. Section 241 of the SEC Act specifically includes those persons set out in Table (2).

TABLE (2)

- A director of a company whose securities are listed on the SET or traded on an OTC (a 'listed company').
- A manager of a listed company.
- A person responsible for the operation of a listed company.
- A person who (together with his spouse and minor children) holds securities in a listed company in an aggregate principal amount in excess of 5 per cent of that company's registered capital.
- State agency personnel, or a director, manager, or officer of the SET (who is in an office or position with access to inside information).

- Any person involved in securities and/or the trading of securities in the SEC Act or in the OTC.

It is conceivable, by virtue of the final limb of the definition of insider in Table (2) *above*, that any investor in the SET or OTC could be deemed an insider if he receives and acts upon inside information.

In theory, individuals and companies or other entities can be insiders. The definition should be regarded as a wide one, with the list set out in Table (2) not intended to be an exhaustive list of all insiders.

2.5 WHAT ARE THE OFFENCES?

2.5.1 Purchasing or selling

Section 241 of the SEC Act makes it an offence for an insider, whether directly or indirectly, which would catch dealing through a nominee or agent, to:

(1) purchase or sell; or
(2) offer to purchase or sell; or
(3) invite any other person to purchase or sell; or
(4) invite any other person to offer to purchase or sell securities in such a way as to take advantage of another person, by using inside information and whether or not such act is done for his own or another person's benefit.

So long as the dealing in question is in securities (as defined in 2.2) it does not matter whether the dealing occurs on or off-market.

In the offence, the word 'invite' should be read loosely (the Thai word can be translated in various ways, eg enlist, entice, encourage, etc). The act of passing on inside information would be an offence provided it is committed with the requisite *mens rea*, ie intentionally or recklessly, even if the insider does not receive any benefit.

There is some ambiguity in s 241 as to whether the act of purchase or sale or offer or invitation must also be 'in exchange for consideration' as for disclosure under 2.5.2 *below*.

2.5.2 Disclosure

Section 241 of the SEC Act also makes it an offence for an insider to disclose inside information in exchange for consideration to another person (who need not be an insider) who then engages in insider dealing, as described in 2.5.1 *above*.

2.5.3 Breach of secrecy

Apart from the sanctions imposed by the SEC Act, an insider may be guilty of violating s 323 of the Thai Criminal Code which deals with breach of secrecy. Under the Code it is an offence where a person, knowing of any secret information by reason of his professional practice, (eg legal counsel or accountant) discloses such information or makes use of it for his own benefit or for the benefit of other persons. This offence is punishable by a term of imprisonment of not more than six months and/or a fine of not more than 1,000 Baht (approximately £30 STG). For the purpose of this offence, secret information is defined as information available to a limited number of specific individuals through the granting of access to it by its proprietor.

2.6 WHAT IS THE TERRITORIAL SCOPE OF THE SEC ACT?

The SEC Act applies only to actions carried out within Thailand.

2.7 WHAT ARE THE DEFENCES?

There are no specific defences provided in the SEC Act.

2.8 WHAT ARE THE PENALTIES AND CONSEQUENCES OF INSIDER DEALING?

Section 296 of the SEC Act sets out the criminal sanctions for insider dealing. It provides that a person convicted of the offence can be sentenced to imprisonment for a period of not more than two years and/or a fine, not exceeding twice the gains which were received or which otherwise would have been received by the insider as a result of such insider dealing, subject to a minimum of 500,000 Baht (approximately £13,000 STG).

In addition, pursuant to s 242 of the SEC Act, the SEC has the right to claim the proceeds illegally gained by an insider from a breach of s 241 of the SEC Act. It states that 'in order that the [insider] shall not receive any benefit from contravention of the first paragraph of s 241, the SEC shall have the right to call on such person to deliver the benefit which he has gained from such trading of securities or from the disclosure of information within a six month period from the date on which he gained access to such information'.

3 NON-STATUTORY REGULATION

Neither the rules of the SET nor the take-over regulations of Thailand specifically address insider dealing.

4 CONCLUSION

The insider dealing legislation in Thailand has not been invoked very often and there is no indication that that position is likely to change in the foreseeable future. As a consequence of the lack of judicial consideration of the SEC Act, the scope of many of its provisions remain unclear.

CASE STUDY

Splash Plc, a company listed on the Stock Exchange of Thailand, manufactures rainwear and umbrellas. Alan, a weather forecaster, on discovering that there is an unseasonable amount of rain due in the next three months, instructs his broker to buy shares in Splash. Meanwhile, Charles, an analyst of the company's shares, is told in a conversation with Jeremy, one of the directors, that the President is expected to be paid a salary of $1 million. Charles knows from his knowledge of the President's service contract (which is available for public inspection) that this salary could only be paid if the company achieved profit in excess of $20 million. Charles revises his profit forecast for the company but before he publishes it he cancels instructions which he had previously given to his broker to sell his Splash shares. Charles also tells his girlfriend, Maggie, that 'things are looking up' for Splash. Maggie then buys shares in the name of her father from an old friend of hers who wanted to sell Splash shares off market to save the payment of a broker's commission. In addition, Owen, an employee of the contracting firm which cleans Splash's offices, finds a draft of the latest management figures, which demonstrate Splash's high profitability, in a wastepaper bin. He immediately buys shares.

Alan
On a strict reading of the SEC Act, Alan may be guilty of an offence in that he has information which is potentially material, price-sensitive and has not been made public. Clearly, the materiality of this information is difficult to assess and there is no reliable Thai judicial interpretation of this. As a man who has a broker, Alan is also potentially an insider, being 'any person involved in securities and/or the trading of securities on the SET' and in any event he may not have to fall into this category to be an 'insider'. It is, however, unlikely that a conviction would be secured on these facts.

Jeremy
Again the information that the President of Splash will be paid US$1 million is potentially material, price-sensitive and not public (thus 'inside'). As the disclosure was not 'for consideration', however, no offence will apparently have been committed unless it could be shown that he 'invited' Charles to purchase or sell. This would probably depend on Jeremy's *mens rea*, ie was the information passed either intentionally or recklessly? Jeremy as a director of Splash may also be guilty of an offence under the Thai Criminal Code (see 2.5.3).

Charles
The information that Charles has may be inside information but as it apparently is not obtained by virtue of his office or position (the two important elements that together constitute the 'inside information' are given to him

in a social situation (the president's salary) and public already (the president's bonus package)). If the information were seen to be 'inside' he might be caught as having 'invited' Maggie to purchase or sell.

Maggie
Although Maggie may have 'inside information', she does not have it 'by virtue of her office or position' (except on a very wide reading of this concept which it is unlikely the Thai courts would take) and it is probable that no offence has been committed.

Owen
If the information which Owen has discovered has not been published, it is likely that it is 'inside' and it is conceivably obtained 'by virtue of his office or position'. The subsequent purchase would apparently amount to an offence, irrespective of whether he is one of the persons categorised in one of the non-exclusive groups at 2.4.

PART 4

Emerging Nations

INDIA
PHILIPPINES
RUSSIAN FEDERATION
INDONESIA
CHINA

India

Dina Wadia, Little & Co, Bombay

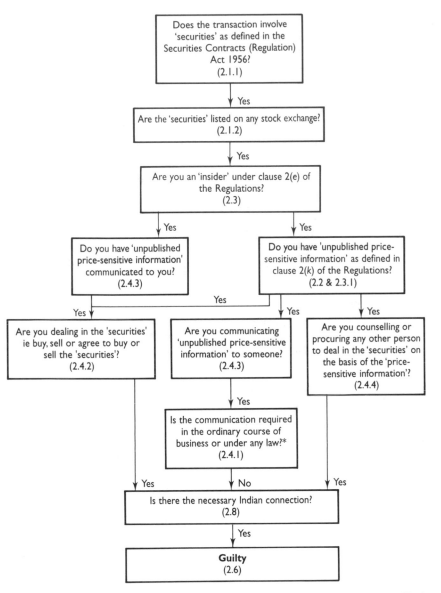

Note: If the information is communicated to a 'connected person' in the ordinary course of business or under any law there can be no offence.

1 INTRODUCTION

Despite the introduction of recent legislation, insider trading is still widely prevalent in India. In the corporate sector a fairly large number of insiders take advantage of their position to make quick returns or avoid losses. In addition, it is widely
recognised that market operators such as stockbrokers and jobbers whilst trans-
acting business for insiders also tend to trade on their own account and pass on
tips to their friends and relatives. This has the effect of increasing speculative
dealing to the detriment of the common investor and undermining the credibility
of the Indian financial market.

The principal anti-insider dealing provisions are contained in the Securities and
Exchange Board of India (Insider Trading) Regulations 1992 (the 'Regulations').
The Regulations are broadly based on the UK Companies Securities (Insider
Dealing) Act 1985 (the 'UK Act'), which was in force immediately prior to the
introduction of the Criminal Justice Act 1993. The Regulations have been recently
supplemented by the Securities Laws (Amendment) Ordinance (the 'Ordinance')
which came into force in January 1995.

Prior to the introduction of the Regulations, attempts to curb insider dealing
were done mainly through the disclosure requirements for company directors
under the Companies Act 1956 (the 'Companies Act') and the Listing Rules of
the Stock Exchanges.

Various expert committees were subsequently constituted from time to time
to review the companies legislation and market practices. These committees
recognised that insider trading was rampant in the Indian securities markets and
made several recommendations to deal with it. Unfortunately these
recommendations were not implemented.

In 1988, the Securities and Exchange Board of India ('SEBI') was constituted
initially as a department functioning under the Ministry of Finance. SEBI has been
constituted on the lines of the Securities and Exchange Commission of the United
States of America. It prepared an approach paper on comprehensive legislation
for the securities market with the objective of a healthy and orderly development
to the securities market and to ensure adequate investor protection. The aim of
SEBI's approach paper was to prevent fraudulent and unfair trade practices in the
market such as price rigging and trading on privileged and price-sensitive information. Subsequently, SEBI released, in 1991, draft Insider Trading Regulations in
which it suggested stringent measures to curb the practice of insider trading and
proposed civil and criminal sanctions for those who indulged in it. SEBI acknowledged that 'insider trading is one of the ills which plague our system today and
there is no legal provision to curb it'.

With the progressive liberalisation of the Indian economy, the capital markets
have undergone dramatic changes in terms of structure, growth and development.

In 1992 the Securities and Exchange Board of India Act (the '1992 Act') came into force by which SEBI became a statutory body with the objective of, amongst other things, regulating the capital markets and to take such measures as it would think fit with a view to protecting the interest of investors. For the first time SEBI had legal power to implement its objectives. This power has been recently supplemented by the 1995 Ordinance, whereby SEBI has been given greater powers to regulate the markets and enforce compliance.

Among the specific objectives of SEBI laid down in the 1992 Act is the power under s 11 to regulate the securities market by providing measures for prohibiting insider trading in securities (s 11(2g)). On 19 November 1992, the Regulations were notified by the government of India and came into force. For the first time, a specific offence of insider trading was created with power to impose a civil penalty as well as a criminal punishment. However, it is widely recognised that in spite of the Regulations insider trading continues to flourish in the Indian stock markets.

2 TO WHICH SECURITIES DO THE REGULATIONS APPLY?

2.1 CLAUSE 3

Clause 3 of the Regulations prohibits dealing in 'securities' by persons who are considered to be insiders on the basis of any unpublished price-sensitive information. 'Securities' are not defined in the Regulations.

2.1.1 'Securities' definition

The word 'securities' has a meaning assigned to it in the Securities Contracts (Regulation) Act 1956 (the 'Securities Act') which defines securities as including:

- shares, scrips, stocks, bonds debentures, debenture stock or other marketable securities of a like nature in or of any incorporated company or other body corporate;
- government securities;
- such other instruments as may be declared by the central government to the securities (none, as yet, have been so notified);
- rates or interest in securities (which includes warrants, share options and other rights over shares).

2.1.2 Marketable securities

There has been considerable judicial debate as to whether the phrase 'marketable securities' is to be taken to mean only listed securities or securities generally, whether listed or not. For instance, some High Courts have held that in order for a security to be marketable it must be freely transferable, a characteristic which is only to be found in securities of public companies. Shares of a private company are restricted with regard to transfer and therefore are not deemed to be marketable. In contrast, other High Courts have held that whatever is capable of being bought and sold in the market is marketable and, therefore, marketable securities would extend to all types of securities. Recently, in an unreported judgment the Bombay High Court has *prima facie* taken the view that a transaction involving the shares of a public company which is not listed on one of the exchanges is not covered by the Securities Act.

Given the recent approach taken by the Bombay High Court and the SEBI's Guidelines of Disclosure and Investor Protection issued in 1992 which were expressed as not applying to the issue of securities by private and unlisted public companies, it would seem that the term 'securities' should be limited to listed securities. In any event, the offence of dealing by insiders may only be committed where listed securities are involved.

Whether other financial instruments, other than those specifically referred to in the Securities Act, will be covered will depend on whether they are of a 'like nature' to shares, scrips, stocks, bonds, debenture or debenture stock. Accordingly, derivatives instruments such as options or warrants, giving the right to acquire or subscribe for shares would seem likely to be covered.

2.2 WHAT IS 'UNPUBLISHED PRICE-SENSITIVE INFORMATION'?

'Unpublished price-sensitive information' has been defined in cl 2(k) to mean:

> any information which relates to the following matters or is of concern, directly or indirectly, to a company, and is not generally known or published by such company for general information, but which, if published or known, is likely to materially affect the price of securities of that company in the market:
> * financial results (both half-yearly and annual of the company);
> * intended declaration of dividends (both interim and final);
> * issue of shares by way of public rights, bonus, etc;
> * any major expansion plans or execution of new projects;
> * amalgamation, mergers and take-overs;
> * disposal of the whole or substantially the whole of the undertaking;
> * such other information as may affect the earnings of the company;
> * any changes in policies, plans or operations of the company.

This is a very wide definition and, in particular, there is no requirement that the information be 'specific or precise', only that such information is of 'concern directly or indirectly to a company'. Accordingly, it would appear that information about market trends or general economic conditions could be covered and, therefore, information that the Indian economy is about to hit recession could constitute unpublished price-sensitive information about all listed companies.

In India, information would be considered to be public if it is widely disseminated among the investing public. This can be through newsletters to shareholders or periodicals or 'open briefings' to inform financial analysts and press representatives. As in the UK, information would be considered public if it is known by market professionals but since India has a very wide shareholder base, it is thought that in order for information to be considered 'public' it would have to be known to those investing shareholders generally. A movement of 5 per cent in the price of securities would probably be considered to be material.

2.3 WHO IS AN INSIDER?

2.3.1 'Insider' definition

Under cl 2(e) of the Regs, an 'insider' means any person who:

- is or was connected with the company; or
- is deemed to have been connected with the company,

and who is reasonably expected to have access, by virtue of such connection, to unpublished price-sensitive information in respect of securities of the company, or who has received or has had access to such unpublished price-sensitive information.

The definition of 'insider' is very wide in its scope. In particular, an insider can be 'any person' which is defined in s 3(4) of the General Clauses Act 1897 as including any company or association or body of individuals whether incorporated or not. Thus, the definition is not limited to individuals and presumably, if the individuals who procurred the insider dealing represent the directing mind and will of the company, then the company will be found guilty of the relevant offence.

In one aspect the definition of insider is much narrower than in a number of other jurisdictions. Those persons who receive information from an insider are not themselves precluded from dealing on the basis of such information unless the person receiving such information is, himself, a 'connected person' or is 'deemed to have been connected with the company'. This is something of a lacuna in the Regulations since, if an insider communicates unpublished price-sensitive information to his friend (who is not otherwise connected with the company), who deals in the securities, the insider will be guilty of an offence but the friend will not be.

TABLE (1)

Who is a 'connected person'? (Primary insiders)
• a director or one who is deemed to be a director of a company;
• an officer or employee of a company who may reasonably be expected to have access to unpublished price-sensitive information in relation to that company;
• a person having a professional or business relationship with the company, if he may reasonably be expected to have access to any unpublished price-sensitive information.

2.3.2 Primary insiders

2.3.2.1 Primary insiders definition

Primary insiders are persons who by virtue of their proximity to or involvement with the company are reasonably expected to have access by virtue of such connection to unpublished price-sensitive information or who have received such information. That is to say some connection with the company is essential.

2.3.2.2 Time limit

A person may not be regarded as an insider unless it is established that he is or was connected with the company. Unlike the UK Act which provided that a person ceased to be connected with the company after a period of six months from the date that the relevant connection ended, the Regulations do not prescribe any time limit and a person may be treated as an insider if, at any time in the past he has had a connection with the company. The draft Regulations had suggested an eight month limit on the past connection which, for some inexplicable reason, has not found a place in the final version. It is generally felt that not prescribing any time limit could lead to extremely absurd situations and further undermines the credibility of the Regulations.

2.3.2.3 Defined categories

The following categories of persons are defined by the Companies Act:

(1) *Directors* A director is defined in the Companies Act as including any person occupying the position of a director by whatever name they are called. This would include a managing, full-time, part-time or nominee Director without exception. Under s 307, any person in accordance with whose directions or instructions the board of directors is accustomed to act is deemed to be a director of the company. It should be noted that under the Companies Act, persons who advise the board in their professional capacity such as auditors or solicitors are not deemed to be directors, but such persons are brought within the scope of the Regulations since such persons may be 'deemed to be connected persons'.

(2) *Officer or employee* The Companies Act definition of the term 'officer' includes any director, manager or secretary or any person in accordance with whose directions or instructions the board of directors or any one or more of the directors is/are accustomed to act. The term 'employee' is to be given its usual meaning. Although there is some judicial authority that to be an officer requires there to be an employment relationship, this issue, in practice, will largely be irrelevant given that persons having a professional or business relationship with the company may be caught. In order that an officer or employee is treated as a connected person, it is necessary to show that he may reasonably be expected to have access to unpublished price-sensitive information in relation to the company. Thus, for example, it is more likely that a manager in the finance department will be an insider than, say, a manager in the personnel department.

(3) *Professional or business relationship* A person having any kind of professional or business relationship may become a connected person and thereby an insider, if he may reasonably be expected to have *access* to unpublished price-sensitive information. Access to unpublished price-sensitive information may be obtained broadly speaking, in one of two ways. First, the information comes to the knowledge of the concerned person as a matter of course by virtue of his professional or business relationship with the company. Second, by virtue of such relationship, the concerned person can lay his hands and be in possession of the information although the information may not come to his knowledge as a matter of course. Moreover, such access may be direct or indirect such as through a director or an officer or employee of the company. Accordingly, this definition would normally cover a company's lawyers and accountants together with those persons who had a business relationship with a company which gave them access to unpublished price-sensitive information, such as a joint venture partner.

TABLE (2)

Who is 'deemed to be a connected person'? (Secondary insiders) (Clause 2(h) of the regulation)
• a company under the same management or group or any subsidiary company thereof;
• an official or a member of a stock exchange or of a clearing house of that stock exchange, or a dealer in securities respectively or any employee of such member or dealing of a stock exchange;
• a merchant banker, share transfer agent, registrar to an issue, debenture trustee, broker, portfolio manager, investment adviser, sub-broker, investment company or an employee thereof, or, is a member of the board of trustees of a mutual fund or a member of the board of directors of the asset management company of a mutual fund or is an employee thereof who have a fiduciary relationship with the company;
• a member of the board of directors, or an employee, of a public financial institution;
• an official or an employee of a self-regulatory organisation recognised or authorised by the board of a regulatory body;
• a relative of any of the aforementioned persons.
• banker of the company.

2.3.3 Secondary insiders

2.3.3.1 Companies under the same management

Generally speaking, under the Companies Act, two bodies corporate are deemed to be under the same management if:

- each has a common managing director;
- if the majority of the board of directors are common to both;

- if at least one-third of the voting power in each company is exercised or controlled by the same individual or body corporate;
- if the management of the holding company is the same as the other body corporate;
- if one or more directors, either themselves or with their relatives, are the common majority shareholders.

The inclusion of subsidiary companies is confusing and it is not clear whether it is intended to cover the subsidiary of a company whose shares are involved in insider trading or, more likely, a subsidiary of any member of the same group.

2.3.3.2 Members and employees of stock exchanges

This enumerates various categories of intermediaries and others associated with the stock market or capital issues in one way or another who will be insiders if they can reasonably expect to have access to unpublished price-sensitive information or have actually received access to such information. The reason for the inclusion of 'broker' in this subclause is not clear. Perhaps it seeks to bring within the net any person who acts as a broker in securities whether he is a member of a recognised stock exchange or not. SEBI has in the past conducted inquiries into alleged insider trading by brokers in certain shares. However, proving that the persons had a fiduciary relationship with the company which has been exploited to some advantage has been extremely difficult to prove.

Problem Area

A broker received an order for the purchase of a large number of securities from a manager of a unit trust. Whilst putting through the order he also purchases a large quantity in the name of one of his relatives. The broker has assumed that if a large unit trust has placed such an order it must be a good buy. He is not aware whether the manager has some special information or whether it is a long term investment decision.

The broker will be an insider since the knowledge of a large buy order by the unit trust will probably constitute unpublished price-sensitive information. But while the broker will have committed an offence, prosecution will be unlikely since it would be difficult to prove that the broker has acted on inside information.

2.3.3.3 Directors and employees of financial institutions

Today in the Indian securities markets, the biggest players and investors are public financial institutions. The scope for such institutions and other big players like mutual funds and portfolio managers to trade on their own account, while in possession of unpublished price-sensitive information, is tremendous and is widely acknowledged to be prevalent. Further, as a result of loans given to companies, many public financial institutions have a nominee director on the board of the company who is privy to confidential information. Accordingly, these persons have been expressly included in the definition.

2.3.3.4 Officers and employees of self-regulatory bodies

This is vague as presently there appears to be no self-regulatory organisation recognised or authorised by the SEBI. One can only surmise that this is a catch-all category to bring future bodies into the regulatory net.

2.3.3.5 Relatives

This seeks to extend the scope of the term 'insider' by bringing into its ambit, relatives of these secondary insiders. Relative is widely defined in the Companies Act and includes the insider's parents, children and grandchildren, together with their spouses. There is an inconsistency with the definition of connected person (see Table (1) *above*) since that definition does not encompass relatives of the persons included in it.

2.3.3.6 Bankers

Bankers of a company are considered as insiders, whilst their officers and employees are not. This is an obvious *lacuna* since it is these persons who can be said to have access to unpublished price-sensitive information by virtue of their position in the banks. Accordingly, it would have to be shown that those who represented the directing mind and will of the bank know or had access to the published price-sensitive information in order for the bank to be considered an insider. The term 'banker' is not defined and in absence of a definition could be construed to include any bank with whom the company has any kind of dealings.

The most glaring omission from the categories of persons deemed to be secondary insiders are government officers and employees of SEBI itself. It would be interesting to see how SEBI would act if one of its own directors or employees was found to have been engaged in insider trading.

2.4 WHAT ARE THE OFFENCES?

2.4.1 Introduction

There are three offences set out in the Regulations:

- no insider shall either on his own behalf or on behalf of any other person, deal in securities of a company listed on any stock exchange on the basis of any unpublished price-sensitive information;
- no insider shall communicate any unpublished price-sensitive information to any person, with or without his request for such information, except as required in the ordinary course of business or under any law;
- no insider shall counsel or procure any other person to deal in securities of any company on the basis of unpublished price-sensitive information.

2.4.2 Dealing

The prohibition against dealing is limited to dealing in securities listed on any of India's 22 stock exchanges. Dealing is defined as 'an act of buying, selling, or agreeing to buy or sell or deal in any securities by any person either as principal or agent'.

Under the Regulations it is not an essential ingredient of the offence that the insider knew that he was an insider or that he knew that the information was unpublished price-sensitive information. Accordingly, it is not necessary for the prosecution to establish '*mens rea*' and a person may be convicted of the offence even if he unwittingly committed it. All that is required to be proved is that he is an insider who did have access to price-sensitive information and that he has committed one of the three acts contemplated by cl 3 that is to say, dealing communicating or counselling.

2.4.3 Communication

Communication may be written as well as verbal and it is irrelevant whether the person who received the information asked for it or not. The person to whom such information is communicated will commit the offence if he uses the information which he has come by to deal in securities but only if he is, in any event, an insider within the meaning of cl 2(e).

2.4.4 Counselling

This subclause prevents a person from encouraging another person to deal, notwithstanding that the actual unpublished price-sensitive information has not been transmitted.

2.5 DEFENCES

There are no statutory defences to the offences outlined in para 5 in the Regulations.

The fact that there are no defences to accommodate accepted market practices threatens the credibility of the current system. For example, a number of jurisdictions expressly legislate that a person's own knowledge of his intended take-over bid for another company will not preclude him from making purchases of the larger shares on the market prior to implementing such a bid. Taken to its logical conclusion, the failure to have such a defence would prevent many take-over bids from occurring. Accordingly, failure to include defences similar to other jurisdictions results in the insider dealing offences becoming draconian in nature with even less chance of prosecution being brought since the Regulations do not have the support of the financial community that they are intended to protect.

2.6 PENALTIES

Though cl 4 states, that any person who commits any of the offences set out in cl 3 shall be guilty of insider trading, the Regulations do not prescribe any penalty for such contravention.

The Ordinance, on the other hand, specifies in a newly added s 15(g), the offences relating to insider trading, mentioned in para 3, and stipulates that if found guilty, SEBI may impose a penalty, on such person, not exceeding Rs500,000 (approximately £9,000 STG).

Any person contravening the Regulations is deemed under s 24 of the SEBI Act to have committed an offence which shall be punishable with imprisonment for a term of up to one year or with a fine or with both. Moreover the amended s 24 stipulates, that failure to pay any penalty imposed by SEBI, pursuant to an adjudication is deemed to be an offence punishable with imprisonment or fine or both. The offence of insider dealing is to be treated as a criminal offence and punishment may only be imposed after SEBI comes to a finding that there has been insider trading and files a criminal complaint under the code of Criminal Procedure 1973. Under s 26 of the SEBI Act, SEBI is authorised to file the complaint which is then to be filed with the magistrate in a court of competent jurisdiction. The Ordinance has removed the previous requirement for the permission of the goverment to be obtained before proceedings could be initiated. There is no time prescribed in the SEBI Act or Regulations for filing such complaint nor, for that matter, any time limit for conducting or completing any enquiry. It should also be noted there is no method by which SEBI can prevent an offence occurring, its powers are limited to investigation once an offence has occurred.

The Ordinance will now allow SEBI to adjudicate on and levy penalties for, *inter alia*, insider trading and related matters. SEBI will now be able, due to its increased powers, to monitor the market and enforce the Regulations more effectively. With these enhanced powers, SEBI has started to monitor aggressively the securities markets and is pursuing issues of price rigging, unusual fluctuations in share prices and insider trading more vigorously.

2.7 INVESTIGATION BY SEBI

SEBI will only act to investigate on the basis of written information in its possession to the effect that an offence may have been committed. It may act on its own or on a complaint being received by it. There is a procedure laid down in the Regulations to be followed by SEBI for conducting an investigation which requires SEBI to give reasonable notice to the insider to produce such account books and other documents and to give reasonable access to the investigating authority to the premises. Naturally, this will limit the effectiveness of the investigation as an alleged insider will have ample time to prepare his defence and may even ensure that such material may be out of SEBI's reach.

SEBI as the investigating authority may also examine or record statements of any director, proprietor, partner or employee of the insider and summon witnesses to examine them on oath. Such persons are required to co-operate with SEBI. After one month of the conclusion of the investigation the investigating authorities are required to give their report to SEBI who may call for an explanation from the insider and direct him to take such measures as SEBI deems fit. In particular, in addition to any criminal sanctions which may be imposed, SEBI may take the following action:

(1) it may direct the insider not to deal in securities in any particular manner;
(2) it may prohibit the insider from disposing of any of the securities acquired in violation of the Regulations;
(3) it may restrain the insider from communicating or counselling a person to deal in securities.

SEBI is now empowered to adjudicate on matters relating to insider trading and related matters and to impose a penalty. Moreover, failure to pay the penalty can lead to imprisonment and/or imposition of further penalties. Appeal against an adjudication of SEBI is to the Securities Appellate Tribunal. In addition, SEBI can direct the insider to disgorge any profits he may have made. Even after holding this disciplinary procedure and passing such orders as it may deem fit the insider is able to appeal to the central government against the directions of SEBI.

Unfortunately, SEBI's powers of investigation are not sufficiently stringent and it has no powers of search and seizure, thereby robbing it of the element of surprise. Further, SEBI may only investigate the insider and in certain respects his associates as specified in Reg 7. SEBI may summon any other person who they may consider to be in a position to give such information and may call upon the insider and his associate to produce such documents which may assist them.

Since the regulations have come into force, SEBI has received complaints and has conducted investigations, but difficulties in proving that an offence has been committed has meant the success rate has been very low.

The Ordinance provides for the establishment of one or more Securities Appellate Tribunals to exercise jurisdiction over matters conferred to it by or under the SEBI Act. The Tribunal is essentially for the hearing of appeals from orders passed by officials of SEBI pursuant to adjudication proceedings.

In the last couple of months, SEBI has suggested a number of procedures to be formulated by the Bombay Stock Exchange (BSE) to facilitate the surveillance of the stock market by SEBI. These include providing SEBI with an on-line (BOLT) terminal at its office to monitor daily trading; directing the Bombay Stock Exchange to generate surveillance reports indicating abnormal price and volume movements in shares on a daily basis and reporting on defaults by brokers and monitoring broker's positions in shares where the abnormality has been noticed. Also the BSE is to strengthen its own surveillance department to attain a degree of self-regulation.

In order to curb market manipulation and price rigging, at a meeting in December 1995 between SEBI and the heads of all the stock exchanges in India, it was decided that the trading of newly listed shares would be monitored from the very first day of their listing (as opposed to the fourth day). This move was to ensure that the four day period was not misused before the price of the share stabilised. The suspension of trading of a particular share for more than one day on account of market manipulation or price rigging would be automatically communicated to all other stock exchanges who would also suspend trading of those shares.

The stock exchanges also agreed to set up a group comprising of representatives of all the stock exchanges to evolve and implement uniform trading practices, specifically those concerning surveillance and market monitoring. In addition individual brokers would also be closely monitored especially with regard to any default in payment or delivery of shares on their part.

2.8 SCOPE AND JURISDICTION

The SEBI Regulations apply to dealings in securities listed on any of the 22 stock exchanges in India which would include the newly set up Over the Counter Exchange of India (OTCEI) and the National Stock Exchange of India (NSE).

3 OTHER REGULATIONS

3.1 STATUTORY DISCLOSURES UNDER THE COMPANIES ACT

Sections 307 and 308 of the Companies Act requires directors to disclose certain information regarding their share dealings. Under s 307 a statutory duty is imposed on every company to maintain a register and, record therein the prescribed particulars in relation to the directors holding in shares and debentures and of the directors dealings in such securities. Section 308 requires directors and managers to disclose particulars prescribed in s 308 to be entered by the company on the register. Any officer of the company who fails to comply with these statutory provisions may be imprisoned for up to two years or fined up to Rs5000 (approximately £100 STG) or both.

3.2 NON-STATUTORY DISCLOSURES

3.2.1 Listing Agreements with the stock exchanges

The Listing Agreements of the stock exchanges in India provide for a number of disclosures to be made by the company at periodic intervals. The more important of these includes the following:

(1) publication of half-yearly unaudited working results and annual audited accounts;
(2) disclosures in relation to take-over bids when the shareholding in the target company exceeds 5 per cent or 10 per cent;
(3) notification without delay of the date of the board meeting recommending declaration of dividend, issue of bonus or rights shares;
(4) notification to the exchange immediately after any board meeting has been held with short particulars of the outcome;
(5) immediate notification of any changes in the nature of its business, composition of its board of directors, and changes in capital structure;
(6) notification by institutional investors intending to sell more than 1 per cent of the shares of any company by press release and thereafter to notify the exchange within a day of the transaction of the price and other relevant information.

3.2.2 Disclosures of 'benami holdings'

Nominee or 'benami' holdings are common in the Indian securities market. Section 187(c) of the Companies Act which requires the person in whose name the shares are registered to disclose the beneficial owner of the shares. This would apply to trusts and other forms of beneficial holdings.

4 CONCLUSION

Despite the Regulations it is still widely perceived that insider trading has gone on in very much the same manner as it was before the Regulations came into force. There is a general feeling that the Regulations are ineffectual and difficult to implement. The effectiveness of any enactment depends largely on the manner of its implementation. Unfortunately, in India while laws are enacted with the best of intentions and look effective on paper they have been found to be difficult to enforce. It is widely acknowledged that SEBI requires many more powers in order to substantially reduce the amount of insider trading currently carried on in India.

However, the Ordinance has vested SEBI with sweeping powers, including the power to adjudicate upon and impose monetary penalties for offences relating to insider trading. As previously mentioned, one of the amendments is the setting up of a Securities Appellate Tribunal to penalise intermediaries for contraventions of the Regulations. While the setting up of the Tribunal is expected to take a few months, it is hoped that with the further powers being granted to SEBI and the hope that all the stock exchanges in India would be computerised by June 1996, it can enforce the Regulations in an effective manner so as to send a clear message to the market intermediaries and other players that investor unfriendly practices will be punished. This would also, to an extent, necessitate a certain amount of re-structuring and re-organising within SEBI which it will surely do to position itself as a more effective watchdog of the Indian capital markets.

Philippines

Simeon Ken R Ferrer and Jose Ma G Hofileña,
SyCip Salazar Hernandez & Gatmaitan, Manila

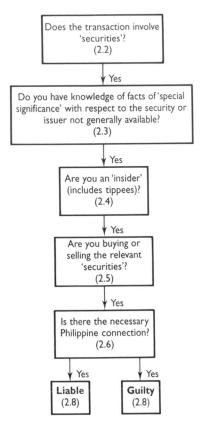

Note: Encouraging and disclosing although not specifically mentioned may give rise to penalties under the general laws of the Philippines (2.5)

1 INTRODUCTION

The principal piece of legislation which defines and imposes sanctions for insider dealing is Batas Pambansa Blg 178 (as amended), more commonly referred to as the Revised Securities Act (the 'RSA'). In general, RSA s 30 prohibits an insider from selling or buying securities of an issuer, if he knows of a fact of special significance with respect to the issuer or the securities which is not generally available. The RSA, adopted on 23 February 1982, totally repealed the original Securities Act (Commonwealth Act No 83), which had been in place since its approval by the then National Assembly on 26 October 1936.

There is little judicial precedent laid down by the Philippine judiciary on insider trading. Moreover, there have been no significant regulations issued by the Philippine Securities and Exchange Commission (the 'SEC') on insider dealing which could assist in the interpretation of the RSA. However, as the RSA is closely based on the US Uniform Sale of Securities Act, the Federal Securities Act of 1933 and the Federal Securities Exchange Act of 1934, Philippine courts and quasi-judicial agencies can be expected to be influenced heavily by American experience and case law when interpreting and applying the RSA.

With the accelerated development of the Philippine capital markets, the SEC, together with the other participants in those markets, is evaluating its insider dealing monitoring and prosecution capabilities with a view to enforcing more effectively the RSA's insider dealing provisions.

2 THE CRIMINAL LAW

2.1 INTRODUCTION

The underlying objectives behind the enactment of the RSA were:

- to require full and fair disclosure of the character of securities to be offered to the investing public;
- to provide for the regulation of securities exchanges and over-the-counter markets and prevent inequitable and unfair practices and transactions; and
- to co-ordinate the securities industry with the monetary and credit policies of the government.

While the RSA serves as the principal legislation prohibiting insider trading, it is supplemented by certain other statutes and legal principles, such as those contained in the Revised Penal Code (Act No 3815, as amended).

Under Philippine law, the duty of an 'insider' to disclose inside information in certain circumstances is not founded solely upon the provisions of the RSA, but also on civil law concepts of fraud and deceit. In the case of Strong v Repide (41 Phil 947 (1909); 213 US 417), the United States Supreme Court, on appeal from the then Supreme Court of the Philippine Islands, applied the provisions of the Civil Code on deceit and fraud and held that a controlling stockholder, director and administrator general of a corporation was guilty of fraud in purchasing the corporation's shares from another stockholder without disclosing the current status of the corporation's negotiations with the Philippine government for the sale of the corporation's property. The duty to disclose did not arise from the bare relationship between director and shareholder 'but because, in consideration of all the existing circumstances [detailed in the decision], it became the duty of the defendant, acting in good faith, to state the facts before making the purchase'.

Finally, the Philippine Stock Exchange ('PSE'), a self-regulating entity which operates and supervises the only functioning stock exchange in the Philippines, has highlighted in a recent notice the basic underlying rationale for the prohibition on insider trading. These are:

(1) the existence of a relationship giving access, directly or indirectly, to information intended to be available only for a corporate purpose and not for the personal benefit of anyone; and

(2) the inherent unfairness involved when a party takes advantage of such information knowing it is unavailable to those with whom he is dealing.

2.2 TO WHICH SECURITIES DOES THE RSA APPLY?

The insider dealing provisions of the RSA can apply in the context of those securities referred to in s 2(a) of the RSA. It is a broad definition and encompasses specific types of securities, such as stocks, bonds, options and warrants as well as all 'interests or instruments commonly considered to be "securities"'. As such, even derivative instruments, while relatively new in the Philippines, would fall within the ambit of the 'securities' definition, as they are considered securities in commercial practice. The width of the statutory definition is also intended to capture such instruments as may be developed in the future and which would be regarded as securities. There is no requirement, for the purposes of applying the RSA's provisions on insider trading, that the security or securities concerned be listed on any stock exchange or that the issuer of the securities be incorporated or domiciled in the Philippines.

2.3 WHAT IS INSIDE INFORMATION?

Under RSA s 30, insider dealing is the selling or buying by an insider of securities if such insider knows of a 'fact of special significance' with respect to the issuer or the security that 'is not generally available'. These two features are considered in turn.

2.3.1 Special significance

Section 30 of the RSA provides that a fact is 'of special significance' if either:

(1) it is material and it would be likely, on being made generally available, to affect
     the market price of a security to a significant extent (there is, however, no
     jurisprudence as to what constitutes 'significant' in this context); or
(2) a reasonable person would consider it especially important under the cir-
     cumstances in determining his course of action in the light of such factors
     as—
     (a) the degree of its specificity;
     (b) the extent of its difference from information generally available previ-
          ously;
     (c) its nature and reliability.

Given that the RSA permits the courts to take into account the nature and
reliability of information it seems likely that, in certain circumstances, market
rumours (which have not at the relevant time been proven to be true) rather than
a 'fact' of special significance could constitute inside information. There is,
however, no precedent on this point.

2.3.2 Generally available

Section 30 of the RSA provides that an offence is not committed where
either:

(1) the accused is able to prove that the fact of special significance is generally
     available; or
(2) if the other party to the transaction (or his agent) is identified, either the
     accused is able to prove that the other party knows such fact or that other
     party in fact knows it from the accused or otherwise.

2.4 WHO IS AN INSIDER?

Section 30 of the RSA defines 'insider' as any of the persons set out in Table (1)
below:

TABLE (1)

Insiders are:
(1) The issuer.
(2) A director or officer of, or a person controlling, controlled by, or
     under common control with, the issuer.
(3) A person whose relationship or former relationship to the issuer
     gives or gave him access to a fact of special significance about the
     issuer or the relevant security that is not generally available.
(4) A person who learns such a fact from any of the persons referred to
     in (1), (2) or (3), with knowledge that the person from whom he
     learns the fact is such an insider.

As the RSA does not draw any distinction between individuals and corporations it follows that the persons referred to in (2), (3) and (4) of Table (1) *above* can be corporate entities. Thus, theoretically it seems possible for a corporate entity to commit an offence of insider dealing by buying or selling securities on the basis of information received by its officers or employees.

Based on the foregoing definition of insider, it is apparent that not only directors or officers but also employees, consultants, lawyers, or other persons who have, or have had, a 'relationship' with the issuer through which facts of special significance became known to them, are considered insiders. In addition, persons not having any direct relationship with the issuer but who have obtained inside information from insiders knowing them to be insiders, are covered by the definition.

It should be noted, however, that the RSA will consider an insider to be such only where knowledge of facts of special significance about the issuer or the security was obtained by virtue of his being an insider. Accordingly, for example, if legal counsel to the issuer learns about special facts, such as major players seeking a position in a specific security through advice given in an informal gathering, there is basis to argue that such information was received by him not in his capacity as an insider (ie as someone having a relationship with the issuer) and, accordingly, any sale or purchase of the issuer's security by him would not be a prohibited form of insider dealing. Problem Area 1 *below* illustrates this point.

Problem Area

Juan, a director of Agricultural Chemicals Co ('ACCo') is aware that ACCo's scientists are on the verge of announcing a new product which when released is likely to render obsolete the current product of Farming Chemicals Co, ACCo's principal industry rival. As a consequence, Juan sells his personal holding of shares in Farming Chemicals Co.

Although clear precedent does not exist, Juan is not likely to be considered an insider with regard to Farming Chemicals Co and as a consequence is not guilty of insider dealing on account of his actions.

Legislation was proposed in 1992 to broaden the scope of the meaning of 'insider' by including in such terms any other person who knows of a fact of special significance about the issuer or security that is not generally available, regardless of such person's relation with the issuer or regardless of the circumstances under which he gained access to the fact of special significance. However, concerns that expanding the definition of 'insider' in the manner proposed was likely to impinge upon *bona fide* researchers and analysts, who piece together information about issuers through independent research, interviews and studies, has meant that the proposed legislation is not being pursued vigorously.

2.5 WHAT ARE THE OFFENCES?

As mentioned earlier, the elements constituting insider dealing are:

- there must be a fact of special significance about the issuer or a security;
- the insider obtains such information by virtue of his being an insider; and
- the insider sells or buys the relevant security.

Under Philippine law, there is no express requirement that the relevant selling and buying takes place on a stock exchange—it can be a private off-market transaction. Moreover, it is not essential that the insider is able to profit from his purchase or sale of securities. Strictly speaking, neither is it an essential feature of insider dealing that the relevant sale or purchase be made specifically on the basis of the facts of special significance. These, however, are significant issues which Philippine jurisprudence has not yet had an opportunity to resolve definitively.

The RSA does not create express offences of encouraging someone else to deal or improperly disclosing inside information. However, encouraging others to breach the RSA may itself be an offence under the general penal laws of the Philippines. In addition, RSA s 44(b) prohibits a direct or indirect violation of the RSA's provisions through or by means of any other person.

2.6 WHAT IS THE TERRITORIAL SCOPE OF THE RSA?

Philippine tribunals have not yet had to consider whether or not an act of selling or purchasing securities must take place in the Philippines in order for such activity to be punishable as insider dealing under Philippine law.

The general position on the territorial nature of penal statutes would suggest that it would be necessary that the acts constituting insider dealing be committed within the Philippines. What is not as clear, however, is whether or not a sale or purchase outside the Philippines of securities issued by Philippine issuers would be considered as having its situs in the Philippines for the purposes of imposing a penal sanction.

2.7 WHAT ARE THE DEFENCES?

The defences to a prosecution for insider dealing would principally consist of an assertion as to the absence of any of the essential elements of the offence. These would be:

(1) that the accused is not an insider within the RSA definition (eg it is not established that the accused obtained information with knowledge that the person from whom the information was received was an insider);

(2) that the relevant information does not constitute a fact of special significance; or

(3) such information was not obtained by the accused in his capacity as an insider.

Under Philippine criminal law, insider dealing, being punishable not by the Revised Penal Code but by a special statute, is classified as *mala prohibita* and, thus, good faith is not a defence and there is no jurisprudence to suggest that the accused can argue that he would have dealt irrespective of knowledge of the significant fact.

2.8 WHAT ARE THE PENALTIES AND CONSEQUENCES OF INSIDER TRADING?

The RSA prescribes both an administrative sanction as well as a penal sanction for insider trading. The imposition of one does not necessarily exclude the imposition of the other. Table (2) *below* sets out those sanctions, which by virtue of RSA s 46, the SEC may impose, in its discretion, for any violation of the RSA.

TABLE (2)

Administrative sanctions which may be imposed on an insider: • Suspension or revocation of its certificate of registration and permit to offer securities. • A fine of no less than P200 (approximately £5 STG) nor more than P50,000 (approximately £1,250 STG) plus not more than P500 (approximately £10 STG) for each day of continuing violation. • Disqualification from being an officer, member of the board of directors or principal stockholder of an issuer whose securities are, or are about to be, registered pursuant to the RSA. • Other penalties within the power of the SEC under existing laws.

On the other hand, Table (3) *below* sets out the penal sanctions that can be imposed under RSA s 56 for violations of the RSA, including insider trading.

TABLE (3)

Penal sanctions: • A fine of no less than P5,000 (approximately £125 STG) nor more than P500,000 (approximately £10,250 STG); and/or • imprisonment of not less than seven years nor more than 21 years.

It should also be noted that companies can be held liable for the actions of their employees and officers.

3 NON-STATUTORY REGULATORS

3.1 SECURITIES AND EXCHANGE COMMISSION/PHILIPPINE STOCK EXCHANGE

The principal regulator of the Philippine securities industry is the SEC, the government agency vested with the power to implement the RSA. It is responsible for regulating the stock exchanges, the regulation of the securities markets, the licensing of securities brokers and dealers, the promulgation of rules and regulations on securities trading, and the issuance of opinions and rulings pertaining to the proper applications of the RSA, the Corporation Code of the Philippines and certain other statutes.

On the other hand, as the operator and supervisor of the only functioning stock exchange in the Philippines, the PSE exercises a degree of regulation over listed securities. In a recent notice, the PSE expressed the view that the basis for its policies against insider dealing is its duty to strengthen itself into an effective and professional self-regulating organisation and to provide one efficient and fair market for the trading of securities.

While at present both the PSE and the SEC have pending investigations of allegations of insider trading, neither of these bodies have currently adopted any formal regulations specifically and directly governing insider dealing and are relying on the RSA, as well as analogous American jurisprudence in their investigations.

The SEC, however, has issued rules to prevent the abuse of inside information. These rules prohibit brokers from dealing in, or otherwise buying and selling, securities listed on a Philippine exchange and issued by any corporation where any stockholder, director, manager, officer, salesman, account executive, floor trader or authorised clerk of the broker is at the time holding office in the issuer as a director, president, vice-president, manager, treasurer, comptroller, secretary or any other office of trust and responsibility (SEC Rule BED No 902-A (1978)).

4 CONCLUSION

Historically, the Philippines has not had significant precedents to rely on in respect of insider dealing. In the determination of whether or not specific acts constitute insider dealing, American jurisprudence is likely to be relied upon as persuasive.

The level of awareness of the participants in the Philippine capital markets as to the adverse consequences of insider dealing is only beginning to rise, albeit gradually, with the growth in those in line markets. In turn, this increase in awareness is likely to lead to further refinements in Philippine insider dealing laws and regulations.

The future challenge, however, lies perhaps not so much in the establishment of the most efficient legal framework for combatting insider dealing but rather in the vigilant enforcement by the regulatory authorities of existing statutes and regulations.

Russian Federation

Dominic Sanders, Linklaters & Paines, Moscow

1 INTRODUCTION

The concept of insider dealing exists in Russian securities legislation but at the time of writing the financial markets are still insufficiently developed for its application to be meaningful in the majority of cases.

Though Russia's mass privatisation programme has resulted in several thousand large and medium sized enterprises incorporating and distributing shares to the public, in particular through a country wide voucher auction process, even shares in the handful of better known issuers are still traded on a random basis on an over-the-counter market albeit rationalised by an electronic quotations system now operational between larger Russian brokers. With limited liquidity and reporting of transactions, a single trade may be negotiated and concluded over a number of days or even weeks. While a contract is settled, the seller assembles a block of shares for the buyer, the buyer is entered on the share register and payment is made. When the lack of basic, independently-verified information about issuers and the uncertain political backdrop is thrown in, regulators and participants in Russia's fledgling financial markets can perhaps be forgiven for not regarding insider dealing as a priority issue: it is too early to draw a real distinction between legitimate arbitrage opportunity and unfair or improper use of inside or confidential information.

2 CIVIL & ADMINISTRATIVE LAW

2.1 INTRODUCTION

The only provision currently in Russian securities legislation which directly relates to insider dealing is contained in para 52 of the Regulation on the issue and circulation of securities and on stock exchanges in the Russian Soviet Federal Socialist Republic ('RSFSR') approved by RSFSR Government Resolution No 78 of 28 December 1991 ('Regulation 78'). The provision states that the completion of transactions in securities with the use of confidential information is forbidden. Confidential information is defined as information about the issuer or its securities which is not 'generally accessible' and the use of which may be used to cause harm to the material interests of the issuer or an investor. Further rules may also apply to particular circumstances, including general provisions on use of information, commercial secrets and confidentiality, the conduct of professional participants in the securities market, restrictions on the entrepreneurial activity of state officials and parliamentary deputies, and duties of directors of joint stock companies (in particular as embodied in the standard constitutional documents adopted by many privatised joint stock companies and more importantly the law on joint stock companies which mostly came into force on 1 January 1996).

2.2 TO WHICH SECURITIES DOES PARA 52 APPLY?

Presidential Decree No 2063 on measures on the state regulation of the securities market in the Russian Federation of 4 November 1994 restricted in particular the categories of securities which may be offered publicly prior to the adoption of a federal law on securities, state securities; registered shares of joint stock companies and banks; options and warrants on securities; bonds, including bonds issued by state and local authorities of the Russian Federation; housing certificates; and other securities, trading in which is permitted in accordance with federal laws or international agreements of the Russian Federation. These it seems are the instruments in which it is most likely that a liquid and information-sensitive market is likely to exist. Formally however, a number of further documentary instruments such as cheques, deposit and savings certificates and promissory notes are also classified as securities by Chapter 7 of the first part of the Civil Code, which came into force on 1 January 1995. Arguably para 52 only relates to the secondary market given that it appears in the section of Regulation 78 dealing with the 'circulation of securities'.

2.3 WHAT IS INSIDE INFORMATION?

Paragraph 52 states that confidential information is information about the issue of securities which is not generally accessible (ie available from the mass media, a securities issue prospectus, periodic reports and information materials published by the issuer) and the use of which may be used to cause harm to the material interests of the issuer or an investor. This wide definition should be seen in the context of the lack of objective information currently available in relation to Russian issuers. Accounts are produced for tax purposes only and are not otherwise designed to present a view of the financial affairs of an issuer. Availability of objective information on issuers is critical to the development of Russia's capital markets. However the wide ambit of the provisions would seem to jeopardise the carrying on of much needed research by independent brokers where such information is then used to deal.

2.4 WHO IS AN INSIDER?

In practice the Russian securities market is filled with insiders. Privatisation involved employees and management acquiring in many cases a controlling stake in their enterprise, with further blocks of shares then being auctioned to the public and to strategic investors. It has been common practice for enterprises to deal and even make a market in their own shares (notwithstanding the limitation, embodied in initial legislation, on domestic investment funds being open-ended).

Commonly the share register is controlled, directly or indirectly, by the issuer or an affiliated broker which is also active in dealing in the securities of that issuer.

This state of affairs makes sensible regulation more difficult to achieve. Unfortunately no attempt is made in para 52 to distinguish use, from abuse of information. The provision applies to use of confidential information, seemingly by any person, which may cause harm to the material interests of the issuer or an investor. It is unimportant how the information is obtained or whether its use is in some sense improper.

2.5 WHAT IS THE TERRITORIAL SCOPE OF PARA 52?

The preamble to Regulation 78 states that it regulates, among other things, the issue and circulation of securities on the territory of the Russian Federation. Currently a significant volume of trading in Russian securities takes place outside Russia and the application of this undetailed provision often creates doubt. Whether Regulation 78 regulates Russian issuers, securities issued or derived from instruments issued by Russian issuers, market participants physically located or registered within Russia or a combination thereof is not clear in all cases.

2.6 WHAT ARE THE SANCTIONS AND CONSEQUENCES OF INSIDER DEALING?

Paragraph 52 does not set out what sanctions apply in the event of any breach. An investment institution, ie a licensed professional participant in the Russian securities market, could probably be fixed with administrative liability by the regulator, the ultimate sanction being withdrawal of the relevant licence. At the time of writing the function of regulator is being transferred from the Ministry of Finance to the Russian SEC.

More serious is the civil sanction set down in art 168 of the first part of the Civil Code which provides that a transaction not complying with appropriate legal requirements is invalid, unless otherwise provided by applicable legislation. On general civil principles it may also be possible for a person to claim damages as compensation for any loss caused whether under contract or, if there is no contractual link, if harm has been inflicted by the person carrying on the insider dealing. On the face of it therefore, the effect of para 52 is potentially to invalidate a large number of transactions in securities concluded on the basis of information which was not generally accessible.

3 SELF-REGULATORY ORGANISATIONS

A number of self-regulatory organisations have now been set up in the Russian securities market including the Professional Association of Participants of the

Financial Market (known as PALLFOR), the Depository & Clearing Company and a number of committees and associations for the protection of shareholders' rights. In addition a number of projects are being run in relation to share registration, the conduct of public equity offers by privatised companies, disclosure of company information and other market infrastructure matters. However, little by way of regulation of insider dealing itself has yet emerged from these initiatives.

4 CONCLUSION

Current regulation of insider dealing on the Russian securities market is in most cases inappropriate. When Regulation 78 was adopted in 1991, Russia's securities markets were hardly existent and para 52 could only imitate similar provisions in legislation governing more developed, foreign markets. With the benefit of hindsight the draftsmen of para 52 should not be faulted for creating a basic concept of insider dealing in the legislation. No one would doubt that in the Russian securities market there is ample opportunity for the misuse of inside information obtained from an office or position of responsibility for personal gain, and that in a more developed, orderly and transparent market this would be perceived as unethical and improper.

Unfortunately the failure of para 52 to recognise that the creation, discovery and use of objective information by market participants is a perfectly legitimate element in the working of a financial market in which issuers compete for the allocation of capital is regrettable. Given the illogical results that will frequently arise from para 52, the overwhelming likelihood is that the majority of market participants simply ignore the provisions, following a by now rich Russian tradition whereby law and practice simply diverge. Paragraph 52 does however provide a pretext for unscrupulous counter parties to seek to invalidate transactions after the event solely on the basis that information was used which was not 'generally accessible'. Given the limited disclosure requirements on Russian issuers and the understandable reluctance of brokers to publish generally their proprietary research, diligent market participants in a difficult market are burdened with further risk in ascertaining whether information used was 'generally accessible'.

The Russian securities market has grown exceptionally rapidly and is by most standards disorderly. As the market develops, it will become more apparent what form of insider dealing regulation is appropriate to support rather than hamper the market. A draft law on the securities market has been adopted by the Russian Parliament but was rejected by President Yeltsin. The State Duma vetoed the President's rejection but the status of the draft is currently unclear. In the meantime, market participants are advised to exercise some care with the existing provisions and are left to ponder a less than orderly process of legal reform which has more often than not assumed, in this case wrongly, that any rule is generally better than no rule at all.

Indonesia

David Simpson and Hoesein Wiriadinata,
Wiriadinata & Widyawan, Jakarta

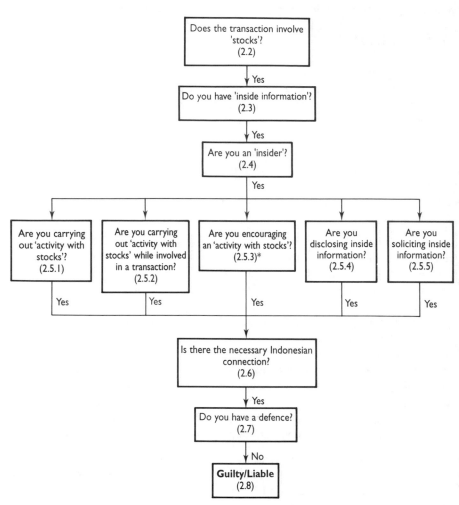

*Note: On a technical interpretation of the encouraging offence you do not need to possess inside information, however, it is unlikely that this couls be relied upon (2.5.3)

1 INTRODUCTION

The law on insider dealing in Indonesia is set out as part of the Indonesian Capital Market Law (the 'Law').

2 THE LAW

2.1 INTRODUCTION

The Law creates various offences which are considered in detail below (see 2.5), and the scope of which depend on a number of key definitions, which are explained first.

2.2 TO WHICH SECURITIES DOES THE LAW APPLY?

The Law is only capable of applying to those types of securities defined in the Law as being 'stocks'. That definition should be construed widely to include those securities set out in Table (1) *below*, which may be issued by either Indonesian companies or other Indonesian non-corporate entities, such as state-owned institutions or public bodies—for example there has been a number of issues of bonds and other debt instruments by Indonesian's seven main state banks. The Law does not apply to stocks issued by foreign issuers.

TABLE (1)

- shares
- bonds
- commercial securities
- credit securities
- debt certificates
- rights
- warrants
- options
- stock derivatives
- instruments stipulated by the Capital Market Supervisory Agency ('Bapepam')—the regulatory agency established by the Indonesian government to ensure the orderly and fair operation of the securities exchanges—to be 'stocks'.

It should be noted that the definition does not appear to include membership rights in investment funds. Stocks need not be listed on any stock exchange in order to fall within the ambit of the Law.

2.3 WHAT IS INSIDE INFORMATION?

'Inside information' means important and relevant information which may influence the price of an issuer's stocks, which information is not available to the public. The essential elements, therefore, are:

- price-sensitivity;
- importance and relevance (which suggest that there could be information which, while price-sensitive, is not important and therefore not to be regarded as inside information);
- unavailability to the public.

These features are considered in turn.

2.3.1 Price-sensitivity

There is no suggestion in the Law that in order for information to be regarded as inside information, that the degree of price-sensitivity attaching to it should be material. The test of whether or not information is price-sensitive is an objective one, rather than a subjective one, however there are no judicial pronouncements which give guidance on the extent to which information must influence the price of a stock in order for it to be regarded as price-sensitive.

2.3.2 Importance and relevance

As to 'relevance', it is submitted that information about one issuer could constitute inside information in relation to a second issuer if it is important, relevant and price-sensitive with respect to that second issuer. This, for example, may be the case where the two issuers are in the same industrial sector and likely to be affected by the information in the same way.

2.3.3 Unavailability to the public

The term 'public' is not defined. If the use of particular information is not otherwise banned, free disclosure of that information (by the issuer) to another party on request (even if not to the public at large) will mean that the information can no longer be regarded as inside information. Apart from disclosure requirements relating to certain important events under the regulations of the Jakarta Stock Exchange, there is no other requirement under Indonesian law to make information available to the public.

As there is no definition of what constitutes 'information' for the purposes of the Law, it is arguable that a rumour which influences the price of stock, but which ultimately turns out to be false, could constitute inside information.

2.4 WHO IS AN INSIDER?

An 'insider' with respect to a company is any of those persons set out in Table (2) *below*.

TABLE (2)

- A commissioner, director or employee of the company or of an affiliate of the company.
- A main shareholder (one holding 25 per cent or more) in the company or in an affiliate of the company.
- A person who, because of his position in, or relationship with, the company or an affiliate, has inside information.
- A person who, within the preceding six months, fell within any of these categories.

An 'affiliate' of a company includes a party which directly or indirectly controls, is controlled by or is under the same control as, that company. It also includes the company's main shareholders. 'Control' is defined as the power to exercise a controlling influence over a company, unless such power is only the result of an official position (an expression which is not defined by the Law) with the company. In the case of a limited liability company, any person having an interest in securities of more than 25 per cent of the total voting rights of the limited liability company, is considered to control the company, unless the person can prove that as a matter of fact he does not exercise control; and a person having an interest in securities of less than 25 per cent of the total voting rights of a limited liability company is considered not to control that company, unless it can be proven that he does exercise control. An affiliate is not necessarily an insider although its directors are.

It is interesting to note that the holders of bonds and other securities (except shares) issued by a company would not be insiders unless, because of their position in or relationship with the company, they are in possession of inside information. However, employees of affiliates are insiders, whether they possess inside information or not. Clearly, however, it is not an offence for such employees to deal if as a matter of fact they do not possess inside information. Both a company which holds 20 per cent of the shares of another company and its directors are insiders with respect to that other company. The third category of insiders in Table (2) *above* catches professional advisers.

The Law does not deem directors to have the inside information of their co-directors nor does it deem a company to be an insider because its employees have inside information.

2.5 WHAT ARE THE OFFENCES?

The Law prohibits a number of specific activities:

2.5.1 Activity with stocks

An insider of a company is prohibited from carrying out an 'activity with stocks' of that company while in possession of inside information. 'Activities with stocks' include the purchase or sale of such stocks or the offering for purchase or sale of such stocks, in each case either in respect of one's own interest or the interests of another party in such stocks.

It follows from the wording of this offence that an insider who does not have inside information, and who has not held inside information during the past six months, is not prohibited from dealing and neither is a person who has inside information but who is not himself an insider. Such a person may deal in stocks without committing this offence, as can a person to whom the relevant information is disclosed (a tippee), unless he is an insider himself.

2.5.2 Activity with stocks while involved in a transaction

An insider with respect to Company A is prohibited from conducting an activity with stocks (as defined in 2.5.1 *above*) of Company B where Company A and Company B are involved in a 'transaction' and that insider has inside information linked to the transaction.

This provision leaves open some interesting questions which have not been resolved as a matter of Indonesian law: What is a 'transaction'? Is it permitted to deal in the stocks of Company B (assuming one is not an insider of Company B) while in possession of inside information that is not linked to the particular transaction? What does 'linked' mean, eg would it extend to information gained in the course of negotiating the transaction but which is not actually relevant to the transaction? Is it possible to be in possession of information linked to a transaction without knowing the transaction is taking place?

2.5.3 Encouraging an activity with stocks

An insider of a company is prohibited from persuading another party to carry out an activity with stocks of a company. This provision does not require the actual possession of inside information by the insider. It could include the case of a director promoting the sale of his company's shares to institutional investors.

2.5.4 Disclosing inside information

An insider of a company is prohibited from giving inside information to a party whom he knows or should know will use that information to carry out an activity with the stocks of the company.

This does not require that the information concerned should relate to the target company, nor does it constrain the party receiving the information.

2.5.5 Soliciting inside information

A person directly or indirectly associated with an insider is prohibited from trying to obtain information for the purpose of carrying out activities with stocks. Persons associated with an insider would probably include those in a family relationship by marriage or descent (to two generations) and may include persons in an employer-employee relationship (both employer and employee). This is a very wide-ranging and, on the face of it, rather severe provision, although there are significant difficulties of proof as to whether an attempt to get information has been made and the actual objective of that attempt. However, it does not prohibit dealing in the stocks concerned, only the attempt to get information.

2.6 WHAT IS THE TERRITORIAL SCOPE OF THE LAW?

The Law only regulates activities in Indonesia in relation to stocks issued by Indonesian issuers. It does not regulate foreign stocks.

2.7 WHAT ARE THE DEFENCES?

The Law provides a number of exceptions to the offences described above:

2.7.1 An activity with a stock

A company may carry out an activity with a stock even if directors or employees of that company have inside information if:

- the decision to undertake the activity is made independently by another party on behalf of the company;
- there is no possibility that the inside information will be obtained by that other party; or
- the other party does not in fact possess the inside information.

These defences allow a company to buy or sell stocks on the basis of a director's resolution, taken at a meeting from which all directors in possession of inside information are excluded, and allow the use of Chinese Walls.

2.7.2 In the course of duty

Company A may carry out activities with the stocks of Company B even though the commissioners, directors, employees or agents of Company A acquire inside information about Company B in the course of their duties, provided that that information is relevant only to the transaction concerned.

2.7.3 Are the defences in 2.7.1 and 2.7.2 unnecessary?

Neither of the defences set out in 2.7.1 and 2.7.2 could have any meaning unless, but for their existence, a prohibition would apply. However, a company is not an insider merely because its employees are insiders so that the prohibition on dealing does not seem to apply anyway.

2.7.4 Carry out activities with an unassociated party

A stockbroker who has inside information about a company may carry out activities with the stocks of that company for an unassociated party, provided the broker acts on 'execution only' instructions and does not give 'special suggestions' to his client in relation to the stocks.

2.8 WHAT ARE THE PENALTIES AND CONSEQUENCES OF INSIDER DEALING?

The Chairman of Bapepam may unwind any transaction if the transaction has been concluded using inside information. In addition, the Chairman of Bapepam may suspend trading in a stock if there are indications that the use of inside information is leading to unreasonable price fluctuations. These powers are derived from the Law.

Breach of any of the offences in the Law is punishable by:

*   imprisonment for up to one year and a fine of up to Rp500,000 (approximately £100 STG), or both, for an intentional violation;
*   imprisonment for up to six months and a fine of up to Rp100,000 (approximately £30 STG) or both, for a negligent violation.

There are also some specific sanctions which may be applied against stockbrokers and investment advisers. For example the Chairman of Bapepam may suspend or revoke their licences for breach of any provision of the Law. An offender is entitled to 15 days' advance notice and has a right to object.

Bapepam is responsible for upholding the effectiveness and integrity of the capital market regulations generally.

There are also rights at general law for persons who have suffered loss to recover damages. However, in practice these would rarely be used.

3 NON-STATUTORY REGULATION

There is no non-statutory regulation dealing with insider dealing.

4 CONCLUSIONS

While provisions to deal with insider dealing are in existence in Indonesia they have not yet been the subject of any judicial ruling. In general, the enforcement of the anti-insider dealing provisions have not been a high priority in a market which is developing so rapidly that there are perceived to be other more pressing issues to be dealt with.

The New Capital Markets Law gives Bapepam enhanced enforcement powers and we will have to wait to see what priority Bapepam attaches to these new powers and the fight against insider dealing.

China

Lucy Warrington, Linklaters & Paines, Hong Kong

1 INTRODUCTION

The Shanghai and Shenzhen stock exchanges were both 'established' in 1990. The re-opening of stock exchanges in China marked an additional step towards opening the Chinese economy to the international community and implementing free market reforms domestically. A similar approach was adopted to the 'experiment' that had been used in opening areas in the coastal region to direct foreign investment and the first private enterprises in the 1980s. Only two exchanges were opened and the scope of business of these stock exchanges was restricted to listing the stocks of companies based in the immediate region. In 1995, they remain the only officially-recognised stock exchanges in China. Recent bids by Wuhan and Tianjin to establish rival exchanges have been discredited for the time being further to crises on local bourses caused by margin lending.

2 THE LAW

2.1 CURRENT LEGISLATION

The first 'A' Shares (shares sold to Chinese persons only) and 'B' Shares (shares sold to non-Chinese persons only) were listed on the Shanghai Stock Exchange (then called the Shanghai Securities Exchange) and the Shenzhen Stock Exchange in 1991 and 1992 respectively. Regulations in relation to securities were promulgated at the local level on 27 November 1990 (Shanghai) and 15 May 1991 (Shenzhen). These local regulations were intended to provide guidelines for the development of the market until sufficient experience was accumulated to issue state level legislation. Thus, both local regulations provide little detail. For example, there are no penalties specified in either the Shanghai or Shenzhen regulations for breach of their respective provisions. These local regulations were followed up with national legislation in 1993 providing greater detail in the definitions of 'insider trading' and 'inside information'. The national measures prevail over the local regulations in case of discrepancy between the two. The following paragraphs provide extracts of the Shanghai and Shenzhen regulations and the national legislation.

2.2 SHANGHAI REGULATIONS

The Administrative Measures of Shanghai Municipality governing Securities Trading provide for prohibition of insider dealing at art 39. This provides that all units (work units are the official term for employees working for a particular organisation or subdivision thereof in China) and individuals trading in securities are forbidden from:

(1) collaborating in secret with two or more units or individuals to buy or sell the same type of securities simultaneously in order to create a false demand and price;
(2) using inside information to trade in securities;
(3) fabricating or spreading information which is false or misleading so as to induce people to participate in securities trading;
(4) continuously forcing up prices by buying or beating down prices by selling off the same types of securities so as to manipulate the market;
(5) directly or indirectly trading one's own securities on the stock exchange without authorisation;
(6) using direct or indirect means to manipulate the market or disrupt market procedures.

Further, art 40 prohibits certain categories of persons for trading in shares directly or indirectly on their own behalf:

(1) relevant personnel working within the authority in charge of securities who are in charge of administering securities matters;
(2) stock exchange administrative personnel;
(3) persons employed by securities operators who are directly involved in share issues and trading;
(4) administrative personnel under the direct administrative jurisdiction of or with an administrative relationship with an issuer;
(5) other persons with inside information in relation to the issuing of and trading in shares.

2.3 SHENZHEN REGULATIONS

In Shenzhen, the Provisional Measures of Shenzhen Municipality on Share Issuing and Trading provide at art 43 that all individuals are forbidden from certain acts when conducting securities trading activities (including centralised trading and over-the-counter trading). These are:

(1) selling shares in great quantities, usually in anticipation of an order or to cause a fall in price;
(2) two or more units or individuals collaborating in secret to buy or sell the same type of securities simultaneously in order to create a false demand and interfere with market prices;
(3) carrying out false transactions without transferring title to the securities in order to disrupt the market;
(4) using inside information to trade in securities;
(5) spreading false or misleading information so as to induce other parties to participate in securities trading and thereby influence the price of securities;

(6) with speculation as one's motive, continuously buy at a high price or sell off at a low price one specific type of security so as to influence market forces;
(7) directly or indirectly trading one's own valued securities on the stock exchange or the trading counter of a securities operator without authorisation;
(8) as a stockbroker, decide on behalf of a client such details as the type of security, amount, price and whether to buy or sell, or accepting a commission to carry out a valued securities transaction in a place outside the stockbroker's own place of business;
(9) conducting illegal trading outside of stock exchange premises;
(10) transferring ownership illegally.

2.4 NATIONAL LEGISLATION

The Provisional Measures on the Prohibition of Deceptive Securities Dealing Activities were approved on 15 August 1993 by the State Council and promulgated on 2 December 1993 by the Securities Committee of the State Council. The fact that these are 'Provisional Measures' suggest that a 'Law' on this subject will be developed based on the effectiveness of these measures and promulgated in due course.

Under the Measures at art 2, 'deceptive securities dealing activities' are described as including 'insider trading, market manipulation, deception of clients, making of false statements in issuing and trading of securities and related activities'.

By art 3, all units and individuals are prohibited from using inside information to conduct the issuing or trading of securities in order to gain interest or reduce loss.

The following arts 4 to 6 define the terms 'insider trading', 'inside information' and 'insiders'.

'Insider trading' is defined to include:

(1) insiders using inside information in the trading of securities or the provision of advice to other persons to trade securities according to inside information;
(2) insiders revealing inside information to other persons resulting in those persons using that information to conduct insider trading;
(3) non-insiders obtaining inside information by unlawful means or by other means to conduct the trading of securities according to that information or provide advice to other persons to conduct trading according to that advice;
(4) other insider trading activities.

'Inside information' means 'major pieces of information which are known by insiders and have not yet been made public and which may influence the prices on security markets'. Major information is defined as including a list of 79 items including major contracts or changes in business of issuer's changes in state policies, a change in control of an issuer and 'other major information'. Information and data used to forecast and analyse the securities markets are specified not to be inside information.

'Insiders' means personnel who may have access to or are able to obtain inside information because they hold the issuers securities or because they have a position within the issuer or in a company which has a close relationship with the issuer, or because of their position as supervisors or professionals supervising or advising the issuer. This extends to secretaries and typists employed by the issuer, to government personnel with access to the issuer and professionals such as journalists who may have working relationships with the issuer.

3 CONCLUSION

The most notable difference between the local and national legislation is that the national measures provide more detail and present it in a legislative format that more closely resembles that of other jurisdictions. The Shenzhen regulations are the most primitive and it is notable that under the original local regulations only an individual (natural person) could apparently commit insider trading.

However, the overriding similarity between the local and national legislation is that all are drafted in a very broad manner. Although 'definitions' are provided in the national legislation, they are open-ended. The scope and application of these regulations are not yet clear; it remains for the trading system to evolve and consequent legislation and case law to establish the scope and consequences of insider trading in China.